# A History of the Ptolemaic Empire

This edition is sponsored by the Austrian Bundesministerium für Wissenschaft und Verkehr, the City of Vienna, Municipal Department 18, Science Group, and the Kunsthistorisches Museum, Vienna.

# A History of the Ptolemaic Empire

Günther Hölbl
translated by Tina Saavedra

London and New York

First published 2001
by Routledge
11 New Fetter Lane, London EC4P 4EE

Simultaneously published in the USA and Canada
by Routledge
29 West 35th Street, New York, NY 10001

*Routledge is an imprint of the Taylor & Francis Group*

Geschichte des Ptolemäerreiches © 1994 by Wissenschaftliche
Buchgesellschaft, Darmstadt

This translation © 2001 Routledge Ltd

Typeset in Garamond by Graphicraft Limited, Hong Kong
Printed and bound in Great Britain by Biddles Ltd, Guildford
and King's Lynn

*British Library Cataloguing in Publication Data*
A catalogue record for this book is available
from the British Library

*Library of Congress Cataloging in Publication Data*
Hölbl, Günther.
  [Geschichte des Ptolemäerreiches. English]
  History of the Ptolemaic empire / Günther Hölbl.
    p.   cm.
  Translation of: Geschichte des Ptolemäerreiches.
  Includes bibliographical references and index.
  ISBN 0–415–20145–4
    1. Egypt—History—332–30 B.C.   2. Ptolemaic dynasty,
  305–30 B.C.   I. Title.
DT92 .H6513   2000
932'.021—dc21                                    00–020437

ISBN 0–415–20145–4 (hbk)
ISBN 0–415–23489–1 (pbk)

To Gen. Dir. Dr Wilfried Seipel,
Promoter of Research

# Contents

# Illustrations

# Foreword

This book has grown in response to the special dilemma faced by a teacher who, when lecturing on Ptolemaic history, is asked for suitable reading material on the subject by his students. Because our topic extends into several modern disciplines, namely, Egyptology, Ancient History, Papyrology and Classical Archaeology, each year a vast amount of specialized work is published that is pertinent to our field, each with its own special focus; and in addition to this there also appears annually an abundant literature of more general studies in Hellenistic history with a cultural–historical focus. Since the appearance of E. Bevan, *A History of Egypt under the Ptolemaic Dynasty*, London, 1927, however, there has not been a comprehensive account of Ptolemaic Egypt. Subjects, such as the recent sub-disciplines of Egyptology (especially demotics) and Papyrology which are today so successful, were at that time still in their infancy and so were not given much attention. Despite this shortcoming, all the relevant references to the ancient authors were incorporated into the monumental history of Ptolemaic Egypt by A. Bouché-Leclercq, *Histoire des Lagides*, I–IV, Paris 1903–1907; this work continues to be useful in the field. Also pertinent to our topic and a good complement to our own efforts is a book currently being prepared by Prof. H. Heinen of Trier, with the provisional title of *Geschichte Ägyptens in hellenistischer, römischer und byzantinischer Zeit*. This book will be published in the series of handbooks on Egyptian history, edited by E. Hornung, Artemis Press, Zurich and Munich.

That this book was ever written is due to discussions I had with the eminent Austrian scholar of the ancient world, Professor Fritz Schachermeyr, before he passed away. When he was acting as the representative of the Egyptian Commission of the Austrian Academy of Sciences, he inspired me to write this book as a service to the profession and he continued to encourage me in every way throughout. I have attempted to incorporate into this account the most recent information from the various disciplines. In keeping with the intended scope of this book, the notes are kept brief; and as a general rule, I cite the most recent work in the field. These more recent publications make the older material more accessible, since in each case they can give us insight into the *status quaestionis* of a particular time. I have written this book from the point of view of an Egyptologist and my concern is to demonstrate the pervasiveness and interdependence of politics, ideology and religious culture in the development of the Ptolemaic empire. For this reason, it was necessary to discuss only very briefly such topics as economics, administration, social relations and Hellenistic scholarship.

Above all, I would like to thank the Wissenschaftliche Buchgesellschaft for accepting the book in their programme, as well as Peter Heitmann who kindly handled the technical problems. I should also like to make special mention of my wife, Ingrid Hölbl, who was supportive and understanding to a fault throughout the years and managed to find funds from the family budget for those scholarly acquisitions which the academy could not finance. Continuous drafting of the manuscript was made possible by Professor Günther Hamann who put his office at the academy at my disposal. Further, I should also like to thank the two women who typed my manuscript into the computer: Ms Maria Braun handled approximately the first third, while Ms Brigitte Akinfenwa typed in the rest and was always willing to include changes and additions. Robert Priewasser studied my lecture notes with great interest and tracked down stylistic shortcomings and typos with zeal. A final word of thanks is due to Professor Gerhard Dobesch who always supported my research on the position of Egypt within the Greco-Roman world with particular interest and provided me with a ready supply of numerous references.

Günther Hölbl
Vienna, September 1993

# Preface

I should like to express my thanks to Routledge and its Senior Editor, Richard Stoneman, for the publication of this English version of my *History of the Ptolemaic Empire*. Tina Saavedra of Quebec has worked industriously to understand my German original and to translate it into easily readable English. As a result, the subject of Ptolemaic history, which leads a shadowy existence in schools and universities, has now a chance of being absorbed into the educational mainstream throughout the world.

A translation of this kind can only come to fruition through financial support. I thank the Austrian Federal Ministry for Science and Culture for the largest part (ATS 60 000) of this subvention; the remainder was provided by the City of Vienna (ATS 25 000) and by the Kunsthistorisches Museum (ATS 15 000). In this way, the book has become a part of Austrian cultural politics. I must at the same time express my gratitude to the general director of the Kunsthistorisches Museum, Hofrat Dr Wilfried Seipel, for supporting my work on the book by guaranteeing the necessary scholarly freedom.

The appearance of this English edition offered the opportunity to eliminate a few errors – for drawing my attention to which I am grateful mainly to my students – and to improve the text by incorporating the latest scholarly views of the last six years. In addition, I was able to add a bibliographical supplement. I am particularly grateful to Routledge that this book could take the form of a revised and upgraded edition.

Vienna June 1999                                                    Günther Hölbl
                                                    Kunsthistorisches Museum

# Acknowledgements

We are indebted to the people and archives cited below for permission to reproduce photographs.

1.1 and 3.4   Deutsches Archäologisches Institut, Berlin (H. Kyrieleis); with kind permission.
2.1   Kunsthistorisches Museum, Vienna, Antiquities collection; with kind permission.
2.2   Nationalmuseet, Copenhagen, Numismatic collection; with kind permission.
4.1 and 9.7   Ägyptisches Museum, Berlin; with kind permission.
7.1   National Museum in Athens; with kind permission.
8.1   Antikenmuseum, Berlin; with kind permission.

3.2, 3.5, 6.1, 9.2, 9.5, 9.8, 9.9 and 9.11   belonging to the author; of these, 3.2 and 6.1 are reproduced with the kind permission of the Egyptian Museum, Cairo (Gen. Dir. M. Saleh).

# Abbreviations and references

The abbreviations for journals and other periodicals used here correspond to those in 'Archäologische Bibliographie' (*Beilage zum Jahrbuch des Deutschen Archäologischen Instituts*, Berlin), 1991. The names of the ancient authors and the titles of their works are abbreviated following those listed in the *Oxford Latin Dictionary* (Oxford 1982) and the *English–Greek Lexicon* (Oxford 1966).

| | |
|---|---|
| Abel (1983) | K. Abel, Polybios Buch 14: Res Aegypti, Historia 32, 1983, 268–286. |
| Alessandria, I (1983)<br>II (1984)<br>III (1984) | Alessandria e il mondo ellenistico-romano. Studi in onore di A. Adriani; hrsg. v. N. Bonacasa u. A. Di Vita, I–III, Roma 1983–84. |
| Alexandrien (1981) | Alexandrien. Kulturbegegnungen dreier Jahrtausende im Schmelztiegel einer mediterranen Großstadt; hrsg. unter Mitarb. v. N. Hinske, Mainz 1981 (= Aegyptiaca Treverensia, 1). |
| Alföldy (1990) | G. Alföldy, Der Obelisk auf dem Petersplatz in Rom, Heidelberg 1990 (= SbHeidelberg 1990, Ber. 2). |
| Alliot (1949)<br>(1954) | M. Alliot, Le culte d'Horus à Edfou au temps des Ptolémées, I–II, Beyrouth 1949–54; Nachdr. 1979 (= Bibliothèque d'Etude, 20). |
| Alliot (1951) | M. Alliot, La Thébaïde en lutte contre les rois d'Alexandrie sous Philopator et Épiphane (216–184), RBPhil 29, 1951, 421–443. |
| Alliot (1952) | M. Alliot, La fin de la résistance égyptienne dans le sud sous Épiphane, REA 54, 1952, 18–26. |
| Alliot (1954) | S. Alliot (1949). |
| Amantini (1974) | L. S. Amantini, Tolemeo VI Filometore re di Siria? RendIstLomb 108, 1974, 511–529. |
| ANRW I, 1 | Aufstieg und Niedergang der römischen Welt, hrsg. v. H. Temporini, W. Haase, I: Von den Anfängen Roms bis zum Ausgang der Republik, 1: Politische Geschichte, Berlin 1972. |

ANRW II, 10, 1      Aufstieg und Niedergang der römischen Welt, hrsg. v. H. Temporini, W. Haase, II: Principat, 10, 1. Halbband: Politische Geschichte (Provinzen und Randvölker: Afrika und Ägypten), Berlin 1988.

AR      Altes Reich, Ägypten.

Arnold (1992)      D. Arnold, Die Tempel Ägyptens. Götterwohnungen, Kultstätten, Baudenkmäler, Zürich 1992.

Badian (1967)      E. Badian, The testament of Ptolemy Alexander, RhM, N.F. 110, 1967, 178–192.

Bagnall (1976)      R. S. Bagnall, The administration of the Ptolemaic possessions outside Egypt, Leiden 1976 (= Columbia Studies in the Classical Tradition, 4).

Bartson (1982)      L. J. Bartson, Cyrenaica in antiquity, phil. Diss., Ann Arbor 1982.

Becher (1966)      I. Becher, Das Bild der Kleopatra in der griechischen und lateinischen Literatur, Berlin 1966.

Beckerath (1984)      J. v. Beckerath, Handbuch der ägyptischen Königsnamen, München 1984 (= Münchner Ägyptologische Studien, 20).

Bengtson (1952)      H. Bengtson, Die Strategie in der hellenistischen Zeit, III, München 1952, Nachdr. 1967.

Bengtson (1977)      H. Bengtson, Marcus Antonius. Triumvir und Herrscher des Ostens, München 1977.

Bergman (1968)      J. Bergman, Ich bin Isis. Studien zum memphitischen Hintergrund der griechischen Isisaretalogien, Uppsala 1968 (= Acta Universitatis Upsaliensis, Historia Religionum, 3).

Bernand (1970)      A. Bernand, Le Delta égyptien d'après les textes grecs, I: les confins libyques, Le Caire 1970.

Bernand (1984)      A. Bernand, Les portes du désert. Recueil des inscriptions grecques d'Antinooupolis, Tentyris, Koptos, Apollonopolis Parva et Apollonopolis Magna, Paris 1984.

Bernand (1989)      A. Bernand, De Thèbes à Syène, Paris 1989.

Bernand (1992)      A. Bernand, La prose sur pierre dans l'Égypte hellénistique et romaine, I–II, Paris 1992.

Beyer-Rotthoff (1993)      B. Beyer-Rotthoff, Untersuchungen zur Außenpolitik Ptolemaios' III, Bonn 1993 (konnte für das vorliegende Buch nicht mehr benützt werden).

BGU      Ägyptische Urkunden aus den Staatlichen Museen Berlin, Griechische Urkunden, I–XV, 1895–1983.

Bicknell (1977)  P. J. Bicknell, Caesar, Antony, Cleopatra and Cyprus, Latomus 36, 1977, 325–342.

Billows (1990)  R. A. Billows, Antigonos the One-Eyed and the creation of the Hellenistic state, Berkeley 1990.

Bingen (1952)  J. Bingen, Papyrus Revenue Laws. Nouvelle éd. du texte, Göttingen 1952 (= SB, Beih. 1).

Bingen (1970)  J. Bingen, Les épistratèges de Thébaïde sous les derniers Ptolémées, ChronEg 45, 90, 1970, 369–378.

Bingen (1978)  J. Bingen, Le papyrus Revenue Laws – tradition grecque et adaption hellénistique, Opladen 1978.

Bloedow (1963)  E. Bloedow, Beiträge zur Geschichte des Ptolemaios' XII, Würzburg, phil. Diss. 1963.

Bonneau (1971)  D. Bonneau, Le fisc et le Nil, Paris 1971.

Boswinkel, Pestman (1982)  E. Boswinkel, P. W. Pestman, Les archives privées de Dionysios, fils de Kephalas (P. L. Bat. 22), Leiden 1982.

Bothmer (1960)  B. v. Bothmer u. a., Egyptian sculpture of the Late Period, 700 BC to AD 100, Brooklyn 1960.

Bresciani (1969)  E. Bresciani, Letteratura e poesia dell'antico Egitto, Torino 1969.

Bresciani (1980)  E. Bresciani, Kom Madi 1977 e 1978. Le pitture murali del cenotafio di Alessandro Magno, Pisa 1980.

Bruneau (1970)  Ph. Bruneau, Recherches sur les cultes de Délos à l'époque hellénistique et à l'époque impériale, Paris 1970.

Brunelle (1976)  E. Brunelle, Die Bildnisse der Ptolemäerinnen, Frankfurt 1976.

BSFE  Bulletin de la Société Française d'Égyptologie.

Burstein (1991)  S. M. Burstein, Pharaoh Alexander: a scholarly myth, AncSoc 22, 1991, 139–145.

CAH VII, 1  F. W. Walbank u. a., The Hellenistic world, 2. Aufl., Cambridge 1984 (= The Cambridge Ancient History, 2. Aufl., VII, 1).

CAH VIII  A. E. Astin u. a., Rome and the Mediterranean to 133 BC Cambridge 1989 (= The Cambridge Ancient History, 2. Aufl., VIII).

Cauville (1987)  S. Cauville, Essai sur la théologie du temple d'Horus à Edfou, I–II, Le Caire 1987 (= Bibliothèque d'Etude, 102).

Cauville, Dechauvelle (1984)  S. Cauville, D. Devauchelle, Le temple d'Edfou, Étappes de la construction, nouvelles données historiques, REg 35, 1984, 31–55.

| | |
|---|---|
| Chamoux (1956) | F. Chamoux, Le roi Magas, Revue Historique 216, 1956, 18–34. |
| Chamoux (1989) | F. Chamoux, Marcus Antonius, der letzte Herrscher des griechischen Ostens, Gernsbach 1989. |
| Chauveau (1990) (1991) | M. Chauveau, Un été 145, BIFAO 90, 1990, 135–168; 91, 1991, 129–134. |
| Christ (1984) | K. Christ, Krise und Untergang der römischen Republik, 2. Aufl., Darmstadt 1984. |
| CIL | Corpus Inscriptionum Latinarum. |
| Clarysse (1978) | W. Clarysse, Hurgonaphor et Chaonnophris, les derniers pharaons indigènes, ChronEg 53, 106, 1978, 243–253. |
| Clarysse, Van der Veken (1983) | W. Clarysse, G. Van der Veken, The eponymous priests of Ptolemaic Egypt, Leiden 1983 (= P. L. Bat., 24). |
| Cleopatra's Egypt (1988) | Cleopatra's Egypt. Age of the Ptolemies, New York 1988 [dt. Ausgabe ohne wiss. Apparat: Kleopatra. Ägypten um die Zeitenwende, Mainz 1989]. |
| C.Ord.Ptol. | M.-Th.Lenger, Corpus des ordonnances des Ptolémées, Bruxelles 1964, Nachdr. mit Suppl. 1980. Bilan des additions et corrections (1964–1988), compléments à la bibliographie, Bruxelles 1990. |
| Crawford (1980) | D. J. Crawford, Ptolemy, Ptah and Apis in Hellenistic Memphis, in D. J. Crawford u. a., Studies on Ptolemaic Memphis, Lovanii 1980, 1–42 (= Studia Hellenistica, 24). |
| CRIPEL | Cahier de Recherches de l'Institut de Papyrologie et d'Egyptologie de Lille. |
| Criscuolo (1989) | L. Criscuolo, La successione a Tolemeo Aulete ed i pretesi matrimoni di Cleopatra VII con i fratelli, in Egitto (1989), 325–339. |
| Criscuolo (1990) | L. Criscuolo, *Philadelphos* nella dinastia lagide, Aegyptus 70, 1990, 89–96. |
| Daressy (1911) (1916/17) | G. Daressy, Un décret de l'an XXIII de Ptolémée Épiphane, RecTrav 33, 1911, 1–8; 38, 1916/17, 175–179. |
| Daumas (1952) | F. Daumas, Les moyens d'expression du Grec et de l'Égyptien comparés dans les décrets de Canope et de Memphis, Le Caire 1952 (= Suppl. aux ASAE, 16). |
| Daumas (1958) | F. Daumas, Les mammisis des temples égyptiens, Paris 1958. |

Dunand (1973)            F. Dunand, Le culte d'Isis dans le bassin oriental
                         de la Méditerranée, I–III, Leiden 1973 (= EPRO,
                         26).

Dunand (1980, 1)         F. Dunand, L'exode rural en Égypte à l'époque
                         hellénistique, Ktema 5, 1980, 137–150.

Dunand (1980, 2)         F. Dunand, Fête, tradition, propagande: Les
                         cérémonies en l'honneur de Bérénice, fille de
                         Ptolémée III, en 238 a. C., in Livre du Centenaire
                         1880–1980, Le Caire 1980, 287–301.

Dunand (1986)            F. Dunand, Les associations dionysiaques au
                         service du pouvoir lagide (IIIe s. av. J.-C.), in
                         L'association dionysiaque dans les sociétés anci-
                         ennes. Actes de la table ronde . . . 1984, Rome
                         1986, 85–104.


Eddy (1961)              S. K. Eddy, The king is dead. Studies in the
                         Near Eastern resistance to Hellenism, 334–31
                         BC, Lincoln 1961.

Edfou I–XIV              Marquis de Rochemonteux, E. Chassinat, Le tem-
                         ple d'Edfou, I–XIV, Paris 1897–1934; 2. Aufl.,
                         hrsg. v. S. Cauville, D. Devauchelle, Iff., 1984ff.

Egitto (1989)            Egitto e storia antica dall'Ellenismo all'età araba.
                         Bilancio di un confronto. Atti del Colloquio Inter-
                         nazionale, Bologna 1987. Hrsg.: L. Criscuolo,
                         G. Geraci, Bologna 1989.

Egypt (1983)             Egypt and the Hellenistic world. Proceedings of
                         the International Colloquium, Leuven 24–26 May
                         1982, ed. E. Van 't Dack u. a., Lovanii 1983 (=
                         Studia Hellenistica, 27).

Ellis (1994)             W. M. Ellis, Ptolemy of Egypt, London 1994
                         (konnte für das vorliegende Buch nicht mehr
                         benützt werden).


Falivene (1991)          M. R. Falivene, Government, management, literacy.
                         Aspects of Ptolemaic administration in the early
                         Hellenistic period, AncSoc 22, 1991, 203–227.

FGrHist.                 F. Jacoby, Die Fragmente der griechischen
                         Historiker, I–III (in 16 Bdn.), Berlin u. Leiden
                         1923–58.

Fraser (1972)            P. M. Fraser, Ptolemaic Alexandria, I–III, Oxford
                         1972.


Gauthier (1916)          M. H. Gauthier, Le livre des rois d'Égypte, IV:
                         De la XXVe dynastie à la fin des Ptolemées, Le
                         Caire 1916.

| | |
|---|---|
| Gauthier, Sottas (1925) | H. Gauthier, H. Sottas, Un décret trilingue en l'honneur de Ptolémée IV, Le Caire 1925. |
| Gehrke (1990) | H.-J. Gehrke, Geschichte des Hellenismus, München 1990. |
| Gera (1987) | D. Gera, Ptolemy, son of Thraseas and the Fifth Syrian War, AncSoc 18, 1987, 63–73. |
| Geraci (1983) | G. Geraci, Genesi della provincia romana d'Egitto, Bologna 1983. |
| Goedicke (1985) | H. Goedicke, Comments on the Satrap Stela, BEgNew York 6, 1985, 33–54. |
| Götte (1986) | K. Götte, Eine Individualcharakteristik ptolemäischer Herrscher anhand der Epitheta-Sequenzen beim Weinopfer, REg 37, 1986, 63–80. |
| Goudriaan (1988) | K. Goudriaan, Ethnicity in Ptolemaic Egypt, Amsterdam 1988. |
| Goukowsky, I (1978) II (1981) | P. Goukowsky, Essai sur les origines du mythe d'Alexandre (336–270 av. J.-C.), I–II, Nancy 1978–81. |
| Grainger (1991) | J. D. Grainger, Hellenistic Phoenicia, Oxford 1991. |
| Green (1990) | P. Green, Alexander to Actium. The historical evolution of the Hellenistic age, Berkeley 1990. |
| Grenier (1983) | J.-Cl. Grenier, Ptolémée Evergète II et Cléopâtre II d'après les textes du temple de Tôd, in Alessandria, I (1983), 32–37. |
| Griffiths (1961) | J. G. Griffiths, The death of Cleopatra VII, JEA 47, 1961, 113–118, Taf. IX. |
| Griffiths (1987) | J. G. Griffiths, Egypt and the rise of the synagogue, *Journal of Theological Studies* 38, 1987, 1–15. |
| Grimm (1981) | G. Grimm, Orient und Okzident in der Kunst Alexandriens, in Alexandrien (1981), 13–25. |
| Gronewald (1982) | M. Gronewald, Ein Brief aus dem sechsten Syrischen Krieg?, in Kölner Papyri 4, bearb. v. B. Kramer u. a., Opladen 1982, 151–163. |
| Gruen (1984) | E. S. Gruen, The Hellenistic world and the coming of Rome, I–II, Berkeley 1984. |
| Grzybek (1990) | E. Grzybek, Du calendrier macédonien au calendrier ptolémaïque. Problèmes de chronologie hellénistique, Basel 1990 (= Schweizerische Beiträge zur Altertumswissenschaft, 20). |
| Günther (1990) | L.-M. Günther, Cornelia und Ptolemaios VIII. Zur Historizität des Heiratsantrages (Plut. TG 1, 3), Historia 39, 1990, 124–128. |

Guéraud (1931–32)  O. Guéraud, ΕΝΤΕΥΞΕΙΣ. Requêtes et plaintes adressées au roi d'Égypte au IIIe siècle avant J.-C., Le Caire 1931–32; Nachdr. Hildesheim 1988.

Habicht (1956)  Chr. Habicht, Gottmenschentum und griechische Städte, München 1956 (= Zetemata, 14).

Habicht (1979)  Chr. Habicht, Untersuchungen zur politischen Geschichte Athens im 3. Jh. v. Chr., München 1979 (= Vestigia, 30).

Habicht (1982)  Chr. Habicht, Studien zur Geschichte Athens in hellenistischer Zeit, Göttingen 1982 (= Hypomnemata, 73).

Haeny (1985)  G. Haeny, A short architectural history of Philae, BIFAO 85, 1985, 197–233, Taf. XXXV–XXXVII.

Hammond (1989)  N. G. L. Hammond, The Macedonian state, Oxford 1989.

Hammond, Walbank (1988)  N. G. L. Hammond, F. W. Walbank, A history of Macedonia, III: 336–167 BC, Oxford 1988.

Harmatta (1963)  J. Harmatta, Das Problem der Kontinuität im frühhellenistischen Ägypten, ActaAntHung 11, 1963, 199–213.

Hauben (1970)  H. Hauben, Callicrates of Samos. A contribution to the study of the Ptolemaic admiralty, Leuven 1970 (= Studia Hellenistica, 18).

Hauben (1983)  H. Hauben, Arsinoe II et la politique extérieur de l'Égypte, in Egypt (1983), 99–127.

Hauben (1989)  H. Hauben, Aspects du culte des souverains à l'époque des Lagides, in Egitto (1989), 441–467.

Hauben (1990)  H. Hauben, L'expedition de Ptolémée III en Orient et la sédition domestique de 245 av. J.-C., ArchPF 36, 1990, 29–37.

Hauben (1992)  H. Hauben, La chronologie macédonienne et ptolémaïque mise à l'épreuve. A propos d'un livre d'E. Grzybek, ChronEg 67, 133, 1992, 143–171.

Havas (1977)  L. Havas, Rome and Egypt in the 60s BC StAeg 3, 1977, 39–56.

Hazzard (1987)  R. A. Hazzard, The regnal years of Ptolemy II Philadelphos, Phoenix 41, 1987, 140–158.

Hazzard (1992)  R. A. Hazzard, Did Ptolemy I get his surname from the Rhodians?, ZPE 93, 1992, 52–56.

Heckel (1992)  W. Heckel, The marshals of Alexander's empire, London 1992.

Heinen (1966)  H. Heinen, Rom und Ägypten von 51 bis 47 v. Chr., Tübingen, phil. Diss. 1966.

Heinen (1969)    H. Heinen, Cäsar und Kaisarion, Historia 18, 1969, 181–203.

Heinen (1972, 1)    H. Heinen, Die politischen Beziehungen zwischen Rom und dem Ptolemäerreich von ihren Anfängen bis zum Tag von Eleusis (273–168 v. Chr.), in ANRW I, 1 (1972), 633–659.

Heinen (1972, 2)    H. Heinen, Untersuchungen zur hellenistischen Geschichte des 3. Jh. v. Chr. Zur Geschichte der Zeit des Ptolemaios Keraunos und zum Chremonideischen Krieg, Wiesbaden 1972 (= Historia, Einzelschr., 20).

Heinen (1974)    H. Heinen, Les mariages de Ptolemée VIII Evergète et leur chronologie. Etude comparative de papyrus et d'inscriptions grecs, démotiques et hiéroglyphiques, in Akten des XIII. Internationalen Papyrologenkongresses, 1971, München 1974, 147–155 (= Münchner Beiträge zur Papyrusforschung und Antiken Rechtsgeschichte, 66).

Heinen (1978)    H. Heinen, Aspects et problèmes de la monarchie ptolémaïque, Ktema 3, 1978, 177–199.

Heinen (1983)    H. Heinen, Die Tryphè des Ptolemaios VIII. Euergetes II. Beobachtungen zum ptolemäischen Herrscherideal und zu einer römischen Gesandtschaft in Ägypten 140/39 v. Chr., in Althistorische Studien, FS H. Bengtson, Wiesbaden 1983, 116–127, Taf. 6–7 (= Historia, Einzelschr., 40).

Holleaux (1908)    M. Holleaux, Etudes d'histoire hellénistique: la chronologie de la cinquième guerre de Syrie, Klio 8, 1908, 267–281 (= id., Etudes d'épigraphie et d'histoire grecques, III, Paris 1968, 317–335).

Huß (1976)    W. Huß, Untersuchungen zur Außenpolitik Ptolemaios' IV, München 1976 (= Münchner Beiträge zur Papyrusforschung und Antiken Rechtsgeschichte, 69).

Huß (1979)    W. Huß, Die Beziehungen zwischen Karthago und Ägypten in hellenistischer Zeit, AncSoc 10, 1979, 119–137.

Huß (1990)    W. Huß, Die Herkunft der Kleopatra Philopator, Aegyptus 70, 1990, 191–203.

Huß (1991, 1)    W. Huß, Gedanken zum Thema '"Staat" und "Kirche" im ptolemaiischen Ägypten', in Hellenistische Studien, Gedenkschrift f. H. Bengtson, München 1991, 55–60.

Huß (1991, 2)          W. Huß, Die in ptolemaiischer Zeit verfaßten
                       Synodal-Dekrete der ägyptischen Priester, ZPE
                       88, 1991, 189–208.
Hutmacher (1965)       R. Hutmacher, Das Ehrendekret für den
                       Strategen Kallimachos, Meisenheim/Gl. 1965
                       (= Beiträge zur Klassischen Philologie, 17).

I. Cret.               Inscriptiones Creticae I–IV, ed. M. Guarducci,
                       Roma 1935–50.
I. Fay.                E. Bernand, Recueil des inscriptions grecques du
                       Fayoum, I–III; I: Leiden, 1975; II–III: Le Caire
                       1981.
IG                     Inscriptiones Graecae.
Ijsewijn (1961)        J. Ijsewijn, De sacerdotibus sacerdotiisque
                       Alexandri Magni et Lagidarum eponymis, Brussel
                       1961.
I. Louvre              É. Bernand, Inscriptions grecques d'Égypte et de
                       Nubie au Musée du Louvre, Paris 1992.
I. Milet.              G. Kawerau, A. Rehm, Das Delphinion in Milet,
                       Berlin 1914 (= Milet III).
I. Philae              A. Bernand, Les inscriptions grecques (et latines)
                       de Philae, I–II, Paris 1969.
I. Priene              F. Hiller von Gaertringen, Die Inschriften von
                       Priene, Berlin 1906.

Junker (1958)          H. Junker, Der große Pylon des Tempels der Isis
                       in Philä, Wien 1958.

Kamal (1904–5)         A. B. Kamal, Stèles ptolémaïques et romaines,
                       I–II, Le Caire 1904–5 (= Catalogue Général des
                       Antiquités Égyptiennes du Musée du Caire).
Kasher (1985)          A. Kasher, The Jews in Hellenistic and Roman
                       Egypt, Tübingen 1985.
Kessler (1989)         D. Kessler, Die heiligen Tiere und der König, I:
                       Beiträge zu Organisation, Kult und Theologie
                       der spätzeitlichen Tierfriedhöfe, Wiesbaden 1989
                       (= Ägypten und Altes Testament, 16).
Kienast (1987)         D. Kienast, Alexander, Zeus und Ammon, in Zu
                       Alexander d. Gr., FS G. Wirth, hrsg. v. W. Will,
                       Amsterdam 1987, 309–333.
Klose (1972)           P. Klose, Die völkerrechtliche Ordnung der
                       hellenistischen Staatenwelt in der Zeit von 280
                       bis 168 v. Chr., München 1972 (= Münchner
                       Beiträge zur Papyrusforschung und Antiken
                       Rechtsgeschichte, 64).

Knibbe (1958)                D. Knibbe, Die römischen Gesandtschaften nach dem Osten in der Zeit von 230–129 v. Chr., Wien, phil. Diss. 1958.

Koenen (1957)                L. Koenen, Eine ptolemäische Königsurkunde (P. Kroll), Wiesbaden 1957 (= Klassisch-philologische Studien, 19).

Koenen (1959)                L. Koenen, θεοῖσιν ἐχθρός. Ein einheimischer Gegenkönig in Ägypten (132/1ᵃ), ChronEg 34, 68, 1959, 103–119.

Koenen (1977)                L. Koenen, Eine agonistische Inschrift aus Ägypten und frühptolemäische Königsfeste, Meisenheim/Gl. 1977 (= Beiträge zur Klassischen Philologie, 56).

Koenen (1983)                L. Koenen, Die Adaption ägyptischer Königsideologie am Ptolemäerhof, in Egypt (1983), 143–190.

Kuhlmann (1988)              K. P. Kuhlmann, Das Ammoneion. Archäologie, Geschichte und Kultpraxis des Orakels von Siwa, Mainz 1988 (= Archäologische Veröffentlichungen des Deutschen Archäol. Instituts, Abt. Kairo, 75).

Kyrieleis (1975)             H. Kyrieleis, Bildnisse der Ptolemäer, Berlin 1975 (= Archäologische Forschungen, 2).

LÄI–VII                      Lexikon der Ägyptologie I–VII, begründet v. W. Helck, E. Otto; hrsg. v. W. Helck, W. Westendorf, Wiesbaden 1975–92.

Lanciers (1986)             E. Lanciers, Die Ägyptischen Tempelbauten zur
        (1987)              Zeit des Ptolemaios V. Epiphanes (204–180 v. Chr.), MDIK 42, 1986, 81–98; 43, 1987, 173–182.

Lanciers (1988, 1)          E. Lanciers, Die Alleinherrschaft des Ptolemaios VIII. im Jahre 164/163 v. Chr. und der Name Euergetes, in Proceedings of the XVIII Intern. Congr. of Papyrology, Athens 1986, II, Athens 1988, 405–433.

Lanciers (1988, 2)          E. Lanciers, Die Vergöttlichung und die Ehe des Ptolemaios IV. und der Arsinoe III, ArchPF 34, 1988, 27–32.

Lanciers (1991)             E. Lanciers, Die ägyptischen Priester des ptolemäischen Königskultes, REg 42, 1991, 117–145, Taf. 2.

La Rocca (1984)             E. La Rocca, L'età d'oro di Cleopatra. Indagine sulla Tazza Farnese, Roma 1984.

Laronde (1987)              A. Laronde, Cyrène et la Libye hellénistique. Libykai Historiai de l'époque républicaine au principat d'Auguste, Paris 1987.

LD                          K. R. Lepsius, Denkmaeler aus Aegypten und
                            Aethiopien, 12 Bde. u. Erg.-Bd., Berlin 1849–
                            58, Leipzig 1913.

LD, Text                    K. R. Lepsius, Denkmäler aus Aegypten und
                            Aethiopien, Text, hrsg. v. E. Naville, 5 Bde.,
                            Leipzig 1897–1913.

Leschhorn (1984)            W. Leschhorn, 'Gründer der Stadt'. Studien
                            zu einem politisch-religiösen Phänomen der
                            griechischen Geschichte, Stuttgart 1984
                            (= Palingensia, 20).

Lewis (1986)                N. Lewis, Greeks in Ptolemaic Egypt. Case studies
                            in the social history of the Hellenistic world,
                            Oxford 1986.

Lichtheim (1980)            M. Lichtheim, Ancient Egyptian Literature, III,
                            Berkeley 1980.


Maehler (1983)              H. Maehler, Egypt under the last Ptolemies, BICS
                            30, 1983, 1–16, Taf. 1–3.

Marasco (1979–80)           G. Marasco, La valutazione di Tolemeo IV
                            Filopatore nella storiograpfia greca, Sileno 5–6,
                            1979–80, 159–182.

Maresch (1991)              K. Maresch, Das königliche Indulgenzdekret vom
                            9. Oktober 186 vor Chr., in Kölner Papyri 7,
                            bearb. v. M. Gronewald u. K. Maresch, Opladen
                            1991, 63–78.

Mehl (1980–81)              A. Mehl, ΔΟΡΙΚΤΗΤΟΣ ΧΩΡΑ. Kritische
                            Bemerkungen zum 'Speererwerb' in Politik und
                            Völkerrecht der hellenistischen Epoche, AncSoc
                            11–12, 1980–81, 173–212.

Mehl (1986)                 A. Mehl, Seleukos Nikator und sein Reich,
                            Lovanii 1986 (= Studia Hellenistica, 28).

Merkelbach (1963)           R. Merkelbach, Isisfeste in griechisch-römischer
                            Zeit, Daten und Riten, Meisenheim/Gl. 1963
                            (= Beiträge zur Klassischen Philologie, 5).

Merkelbach (1981)           R. Merkelbach, Das Königtum der Ptolemäer
                            und die hellenistischen Dichter, in Alexandrien
                            (1981), 27–35.

Merker (1970)               I. L. Merker, The Ptolemaic officials and the League
                            of the Islanders, Historia 19, 1970, 141–160.

Michaelidou-               I. Michaelidou-Nicolaou, Prosopography of
   Nicolaou (1976)          Ptolemaic Cyprus, Göteborg 1976 (= Studies in
                            Mediterranean Archaeology, 44).

Mitteis, Wilcken            L. Mitteis, U. Wilcken, Grundzüge und
                            Chrestomatie der Papyruskunde, I–II (in 4 Bdn.),
                            Leipzig 1912.

Mooren (1974)      L. Mooren, The governors general of the Thebaid in the second century BC (II), AncSoc 5, 1974, 137–152.

Mooren (1975)      L. Mooren, The aulic titulature in Ptolemaic Egypt. Introduction and Prosopography, Brussel 1975.

Mooren (1977)      L. Mooren, La hiérarchie de cour ptolémaïque, Lovanii 1977 (= Studia Hellenistica, 23).

Mooren (1979)      L. Mooren, Antiochos IV. Epiphanes und das ptolemäische Königtum, in Actes du XVe Congrès Intern. de Papyrologie, Bruxelles 1977, IV, Bruxelles 1979, 78–86.

Mooren (1981)      L. Mooren, Ptolemaic families, in Proceedings of the XVI Intern. Congress of Papyrology, New York 1980, Chicago 1981, 289–301.

Mooren (1985)      L. Mooren, The Ptolemaic court system, ChronEg 60, 119–120, 1985, 214–222.

Mooren (1988)      L. Mooren, The wives and children of Ptolemy VIII Euergetes II, in Proceedings of the XVIII Intern. Congress of Papyrology, Athens 1986, II, Athens 1988, 435–444.

Mørkholm (1966)    O. Mørkholm, Antiochos IV of Syria, København 1966.

Mørkholm (1975)    O. Mørkholm, Ptolemaic coins and chronology, the dated silver coinage of Alexandria, MusNotAmNumSoc 20, 1975, 7–24.

MR                 Mittleres Reich, Ägypten.

Müller, B.-J. (1968)  B.-J. Müller, Ptolemaeus II. Philadelphus als Gesetzgeber, Köln 1968.

Müller, W. (1966)  W. Müller, Kleopatra Berenike III. – θεὰ Φιλοπάτωρ, ZÄS 93, 1966, 93–96.

Müller, W. M. (1920)  W. M. Müller, Kgyptological researches, III: The bilingual decrees of Philae, Washington 1920.

Nock (1928)        A. D. Nock, Notes on ruler-cult I–IV, JHS 48, 1928, 21–43 (= id., Essays on religion and the Ancient World, I, Oxford 1972, 134–157).

NR                 Neues Reich, Ägypten.

OGIS I–II          W. Dittenberger, Orientis Graeci inscriptiones selectae, I–II, Lipsiae 1903. Vgl. dazu stets: E. Bernand, Inscriptions grecques d'Egypte et de Nubie: répertoire bibliographique des *OGIS*, Paris 1982.

Olshausen (1963)   E. Olshausen, Rom und Ägypten von 116 bis 51 v. Chr., Erlangen, phil. Diss. 1963.

Onasch (1976)            Chr. Onasch, Zur Königsideologie der Ptolemäer
                         in den Dekreten von Kanopus und Memphis
                         (Rosettana), ArchPF 24–25, 1976, 137–155.
ORF                      H. Malcovati, Oratorum Romanorum fragmenta
                         liberae rei publicae, 4. Aufl., Aug. Taurinorum 1976.
Orrieux (1983)           Cl. Orrieux, Les papyrus de Zenon, Paris 1983.
Orth (1977)              W. Orth, Königlicher Machtanspruch und
                         städtische Freiheit, München 1977 (= Münchner
                         Beiträge zur Papyrusforschung und Antiken
                         Rechtsgeschichte, 71).
Otto, E. (1964)          E. Otto, Gott und Mensch nach den ägyptischen
                         Tempelinschriften der griechisch-römischen Zeit,
                         Heidelberg 1964 (= Abh Heidelberg, Jg. 1964, 1).
Otto, W. I (1905)        W. Otto, Priester und Tempel im hellenistischen
      II (1908)          Ägypten, I–II, Leipzig 1905–1908.
Otto, W. (1928)          W. Otto, Beiträge zur Seleukidengeschichte des
                         3. Jh. v. Chr., München 1928 (= Abh München,
                         34, 1).
Otto, W. (1934)          W. Otto, Zur Geschichte der Zeit des 6. Ptolemäers,
                         München 1934 (= AbhMünchen, N.F., 11).
Otto, Bengtson          W. Otto, H. Bengtson, Zur Geschichte des
    (1938)               Niederganges des Ptolemäerreiches. Ein Beitrag
                         zur Regierungszeit des 8. und des 9. Ptolemäers,
                         München 1938 (= AbhMünchen, N.F., 17).

Paci (1989)              G. Paci, Per la storia del dominio tolemaico in
                         Cirenaica: nuovo basamento in onore dei dinasti
                         alessandrini dall'agorà di Cirene, in Egitto (1989),
                         583–593.
Parmentier (1987)        A. Parmentier, Phoenicians in the administra-
                         tion of Ptolemaic Cyprus, Studia Phoenicia 5,
                         1987, 403–412.
Passoni Dell'Acqua       A. Passoni Dell'Acqua, Le testimonianze
    (1986)               papiracee relative alla 'Siria e Fenicia' in età
                         tolemaica (i papiri di Zenone e le ordonanze reali),
                         Rivista Biblica Italiana 34, 1986, 233–283.
PCZ                      Catalogue général des Antiquités égyptiennes du
                         Musée du Caire. Zenon Papyri, ed.: C. C. Edgar,
                         5 Bde., Le Caire 1925–1940.
Pelling (1988)           C. B. R. Pelling, Plutarch. Life of Antony, Cam-
                         bridge 1988 (die Untergliederung der Kapitel
                         folgt dieser Ausgabe).
Peremans (1973)          W. Peremans, Égyptiens et étrangers dans le
                         clergé, le notariat et les tribunaux de l'Égypte
                         ptolemaïque, AncSoc 4, 1973, 59–69.

Peremans (1975)   W. Peremans, Ptolémée IV et les Égyptiens, in Le monde grec, FS Cl. Préaux, ed.: J. Bingen u. a., Bruxelles 1975, 393–402.

Peremans (1978)   W. Peremans, Les revolutions égyptiennes sous les Lagides, in Ptol.Äg. (1978), 39–50.

Peremans (1980/81)   W. Peremans, Étrangers et égyptiens en Égypte sous le règne de Ptolémée Ier, AncSoc 11/12, 1980/81, 213–226.

Peremans (1983)   W. Peremans, Le bilinguisme dans les relations gréco-égyptiennes sous les Lagides, in Egypt (1983), 253–280.

Pestman (1965)   P. W. Pestman, Harmachis et Anchmachis, deux rois indigènes du temps des Ptolémées, ChronEg 40, 1965, 157–170.

Pestman (1967)   P. W. Pestman, Chronologie égyptienne d'après les textes démotiques (332 av. J.-C. –453 ap. J.-C.), Leiden 1967 (= P. L. Bat., 15).

Pestman (1977)   P. W. Pestman, Recueil de textes démotiques et bilingues, I–III, Leiden 1977.

Pestman (1980)   P. W. Pestman, Greek and Demotic texts from the Zenon Archive, 2 Bde., Leiden 1980 (= P. L. Bat., 20).

Pestman (1981)   P. W. Pestman, A guide to the Zenon Archive, 2 Bde., Leiden 1981 (= P. L. Bat., 21).

PM   B. Porter, R. L. B. Moss, Topographical bibliography of ancient Egyptian hieroglyphic texts, reliefs and paintings, 7 Bde., Oxford 1927–52, 2. Aufl. 1960ff.

P. Oxy.   The Oxyrhynchus Papyri, ed. B. P. Grenfell, A. S. Hunt u. a., London 1898ff. (noch nicht abgeschlossen).

PPI–IX   W. Peremans, E. Van 't Dack, Prosopographia Ptolemaica, I–IX, Lovanii 1950–81 (= Studia Hellenistica, 6. 8. 11.–13. 17. 20. 21. 25.).

Préaux (1936)   C. Préaux, Esquisse d'une histoire des révolutions égyptiennes sous les Lagides, ChronEg 11, 1936, 522–552.

Préaux, I (1978)   C. Préaux, Le monde hellénistique. La Grèce et
    II (1988)   l'Orient (323–146 av. J.-C.), I, Paris 1978, II, 2. Aufl., Paris 1988 (= Nouvelle Clio, 6).

PSI   Papiri greci e latini. Pubblicazioni della Società Italiana per la ricerca dei Papiri greci e latini in Egitto, Firenze 1912ff.

Ptol.Äg. (1978)   Das ptolemäische Ägypten. Akten des internationalen Symposions 27.–29. Sept. 1976 in

Berlin, hrsg. v. H. Maehler u. V. M. Strocka, Mainz 1978.

Quaegebeur (1971, 1)    J. Quaegebeur, Documents concerning a cult of Arsinoe Philadelphos at Memphis, JNES 30, 1971, 239–270.

Quaegebeur (1971, 2)    J. Quaegebeur, Ptolémée II en adoration devant Arsinoé II divinisée, BIFAO 69, 1971, 191–217.

Quaegebeur (1978)    J. Quaegebeur, Reines ptolémaïques et traditions égyptiennes, in Ptol.Äg. (1978), 245–262.

Quaegebeur (1979)    J. Quaegebeur, Documents égyptiens et rôle économique du clergé en Egypte hellénistique, in State and Temple Economy in the Ancient Near East, II, Louvain 1979, 707–729 (= OLA, 6).

Quaegebeur (1980)    J. Quaegebeur, The genealogy of the Memphite high priest family in the Hellenistic period, in D. J. Crawford u. a., Studies on Ptolemaic Memphis, Lovanii 1980, 43–81 (= Studia Hellenistica, 24).

Quaegebeur (1988)    J. Quaegebeur, Cleopatra VII and the cults of the Ptolemaic queens, in Cleopatra's Egypt (1988), 41–54.

Quaegebeur (1989, 1)    J. Quaegebeur, The Egyptian clergy and the cult of the Ptolemaic dynasty, AncSoc 20, 1989, 93–115.

Quaegebeur (1989, 2)    J. Quaegebeur, Une scène historique méconnue au grand temple d'Edfou, in Egitto (1989), 595–608.

Quaegebeur (1991)    J. Quaegebeur, Cléopâtre VII et le temple de Dendara, GöttMisz 120, 1991, 49–72.

Quirke, Andrews (1988)    S. Quirke, C. Andrews, The Rosetta Stone. Facsimile drawing with an introduction and translations, London 1988.

Ray (1976)    J. D. Ray, The Archive of Hor, London 1976.

Ray (1978)    J. D. Ray, Observations on the Archive of Hor, JEA 64, 1978, 113–120.

RE    Pauly's Realencyclopädie der classischen Altertumswissenschaft, Stuttgart 1893–1978.

RecTrav    Recueil de travaux rélatifs à la philologie et à l'archéologie égyptiennes et assyriennes, Paris.

Reinhold (1981/2)    M. Reinhold, The declaration of war against Cleopatra, CIQ 77, 1981/2, 97–103.

Reinhold (1988)    M. Reinhold, From republic to principate. An historical commentary on Cassius Dio's *Roman History* books 49–52 (36–29 BC), Atlanta 1988.

Reymond (1981)　　　E. A. E. Reymond, From the records of a priestly family from Memphis, Wiesbaden 1981 (= Ägyptologische Abhandlungen, 38).

Ricketts (1980)　　　L. M. Ricketts, The administration of Ptolemaic Egypt under Cleopatra VII, Diss. Univ. Minnesota, Ann Arbor 1980.

Ricketts (1982/3)　　L. M. Ricketts, The epistrategos Kallimachos and a Koptite inscription: SB V 8036 reconsidered, AncSoc 13/14, 1982/3, 161–165.

Ritter (1965)　　　H.-W. Ritter, Diadem und Königsherrschaft. Untersuchungen zu Zeremonien und Rechtsgrundlagen des Herrschaftsantritts bei den Persern, bei Alexander dem Großen und im Hellenismus, München 1965 (= Vestigia, 7).

Roeder (1959)　　　G. Roeder, Die ägyptische Götterwelt, Zürich 1959.

Roeder (1960)　　　G. Roeder, Kulte, Orakel und Naturverehrung im alten Ägypten, Zürich 1960.

Rostovtzeff, I–II (1955)　M. Rostovtzeff, Die hellenistische Welt.
　　　III (1956)　　Gesellschaft und Wirtschaft, I–III, Tübingen 1955–56.

Rowe (1946)　　　A. Rowe, Discovery of the famous temple and enclosure of Serapis at Alexandria, Le Caire 1946 (= Suppl. aux ASAE, 2).

Rübsam (1974)　　　W. J. R. Rübsam, Götter und Kulte im Faijum während der griechisch-römisch-byzantinischen Zeit, Marburg/Lahn 1974.

Samuel (1962)　　　A. E. Samuel, Ptolemaic chronology, München 1962 (= Münchner Beiträge zur Papyrusforschung und Antiken Rechtsgeschichte, 43).

Samuel (1989)　　　A. E. Samuel, The shifting sands of history: interpretations of Ptolemaic Egypt, Lanham 1989 (= Publications of the Association of Ancient Historians, 2).

SB　　　　　　Sammelbuch griechischer Urkunden aus Ägypten, I–XVI, 1913–88 (durchgezählte Numerierung).

Schachermeyr (1970)　F. Schachermeyr, Alexander in Babylon und die Reichsordnung nach seinem Tode, Wien 1970 (= SbWien 268, 3).

Schmitt (1964)　　　H. H. Schmitt, Untersuchungen zur Geschichte Antiochos' des Großen und seiner Zeit, Wiesbaden 1964 (= Historia, Einzelschr., 6).

Schmitt (1969)　　　H. H. Schmitt, Die Staatsverträge des Altertums, III, München 1969.

SEG — Supplementum epigraphicum Graecum, Leiden 1923ff.

Seibert (1967) — J. Seibert, Historische Beiträge zu den dynastischen Verbindungen in hellenistischer Zeit, Wiesbaden 1967 (= Historia, Einzelschr. 10).

Seibert (1969) — J. Seibert, Untersuchungen zur Geschichte Ptolemaios' I, München 1969 (= Münchner Beiträge zur Papyrusforschung und Antiken Rechtsgeschichte, 56).

Seibert (1981) — J. Seibert, Alexander der Große, Darmstadt 1972 (2., unver. Aufl. 1981) (= Erträge der Forschung, 10).

Seibert (1983) — J. Seibert, Das Zeitalter der Diadochen, Darmstadt 1983 (= Erträge der Forschung, 185).

Seibert (1985) — J. Seibert, Die Eroberung des Perserreiches durch Alexander den Großen auf kartographischer Grundlage, Wiesbaden 1985 (= Beihefte zum Tübinger Atlas des Vorderen Orients, R. B, 68).

Seibert (1991) — J. Seibert, Zur Begründung von Herrschaftsanspruch und Herrschaftslegitimierung in der frühen Diadochenzeit, in Hellenistische Studien, Gedenkschrift f. H. Bengtson, München 1991, 87–100.

Seidl (1962) — E. Seidl, Ptolemäische Rechtsgeschichte, 2. Aufl., Glückstadt 1962 (= Ägyptologische Forschungen, 22).

Sethe (1917) — K. Sethe, Die historische Bedeutung des 2. Philä-Dekrets aus der Zeit des Ptolemaios Epiphanes, ZÄS 53, 1917, 35–40.

Shatzman (1971) — I. Shatzman, The Egyptian question in Roman politics (59–54 BC), Latomus 30, 1971, 363–369.

SIRIS — L. Vidman, Sylloge inscriptionum religionis Isiacae et Sarapiacae, Berlin 1969 (= Religionsgeschichtliche Versuche und Vorarbeiten, 28).

Skeat (1969) — Th. C. Skeat, The reigns of the Ptolemies, 2. Aufl., München 1969 (= Münchner Beiträge zur Papyrusforschung und Antiken Rechtsgeschichte, 39).

Smith, H. S. (1972) — H. S. Smith, Dates of the obsequies of the mothers of Apis, REg 24, 1972, 176–179, Tabelle 1–8.

Smith, R. R. R. (1988) — R. R. R. Smith, Hellenistic royal portraits, Oxford 1988.

Sonnabend (1986) — H. Sonnabend, Fremdenbild und Politik. Vorstellungen der Römer von Ägypten und dem

Partherreich in der späten Republik und frühen Kaiserzeit, Frankfurt/Main 1986.

Spiegelberg (1904)
(1932)
W. Spiegelberg, Die demotischen Denkmäler, I, Leipzig 1904; III, Berlin 1932.

Spiegelberg (1922)
W. Spiegelberg, Der demotische Text der Priesterdekrete von Kanopus und Memphis (Rosettana), Heidelberg 1922; Nachdr.: Hildesheim 1990.

Spiegelberg, Otto (1926)
W. Spiegelberg, W. Otto, Eine neue Urkunde zu der Siegesfeier des Ptolemaios IV. und die Frage der ägyptischen Priestersynoden: SBMünchen, Jg. 1926, 2. Abh.

Sullivan (1990)
R. D. Sullivan, Near Eastern royalty and Rome, 100–30 BC, Toronto 1990.

Swinnen (1973)
W. Swinnen, Sur la politique religieuse de Ptolémée I$^{er}$, in Les syncrétismes dans les religions Grecque et Romaine, Paris 1973, 115–133.

Syll. I–IV$^3$
W. Dittenberger, Sylloge inscriptionum Graecarum, I–IV, 3. Aufl., Leipzig 1915–1924.

Taeger, I (1957)
II (1960)
F. Taeger, Charisma. Studien zur Geschichte des antiken Herrscherkultes, I–II, Stuttgart 1957–60.

TAM
Tituli Asiae Minoris, Iff., Vindobonae 1901ff.

Thissen (1966)
H.-J. Thissen, Studien zum Raphiadekret, Meisenheim/Gl. 1966 (= Beiträge zur Klassischen Philologie, 23).

Thomas (1975)
J. D. Thomas, The epistrategos in Ptolemaic and Roman Egypt, I: The Ptolemaic epistrategos, Opladen 1975 (= Papyrologica Coloniensia, 6).

Thompson, D. B. (1973)
D. B. Thompson, Ptolemaic oinochoai and portraits in faience. Aspects of the ruler-cult, Oxford 1973.

Thompson, D. J. (1988)
D. J. Thompson, Memphis under the Ptolemies, Princeton 1988.

Thompson, D. J. (1989)
D. J. Thompson, Pausanias and protocol: The succession to Euergetes II, in Egitto (1989), 693–701.

Thompson, M. (1964)
M. Thompson, Ptolemy Philometor and Athens, MusNotAmNumSoc 11, 1964, 119–129.

Török (1986)
L. Török, Der meroitische Staat, I, Berlin 1986 (= Meroitica, 9).

Török (1988)
L. Török, Geschichte Meroes, in ANRW II, 10, 1 (1988), 107–341.

Tondriau (1946)
J. Tondriau, Les thiases dionysiaques royaux de la cour ptolémaïque, ChronEg 21, 41–42, 1946, 149–171.

Tondriau (1948, 1)         J. Tondriau, Princesses ptolémaïques comparées
                           ou identifiées à des déesses (IIIᵉ–Iᵉʳ siècles avant
                           J. C.), Bulletin de la Société Royale d'Archéologie
                           – Alexandrie 37, 1948, 12–33.

Tondriau (1948, 2)         J. Tondriau, Rois lagides comparés ou identifiés
                           à des divinités, ChronEg 23, 45–46, 1948, 127–
                           146.

tondriau (1950)            J. Tondriau, La dynastie ptolémaïque et la reli-
                           gion dionysiaque, ChronEg 25, 49–50, 1950,
                           283–316.

Tondriau (1953)            J. Tondriau, Dionysos, dieu royal: du Bacchos
                           tauromorphe    primitif    aux    souverains
                           hellénistiques Neoi Dionysoi, AlPhOr 12, 1952
                           (1953), 441–466 (= Mél. H. Grégoire).

Tory (1986)                L. Troy, Patterns of Queenship in ancient Egyptian
                           myth and history, Uppsala 1986 (= Boreas, 14).


UPZ                        U. Wilcken, Urkunden der Ptolemäerzeit (ältere
                           Funde), I–II, Berlin 1927–57.

Urk. II                    K. Sethe, Hieroglyphische Urkunden der
                           griechisch-römischen Zeit, 1–3, Leipzig 1904–
                           1916 (= Urkunden des aegyptischen Altertums,
                           begr. v. G. Steindorff, Abt. II).


Van 't Dack (1973)         E. Van 't Dack, Les commandants de place lagides
                           à Théra, AncSoc 4, 1973, 71–90 (= Van 't Dack,
                           1988, 124–145).

Van 't Dack (1981)         E. Van 't Dack, Le proplème des commandants
                           de place lagides à Théra réexaminé, in Scritti in
                           onore di O. Montevecchi, hrsg. v. E. Bresciani u.
                           a., Bologna 1981, 419–429 (= Van 't Dack,
                           1988, 146–156).

Van 't Dack (1983, 1)      E. Van 't Dack, L'armée romaine d'Égypte de 55
                           à 30 av. J.-C., in Das römisch-byzantinische
                           Ägypten. Akten des internationalen Symposions
                           26.–30. Sept. 1978 in Trier, Mainz 1983, 19–
                           29 (= Aegyptiaca Treverensia, 2) (= id., 1988,
                           185–213).

Van 't Dack (1983, 2)      E. Van 't Dack, Encore le problème de Ptolémée
                           Eupator, in Althistorische Studien, FS H.
                           Bengtson, hrsg. v. H. Heinen u. a., Wiesbaden
                           1983, 103–115 (= Van 't Dack, 1988, 157–174).

Van 't Dack (1983, 3)      E. Van 't Dack, Les relations entre l'Égypte
                           ptolémaïque et l'Italie, in Egypt (1983), 383–
                           406.

Van 't Dack (1988)  E. Van 't Dack, Ptolemaica selecta, Lovanii 1988 (= Studia Hellenistica, 29).

Van 't Dack u. a. (1989)  E. Van 't Dack u. a., The Judean-Syrian-Egyptian conflict of 103–101 BC A multilingual dossier concerning a 'war of scepters', Brussel 1989 (= Collectanea Hellenistica, 1).

Van 't Dack, Hauben (1978)  E. Van 't Dack, H. Hauben, L'Apport égyptien à l'armée navale lagide, in Ptol.Äg. (1978), 59–94.

Vandorpe (1986)  K. Vandorpe, The Chronology of the reigns of Hurgonaphor and Chaonnophris, ChronEg 61, 122, 1986, 294–302.

Vandorpe (1988)  K. Vandorpe, Der früheste Beleg eines Strategen der Thebais als Epistrategen, ZPE 73, 1988, 47–50.

Vittmann (1981)  G. Vittmann, Zu den ägyptischen Wiedergaben von 'Eupator', GöttMisz 46, 1981, 21–26.

Volkmann (1959)  H. Volkmann: RE XXIII, 2, 1959, 1592–1767 (s. v. Ptolemaios, Nr. 1–61).

Wace u. a. (1959)  A. J. B. Wace u. a., Hermopolis Magna, Ashmunein, The Ptolemaic sanctuary and the basilica, Alexandria 1959.

Walbank, I (1957)  F. W. Walbank, A historical commentary on
     II (1967)  Polybius, I–III, Oxford 1957–79.
     III (1979)

Walbank (1980)  F. W. Walbank, The surrender of the Egyptian rebels in the Nile Delta (Polyb. XXII, 17, 1–7), in φιλίας χάριν. Miscellanea di studi classici in onore di E. Manni, VI, Roma 1980, 2187–2197.

Wb  Wörterbuch der ägyptischen Sprache, hrsg. v. A. Erman u. H. Grapow, 6 Bde., Berlin 1926–31, 2. Aufl. 1957.

Whitehorne (1994)  J. Whitehorne, Cleopatras, London 1994 (konnte für das vorliegende Buch nicht mehr benützt werden).

Wilcken (1895)  U. Wilcken: RE II, 1, 1895, 1281–1289 (s. v. Arsinoe, Nr. 25–28).

Wilcken (1928)  U. Wilcken, Alexanders Zug in die Oase Siwa, SbBerlin Jg. 1928, 576–603.

Wild (1981)  R. A. Wild, Water in the cultic worship of Isis and Sarapis, Leiden 1981 (= EPRO, 87).

Will, I (1979)  E. Will, Historie politique du monde
     II (1982)  hellénistique (323–30 av. J.-C.), I–II, 2. Aufl., Nancy 1979–1982.

| | |
|---|---|
| Will u. a. (1990) | E. Will u. a., Le monde grec et l'Orient, II, 3. Aufl., Paris 1990. |
| Winkler (1933) | H. Winkler, Rom und Aegypten im 2. Jahrhundert v. Chr., Leipzig 1933. |
| Winnicki (1989) (1991, 1) | J. K. Winnicki, Militäroperationen von Ptolemaios I. und Seleukos I. in Syrien in den Jahren 312–311 v. Chr., I–II, AncSoc 20, 1989, 55–92; 22, 1991, 147–227. |
| Winnicki (1990) | J. K. Winnicki, Bericht von einem Feldzug des Ptolemaios Philadelphos in der Pithom-Stele, JJurP 20, 1990, 157–167. |
| Winnicki (1991, 1) | S. Winnicki (1989). |
| Winnicki (1991, 2) | J. K. Winnicki, Der zweite syrische Krieg im Lichte des demotischen Karnak-Ostrakons und der griechischen Papyri des Zenon-Archivs, JJurP 21, 1991, 87–104. |
| Winter (1978) | E. Winter, Der Herrscherkult in den ägyptischen Ptolemäertempeln, in Ptol.Äg. (1978), 147–160. |
| Winter (1981) | E. Winter, Ergamenes II, seine Datierung und seine Bautätigkeit in Nubien, MDIK 37, 1981, 509–513. |
| Wörrle (1977) | M. Wörrle, Epigraphische Forschungen zur Geschichte Lykiens, I: Ptolemaios I. und Limyra, Chiron 7, 1977, 43–66. |
| Wörrle (1978) | M. Wörrle, Epigraphische Forschungen zur Geschichte Lykiens, II: Ptolemaios II. und Telmessos, Chiron 8, 1978, 201–246. |
| Wörrle (1979) | M. Wörrle, Epigraphische Forschungen zur Geschichte Lykiens, III: Ein hellenistischer Königsbrief aus Telmessos, Chiron 9, 1979, 83–111. |
| Zauzich (1983) | K.-Th. Zauzich, Die demotischen Papyri von der Insel Elephantine, in Egypt (1983), 421–435. |

# Introduction

Any account of a specific period of ancient Egyptian history seeking to respect the perspective of the Egyptians themselves must take into consideration the relevant religious conditions and developments. Political and religious-cultural events were always mutually dependent, closely connected and affected by one another. This fact is one of the most striking features of ancient Egyptian history from the beginning of the dynastic era in *c.* 3000 BC to the end of Egyptian religion *per se* in late Roman times. The historical events are crystallized in the person of the king who, by virtue of holding the throne, appeared as 'Horus' (i.e. the earthly form of this god) and as the 'son of Re'. The king was, therefore, primarily defined in religious terms; his activities are basically cultic actions whose purpose is to construct anew and preserve continually the world order (Maat) which was brought about by the Creator. The cultic activities in the temples did as much to protect this order as did the defeat of an external foe; for there was virtually no difference in how they were conceived. Consequently, the highest political authority of the country is at the same time its foremost religious representative, and, by virtue of his office, is the only one capable of associating with the gods and mediating between the human and divine worlds. The ancient Egyptian king is, in this regard, the only true priest, while the other priests are merely his deputies whose task is to carry out the required cultic duties.

Given that the maintenance of order depended on the existence of a legitimate pharaoh, the Egyptians were obliged to recognize the prevailing ruler as their Horus-King, for as long as he could not be replaced by another king. Conversely, foreign rulers also had to assume the religious role of the pharaoh, if they were to secure their success. This holds true both for the Persian kings as well as for the Roman emperors. Alexander the Great and the Ptolemies took particular care to act as cultically relevant kings and, thus, gain acceptance (whenever possible) as the central figure of Egyptian religion. One can say, therefore, that the state system of an absolute monarchy controlled in all matters by the king, as exemplified by the Ptolemaic (and Seleukid) empire, corresponded in great measure to the ancient Egyptian ideology of the king.

Like the king, his subordinates in the administration of the state were defined in equal measure in both religious-cultic and political terms. Throughout history, the priesthoods represented not only an extraordinary spiritual concentration of power but an economic one as well. The internal development from the eighteenth dynasty to the end of the so-called Third Intermediate Period (in the late eighth century) was characterized by continuous conflict between the priesthoods and the king for hegemony. During the late Ramesside period, a state-within-a state was created in Thebes under the political, military and spiritual leadership of the high priest of Amun. The so-called 'Divine State' of Amun marked the high point of political power for the Theban priesthood, while in the north a weak king of the twenty-first dynasty ruled in Tanis. This was the last phase of development carried out by the Egyptians in a purely political sense.

Afterwards, a series of kings of Libyan descent followed as the twenty-second to the twenty-fourth dynasties, roughly from the middle of the tenth century until the late eighth century. While Libyans had for centuries pushed their way or filtered into Egypt or were settled there after suffering defeat, they maintained their old tribal structures. The first Libyan tribal chief of this sort was a certain Sheshonk (I). Sheshonk and those who followed him succeeded gradually in assuming pharaonic honours and even maintaining an ideological continuity with the past (especially through marriage). The Libyan component of the population would from then on become the major political element of the ancient Egyptian nation. The Libyans were so strongly Egyptianized that they were not perceived as being foreign rulers.

The first military conquest of the Late Egyptian Period began in Nubia: Piankhi established sovereignty; his brother and successor Shabaka secured direct control of the twenty-fifth dynasty in Egypt. Although Nubia and its royalty had been thoroughly imbued with Egyptian culture, these kings also sought to achieve complete cultic legitimization as pharaohs. A number of such measures marked the political ideology of Piankhi: the bestowal of authority by Amun; after the seizure of every city, religious celebrations were held in order to secure the benevolence of the gods (i.e. in reality, the goodwill of the local priesthoods); the performance of the royal ritual in Memphis (temple of Ptah) and Heliopolis, which amounted to a coronation. Piankhi, in the manner of a 'great king', allowed the Libyan 'kings' to continue in Egypt, but the supremacy of the twenty-fifth dynasty was continually exposed to Libyan opposition in the north.

Egypt of the twenty-fifth dynasty fell victim to the Assyrian empire in the seventh century. For the first time, Egypt was placed under the sovereignty of an Asian world power; the ruler lived outside the country and showed no interest in becoming pharaoh. For this reason, the Egyptian lists of kings recognize no Assyrian period. The Egyptians benefited from their remote location as well as from the deserts of the Arab region and the Levant, because these served to screen the land of the Nile from the centre of the Assyrian empire. In the long run, even the Assyrian kings could not

afford to finance the costly distant expeditions necessary for Egypt's subjugation. As a result, Assurbanipal took appropriate measures by setting on the
throne the kings of the twenty-sixth dynasty, Necho and his son Psamtik I.

The new dynasty, clearly of Libyan descent, with its base in Sais (hence
the Saite dynasty), occasioned a national renaissance for Egypt, especially in
the cultural domain. With the fall of the Assyrian empire in the seventh
century, the Asian policy had also failed. Nevertheless, the Saites felt themselves bound to the very end to the Assyrian empire, and had wished to
maintain it as a buffer-state. Its demise, however, now caused Egypt to turn
its gaze more and more often to the Mediterranean and the Greeks. King
Amasis (570–526) was perceived as a particularly good friend of the Greeks;
he bestowed the legal status of a polis upon the Greek settlement in Naucratis
(in the Delta). At that time, Cyprus belonged to the Egyptian empire and an
agreement of friendship existed with Cyrene.

This active, economically driven policy in the Mediterranean was interrupted as a result of Egypt's subjugation at the hands of the Persian king,
Cambyses (525). Egypt became a satrapy of the Persian empire. Much had
changed since the Assyrian period: the Persian empire had far greater economic and military resources at its disposal, allowing it to introduce the
land of the Nile country permanently into its world empire. Egypt was,
moreover, directly administered by the Persians, following the model of the
other satrapies. A historically farsighted and successful political arrangement
was instituted following the Persian incursion: the 'Great King of all foreign
lands', presumed a priori to be the enemy of Egypt, was now made the
Egyptian king. This solution made him responsible for the well-being of
the people, and particularly for the management of the cults and the gods.
The priest of Neit and physician, Uzahorresneit, well known from his statue
in the Vatican, was able to persuade Cambyses of his ideological duty. The
former composed a royal titulary and organized the solemn entry of the
Persian king into Sais as pharaoh. In this way, Uzahorresneit did much to
protect Egypt not only by keeping it from being plundered but also by
bringing the culture and political structures of Egypt into line with the
times.

Despite this successful tactic, Cambyses subsequently underestimated the
power of the local priesthoods; instead of providing them with endowments
or initiating building projects, he actually reduced their revenues. The priests
reacted to this by branding Cambyses as a moral transgressor and criminal.
His successor, Darius I (522–486), already acquainted with Egypt from
earlier times, learned from these mistakes. He sought a reconciliation with
the priesthoods and even erected the magnificent temple to Amun of Hibis
in the El Karga oasis. As a result, Darius I the Great went down in history
as a virtuous and esteemed pharaoh. The fact that he was a foreign ruler,
ruling Egypt from afar most of the time, was of little moment. His reputation and acceptance stemmed from the fact that he had fulfilled the requirements of the Egyptian office of king in both religious and ideological terms.

The successors of Darius, however, paid scant attention to these matters; the result was that the priests sought revenge by means of character assassination.

Shortly before 400, a Libyan dynast by the name of Amyrtaeus (404–399), finally succeeded in wresting Egypt from the Persians and bringing about a lasting period of national independence. A dynastic crisis in the Achaemenid empire assured its success. In the eyes of the Persians, Egypt had always been a rebellious satrapy in the period treated in the king-lists as the twenty-ninth and thirtieth dynasties – with Amyrtaeus counting as the twenty-eighth dynasty. Egypt held its ground against four failed Persian attempts at reconquest only with the continuous aid of the Greeks and by adopting a very complex policy with respect to Greece. Internal stability could only be maintained by those kings who expected no concessions from the priesthoods and who made a name for themselves by building places of worship and promoting animal cults in particular. Nectanebo I (380–362) and II (361/60–343) were especially active in this regard. Nectanebo II was considered the last native king and went down in history because of a victory over the Great King. Alexander the Great was then able to establish a direct ideological connection to the last king.[1]

With the Persian invasion of 343, Egypt finally capitulated. As before, Artaxerxes III and Darius III paid not the slightest attention to any sort of pharaonic duties. The regime was, therefore, completely spurned, but for dating purposes they could not avoid placing Darius III's name in the royal cartouche.

It is worth pointing out that many basic elements of Ptolemaic society, politics and religion were already present before the Hellenistic period, though the emphasis placed on them and their relative importance changed with time. In politics, such points of similarity were the fact that membership in the great empire was rejected, measures in the Near East were determined by a need for safety, a distinct policy was adopted with respect to Greece, the relationship with Cyprus and Cyrenaica was privileged.[2] In terms of its inhabitants, since the time of the Saite dynasty Egypt increasingly had begun to take on 'two faces'.[3] Owing to its close relationship with Greece, along with the influx of Greek soldiers and tradespeople, the Hellenistic element became ever stronger in Egypt; Greeks could even penetrate into the administrative bureaucracy.[4] The Greek military leaders had more and more influence on the last native kings in questions of national defence. In this manner, the ground was slowly laid for the later dominance of the Greeks as the country's elite. With regard to religion, the Greeks had delved into Egyptian religion for some time and even revered some Egyptian gods, in particular Osiris-Apis (Ὀσορᾶπις or the like) in Memphis.

Conversely, Greek temples could be found in Naucrautis, and King Amasis – here too a forerunner of the Ptolemies – dedicated votive offerings at Greek sanctuaries.

A clear line of continuity can be traced then from Saite Egypt to the last native dynasties and finally to the Ptolemaic period. During the Hellenistic era, as pharaoh and basileus the king – now of Macedonian stock – joined together in his person by his twofold legal position the two main character-istics of the empire. In the one capacity, he is seen offering to the ancient Egyptian gods on temple reliefs and, in the other, he becomes himself an object of cult within Hellenistic ruler-worship.[5]

## Notes

1  See p. 78f. on the titulature and the Alexander Romance. King Khababash was able to pull Egypt out of the Great Empire for a short time during the second period of Persian rule (winter 337/6 to winter 336/5); there is even evidence for him from an Apis burial. Nonethetheless, he is passed over in the official history, although the Satrap Stele (see p. 83f.) emphasized that he was a good and legitimate king.
2  See p. 28.
3  I use the expression 'two faces' ('Doppelgesichtigkeit') here in memory of the master of Austrian scholarship, Fritz Schachermeyr. A few days before his death (December 1987), Schachermeyr repeatedly used this term in discussions on this topic with me and the phrase nicely illustrates his characteristic accuracy.
4  Falivene (1991), 205.
5  At this point, the reader is referred to two general, recent works on Hellenistic history which are particularly important: Will, I–II (1979–82); Green (1990). Otherwise, see the bibliography in Gehrke (1990), 215–263 which has been categorized thematically. Specific topics of every kind can be found in *Der Kleine Pauly. Lexicon der Antike in fünf Bänden*, Munich 1975 (paperback edition 1979) and in the LÄ. I almost always follow the terminology used in both lexica; see the prefacing remark to the list of abbreviations and references.

# Part I

# The beginning and the golden age of Ptolemaic rule

Part II

The beginning and
the golden age of
Ptolemaic rule

# 1 Alexander the Great and Ptolemy I Soter (332–282)

## ALEXANDER AND EGYPT (332–323)

After his great victory at Issos in November 333, Alexander the Great conquered Tyre in 332 following a seven month-long siege. Afterwards, he moved southwards with his army against Egypt. Only Gaza put up two months of stubborn resistance. From there, after marching for several days in the desert, Alexander reached the border fortress of Pelusion, where without encountering any resistance, he set up a garrison. Egypt was drained of troops because the satrap had gone with a large levy to Issos and he himself fell there (Arr. *An.* II.11.8). The commander of the rest of the armed forces, Mazakes, who had been made satrap by the Great King himself after Issos, could not contemplate resistance. He therefore received Alexander in a friendly manner and handed the country over to him (Arr. *An.* III.1.1–3).

Alexander's motives for not pursuing the Great King eastwards but instead turning toward the land of the Nile will have been manifold.[1] As the history of Persian Egypt showed, the establishment of a national dynasty was essential. The east-Mediterranean empire that Alexander had up to this point founded could be considered a complete entity, both from a political and an economic point of view (the latter on account of Egyptian grain export), only with the integration of Egypt. Furthermore, Alexander's grand design will slowly have come to encompass the idea that all peoples were to be subjugated for the formation of a new world order; for this purpose, the Egyptian pharaonic system presented a very suitable ideology that was well established and has been accepted for millennia.

In Egypt, therefore, Alexander observed the traditional protocol associated with a pharaoh's accession to power: he visited Heliopolis, the city of the sun god, and the capital, Memphis, where he sacrificed to the gods in the shrines and especially to the royal god, Apis, in the precinct of the temple of Ptah. Since, in Egypt, making offerings to the gods was taken to be a pharaoh's prerogative, it was an inextricable part of Alexander's accession as an Egyptian king, as the Alexander Romance reports (Ps. Kallisthenes I.34.1). Alexander did not take the time for an extravagant coronation ceremony, something which would have required rather elaborate preparations.[2] He nonetheless held athletic and musical contests following Greek tradition (Arr. *An*. III.1.3–4). After Alexander assumed power and until 323, official documents in Egypt were dated according to the year of his reign.

At the beginning of 331, the king went down the Canopic branch of the Nile with a small detachment of troops and gave orders for the founding of the city of Alexandria near the site of Rhakotis,[2a] probably an Egyptian settlement at an especially favourable location on the isthmus between the ocean and Lake Mariut. True to his nature, Alexander himself apparently laid out the plans for the most important streets on a grid system as well as the position of the market square and individual temples (Arr. *An*. III.1.4–5; cf. Ps. Kallisthenes I.31.5–32.6). The rest of the urban planning, however, was delegated to the architect Deinokrates of Rhodes (Vitr. II, *praef.* 4).[3] The foundation date for Alexandria was traditionally celebrated on the 25th of Tybi (Ps. Kallisthenes I.32.7); this fell on 7 April 331.[4] The new city rapidly became Egypt's gateway to the Mediterranean world, since it bound the Nile country completely to the network of commercial and political relations between Mediterranean peoples.

At the beginning of 331, even before the foundation date of the city, Alexander undertook his journey to the world-famous oracle of Amun (in Greek, Ammon or better still, Zeus-Ammon) in the Siwah oasis. He first went along the Libyan coast westwards towards Paraitonion (today, Marsa Matruh), where envoys from Cyrene brought gifts. Alexander formed a pact with them and in this way apparently guaranteed the city its independence as a free polis (Diod. XVII.49.2–3; Curt. IV.7.9).

At Siwah, Alexander wanted to ask the oracle both about the future and about his own personal nature, 'since he traced a part of his ancestry to Ammon, just as the myths traced the descent of Herakles and Perseus (fore-fathers of the Macedoniaian royal house of the Argeads) to Zeus' (Arr. *An*. III.3.2). As the analogy to both sons of Zeus shows, Alexander was probably not thinking of a distant lineage but of a father–son relationship. In any case, his motivation for the journey was explicitly to obtain more information on his birth (Arr. *An*. III.3.2.; cf. Curt. IV.7.8.), and, in view of the timely arrival in Memphis of the embassies from the oracle in Asia Minor[5] the objective of his expedition must have previously been discussed with Alexander. Nonetheless, Philip II was still then as before credited with being his mortal father.

Zeus-Ammon of Siwah and Cyrene, an offshoot of the Theban Amun, represented, furthermore, the best link to Macedonia in the cultic-religious domain: he was honoured in all of Greece as Libyan Ammon and had a cult from the late fifth century onwards in Macedonian Aphytis (Chalkidike), where the temple has been excavated;[6] Alexander was thus visiting the god in his original home.

Alexander's personal belief in his own divine nature easily harmonized with the Egyptian conception of the pharaoh as son of god. The title 'son of

Re' and the notion that the successor to the throne was begotten by Amun, an idea which was especially widespread in the New Kingdom, gave legitimacy to the idea that the king was divine and a representative of the gods on earth. No doubt the trip to Siwah was undertaken to have Alexander declared the son of Amun and thereby legitimize the Egyptian regal titles soon to be conferred on him.[7]

And so Alexander moved with his train (among whom was Ptolemy, who himself later wrote about the trip) from Paraitonion southwards through the desert; owing to divine providence, there was sufficient rainwater and the way was found (Arr. *An.* III.3.3–6).[8] Having reached Siwah, the companions had to remain outside of the temple of Amun-Re which lay on the hill of Aghurmi. Only Alexander himself was led into the inner sanctum, to the cult image, after one or several priests betook themselves into the secret chamber above the sanctuary (whose existence has since been confirmed by archaeologists) to listen to the questions put to the oracle. This was a kingly oracle and so it was carried out in accordance with ancient custom, in which the king alone could ask his questions of the godhead. Afterwards, Alexander will have been taken back by the priests and led into the neighbouring room. The high priest entered there and he greeted the king as son of Zeus (-Ammon), by which he explicitly indicated that what followed were the words of the god; then he announced to Alexander the rest of the oracle's words (Kallisthenes: FGrHist. 124 F 14 in Strabo XVII.1.43; Diod. XVII.51). Thereafter followed the public oracular procession for Alexander's companions: the boat with the aniconic image of Amun,[9] which was adorned (Diod. XVII.50.6) and similar to an umbilicus (Curt. IV.7.23), was carried by 80 priests from Aghurmi on the street going straight to the temple of Amun of Umm ʿUbayda which lay opposite it; in this way, the boat answered the various questions by means of corresponding movements.

Alexander could be well content with the oracular achievement of the priesthood of Amun of Siwah. He returned to Memphis and organized sacrifices in honour of 'Zeus Basileus' (i.e. to Amun as king of the gods) accompanied by a ceremonial parade of his troops as well as a second athletic and musical Agon (Arr. *An.* III.5.2). Alexander kept mostly to himself the revelations of the oracle, but not his ideologically significant status as son of god. There is evidence for two other questions put to the oracle (e.g. Plu. *Alex.* 27), but while these may not be as certain, they are that much more politically important. These had to do with the question of world domination and with the issue of whether the murder of Philip II had already been avenged; with the latter question, Alexander will have wished to free his mother from suspicion of having instigated the act. It is important to realize that soon after Alexander's return from Siwah, envoys from the oracle of Apollo at Didyma (near Miletus) and from the Sibyl at Erythrae arrived at the court in Memphis to confirm his divine birth (Kallisthenes: FGrHist. 124 F 14). It was no coincidence that all these events took place at the same time and so it follows naturally that these envoys had been given their orders already some time before the journey to Siwah and that Alexander had brought with him there the idea that he was the son of Zeus(-Ammon).[10]

Alexander had rearranged the administration of Egypt and in this he encouraged the separation of powers (Arr. *An.* III.5): two governors for civil matters, Doloaspis (perhaps an Iranian and already a functionary in the Persian administration) and the Egyptian Peteisis, were to have divided their responsibilities geographically (probably between Upper and Lower Egypt); a short time thereafter Peteisis resigned and Doloaspis took over the whole area. From this territory, both the western deserts with their oases and the eastern deserts including the eastern delta were separated off as their own administrative areas. The local nomarchs were expressly left to carry on in their functions. Conversely, the military command came under Macedonian control: two strategoi (Balakros and Peukestas) commanded the occupying forces which had been left behind; the garrison commanders of Memphis and Pelusion were probably subordinate to them.[11]

Kleomenes of Naucratis obtained the most important position: he took over the direct administration of the eastern border area of Arabia, had overall control of the finances of all of Egypt and was entrusted with the construction of Alexandria; it seems he was promoted to satrap with comprehensive powers fairly quickly.[12] In the matter of the collection of money, Kleomenes acted in the ensuing period with a great lack of consideration for the native inhabitants. It was no doubt the propaganda of his opponents, provoked by his corrupt conduct, that gave rise to the tradition that Kleomenes threatened to close the temples in order to be dissuaded by bribes (Arist. *oec.* II.2.33).[13] Complaints against him seem to have reached Alexander immediately (Arr. *An.* VII.23.6–8), but the king did not withdraw his favour.

In the first days of the spring of 331 (Arr. *An.* III.6.1), Alexander set out from Memphis on his campaign of conquest. Early in 323, Alexander returned to Babylon and died suddenly on 10 June 323 in the middle of hectic preparations for his ambitious plans (28 Daisios: Plu. *Alex.* 76.9). On his deathbed, he publicly expressed his desire to be buried in the Ammoneion of Siwah (Diod. XVIII.3.5).[14] He had handed over his royal signet ring to the highest-ranking general and somatophylax ('bodyguard') Perdikkas.

With the death of Alexander, who was nothing short of a fanatical autocrat, the enormous empire, unprepared for such an eventuality, lost its leadership. The feeble-minded half-brother of the dead king, Arrhidaios, was not capable of ruling; Roxane, daughter of a nobleman of Sogdiana, whom Alexander had married in 327 in her homeland, was expecting a child. The army and the generals, therefore, had to find an immediate solution. Thus, after settling disputes which had flared up, the *settlement at Babylon* (323)[15] was concluded.

At the very beginning of these deliberations, one of Alexander's best and most loyal friends, Ptolemy, presented a detailed and historically far-sighted model to the royal council: he suggested doing away with a mere token Argead kingdom and dividing the empire into loosely united satrap-states; a council of the satraps was occasionally to pass supra-regional resolutions

(Just. III.2.12; Curt. X.6.15). Ptolemy's proposal to break with tradition did not gain acceptance.

The military assembly eventually adopted the following resolution: Arrhidaios, who had just been acclaimed king by the infantry, was recognized as king under the name of Philip, and the unborn child of Roxane, if he were male, would be named joint king. A triumvirate took over the government. Antipatros, the erstwhile confidant of Philip II, whom Alexander had left behind in Macedonia as regent, was to continue to rule as the autonomous strategos of Europe. Perdikkas, by virtue of his role as chiliarch,[16] i.e. as commander of the royal cavalry, then took over the supreme command of the remaining royal army. The third member was Krateros, a reliable field commander, who was at that time in Cilicia because Alexander had given him the task of relieving Antipatros and leading the veterans back to Macedonia; he was chosen to act as the representative of the crown (*prostates*) and of the alleged final wishes of the king.[17] The satrapies were to be divided among the highest-ranking philoi and somatophylakes of the dead king (Dio. XVIII.2.4); the body of Alexander, in accordance with his own wishes, was prepared for conveyance to the Siwah oasis (Just. XIII.4.6).[18]

A few months later, Roxane gave birth to a son, who was named Alexander and, as had been planned by the military assembly, was acclaimed joint king. In Egypt, the 'pharaonic' monuments and papyrological documents now bore the names of absentee token-kings who were never crowned; first there was the 'pharaoh' Philippos III (323 until the beginning of 316) and then there was Alexandros IV (316 until the beginning of 304).[19]

The settlement at Babylon was far from being a solution to the fundamental problems of the empire. Perdikkas took over temporarily the *prostasia* of the absent Krateros; it became a permanent condition and this elevated him to regent with sweeping powers (Epimeletes: Diod. XVIII.2.4). His jurisdiction over the satraps remained unclear. The tension between the original idea of maintaining a centrally controlled greater empire and the endeavours of some successors to rule their own areas independently and wherever possible to expand their territories was a decisive factor in the clashes of the years to come.

In the division of the satrapies, Ptolemy was allotted the best share, namely Egypt, which was rich and, because of its location, virtually independent; the acting satrap, Kleomenes, was subordinate to him as *hyparchos* (subruler). Of the other so-called *diadochoi* (successors of Alexander the Great) who were significant in the following years, Antigonos Monophthalmos (the one-eyed) took possession of Pamphylia and Lycia in addition to his own satrapy of Great Phrygia; Eumenes of Cardia, a follower of Perdikkas, received Paphlagonia and Cappadocia and the somatophylax Lysimachos got Thrace, which had again become separate from Macedonia. The young Seleukos had originally joined Alexander as his officer and hetairos ('companion') and by the time of the campaign against Babylon, before Alexander's death, he was numbered among his closest friends. However, he did not receive a satrapy at this time; Perdikkas handed the command of the royal cavalry over to him.[20]

## PTOLEMY THE SATRAP (323–306)

## The period of the last Argead kings (323–311)

### *Maintenance of the independent satrapy; spread of power in the West and Northeast*

Next to Seleukos, Ptolemy proved himself to be the most important figure in the course of the history of the successors. Born in 367/6 as the son of a certain Lagos (hence the Lagid dynasty), who belonged to a respected Macedonian family, and Arsinoe, who even had family connections to the royal house, Ptolemy witnessed the rise of Philip II of Macedon and took part in Alexander's conquest of the Persian empire right from the beginning. In Egypt, as one of the designated companions of the king, he visited the oasis of Ammon. Since the autumn of 330 he had, by virtue of being a *somatophylax*, more and more opportunities to distinguish himself. As a result, he succeeded, among other things, in capturing Bessos, the murderer of Darius (Arr. III.29.7–30.5). In the successful campaigns of 327 against the mountain peoples of Pakistan, Ptolemy commanded approximately one-third of the army (Arr. IV. 24.8–25.4) and we find him among the commanders (as trierarch) of the Indus fleet built on the Hydaspes (Arr. *Ind.* 18.5). At the mass wedding of 324 in Susa (Arr. *An.* VII.4.6), Ptolemy married a distinguished Persian woman, Artakama, whom he divorced shortly after Alexander's death; the other successors, with the exception of Seleukos, had done the same kind of thing. During the long period of his rule in Egypt, Ptolemy composed a history of Alexander (FGrHist. 138),[21] in which he placed special emphasis on his own achievements; this work was to be the main source for Flavius Arrianus, the Alexander historian of the second century AD. As satrap and later as king, Ptolemy I contributed to the formation of the empires of the diadochoi as well as to the slow consolidation of the Hellenistic states and thus decisively influenced world history.

In 323, Ptolemy went to Egypt as the new satrap. Kleomenes obediently took on the position of hyparch but clearly sought the support of the central government. Therefore, Ptolemy quickly removed this widely disliked man[22] a move which could only have won him friends (Diod. XVIII.14.1; Paus. I.6.3).

Ptolemy began his foreign policy in 322 by intervening in Cyrene (Diod. XVIII.21.6–9; Arr. FGrHist. 156 F9. 17–18; Marmor Parium: FGrHist. 239 B 10–11). In the course of internal unrest, the oligarchs had been driven out of the city. They turned to Ptolemy and asked him to help them be reinstated in their polis. The satrap gave them his support and sent his field-general Ophellas to Cyrene, which was being supported by the Spartan mercenary leader Thibron. Ophellas conquered Cyrene and led the exiles back; the captured Thibron was executed in the Cyrenian city of Taucheira. Afterwards, Ophellas took control of the remaining cities of Cyrenaica, probably set up some garrisons there and remained as Ptolemaic governor. The conflict between the partisans of Ophellas and his opponents, however, was not settled. For this reason, Ptolemy had to find a solution which assured both the self-administration of the city of Cyrene as well as his own influence there. To this end, after the Settlement of Triparadeisos,[23] he supposedly went to Cyrene in person and promulgated guidelines which were based on constitutional principles for the future organization of the city: the so-called *diagramma* of Cyrene (321/20).[24] In this plan, the aristocrats who had asked the satrap for help regained their local authority while Ptolemy, by virtue of his position as permanent strategos and supreme justice and on account of other privileges, was given supreme authority backed by military occupation. Through these measures, Cyrene no longer enjoyed the status of a free city, a standing which Alexander had conferred upon it, but through the efforts of Ptolemy it had become the first large foreign territory of his empire.

In the meantime, Krateros, Antipatros and Lysimachos formed a coalition on account of their displeasure with Perdikkas' autocratic style (winter 322/1). Ptolemy joined them, possibly because by executing Kleomenes and annexing Cyrenaica he had come into conflict with the central government.

There followed a conflict over Alexander's body (Diod. XVIII.26–28; Paus. I.6.3) which had been embalmed in Babylon. The funeral carriage, which had taken two years to make, was now under Perdikkas' control. Disregarding the settlement reached at Babylon, he ordered that the body be brought to the ancient tombs of the Macedonian kings at Aigai. Ptolemy, who hoped to increase his status by taking possession of the dead Alexander, intercepted the burial train in Syria and compelled those on duty to bring the deceased to Egypt. But for Ptolemy it was more important to have Alexander's corpse in his own residence than to respect the last wishes of the deceased. He thus initially had him buried in the ancient capital of Memphis and later on – probably still in the reign of Ptolemy I – the dead conqueror was taken to a new tomb (*sema* or *soma*) in Alexandria.[25]

The brazen provocation in intercepting the funeral cortège accelerated the outbreak of a war which Perdikkas had already been planning against the allies. Around that time at the very latest, the son of Lagos also allied himself with some Cypriot kings (Nikokreon of Salamis, Pasikrates of Soloi, Nikokles of Paphos and Androkles of Amathus) (Arr. FGrHist. 156F 10.6). The growing power and independence of Ptolemy probably prompted Perdikkas to strike at Egypt first. He lost two battles there, however, and was killed by his own officers in the field-general's tent (probably in the summer of 320) after suffering heavy losses when crossing the Nile. Through a show of goodwill and a careful distribution of food to the opposing army, Ptolemy won general admiration. But remaining true to his old principles,

he nonetheless refused the regency which was offered to him at that time
(Arr. FGrHist. 156 F 9.28–29; Diod. XVIII.34.6–36.6) While these events
transpired in Egypt, Eumenes, who as a follower of Perdikkas was the strongest
advocate of a great empire in Alexander's sense of the word, defeated Krateros
in Asia Minor; the latter met his death there. This was the First War of the
Successors (also known as the First Coalition War).[26]

With the deaths of Perdikkas and Krateros, the empire lost the head of its
government. As a result, the victorious diadochoi of the coalition were united
once again, probably in the autumn of 320, by the Settlement of Triparadeisos
in northern Syria (Diod. XVIII.39; Arr. FGrHist. 156 F 9.30–38):[27] Antipatros
was named regent (epimeletes). In this capacity, he named Antigonos satrap
of Greater Phrygia, appointed him field commander and strategos of Asia
and bestowed upon him the mission of ending the war with Eumenes, who
had been condemned to death; he made his own son Kassandros chiliarch of
the cavalry to accompany Antigonos. Eumenes was eventually defeated and
executed in the winter of 316/15. At Triparadeisos, Ptolemy had his satrapy
confirmed; his acquisition of the Cyrenaica ('Libya') and his annexation of
the territory lying to the west of it were legitimized. Moreover, he was granted
the right of further conquest in the West. Seleukos, the former deputy of
Perdikkas who had been one of his assassins, received Babylon.

Antipatros took the kings with him to Europe, where the 80-year old
regent had only a short time to live. Shortly before his death in the autumn
of 319, he appointed the former general of Alexander the Great, Polyperchon,
regent and strategos of Europe. The diadochoi, however, mindful of their
own autonomy, especially Kassandros, Antipatros' son, were dissatisfied with
him. Kassandros, therefore, immediately formed a coalition with Ptolemy,
Antigonos and Lysimachos against Polyperchon. The ensuing military conflicts constitute the Second War of the Successors (319–315).

Ptolemy, whose policy always aimed at a strengthening and securing of
his satrapy, annexed Syria and Phoenicia after Antipatros' death (319/18)
(Diod. XVIII.43; App. *Syr.* 52.264; Marmor Parium: FGrHist. 239 B 12),
withdrew his army soon thereafter and left only garrisons in a few cities. He
was quick, therefore to address the problem of the creation of military and
economic buffer-zones around Egypt.[28]

### The end of Philip III (317) and the interned 'pharaoh' Alexander IV

The ensuing clashes led to the downfall of the Argeads, which had been a
glorious ruling dynasty under Philip II and Alexander the Great, not least
because of two ambitious women in the family who pursued their aims at
cross-purposes to each other: one was Olympias, the mother of Alexander
the Great who resided in Epiros and had been invited officially by Polyperchon
to share in the highest administration of the empire; the other was Eurydike,
the wife of the half-witted Philip III Arrhidaios. Eurydike, together with
Philip, went over to Kassandros' side, deposed Polyperchon by means of a

decree issued by her royal consort and had Kassandros named regent (317). In response to this, Olympias led an army out of Epiros towards Macedonia. Olympias was able to take as prisoners both Eurydike and Philip, Alexander's half-brother whom she despised; the king was murdered at her command, Eurydike was compelled to commit suicide and a hundred prominent Macedonians were chosen for execution (autumn 317). With this crime, however, Olympias condemned herself to a similar fate: largely abandoned by her troops, Olympias was forced to surrender to Kassandros who had hastened to the scene and she was condemned to death by a military assembly (early in 315) (Diod. XIX.35–36, 49–51; Just. XIV.5–6).[29]

At the beginning of 316, Alexander IV was the only remaining king. In Egypt, the priests devised a new royal title in hieroglyphics and from now on had 'Alexandros' written in the cartouche bearing the birth name of the pharaoh. The boy was, to be sure, a hostage in the hands of the new ruler of Macedonia, Kassandros, who kept him henceforth in custody with his mother Roxane in Amphipolis.

## The annexation of Cyprus, wars in Cyrenaica and in Syria/Phoenicia

In the winter of 316/15, Antigonos Monophthalmos, strategos of Europe, finally defeated Eumenes after years of warfare. This cleared the way for Antigonos to expand his power in the East at his own discretion. In the summer of 315, he arrived in Babylon and demanded of Seleukos, the satrap, that he give him an account of the administration of the satrapy. Seleukos refused to do as he was asked, but he feared for his life and so fled to Ptolemy who received him with honour (Diod. XIX.55–56.1).

With this show of force, Antigonos, who at least since Triparadeisos was equipped with outstanding military resources, seemed to be emulating Perdikkas' attempt to establish a central authority within Alexander's empire. Seleukos, however, managed very quickly to form a coalition against Antigonos made up of Ptolemy, Kassandros and Lysimachos[30] with the express purpose of hindering the latter's attempt at domination. Antigonos did not comply with their final demands and started the Third War of the Successors (also known as the Second Coalition War: 314–311) (Diod. XIX.56–62).

Antigonos entered into a pact with some of the Cypriot kings; the others, in particular Nikokreon of Salamis, were allies of Ptolemy – either dating from the First Coalition War or from some later time. Bent on his purpose, Antigonos was able to extend his powers in all of Asia Minor and Syria; only in Tyre did the Ptolemaic garrison put up some resistance and then only to surrender after a year-long siege. From his camp in front of the city, Antigonos proclaimed a wide-ranging resolution of his military assembly which, among other things, granted him the title of 'epimeletes of the king' and announced the Greek cities' autonomy. In answer to this, Ptolemy replied with a declaration granting freedom of the Greeks which no doubt was intended as propaganda and not meant in earnest.

The driving force of the Ptolemaic war machine was Seleukos who had nothing left to lose. Together with Menelaos, the brother of Ptolemy, he was the leader of operations on Cyprus, which in 313 was won for the Ptolemaic empire. Ptolemy made his long-time ally Nikokreon, the king of Salamis, strategos over the entire island and added to his empire a series of city-kingdoms that had attempted to oppose Ptolemaic domination (Diod. XIX.79.5). As a general principle, however, the city-kingdoms continued to enjoy a limited sovereignty.

In addition to this, difficulties arose in Cyrenaica. Ptolemy had extended the area under his control westwards along the coast of the Great Syrtis as far as Euphrantas Pyrgos (today called Sirte at the mouth of the Wadi Tamet) so that he would have under his control the caravan routes coming from the interior of Libya. In this way, he managed to gain control over the profits from Central African trade, which otherwise would have been controlled by the Greek cities on the coast of Northern Africa. He had, besides this, strongly asserted his political supremacy in this region, as is shown by the coins minted in Cyrene in 314. Perhaps in reaction to this, the Cyrenians revolted in 313 and laid siege to the garrison on the citadel. Ptolemy sent both an army and a fleet against the rebels and thus re-established order (summer 312) (Diod. XIX.79.1–3). Ophellas remained in office.[31]

Soon thereafter, Ptolemy and Seleukos united their respective military interests in an expedition to Syria (Diod. XIX.80–85);[32] the one wished to regain lost territory, the other to advance as far as Babylon. Thus, a battle took place in the autumn of 312 at Gaza against the son of Antigonos, Demetrios, who was active in the area. Ptolemy had, at that time, a large levy of Egyptians in his army (Diod. XIX.80.4). Although Ptolemy and Seleukos were victorious in this battle,[33] Ptolemy had to retreat (after his general Killes was defeated by Demetrios in the spring of 311) when faced with an advance by the superior forces of Antigonos (Diod. XIX.93.2–7). The latter gained control of all of Syria once again. At the same time, Seleukos was able to move with a small expeditionary corps beyond Petra to Mesopotamia. In August of 311, he recaptured his satrapy of Babylon and with it an entirely new situation emerged in Asia. From 308, Seleukos, unimpeded by Antigonos, was able to build up the Seleukid empire by capturing all of the eastern part of what was once Alexander's empire as far as India.

Around the beginning of the autumn in 311, a peace was concluded (Diod. XIX.105) in which the *status quo* was given official recognition. Antigonos' power was confirmed in 'all of Asia', but apparently no mention was made of Seleukos' activities.[34] Ptolemy's foreign territories, Cyprus and Cyrenaica, were also not part of the settlement.[35] The autonomy of the Greek poleis was restated, though none of the parties to the settlement was willing to accept this in their own area. A fact of some significance was that Kassandros was to be strategos of Europe until Alexander IV reached adulthood. Thus, in 311 the empire of Alexander was legally preserved as a hereditary monarchy.

## Years of change without a living king (310/9–306)

For many years, Kassandros' position was made valid and legitimate by virtue of the fact that he had in his power the recognized king and the king's mother. Alexander IV's fourteenth year approached and he would soon join the ranks of the royal pages (βασιλικοὶ παῖδες). This must have given the youth an increasing appearance of individuality in the eyes of those wishing to see an offspring of the ancient Macedonian house of the Argeads on the throne. He thereby became all the more dangerous to Kassandros. For this reason, Kassandros had Alexander and Roxane quietly eliminated in 310 or 309 (Diod. XIX.105.2; Just. XV.2.5).[36] It was at this point that the interregnum period began and it lasted until the diadochoi took on the title of king (306). After the death of Alexander IV, dates continued to be reckoned as though he were still reigning; this was true of both Egypt and the Seleukid empire.[37]

The peace of 311 was probably not satisfactory to Ptolemy. Under the slogan of freeing the Greek cities in 'Rough' Cilicia from the rule of Antigonos, he sent a military expedition there, obviously motivated in this by Cilicia's favourable location opposite Cyprus. The undertaking foundered in the face of a retaliation by Demetrios, the son of Antigonos, who later received the epithet 'Poliorketes' (Diod. XX.19.2–5).

An event that ran parallel to this expedition was the inclusion of Cyprus in the Ptolemaic empire. In 311/10, Nikokreon of Salamis died (Marmor Parium: FGrHist. 239 B17) and his successor in Cyprus was Ptolemy's brother, Menelaos, who had already enjoyed much success there. He took office as governor (*strategos*) of the island and as king of Salamis; it was under the latter title that he minted his own coins. It may be that Nikokles, the king of Paphos, who had long been allied with Ptolemy, was unwilling to submit to the authority of Menelaos: he thus fell under suspicion for having formed a treaty with Antigonos and was compelled to commit suicide together with his family (Diod. XX.21.1–3).[38]

Ptolemy would not admit to defeat in Asia Minor: in 309, he initiated his 'liberation campaigns' in the West (Lycia and Karia) and was able to win over to his side Xanthos, Kaunos, Myndos and apparently Iasos.[39] In 309/8 the Lagid royal household set up its winter quarters on the island of Kos (Diod. XX.27.1–3). In front of Halikarnassos, however, Demetrios once again put a stop to the Ptolemaic advance. The Ptolemaic naval expedition to Greece of 308[40] proved, in the end, to be a short-lived event: Corinth, Sikyon (Diod. XX.37.1–2) and Megara (D. L. II.115) were garrisoned for the time being and this cast serious doubt on the policy of liberation put forth by Ptolemy; up until 303 these bases were gradually lost, however, to Kassandros and Demetrios. Hence also in the North, Ptolemy's attempts at territorial gain and influence led to the creation of military outposts for the protection of Egypt in future clashes; this policy was mostly aimed at Antigonos, who, at the same time, presided over the union of Greek islands called the League of Islanders.[41]

In about 309/8, the governor of the Cyrenaica, Ophellas, undertook from Cyrene a campaign against Carthage (Diod. XX.40–43) in support of Agathokles of Syracuse. Judging by the size of his army, he probably dreamed of a North African empire at the expense of the Carthaginians. This action no doubt made Agathokles uneasy and so he betrayed Ophellas and had him executed in the autumn of 308 somewhere in the vicinity of the Punic metropolis. It remains unclear whether or not Ophellas had acted independently of Ptolemy or whether he had proceeded with the latter's consent. At any rate, it was only after a five-year-long revolt of Cyrenaica that the stepson of Ptolemy, Magas, was made governor there in 300 (Paus. I.6.8).[42]

In 306, the conflict between Antigonos and Ptolemy first came to a head in the most important sea battle of the wars between the diadochoi: Demetrios, having been put in charge of the major offensive against Cyprus, dealt Ptolemy a crushing defeat at Salamis and in the battle most of the Egyptian fleet and half of the transportation ships were lost (Diod. XX.46–52; Plu. *Dem.* 15–16; among others).[43] Perhaps Ptolemy and Menelaos were rather hasty in ceding the island to Demetrios since for the 12 years that followed he was able to maintain control of it (306–295/4).

After his son's victory at Salamis, Antigonos became the first of the diadochoi to assume the title of king (βασιλεύς), conferred upon him by the military assembly and the *philoi*, and he made Demetrios his co-ruler. Hoping to eliminate the other diadochoi without effort, Antigonos claimed in this way to be the successor within the empire of Alexander. In response to this, Ptolemy was in turn acclaimed king by his own army in the late summer or autumn of 306 (Plu. *Dem.* 18.2; App. *Syr.* 54.276; Just. XV.2.11). The other diadochoi, Seleukos, Kassandros and Lysimachos, quickly followed his example. (Diod. XX.53.2–4).[44]

Antigonos and Demetrios now advanced together (end of October 306) from Gaza toward Egypt – Antigonos with ground troops, Demetrios with a fleet. The direct attack on Alexandria was intended to begin from Pelusion. The march through the Nile delta, with its swamps and many tributaries, however, proved to be a hopeless undertaking. Ptolemy was able to fend off Demetrios' attempt at landing. Antigonos eventually had to call off the venture at the end of November 306 because of difficulties with the provisions for the army (Diod. XX. 73–76; Plu. *Dem.* 19.1–3; Paus. I.6.6).

## THE RULE OF PTOLEMY I SOTER AS KING (306/4–283/2)

### The establishment of the empire in Syria/Phoenicia, Cyprus and Anatolia (until 295/4)

With his elevation to basileus, Antigonos officially put an end to the Argead dynasty. By taking on the same title, the other diadochoi showed that their status was equivalent to Antigonos' and in so doing they also founded new

*Figure 1.1* Silver tetradrachm of Ptolemy I with royal diadem; privately owned; Kyrieleis (1975), 4f., plates 1 and 2.

dynasties. Nevertheless, an important distinction must be borne in mind: while Antigonos laid claim to the entire kingdom of Alexander the Great, the others recognized each other as equals,[45] even though they also based their kingships on their association with Alexander. For this reason only Kassandros bore the title 'King of the Macedonians',[46] since he ruled over Macedonia; Ptolemy and Seleukos merely called themselves 'basileus' and proclaimed in this way their personal kingship, which, to be sure, followed Macedonian tradition in emulation of Alexander. Soon after his coronation, a realistic image of Ptolemy began to appear on the coins he had minted (Fig. 1.1).

It is obvious that Ptolemy explicitly associated himself with Alexander by means of his coronation as Egyptian pharaoh. So, after resolving the problems following Antigonos' attempted invasion of Egypt in the autumn of 306, he chose for his coronation feast the next anniversary of Alexander's death. This was on the 28th of the month Daisios, i.e. the 12th of January in 304, on the assumption of the intercalation of a Macedonian month.[47] As a result of this, the year 305/4 is counted in the demotic papyri as the first year of Ptolemy's rule; other chronographic sources such as the Marmor Parium (FGrHist. 239 B 23) also take that year to be the first of his reign as king. According to the Greek sources (papyri as well as inscriptions), however, Ptolemy retroactively had his years as satrap, starting with the death of Alexander the Great, included in the reckoning of dates throughout the empire.[48] In the Ptolemaic kingdom, therefore, one must distinguish between the personal figure of the 'basileus' and the honours of the ancient Egyptian monarch which were bound to territory and nation. The same can be said of the Babylonian kingship in the Seleukid kingdom from the time of Antiochos I.[49]

Those of the diadochoi who took on the title of king and thereafter recognized each other as equals dissolved the unity of Alexander's empire. Antigonos had to accept this but he continued fighting for further territorial possessions.[50]

After the failed Egyptian campaign, Antigonos sent his son and co-regent, Demetrios, to conquer Rhodes. Already by the end of the fourth century, the island republic had become one of the most important commercial centres for Egyptian grain and was a point of transit for all manner of goods shipped to the Nile country. The Rhodians had immediately recognized Ptolemy's royal title, since it seemed advantageous to them for economic reasons.[51] Success was to prove them right: in the well-known siege of 305/4 BC, in which Demetrios acquired the epithet of Poliorketes, the Rhodians were able to put up a successful resistance, not least because of the military contingents and the food supplies shipped by Ptolemy (Diod. XX.81–88, 91–100.4; Plu. *Dem.* 21–22). To commemorate the fortunate outcome, they erected a large statue to Helios, the famed Colossus of Rhodes, at the entrance to the harbour and offered extravagant honours to Ptolemy.[52] In this way, Rhodes' increasing importance as the commercial centre of the Hellenistic world was assured, as was its long-lasting friendship with the Ptolemaic kingdom.[53]

In view of the fact that the power of Antigonos and Demetrios was still great, the other diadochoi immediately formed a new coalition: in 301, Antigonos lost the last battle at Ipsus (Phrygia) and died in combat (Fourth War of the Diadochoi: 303–301). Demetrios was able to escape and retained Cyprus as well as his positions in Greece. In this way, he remained a power to be reckoned with, possessing as he did the largest fleet in the Mediterranean basin. Ptolemy himself was not present at Ipsus. Pursuing his old plans in the East, however, he occupied the south coast of Syria (temporarily in 302 and permanently in 301) together with a certain amount of territory north-wards as far as the river Eleutheros (Diod. XX.113.1–2). His most northerly city of considerable size was Byblos; he may also have seized Damascus. Sidon and Tyre remained enclaves in the possession of Demetrios.

Antigonos' empire was divided among the three victors at Ipsus (Plb. V. 67.8; XXVIII.20.7; Plu. *Dem.* 30.1; App. *Syr.* 55.280): Lysimachos received Anatolia as far as Taurus, with the exception of coastal sites already under Ptolemy's control and Cilicia, which went to Kassandros' brother, Pleistarchos. Seleukos was to have received all of Syria from the Euphrates until the Mediterranean but he refrained from pressing his claims to Ptolemaic Syria in view of his friendship with Ptolemy without, however, surrendering the

Seleukid rights to it (Diod. XXI.1.5).[54] This conflict would be one of the major causes for the armed encounters between the Ptolemaic and Seleukid kingdoms in the third and second centuries known as the Syrian Wars.

Ptolemaic Syria, officially known as the province of 'Syria and Phoenicia' and by modern scholars as Coele Syria (Κοίλη Συρία),[55] was over the long term the second largest foreign possession of the Nile empire next to Cyrenaica. Aside from the value of this area as a military buffer-zone, the Ptolemies thus also had access to the very valuable cedar trees of Lebanon and controlled the caravan trails, the so-called spice-route, which began in Saudi Arabia and ended in Coele Syria. The country itself was rich in agricultural products such as grain, oil and wine.

An opportunity for further expansion in the North was soon to present itself to Ptolemy whose diplomatic skill allowed him to make the most of favourable circumstances. A treaty of friendship between him and Demetrios (Plu. *Pyrrh.* 4.5) did not endure. As a result of the treaty, however, a follower of Demetrios, Pyrrhos of Epiros, was held hostage in Alexandria. There, Pyrrhos and Ptolemy formed a close friendship so that about a year later Pyrrhos was able to regain his Molossian kingdom with the help of Ptolemy (Plu. *Pyrr.* 5.1).

In the same year (297), Kassandros died. In the resultant turmoil among his sons, Demetrios managed to have himself acclaimed king in Macedonia in 294. His unrelenting activities, however, had alarmed the other kings, Lysimachos, Ptolemy and Seleukos. They attacked Demetrios' scattered possessions in Asia: Lysimachos took the western cities of Asia Minor[56] and Seleukos Cilicia. In 295/4, Ptolemy was finally able to make the island of Cyprus, which he had coveted for a long time, a part of his empire. The island was of strategic importance for the Ptolemies, owing to its geographical position as well as its natural resources (metals and agricultural products). All of Lycia came under Ptolemaic rule, at the latest in the aftermath of the events just mentioned: two oikonomoi (administrators of finance) are attested at the end of 288.[57] The same could be said for Pamphylia,[58] where there is evidence of a Ptolemaic governor, the Pamphyliarch, but in this case only in the reign of Ptolemy II at the end of 278.[59] Sidon and Tyre also came under Ptolemaic control in 295/4. At that time (if not earlier), Philokles, a Phoenician by birth, was the Sidonian king. History, however, was to prove this man an extraordinary general and an able organizer of the Ptolemaic dominion in the Aegean and in Asia Minor up until the early years of Ptolemy II's reign.[60]

## Greek policies and the Island League in the 280s

Friendship with Athens represented a constant element of Ptolemaic policy in the third century. For the time being, however, the Ptolemaic fleet could not prevent Demetrios Poliorketes from conquering the city early in 294; 150 Ptolemaic ships had attempted to disperse the blockade at Aegina in front of

Athens (Plu. *Dem.* 33–34).[61] Six years later (288), we find Ptolemy allied with Lysimachos, Seleukos and Pyrrhos of Epiros in a coalition meant finally to bring down Demetrios (Fifth War of the Successors) (Plu. *Dem.* 44; *Pyrrh.* 10–11). The Egyptian king had set up a strongly fortified base on the Cycladic island of Andros. Athens prepared itself to shake off Demetrios' hegemony with Ptolemy lending assistance once again. The commander of his troops, the Athenian Kallias from the deme of Sphettos, arrived in Attika with 1,000 Ptolemaic soldiers from Andros and actively took part in the Athenian rebellion of June 287. Shortly thereafter, however, Ptolemy concluded a separate peace by means of his negotiator, the architect and diplomat Sostratos of Knidos,[62] a man who was highly and widely esteemed. The Piraeus and other fortifications in Attika remained under the control of the Antigonids. Athens joined in the peace and Ptolemy resigned from the coalition for this reason.[63]

At the latest in 287, Ptolemy was finally able to take over the protectorate of the Island League, originally founded by Antigonos.[64] Control of the islanders resulted in a Ptolemaic hegemony in the Cyclades for the next three decades. The situation of Athens remained precarious given the presence of an Antigonid garrison in the Piraeus, but in the following years it received support from the Ptolemaic empire in the form of grain and money (286/5, 282/1).[65] In 285, Demetrios Poliorketes fell into the hands of Seleukos and died in his custody in 283. His son, Antigonos Gonatas, had remained behind in Antigonid territory in Europe.

## Family politics

A good part of the politics of the diadochoi was developed through unions by marriage. In this domain as well, Ptolemy I was very successful. Only the most important details from the family's history in the years following Alexander's death will be mentioned: between 322 and 319, Ptolemy I, then satrap, married Eurydike, daughter of the regent Antipatros. The marriage produced Ptolemy Keraunos ('lightning') and Meleager, both of whom were destined to become Macedonian kings for a short time.[66] It also produced a third son, as well as two daughters, Lysandra and Ptolemais,[67] perhaps also Theoxene (see Stemma 1). Together with Eurydike, the newly widowed Macedonian, Berenike, had arrived at the Lagid court; she soon became Ptolemy's mistress and then his third wife (Berenike I), after Eurydike had been pushed aside. Already in 316, she gave birth to a daughter named Arsinoe, later referred to as Arsinoe II. In 308, during her stay on Kos, she delivered a son, who was later to be Ptolemy II, and at least one more daughter named Philotera. Berenike eventually managed to have Ptolemy Keraunos removed from the line of successors in favour of her own son Ptolemy. Perhaps shortly before 287, Eurydike and Ptolemy Keraunos left Egypt; the latter then appears at the courts of Lysimachos and Seleukos.[68] Ptolemy II was accordingly named co-regent in December or January of

285/4.[69] His sister Arsinoe (II), who was approximately eight years older than he, had married Lysimachus of Thrace by the year 300; for him, already over 60, it was his third or fourth marriage.[70] Lysimachos, in turn, married off his own daughter from his first marriage to Ptolemy II, either while Ptolemy I was still living or after his death.[71] This woman was referred to as Arsinoe I in the royal house of the Ptolemies.

## The situation in Egypt

The clashes between Ptolemy I and the other successors along with the task of building up an empire represent only one of the two main sets of political problems with which the former had to deal. The second, very heterogeneous set of problems was the question of how he was to proceed within Egypt. Here his foremost concern was to gain acceptance as ruler from the Egyptian people; the measures taken to this end have to do with questions of religious policy and the royal ideology, and the development of these will be discussed in Chapter 3. A further problem was that a *modus vivendi* had to be implemented which would ensure harmony between the Macedonian and Greek immigrants on the one hand and the native population on the other.

First of all, it is important to emphasize the fact that no major changes had been made to the socio-economic realities of Egyptian society or to the organization and administration of the Egyptian state since the time of the Persians.[72] The same units for the administration of land had been retained: namely, the nomes (νομοί) along with their sub-divisions (τόποι or τοπαρχίαι) and the villages (κῶμαι). The separation of the civil and military administration of the nomes in the person of nomarchs and strategoi[73] was also retained. As in former times, half-free royal farmers (βασιλικοὶ γεωργοί) tilled the royal estates (γῆ βασιλική); in addition, there were the great areas of temple land (γῆ ἱερά).

A variety of complex problems and changes resulted from the ever-increasing numbers of Greeks who had settled in Egypt since the time of Alexander the Great. Directly related to this was an increase in new Greek settlements in many areas of the land of the Nile. These people took over important administrative and economic positions; the Greek language soon became the dominant one in public life, although no one was forced to speak it.[74] The change was not effected suddenly. Rather, Ptolemy I carried it out step by step in a shrewd and pragmatic fashion. Hence, the paying out of taxes to the high priests of Amun in Thebes was continued by the Argead kings.[75] The Ptolemaic state with its Greek bureaucracy was perfected only in the third century under Ptolemy II. The standing army, conversely, had, since the time of Alexander the Great, consisted of Greeks and Macedonians, with the exception of the Egyptians who fought alongside them at Gaza.[76]

The seat of Ptolemy as satrap remained for the time being at Memphis, out of respect for tradition and owing to practical considerations. On the other hand, Memphis was hardly suited to the kind of governance which Ptolemy had in mind for his kingdom in the context of the Hellenistic world. It was not a convenient location from which to administer foreign interests, nor was it a likely site for a world capital of economic and commercial activity.

In the Satrap Stele (Fig. 3.2) of 311,[77] the transfer of the residence to Alexandria is reported as completed.[78] From that time on, it was from this city that the Ptolemies carried out their complex Mediterranean policy. Greeks experienced in financial matters and in commercial relations took over these new tasks.

This 'superstructure' of influential Greeks[79] in the Ptolemaic empire came to require its own spiritual centre in learning and poetry, a counter-weight both to ancient Egyptian science and culture and to the other Greek centres of learning such as Athens. To fulfil this need, the Museion was established in Alexandria (see Map 3), a centre for teaching and research, following the example of the peripatetic school of Aristotle and of Theophrastus in Athens. The Alexandrian Museion became the first scholarly academy in the western sense of the word. The library of the Museion became an institution of great importance because of the hundreds of thousands of papyrus rolls housed within it, serving as they did as the basis of Alexandrian philology. Although Ptolemy II is traditionally credited with being the great creator of this academic institution, the planning and the first phase of construction certainly took place already under his father. We may therefore rightly assume that the idea, foundation and organization of the Museion and its library go back to the recommendations of Demetrios of Phaleron.[80] Theophrastus had been in Egypt, perhaps even in pre-Ptolemaic times, and thereafter had close ties with Ptolemy I.[81] His student, Demetrios of Phaleron, Athenian statesman, peripatetic philosopher, legal scholar and rhetorician, had been driven out of Athens by Demetrios Poliorketes in 307. In 297, he arrived in Alexandria and was cordially received by Ptolemy and promoted to royal counsellor in cultural affairs.[82] As such, he was also a member of a legislative commission formed by Ptolemy I (Ael. *VH* III.17).

The culturally receptive environment cultivated by Ptolemy I, who indeed made a name for himself as a historian,[83] also drew in scholars, writers and philosophers, some of whom gained entry at court, such as, for example, the philosophers Theodoros Atheos of Cyrene or Straton of Lampsakos, tutor of Ptolemy II.[84] Already in the time of Ptolemy I, a number of Greeks were even visiting the venerable site of Thebes; thereafter, several wrote Egyptian 'histories', among whom was the philosopher, historian and grammarian Hekataios of Abdera (Diod. I.46.8).[85]

From a legal point of view, there were three[86] Greek cities in Hellenistic Egypt: the ancient colony of Naukratis, Alexandria and the city founded by Ptolemy I, Ptolemais Hermaiou in the Thebaïd.[87] This new city replaced the ancient Egyptian city of Thinis as a centre and was perhaps intended as a counter-weight to Thebes in the sphere of domestic politics. All three poleis had their own legal status as a city, the usual administrative organs (prytanies, boule, assembly) and the concomitant estates (γῆ πολιτική); the king controlled the poleis through his supervisory bodies.[88]

Alongside the influential minority of Greeks and other groups of foreigners (e.g. the Jews) were the Egyptians who formed the great majority of the population. There was a small elite of the latter, composed mainly of priests, distinguished from the mass of farmers by being the carriers of national tradition and ancient Egyptian culture. On the farmer's work depended the economic riches of the land as well as the income derived from taxes, the latter providing the funds with which the army and foreign undertakings had to be paid. As far as the native ruling elite is concerned, it is important to remember that at the beginning of Macedonian–Greek rule, Alexander the Great had left the Egyptian nomarchs in office. We also know, moreover, of a group of native officers from the third century, mostly under Ptolemy I, who now and then bear important-sounding titles in their hieroglyphic inscriptions. It is, however, not possible to define their precise functions.[89] The best-known of these is the grandchild of a sister of the pharaoh Nectanebo I (380–362), also named Nectanebo; on his sarcophagus he identifies himself as nomarch of the lower-Egyptian district of Sebennytos and Sile in the northeast, where he is said to have been responsible for the protection of the borders as the 'great first-ranking officer of the army for his majesty'.[90]

The first member of the priestly aristocracy worthy of mention is Somtutefnakhte, 'head of the priests of Sakhmet' and as such a doctor. He had fought alongside the Persians at Issos and was able to return to his paternal city of Herakleopolis Magna (Middle Egypt) where, held in high honour, he continued to perform his duties.[91] Changing circumstances between the time of the second Persian domination and the consolidation of Greek rule are also reflected in the texts of Petosiris, high priest of Thoth of Hermopolis which are found in his splendidly painted mausoleum; the latter became a religious centre of the local necropolis (near Tuna el-Gebel in Middle-Egypt).[92] The Greek influence in the grave-reliefs indicates that the deceased as well as the son and grandson, who completed construction of the monument under Ptolemy I, were receptive to the culture of the new masters. The name Manetho, especially, evokes the sometimes fruitful exchange between the Greek and Egyptian worlds: this Egyptian priest from Sebennytos was one of Ptolemy I's counsellors and significantly influenced his religious policies.[93] He later composed a history of the pharaohs to the end of the thirtieth dynasty in the Greek language, at Ptolemy II's bidding, which is preserved in excerpts; he had at his disposal authentic documentary sources and kings' lists. The modern conventional division of the dynasties depends on that work.[94]

## The historical achievement of Ptolemy

In the winter of 283–2, Ptolemy I died at the age of 84.[95] An assessment of his achievements must be based on a consideration of general events in

Egypt and in the Ptolemaic kingdom during his reign and not of a few unfortunate and isolated incidents.[96] In contrast to those of the successors who
promoted a central administration within a greater empire, Ptolemy always
acted with a view to Egypt's autonomy and in so doing determined the basic
features of Ptolemaic foreign policy for the remainder of the third century.
This policy had two main directives: a primary policy directed at Asia; and a
northern policy, mainly concerned with Greece and the Aegean Islands. The
result of this, as the case of Ptolemy I illustrates, was a Ptolemaic thalassocracy
in the eastern Mediterranean having as its strategic objective the protection
of Egypt from external attacks (such as those of Perdikkas and Antigonos).

Basically, Ptolemy was drawing upon the Saite idea of a state, although in
his adaptation of it he combined older and more recent elements. Necho II
had, already, from 609–605, been forced to make Egypt a hegemonic power
in Western Syria as far north as Karkemish in order to protect the land's
vital interests against Asiatic powers. Just as Amasis did in the later Saite
period, so Ptolemy managed Egypt as a Mediterranean state which was
closely connected to the Greek world, and in this he was much more exhaust-
ive than the former. Cyprus, at one time occupied by Amasis, once again
became Egypt's power-base in the Mediterranean.[97] Egypt's annexation of
Cyrene replaced an earlier pact made between the two under Amasis and
then Alexander the Great. In a kind of defensive imperialism (cf. Plb. VI.34.2–
9), Ptolemy I succeeded in forming a direct territorial protective boundary
for Egypt by means of Cyrenaica, Cyprus, Coele Syria and several large
Phoenician harbour-cities.

Ptolemy had also initiated his own offensive policy in the Aegean in his
battles with the Asian empire of Antigonos. Later, he was able to deprive
Demetrios Poliorketes of important bases of operation by taking over the
protectorate of the islanders, i.e. the Cyclades, and thereafter he opposed his
own might to that of Lysimachos, who controlled Thrace, Macedonia and
western Asia Minor. With an attempt at seizing parts of the Anatolian coast
(at least Lycia and parts of Karia),[98] Ptolemy started establishing a foreign
protective zone with bases designed to protect Cyprus and to safeguard
communication with the Aegean.

Although there are few papyrological sources describing the organization
of the state in the reign of Ptolemy I,[99] they do, nevertheless, tell us that the
basic features of Ptolemaic economic policy must have been developed in
co-ordination with the objectives of foreign policy. This economic policy of
the Ptolemaic empire provides us with the first known example of true state
mercantilism.[100] Even if a good part of the raw materials necessary for carrying
out the Greek–Macedonian wars could be supplied from foreign territories
(Cyprus was rich in metals and forests, the coveted cedars grew in Coele
Syria), the need for coined silver to pay the soldiers was especially urgent. A
favourable balance of trade, therefore, had to be achieved through a surplus
of agricultural produce. Ptolemy I's monetary policy was conceived in light
of this. After trying a variety of measures, he created in the later years of his

rule a unified monetary policy for the grain-bearing countries (Egypt, Cyrenaica, Cyprus, Coele Syria) and so set them off economically from the rest of the Hellenistic world. The circulation of any currency other than that issued by the royal house of the Ptolemies was forbidden in those areas; the exchange of currency that this restriction imposed was made into a state-run monopoly probably already in the time of Ptolemy I.[101] The importance that Ptolemy attached to this economic policy may be measured by the extent to which he brought support to the island of Rhodes against Demetrios Poliorketes. His intention was, of course, to maintain the independence of this trading centre so vital to Egypt's commercial interests.

Through difficult battles and a keen political sense, Ptolemy I forged from a satrapy subject to tribute an independent kingdom that went on to become a leading player in the politics of the ancient world. Since the land of the Nile itself was generally spared the burden of war, his 40-year reign was marked by a peaceful development in which the foundations of Ptolemaic policy towards the local populace were laid down. Ptolemy I, therefore, initiated a new epoch in the history of Egyptian art, culture and intellectual achievement, one that was of a relatively uniform character for the 300 years of its duration.

## Notes

1  Seibert (1981), 109–111.
2  On the problem of Alexander's coronation see most recently Burstein (1991); cf. also Bergman (1968), 92–99.
2a  Recently, it has been pointed out that the name 'Rhakotis' means 'building site'/'construction place' (see Chauveau, bibliographical suppl.) but this does not necessarily mean that Rhakotis was an empty site at the time of Alexander the Great.
3  G. A. Mansuelli, 'Contributo a Deinokrates', in *Alessandria*, I (1983) 79–80.
4  It is therefore disputed whether he founded the city before or after the visit to Siwa. See Seibert (1985), 85, footnote 35. Is it necessary to assume that Alexander himself was present at the ceremonies for the founding of the city or that he was present at all in Egypt at the time? Our account follows the chronological order in Arr. *An.* III.1–5.
5  See pp. 11–12.
6  G. Hölbl: *LÄ* VI, 1986, 920–922 (s.v. Verehrung ägyptischer Götter im Ausland).
7  Kuhlmann (1988), 154f.
8  Our account of the order of events follows Kuhlmann (1988), 144f.; for the facts and sources see Wilcken (1928); P. Langer, 'Alexander the Great at Siwah', *Ancient World* 4, 1981, 109–127; for research in this field see Seibert (1981), 116–125.
9  Probably the veiled Min-Amun of which only the head was exposed, cf. Kuhlmann (1988), 119–123.
10  A. B. Bosworth, 'Alexander and Ammon', in Festschrift für F. Schachermeyr (ed.) *Greece and the Eastern Mediterranean in Ancient History and Prehistory*, Berlin, K. H. Kinzl, 1977, 51–75.

11 For Memphis cf. E. G. Turner, 'A commander-in-chief's order from Saqqâra', *JEA* 60, 1974, 239–240. On Balakros: Heckel (1992), 335. On the adminis-tration of Egypt under Alexander: Falivene (1991), 207–215.

12 J. Vogt, 'Kleomenes von Naukratis – Herr von Ägypten', *Chiron* 1, 1971, 153–157; Seibert (1969), 39–51; J. Seibert, 'Nochmals zu Kleomenes von Naukratis', *Chiron* 2, 1979, 99–102. The title 'satrap' on an ostrakon from Memphis in the demotic script probably refers to Kleomenes: H. S. Smith, 'A Satrap at Memphis', in J. Baines *et al.* (eds) *Pyramid Studies and Other Esays Presented to I. E. S. Edwards*, London, 1988, 184–186; The 'Peteisis' mentioned on the same ostrakon is probably that high public official of the same name before his resignation; Alexander himself (line 1) did not yet have a cartouche, cf. Burstein (1991), 141.

13 A. Andréadès, 'Antimène de Rhodes et Cléomène de Naucratis' *BCH* 53, 1929, 10–18; Eddy (1961), 269.

14 Bosworth (cf. note 10), 55–57; for a contrary view cf. Hammond, in Hammond, Walbank (1988), 96, 131. On the date of Alexander's death cf. Grzybek (1990), 29–35, 53–56.

15 Schachermeyr (1970), 79–186; Seibert (1983), 84–91. For the ensuing history of the successors to Alexander see also Billows (1990).

16 On Perdikkas' command as chiliarch: Schachermeyr (1970), 171–184; Heckel (1992), 366–370, also 134–163 (on the life of Perdikkas).

17 Schachermeyr (1970), 164–171; Heckel (1992), 107–133.

18 Schachermeyr (1970), 127, 139; for an opposite view cf. Hammond, in Hammond, Walbank (1988), 106.

19 For the chronology based on these documents cf. Pestmann (1967), 10–13.

20 In so far as our account deals with Seleukos, we generally follow Mehl (1986); compare with this the general overview in J. D. Grainger, *Seleukos Nikator*, London, 1990. On the successors mentioned in the work just cited cf. the 'lives' in Heckel (1992).

21 A late date is usually posited for the time of composition: Seibert (1969), 1–26; id. (1981), 19–21; G. Wirth, *Tyche* 4, 1989, 203, footnote 43; R. M. Errington, 'Bias in Ptolemy's history of Alexander', *CIQ* 19, 1969, 233–242 (for a composition date shortly after 320); J. Roisman, 'Ptolemy and his rivals in his history of Alexander', *CIQ* 34, 1984, 373–385.

22 See p. 12.

23 See p. 16*f*.

24 *SEG* IX, 1; P. M. Fraser, *Berytus* 12, 1959, 120–127; Bagnall (1976), 28f.; M. A. Laronde, 'La date du diagramma de Ptolémée à Cyrène', *REG* 85, 1972, XIIIf.; id. (1987), 85–128, 254. On Ophellas see *PP* VI, 15062.

25 Seibert (1981), 115f.; Fraser (1972), I, 16.

26 H. Hauben, 'The first war of the successors (321 BC)', *AncSoc* 8, 1977, 85–120.

27 For the chronology of the early years of the successors, we follow here the so-called lower chronology which in the last decade has been generally preferred. There is a discussion of this in the following: R. M. Errington, 'From Babylon to Triparadeisos, 323–320 BC', *JHS* 90, 1970, 49–77; id., 'Diodorus Siculus and the chronology of the early Diadochoi, 320–311 BC', *Hermes* 105, 1977, 478–504; B. Gullath, L. Schober, 'Zur chronologie der frühen Diadochenzeit: die Jahre 320–315 v. Chr.', in *Studien zur alten Geschichte*, Festschrift für

Laufer, I, Rome, 1986, 331–378; E. M. Anson, 'Diodorus and the date of Triparadeisus', *AJPh* 107, 1986, 208–217. A. B. Bosworth, 'Philip III Arrhidaeus and the chronology of the successors', *Chiron* 22, 1992, 55–81, advances very plausible arguments in favour of the so-called higher chronology which dates Triparadeisos in the year 321 and for ensuing events gives a date that is one year earlier than the other chronology (for example the spring of 316 is given as the date for the death of Olympias). The deaths of Antipatros in the autumn of 319 and of Philipp Arrhidaios in the autumn of 317 remain the same in both chronologies.

28  It remains unclear whether Ptolemy first invaded Syria and Phoenicia and then entered into the coalition in an attempt to consolidate this move or whether he undertook this conquest when he was already under the protection of the coalition. See Seibert (1969), 130–132; *CAH* VII, 1, 41f.

29  Hammond, in Hammond, Walbank (1988), 136–144. Polyperchon may have stayed in the Peloponnese until the last decade of the fourth century, but if so he was no longer of any significance to the history of the Ptolemaic kingdom.

30  Seleukos himself was not a partner in this alliance. See Mehl (1986), 76f.

31  O. Mørkholm, 'Cyrene and Ptolemy I', *Chiron* 10, 1980, 154–159; Laronde (1987), 199–218, 350–356.

32  Satrap Stele, ll. 5–6: Urk. II, 15, ll. 2–7. On the sequence of events see Winnicki (1989 and 1991, 1).

33  On the elephants used in this battle see p. 55; on Ptolemy I's advance on Jerusalem possibly at the beginning of 311 see p. 189.

34  Mehl (1986), 127.

35  E. Will, 'La Cyrénaïque et les partages successifs de l'empire d'Alexandre', *AntCl* 29, 1960, 369–390; Mehl (1986), 121f.

36  On the chronology and the background of events see Hammond, in Hammond, Walbank (1988), 164–167.

37  See p. 17; Mehl (1986), 139–147. To be sure, it remains an open question when the death of Alexander IV became known.

38  H. Gesche, 'Nikokles von Paphos und Nikokreon von Salamis', *Chiron* 4, 1974, 103–125; Bagnall (1976), 39–42. In the ancient tradition, there is confusion between Nikokreon and Nikokles and so, in the more recent literature, this tragic end is most often ascribed to Nikokreon. Cf. V. Karageorghis, *Cyprus From the the Stone Age to the Romans*, London, 1982, 168–170; F. G. Maier, V. Karageorghis, *Paphos*, Nicosia, 1984, 224.

39  Wörrle (1977), 51, footnote 46; Bagnall (1976), 89–91; H. Hauben, 'On the Ptolemaic Iasos Inscription', *IGSK* 28. 1, 2–3, *EpigrAnat* 10, 1987, 3–5.

40  G. Horat Zuffa, 'Tolemeo I in Grecia', *Atti Venezia* 130, 1971–72, 99–112.

41  Seibert (1983), 117.

42  Bagnall (1976), 25f.; Seibert (1983), 133–136; on Magas: PP VI, 14533.

43  H. Hauben, 'Fleet strength at the battle of Salamis (306 BC)', *Chiron* 6, 1976, 1–5.

44  On the motives and on the chronological sequence of events the fundamental discussion is now: G. A. Lehmann, 'Das neue Kölner Historiker-Fragment (P. Köln Nr. 247) und die χρονικὴ σύνταξις des Zenon von Rhodos (FGrHist. 523)', *ZPE* 72, 1988, 1–17; somewhat different from our own account: Billows (1990), 155–160, 351f.; Seibert (1991), 88, note 8. The Babylonian catalogue

of kings gives 305/304 as the first year of Seleukos I's reign; cf. E. Grzybek, 'Zu einer babylonischen Königsliste aus der hellenistischen Zeit (Keilschrifttaffel BM 35603)', *Historia* 41, 1992, 193.

45  In any event, this became a fact in a very short time, even though the 'parity' that Ptolemy made a show of *vis-à-vis* Antigonos with his accession to the throne sought to be 'unrestricted' in practice (Lehmann, loc. cit., 8); cf. Hauben (1992), 158.

46  D. Pandermalis, in Πρακτικὰ τοῦ Η' Διεθνοῦς Συνεδρίου Ἑλληνικῆς καὶ Λατινικῆς Ἐπιγραφίας, Athen, 1984, 271; Hammond, in Hammond, Walbank (1988), 173f.

47  Following Grzybek (1990), 90, 96f. On the coronation date of Ptolemy I cf. also Merkelbach (1963), 45f.; Koenen (1977), 57 (6 January); on the continuity in ideology from Alexander to Ptolemy I expressed through the throne name see p. 80. The long period of time between Ptolemy's adoption of the title of basileus and the establishment of a calendar on the basis of his reign as pharaoh clearly shows that the coronation ceremony was planned in every detail. The coronation of the first four Ptolemies as pharaoh is in our opinion unjustifiably rejected in many cases, cf. *REg.* 38, 1987, 103, footnote 85; Burstein (1991), 140f.; in response to the last see p. 35 together with note 1.

48  Samuel (1962), 11–24; Wörrle (1977), 45; D. Hagedorn, *ZPE* 66, 1986, 68f. For an analogous course of action in Seleukos I's kingdom see Mehl (1986), 144–147.

49  Mehl (1986), 152–154; see also p. 91.

50  Cf. Klose (1972), 22; G. Wirth, *Tyche* 3, 1988, 243f.

51  As expressly stated by the historian of the Kölner Papyrus.

52  See p. 91.

53  H. Hauben, 'Rhodes, Alexander and the Diadochoi from 333/332 to 304 BC', *Historia* 26, 1977, 307–339.

54  Mehl (1980–81), 197; id. (1986), 207–212.

55  Literally 'hollow Syria' possibly from the Semitic *kol surija* 'the whole of Syria': E. Bikerman, 'La Coelé-Syrie', *RBi* 54, 1947, 256–268; W. Röllig in *Der Kleine Pauly* III, 1975, 267 (s.v. Koile Syria).

56  On Miletus see p. 38.

57  Wörrle (1977).

58  Bagnall (1976), 111–113; Mehl (1986), 273.

59  See p. 38.

60  PP VI, 15085; J. Seibert, 'Philokles, Sohn des Appollodoros, König der Sidonier', *Historia* 19, 1970, 337–351; Merker (1970), 143–150; Wörrle (1978), 225–230; H. Hauben, 'Philocles, King of the Sidonians and general of the Ptolemies', *Studia Phoenicia* 5, Leuven 1987, 413–427; Hauben (1992), 164.

61  Habicht (1979), 2–8.

62  PP VI, 16555; Mooren (1975), 56f. (08); see p. 65.

63  The source for these events is the Athenian decree in honour of Kallias of Sphettos (270/269): *SEG* XXVIII, 60; Habicht (1979), 45–67; M. J. Osborne, 'Kallias, Phedros and the revolt of Athens in 287 BC', *ZPE* 35, 1979, 181–194; L. Robert, *REG* 94, 1981, 394–400.

64  Seibert (1983), 117–120.

65  *IG* II². 650 (the decree of Zenon); *IG* II². 682 (the decree of Phaidros); *SEG* XXVIII, 60, l. 44–55 (the decree of Kallias); Habicht (1979), 49f., 59.

66 See p. 35f.

67 Heinen (1972, 2), 8, footnote 21; H. Volkmann: *RE* XXIII, 2, 1959, 1867 (s.v. Ptolemais, 2).

68 Heinen (1972, 2), 3–20; on the chronology see more recently Hazzard (1987), 149.

69 Koenen (1977), 51–53, 62, 101; Grzybek (1990), 131, 171, 175. On the question of the co-regency (a later invention of Ptolemy II against the claims of Keraunos?) cf. Hazzard (1987), 148–152.

70 Seibert (1967), 95f.

71 Ibid., 78.

72 Harmatta (1963).

73 Bengtson (1952), 24–29.

74 Peremans (1983), 272.

75 Quaegebeur (1979), 726f.; Peremans (1980/81), 222f.

76 See p. 18; see also the indigenous 'officers' p. 27 and the mention of a very few simple soldiers in the time between Ptolemy I and Ptolemy III in W. Peremans, 'Les indigènes Egyptiens dans l'armée de terre des Lagides', *AncSoc* 9, 1978, 83–100, esp. 94f. Alexander himself had obviously planned also to recruit a great number of Egyptians in the imperial army, since he had 6,000 Egyptian youths trained for the corps of royal pages: Suda, s.v. βασίλειοι παῖδες; N. G. L. Hammond, 'Royal pages, personal pages, and boys trained in the Macedonian manner during the period of the Temenid monarchy', *Historia* 39, 1990, 261–290, esp. 276.

77 See p. 83f.

78 The Satrap Stele, l . 4: Urk. II, 14, 12–16; on this topic see D. Lorton, 'The names of Alexandria in the text of the Satrap Stele', *GöttMisz* 96, 1987, 67–70. On the date for the transfer of the capital city which took place before the Syrian campaign, researchers hesitate between 320/319 (Swinnen [1973], 116 footnote 2, 120; Fraser [1972], I, 7, II, 12, footnote 28) and 313 (*CAH* VII, 1, 127 [Turner]).

79 Rostovtzeff, I (1955), 205.

80 Fraser (1972), I, 312–335.

81 PP VI, 16764.

82 PP VI, 16742; of the works cited here, see above all the collection of texts in F. Wehrli, *Demetrios von Phaleron*, 2nd edn, Basel, 1968.

83 See p. 15.

84 PP VI, 16761, 16786.

85 PP VI, 16915.

86 The legal status of Paraitonion, on the northwest coast of the Cyrenaica, seems uncertain: H. Kees, *RE* 36, 2, 1949, 1182–1184 (s.v. Paraitonion); Rostovtzeff, I (1955), 253. On the map of H. Heinen, *Ägypten in hellenistisch-römischer Zeit* (Tübingen, 1989) (=Tübinger Atlas des Vorderen Orients, B V 21) the site of Paraitonion is not indicated as a polis.

87 G. Plaumann, *Ptolemais in Oberägypten*, Leipzig, 1910. On the organization of power in the cities cf. Bernand (1992), Nr. 2, 4–7.

88 Bengtson (1952), 128–133. On the political and legal status of Alexandria and the surrounding region see A. Jähne, 'Die Ἀλεξανδρέων χώρα', *Klio* 63, 1981, 63–103; on the question of the boulé which was taken from the city for the first time by Octavian see Geraci (1983), 176–182.

89  W. Peremans, 'Un groupe d'officiers dans l'armée des Lagides', *AncSoc* 8, 1977, 175–185, esp. 184; id., 'Les Egyptiens dans l'armée de terre des Lagides', in Festschrift für H. Bengtson (ed.) *Althistorische Studien*, H. Heinen, Wiesbaden, 1983, 92–101, esp. 95.

90  Urk. II, 24–26; PP I, 285; II, 2122.

91  Urk. II, 1–6; Roeder (1959), 214–219; Lichtheim (1980), 41–44; O. Perdu, 'Le monument de Samtoutefnakht à Naples', *Reg* 36, 1985, 89–113. His biography can be read on the man's Stele which was found at the Iseum in Pompeii but originally was set up in the temple of Harsaphes at Herakleopolis Magna.

92  Lichtheim (1980), 44–49; S. Nakaten: *LÄ* IV, 1982, 995–998 (s.v. Petosiris); PP III, 5406.

93  See p. 100.

94  *FGrHist.* 609; W. G. Waddell, *Manetho*, London, 1940 (Text); W. Helck, *Untersuchungen zu Manetho und den ägyptischen Königslisten*, Berlin, 1956; PP III, 5395; VI, 16934.

95  On the time of death see Samuel (1962), 28–30; Koenen (1977), 43, 52 (early in 282); Grzybek (1990), 97–99 (November 283). On his age see Heckel (1992), 205, 222.

96  Cf. E. Olshausen, *Gnomon* 48, 1976, 466–477 (Review of Seibert [1969]).

97  For an assessment of this role played by Cyprus see H. Hauben, 'Cyprus and the Ptolemaic navy', *RDAC*, 1987, 213–226.

98  See p. 19; for Karia cf. a decree from the city of Amyzon in the time of Ptolemy I's reign: J. and L. Robert, *Fouilles d'Amyzon en Carie*, I, Paris, 1983, 127f. (Nr. 6).

99  Cf. J. Harmatta, 'Zur Wirtschaftsgeschichte des frühptolemäischen Ägyptens', in H.-J. Diesner *et al.* (eds) *Sozialökonomische Verhältnisse im Alten Orient und im Klassischen Altertum*, Berlin/DDR, 1961, 119–139 (cites an Aramaic papyrus on the commercial relations between two Jewish merchants, probably from around 310 BC). For the time of Argead kings see J. Quaegebeur, 'De nouvelles archives de famille thébaines à l'aube de l'époque ptolémaïque', in *Actes du Xve Congr. Intern. de Papyrologie*, 4e partie, Bruxelles, 1979, 40–48.

100  Will, I (1979), 168.

101  Proof of this in *PCZ* 59021 for 258 BC. On the monetary policies of Ptolemy I and II see Bagnall (1976), 176–212; Will, I (1979), 175–179; Orrieux (1983), 28f.

# 2 The empire under the second and third Ptolemies (282–222)

## POLITICAL DEVELOPMENT UNDER PTOLEMY II PHILADELPHOS (282–246)

### The Ptolemaic family during the first years of rule

After about two years as joint-ruler, Ptolemy II assumed sole command and was crowned pharaoh probably on 7 January 282.[1] At first, he counted the years of his reign as of that date but later he included the period of his joint-rule (from 285/4) in this reckoning.[2]

At the beginning of his reign, the pharaoh was married to Arsinoe, daughter of the successor, Lysimachos of Thrace, and she gave birth to a Ptolemy (who would later be the third king of the dynasty), to a Lysimachos and to a Berenike. Another Ptolemy, referred to as the 'son' and known to have been the official co-regent of the years 267–259,[3] was probably the oldest son of the royal couple.

Around the year 300, the sister of Ptolemy II, Arsinoe, had begun to live at the Thracian court as the spouse of King Lysimachos. From the year 285, the latter controlled all of Macedonia as well. At his court, Arsinoe became increasingly ruthless and hungry for power and she succeeded, in particular, in having the successor to the throne, Agathokles, killed (283/2). The widow of Agathokles, Lysandra, daughter of Ptolemy I and Eurydike, fled to Seleukos with her children and her brothers, among them Ptolemy Keraunos, who had been staying at the court of Lysimachos. Numerous followers of Agathokles also went there and they eventually managed to launch a war against Lysimachos (Sixth War of the Successors). Lysimachos lost his life in a battle at Korupedion in Lydia at the beginning of 281. This battle also marked an end to the history of the successors, since 281 was the last time that two former officers of Alexander the Great clashed. In late summer of the same year, Seleukos crossed over to Europe with his victorious army. On his way to the Thracian residence at Lysimacheia, however, he was assassinated single-handedly by Ptolemy Keraunos. By this treachery Keraunos sought to acquire the power of his former protector. His next act was to rush to Lysimacheia, assume the diadem and have himself acclaimed king by Seleukos' army (Memnon: FGrHist. 434 F8).

Keraunos' half-sister, Queen Arsinoe, had taken refuge in the city of Kassandreia (Chalkidike) after the battle at Korupedion. Her children by Lysimachos were a threat to the usurper since they were legitimate heirs and so in an attempt to lay his hands on them he induced Arsinoe to marry him and made her queen for a second time in the presence of the Macedonian military council. After the city of Kassandreia came under his control, however, Keraunos revealed his true colours: the two sons of Arsinoe, both of whom had remained in the city, were killed and Arsinoe herself was allowed to flee. At first she travelled to Samothrace and from there she went to her brother Ptolemy II in Egypt in about 279 (Just. XVII.2; XXIV.2–3).

Here she once again took to intrigue and this time she directed it against Arsinoe I who stood in the way of her plans to become queen for a third time. Shortly thereafter, Arsinoe I was banished to Koptos and Ptolemy II and Arsinoe II (Fig. 2.1), who were full siblings, married. The union between brother and sister was taboo and a scandal of the first order for traditional Greeks and Macedonians. The poet Sotades (Ath. XIV.621 a–b), who made fun of the royal couple, was forced to leave and later paid for his mockery with his life.[4] The court poet, Theocritus, on the other hand, celebrated this union of brother and sister by likening them to the gods (*Id.* XVII)[5] and thus reaped great renown.

The accession of Ptolemy II did not go uncontested. Demetrios of Phaleron was expelled from Alexandria after the death of Ptolemy I because he had supported the succession of the children of Eurydike; he died not long after of a snake bite (D. L. V.78f.; cf. Cic. *Rab. Post.* 23). If we believe the account of events in Paus. I.7.1, the execution of two of his 'brothers'[6] by Philadelphos early in his reign may well stem back to Arsinoe II's influence. Even Magas, son of Berenike I from the first marriage and from 300 governor of Cyrenaica, assumed the title of king; Ptolemy II could do nothing about it.

Ptolemy Keraunos gave up his claims in Egypt in writing after he was acclaimed king (Just. XVII.2.9f.). He was not to enjoy a long reign in Macedonia, however, since in January/February of 279 he was captured and killed in battle against a Celtic army. His brother, Meleager, was subsequently elected king but after only two months was replaced by Antipatros, a nephew of the successor Kassandros (Porph.: FGrHist. 260.3.10). Macedonia fell into utter disarray. Only in 277 was the son of Demetrios Poliorketes, Antigonos Gonatas, able to defeat the Celts at Lysmacheia from his bases in Greece. Afterwards he arrived in Macedonia to take over the kingdom (276) as its victor and saviour. It was of this date that the successor kings decisively consolidated their power; the most significant leaders being Ptolemy II, the Seuleukids Antiochos I (281–261) and II (261–246) as well as the Macedonian king Antigonos II Gonatas (276–239).

*Figure 2.1* Ptolemaic cameo of Indian sardonyx with image of the second Ptolemaic couple; the nearer profile shows Ptolemy II with Attic helmet, above it a snake (perhaps a transposition of the Egyptian Uraeus-snake), on the neck-piece an image of Zeus-Ammon with ram-horn winding about his ear; behind the king's profile is that of Arsinoe II with a cap-like crown and veil (sometimes interpreted as a bride's adornment); datable to some time during the 270s; height: 11.5 cm; found in the thirteenth century as an adornment on the Shrine of the Three Kings at Cologne; Vienna, Kunsthistorisches Museum, AS-Inv. IX A 81; Kyrieleis (1975) 19: 81; W. Oberleitner, *Geschnittene Steine, die Prunkkameen der Wiener Antikensammlung*, Vienna 1985, 32–35.

## The 'Syrian War of Succession'; territorial gains in Anatolia

In 281, Seleukos I Nikator had bequeathed to his son Antiochos I Soter a huge tract of land which had been increased substantially by the addition of territories taken from Lysimachos and which now stretched from the Dardanelles to India. Upon his accession, however, the new king found himself facing unrest in the north of Syria (around the state capital of Seleukia in Pieria). This situation temporarily weakened the Seleukid king and Ptolemy II was quick to exploit it. He was thereby able to further Ptolemaic control in Anatolia (in the so-called Syrian War of Succession:[7] 280–79) and did so without risk because Ptolemy Keraunos had won the army of Seleukos over to his side.

Although very little is known about the Ptolemaic campaigns, epigraphic sources do provide us with the following picture. Ptolemy II gave a piece of land[8] to the city of Miletus, where in 280/79 Antiochos I was still hailed as 'stephanephoros',[9] and he probably renewed the treaty of alliance and friendship initially made by Ptolemy I in about 294.[10] The beginning of Ptolemaic domination on the island of Samos, which had belonged to Lysimachos prior to Korupedion, is marked by the fact that Philokles of Sidon called a gathering of the Island League there in 280/79.[11] During the period of Ptolemaic occupation, Samos served as an important base for the naval fleet. Following the epigraphic sources for the cities of Stratonikeia, Amyzon, Halikarnassos and Myndos, a consequence of the so-called Syrian War of Succession was that Ptolemaic rule in this area spread as far as Karia and was partially organized by the above-mentioned Philokles.[12] Evidence for a Ptolemaic garrison in Halikarnassos dates from 270/69.[13] Numerous inscriptions mention Ptolemaic territorial expansion into Lycia, which had already been won by Soter.[14] Close to the city of Telmessos,[15] a Ptolemy, the surviving son of the successor, Lysimachos, and Arsinoe (II), received his own province from Philadelphos. Later (240), Ptolemy III gave him control over Telmessos, where he proved himself to be a judicious legal and tax reformer. At the end of 278, the pamphyliarch previously mentioned[16] is already documented as administrator of Pamphylia in Termessos. Since Ptolemaic territorial gains resulting from the First Syrian War at the end of the 270s are very uncertain, the acquisition of Cilicia should also belong within the timeframe of the so-called Syrian War of Succession.

In 279, peace returned between the Ptolemaic and Seleukid empires, without Antiochos I being able to do anything about Ptolemaic conquests in Asia Minor; instead he had to concentrate all his forces on dealing with an alliance of his enemies to the north (Bithynia, Byzantium, among other cities, as well as Antigonos Gonatas) simply to ensure his succession to his father's kingdom. In Alexandria, however, there was a general expectation of some retaliation on the part of Antiochos I as soon as calm returned to the region. Ptolemaic possessions at the end of the 270s are summed up in a poem by Theocritus (*Id.* XVII.86–90): in Anatolia he names Pamphylia, Cilicia, Lycia and Karia.

## The conflict with King Magas and the First Syrian War (274–271)

It took a few years for Antiochos I to solve his problems in Asia Minor. New powers to be reckoned with in the region were Bithynia, Pontus, Cappadocia, Pergamon and the Galatians who had migrated there since 278. The last of these invaded Ptolemaic Lycia at a later time but were eventually defeated (St Byz. s.v. Ἀγρίαι). Relations were established between Antiochos I and

Antigonos Gonatas in 278 and in 276, upon the accession to the throne of Antigonos in Macedonia, and developed into a friendship between the two dynasties. This was dangerous for the Ptolemaic state, since with it came the possibility of a conflict on two major fronts.

The military conflicts which followed were triggered by a crisis within the Ptolemaic dynasty. Magas, self-appointed king of Cyrenaica, was able to gain support in the house of the Seleukids against Ptolemy II through his marriage to Apame, daughter of Antiochos I (Paus. I.7.3).[17] It seemed inevitable that Egypt would be faced with a war on two fronts, but co-ordination was lacking. Magas took possession of the coastal city of Paraitonion in the mid-270s and quickly marched upon Alexandria, evidently to oust his half-brother from the throne. He was, however, forced to turn back, because a revolt of Libyan nomads had broken out in his absence. Magas was able to quell the rebellion but any further action against Egypt was now out of the question. For his part, Ptolemy II was prevented from pursuing Magas by a rebellion of his Celtic soldiers. In response to this, he lured them to a deserted island on the Nile where they were destroyed (Paus. I.7.2; Call. h.IV.185–187 and Schol. to 175–187 p. 70f., Pf.).[18] Philadelphos' half-brother thus continued to rule as king in Cyrene and to mint his own coins, but his relations with the Ptolemies in Alexandria remained strained for more than two decades. Under Magas there was a cultural awakening in Cyrene which rivalled that of Alexandria. The young Callimachus praised the king and the holy shrines of his native Cyrene by name in his hymns.[19]

The great ceremonial procession described by Kallixeinos of Rhodes[20] may be attributed to the period following Magas' campaign and Philadelphos' success with the Celts. Accordingly, it would act as an expression of the mood of discord before the clash with the Antiochus I, on the occasion of the dynastic festival of Ptolemaia[21] in the winter of 275/4. In the procession, a good example of the incomparable luxury of the Ptolemies, there were segments honouring the various dynastic gods (Dionysos, Zeus, other Olympian divinities, Alexander the Great as well as the first Ptolemaic couple) together with figures representing the 'free' Greek cities, led by the personification of Corinthian; in this way, Philadelphos presented himself as a champion of the Panhellenic idea of freedom. The main part of the procession was dedicated to Dionysos returning as world conqueror from India with immeasurable treasures. Related to this theme was the endless parade of exotic animals from Africa, Arabia and India, especially the 24 elephant-wagons, several types of antelopes, ostriches, wild asses, zebus, leopards as well as rarities like a giraffe and a rhinoceros. Many of the countless camels were burdened with the bounty of the incense country; they were followed by tribute-bearing Africans (or dark-skinned Nubians). One is reminded of the 'tribute–bearers' from all over the world found in the Theban tombs of the New Kingdom – a thousand times surpassed, to be sure, by the lavishness of the Ptolemaic display. There was also a huge parade of over 80,000 men from the Ptolemaic army. Beside the areas laid out for the refreshment of the soldiers and guests, was the large and splendid tent of Ptolemy II. It was set up within the walls of the citadel for the royal symposium and could seat 130 guests; an approximate reconstruction of the structure is possible.[22]

Ptolemy Philadelphos himself initiated the so-called First Syrian War (274–271)[23] by undertaking a military campaign against Seleukid Syria; his troops retreated, however, in the face of an advance by Antiochos who mobilized new units in Babylon and even demanded 20 elephants from Baktria. The Egyptian administration thus had to take all steps to prevent an imminent invasion perhaps both by sea and by land (Theoc. *Id.* XVII.98–101). In 274/3, Ptolemy II and his spouse Arsinoe II went personally to the border of the east Delta to organize defences there.[24] The armed forces in Babylon were beset by a serious economic crisis and, at the same time, a plague was raging there. In 271, Antiochos abandoned his plans for conquest[25] and Philadelphos suddenly and unexpectedly emerged as the victor. The peace which was agreed upon in 271 was essentially based on the *status quo* and so large territorial changes seem quite unlikely; Damascus remained Ptolemaic, though it was one of the points of contention in the war.[26] The atmosphere of rejoicing in Egypt was proclaimed by Theocritus in his poem dedicated to Ptolemy II (*Id.* XVII) which he had probably presented at the Ptolemaia of 271/70 and for which he probably won the musical contest.

Arsinoe II was the first significant female figure in Ptolemaic history. During her lifetime, she was not only a counterpart to her brother-spouse in the cult-worship of the ruler,[27] but she also took an active role in the defence of Egypt. In the 260s, the Greeks attributed to her a strong influence on Ptolemaic foreign policy which was now strongly anti-Macedonian and eventually led to the Chremonidean War.[28] Arsinoe II passed away in July of 270.[29] The religious and historical consequences of her death will be discussed in Chapter 3.

## The Chremonidean War (267–261) and the Ptolemaic bases in the Aegean

The policies of the second and third Ptolemies towards Greece were determined by their rivalry with the Antigonids in Macedonia, especially regarding their influence in the Peloponnese and the Aegean Islands. At the time of the First Syrian War, Antigonos Gonatas defeated Pyrrhus and then strengthened Macedonian influence in Greece; a large part of Greece was subjugated by means of Macedonian occupation or through tyrants set up by Antigonos. A new version of Demetrios Poliorketes' former domination of the seas would have directly threatened the Ptolemaic thalassocracy, based largely as it was on its protectorate of the Island League,[30] and so would have been a direct menace to the security of the kingdom. This was all the more disturbing given the good relations between Antigonos and the Seleukid kingdom.

Philadelphos' naval campaign in the Black Sea in support of Byzantium at an uncertain date may be best understood in light of the political situation described above and of the balance of power after the First Syrian War. Ptolemy II granted the city new territory in Asia as well as a large supply of grain, arms and money. For this reason, he was paid the highest homage a city could grant: a cult and a temple were founded in his honour (St Byz. s.v. Ἄγκυρα; Dion. Byz.: *Geogr. Graeci Min.* II.34).[31] Ptolemy II thus carried out an interventionist policy in the northern Aegean but continued to rely completely on naval supremacy. Ptolemy III would later discover the setbacks to which such a thalassocracy could easily be exposed.

Macedonian naval power will have been the most significant impetus for Ptolemy II to provoke the Chremonidean War (267–261),[32] named after the Athenian Chremonides. As early as the great procession in 275/4 (?), Philadelphos had made known his policy in favour of panHellenic freedom. In the years which followed, the Hellenic anti-Macedonian league based in central Greece (Plataea) was able to rely on the support of the Ptolemaic king.[33] The friendship between Athens and the Ptolemaic empire had also been further cultivated in the 270s. Envoys travelled back and forth and the king brought aid to Athens in the form of donations of money and grain.[34] Shortly before the Chremonidean War, Philadelphos almost certainly had concluded anti-Macedonian treaties with Athens and Sparta. After several failed attempts, Athens could finally hope to regain the Piraeus which doubtless had been under continued Macedonian occupation since 294.[35] Sparta, for its part, saw its advantage, since historically it had always nurtured the dream of gaining supremacy in the Peloponnesus. At the request of Chremonides, a treaty of alliance and friendship was formed between Athens on the one side and Sparta with its Peloponnesian allies on the other.[36] Together with earlier bilateral agreements, a threefold alliance between the Ptolemaic empire, Athens and Sparta was now firmly in place and directed against Antigonos Gonatas.

Antigonos opened the hostilities soon afterwards (perhaps early in 267). The Ptolemaic fleet, under the command of a Macedonian-born strategos Patroklos,[37] arrived in Attika. Patroklos' actions in the Aegean and his efforts in setting up bases throughout the Aegean Islands are more important in terms of Ptolemaic history as a whole than for the course of the Chremonidean War – we will return to this topic at a later point. Antigonos was quicker to reach the limits of Attika and could easily block off access to the Piraeus with the garrison he already had there. Patroklos had to resort to other harbours facing and along the Attic coast, where he benefited from the co-operation of Athenian patriots. He set up his main base on the small island of Gaiduronisi (Paus. I.1.1; Str. IX.1.21) facing the southern point of Attika. The island was given the name 'Patroklos' Island' or 'Patroklos' Camp' and it is still today called Patróklu. Other bases were Koroni (east coast)[38] or Rhamnus (northeast coast).[39] Methana, lying across from Attika, off the southern coast of the Saronic Gulf, was made into a Ptolemaic foreign territory no doubt during the course of the war; perhaps it was Patroklos who gave the city its new name of 'Arsinoe'.[40] By blockading the Saronic Gulf,

Patroklos may have been able to cause Antigonos some damage but he was not able to influence the outcome of the war in any decisive way. Indeed, at the beginning of its campaign, the Ptolemaic fleet was not once able to shield the Attic people from the marauding pirates who were obviously in Antigonos' pay.[41] Thus, Ptolemy II conducted this war only to the extent that it benefited his political interests and so never deployed the full resources of his empire. Patroklos, who had no expeditionary force with him, operated only from his sea bases and avoided any confrontation on land, given that a good proportion of his troops were Egyptian by birth (Paus. III.6.4–6).[42] Such a half-hearted venture could not possibly succeed.

In land operations, the Macedonian army proved itself to be superior to the allied forces of Spartans and Athenians. The Spartan king, Areus, died in battle at Corinth (265). Athens came under siege and was forced to capitulate (early in 261). Chremonides and his brother Glaukon found refuge in Egypt as Philadelphos' advisers (Teles. *De fuga*, 46f., ed. O'Neil, p. 22f.) Chremonides[43] attained the rank of a Ptolemaic fleet commander and his brother[44] appears in 255/4 as a priest of Alexander enjoying much favour; Ptolemy III later had a statue in his honour erected at Olympia. In Athens, aside from the Piraeus, the hill of the Museion was also occupied by the Macedonians and the city itself came under the command of a royal Macedonian commissar (261).[45] Although Antigonos withdrew his troops from the city in the mid-250s and thus legally re-instituted its freedom, nonetheless the city's position was compromised by the presence of garrisons in the Piraeus and in Attika. Athens' greatest loss was the ensuing decline of its status as a cultural and intellectual centre, a role which would henceforth be taken over by Alexandria.

The Ionian coast became a secondary theatre of war in the late 260s where the king's son and co-regent, Ptolemy, had taken on supreme command. Miletus was seriously affected and even directly threatened by military action. Ptolemy II, however, could justifiably praise the city's loyalty and urge its citizens to remain loyal (262/1).[46] In about 262, Ephesos and perhaps also the island of Lesbos[47] came under Ptolemaic control. But Ptolemaic hegemony would soon suffer serious setbacks in this very region owing to the Chremonidean War which had weakened it.

Ptolemaic rule remained unbroken in the central Aegean owing to a few island bases set up by Patroklos partly on his way to Attika and partly during the course of the ensuing military campaign. These bases went on to become lasting military strongholds and were instrumental in upholding the Ptolemaic protectorate over the Cyclades, i.e. over the Island League.

On the way north, Patroklos stopped over in the east-Cretan city of Itanos. Inspired by a decree in his honour,[48] he organized the city's internal affairs and foreign relations, for which he was made a citizen of Itanos. Patroklos probably left behind a garrison to safeguard the city which went on to become one of the most important Ptolemaic bases in the Aegean. In Olus (on the west coast of the bay of Mirabello in eastern Crete), Patroklos, his admiral Kallikrates of Samos and other Ptolemaic officers were given the titles of 'proxenos' (guest-friend of the state) and 'euergetes' (benefactor). Finally, it should be mentioned that on the small island of Kaudos, facing the southern coast of Crete, the poet Sotades, who had been forced into exile because he had mocked the royal pair, was apprehended and drowned in the sea (Athen. XIV.621a).[49]

Lying further to the north, the island of Thera seems to have become a significant Ptolemaic bastion from this point on. Patroklos installed a garrison there and made a certain Apollodotos its commander (*epistates*) in 267/6.[50] One of the troops' most important duties was to ward off the pirates. Most of the evidence relating to Ptolemaic activities on Thera, dates only from the reign of the sixth Ptolemy (180–145). We do know, however, that at this later date soldiers on Thera as in Egypt were recruited from the social classes of the poorer *machimoi* and the superior *stratiotai*; in other words that in the second century, Greek soldiers together with soldiers from the Egyptian peasantry were stationed on Thera.[51] During the reign of Ptolemy VI, Itanos, Thera and Methana (cf. the context in which Fig. 7.1 was found) were the last three strongholds of the Ptolemies in the area and they formed a single administrative unit in both military and civic terms.[52] After he acceded to the throne in 145, Ptolemy VIII gave up the three bases and withdrew the troops stationed there.

The island of Keos, lying to the southeast of the southern point of Attika, is also worthy of mention. As early as the 280s or 270s, The Ptolemies had involved themselves in the internal affairs of the island through their representatives Philokles of Sidon and the nesiarch Bakchon.[53] During the Chremonidean War, Patroklos drew it and Methana into his plans against Antigonos Gonatas. The new military commander established his quarters in the harbour city of Koresia which was renamed 'Arsinoe' and may also have been Patroklos' main base during the war.[54] The Ptolemaic administration and military presence lasted until the end of the third century.

In conclusion, Ptolemy II Philadelphos, together with his allies, lost the Chremonidean War against Antigonos Gonatas but several important Ptolemaic bases were established during the course of the conflict. These were to become the military backbone of Ptolemaic policy in Greece during the rest of the third century and, to some extent, for the first half of the second century.

## The Second Syrian War (260–253)

During the Second Syrian War, the third Seleukid ruler, Antiochos II, came into conflict with the Ptolemaic king; rather exceptionally, the former was supported by the island of Rhodes, although the Rhodians always took care to maintain close relations with the Ptolemaic empire owing to the important commercial relations between the two and because Rhodes was surrounded by Ptolemaic harbours.

Conflicts which had barely been settled in western Asia Minor (around Miletus and Ephesos in the late 260s) undoubtedly triggered the war – tensions which were clearly carried over to the Ptolemaic royal family. The successor to the throne, Ptolemy, who was operating in Ionia, revolted against his father. The Aetolian Timarchos attached himself to the revolt and proclaimed himself tyrant of Miletus (Trog. *prol.* 26); he implicated Samos in his affairs by killing the Ptolemaic general stationed there (Fron. *Str.* III.2.11).[55] After the spring of 259, Ptolemy, 'the son', no longer figures in the Egyptian dating formula and so, we can assume, was divested of the co-regency. His own rule and Timarchos' rule did not last long: in 259/8, Antiochos II gained control of Miletus (App. *Syr.* 65) and Samos.[56] Matters came to a head shortly thereafter in the sea battle of Ephesus (that is, probably still before the mid-250s) in which the Rhodians defeated the Ptolemaic fleet under the command of the Ptolemaic nauarch Chremonides;[57] Ephesus was taken.[58] A Seleukid presence is again attested in inscriptions dating to 254/3.[59]

Antigonos Gonatas had probably also supported the Seleukid king; this is certainly true of the naval battle at Kos if we take this to be a part of the Second Syrian War. If so, it was in the spring of 255 that Antigonos inflicted a serious defeat on the Ptolemaic admiral Patroklos in that battle, known to us from the Chremonidean War (Plu. *Mor.* 545B; Athen. V. 209e, VIII.334a).[60] It may be that as a result of further engagements, the Ptolemaic thalassocracy went on to suffer other serious losses in the Aegean into the mid-250s. For the year 255, however, peace is attested in the Cyclades region.[61] The Ptolemaic protectorate over the Island League came to an end at this time; the koinon, in any case, disappears from historical sources in the mid-third century. The island of Andros was certainly in Antigonos' possession by the end of the 250s (Plu. *Arat.* 12.2).[62]

Antiochos II was *de facto* the victor in Anatolia. Aside from his successes in Ionia (Miletus, Samos, Ephesos), he was able to regain a large share of territories in Cilicia and Pamphylia which had been lost in the Syrian War of Succession. What transpired in Syria itself remains unknown; we hear only that Philadelphos undertook a campaign there in the spring/summer of 257.[63]

Peace was concluded before the summer of 253[64] owing to the deft diplomacy of the Ptolemies and it was strengthened by a marriage between Antiochos II and the daughter of Ptolemy II, Berenike. Antiochos had previously repudiated his wife Laodike. Some details are known of preparations for the bride's journey at the end of 253. In the spring of 252, Philadelphos accompanied his daughter to Pelusion, on which occasion he is said to have brought vast quantities of silver and gold, ostensibly a 'dowry' but probably indemnities for the war (Porph: FGrHist. 260F 43). The dioiketes, Apollonios, who was the highest administrative official in the empire, then brought the bride to Antiochos as far away as the border of the empire north of Sidon.[65] We may infer from this destination that Philadelphos did not surrender any land in this region and that the Eleutheros continued to represent the border between Ptolemaic and Seleukid Syria.

## Greek policy in the later years

During the last decade of his life, Ptolemy II continued to pursue his anti-Macedonian policy in Greek areas. In about 250, the Ptolemaic fleet was even able to defeat Antigonos in a naval battle (Ps. Aristeas 180; J. *AJ* XII.93) and thereby vindicate to a certain extent its defeat at Kos. Philadelphos appears then to have strengthened his influence in the Cyclades once again; in 249 he sponsored a festival at Delos in honour of the Delian gods (the so-called Second Ptolemaia).[66] Ptolemy III would later declare that the Cyclades were included in the territories he had inherited from his father, although this was certainly exaggerated.[67]

During the second half of the third century, the Hellenic leagues on the mainland, the Aetolian League in central Greece and the Achaean League in the northern Peloponnese, take on a new and greater significance for the Ptolemies. The Achaean League, especially since its reorganization in 280, pursued the same political aims as the Ptolemies in their decades-old struggle against the Macedonian hegemony. Philadelphos, therefore, began giving the league financial support. In the winter of 250/49, Aratos, leader of Sikyon, reached Alexandria after an eventful voyage and once there was able to negotiate Ptolemaic subsidies in several instalments (Plu. *Arat.* 9–15). On the whole, one can discern a slow revival of Ptolemaic influence in the Aegean in the mid-third century.

## The reconciliation with Magas, and Cyrenaica after his death

While the wars brought economic difficulties upon the Alexandrian court, Cyrene managed to steer clear of the crisis of that period. The end of the 250s was a time in which Philadelphos strove to unite once again the economically powerful Cyrene with his own empire by diplomatic means. The ageing Magas is said to have enjoyed the fruits of his wealth by indulging in the luxuries and banquets that acompanied court life (Athen. XII.550b–c). His own desire to join his family once again with that of the Egyptian dynasty was the perfect complement to Ptolemy II's wish for a reconciliation; the Egyptian successor to the throne, who would later be Ptolemy III, was thus engaged to Berenike, daughter of Magas (Just. XXVI.3.2). In about 250, Magas died after a reign of 50 years.

The widow of Magas and daughter of Antiochos I, Apame, was, however, opposed to the impending renewal of ties with the Ptolemaic empire. The marriage would invalidate the very purpose of her own marriage, namely that of making an independent Cyrenaica a base for the Seleukid kingdom. She therefore dissolved the engagement and summoned Demetrios the Fair of the Antigonid dynasty from Macedonia.[68] The Antigonids were now friendly toward the Seleukids and so there was much greater advantage in offering him her daughter's hand in marriage. Demetrios arrived and was able to obtain not only the city of Cyrene but also the Libyan territory which was associated with it. In this, he was assisted by the local party whose aim was to put into place the policies and government of the previous decade (250–249/8) (Eus. I.237f. Schöne). Berenike did not accept this set-back and headed her own opposition party; Demetrios, surprised in the bedroom of his future mother-in-law, was then murdered on Berenike's initiative (Just. XXVI.3.3–6; Catul. 66.25–28). As a result of this, the former engagement became valid once again and the joining of Cyrenaica with the Ptolemaic kingdom was assured. It appears, however, that in the coming years Berenike was not able to exercise her newly acquired power.

A third, i.e. 'republican' party managed to gain the upper hand in Cyrene. The Cyrenians invited two legislative reformers, Ekdelos and Demophanes, to take over the direction of their state; the two were able to acquire the reputation of having set up a fair government and of having preserved the 'freedom' of Cyrene (249/8–246) (Plb. X.22.3; Plu. *Phil.* 1.4). This situation did not dissuade either Berenike or the politicians in Alexandria from giving up their plans for a reunification of the two realms. The union of two dynastic houses was solemnized through wedlock, either shortly before or at the accession of her spouse, and the daughter of Magas consequently conferred her rights and privileges on the royal house of Lagos. As a result of this, Ptolemy III would later consider 'Libya' as having been (at least formally) inherited from his father.[69]

## POLITICS AND IMPERIAL HISTORY UNDER PTOLEMY III EUERGETES I (236–222)

### Change of reign; return of Cyrenaica

Ptolemy II Philadelphos died early in 246. His private life was not conducted in nearly as serious a fashion as his political and cultural achievements might allow us to believe. His extravagance in maintaining the court as well as the provisions for his mistresses[70] must have consumed vast amounts of tax money; the dwellings of the ladies were thought to be the most beautiful in Alexandria (Plb. XIV.11).

On 28 January, Ptolemy III took over the 'office of king from his father', that is, he was probably crowned pharaoh on that day.[71] In his royal title, he styled himself as the son of Ptolemy II and Arsinoe II, the Theoi Adelphoi (brother-sister gods), with the result that his real and exiled mother, Arsinoe I, does not appear officially as one of the ancestors of the Ptolemaic kings. For her part, Berenike II, who had already minted coins in Cyrene, was able

*Figure 2.2* Gold octadrachmon of Berenike II, dating from the beginning of
Ptolemy III's reign; obverse (left): bust of the queen with veil and diadem on
her head; the highly individualized facial features seem quite youthful; reverse
(right): cornucopia joined with a royal diadem and the legend ΒΕΡΕΝΙΚΗΣ
ΒΑΣΙΛΙΣΣΗΣ; Copenhagen, Nationalmuseet; Kyrieleis (1975): 95, Table 82.2;
Sylloge Nummorum Graecorum, Danish National Museum, Egypt: *The Ptolemies*,
ed.: A. Kromann, O. Mørkholm, Copenhagen 1977, nr. 169.

to continue doing so even in the rest of the empire during the Asian campaign
of her spouse owing to her status as the foremost lady of the Ptolemaic
house. Her imperial coins (e.g. Fig. 2.2) are among the finest Hellenistic
coin portraits and were already renowned in antiquity (Plb. IX.85).

The new royal couple re-established Ptolemaic authority in the Cyrenaica
right from the start and clearly could do so effectively by having behind
them the weight of a great empire. A comprehensive re-organization of the
country ensued (about 246): the harbour of Barke was re-founded as Ptolemais
(modern Tolmeta) and it eliminated the role of the old city as administrative
centre. Near modern Benghasi, the new harbour-city of Berenike was formed
and fitted out with defensive structures; it replaced the neighbouring old
city of Euhesperides. Taucheira (modern Tocra) was founded anew *in situ* as
Arsinoe. As an attempt to reconcile the recent Ptolemaic hegemony with the
Greek taste for self-administration and decentralization, a political solution
in the form of a city-league was devised (league of Cyrene, Ptolemais, Arsinoe
and Berenike). At the same time, this decentralization also served to keep in
check Cyrene's traditional proponderance over its neighbours. The league
struck its own coins with the legend 'KOINON' during the time of Ptolemy
III. It may be that the Libyarch who is attested only from the end of the
third century already served as the king's representative with the founding
of the koinon (Plb. XV.25.12). The disappearance of the koinon currency, at
the latest by the end of Ptolemy III's rule, may be a sign of the further
strengthening of Alexandria as a central power at that time.[72]

## The Third Syrian War (246–241): the empire in its greatest extent

The seeds of the subsequent clash with the Seleukid empire had already been sown in the aftermath of the Second Syrian War when Antiochos II had married a daughter of Ptolemy II called Berenike. Antiochos II died under suspicious circumstances in 246 at the residence of his former wife Laodike in Ephesos, only a few months after the accession of Ptolemy III. Also with Laodike were her two sons from the marriage with Antiochos II, Seleukos and Antiochos. The former queen maintained that on his deathbed the king had named one of her sons, Seleukos II (246–226/5), as his successor and thus had passed over his young son from his union with Berenike. Berenike, who was living in Antioch, refused to go along with this and thus proclaimed her own son as king (his name remains unknown) and appealed to Ptolemy III for help. This situation led to the outbreak of another war, the Third Syrian War, also known as the Laodicean War (Λαοδίκεως πόλεμος).[73] Seleukos II was only recognized in large parts of Seleukid Asia Minor and even there not entirely. The procurator of Ephesos, Sophron, decided in favour of Berenike's son and probably fled to Ptolemy III who took up the challenge.

The most important source for the initial phase of the war is a report obviously published by the Ptolemaic king himself (papyrus from Gurob, see footnote 73). To begin with, Berenike ordered a naval expedition to Cilicia. With the help of the citizens of Cilician Soloi, the expeditionary force succeeded in taking the city as well as its citadel. The Seleukid governor of Cilicia, Aribazos, would no doubt have wanted to bring the local treasure, worth 1,500 talents, to Laodike in Ephesos and so it was seized and transported to Seleukeia. Aribazos was murdered in the Tauros by local inhabitants while attempting to flee and his head was sent to Antioch. The heart of the Seleukid empire around Seleukeia and Antioch remained firmly in the hands of Berenike.

In addition to this, in his report Ptolemy III gave news of his own expedition to Seleukeia with a small fleet. There he was enthusiastically received by 'the priests, the city-magistrates, the remaining citizens as well as officers and soldiers, who had garlanded with wreaths the streets leading to the harbour'. Even the Seleukid satraps and strategoi are said to have paid their respects to the king; perhaps Berenike herself had hastily summoned them there. The reception in Antiocheia that followed was even more enthusiastic much to the surprise of the king; the satraps and other functionaries were again at hand. In the evening he betook himself to his 'sister' and arranged various matters in the palace. The literary tradition unanimously asserts, however, that Berenike and her son had already been murdered by Laodike's thugs before the arrival of the Ptolemaic king. It is possible that Ptolemy III first learned of their murder when he entered his sister's chamber, kept quiet about it for a while and took up official duties in the name of Berenike and the boy (as per Polyaen. VIII.50).

Having begun a huge campaign, Ptolemy suddenly found himself faced with an entirely new situation once he arrived in Antioch. Despite the sympathy shown to him by many, even if it was orchestrated by supporters of Berenike, the new situation brought on by the death of his sister still meant that he would have to go home empty-handed. But he refused to do this. Instead, he led a campaign through Syria, which the sources claim was the most successful one in Ptolemaic history, and reached Mesopotamia without fighting a single battle. The Adulis inscription (see note 73) describes the trail of conquest of the 'Great King Ptolemy' as a pharaonic enterprise in the manner of the eighteenth dynasty and thus alleges that he subjugated the Seleukid empire as far as Baktria; Polyaenus (VIII.50) declares that his empire extended as far as India. To be sure, Ptolemy may have received the homage of the satraps (or their envoys) already in Seleukeia or Antioch (cf. the account of the Gurob papyrus) or, later on in Babylon, and this could have been interpreted in the tradition as tantamount to the establishment of a Ptolemaic hegemony.

It is quite certain that Ptolemy III broke off the campaign in Mesopotamia as early as the first half of 245, set up another governor (strategos) for the region 'on the other side' of the Euphrates[74] as well as one to administer the newly acquired territory of Cilicia[75] and finally returned home with an enormous quantity of spoils. As part of a propaganda campaign meant to portray him as a victorious pharaoh in full enjoyment of religious legitimacy,[76] he took on the cult title of Euergetes ('benefactor'). The royal couple appeared as the 'Theoi Euergetai' from 243.[77]

Ptolemy III was in sore need of a title of ideological significance such as 'benefactor', since his sudden return to Egypt had been occasioned by an uprising of the local Egyptians, the first of its kind in Ptolemaic history (Just. XXVII.1.9; Porph: FGrHist. 260F 43).[78] During the Second Syrian War, Philadelphos had already been forced to increase pressure on the Egyptian populace to put at the state's disposal as much of the land's resources as possible. During the first years of Euergetes' reign, social equilibrium was seriously threatened because of the injustices that the economic and administrative system visited upon Egyptian workers and farmers. The uprising, triggered by the demands of his campaign and encouraged by the king's absence, was quickly put down by the pharaoh and this in spite of the additional problems caused by inadequate flooding of the Nile in 245. As a special recourse, grain had to be imported to Egypt 'from Syria, Phoenicia, Cyprus and many other lands at great cost'.[79]

Apart from the situation in Egypt, Ptolemy III must have soon realized that a Ptolemaic government in eastern Syria, let alone in Mesopotamia, could only be of an ephemeral nature. Indeed, Seleukos II quickly went on the counter-offensive and was recognized as ruler in Babylon by July of 245.[80] The news of the death of Berenike's son probably also influenced a change of opinion in favour of the legitimate Seleukid; Ptolemy III could now have even fewer hopes of being successful against the opposition of the local rulers. In view of this, the triumphant campaign to Mesopotamia was without any long-term results and thus would be more accurately described as an exercise in plundering and pillaging. Toward the end of the war (242/1) there was some fighting near Damascus, the outcome of which is unclear (Porph: FGrHist. 260F 32.8). It is even said that Seleukos II attempted an attack on Egypt (Just. XXVII.2.5).

In terms of his designs to create an eastern Mediterranean hegemony, the Seleukid territories on the Anatolian coast and in Thrace will have been more important to Ptolemy than the eastern campaign. The Ptolemaic fleets achieved lasting victories on these coasts, even though they obviously suffered a serious set-back at the hands of the Macedonian king who was reacting to what he saw as disturbing developments in the area.

The Adulis inscription, a work of propaganda given to some exaggeration, lists Cilicia, Pamphylia, Ionia, the Hellespont and Thrace (cf. Plb. V.24.7–8) as having been acquired and even more specifically as having been won back during the Third Syrian War. The epigraphic evidence tells us two very important things about this event: (1) it is evident that the south Thracian cities of Ainos and Maroneia, if not others, were under Ptolemaic rule as of 243, and furthermore in Ainos, a 'priest of the king' is attested;[81] (2) a certain Ptolemy Andromachos (or so-called son of Andromachos) conquered various places in Thrace, among which Ainos is explicitly mentioned.[82] It appears reasonable then to place the activities of this Ptolemy in the early stages of the Third Syrian War. He actually was the son of Philadelphos and was probably an illegitimate offspring born to one of the king's mistresses, although he may have been raised under the assumed name of 'son of Andromachos'. He is, at any rate, clearly the same person who was the priest of Alexander in 251/50.[83]

Ptolemy Andromachos, we may assume, was able to procure the city of Ephesos for the Ptolemaic empire already in 246 and this without too much of a struggle owing to the desertion of the Seleukid commander. He then set up a substantial garrison there for which there is still testimony at the time of the reign of the fourth Ptolemy (Plb. V.35.11). Ephesos remained a cornerstone of the Ptolemaic hegemony in the Aegean until 197.

This extremely successful Ptolemy, nonetheless, lost a significant naval battle against Antigonos Gonatas at Andros.[84] Some time thereafter he was killed by his own Thracian soldiers (Athen. XIII.593 a–b).[85]

In 241, a peace was agreed upon which was very favourable for the Ptolemies (Just. XXVII.2.9). The Seleukid empire had been shaken by some serious upheavals. Soon after the mid-third century, the satraps of Baktria and Parthia had become practically independent. A Greek-Baktrian kingdom arose in Baktria; the former satrap bore the title of king as of 239/8. The Parnians who had invaded Parthia took power there under a new name, the Parthians. The Ptolemaic empire emerged from the Third Syrian War as the most powerful Hellenistic state without much effort because of the weaknesses of the Seleukid empire. With the exception of Pamphylia, which in Euergetes' reign was lost once again, the empire remained basically the same until the end of the third century. Epigraphic, papyrological and literary sources for Ptolemaic domination or influence in Cilicia,[86] Lycia,[87] Caria, Ionia,[88] in the Dardanelles and Thracia are widely scattered in chronological terms.[89] One of the most significant territories acquired in the Third Syrian War is the Ptolemaic enclave surrounding Seleukia in Pieria (northern Syria) (Plb. V.58.10). Seleukia was one of Seleukos I's residential cities (until 281) and next to Laodikeia the most important harbour-city of the Seleukids. Analogous to Alexandria, Seleukia was the Seleukid gateway to the Mediterranean, a final stop for distant trade routes, an excellent fortress and naval base, in whose shipyards ships would now be constructed for the Ptolemies. By taking over the city with its convenient connections by sea to the newly conquered territories of Cilicia and Pamphylia, as well as to Ptolemaic Cyprus and Coele Syria, Ptolemy III hit a vital nerve in the Seleukid empire.[90] Ptolemy III's empire now encompassed, with only a few gaps, the whole of the eastern Mediterranean basin from the eastern part of the Greater Syrte in Libya up to Thrace where it directly bordered on Macedonia (cf. Plb. V.34). In poetic accounts as brief as they are to the point, Callimachus and after him Catullus[91] both describe the 'conquest of Asia' as well as its annexation to the Egyptian empire.

## Greek policy (243–222)

Ptolemy III continued the interventionist policy in Greece which had been begun by his two predecessors. The Achaeans, under the bold leadership of their strategos Aratos (who first took on the office in 245), had come into conflict with the Aetolians and had been able to increase their territory at the expense of the Macedonians in particular. These circumstances led to a rapprochement between the Achaean League and the Ptolemaic empire. Ptolemy III was chosen in 243 to be the hegemon of the league and had honorary command of the forces over sea and land (Plu. *Arat.* 24.4); this put an official seal on the friendship between the Ptolemies and the league. The king thereupon supported Aratos by means of yearly payments (Plu. *Arat.* 41.5). Probably in 240, a peace was brokered between the Achaeans on one side and the Aetolians together with their ally Antigonos on the other. Antigonos Gonatas in all likelihood died in the spring of 239 after ruling for approximately 40 years; his death marked the end of an era in Macedonia. His son Demetrios II (239–229) succeeded him.

Right at the onset of Demetrios II's rule, the Aetolians switched camps and went to the side of Aratos, who then attacked Argos and Attika, the Macedonian outposts in the south (this conflict is known as the Demetrian War: 238/7–234/3.[92]) The son of Demetrios the Fair, Antigonos Doson (229–221), succeeded Demetrios II as ruler of Macedonia; he was first named as strategos and as guardian of the nine-year old Philip V (son of Demetrios II) and then given the title of king from 227.

Soon after his accession to power, Antigonos Doson found himself faced with an insurrection in Thessaly which clearly had been provoked by the Aetolians. In the war that followed (229/8), Antigonos was able to defeat the Aetolians in spite of the aid they had received from Ptolemy III (Fron. *Str* II.6.5). There is explicit evidence for a military pact (symmachy) between the Aetolians and the Ptolemies in this period (229/8).[93] It was clearly as a result of this symmachy that statues were erected in honour of the Ptolemaic family in Thermos, the meeting place of the council of the Aetolian League, as well as in Delphi.[94] It may be that the city of Ptolemais in Aetolia came into existence at this time.[95]

In 229, Athens, with the help of Aratos, was able to secure the retreat of the Macedonian occupation troops from Attika for a fee. Although Athens pursued a policy of neutrality, it still attempted to gain support, especially from Euergetes, given the traditional friendship between Athens and the Ptolemaic empire.

In the same year, 229, hostilities broke out between Sparta, under the rule of King Kleomenes III, and the Achaeans and this led to the war now known as the War of Kleomenes (229/8–222) (Plb. II.46–71). The revolutionary reforms of Kleomenes (227) in social and military matters suddenly made Sparta powerful beyond anyone's expectations. In the uncertainty of the moment, Aratos committed a volte-face and now sought support from Antigonos Doson (winter 227/6). In his encounters with the Achaean League, Kleomenes soon achieved several victories (226/5). Consequently, Ptolemy III, undoubtedly conscious of the new rapprochement between Aratos and the Macedonians, discontinued his subsidies of the League and instead diverted them to Sparta, probably still in the winter of 226/5.[96] This was to be expected, since Ptolemaic policies in the area had always had as their principal aim the limitation of Macedonian power. There was nothing left for Aratos to do except formally to ask Antigonos for help (225/4). The Macedonian king was officially named hegemon of the Achaean League, a position formerly held by Ptolemy III, and he then advanced southwards with his troops.

This dangerous situation led to greater unity among the Aetolians, Athens and the Ptolemaic empire. Athens was probably given positive assurances of safety by Euergetes. Already in 226, the city honoured a courtier (*philos*) of the king.[97] The year 224/3 saw the creation of a new phyle in Athens called 'Ptolemais' to honour the royal pair (Paus. I.5.5) as well as a deme called 'Berenikidai' (Steph.Byz. s.v. Βερενικδαι). As the hero of the phyle, Euergetes received his own cult with priests (this same cult also honoured Berenike) as well as a statue in the Athenian agora and another in Delphi (Paus. X.10.2). From 224/3, the 'Ptolemaia' festival was celebrated every four years in Athens. Furthermore, a gymnasium was erected not far from the Athenian agora which was called 'Ptolemaion' to honour Ptolemy III who had financed its construction.[98]

In the autumn of 224, Antigonos Doson arrived at Aigion in Achaea and created the Hellenic League (a symmachy) which would be under Macedonian hegemony. Most of Greece was united under its aegis (Achaeans, Thessalians, Akarnanians, Boeotians, Phokians and later still others). The Aetolians and the Athenians, however, as well as a few others who were allied with Euergetes did not join.

At the end of 224, Kleomenes asked the Ptolemaic king for financial assistance for the recruitment of troops. The king of Sparta had, in exchange, to send his mother and children as hostages to Alexandria. An attempt by Antigonos in Alexandria to prevent these payments had for the time being no effect (Plu. *Cleom*. 22.4–10). Only after the battles in 223 did Ptolemy no longer consider Kleomenes worth supporting. It is possible that an arrangement was made between the Ptolemies and Macedonians in which Kleomenes was to be sacrificed; he could only have been kept in power by a substantial deployment of Ptolemaic forces – an action which would have gone contrary to the spirit of Ptolemaic policy in Greece. Only a little earlier in the spring of 222, Antiochos III had ascended the Seleukid throne. Asia required all of Euergetes' attention.[99] The possibility of a direct Seleukid attack on Coele Syria was, moreover, a continual threat in the last months of Ptolemy III's reign (Plb. V.41.6–42.6).

Early in the summer of 222, Antigonos marched into Lakonia with his army. There Kleomenes received the disappointing news from Alexandria that his support was cut off and he should sue for peace (Plb. II.63.1). Kleomenes engaged in battle at Sellasia ten days later and lost (Plb. II.65–69). Antigonos marched into Sparta as victor and Kleomenes fled to Alexandria where Euergetes received him honourably and promised him aid in regaining his throne (Plu. *Kleom*. 29–32). The emptiness of this promise only became evident in the reign of Ptolemy IV. For the future, the Ptolemies renounced any policy of intervention in Greece which would oppose Macedonia.

Euergetes continued to cultivate good relations with Rhodes. When a severe earthquake struck the island, in which the famous Colossus collapsed into rubble, he sent vast amounts of supplies (grain, sailing cloth, wood for ships, monetary aid, labour forces, etc.) as did the other dynasties, including Antigonos and Seleukos II (Plb. V.89). He wished by his unsurpassed generosity to underscore the supremacy of his kingdom.

## Ptolemaic policy in Asia Minor until the death of Euergetes I (turn of 222/1)

Antiochos Hierax, brother of Seleukos II, was still co-ruler with his mother Laodike, and had been entrusted with an almost independent control over Seleukid Asia Minor. There is no evidence that Ptolemy III supported any one side in the war between the Seleukid brothers (*c.* 241/239); but considering the fact that the main feature of Ptolemaic policy in Asia was opposition to the Seleukid central government, the sympathies of Ptolemy probably favoured Antiochus Hierax. Euergetes did aid the latter by sending him soldiers to put down a rebellion of his Galatian troops in Magnesia (Porph: FGrHist. 260F 32.8).

In keeping with this policy, Ptolemy III, at the end of his life, evidently supported the ruler of Pergamon, Attalos I, who had acquired the lion's share of Seleukid Asia Minor as a result of battles with Hierax.[100] In the Seleukid empire, the short rule of Seleukos III (226/5–222) was followed by that of his brother Antiochos III (222–187). His relative, Achaios, took on the task of regaining Asia Minor. For this reason, Ptolemy III sent his son, Magas (see Stemma 1), to Asia Minor with a comprehensive military command,[101] but the latter was not able to prevent Seleukid troops from pushing Attalos back within the former borders of Pergamon. The Ptolemaic mission soon came to an end but it may well have been one of the causes for the outbreak of the Fourth Syrian War under Ptolemy IV.[102]

Euergetes died from some illness at the turn of the year 222/1 (Plb. II.71.3). No scandalous behaviour has been reported of him in the sources.


## PTOLEMAIC ACTIVITIES OUTSIDE THE EASTERN MEDITERRANEAN

### Relations with Carthage and Rome

From about the mid-270s, close relations existed between Ptolemaic Egypt and Carthage. Political issues which stemmed from the clashes with King Magas together with economic considerations (and these perhaps were the deciding factor) may well have tipped the balance in favour of friendly relations.[103] As a result of their good relations, Philadelphos' naval commander, Timosthenes of Rhodes, was able to carry out an expedition unobstructed through Punic waters as far as the western edge of the Mediterranean.[104]

In 273, Philadelphos took the initiative in organizing a formal exchange of envoys with Rome (D.H. *Ant.* 14.1f.; Liv. *Per.* XIV among others).[105] This resulted in the formation of friendly political relations (an *amicitia*) between Rome and Alexandria. Owing to this development, Philadelphos remained completely neutral during the First Punic War (264–241). When Carthage, which was on equally amicable terms with Philadelphos, asked him for a loan of 2,000 talents, he refused (App. *Sic.* 1).

The year 241 brought with it not only the end of the Third Syrian War but also a decisive Roman victory over Carthage near the Aegatian Islands. It is clear that at this point the Roman senate would have wished to re-affirm its old relations with the great power in the East. A Roman embassy appeared in Alexandria after the end of the First Punic War, probably out of gratitude for the goodwill shown by the Ptolemies (Eutr. 3.1).

At this early stage, very few people of Roman or Italian extraction were actively involved in the Ptolemaic army. Only a few Roman mercenaries or even emigrating kleruchoi from Rome or Italy could be found in the Ptolemaic army of the third century.[106] We first find a Roman occupying a high-ranking military position under Ptolemy IV; he was the garrison commander of Itanos (Crete) in about 221/09.[107]

## Nubia, Arabia and the Red Sea

From the time of the expulsion of the twenty-fifth dynasty from Egypt, Nubia became an independent and important kingdom in terms of its culture, economics and, at times, politics. It was known as the Meroitic empire, after its capital, Meroe located between the fifth and sixth Nile cataract, approximately 200 km north of Khartoum. The area where Nubia and Egypt bordered on each other was Lower Nubia, a zone between the first and second cataract, that is, between the southern Egyptian border at Elephantine/Syene (today Aswân) and near the modern-day Wadi Halfa. This area is known as the 30-mile district (Triakontaschoinos), the northern part of which, the 12-mile district (Dodekaschoinos), was of particular historical significance for Ptolemaic and Roman Egypt. The most important contemporary of Ptolemy II in Meroe was King Ergamenes I (Arkamaniqo; perhaps *c.* 270–260), who is said to have enjoyed the privilege of a Greek education (Diod. III.6.3).

The border area near Syene probably suffered from incursions of Lower Nubian nomads[108] and these may have been the reason for the rather large expedition to Lower Nubia carried out by Ptolemy II in approximately 275 (Agatharchides frg. 20; Diod. I.37.5).[109] It is not known how far the expedition got and what sort of resistance Meroe put up. The Nubians and the African beasts led in Philadelphos' large procession may bear some relation to that expedition. In the reign of Philadelphos, a list was displayed in the temple of Isis at Philae detailing the names of the Nubian districts[110] and no doubt publicizing the claims of Ptolemaic sovereignty and administrative authority at least over the Dodekaschoinos; this is confirmed in an idyll of Theocritus (*Id.* XVII.87). The goldmines in the mountains of Wadi Allaqi (which is near the southern end of the Dodekaschoinos and extends from the eastern deserts into the Nile valley) probably also came under Ptolemaic power at Philadelphos' initiative (Diod. III.12). There the king may have founded a city, the impressive location of which has recently been uncovered,[111] lying far to the west of the Nile in Wadi Allaqi and perhaps the same as the city called Berenike Panchrysos ('all-gold Berenike') by Pliny (*Nat.* VI.170). Ptolemy II's campaign then was meant not only to bring peace to the southern border of the empire but also to further Egypt's economic interests.

Aside from commercial relations and the acquisition of gold, the economic interests advanced in the campaign also had to do with securing a supply of war-elephants from the Nubian region. These were among the most important war matériel in the Hellenistic period and, therefore, we can understand why it was such a great achievement for Ptolemy I to be able to keep all 43 elephants belonging to Demetrios after the battle of Gaza (312) (Diod.

XIX.83.2; 84.4). At any rate, the Ptolemies had to attempt, by means of the African elephants, to balance the Indian elephants of the Seleukid army which were far superior for military purposes.[112] These war-elephants could be acquired either from an area south of the fifth Nile cataract (in the area around Meroe) or from the southern shores of the Red Sea. To this end, expeditions to capture the animals were mounted by the second to the fourth Ptolemies (Agatharchides frg. 85).[113] Reconaissance trips for gathering information were also organized either before or at the same time as these expeditions. The first known undertaking of this nature was that of Philon who visited Meroe and an island in the Red Sea during the transitional period between the rule of the first and second Ptolemies; like many of his successors, he wrote a travel commentary afterwards (the so-called *Aethiopica*) (FGrHist. 670).

The organization and safeguarding of travel around the Red Sea and the Arabian peninsula as well as the colonizing activities of Ptolemy II and III in these areas also had as an ulterior motive the acquisition of elephants for war and other economic concerns. In 270/69, Philadelphos had the precursor of the Suez Canal, which had been silted over since the time of the Persians, reconstructed. It ran from the eastern Delta not far from Bubastis through Wadi Tumilat, went by Pithom/Heroonpolis (modern Tell el-Maskhuta) through Lake Timsah and the Bitter Lakes to the Gulf of Suez. By the mouth of the canal near modern-day Suez, the king also founded the city of Arsinoe (later Kleopatris).[114] Soon after the canal was re-opened, the king sent two reconnoitring expeditions south, one along the Arabian coast, the other along the Egyptian coast.[115]

Under Ptolemy II, Ptolemaic troops probably occupied a settlement situated in the area between what would now be the cities of Eilat and Aqaba and founded a new colony there called 'Berenike' (J. *AJ* VIII.163–164). Also recently founded, and this time clearly with the help of the Milesians, was the new colony of Ampelone, situated on the Arabian coast north of modern-day Jeddah (Plin. *Nat.* VI.159). The incense trade-route also had to be protected, since it went deeper into the interior of the Arabian peninsula. For this reason, there had to be co-operation with the south Arabian Minaeans and Sabaeans who transported their wares along this route. The northern section near Petra on the Mediterranean and especially towards Gaza was controlled by nomads and the semi-nomadic Nabataeans who had set up way-stations equipped with proper cisterns for their caravans in the central Negev (Diod. XIX.94.4–8). In this way, the Nabataeans in the eastern and southern border regions of Coele Syria found themselves caught between the Ptolemaic and Seleukid spheres of influence. Armed clashes between Nabataean pirates and the Ptolemies in the Red Sea may have first occurred only in the second century (Agatharchides frg. 90).[116]

Following the Arabian coast from the Suez Gulf to the Bab el-Mandeb road, up to about 270 harbours and bases were constructed as the sites of future cities (Str. XVI.4.5; Plin. *Nat.* VI.168). The series of harbours, from north to south, begins with the ancient site near modern-day Abu Shaᶜr, north of Hurghada. Two caravan routes coming from the region of the Nile valley (at modern-day Qena) and which were already in use during the time of the Ptolemies led to this important harbour. One of these went north going by Mons Porphyrites, and a second southern route passed by Mons Claudianus; on this latter route, near Abu Zawal, gold was obtained during the third and second centuries.[117] At the mouth of the Wadi Gawasi (Gasus; approximately 22 km south of modern-day Safaga Harbour), on the site of an earlier Middle Kingdom colony, Philotera(s) was now founded by a certain Satyros, who had been sent by Ptolemy II to explore the coast and hunt for elephants; the city bore the name of one of Philadelphos' sisters (see Stemma 1). Southwards, by the outlet of the Wadi Hammamat, at the end of the shortest path between the Red Sea and the Nile, was the Ptolemaic port of Myos Hormos (modern-day Quseir). The sites of Leukos Limen and of Arsinoe Trogodytiké, probably founded by Philadelphos, are not known; the epithet Trogodytiké comes from the people of the same name, the Trog(l)odyti, who lived in the western desert. Roughly on the same latitude as Aswan, Ptolemy II founded Berenike Trogodytiké (modern-day Berenice). Named after the king's mother, the city became the point of departure of an important caravan route put into place by Philadelphos, which then went through the eastern deserts as far as Koptos. Set up by Ptolemy II as a military colony and a base for elephant hunts, Ptolemais Theron became perhaps the most important settlement outside of the limits of the empire (probably at modern-day Aqiq south of Port Sudan) (Agatharchides frg. 86; Str. XVI.4.8; Plin. *Nat.* VI.171).[118]

Since Euergetes continued with his father's policy as a result of the need for war-elephants (cf. Diod. III.18.4), he founded more bases on the coast, among them Adulis on the island of Massawa (Eritrea),[119] which later went on to be of great importance for trade between the Romans and the Aksumites. Directly along the Bab el-Mandeb road, lay still other Ptolemaic fortifications, such as Berenike Epi Dires, but their foundation dates remain uncertain.

As far as Ptolemaic trade in the south and southeast is concerned, three main routes can be discussed briefly: one followed the Nile upstream into the Meroitic empire;[120] the second led to the Red Sea by ship and then from the coast by various land routes (which could be avoided by going through the canal) to the Nile. Finally, the third was the so-called incense route on the Arabian peninsula: to use this, it was essential that the Ptolemies keep control of Coele Syria. In addition to the trade in such products as ivory, incense and spices from the interior of Africa and from the southern part of the Arabian peninsula, there was trade with India. Already in the great procession of the 70s, one could find Indian women as well as Indian dogs and cattle (FGrHist. 627F 2, symbol 32). Embassies were exchanged with the Maurya king Asoka (*c.* 270–235) (Pliny, *Nat.* VI.58); one of his inscriptions from 251/248 mentions diplomatic contacts with, among others, Ptolemy II, Antiochos II, Antigonos Gonatas and even King Magas of Cyrene. During

the third century and a greater part of the second, the journey to India followed the dangerous rocky coasts, since the monsoon was still unknown.[121]

## SITUATION WITHIN THE EMPIRE

## Government and administration

As the historical evidence shows, the Ptolemaic king ruled his empire in the
same manner as the Seleukid king (the Antigonids, on the other hand, were
restricted by Macedonian tradition). He ruled absolutely at every level, helped
by a staff of close, trusted men, the so-called philoi ('friends of the king')
who were the Hellenistic equivalent of the old Macedonian hetairoi and of
the Persian king's retinue. The philoi came from very different backgrounds;
only a few were Macedonian, just as there were few Macedonians among the
administrative officials of the empire.[122] As for the traditional Macedonian
military council, it continued to exist in the form of the court bodyguard
in Alexandria and its members were known as the 'Macedonians'; the corps
had lost the important political powers which it had exercised just after the
establishment of the dynasty during the period of the Successors, but at the
end of the third century, during the crisis following the death of Ptolemy
IV, it once again emerged as a decisive political force (Plb. XV.25–32).

At the top of the administrative hierarchy was the royal secretary for
diplomatic affairs (epistolographos), the chief secretary (hypomnematographos),
the drafter of royal edicts (ὁ ἐπὶ τῶν προσταγμάτων), the top military leaders
and the dioiketes, who was responsible for all departments of the civil
administration. During the third century, the post of dioiketes was often
filled by more than one person. There may be evidence for a college of
officials[123] at the time of the Apollonius[124] known to us from Berenike's
bridal journey in 252.

The duties and activities of Apollonius are known from the most comprehensive archive yet uncovered in Egypt, the so-called Zenon archive, one of
approximately 50 known archives dating to the Ptolemaic period. Roughly
3,000 papyri, of which 1,750 are legible, come from Philadelphia (modern-
day Kom el-charaba el-kebir), a village founded by Ptolemy II on the north-
eastern shore of the Fayum. The archive includes documents dating to the
years 261–229/8 and is today divided among many collections (Cairo, London,
New York, Michigan, Florence, Manchester, and elsewhere).[125] Apollonius
was at once dioiketes (c. 262–245) and an important merchant and land-
owner. He had ships at his disposal which transported goods from Syria and
Asia Minor. Zenon himself, a Karian from Kaunos who put together the
documents, was appointed by Ptolemy II to be a trusted adviser to Apollonius.
In this capacity, during the Second Syrian War from 260–258, he toured
the region of Coele Syria, where Apollonius had a large estate mainly with
vineyards in Bēt ᶜAnāt (Galilee). The Zenon papyri therefore provide us with

a special glimpse of details concerning the economy, administration and population of the province; as far as questions of land ownership are concerned, it is important to note the existence there of crown land on the Egyptian model. After his journeys in Asia, Zenon accompanied the dioiketes on his inspection trips throughout Egypt and finally became administrator of the approximately 2,500 ha *dorea*[126] belonging to Apollonius in the area around Philadelphia.

The local bodies in the civil administration of the nomes were also subordinate to the dioiketes:[127] the nomarch together with his subordinates in the smaller units, the toparchs and komarchs, oversaw agricultural production; the oikonomos was in charge of the financial management of the nome and was thus responsible for the handling of transactions in coin and kind as well as all related issues; the basilikos grammateus ('royal scribe') with his staff, the topogrammateis and komogrammateis, was charged with the administration and registration of estates and land. This section of the local civil administration remained mostly in Egyptian hands; this was especially true of organization at the village level (komarch, komogrammateus) but was also true of the offices of the oikonomos and the 'royal scribe'.[128] The number of nomes was raised by Philadelphos from 36 to 39.[129] In this way the Fayum became its own nome and was named 'Arsinoites', after the deified sister-wife of the king.

From the beginning of Ptolemaic rule, the troop commander in the nome was a 'nome-strategos", subordinate to the dioiketes and probably directly appointed by the king. Under Ptolemy III in the latter half of the 240s, these strategoi acquired increasingly greater influence in civil matters until they eventually occupied the top position in the administration of the nome in addition to their military duties (evidence from 229/8 onwards).[130] The nomarch saw a corresponding decline in the importance of his office so that by around the mid-second century at the latest he became a minor civil servant dealing with financial matters. The strategos later had less military importance and in Roman times became a purely civilian administrator for the nome.

A bureaucratic system to control the foreign territories[131] was only established after the wars of the successors. Its development was still not fully realized under Ptolemy III and it was only under his successor that it reached a tentative completion. Thus, it was in the reign of Euergetes that the league (koinon) of cities in the Cyrenaica came into existence.[132] In Cyprus, local Phoenicians had ruled as Ptolemaic governors[133] since the reconquest of 295/4 and it was only under Ptolemy IV that the island was re-organized as a military base. From 217, we know of a complete succession of select strategoi who were of Greek or Macedonian origin and were sent from Alexandria. The first evidence for a provincial strategos in 'Syria and Phoenicia' also dates from the early years of Ptolemy IV's reign. Despite this rapid pace of development in the provinces, Cyrenaica, generally called 'Libya', Cyprus and Coele Syria, being together with Egypt, the grain-producing lands of the empire were of vital importance and accordingly were organized along very similar lines. They formed a single monetary zone;[134] the civil servants of the central administration had to ensure an optimal exploitation of resources throughout these provinces, especially in view of the abundant primary and secondary goods which Egypt lacked. Taxes were directly administered by royal representatives.

On the 'periphery' of the empire, strategoi are already attested as provincial procurators under Ptolemy II and III in Cilicia,[135] Karia,[136] Thrace and the Hellespont. Philadelphos appointed a pamphyliarch in Pamphylia, but the exact nature of his function remains unclear. The nesiarch remained outside the royal administrative system,[137] but it was through this office that the king was able to exercise his protectorate over the League of Islanders; he was able to have his decisions carried out through the assistance of a local executive body. The territories in Anatolia and in the Aegean lay outside of the Ptolemaic monetary zone and thus the tendency in these areas was to act through the intermediary of the city governments.

There were military garrisons in every important city and in strategic points of the empire. Ptolemy III appointed the strategos Hippomedon to administer Thrace and the Hellespont and in this capacity the latter's authority extended over both military and economic matters and he even managed the public finances in his region.[138] There remained a few oikonomoi who, like their counterparts in Egypt, were probably under the direct control of the dioiketes in Alexandria and who were responsible for the finances of the provinces.[139] The individual hyparchiai in Coele Syria, which were in this province the administrative units of first order, each had an oikonomos to oversee the public revenue. The oikonomoi were also subordinate to a dioiketes for 'Syria and Phoenicia' who was in turn directly answerable to the dioiketes in Alexandria.

The development of cities, in the full legal sense of the word among the Greeks, varied throughout the empire. In comparison with only three poleis in Egypt,[140] there were about 13 in Cyprus, each enjoying complete civic autonomy. The old city of Marion on the west coast of the island, which had been destroyed by Ptolemy I in 312, was founded anew by Philadelphos as 'Arsinoe'. There were two other cities founded by the Ptolemies on Cyprus which bore the same name (Str. XIV.6.3). In Coele Syria, especially in the coastal cities of Phoenicia, Hellenism enjoyed an increasing popularity. New 'Hellenistic' cities founded in the reign of Philadelphos include: Ptolemais (Ake/Akko), Philadelphia (Rabba<u>t</u> ᶜAmmôn, modern-day Amman) and Philoter(i)a (modern-day Beth Yerah? on lake Tiberias) named after the sister of Philadelphos).[141] A few new cities were also founded in Asia Minor such as Arsinoe (the old Patara) and Philotera (still unidentified) in Lycia, Ptolemais (between Side and Alanya) and Arsinoe (presumably east of Alanya) in Pamphylia, yet another Arsinoe (east of Anamur) and the city of Berenike (still unidentified) in Cilicia.[142] The cities of the empire were usually under the control of Ptolemaic governors; a city's self-administration and royal administration were inseparably bound to one another.

After an earlier experimental phase under his father, Philadelphos further organized the administrative system of the empire in a flexible and pragmatic fashion; by his readiness and ability to adapt it to local conditions, he conferrred upon it a lasting stability. Below the king, no one was given too much power; even the comprehensive authority of provincial governors was limited by the powers of the oikonomos and those of garrison commanders directly appointed by the king and subordinate to him. For this reason, revolutions such as the one incited by Magas in Cyrene or those by the crown prince Ptolemy in western Asia Minor were extremely rare and could only cause limited damage.

## Economic aspects

To obtain effectively the funds for his foreign policy (i.e. for military expeditions and for the purchase of imported goods so vital to Egypt), the king had to have full control over the economic life of his kingdom and indeed over all those other realms that fell under his authority. Both in theory and in practice, then, we can see this as an extension of the ancient Egyptian model of sovereignty in which the pharaoh (following what is known as the royal dogma) was the sole proprietor in Egypt and correspondingly all land and its products were said to belong to him. This notion of the king as the ultimate owner of all property seems to come to the fore in the concept of 'borrowed land' (γῆ ἐν ἀφέσι) – i.e. all land outside of the royal estates,[143] a term which still appears in the Amnesty Decree of 118.[144] Apart from temple precincts and city property,[145] other land-holdings not considered to be part of the royal estates were royal fiefs and personal property.

Large estates (δωρεαί; γῆ ἐν δωρεᾷ), such as those of Apollonius,[146] were conferred upon deserving officials by the king, but, as soon as the beneficiary had been discharged from his office, the land reverted to the crown; this was also true of the domains allotted from royal land in Persian Egypt.[147] Smaller lots of land (κλῆροι; γῆ κληρουχική) were assigned to soldiers on active duty to provide income for themselves and their families. This system of allotting land to military settlers probably spread over all the grain-producing lands of the Ptolemaic empire and, outside Egypt, was especially common in Coele Syria.[148] The kleruchs were mostly descendants of soldiers who were in the army of Ptolemy I during the two decades that he was satrap and so the majority of them were either Macedonian or from other parts of the northern Balkans.[149] At the end of the Second Syrian War, when Philadelphos distributed much new kleruchic land in the Fayum, he personally went to Memphis in July of 253 for this purpose.[150] Scattered over the entire country, the kleruchs introduced Greek ideas and technology into the agricultural environment in which they were living. During a military campaign, they were naturally away and supervision of their estate had to be entrusted to others. Kleruchic land, in contrast to the dorea, remained within the family and was inherited. While the kleruchy originated in classical Greece and continued to be a common practice in Hellenistic times, it also had antecedents in the

Egyptian New Kingdom. Phenomena of this kind, with roots in both cultures, were absolutely characteristic of Ptolemaic Egypt. As in the time of the pharaohs, there was also private land (γῆ ἰδιόκτητος) which was treated in the same way as private property and provided the conditions under which officials could be rewarded for the success of their service.

Thus, the idea of Egypt as a royal 'patrimony' was limited in scope by the existence of non-royal estates, private enterprise and the possession of private capital (this was even encouraged).

Agriculture, especially the production of grain, provided the basis of Egyptian wealth. The demands of foreign policy required that measures be taken to increase agricultural yield. Significantly, at the beginning of the Second Syrian War, Ptolemy II ordered that stock be taken of all Egyptian territory from Elephantine to the Mediterranean (this encompassed all fields, the systems of irrigation, the canals, its afforestation, etc., all itemized according to the different categories of land) in order to determine the economic potential of the land. The 'general inventory' of Egypt was entrusted to the dioiketes in the autumn of 258. These measures concerned with domestic issues were thus ultimately inspired by the needs of foreign policy and the security of the state.[151]

Measures incorporated in the document known as the Revenue Laws Papyrus[152] of 259 also served a similar purpose, seeking as they did to increase the yield from taxes in the various areas of economic life. In the first section, the papyrus contains general rules governing the leasing out of tax-collection and in particular deals with the yields from wine, fruits, and plant-oils as well as banking. At least in Egypt and in 'Syria and Phoenicia', direct taxation was carried out with the help of tax-farmers (τελῶναι); this was inspired by a practice long in use in Classical Greece and particularly in Athens. These tax-farmers, who were members of organizations that had a great deal of capital at their disposal, were intermediaries between the tax-payer and the tax-collecting officials. They were under obligation to render to the king the tax-revenues stipulated in their contract and thus were a very effective means of controlling state officials, since they had to make up losses due to bureaucratic corruption from their own capital. A surplus, however, was credited to them as profit. For the tax-payer, on the other hand, there was scarcely a loophole by which they could evade the authorities.

Particular attention was given to the fertile land of the Fayum, the newly created Arsinoite nome, which was linked to the Nile valley through an old tributary (modern-day Bahr Yussuf). This river-access to the Fayum valley was closed off in early Ptolemaic times, perhaps already under Ptolemy I, by a dam at el-Lahun so that the amount of arable land could be increased. This artificial control of the water supply permitted a reduction in the water levels of the oasis lake there (modern-day Birket Qarun). Moreover, under Philadelphos the irrigation of the edges of the desert proceeded at the hands of newly settled Greeks. Approximately 30–40 relatively large settlements now sprung up in formerly uninhabitable areas of the Fayum. Names such as

Arsinoe,[153] Philadelphia, Theadelphia, Philoteris clearly reflect the time of their foundation. The installation of an artificial lake in the southern Fayum, which probably took place under Ptolemy II, was a masterful achievement in hydraulic engineering. Its surface was 114 km² and its reservoir had a capacity of 275 million m³, from which arable land of about 150 km² could be watered for a second harvest in the spring. A concomitant variety of improvements and experiments were also put into effect to raise the agricultural yield, a pursuit to which Ptolemy II was personally committed. In this regard, Zenon was charged with watering the land on the estates of Apollonios in the Fayum a second time by means of certain technical aids for a period of five days and then to sow wheat that could be harvested in three months.[154] With measures such as these, the Fayum became an agricultural wonder of the first order. In September of 254, the king even sent the embassies that had arrived from the Bosporan kingdom and from Argos on an inspection tour of the oasis.

Even the royal legislation on slaves was dictated by their utility to the state and their value in maintaining the workforce. In 260, Philadelphos thus prohibited, in a decree (prostagma) issued for 'Syria and Phoenicia', that in the future free-born people should become *de facto* slaves as a result of private debt.[155]

All of this invites the conclusion that the economic and administrative system of the Ptolemaic kingdom functioned most perfectly under Philadelphos. It is also true to say that this empire far outshone all other Hellenistic states because of the stability of its finances. At the same time, however, this economic policy based on the development of every taxation source and the exploitation of the workforce contained the seeds of an eventual instability in this society which would lead to a revolt under Euergetes and would shake the empire to its roots for the first time.

## Alexandrian scholarship[156]

In the realm of cultural history, the greatest contribution of the Ptolemaic kings was the establishment and development of Alexandria as an intellectual centre. Not only were there new cultural and scholarly achievements, but, more importantly, the literary and intellectual heritage of ancient Greece was collected and edited in Alexandria and ultimately prepared for transmission to posterity.

From the dynasty's beginnings, the Ptolemaic princes were educated by the best scholars of the day. At the court of Ptolemy Philadelphos, these were Straton of Lampsakos,[157] a natural philosopher and thinker of wide interests; the poet and philologist, Philetas of Kos, as well as the Homeric scholar and first director of the Museion library, Zenodotos of Ephesos. The latter's successor was Apollonios of Rhodes, who composed the epic 'Argonautica' and taught the later Euergetes. Raised in this intellectual environment, the kings made an effort to seek out talented men in the Greek world and to invite them to Alexandria or, if these latter already happened to be in the city, they were offered the possibility of work. The new Alexandrian intelligentsia, naturally enough, most often came from areas within the Ptolemaic sphere of influence (especially from Cyrene, Kos or Samos). With the exception of the historian Manetho, there were no Egyptian scholars at court in the third century.[158]

A priest of the muses was directly appointed by the king to preside over the Museion[159] which was within the royal precinct of Alexandria. Members of the Museion were paid by the treasury and had to dedicate themselves primarily to scholarship but also to education. Research in the sciences (in the broadest sense of the word) was carried out in all those areas dealt with in the corpus of Aristotle, and in addition to this there was also a great deal of literary and philological scholarship. To complement the Museion library, Euergetes had a second very important library built in the newly erected Serapeion.[160] It was a temple library very much like the later library of Pergamon, which was located in the precinct of Athena Polias, and it reflected a long-standing tradition of temple libraries in Egypt. Alexandria's library collection was procured from the best book-markets of the time, namely those in Athens and Rhodes (Athen. I.3b). Euergetes' craze for books is said to have been so acute that he would have them searched out and confiscated on the ships in Alexandria's harbour and then would return to the owners a specially prepared copy (Gal. *comm. in epidem.* III. ed. Kühn XVII.I.606).

The first physician to come was Praxagoras of Kos, who as early as the end of the fourth century brought the Hippocratic tradition to Alexandria. His student, Herophilos of Chalkedon, became the most important doctor in Alexandria during the first half of the third century; he made dissection a regular practice, accomplished groundbreaking work in medical terminology and wrote commentaries on parts of the Hippocratic Corpus.

Already in the time of Ptolemy I, Euclid (d. *c.* 270) came from the Platonic school in Athens and taught in Alexandria; he was certainly one of the most eminent mathematicians and geometrists of any period. Of his numerous writings, the most important are the 13 books entitled 'Elements' (Στοιχεῖα) outlining the basics of geometry. In the first half of the third century, the astronomer Aristarchus of Samos (d. *c.* 230 at about 80 years of age) was active in Alexandria. He became famous particularly for his heliocentric system which was handed down to posterity by Archimedes; in it the sun and fixed stars are said to be stationary and the planets including the earth to be in motion around the sun. Archimedes of Syracuse was also in Alexandria for some time and when he was in Syracuse he corresponded with Alexandrian scholars. Among them was Konon of Samos who is credited with the theory of conic sections, and the universal scholar, Eratosthenes of Cyrene (*c.* 284–202).

Eratosthenes, when he was already a well-known scholar at about the age of 40, was invited by Euergetes to come to Alexandria from Athens and was entrusted with the direction of the Museion library as the successor of Apollonios Rhodios. In this position he was destined to become the tutor of the crown prince Ptolemy (IV). Eratosthenes' greatest achievement was his calculation of the earth's circumference using a method that was quite accurate in its theoretical assumptions: he knew that during the summer solstice the midday sun was directly over Syene, because it reflected itself in a fountain there; by measuring the angle of incidence of the sun in Alexandria at the same time and the distance between the two cities, he was able to calculate the circumference. Eratosthenes' fountain was probably on the island of Elephantine on the Nile, since quite suddenly from the time of Ptolemy III the Egyptian name of the island (ᶜbw) could be written in hieroglyphics representing two geometric tools: the protractor and the plumb-line. This measurement of the earth's circumference was also seen as a great achievement by local Egyptian intellectual circles.[161] Finally, Eratosthenes also made a name for himself as a historian, geographer and poet.

The last great mathematician and geometrist to be in Alexandria was Apollonius of Perge who had studied there and taught under Euergetes.

Built in about 280, the Pharos lighthouse erected on an island facing Alexandria was an outstanding engineering feat. It cannot be determined whether Sostratos of Knidos was its architect or its sponsor, though it does seem unlikely that one of the great wonders of the world could have been privately financed.[162] The lighthouse collapsed in the fourteenth century as a result of two earthquakes.

The court poets Theocritus and Callimachus are of particular historical interest, since they put their talents at the disposal of Ptolemaic ideology. Theocritus of Syracuse,[163] the first bucolic poet whose work has survived in part, wrote poems called the 'Idylls', among which is Id. XVII, an encomium of Ptolemy II. He also composed epigrams and some lost works.

Callimachus of Cyrene apparently came to Alexandria in the 270s, where he was first active as a teacher in the area of Eleusis. Later he was called to court and rose to become one of the most influential figures of intellectual life. In the Cyrenaica, he had honoured the kingship of Magas and now he wrote a poem on the occasion of Arsinoe's deification.[164] He became the most important representative of Hellenistic elegy through his magnum opus, a four-volume work called 'Aitia', in which he dealt with the origins of cults, customs, festivals, sanctuaries, names of gods and heroes and similar matters. The collection ended with a poem, the 'lock of Berenike',[165] known to us through Catullus' version of it (*carm.* 66). Other poetic works of his are above all else his iamboi (a series of individual poems), an epyllion *Hekale,* and hymns – to name only a few. Callimachus was also a great scholarly historian attached to the Museion library; he wrote a universal biography of scholars from all academic branches with lists of their writings (*pinakes*) in 120 books. For the most part, only fragments remain of this scholarly poet's voluminous work.

## MAIN ELEMENTS OF THE POLICIES OF THE SECOND AND THIRD PTOLEMIES

Ptolemy II pursued the same aims in foreign policy as his father in a consistent manner, even if, after initial territorial gains in Asia Minor, he began to suffer setbacks there and in Greece. The two basic trends of his foreign policy were now more accurately defined as anti-Seleukid and anti-Macedonian. For Egypt to maintain its military strength and its naval dominance in particular, it had to perfect as much as possible the functioning of its domestic economy as well as commercial activity throughout the empire. Quite in keeping with these aims, the Ptolemies expanded their power and influence as far as Nubia and the southern coast of the Red Sea.

Philadelphos' policy in Greece, which was designed to counter Macedonian influence, shows clearly that he preferred to suffer setbacks outside the heartland of his empire and incur the ill-repute of having been negligent in his support of the league members (Paus. I.7.3) rather than bleed the wealth of Egypt to death. In this respect, Soter, Philadelphos and Euergetes were consistent in their policy towards Greece until 222, this despite many diplomatic reversals.

It appears, however, that inspired by imperial ambitions Euergetes strayed for a short time from the considerations of security and the striving for hegemony of his two predecessors. Otherwise he would not have placed yet another governor in the Euphrates area. It is quite possible that he was seduced by the idea of an eastern Mediterranean empire, as Darius III had formerly been when he had offered Alexander the Great a portion of his empire with the Euphrates serving as its border.[166] In fact, Euergetes did succeed in expanding his empire to include within it the eastern Mediterranean; by virtue of his office as hegemon of the Achaean League he also held a key position in Greece itself.

It is important to remember that the Ptolemaic thalassocracy was seriously weakened in the Chremonidean War (which the Ptolemies lost) and in the naval battles of Ephesos and Kos, and that this made it necessary to set up bases on land as close as possible to the interior of Macedonia. Finally, one must also recall that, in addition to wielding superior power at sea in the northern Aegean during the 270s, Philadelphos also deliberately carried out a policy of aggression during his campaign in Pontus on the eve of the Chremonidean War. Seen from this perspective, Ptolemy III's expansion into Thrace was just a continuation of this same policy at an opportune moment. In the eastern Mediterranean, Euergetes succeeded, as had his father in the 270s, in uniting hegemonic influence, a thalassocracy and territorial rule. The realization that a sea-power relying on only a few strongholds remained quite vulnerable, however, was probably what led him to expand his territories in the east and north of the Aegean.[167] The historian Polybius saw that the main motivation for the build-up and organization of Ptolemaic power from southeast Anatolia as far as Thrace was the creation of an extensive buffer-zone for the 'Egyptian kingdom' (Plb. V.34.2–9). As far as this end is concerned, Euergetes brought to completion what was begun by his grandfather. With the acquisition of Seleukia in Pieria, he formed a bridge between Ptolemaic Anatolia, Cyprus and Coele Syria; a significant portion of the Seleukid trade in the Mediterranean thus came into Ptolemaic hands. The part still left to the Seleukids now had to accommodate itself to the conditions established under Ptolemaic hegemony. Only under Ptolemy IV did the Egyptian empire have to give up its hegemonic ambitions in favour of a policy advocating a balance of power, which was pursued by some very able politicians.[168]

The success of the Ptolemies is most evident in the fact that they managed to keep the Egyptian homeland untouched by war. They also succeeded in securing a dynastic succession and thereby were once again able to lay claim to Cyrenaica. The continuation of the policy of Ptolemy I is also true of many measures adopted on domestic issues (e.g. the cultivation of land and colonization by kleruchs, the promotion of Alexandrian scholarship, etc.). Under Philadelphos there was great progress in many areas: one need only think of the many cities founded and especially re-founded by him (among them a dozen bearing the name of 'Arsinoe') or of his religious policies which are the subject of the next chapter. To the dynasty's splendour and the pre-eminence of its power in international affairs was added the crowning achievement of 20 years of peace under Euergetes.

## Notes

1 On the 7th of Hathyr according to the Pithom Stele which in reference to Ptolemy II describes the festival commemorating the beginning of ʿnḫ-wdꜣ-snb (ie. the happy epoch initiated by Ptolemy II); cf. G. Hölbl, *Tyche* 7, 1992, 119f. with Grzybek (1990), 81–86; also Koenen (1977), 52, 56–58, 62, 101; see note 47 on p. 32.

2 On the problem of the ante-dating (occurring, no doubt, at different points in time) of Ptolemy II's reign in Macedonia and in Egypt, cf. Koenen (1977), 43–45; Wörrle (1978), 215; Clarysse, Van der Veken (1983), 5 (17–21); Hazzard (1987); Grzybek (1990), 115–134; Hauben (1992), 162–167. On the comparable but still different reckoning of both systems in the case of Soter see p. 20–1.

3 Pestman (1967), 16, together with footnote c; J. and L. Robert, *Fouilles d'Amyzon en Carie*, I, Paris 1983, 124–127 (The Xanthos Decree from the winter of 260/259).

4 See p. 42f.

5 See p. 111.

6 One of these, whose name is unknown, was a son of Ptolemy I by Eurydice. The other, Argaios, may have been the son of Berenike I or of a concubine; see Stemma 1.

7 *OGIS* I, 219 (the Ilion Decree); Memnon: *FGrHist.* 434 F 9, 1; on this subject see Otto (1928), 17–21. On account of the few sources for this war, it is not taken into account in older research into the chronology of the Syrian Wars.

The traditional terminology, however, is retained here and so the title 'The First Syrian War' is ascribed only to the next military confrontation in this area. For recent critics on the so-called War of Succession, see Mastrocinque (bibliographical supp.).

8   I. Milet. 123, 38–40.

9   I. Milet. 123, 37.

10  I. Milet. 139, 28f. J. Seibert, 'Ptolemaios I und Milet', *Chiron* I, 1971, 159–166; Bagnall (1976), 173; Wörrle (1977), 55f.; Orth (1977), 23–31. With respect to Herakleia on the Latmian Gulf near the Karian border see M. Wörrle, 'Inschriften von Herakleia am Latmos', *Chiron* 18, 1988, 434f.

11  Syll. I³, 390, see p. 24 together with note 60.

12  L. Robert, *Opera Minora Selecta* V, Amsterdam 1989, 449–568 (Stratonikeia, 9th year = 277/6); J. and L. Robert, *Fouilles d'Amyzon en Carie*, I, Paris 1983, 118–124 (Nr. 3: Source for the strategoi of Karia in the 9th year); Bagnall (1976), 89–102; *SEG* I, 363. On the history of Karian Mylasa and of the sanctuary of Labraunda (267: Ptolemaic; under Antiochos II once again Seleucid) see G. Le Rider, 'Antiochos II à Mylasa', *BCH* 114, 1990, 543–551.

13  *SEG* XXVIII, 60, ll. 71–78 (The Decree of Kallias of Sphettos, see p. 69 note 34 and p. 117 note 90); L. Robert, *REG* 94, 1981, 398.

14  See p. 19. *Ptolemaios* appears in Lycian inscriptions (TAM I, 35; 65, Zl. 8) as *pttule* (for this reference I would like to thank Prof. J. Borchhardt in Vienna); TAM I, dated to the 4th year of the king *pttule*, deals with Ptolemy II (and so refers to the year 282/1 according to Hazzard, 1987), since in the Greek chronology of Ptolemy I, which is probably also used in Lycian inscriptions, there is no 4th year (see p. 21 together with footnote 48).

15  Wörrle (1978); TAM II, 1. On Lissa see TAM II, 158f.

16  Page 23; Bagnall (1976), 111.

17  Seibert (1967), 51–53.

18  Chamoux (1956); Huß (1979), 128f. (on the eventual involvement of Carthage); Koenen (1983), 178–181. The infamous suppression of the rebellion of the Celtic soldiers was made over into a victory by the propaganda of the court and so became a much treated theme in the visual arts: H. P. Laubscher, 'Ein ptolemäisches Gallierdenkmal', *AntK* 30, 2, 1987, 131–154, Plates 20–21.

19  Chamoux (1956); 32f.; Laronde (1987), 362–370, interprets convincingly hymns I (to Zeus), II (to Apollo) and VI (to Demeter) in this sense. In the hymn to Apollo, one may also discern the likening of Ptolemy II to the god.

20  V. Foertmeyer, 'The dating of the Pompe of Ptolemy II Philadelphus', *Historia* 37, 1988, 90–104; Gehrke (1990), 200; cf. also H. Maehler, *JEA* 74, 1988, 290–292, with E. E. Rice, 'The grand procession of Ptolemy Philadelphus', Oxford 1983.

21  See p. 94.

22  G. Grimm (1981), 14–17; R. A. Tomlinson, in *Alessandria* II (1984), 263f.

23  The most important source for the war from the Seleucid point of view is a cuneiform text in the British Museum: A. J. Sachs, H. Hunger, *Astronomical Diaries and Related Texts from Babylonia*, I, Vienna 1988, 335–348 (Nr. 273); the historical passage on Nr. 273 B, v. ll. 29–38; on this subject see P. Bernard, *BCH* 114, 1990, 532–536. From the Egyptian perspective, the Pithom Stela, ll. 10–11 (=Doc. II, 91, 6–7), reports on the prelude to the war: 'The king came to the district (tšyt) of Asia and reached Palästina (or Philistaea).' On this

subject see D. Lorton, 'The supposed Expedition of Ptolemy II to Persia', *JEA* 57, 1971, 160–164; Winnicki (1990); Paus. I, 7, 3.

24 Pithom Stele, ll. 15–16 = Doc. II, 94, 5–15.

25 For the Babylonian year April 271/March 270, a cuneiform text reports that Antiochus I was still on the field: Sachs, Hunger, op. cit., 355 (–270 B, v. l. 18).

26 Bagnall (1976), 12.

27 See p. 94 together with note 96.

28 Syll. I³, 34/35, 4l. 17; on this see Hauben (1983).

29 Mendes Stele, l. 11 = Doc., II, 40, 8–9; Kall. frg. 228, 5–16 (Pf.). H. Cadell, 'A quelle date Arsinoé II Philadelphe est-elle décedée', in, Le culte du souverain dans l'Eypte ptolémaïque au IIIe siècle avant notre ère, ed. H. Melaerts (Leuven 1998), 1–3. cf. St M. Burstein, 'Arsinoe II Philadelphos: a Revisionist View'; in *Philip II, Alexander the Great and the Makedonian Heritage*, Washington 1982, 197–212.

30 See p. 24.

31 Habicht (1956), 116–121; M. Wörrle, *Chiron* 5, 1975, 69, footnote 45 (date: the early 70s); Will, I (1979), 147 (date: 271/70).

32 Sources: Paus. I, 1, 1 and 7, 3; III, 6, 4–6; Just. XXVI, 2, 1–8. A detailed account in Heinen (1972, 2), 95–213, whose dating we follow, because of the futile discussion of chronology in the last decade. On this see Hauben (1992), 162.

33 R. Etienne, M. Pierart, 'Un décret du Koinon des Hellènes à Platée en l'honneur de Glaucon, fils d'Etéoclès, d'Athènes, *BCH* 99, 1975, 51–75; G. A. Lehmann, 'Der "Lamische Krieg" und die "Freiheit der Hellenen" ' *ZPE* 73, 1988, 144–149.

34 *SEG* XXVIII, 60, ll. 40–78 (The Decree of Kallias, see p. 68, footnote 13); J. and L. Robert, *REG* 94, 1981, 396–398; Habicht (1979), 85.

35 Habicht (1979), 95–112.

36 Syll. I³, 434–435; Schmitt (1969), 129–133 (Nr. 476); The dating here follows Hauben (1992), 162.

37 PP VI, 15063. A priest of Alexander before the war: Clarysse, Van der Veken (1983), 4, Nr. 20.

38 E. Vanderpool *et al.*, 'Koronoi: A Ptolemaic Camp on the East Coast of Attica', *Hesperia* 31, 1962, 26–61, Plates 13–23; id. *et al.*, 'Koroni: The Date of the Camp and the Pottery', *Hesperia* 33, 1964, 69–75, Plate 10; J. and L. Robert, *REG* 77, 1964, 160f.

39 *SEG* XXIV, 154; Heinen (1972, 2), 152–159.

40 Bagnall (1976), 135f.

41 Heinen (1972, 2), 157f.

42 Van't Dack, Hauben (1978), 87–89.

43 PP VI, 14636.

44 PP VI, 14596; Clarysse, Van der Vecken (1983), 8, Nr. 36; J. Pouilloux, 'Glaucon, fils d'Eteocles, d'Athènes', in *Le monde grec*. FS Cl. Préaux, ed. J. Bingen *et al.*, Bruxelles 1975, 376–382.

45 Schmitt (1969), 134 (Nr. 477); Heinen (1972, 2), 180; Habicht (1979), 101; id. (1982), 19.

46 I. Milet. 139; C. B. Welles, *Royal Correspondence in the Hellenistic Period*, New Haven 1934, 71–77 (Nr. 14); Ptolemy the 'son' is also mentioned here (see p. 67, footnote 3).

47  P. Brun, 'Les Lagides à Lesbos: essai de chronologie', *ZPE* 85, 1991, 99–113. On the Seleucid control of Ephesus in the 260s see OGIS I, 222, new edition by F. Piejko, 'Decree of the Ionian League in Honor of Antiochus I', *c.* 267–262 BC, *Phoenix* 45, 1991, 126–147.

48  I. Cret. III, 4, 2 and 3.

49  M. Launey, 'L'exécution de Sotadès et l'expédition de Patroklos dans la Mer Egée (266 av. J.-C.), *REA* 47, 1945, 33–45.

50  Van't Dack (1981), 419.

51  *OGIS* I, 102, 11–14; Bagnall (1976), 130; Goudriaan (1988), 123.

52  Bagnall (1976), 123, 125f., 131, 136.

53  *IG* XII, 5, 1065; PP VI, 15038; Bagnall (1976), 144f. On the role of the nesiarch see p. 60.

54  *IG* XII, 5, 1061, ll. 2–4; L. Robert, 'Arsinoè de Kéos', *Hellenica* 11–12 (1960) 146–160; Bagnall (1976), 141–145.

55  Bagnall (1976), 80f., 174.

56  Habicht (1956), 104, 231; Orth (1977), 153–156; Bagnall (1976), 81 (on *SEG* I, 366).

57  See p. 41f.

58  On the problems and sources see J. Seibert, 'Die Schlacht bei Ephesos', *Historia* 25, 1976, 45–61; Orth (1977), 131f.; Will, I (1979), 235, 237, 369; A. N. Oikonomides, 'The Death of Ptolemy "the son", at Ephesos and P. Bouriant' 6, *ZPE* 56, 1984, 149. The common association of the rebellious successor to the throne, Ptolemy, with the commander killed in Ephesus, also called Ptolemy and the so-called son of Andromachos, is here avoided following the example of Hammond, Walbank (1988), 588–592. The association of the latter with the priest of Alexander of 251/50 seems more probable; see p. 50.

59  Th. Wiegand, *Didyma*, II: A. Rehm, Die Inschriften, Berlin 1958, 291–295 (Nr. 492).

60  This date is suggested by Hammond, Walbank (1988), 595–599. However, there is the possibility that the sea battle at Kos was fought earlier at the end of the Chremonidian War (261), see Heinen (1972, 2), 193–197.

61  *IG* XI, 2, 11.

62  Walbank, in Hammond, Walbank (1988), 294.

63  E. Bresciani, 'La spedizione di Tolomeo II in Siria in un ostrakon demotico inedito da Karnak', in *Ptol. Äg.* (1978), 31–37; ead., 'Registrazione catastale e ideologia politica nell'Egitto tolemaico', *EgVicOr* 6, 1983, 15–31; for corrections to the preceding see K.-T. Zauzich, *Enchoria* 12, 1984, 193f.; Winnicki (1991, 2).

64  W. Clarysse, 'A royal visit to Memphis and the end of the Second Syrian War', in D. J. Crawford *et al.*, *Studies on Ptolemaic Memphis*, Lovanii 1980, 83–89 (= *Studia Hellenistica*, 24).

65  *PCZ* II, 59242 = *SB* 6745; II, 59251 = *SB* 6748; Orrieux (1983), 49f. On Apollonios see p. 58.

66  See p. 98 and p. 117, footnote 94.

67  *OGIS* I, 54, 8.

68  Demetrios the Fair was the half-brother of Antigonos Gonatos and son of Demetrios Poliorketes and Ptolemais, daughter of Ptolemy I.

69  *OGIS* I, 54, 6. Our account essentially follows Laronde (1987), 381f.; for a contrary view see Bartson (1982), 489–491.

70 Listed by Ptolemy VIII in his *Hypomnemata*: *FGrHist*. 234 F 4.
71 On the 25th of the month Dios, according to the Canopus Decree, in Greek, l. 4 (Hisn.) especially 6 (Tanis); demotic A(Hisn), l. 2, B(Tanis), l. 7; hieroglyphic, ll. 3–4; doc. II, 127, 4; Spiegelberg (1922), 5, 66; the text of the Canopus Decree see p. 121, footnote 186; on the dates for the beginning of his reign see Koenen (1977), 67, 72, 75 and plate on p. 106. A papyrus from Elephantine still gives the date in February of 246 as though it were during the reign of Philadelphos: Skeat (1969), 31, (6). cf. also Pestman (1981), A, 216 (somewhat different from Koenen).
72 On the events in Cyrenaica see Laronde (1987), 382–415.
73 I. Priene 37, 134. The most important sources for the war: a papyrus from Gurob: *FGrHist*. 160, new edition and commentary by F. Piejko, 'Episodes from the Third Syrian War in a Gurob Papyrus', 246 B. C., *ArchPF* 36, 1990, 13–27; *OGIS* I, 54: an inscription, known as the Monumentum Adulitanum, which the merchant and extensive traveller of the sixth century AD, Kosmas Indikopleustes, found at Adulis and of which a copy was made for posterity in his *Christian Topography*. For the historiographical literature on this see App. *Syr*. 65, 345–346; Just. XXVII, 1–2; Polyain. VIII, 50; Porph.: *FGrHist*. 260 F 43; Plb. V, 58, 10f.; Kall. frg. 110 Pf.; Catull. 66. For a discussion of all the problems see Hauben (1990).
74 PP VI, 15060; on this Xanthippos cf. H. Hauben, 'Triérarques et triérarchie dans le marine des Ptolémées', *AncSoc* 21, 1990, 120 (Nr. 2), 135–138.
75 PP VI, 14584; Mooren (1975), 61f. (014).
76 See p. 81.
77 Pestman (1967), 134f.; J. Bingen, *ChronEg* 67, 134, 1992, 326.
78 For more see P. Haun. 6, Fr. 1, ll. 14–17; in response to this see J. Schwartz, *ZPE* 30, 1978, 95–99; A. Büllow-Jacobsen, 'P. Haun. 6. An Inspection of the Original', *ZPE* 36, 1979, 93; W. Huß, 'Eine Revolte der Ägypter in der Zeit des 3. Syrischen Krieges', *Aegyptus* 58, 1978, 151–156; W. Peremans, 'Sur la *domestica seditio* de Justin (XXVII, 1, 9), *AntCl* 50, 1981, 628–636.
79 Kanopos Decree, hieroglyphics, ll. 7–10, Greek, ll. 10–14 (Dom el-Hisn): Doc. II, 130–132, Bernand (1970), 990f., 994; Bonneau (1971), 126–129; Hauben (1990), 34.
80 Hauben (1990), 32.
81 R. Herzog, G. Klaffenbach, 'Asylieurkunden aus Kos', *AbhBerlin* 1952, H. 1, Nr. 8–9; Habicht (1956), 122f.; F. W. Walbank, in Hammond, Walbank (1988), 307, 319.
82 P. Haun. 6, Fr. 1, ll. 4–7 = Bülow-Jacobsen, *ZPE* 36, 1979, 92.
83 Clarysse, Van der Veken (1983), 8, Nr. 40. At the same time, the mistress Belistiche (PP VI, 14717) discharged the priestly office for Arsinoe Philadelphos (see p. 103). Was she the mother? On these problems and on the battle of Andros mentioned in the text that follows see Hammond, Walbank (1988), 587–595.
84 This according to P. Haun. 6, Fr. 1, ll. 8–9 (*ZPE* 36, 1979, 92f.). The historiographical tradition (Plu. *mor*. 183 C, 545 B; Plu. *Pelop*. 2; Trog. *prol*. 27) ascribes this position to Admiral Opron who accordingly must have been put under the command of the king's son; cf. A. N. Oikonomides, 'Opron and the sea-battle of Andros', *ZPE* 56, 1984, 151f.
85 On this see P. Haun. 6, Fr. 1, ll. 11–13 (*ZPE* 36, 1979, 93).

86  E. Kirsten, I. Opelt, 'Eine Urkunde der Gründung von Arsinoe in Kilikien', *ZPE* 77, 1989, 55–66; C. P. Jones, Ch. Habicht, 'A Hellenistic Inscription from Arsinoe in Cilicia', *Phoenix* 43, 1989, 317–346.

87  For Xanthos at the time of the third and fourth Ptolemies see J. Bosquet, 'Lettre de Ptolemée Evergète à Xanthos de Lycie', *REG* 99, 1986, 22–32.

88  Apart from Ephesos, here Lebedos (under the name of Ptolemais), Kolophon with Klaros (see L. Robert, *Opera minora selecta*, IV, Amsterdam 1974, 183f.), Priene and Samos may be referred to; Ptolemaic influence on Miletos no longer being tenable.

89  Summary of this problem in Huß (1976), 188–213; Bagnall (1976), 80–116, 159–175. The island of Samothrake was also under the control and influence of the strategoi of Thrace and the Hellespont but was not occupied militarily by the Ptolemies: Bengston (1952), 178–181; on this see PP VI, 14605.

90  A. Jähne, 'Die "Syrische Frage", Seleukia in Pierien und die Ptolemäer', *Klio* 56, 1974, 501–519; on the discoveries of Ptolemaic coins on this site see Will, I (1979), 259; on all aspects of this issue see J. D. Grainger, *The Cities of Seleukid Syria*, Oxford 1990, *passim*. What is more, a Ptolemaic base at Cape 'Ras Ibn Hani', a few kilometres north of Laodikeia, seems to have had control over access to this Seleukid Port: J.-P. Rey-Coquais, 'Inscription grecque découverte à Ras Ibn Hani: stèle de mercenaires lagides sur la côte syrienne', *Syria* 55, 1978, 313–325.

91  Catullus 66, 35f.: is haut in tempore longo captam Asiam Aegypti finibus addiderat. A hieroglyphic text, formerly on a wall of the small Chnum temple north of Esna which was destroyed in the nineteenth century, gives in a certain way information which supplements that in the Adulis inscription (see note 73). In the former, the lands conquered by Ptolemy III are listed as Makedonia, Thrace, Persia and Elam among others: Doc. II, 158.

92  M. J. Osborne, *ZPE* 78, 1989, 226.

93  Chr. Habicht, 'Bemerkungen zum P. Haun. 6', *ZPE* 39, 1980, 1–5.

94  *IG* IX, 12, 56 (Thermos), 202–203 (Delphi); W. Huß, 'Die zu Ehren Ptolemaios' III. und seiner Familie errichtete Statuengruppe von Thermos', *ChronEg* 50, 99–100, 1975, 312–320.

95  Syll. II³, 545, 6.

96  Schmitt (1969), 208f. (Nr. 505).

97  PP VI, 14608.

98  On the religious aspects of these honours see p. 93. On all the measures taken and their political affinities see Habicht (1982), 79–117.

99  See p. 54.

100  Antiochus Hierax met with an unfortunate end in Thrace, after having been detained in Egypt as a prisoner of state while he was there in temporary exile (around 227). See Just. XXVII, 3, 9–11.

101  P. Haun. 6, Fr. 1, ll. 19 and 28–31 = *ZPE* 36, 1979, 93f. Our dating is based on the postulate of the earliest possible date for Antiochus III's accession to power (i.e. after 9th April in the spring of 222) in Grzybek, loc. cit. (p. 31, footnote 44), 195–197.

102  W. Huß, 'Eine ptolemäische Expedition nach Kleinasien', *AncSoc* 8, 1977, 187–193; Chr. Habicht, 'Bemerkungen zum P. Haun. 6', *ZPE* 39, 1980, 3f.

103  Huß (1979), 128f.; Rostovsteff, I (1955), 308–310; Fraser (1972), I, 152f.

104 The result of this was a ten-volume work titled *On the Ports* which was used by Eratosthenes: Fraser (1972), I, 152, 522.

105 Ptolemy II may have felt himself compelled to take this measure, since he (and not Ptolemy Keraunos) was the Ptolemy who, during the Pyrrhos' campaigns in Italy, had stationed a strong military contingent in Epiros in order to protect the Molossian kingdom; cf. N. G. L. Hammond, 'Which Ptolemy gave troops and stood as protector of Pyrrhus' Kingdom?', *Historia* 37, 1988, 405–413.

106 PP II, 3878 (a Roman and common soldier; 252/1); 3957 (a Syracusan and Kleruch, on the latter see p. 61f; 237/6), 4171 (from Campania, *c.* 225/4).

107 PP VI, 15117. On this subject see W. Peremans, E. Van't Dack, 'Sur les rapports de Rome avec les Lagides', in *ANRW* I, 1, 1972, 660–667; Heinen (1972, 1), 634–639; D. Vollmer, *Symploke, das Übergreifen der römischen Expansion auf den griechischen Osten*, Stuttgart 1990, 24f.

108 SB 5111 = Török (1986), 207, Nr. 27: a letter to a Ptolemy (possibly Ptolemy II) on an attack against Elephantine from the south.

109 S. M. Burstein, 'The Ethiopian War of Ptolemy V: a Historical Myth?', *Beiträge zur Sudanforschung* I, 1986, 17–23; id., *Agatharchides of Cnidus, On the Erythraean Sea*, London 1989, 7, 25 (here and in what follows the Agatharchides-Fragments are cited from this edition).

110 Doc. II, 120, 12–17; on the procession just mentioned see p. 39f.

111 A. and A. Castiglioni, G. Negro, 'A la recherche de Berenice Pancrisia dans le désert oriental nubien', *BSFE* 121, 1991, 5–24.

112 The account in the Adulis Inscription is very instructive: *OGIS* I, 54, 10–13, 16.

113 Many of the leaders and participants in the expeditions are known: PP II, 4419–4511; cf. Mitteis, Wilcken, I Nr. 451–452.

114 The canal works and founding of the city are mentioned in the Pithom Stela, ll. 16, 20–21 = Doc. II, 95, 2–11; 100, 4–11; on this see Diod. I, 33, 11f.; Plin. *nat*. VI, 29, 165–167. On later developments cf. K. W. Butzer: *LÄ* III, 1980, col. 312f. (s.v. Kanal, Nil-Rotes Meer) and H. Goedicke: *LÄ* VI, 1986, col. 1125 (s.v. Wadi Tumilat) with H. Heinen *et al.*, *Ägypten in hellenistisch-römischer Zeit, Tübinger Atlas des Vorderen Orients*, Map B V 21, Wiesbaden 1989 (Ptolemaios potamos).

115 Fraser (1972), I, 177; II, 299f. (footnote 348f.).

116 F. Altheim, R. Stiehl, *Die Araber in der alten Welt* I, Berlin 1964, 65–79 ('Ptolemäer und Nabatäer'); R. Wenning, *Die Nabatäer – Denkmäler und Geschichte*, Freiburg/CH 1987, 126–128; M. Evenari, 'Die Nabatäer im Negev', in *Petra und das Königreich der Nabatäer*, ed. by M. Lindner, 5th edition, München 1989, 164–166; Winnicki (1991, 1), 185–198.

117 M. J. Klein, *Untersuchungen zu den kaiserlichen Steinbrüchen an Mons Porphyrites und Mons Claudianus in der östlichen Wüste Ägyptens*, Bonn 1988, 18–20, Illustration 1.

118 Report of the founding and an elephant hunt on the Pithom Stela, l. 23f. = Doc. II, 101f.

119 L. Casson, 'The Location of Adulis (Periplus Maris Erythraei 4), in *Coins, Culture, and History in the Ancient World*, FS L. Trell, Detroit 1981, 113–122.

120 Elephant expeditions also took this route as the evidence in Abu Simbel shows: PP II, 4461, 4462, 4483; certainly in the third century, see Fraser (1972), II, 309, footnote 375.

121  On this whole subject see H. Kortenbeutel, *Der ägyptische Süd- und Osthandel in der Politik der Ptolemäer und römischen Kaiser*, Berlin 1931; Fraser (1972), I, 173–184.

122  On the circle of philoi during the entire Ptolemaic period see Mooren (1975), 52–80; on the Macedonians in their number: 53 (04), 54 (06), 60f. (011); see id., 'Macht und Nationalität', in *Ptol.Äg.* (1978), 51–57. An exception among the high-ranking Ptolemaic officials was Patroklos, the famous admiral in the Chremonidean War; he was a Macedonian by birth, but did not belong to the *philoi*.

123  See p. 70, footnote 63 (quotations from Bresciani and Zauzich), on this see PP I, 51; J. D. Thomas, 'Aspects of the Ptolemaic Civil Service: the Dioiketes and the Nomarch', in *Ptol.Äg.* (1978), 189–192; On the question of the dioiketes for specific regions during the entire period of Ptolemaic history see Mooren (1977), 136–158.

124  See p. 45.

125  Pestman (1980); id. (1981); Cl. Orrieux, 'Zénon de Caunos, parépidémos, et le destin grec', Paris 1985; a good account worth reading of the range of themes covered in this archive can be found in Orrieux (1983); on the relationship with Coele Syria see Passoni Dell'Acqua (1986).

126  See p. 61.

127  On local organization see p. 25. In general, the jurisdiction of the nomarch was connected to a district (nome). However, there were also toparchs who had jurisdicition over a nome and nomarchs who governed only a part of a district (nome); see Thomas (footnote 124), 192f. On the relations between the dioiketes and the nomarch see Falivene (1991), 209–215.

128  W. Peremans, 'Egyptiens et étrangers dans l'administration civile et financière de l'Egypte Ptolémaïque', *AncSoc* 2, 1971, 33–45; Falivene (1991), 217–224 (on the question of the Greek or Egyptian character of certain offices).

129  Only in the temple-lists of Greek and Roman Egypt was reference still made to the old 42 districts. Nothing is known about the administration of the oases during the Hellenistic period; Siwa remained independent under the control of local priest-kings.

130  Bengston (1952), 32–35; Thomas (footnote 124), 192–194. On the military administration of southern Egypt during the entire period of Ptolemaic history see J. K. Winnicki, *Ptolemäerarmee in Thebais*, Wroclaw 1978.

131  On the following see Bagnall (1976).

132  See p. 47.

133  Parmentier (1987), 403–412.

134  See p. 29.

135  See note 86 of this chapter.

136  See p. 68, footnote 12; Chr. Marek, 'Ein ptolemäischer Stratege in Karien', *Chiron* 12, 1982, 119–123.

137  Merker (1970).

138  Syll. I³, 502 (= P. M. Fraser, *Samothrace, II, 1: The Inscriptions on Stone*, New York 1960, 39f.)

139  Attested for Cyprus, Syria, Lycia, Karia, Thera; the nesiarch also had with him an oikonomos.

140  See p. 26f.

141  Passoni Dell'Acqua (1986), 278f.

142 Bagnall (1976), 108, 113–115; 119 and 201 on an Arsinoe in Crete (Rhethymnon?) of which the chronology remains unclear; Wörrle (1979), esp. 104–106; for Arsinoe in Cilicia see the works cited in note 86 of this chapter; the 'Arsinoe in Pamphylia' can be attributed together with Korakesion (modernday Alanya) lying west of it to Cilicia (Str. XIV, 5, 3), on this see p. 138.

143 So Rostovsteff, I (1955), 215; Bagnall (1976), 5; but see Siedl (1962), 127.

144 See p. 201f.

145 See p. 27.

146 See p. 58.

147 Harmatta (1963), 203; Seidl (1962), 110.

148 Bagnall (1976), 17.

149 R. S. Bagnall, 'The Origins of Ptolemaic Cleruchs', *BAmSocP* 21, 1984, 7–20.

150 Clarysse, loc. cit. p. 290, footnote 64.

151 The text in demotic on an ostrakon from Karnak: see sections in Bresciani mentioned in note 63 of this chapter.

152 Bingen (1952); id. (1978). On the leasing out of tax-collection outlined in what follows see Müller, B.-J. (1968), 19–38.

153 The toponym 'Arsinoe' in the Fayum is in the papyri associated with two villages of Arsinoites. The district capital, Krokodilopolis, is referred to as 'Arsinoe' only by the geographers from the time of Strabo (XVII, I, 38) onwards; cf. L. Casarico, *Aegyptus* 67, 1987, 127–170.

154 *PCZ* 59155 dated 27/12/256; R. Johannsen, 'Ptolemy Philadelphus and Scientific Agriculture', *ClPhil* 18, 1923, 156–161; Orrieux (1983), 79–93 (92f. the document on what was subsequently called the tour of inspection). On the hydraulic installations see G. Garbrecht, H. Jaritz, *Untersuchungen antiker Anlagen zur Wasserspeicherung im Faym/Ägypten*, Braunschweig 1990 (= Bulletin from the Leichtwieß-Institut für Wasserbau at the Universität Braunschweig, 107).

155 *C.Ord.Ptol.*, Nr. 22; for the legislation on slavery see Müller, B.-J. (1968), 70–86.

156 For a very detailed discussion of all the issues related to this theme see Fraser (1972) I, 305–793. For a general account of the different aspects of Alexandrian culture see Chr. Jacob *et al.*, *Aléxandrie IIIe siècle av. J.-C. Tous les savoirs du monde ou le rêve d'universalité des Ptolémées*, Paris 1992.

157 See p. 26.

158 W. Peremans, 'Egyptiens et étrangers dans le milieu d'Alexandrie au temps des Lagides', *AncSoc* 7, 1976, 167–176.

159 See p. 25.

160 See p. 100.

161 E. Winter, 'Weitere Beobachtungen zur "Grammaire du temple" in der griechisch-römischen Zeit', in *Tempel und Kult*, ed. v. W. Helck, Wiesbaden 1987, 72–75.

162 On Sostratos see p. 24f. above together with footnote 62; on this issue see Fraser (1972), I, 18–20, II, 50f., footnote 111.

163 On Theocritus see p. 36, 38, 40 and p. 111. On the encomium of Ptolemy II see M. A. Rossi, *Theocritus' IDYLL XVII: A Stylistic Commentary*, Amsterdam 1989.

164 See p. 39 together with footnote 19 and pp. 101–103, also p. 69, footnote 29 and Laronde (1987), 379. On other poets see p. 105 together with footnotes

177–181. He came into conflict with Apollonius Rhodes: M. R. Lefkowitz, 'The Quarrel between Callimachus and Apollonius', *ZPE* 40, 1980, 1–19.

165 See p. 105.

166 R. Bernhardt, 'Zu den Verhandlungen zwischen Dareios und Alexander nach der Schlacht bei Issos', *Chiron* 18, 1988, 181–198.

167 Cf. H. Braunert, 'Hegemoniale Bestrebungen der hellenistischen Großmachte in Politik und Wirtschaft', *Historia* 13, 1964, 80–104.

168 Cf. H. H. Schmitt, 'Polybios und das Gleichgewicht der Mächte', in F. W. Walbank *et al.*, *Polybe*, Genève 1974, 65–102, esp. 76. The much cited balance of power between the three Hellenistic kingdoms existed *de facto* only by virtue of the fact that none of these was able to eliminate either both or even one of the others. The resurgence of the Seleucid kingdom which had been to a great extent expelled from the Mediterranean region was not long in coming.

# 3 Royal ideology and religious policy from Alexander the Great to Ptolemy III

## THE PHARAOH – EGYPTIAN PRIESTS AND TEMPLES

### Pharaonic image of the Macedonian foreign rulers

The argument advanced at the end of the Introduction was that the ancient Egyptian king ruled as the earthly manifestation of Horus and as the 'son of Re'. From this idea follows the concept that the gods acted as the actual rulers of the world from an Egyptian viewpoint, embodied the political unity of Egypt and accepted the king as their legitimate representative only after the coronation rituals had been performed. The more belief in the legitimacy and cultic significance of the earthly rulers declined during the course of later Egyptian history, the more the conqueror Alexander and the new foreign dynasty had to strive to obtain legitimacy for themselves. The burden was on them to assimilate and restore in the best possible way the ancient Egyptian ideology of the king. Only in this way could they give the impression that in their actions both at home and abroad they were simply complying with the requirements of a cult whose function was the preservation of world order. Quite in keeping with these notions, the legitimate pharaoh had to be one who was recognized as such by the gods. In addition, the new pharaoh had to carry out the rituals required for the transmission of power as the son or the nominal son of his deceased but equally legitimate predecessor.

These religious aspects were duly transferred to Alexander, to some extent perhaps only after his departure from Egypt, if the official depiction of Alexander's coronation as pharaoh on the temple reliefs does not represent ceremonies which had actually been carried out. Alexander was quite justified, at any rate, in laying claim to the fulfilment of the ancient pharaonic duty of driving away the preceding chaos and of repeating the act of creation through the re-establishment of Maat; he had in effect put an end to the ten years of much detested Persian rule which had preceded him (Diod. XVII.49.2; Curt. IV.7.1–4) In choosing Memphis as the setting for his accomplishments as king, Alexander achieved two objectives: first, he associated himself with the foundation of the united Egyptian state traditionally attributed to King Menes; second, by choosing Memphis as the pharaoh's official city of residence he reflected a trend of emulating Old Kingdom tradition which had emerged in the course of later Egyptian history. At the same time, he became associated with certain facets of the ideology of the king specific to Memphis. There the pharaoh enjoyed the special privilege of being linked to the national god, Ptah, who was also described as a primordial god and a god of creation, as 'Lord of Maat', 'Father of the Gods', and 'King of the two Lands'. The Ptolemies followed Alexander's example inasmuch as they, like him, chose to be crowned in Memphis. Thus, from the beginning, a relationship of co-operation existed between the priesthoods of Memphis and the Ptolemaic royal house; the high priest of Ptah who carried out the rite of coronation represented the Egyptian priesthoods as a whole.[1]

Alexander endeavoured to take over the Persian empire and yet in Egypt he had to distance himself from his Persian predecessors so as to appear as a liberator of the land and not yet another conqueror. In view of this dilemma, an official summons by a royal oracle to assume the office of pharaoh seemed the most expedient option available to him. Through the oracle's pronouncement of his mythical descent from an Egyptian god, Alexander was recognized as a legal successor of the *native* Egyptian pharaohs. This mark of legitimacy was obtained by him in Siwah and not in Thebes. The reason for this choice was because Amun of Siwah (in his guise as Zeus-Ammon) permitted a convenient union of the Egyptian myth of divine lineage with the Greek idea of descent from Zeus. Moreover, an announcement from Siwah would be binding not only on Egypt but also on the entire Greek oikumene. As we shall see,[2] the oracular utterances from Siwah did in fact grant legitimacy to the Greek ruler cults established outside Egypt.

In addition to Alexander's actual father, Philip II, and his mythical one, Amun/Zeus-Ammon, he was to be provided with a third father (i.e. Egypt's last native king, Nectanebo II) for reasons of ritual once he became pharaoh. The prospect of establishing this kind of ideological link to Nectanebo II appeared very promising owing to the latter's reputation as a favourite of the gods;[3] it was a distinction conferred upon him because of the achievements of his building programme, his devotion to animal cults, the gifts of land he made to temples, his programme for the restoration of cult statues and the foundation of *naoi*, but above all because of his surprising victory over the Persian Great King in 350.[4] In the story known as the 'Deception of Nectanebo' (ps. Kallisthenes I.1–8) which is found in the Alexander Romance, Nectanebo is said to have defeated the dastardly foreign rulers precisely because he was the father of Alexander – although he was forced to flee in the winter of 343/2 in the face of the Persian invasion. In the account, Nectanebo, who is well-versed in the magical arts, betakes himself in the guise of an Egyptian priest to the court at Pella. In a reflection of the high standing which Egyptian soothsaying enjoyed abroad, Nectanebo predicts the queen's future while Philip is away. He foretells her mystical union with the Libyan Ammon and the birth of Alexander which would result from it.

In keeping with Egyptian myth, Nectanebo then spent the night with Olympias in the guise of a god and thus brought into the world the future vanquisher of the Persians as well as his legitimate Egyptian successor (as Harendotes 'Horus, avenger of his father' cf. Ps. Kallisthenes I.8.3).[5] In view of the later date of the Alexander Romance, its attempt to associate Alexander with Nectanebo II[6] is clearly evidence that the Ptolemies appropriated this element of pharaonic ideology. In essence, it was meant to convey the message that the Argead and Ptolemaic kings continued the line of native Egyptian kings; the ten-year period of the second Persian domination was to be disregarded as a time of chaos and of the enemies of the gods.

The royal titularies on the hieroglyphic monuments represent the most fundamental precondition for the pharaonic function. The five names express specific relationships of the king to the divine world, but given the cultic nature of historical events these names can also reflect them. This is particularly true of the short and concise titularies from the time of Alexander until Ptolemy II.[7]

Alexander appeared as 'protector of Egypt' on account of his Horus-name, a name which describes the king as the representative of Horus. The same was implied by the so-called 'Nebty-name' (the Two Ladies Name) of the kings of the nineteenth and twentieth dynasties from the time of Ramses II onwards; the 'Nebty-name' was the second component of the royal titulary; in the case of Alexander, it was appended to the Horus-name of Nectanebo II. Even the phrase 'he who drives out the foreigners' (tkn-ḫꜣswt) which appears in a certain variant of Alexander's Horus-name was taken from Nectanebo's Nebty-name and referred in both cases to the Persian empire; related to this was the Nebty-name of Philip Arrhidaios 'ruler of the foreign lands' (ḥqꜣ-ḫꜣswt) which had once been used by the Hyksos in addition to their Egyptian royal titles. Officially, the expression could only mean 'conqueror of the (previously hostile) Persian empire'; however, for an informed and nationally minded Egyptian the title might have suggested the hated Hyksos themselves. Since Alexander's empire hardly existed even on paper, thereafter, special care was given to maintaining at least the appearance of Alexander IV's legal right to rule: in his Nebty-name he was expressly referred to as 'he to whom the office of his father was given'. His golden-name (the third part of the titulary) depicts him as '(strong?) ruler over the whole land'; since this term is unique in the history of the names of Egyptian kings, the translation 'ruler over the entire empire' seems to suggest itself in this particular instance.

Both parts of Alexander the Great's throne-name refer to the special circumstances of his legitimation: 'the one whom Re (or Amun) chose, beloved of Amun (i.e. Re)'; in themselves, they were common additions to the royal throne-names of the New Kingdom but they would never have constituted a complete throne-name in and of themselves. These additions state the essential elements of divine lineage in the context of the concrete and historical circumstances by which the Macedonian rulers became pharaoh: Alexander and his successors, Philip and Ptolemy I, who both went under a similar throne-name, appear as 'chosen' by god and the 'beloved' son, namely as the desired and legitimate successors of the gods in their office. By these measures, divine support of the government seemed to be secured, but this also meant that the ruler now had to observe certain religious duties such as showing piety in office, erecting sanctuaries and fostering the cults of the gods.[8]

The throne-name, which traditionally evoked the essential character and activities of the king in relation to the god of creation, was meant to mark an ideological continuity between the line of Argead kings and the Ptolemaic dynasty. At the same time, the Horus-name and Nebty-name of Ptolemy I also marked the beginning of a new dynasty: the former satrap of the Satrap Stele of 311,[9] who had already been acting as a pharaoh, appears now in the guise of Horus 'great in strength, strong king (*nswt*)'; in the Horus-names of the earlier periods an address to the ruler as king is extremely rare[10] and the concise version found here is unique. The assumption of the office of Egyptian king is shown as a legally important step; the Nebty-name which was created for Ptolemy I with its reference to the two protective snakes of the crown of Upper and Lower Egypt gives the reason for this process: 'the one who conquers with power, a virtuous ruler'. The golden-name of Ptolemy II, naturally enough, makes reference to 'he whom his father crowned'. This manner of legitimizing by succession was to be continued in future titularies of Ptolemaic kings and so was a convenient vehicle for outlining the particular circumstances of family history. The passing on of royal power is clearly represented on the scenes of ancestor worship in temple-reliefs.[11]

With Ptolemy III, complex royal names begin to appear laden with elaborate religious components and epithets of praise. In epithets such as 'lord of the jubilee-festivals as well as Ptah Tatjenen' (in the golden-name of Ptolemy III), the pharaoh is, henceforth and until the time of Ptolemy XII, regularly compared with 'king' Ptah who is at the head of the dynasty of the gods in the list of kings (Royal Papyrus of Turin, Manetho): this is a definite sign of the transfer of the king's ideology onto the Ptolemies and comes as a consequence of the increasing importance of the priesthood of Memphis; Amun, who was progressively mentioned only in passing, was replaced by Ptah as the god of Egyptian kings and at the end of the third century went on to become the patron god of the insurgent Theban kings. In Euergetes I's Nebty-name ('strong is the protector of the gods, a mighty wall for Egypt), there is a clear reference to his successful policy of making Egypt into a great power and this is interwoven with the traditional theme of the cultic role of the king as a protector; what is more, the allusion to his role as protector of Egypt is a direct reference to Alexander the Great.

The image of the pharaohs in later times was shaped above all in Memphis. This was due to a number of factors: first, from a theological point of view, Apis of Memphis was related to the king by virtue of the fact that the latter held a divine office; second, Apis played an especially important role in the royal year festivals and coronation festivals and, as the city-god on the standard of the king, he was the protector of the king at his coronation. If one had the intention of propagating a complete break between the world of the gods and the actual ruler of Egypt, one imputed to the latter crimes against the gods, such as, in the case of the Persian conquerors Cambyses (Hdt. III.29) and Artaxerxes III (among others Plu. *de Iside* 11), the most infamous deed of killing the Apis bull. Thus, in stark contrast to the loathed Persian conquerors, Alexander was careful to have himself seen sacrificing to Apis and he thereby set a precedent which would be followed by the Ptolemies in their anti-Persian royal ideology.

The expulsion of the Persians eventually took on the same ideological significance as the banishment of the Hyksos before them. The recovery of the sacred statues of the gods, said to have been stolen by the Persians, was a persistent topos in the efforts by the early Ptolemies to represent themselves as ancient Egyptian pharaohs. Prior to the Ptolemies and probably with reference to the twenty-ninth dynasty,[12] the accomplishment of this pious deed had already been promulgated in the so-called 'prophecy of the lamb'[13] which was partially preserved in demotic. (In this instance it refers to the chapels which the Assyrians had supposedly taken back to Nineveh.) Under the first four Ptolemies, the act is mentioned each time in connection with a Syrian campaign, during which the cult images are said to have been unearthed. This was already true of the satrap Ptolemy after the battle at Gaza (312).[14] One may infer from the report on the Pithom Stele (Fig. 3.1),[15] that, following a campaign in the Near East which marked the onset of the First Syrian War in 274 the cult images were consequently returned to their temples. In celebration of their return, Ptolemy II held lavish cultic festivities with priests chosen from all of Egypt. After the great Asian campaign of Ptolemy III, the return of cult images once stolen by the Persians is included among the deeds for which the king was honoured;[16] according to the classical sources, which mention 2,500 *simulacra deorum* (Porph: FGrHist. 260 F 43), a sum worthy of the Ptolemaic Great King,[17] he received the name Euergetes just for this accomplishment. Finally, in 217 the priests who had gathered in Memphis confirmed that Ptolemy IV had successfully concluded a search for such statues of the gods in the reconquered land of Coele Syria and then had them brought back to Egypt.[18] It is clear from all of this that Ptolemaic propaganda effectively used anti-Persian nationalism against the Seleukids who were, after all, the direct heirs to the Achaemenid empire; in other words, the Ptolemies used this ideological message to obtain the support of the priesthoods for the stringent economic policy necessary to carry out the Syrian wars. In a similar vein, it is noteworthy that Seleukos I is said to have actually restored the statue of Apollo to the sanctuary at Didyma (in about 300/299) which had been carried off by the Persians at an earlier date (Paus. I.16.3; VIII.46.3).[19]

As we have seen, during his satrapy Ptolemy I had already taken on this new anti-Persian image and had embraced the religious duties that came

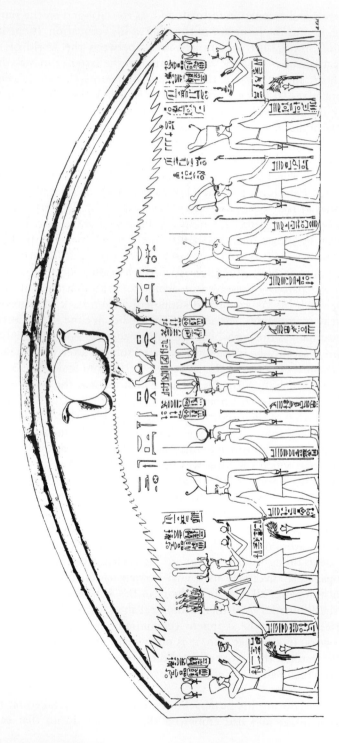

*Figure 3.1* Top part of the Pithom Stele, reproduced from Grzybek (1990) plate on p. 212 (after E. Naville); see p. 113, note 15. Three sacrifice scenes beneath winged sun: (right) Ptolemy II before Atum, Osiris, Horus, Isis and Arsinoe II; (centre left) Ptolemy II facing Atum, Isis and Arsinoe II; (far left) Ptolemy II facing his 'father'.

*Figure 3.2* Rounded upper portion of the so-called Satrap Stele of 311; beneath the winged sun are two sacrifice scenes of a king with blank cartouches facing the gods of Buto: to the left he faces the falcon-headed Horus who is wearing a double crown, to the right he is facing the goddess Uto wearing the crown of Lower Egypt; black granite; total height: 1.85 m; Cairo, Egyptian Museum, Cat. Gén. 22181.

with the office of pharaoh. The Satrap Stele (Fig. 3.2),[20] already mentioned several times,[21] confirms this. The stele, dated to the 1st of Thoth in the seventh year of Alexander IV (9 November 311) was used as building material for a mosque in Cairo and was perhaps originally erected in a temple in Sais. Quite in keeping with the characterization of 'Ptolemy the great ruler of Egypt' as a brave warrior and victorious general after the manner of the great pharaohs, the stele mentions among other things that he returned from his Syrian campaign in 312/1 and landed on the coast, north of Buto. There he confirmed that the revenues from that area were reserved for the gods of Buto (i.e. the local priesthoods); they had been robbed of them by the 'enemy Arses' or 'Xerxes' and king Khababash[22] had restored them once again. The cartouches in the upper field of the stele remained empty; the fact that Alexander IV, who was held hostage in Macedonia, is mentioned only in the part of the text which gives the date clearly indicates to what extent this king's name had lost its historical and cultic significance. Ptolemy was the single important historical figure of the time. Perhaps the empty cartouches in the scene of the gods are meant to suggest that the one sacrificing could also be Ptolemy.

*Figure 3.3* Upper portion of the Mendes Stele, after Roeder (1959), 172, Fig. 26;
see p. 113 note 23. Beneath the winged sun and the sign of the sky – in the left
half, the royal family sacrificing: Ptolemy II, Arsinoe II (long deceased before the
stele was produced) and the crown prince Ptolemy 'the son' – in the right half,
the divinities being worshipped: the newly installed ram of Mendes (depicted as
'king of Lower and Upper Egypt'), Harpokrates, the deceased ram of Mendes
(anthropomorphized with a ram's head), Hatmehit (district goddess of Mendes
carrying as her attribute the district standard with a fish on her head), finally the
new goddess Arsinoe II. The hieroglyphic text has been omitted in our figure.

Soon after his accession to the throne, Ptolemy II fulfilled his religious
duties as pharaoh by visiting important sanctuaries, especially those devoted
to animal cults. According to the evidence of the so-called Mendes Stele[23]
(Fig. 3.3), one of his first destinations was the temple of the ram of Mendes
(Delta) where, in keeping with the custom of 'earlier kings', he personally
performed the rituals connected to the procession of the ram on water and
made arrangements for the completion of the temple. At the beginning of
279 on the day of the jubilee of his reign, Ptolemy II presided over the
inauguration of a temple in Pithom (eastern Delta).[24] His son and co-regent
also had to take on the role of pharaoh before he set himself against his
father in 260/59. In 265/4, the crown prince performed the dedication of the
temple in Mendes;[25] in the upper field of the Mendes Stele he can be seen
behind the royal couple of Ptolemy II and Arsinoe II with cartouches which
are the same as his father's.[26]

The queens also were increasingly involved in the religious office of the pharaoh. Arsinoe II was the first to receive posthumously a new throne-name in her cartouche added to her birth name. Already in ancient Egypt from the time of the Middle Kingdom, cartouche names were common for queens but, since officially they were merely royal consorts, they never received a title from the royal titulary. Exceptions were women who ruled in their own right such as Hatshepsut or Tauseret or the so-called consorts of the gods, the high priestesses in Thebes in the later history of Egypt. Later, Berenike II became the first spouse of a king in Egyptian history with a royal titulary in her lifetime which was drawn from the Horus-name and her birth name.[27] Berenike II appears in the temple reliefs as a companion of her husband enjoying equal rank, something which in earlier times occurred only exceptionally such as with Nofretete and Nofretari, the spouses of Akhenaten and Ramses II. Berenike is seen worshipping the gods at the king's side and wears the ceremonial coat characteristic of the Ptolemaic kings. She even stands next to her husband in the scene of the bestowal of power by the god Thoth. Alongside the only full priest of Egypt and of the Egyptian religion, the king's spouse appears as a priestess of equal rank. Consequently, Berenike II appears sometimes in the dating protocol of demotic sources as the 'pharaoness Berenike' (*t3 Pr-ᶜ3t Brnjg3*).[28] The infiltration by the dynastic women into both political and cultic spheres will be an important feature in the development of Ptolemaic history of the second and first centuries BC.

## The king and the temples

The sacred building programmes are the clearest outward expression of the pharaonic reign of the Ptolemies and its concomitant religious policy. The building projects undertaken in the name of Alexander the Great were at once a prelude to similar efforts by the Ptolemies as well as a continuation of the construction of temples which flourished in the thirtieth dynasty. To these belong, in particular, the construction of a new boat shrine in the temple at Luxor and the renovation of a sanctuary in the festival temple of Tuthmosis III in Karnak; here Alexander is to be seen in parallel with his great predecessor and thus gives the appearance of being a new Tuthmosis III.[29] Of some interest is also the temple 'Qasr el-Megisba' at ᶜAin el-Tibanija in the oasis Bahariya for Amun-Re and Horus.[30] What is more, Alexander sponsored construction of a temple of Isis in Alexandria (Arr. *An.* III.1.5). It was evident to the king just how important Isis and Osiris were in late Egyptian religion, especially in their popular representations. Already prior to 333, an Isis temple existed in the Piraeus[31] which had been founded by Egyptian traders and so by the time of Alexander one could foresee the expansionist potential of the religion of Isis. No doubt the Alexandrian temple of Isis was also intended for the Greek population and it prepared the way for the religious policy of Ptolemy I who, after the death of Alexander the Great, continued building activity in the name of the last Argead 'pharaohs'. The bark shrine in the temple of Amun at Karnak and even the large hypostyle hall added to the temple of Thoth in Hermopolis (Middle Egypt) – which was still standing in the nineteenth century but today is in ruins[32] – were fitted out with the cartouche of Philip Arrhidaios; the construction of the temple had been begun by Nectanebo I at an earlier date. The monumental gate of the temple of Khnum on the island of Elephantine as well as the small grotto of Speos Artemidos in Middle Egypt both date from the time of Alexander IV.[33]

The material evidence for Ptolemy I's building activities as pharaoh[34] is no doubt eclipsed by the remains of the great works undertaken by the later Ptolemies. Nonetheless, there are remains of buildings erected by Ptolemy I scattered throughout the entire country and they show that the king founded many sanctuaries; in the Delta, an example of this is the temple of Hathor in Terenuthis, another is the temple of Amun (in the guise of a ram) in the native quarter of Naukratis;[35] in the Fayum, one instance is the temple of Soknebtunis in Tebtunis; in Middle Egypt, there is the Ptolemaic temple in Kom el-Ahmar/Sharuna and certainly the temple in Oxyrhynchos of which the reliefs of Ptolemy I offering Maat have been preserved.[36] In the necropolis of Tuna-el-Gebel at Hermopolis, two cult chapels bear the cartouches of Ptolemy I.

Because of his construction of the temple of Isis on the island of Philae, Ptolemy II went down in history as the first great builder worthy of special mention among the Ptolemies: the entire naos, that is the temple behind the hypostyle hall with the inner sanctum (Fig. 9.1A), was erected and decorated during his reign. The so-called donation of the Dodekaschoinos or, more specifically, the allotment of the taxes from the 12-mile district to the temple of Isis can only, in view of the political circumstances surrounding it, be attributed to Ptolemy II,[37] even if the temple that existed there before it, which dated from the time of Amasis, acquired a few fields on behalf of the satrap Ptolemy.[38] This donation of the Dodekaschoinos, which greatly aggrieved the priests of Khnum in Elephantine[39] was often confirmed and renewed up until Roman times. North of Aswan, one may also mention the small sanctuary of Isis at el-Qubaniye.[40]

In Thebes, the Ptolemaic gate in the enclosure wall of the temple of Muth in Karnak is linked with the name of Ptolemy II;[41] during his reign and his son's, the late decorative work on the pre-Ptolemaic temple of Opet in Karnak was begun.[42] In Dendera, the birth house (the sanctuary erected under Nectanebo I for the rituals associated with the birth, the rearing and enthronement of the divine child in the local triad of gods) was expanded into a small temple with a room for making offerings and a colonnaded vestibule.[43] Since Koptos was the terminus of the desert route coming from Berenike which was so important to Philadelphos, it was here that a temple to the desert god Min was constructed. Evidence for Ptolemaic interest in the Fayum at this time can be found in the temple of Pnepheros in Theadelphia[44] and most probably in the early Ptolemaic additions to the temple of Isis-Renenutet in Medinet Madi.[45] The early Ptolemaic construction phase of the Anubieion in Saqqâra also began under Ptolemy II.[46] In the Delta area, the decorative work on the main sanctuary of Isis in Behbeit el-Hagar continued under Ptolemy II and III and similar work on the temple of Onuris-Shu in Sebennytos was completed under Ptolemy II. Work on both temples which originally had been undertaken in the time of the thirtieth dynasty had come to a halt during Persian rule as of 343. Finally, one should mention the construction activities in the precinct of Darius' temple of Amun in the Kharga oasis.[47]

These diverse building activities were continued by Ptolemy III. A birth house (Fig. 9.1E), which had long been planned for the temple of Isis at Philae, was finally constructed; it consisted of two rooms with a vestibule and a colonnaded ambulatory.[48] Moreover, an additional sanctuary for Isis and Harpokrates was built on the island.[49] A temple of Isis was begun in Syene/ Aswân (here on the southern border where Isis was honoured as patroness of the army) which was continued under Ptolemy IV.[50]

On 23 August 237, after ceremonial foundation rituals, construction was begun on the finest building of the Ptolemaic period, the temple of Horus at Edfu (Fig. 9.5); it is today the best preserved temple in the ancient Egyptian style. The inscriptions place special emphasis on the actual presence of the king during the ceremonies, although this remains uncertain. They also report that using a rope and pointer he marked out the measurements of the chapels with the aid of Seshat, the goddess of writing, calculation and construction.[51] It is probably correct to view the foundation of the temple as a reaction by Ptolemy III to the tense political situation at home over the last 40 years and as an event related to a synod of the priests at Canopus[52] the year before. Construction was continued on the temple until its consecration in the year 70. The temple was thus a harmonious structure built according to a concerted plan and as such became an outstanding testimony to the high period of Ptolemaic architecture.

The small temple of Khnum in Esna has already been mentioned.[53] In Karnak, a marvellous entrance, known as the gate of Euergetes, was added to the temple of Khonsu, while a brick retaining-wall[54] was built around the temple of Month. To the latter was also added an equally impressive gate on the north side, construction of which continued under Ptolemy IV. In Medamud, a sanctuary was constructed on the southern side of the large temple of Month near the sacred lake built by Ptolemy III.[55] In the north near Alexandria, especially noteworthy is the foundation of a temple of Osiris in Canopus.[56] The oasis of Kharga also deserves mention. Here the temple of Qasr Gueida consecrated to the Theban triad, formerly begun by Darius I, was now decorated under Ptolemy III.

This brief overview clearly shows that this period covering the reign of the second and third Ptolemies, that was so decisive for the politics of the empire, was also a time in which many temples were founded and an intense building programme was pursued.

From the beginning of their reign in Egypt, the Macedonian kings had understood that they were obliged to tend to and assist the local temples and cults in order to win over the intellectual elite of the country (i.e. the priesthoods) and thereby ensure a peaceful development of domestic conditions. Accordingly, the Pithom Stele (Fig. 3.1) depicts Philadelphos making numerous payments to the sanctuaries in all of Egypt, and particularly to the temple of Amun in Pithom. Even Alexander had been anxious to see that Egyptian customs and religious institutions were observed (Curt. IV.7.5). His strategos Peukestas had forbidden the Greek troops to trespass on the precinct of the priests around temples as well as on the animal necropolis in North Saqqâra.[57] The satrap Ptolemy respected the original land holdings of the temples. Once he became the new king, he made himself the patron of Egyptian sanctuaries by issuing a decree forbidding the alienation of sacred precincts or temples and established sanctions to be visited upon those transgressing the decree.[58]

For the Ptolemies, an important consequence of assuming the office of pharaoh was admittance into the ancient Egyptian ruler cult, that is, into the statue and festival cults. The statue cult involves the worship of the divine forces of the king, especially the royal Ka, but not of the king represented as a person; for this reason, the statues of living Ptolemies in Egyptian temples should not be taken a priori as positive proof of the introduction of Hellenistic ruler cults into the ancient Egyptian temple cults. The restoration of the sanctuaries in the principal Theban shrines at Luxor and Karnak (under the first two Argeads) indicates that from the beginning of their reign the cult of the royal Ka practised there was transposed onto the new rulers. According to Theban convention, this made them the legitimate representatives of Amun on earth.

During the course of the festival of the new year, the king was united with the appropriate father-god (Ptah in Memphis, Amun in Thebes, the ram in Mendes, etc.) in order to take part in the cyclical rejuvenation of the god and himself take on the appearance of the youthful Horus-King. From Ptolemy II onwards, the Macedonian pharaohs were included during their lifetimes in this yearly cultic festival. In Memphis, the high priest of Ptah performed the appropriate rituals for the statues of the Ptolemaic kings in the precinct of the temple of Ptah. Once the ruler had died, his ritual deification followed in accordance with ancient tradition in the temples of the dead. Among these was the east temple within the Serapeion of Memphis which had been built by Nectanebo II on the eastern end of the dromos opposite the gallery of Apis. At least from the time of Ptolemy II, the statues of the deified Ptolemies were placed there, next to the statues of the living Apis and other gods.

Designated ritual beasts were also a part of the ritual of rejuvenation of city-god and king symbolizing the cycle of death, deification and rebirth as well as denoting the soul ('Ba') of the god. The most important of the zoomorphic gods connected to the royal office was Apis who accompanied the pharaoh in his festival of rejuvenation; the Apis bull belonged to the god and lived within the temple of Ptah to be led out for the festivals. From the beginning, the Ptolemies displayed great interest in the Egyptian cult of the king and with this came a concomitant interest in the animal cemeteries. Already under Ptolemy I, the significance of the sacred animals for the holy office of the ruler increased significantly. The state officially bore the expense of the mummification of the animals; under Ptolemy II, 100 talents[59] were reserved for the preparation of a Hesat cow, while under Ptolemy I, 50 talents were added to the already large amount of money set aside for the burial of an Apis (Diod. I.84.8). In this way, the king was ideologically represented as the main promoter of the cults but those who belonged to the relevant temple precincts and were subordinate to the royal treasury as tax-payers, were the ones who in reality assumed the burden of all expenditures, both those incurred on normal occasions and those arising from special events.[60]

The priests in northern Egypt were in continuous contact with the royal house, especially the priests in Memphis, while the Ptolemaic kings were themselves often present in the religious capital of Memphis. Conversely, from the beginning of the Hellenistic era, the festival liturgy in the temples of the south developed in an increasingly independent way. The evidence from Edfu in particular indicates that, in the sanctuaries there, one no longer made a substitution for the king if he happened to be absent. Rather, a local high priest usually took the title of '(priest of the) king' and thus replaced the actual pharaoh who thereby was no longer absent but present as a ritual figure. Here, the figure of the king was by this action completely divested of any historical content. Nevertheless, in temple reliefs dating from the Greco-Roman period, the king is still depicted in a cultic context which, with the exception of a few innovations, follows age-old motifs: he is shown interacting with the gods and performing numerous rituals; and the individual cartouches bearing the names of the rulers were still regularly appended in early Ptolemaic times.

It is beyond the scope of the work to consider properly the themes of the Egyptian temple as a focal point of scholarship and art, as an important economic centre which amassed considerable revenues and as the heart of public life – even insofar as they concern the Ptolemaic period.[61] It is important, however, to emphasize the fact that 'god's house' of the regional god remained completely autonomous within its precincts and had its own high clergy and estates. The supply of sacrificial animals was a matter dealt with by means of contracts of donation between the pharaoh and the deity; even during the Ptolemaic period, taxes were not paid in this domain. The remaining areas of the temple precinct (which included the various sanctuaries, workshops, etc.) had all been brought under state management from the time of the New Kingdom. The priests who worked in those areas as well as the civil employees all paid taxes; the lands themselves were subject to the tax regulations of the nome administration. To ensure the livelihood of those assigned to royal institutions in temple precincts, the state distributed sums of money (syntaxis) to them each year.[62] The interests of the king within the temple were managed by administrative bodies of the state. Members included, for instance, the well-known Petosiris of Hermopolis under Ptolemy I[63] or the high priest of Ptah himself in Memphis under Ptolemy III.[64] Temple wealth allowed priests to finance in their own right many of the construction projects. Autobiographical texts demonstrate, moreover, that often enough individual priests of some affluence contributed substantially to such projects of their own initiative or erected chapels in their own names.[65]

## BASILEUS, HELLENISTIC RULER CULT AND THE GREEK GODS

### The ideology of the basileus

Alexander the Great as king of Macedon set out on an eastern campaign which eventually made him pharaoh in Egypt and afterwards procured for him the succession to the line of Persian kings. Though he adopted from the ceremonial of the Persian court certain conventions and sacred symbols (such as the sacred fire) and tried to incorporate his Macedonians into Achaemenid tradition, he nonetheless succeeded in imposing in Asia his own personal brand of monarchy. Correspondingly, he did not assume royal titles typical of Persian monarchs, such as 'Great King' or 'king of kings', but instead used the simple title of 'basileus' (king). As such, Alexander exercised his own individual form of sovereignty over a land he had 'won by spear', ruling it at his own discretion.[66]

In short, Alexander had by these measures created a kind of 'supranational' kingship whose legitimacy rested on military victory. He governed his subjects as a charismatic ruler who fostered adherence by the force of his exceptional character and was thus spontaneously recognized as king by them. This kingship was not circumscribed by national barriers (defined by either a specific people or land) but, instead, it encompassed the most diverse peoples and cities whose number and composition varied with changes in the political landscape. By taking on the title of 'basileus' in 306 BC, the successors associated themselves with this very personal kingship of Alexander.

It is from that time onwards that we can trace the development of the Hellenistic monarchies all of which, while following the model established by Alexander, also took on special characteristics insofar as they were strongly influenced by traits of the pre-existing national kingdoms. These two components of the kingship (i.e. the king as Hellenistic basileus and as local pharaoh) were most evident in the Ptolemaic kings,[67] and led to a variety of measures to harmonize them. Conversely, the Antigonid monarchy was from 276 mainly Macedonian in nature and only took on the 'personal' stamp of the Hellenistic basileus in matters outside of Macedonia. The case of the

Seleukids was the direct opposite of the Antigonids, since the local Babylonian form of kingship only had a bearing on a small proportion of the population in the empire. In the end, however, the Hellenistic kings always preserved their Macedonian roots as well as the Macedonian tradition of their rule, bound as they were to the Macedonian court troops.[68]

While the sovereignty of the pharaoh was mitigated by the legally autonomous and influential collective of Egyptian priests (Chapter III.3.3; VI.2), the Ptolemaic basileus, like his Seleukid counterpart, embodied the principle of the state entirely in his own person. To the extent that the latter concept prevailed, there could be no question of collective interests or affairs but only of those of the king. The principal quality of the Ptolemaic kingship, inspired as it was by Hellenistic ideology, consisted of a charismatic invincibility which was upheld by the gods and which had to be proven if recognition by the kingdom's subjects was to be secured. This was essentially different from the sovereignty of the ancient Egyptian pharaoh, since the latter's invincibility, affirmed in his role as the victorious Horus, was principally understood in cultic and mythic terms. It was of little consequence whether he fulfilled the obligations of this role on campaign outside Egypt or in a temple ritual with a priest acting as his representative.

While the basileus, whose duty is success, is not accountable to any institution, he nonetheless had to comply with the image befitting a king. This model was in part derived from the ancient Greek kingship itself, partially from Greek philosophy of the fourth century (e.g. Arist. *Pol.* III.14.1[1284b 35ff.]); Plat. *Lg.* IV.711e–712a; *Plt.* 294a; *R.* V.473d) and finally also in many ways from the ideal image of the citizen of a Greek polis. In this regard, the ideology of the king transformed him into a saviour, liberator (especially of Greek cities), protector and begetter and guarantor of fertility and affluence. These qualities were expressed in epithets such as Soter and Euergetes and were exemplified in action by donations to cities and benefactions to temples; among such deeds were the grain donations from the Ptolemies to Athens and Rhodes or their gifts to the sanctuaries on Delos.[69] Theocritus, in particular, extolled the good fortune of Ptolemy II's subjects in his encomium to the king (*id.* XVII.96–120) where he describes Ptolemaic rule as a Homeric military kingship.[70] The attempts by the Ptolemies to make of Alexandria the foremost centre of Greek learning should in ideological terms be understood as an effort to promulgate the exemplary wisdom expected of the king.

Hellenistic monarchy, by virtue of its peculiar model of sovereignty, in all instances carried with it a very important sociological component, namely, if the basileus knew how to measure up to the requirements of ideology by his successes and propaganda then he would gain the adherence of his subjects. In the heyday of Ptolemaic rule, the relationship between king and subjects had not yet been stifled by the bureaucratic structure; the many petitions directed to the king[71] which have survived from that time indicate that the king was recognized as the source of justice and as a direct partner in a dialogue.

The king's wealth was the material basis of his success as a ruler and so it had to be put on display; at times this was pushed to the level of megalomania as illustrated by the scale of expenses incurred by palaces, maintenance of the court, festival processions,[72] banquets, etc. Ptolemy III was the first to take on the epithet of 'Tryphon' (the one who makes a show of splendour and magnificence) and in this way promulgated the notion of *tryphé* (τρυφή), splendour and magnificence, as the ideal image of the wealth and good fortune produced by Ptolemaic rule. In keeping with this image of extravagance, the Ptolemies laid special emphasis on their proximity to Dionysus, who was an ancestral father of the dynasty, and on the Dionysiac components of the ruler-cult.[73]

## Hellenistic ruler cult: Alexander and the first Ptolemies; Greek religious policy

While the Egyptian pharaoh was the mortal bearer of a divine office during his lifetime and was the king carrying out the role of a god and mediator between the mortal and divine worlds, the charisma of the Hellenistic basileus alone was enough to transform him into a god.[74] The superhuman qualities required of a basileus brought him into the company of the gods.

No doubt this last element of the ruler cult had its origin in the Greek practice of worshipping outstanding individuals as heroes after their death in order to retain for the future the strength they radiated. True to this practice, the oracle of Siwah allowed Hephaistion, the deputy of Alexander the Great, who died in 324 in Ekbatana to be worshipped only as a hero. To this end, Kleomenes was to erect heroa for Hephaistion in Alexandria and on the island where the Pharos later stood (Arr. *An.* VII.23.7).[75]

Moreover, in the Greek world, from time immemorial the historical founders of cities received an official cult of the dead as heroes. From the abundant source material dating to the Roman period, one may almost certainly assume that, if not during Alexander's lifetime then at the latest upon the construction of the sema for Alexander, a cult was set up for him as ktistes (founder) of the city of Alexandria. This cult was to be maintained side by side with the cult of Alexander as imperial god which soon overshadowed all else.[76] The city cult for Ptolemy I in the city of Ptolemais in the Thebaid (which he founded) belongs to this same tradition. It is, however, quite possible that, in this place which he had founded, he was as such immediately elevated to a 'god' either during his lifetime or posthumously. At any rate, he appears as a god in sources of the Hellenistic and Roman periods.[77] Yet, one must carefully distinguish between the founder cult and the dynastic cult established by Ptolemy IV for Ptolemy Soter and the ruling couple.

As a result of the unclear distinction between god and man in the Greek mind, cultic honours were occasionally given to living individuals even before Alexander, for example, to the Spartan general Lysander in Samos, later to the Macedonian king Amyntas III in Pydna and to Philip II in

Amphipolis. Alexander also received city cults in Asia Minor, Athens and Sparta during his lifetime and these corresponded with Alexander's view of himself at the time. The scepticism which developed with respect to the old Olympian gods formed the background out of which the ruler cults decreed by cities arose and proliferated. Contrary to the obsolete cults of the old religion, the latter offered a direct experience of the power of those who were worshipped. The Athenians expressly mention feelings of this type in a hymn to Demetrios Poliorketes from the year 290 (Duris: FGrHist. 76 F13).[78] As early as 307 after Athens had been freed from the authoritarian regime of Demetrios of Phaleron, Antigonos and his son Demetrios were portrayed there as kings and were at the same time elevated to the rank of saviour-gods (θεοὶ σωτῆρες) (Plu. *Dem.* 10.3–4). Thus, in the early Hellenistic period, they led the way in shaping the idea of a close connection between the ruler cult and the obligation of success that this imposed on a kingship. The establishment of a cult was the only way for a city to express its gratitude to a ruler for benefactions that otherwise could only be expected of gods.

The Rhodians were the first to establish a cult honouring Ptolemy I as a *god* in 304, out of gratitude for his aid against Demetrios Poliorketes. Accordingly, they erected a sanctuary in his honour known as the *Ptolemaion*; on this occasion, the oracle at Siwah was consulted and acquiesced in his being worshipped with the status of a *Theos* (Diod. XX.100.3–4; Paus. I.8.6).[79] In about 287/6 the Island League thanked Ptolemy for his contribution to the expulsion of Demetrios and the restoration of the old constitution by alloting him 'divine honours' together with the erection of an altar at Delos.[80] As already mentioned,[81] Byzantium and Athens later resolved to set up cults for Philadelphos and Euergetes I respectively.

By associating himself with Alexander, Ptolemy also tried to procure divinity for himself. For this reason, he made every effort to ensure that he would receive the corpse of the great king in his capital city. Alexander had considered himself to be the son of Zeus-Ammon and had had coins minted which assimilated him to Zeus[82] and even appeared with the various attributes of the divinities, such as the horns of Ammon (Ephippos: FGrHist. 126 F5). Thus, during his satrapy, Ptolemy re-issued coins of Alexander bearing the attributes of Dionysos, Ammon and Zeus. In being depicted with the horns of Ammon on his head, Alexander was placed in a tradition of pharaonic representations which went back to the New Kingdom (Tuthmosis III, Amenophis III, Ramses II) and which expressed the ritual unification of the Egyptian king with the sun-god Amun-Re.[83] When Ptolemy I, in turn, had himself portrayed on coins and monuments with the characteristic attributes of Ammon, Zeus, Helios, Dionysos or even Pan, he appropriated for himself as well as for his dynasty Alexander's divinity. The fact that he likened himself to the various gods was not so strange for an Egyptian, because of the manifold aspects of Amun himself.[84] At the same time, for the Greeks such a comparison expressed the specific traits and abilities that the king was expected to assume with his office. In a similar vein, Ptolemy I's assimilation to Dionysos also made the link with Alexander quite explicit; soon after the latter's death, Alexandrian propaganda associated the theme of his divinity with his conquests in India and so brought together the myths of Alexander and Dionysos.[85] The tradition of depicting rulers with the horns of Ammon continued to exist right into the Roman period and was even expanded to include female members of the dynasty, such as Arsinoe II and Berenike II.[86]

Ptolemy I took the decisive step in making the deification of the Ptolemaic dynasty a state matter. This was done by elevating the dead Alexander to the level of a state god and by making the priest at the head of this purely Greek cult the highest state priest in the land. The priest of Alexander, as a so-called eponymous priest, was named directly after the king in dating formulae in both Greek and demotic documents as well as in the hieroglyphic versions of decrees made by the priests. Owing to the nature of the office, it was naturally reserved for the most prominent Macedonian and Greek or Hellenized inhabitants of the kingdom;[87] there is no evidence for a single Egyptian holding the office. In 284/3 the brother of the king, Menelaos, actually held the office for the fifth time.[88]

Ptolemy II was the most active in developing a state-run ruler cult. He may have already elevated his deceased father to the rank of 'theos soter' at the beginning of his reign;[89] he instituted the lavish festival of the Ptolemaia in Alexandria to honour his father, a festival which was to take place every four years. When Berenike I died in 279, she was incorporated into the cult of the first Ptolemaic couple which was jointly worshipped in the temple of the Theoi Soteres in Alexandria. Both, it seems, also received individual cults, since there is evidence for the existence of a temple to Berenike, the Berenikeion, in Alexandria in about the mid-270s (Kallixeinos: FGrHist. 627 F2, p. 176, l.8).

The Ptolemaia were celebrated for the first time in 279/8.[90] The festival was to rival the Olympic games in renown. As such, it included not only processions (such as the pompé described by Kallixeinos),[91] extravagant sacrifices and lavish banquets, but also all sorts of competitions.[92] The festival became more and more elaborate with each new Ptolemy and so it developed into the quintessential festival of the Ptolemaic dynasty, at the same time making Alexandria shine as the centre of the new world. Since almost all Greek states were invited to participate, it is probably the best example of the use of the ruler cult in the arena of world politics.

Ptolemaia festivals were established in a variety of places throughout the Greek world during the course of the third century,[93] a fact attesting to the high standing of the Ptolemaic royal family. On Delos, the Island League celebrated the Ptolemaia as a League festival already in the early 270s, at a time when Philadelphos had not yet married Arsinoe II. What is more, in the cult of this festival the king was associated with his deceased father.[94]

When Philadelphos decided to join the living royal couple to the cult of Alexander with the special cult title of Theoi Synnaoi, he determined the nature of this cult for the future. This decision probably came into effect in

272/1.[95] The priest of Alexander had formerly simply been called ἱερεύς but was now known as the 'priest of Alexander and of the Theoi Adelphoi'[96] (i.e. the brother-sister-gods). This latter title, of course, referred to the sibling marriage of the second Ptolemaic royal couple, which was meant to be understood as a *hieros gamos* following the example of Zeus and Hera (Theoc. *id*. XVII.131–34). During the Third Syrian War, Ptolemy III and Berenike II were incorporated into the cult as the Theoi Euergetai[97] and the title of the priest of Alexander was correspondingly extended.

It is clear, then, that the state cult for Alexander the Great developed into a collective dynastic cult, once the worship of the individual Ptolemaic couples beginning with Philadelphos was officially added to it. Its development, however, was only complete under Ptolemy IV who added to it the cult of the Theoi Soteres, one which had been established by Philadelphos and had remained independent of it up to this time. Thus, all of the Ptolemaic couples appeared in the title of the priest of Alexander in their historical order including the current ruling couple.[98]

The institution of the dynastic cult was at that point unique and otherwise known only in the Seleukid kingdom (in more limited form) and later in Commagene. The nature of the cult implied an almost automatic deification of the kings and, in the end, it was not so much the person of king as the king's function within the family (which embodied the state) that was worshipped. This was quite distinct from the city ruler cults previously mentioned which, at least initially, were meant for the worship of one deserving ruler who was not a native of that polis. The dynastic cult elevated the charisma of the triumphant basileus to a theological plane which was then passed on to all of his successors on a permanent basis. In this way, the dynastic cult strengthened each king's claim to legitimacy and later during the decline of the empire it became a substitute for the victories and services which normally gave the king the official recognition that he needed. By means of the dynastic cult in Alexandria and the other ruler cults organized by the state, the Ptolemies actually succeeded during the third century in subordinating various aspects of the state to the person of the king, that is, to the dynasty. These aspects encompassed the heterogeneous state apparatus, the philoi, soldiers and civil servants (all of whom no longer belonged to one polis with its own gods and cults) and even the various peoples of the kingdom. Even the Egyptian priesthoods were bound to the king on the basis of their ancient cult of the king. In this way, the dynastic cult became an essential component of the Ptolemaic monarchy.

Philadelphos knew no bounds to the development of cults for relatives and those close to the dynasty. Aside from the posthumous elevation of Arsinoe II to the status of an individual goddess,[99] something which transcended the bounds of the collective cult, he went so far as to identify his favourite mistress Belistiche[100] with Aphrodite and dedicated sanctuaries to her (ἱερά and ναοί, Plu. *Mor*. 753 F). He immortalized another mistress in statues which he had placed in the temples of Alexandria (Pol. XIV.11).

The Ptolemaic model influenced Cyrene where a priest administered the cult for King Magas.[101] Later cults were also set up for the the individual Ptolemies as well as for their spouses.[102]

As an extension of the practice established during the period of the successors, numerous Ptolemaic cults continued to be founded (mostly by cities) throughout the empire and with time this sort of honour lost much of its significance and gradually became a mere formality. For example, under Philadelphos there was a priest of Ptolemy I in Lapethos on Cyprus[103] in about 274, a Ptolemaic priest in Methymna on Lesbos[104] and even an organization of the so-called basilistai (βασιλισταί) on Thera[105] responsible for the cult of the king. In addition to this, the podium structure in Limyra (Lycia) may also be dated to his reign; the podium should most probably be interpreted as a Ptolemaion: a columned tholos was raised over a foundation consisting of a massive square floor-plan with the statues of the rulers placed in the cella of the tholos.[106] Following Ptolemy III's accession to the throne, the town of Itanos, garrisoned by Ptolemaic troops, decreed that a temenos be consecrated to him and to his spouse Berenike II.[107] Immediately after the acquisition of southern Thrace, a priest of the king held office in Ainos in 243.[108] Sanctuaries of the ruler cults were sometimes financed by private individuals or by groups such as the small sanctuary in Thera[109] dedicated to the third Ptolemaic couple or the entire building complex in Hermupolis Magna in Middle Egypt. The latter was dedicated by the cavalry stationed there to the theoi euergetai (named in the first place in the inscription) and to the Theoi Adelphoi for the benefaction (εὐεργεσία) bestowed upon them.[110]

The likening of the Ptolemies to different gods is a trend that is significantly developed in the various official representations of the kings.[111] The club of Herakles[112] becomes an attribute of the king as of the time of Philadelphos. Herakles had already been an ancestor of the Argeads and later Theocritus ascribed this same lineage to the Ptolemies (*id.* XVII.20–27). In the Adulis inscription, Euergetes I declares that his origins stem from Herakles on his father's side and from Dionysos on his mother's side, both of whom were sons of Zeus[113] (cf. Fig. 3.4). By pursuing this same theme, it was easy to form similar links with Egyptian religion. Thus, we find images of Ptolemy III representing him as Hermes with a lotus leaf on his head, i.e. as the Egyptian Hermes-Thoth. Oktodrachmae of Ptolemy IV represent Ptolemy III with a variety of attributes which identify him as the divine Euergetes, fruit-bearing Aion (Aion Plutonios) or as Osiris (and thus also as Sarapis).[114]

It is not known to what extent the divinity of the basileus made an impression on his subjects. The many dedicatory inscriptions attest to the fact that it fulfilled a deep need. The dedications to certain gods which begin with the formula 'on behalf of' (ὑπέρ) the royal house mark the transition to the worship of the ruler as a divinity. In such cases, although the ruler is associated with the gods, he does not quite have the rank of a god who is referred to in the dative case in the dedication. From the reign of Euergetes I onwards, we do know of a large number of private dedications to

*Figure 3.4* Marble head of Ptolemy III with a diadem in his hair and small bull-horns which liken him to Dionysos; possibly from Crete: 24 cm. Copenhagen, NY Carlsberg Glyptothek. Inv. 573; Kyrieleis (1975), C 3 (p. 32ff.; 168), Table 20.1; for interpretation see Laubscher, loc. cit. (see p. 117, note 84), 349, note 87.

the ruling royal couple as well as to other gods, most often Isis, Sarapis and sometimes also Harpokrates or the Nile.[115]

While the deification of the kings arose from a scepticism about the old gods, it could not entirely replace traditional forms of religion. The royal dynasty could not, therefore, afford to neglect the cults of Greek gods. Dionysos was given preference,[116] because through his worship the various elements pertaining to the cults of the gods, the ruler cults and the ideology of the king could be bound together. It is hardly surprising then that Dionysos should already appear as the most important god in the pompé of Philadelphos. The deification of the queen, on the other hand, pushed Aphrodite to prominence. To this end, Arsinoe II had a play staged in the royal palace which portrayed the love between Aphrodite and Adonis (Theoc.

*Id.* XV.22–24); Aphrodite herself is said to have elevated Berenike I to the status of goddess (ibid. 106–8).

The Ptolemies also pursued religious policies in the Greek world outside their kingdom as part of an effort to consolidate their close relations. Ptolemy I already made his influence felt in many Greek cities such as Athens, Corinth, Epidauros, Olympia, Thebes or Miletus, by dedicating statues and other gifts or participating in festival games.[117] Special note should also be made of the building policy of Philadelphos to the benefit of Greek sanctuaries. In particular, he enthusiastically supported the new building of the temple of Apollo at Didyma, donated a temple for the acropolis of Herakleia on the Pontos and a propylon for the sanctuary of the great gods at Samothrake, as well as the so-called 'oblation of the Ptolemies' to Olympia; moreover, Philadelphos sponsored temple B in the Asklepieion on the island of Kos, where he was born.[118] On Delos, Ptolemy II and III founded festivals honouring the Delian gods, known as Ptolemaia II (249) and III (246) respectively.[119]

## THE SEARCH FOR VALUES TO BIND TOGETHER THE PEOPLES OF THE KINGDOM

### Graeco-Egyptian gods

#### *Zeus-Ammon*

Zeus-Ammon of Siwah was a god who, already in the fifth and fourth centuries BC, served to bring people of different ethnic origins together. He could do this because he was of Egyptian origin, had sacred sites dedicated to him in Greece and Macedonia[120] and, at the same time, he enjoyed the highest standing in the entire world owing to the oracle in the Siwah oasis. It seems quite likely, therefore, that Alexander chose this god specifically as the authority to lend credence to the ideology of his divine lineage.

The figure of Zeus-Ammon (cf. Fig. 2.1) was, in the Egyptian manner, the sum of a fusion of different gods, alongside which the individual components each existed as an independent entity. In a simplistic interpretation (Hdt. II.42), however, the various components were generally felt to correspond to each other. For this reason, it presented no difficulty when Alexander[121] emphasized his own original preference for Zeus, even when speaking of his ancestry (Plu. *Alex.* 33.1). Conversely, he was criticized by his Macedonian friends precisely for dubbing himself the son of Ammon (Plu. *Alex.* 50.11). It was clear to them that Alexander's divine parentage had already been confirmed in Siwah and was most strongly supported by pharaonic ideology. When in 324 the offended soldiers called on their king in Opis to discharge them and carry on the war alone with his father Ammon, one is struck by the parallel with the Egyptian ideology of the king and with Ramses II in Kadesh: there the latter was said finally to have achieved his 'victory' without the help of his soldiers but instead alone with Ammon's assistance.[122] Alexander himself could, in one breath, call on 'Zeus of the Greeks and Ammon of the Libyans' (Arr. *Ind.* 35.8).

Once Alexander had arrived in the Indus valley, the oracle from Siwah predicting his conquest of the world was clearly confirmed and it was then that the god Ammon became more prominent. Not only did Alexander sacrifice to him along with the other gods (Arr. *An.* VI.3.2), but later, in the delta of the Indus, it was the oracular god Ammon himself who revealed to the king to which gods he should sacrifice (Arr. *An.* VI.19.4–5). Alexander may have felt that the Nile and Indus were direct counterparts at opposite ends of his world empire and so, there on the Indus, Ammon would have acquired a special significance for Alexander. The god remained the highest authority in oracular matters until the death of the king;[123] he had even chosen as his final resting place the Ammoneion of Siwah.[124]

The fact that Alexander visited Zeus-Ammon at Siwah and did not consult, for example, the oracle of Amun at Thebes is very telling. For his choice indicates, in my opinion, the extent to which he wanted the sacral elevation of his office as king and of his person to be perceived as binding for the entire empire. The apotheosis of Alexander as Ammon may subsequently have laid the framework for the deification of the Ptolemies,[125] but, from his own point of view, it was simply a matter of survival. After the collapse of the Great Empire, Ptolemaic religious policy could easily dispense with a god who was also at home in Greece and Macedon. Thus, as a result of the breakup of the empire, Zeus-Ammon no longer played the broad historical role intended for him by Alexander.

## Sarapis

From the time Ptolemy I took over the Egyptian satrapy, one of the most important goals of his religious policies must have been to draw together the Greek and Egyptian peoples in one religious sphere. At the same time, he found that Greeks already settled in Memphis worshipped the great god in the Serapeum located in the necropolis district.[126] The political shrewdness of the first Ptolemies can be seen in his recognition and cultivation of the possibilities inherent in this situation.

The precinct of the Serapeum had experienced enormous development and growth in the late Egyptian period. The galleries of Apis with the temple of Osiris-Apis and the East temple[127] constituted the southern central part of the precinct (Fig. 9.12. no. 1); in the northern half was the temple of Isis, mother of Apis (the latter was the theological form taken by cows that were deified on their death because they had given birth to the Apis bull). These three temples had been constructed in the thirtieth dynasty. Associated with the sanctuary of Isis were the burial sites of the sacred cows, baboons and falcons. Connected to the Serapeum were the Bubasteion and Anubieion, temple precincts for Bastet and Anubis on the eastern slope of the desert plateau which had been erected by Amasis.

The royal god Apis, to whom the bull Apis belonged as a ritual beast, went through various transformations in theological form from the time of the New Kingdom. Multitudes of Apis bulls were transmuted after their death into the god of the underworld Osiris-Apis (Egyptian Wsjr-Ḥp, in Greek Ὀσορᾶπις or the like), a form of Osiris unique to Memphis. Theologians distinguished this form from that of the solar, royal Apis who is the god of heaven (Apis-Osiris).[128] This god, whose complex nature and mysterious transformations only the Egyptian scholars could fully appreciate, had already been Hellenized in the early years of Ptolemy I's satrapy. In this Hellenization, he assumed the names, characteristics and powers typical of Greek gods and came to be portrayed after the Greek fashion.

The Egyptian priest and historian Manetho is said to have made an important contribution to the creation and interpretation of the new cultic figure Sarapis[129] (Plu. *de Iside* 28).[130] While Egyptian theology constructed Sarapis from his roles of Osiris and Apis as king and fertility god respectively as well as from Osiris' role in particular as lord of the underworld, from a Greek perspective, the god was seen as Dionysos in his guise as chthonic god and as Zeus-Hades.[131] Coins of Ptolemy II–IV illustrate his relation to Osiris by depicting Sarapis as Zeus with the Atef crown[132] The Roman imperial copy from Alexandria of the famous, indeed canonical, cult image of Sarapis, which portrays him as a paternal god (seated, bearded, with a kalathos on his head) was ascribed to the sculptor Bryaxis from the second half of the fourth century.

In keeping with his religious connection to Osiris, Sarapis was also associated with Isis to whom Alexander had already dedicated a temple in Alexandria.[133] Now Ptolemy I had the first Serapeum of Alexandria constructed on Rhakotis hill, also in Alexandria (see Map 3). Since Sarapis was the god of the king and Isis was conceived of as a queen by Egyptians, it is hardly surprising that the divine pair rose quickly to become gods of the Ptolemaic dynasty.[134] An altar in the oldest temenos of the Serapeum is dedicated to the second Ptolemaic couple as '(descendants) of the Theoi Soteres'.[135] Euergetes pursued the religious policy of his grandfather and initiated the large-scale new building of the Hellenistic Serapeum with cellae for Sarapis and Isis, the Nilometer, as well as two subterranean galleries which suggest Egyptian influences on the cult and, finally, a library.[136] The bilingual foundation plaques of the sanctuary of Sarapis indicate that the Egyptian name Osiris-Apis was the official counterpart of the Greek. The god remained linked to the Ptolemaic royal family in the new sanctuary, as the images of the third and fourth Ptolemies erected there confirm.[137]

On the one hand, Isis and Sarapis were seen as Hellenistic gods integrated into the Greek world but, on the other, they were also viewed as ancient Egyptian divinities. Their dual nature thus corresponded nicely to the twofold aspect of the Ptolemaic king. For the Egyptians, Sarapis was and remained the form attributed to Osiris in Memphis or merely the Greek name for the ancient Osiris. Contrary to the expectations of the religious policy which engendered it, there was little response in Egypt to the figure of Sarapis. By contrast, the religion of Isis and Sarapis spread quickly throughout the eastern Mediterranean from the end of the fourth century onwards. Interestingly enough, this was accomplished mostly through private initiative even outside the kingdom of the Ptolemies and of the other Hellenistic realms.[138] Within the Ptolemaic empire (Thera and Cyprus), there is occasional evidence of the association of this cult with the cult of the Ptolemies.[139]

## The queen as Egyptian and Greek goddess

### Arsinoe II

From the Mendes Stele[140] (Fig. 3.3), we learn that the deceased Arsinoe was received into the world of the immortals as a *goddess* and as *living Ba* (roughly, a powerful divine being). Already in her lifetime, she had been the priestess of the ram of Mendes This transformation followed as a result of the ancient Egyptian burial and deification rites which had been performed for Arsinoe in Mendes. Ptolemy thereupon decreed that her image be placed in all of the houses of the gods (ḥwt-nṯr). Consequently, statues of the new goddess were made in every nome. She herself was given the cult name of 'beloved of the ram,'[141] brother-loving goddess,[142] Arsinoe'.[143]

This meant that from now on Arsinoe II would be placed in all of the country's sanctuaries beside the main god as a guest-goddess (in Greek: σύνναος θεά). She was placed next to the ram of Mendes, Ptah in Memphis, Sobek in the Fayum, to name only a few.[144] The upper field of the Mendes Stele illustrates this fact: the royal family[145] is shown offering before the gods of Mendes with the goddess Arsinoe among them, thus implying that Arsinoe is fictitiously offering to herself.[146] In addition, Ptolemy II is himself prominent in the worship of the new goddess on Egyptian reliefs and stelae;[147] perhaps the loveliest piece depicting such a scene is the gate of Philadelphos in front of the first Pylon of Philae (Fig. 9.1, O), where in one scene the king sacrifices to Isis and Arsinoe (Fig. 3.5) and in another to Nephthys and Arsinoe.[148]

It is important to understand that the decision to deify the deceased Arsinoe II as a measure of religious policy did not go against ancient Egyptian tradition in any fundamental way, despite the spectacular manner in which it was carried out. The Mendes Stele shows quite clearly that the priests considered the erection of statues of Arsinoe in the temples to be quite acceptable. There is proof that in Ptolemaic Memphis itself there were a number of cults for deceased pharaohs each with its own priests. These pharaonic cults include those of Menes, Snofru, Teti, Ramses II, Merenptah, Amasis and of particular importance the one devoted to 'Nectanebo II the falcon'.[149] One could attach oneself to this tradition, as illustrated by the case of the high priest of Ptah, Nesisty II, who in the first half of the third century combined among his many duties that of 'prophet . . . in the shrine of Ramses II' as well as 'prophet of Arsinoe II'.[150]

*Figure 3.5* Relief from the gate of Philadelphos in front of the first pylon of the temple of Isis at Philae; Ptolemy II with the crown of Upper Egypt sacrifices before the goddesses Isis and Arsinoe II.

In like manner, Ptolemy II had temples constructed exclusively for Arsinoe as an independent Egyptian goddess. For example, in Memphis there was an Egyptian Arsinoeion that was closely connected to the temple of Ptah.[151] There, in the third century the high-priest of Ptah was also the priest of Arsinoe. Even in Berenike, which Philadelphos had founded by the Bitter Lakes and named after his daughter, there was an Arsinoeion where the deified queen was worshipped as an Egyptian goddess. To this fact attest the foundation rites carried out by the priests of Atum of Pithom according to ancient Egyptian tradition.[152] Statues of the Theoi Adelphoi were also placed in the sanctuary. This indicates that in Egyptian communities just as in Greek ones the cult of Arsinoe was kept separate from that of the Theoi Adelphoi, although Arsinoe did have some connection to the latter cult.

From an Egyptian point of view, Arsinoe could be identified with Isis in many ways, not only in native Egyptian communities[153] but even in the more Hellenized environment of Alexandria.[154] Arsinoe's intermediate position as an Egyptian-Greek goddess must have been particularly prominent in the Fayum, where she became the nome-goddess for both ethnic groups in the newly established Arsinoite nome.[155]

Along with her elevation to the status of an Egyptian goddess, Arsinoe also became a Greek goddess; this is the subject of Callimachus' poem ''Εκθέωσις 'Αρσινόης' (frag. 228, Pfeiffer). In Alexandria she had an annual eponymous priestess with the title of kanephoros or 'basket-carrier' (κανήφορος 'Αρσινόης Φιλαδέλφου) who is attested from March 269;[156] the kanephoros was from that time on mentioned in documents after the priest of Alexander. A lavish sanctuary was erected on the wharf of the old harbour (Arsinoeion; see Map 3). It is said that the architect planned the construction of a round portrait of Arsinoe made of iron which was to hang in the inner sanctuary suspended by means of magnetism (Plin. *Nat.* XXXIV.148). An obelisk from Heliopolis was placed within the cult precinct (Plin. *Nat.* XXXVI.67–69) to emphasize the Egyptian character of the place. As a Greek goddess, Arsinoe was identified with Hera, Demeter and other goddesses but, above all, with Aphrodite.[157] It was in this connection that the well-known admiral Kallikrates of Samos financed a small sanctuary to her as Aphrodite Euploia, the patroness of sailing, on cape Zephyrion east of Alexandria. The sanctuary was praised in epigrams by Callimachus and other poets of the age.[158]

Probably in the wake of Arsinoe, her sister Philotera, who had passed away before her, also obtained her own Egyptian and Greek cults. Nesisty II, in addition to his functions mentioned above, was also 'prophet of the goddess Philotera, daughter of the king and sister of the king'.[159] A woman, Heresankh,[160] is likewise attested as having held the office of this priesthood; she was a member of the family of the high priest of Memphis. The Greek literary tradition mentions the combined worship of both sisters Arsinoe and Philotera (FGrHist. 613 F5). Several sites were named after Philotera, although the list of cities called Arsinoe is about three times as long.[161]

Philadelphos took every step to ensure that the decree regarding his sister-spouse's deification should be carried out and that the cult should become popular. To this end, coins were minted bearing the portrait of the queen, on which she wears the ram's horns of Amun, among other features. These representations of her on coins reveal a carefully thought-out iconography of the deification which would have been equally significant for both the Egyptians and the Greeks.[162] To ensure that the cult was on a sound economic footing, beginning in 263, the king allotted a considerable portion of the religious tax (apomoira), which was raised on the fruit and vineyard production of the entire country, to the cult of Arsinoe.[163] The success of this religious policy can be seen from the number of cult sites; more than 25 are attested to. Naturally enough, the majority of these are in the north, but Thebes is also represented. In Memphis, the loyalty and co-operation of the priesthoods is evident in the widespread use of 'Arsinoe' and 'Berenike'[164] as proper names for women. These are the only two Greco-Macedonian names to be found among the families of Egyptian priests.

Festivals in honour of the goddess Arsinoe, known as Arsinoeia, served to enhance her popularity.[165] These took place both in the rural areas (Chora) as well as in Alexandria. In the capital, a procession led by the kanephoros took place during the festival; according to one source, on those streets where the procession bearing the cult image of Arsinoe passed, residents erected their own altars and brought victims for sacrifice.[166] There was a certain amount of coercion implicit in these festivities, since by their participation people demonstrated their loyalty to the royal house.

The cult of Arsinoe as the patroness of sailing established itself quickly in numerous harbour-cities of the eastern Mediterranean. The cities were either a part of the empire or were in places where the Ptolemaic fleet could make their presence felt. This was particularly true of the cities named Arsinoe.[167] At Kition on the island of Cyprus, an eponymous kanephoros for Arsinoe was established whose presence is confirmed from 255/4.[168] On the island of Delos, the nesiarch Hermias established a festival called Philadelpheia in which he associated Arsinoe Philadelphos with Apollo, Artemis and Leto;[169] epigraphic sources also testify to a Philadelpheion which was probably built on the island soon after the death of the queen.[170] In addition, there is evidence for the celebration of the Arsinoeia on the island of Thera as of the reign of Ptolemy II/III.[171] Even outside Egypt, Arsinoe was often worshipped together with Isis and Sarapis.[172] The best evidence that the new goddess actually had an impact on the emotional lives of people is furnished by the dedication plaques and house altars on which her name is inscribed; many have been found on sites throughout the Aegean and on the island of Cyprus.[173]

Through the posthumous deification of Arsinoe II, Ptolemy II succeeded in creating a goddess who had emerged from the ruling family and who would be recognized in all of the eastern Mediterranean basin. At the same time, the dynasty began its first and most successful attempt at introducing a deceased member of the family into the Egyptian pantheon. The decree raising Arsinoe's status to that of a σύνναος in the temples of the native gods indicates that her cult was not intended as just another addition to those already in existence. In comparison with this, the move to associate Arsinoe with Isis was only of secondary importance and was probably meant to widen her significance. The identification with Aphrodite will have served a similar function within the framework of Greek religion. There, a strong religious need, which conveniently became entwined with the religious policy of the Ptolemaic state, was a driving force in the widespread diffusion of Arsinoe's cult.

*Berenike II*

Apart from the worship of Berenike II in conjunction with her spouse, her individual cult was far less significant than that of Arsinoe II. Its development, however, already began during her lifetime.[174] When Ptolemy III embarked on the Third Syrian War, Berenike pledged that she would dedicate a lock of her hair to the gods in the temple of Arsinoe on Cape Zephyrion, should the king return safely. She fulfilled her promise but the lock disappeared on the next day. The mathematician and astronomer, Konon of Samos,[175] thereupon found the lock once again in the form of a celestial constellation (Call. '*Lock of Berenike*': frg. 110 Pf.: Catul. 66).[176] In performing this act, Berenike II was not only inspired by Greek tradition[177] but was also influenced by certain deeds attributed to Isis in Egyptian mythology. The story was that in Koptos Isis had dedicated a lock of hair while mourning her husband, Osiris (Plu. *De Iside* 14). Indeed, a thick tuft of hair was shown as a relic to visitors to Koptos. For this reason, Isis of Koptos was viewed in the Greco-Egyptian period as the 'goddess of hair-growth (τρίχωμα)'; the lock of Isis signified resurrection and rebirth.[178] To mark the favourable outcome of the Third Syrian War, seals were made in the Greek style depicting the head of Berenike. The queen who, from 243 was named Thea Euergetis, was depicted with shorn hair and bearing the fertility attributes of Demeter-Isis.[179] In addition, in Callimachus' poem the 'Victory of Berenike'[180] the queen was associated with Io, the beloved of Zeus who had been driven to Egypt. This reference also connected her to the world of the gods, since Io had long since been identified with Isis (Hdt. II.41.2; Diod. I.24.8).

There is reliable evidence for the cult of a Berenike in the Fayum during the reign of Ptolemy III which was distinct from that of the king; presumably Berenike II is meant, since the sources use the cult name 'Aphrodite'[181] in reference to her and they also equate her with 'Isis, mother of the gods'.[182]

The continuation of the cult of Berenike II after her death as 'benevolent goddess' as well as as '(Isis) protectress in disasters at sea' (σῴζουσα) must be placed in the period from Ptolemy IV onwards.[183] Apart from the Egyptian forms of common cult for the Ptolemaic couple, the worship of Berenike II remained within a Greek setting, even when she was identified with Isis.

### The priestly Decree of Canopus and the development of the Egyptian cult of the king to the dynastic cult of the Ptolemies

In the second half of the third century, it was the duty of the high-ranking Egyptian priests to come from all parts of the country once a year and gather at the king's court;[184] the dates were fixed according to special events such as the coronation of the king, his birthday, a victory celebration or festivals of national importance. At these synods, matters regarding cults and temple organization were primarily discussed. With the growing importance of the native representatives, problems related to the finances, rights and privileges of the priests were also considered. In this regard, the assembly clearly had to fulfil court duties on a regular basis, among which were the royal festivals and honours due to the royal pair. In important cases, the resolution (ψήφισμα; hierogl: *sḫȝw*) was composed in hieroglyphic, demotic and Greek, according to the final resolution. Usually, it was then inscribed on stelae which were erected in the outer courtyards of all important temples so as to make their contents available to everyone. It is therefore possible to conclude that these synodic resolutions were intended for both Egyptians and Greeks alike.

These priestly decrees were, therefore, an expression of the Ptolemaic ideology of the king as a whole. In essence, their main concern was to create a single ideological and cultic image from the distinct figures of the basileus and the pharaoh. We have seen that the Ptolemies attempted to use the authority of the Egyptian clergy to their own advantage. To this end, they encouraged the clergy to express its loyalty openly as a means to gain support for their regime and to counteract the resentment of the native population toward a foreign dynasty. This policy is still very much evident in the Canopus Decree of 238. However, in the time between the Raphia Decree of 217 and the Rosetta Stone of 196 the importance of the king's role as a Hellenistic ruler gradually decreased in favour of his status as an ancient Egyptian monarch. The priests, for their part, increasingly came to expect concessions from the king during this period. The three decrees just mentioned along with the two so-called Philae decrees of 186 and 185 are the most important documents of their kind for the history of the Ptolemaic kingdom; in all, we know of some 15–17 priestly synods dating to the third and second centuries.[185]

While the crown had established the councils of priests and in many ways was able to influence the content of their resolutions, it is nevertheless true that the priests presented themselves as an autonomous body. They cast themselves as an independent legal body which formulated resolutions concerning all of Egypt and made official decisions at the king's side. The decrees of the priests, however, stand in contrast to the προστάγματα and διαγράμματα of the kings – these were the decrees and legal norms issued by the king. While the religious orders always paid tribute to the power of the king and especially of the royal couple, the synodic decrees show the tensions between the king and the priesthoods. The history of these tensions goes back hundreds of years and the efforts of the Ptolemies to gain their acceptance only seems to have resolved this problem on a superficial level.

Late in the winter of 238, the priests arrived in Alexandria after having been summoned to a synod. The occasion was Ptolemy III's birthday as well as the jubilee of his rule which was to take place 20 days later. Since the celebrations are described in the second part of the decree, we know that the concluding session, at least, took place on 7 March 238 in the suburb of Canopus, on the coast northeast of Alexandria.

*Figure 3.6* Canopus Decree: upper portion of the stele from Kom el-Hisn (Egyptian: Jm3w: Greek: Momemphis; capital of the third Lower Egyptian nome) after Roeder (1960), 151, Fig. 34; see p. 121, note 186. Below the winged sun: Left half: Ptolemy III followed by Berenike II, Thoth, Seshat, the second Ptolemaic pair and finally the first royal pair.
Right half: the goddess of the third nome of Lower Egypt, Hathor, Sakhmet, Sekhat-Hor, Amun-Re, a form of Horus, the last two figures not visible because of damage to the stele. The hieroglyphic inscriptions have been omitted.

Six copies of the decree (Fig. 3.6) have survived, two of which have been completely preserved.[186] The first part of the decree consists of honours for the ruling royal couple. The benefactions performed by the couple are given as evidence that they have shown themselves to be 'beneficent gods'. Deeds of this type were a common theme in the ideology of the ancient Egyptian king; the Ptolemies had subsequently appropriated this motif for their own purposes and had promulgated the message of their accomplishments by means of the priests. The benefactions mentioned in the decree include: care of the animal cults, especially donations for Apis and Mnevis; the recovery of the sacred statues of the gods once stolen by the Persians;[187] military protection of the country by means of battles outside Egypt; just execution of the law by the judiciary and relief for the famine which had arisen as a result of insufficient Nile flooding.[188]

One of the honours conferred upon the royal couple in the decree was the pledge of an organizational reform of the $w^cb$-priests. A fifth section of priests was to be added to the four already in existence in all of the $r$-$pr$ sanctuaries (the royal cultic institutions within temple precincts)[189] and it was to be called 'phyle of the beneficent gods'. All of the $w^cb$ priests who were about to take office or who had taken office in the first nine years of Ptolemy III's rule were to be incorporated into this fifth phyle. This group of priests appointed exclusively by Euergetes I, and therefore loyal to him, increased the king's authority and his influence within the clergy.

A monthly festival of the Theoi Euergetai had already been established in an earlier decree, but now further celebrations, including five-day-long processions, were decreed in honour of the royal pair. The festival was to be held in conjunction with the reappearance of the star Sothis in the early-morning sky. According to ancient Egyptian scholarly tradition ('in agreement with the writings of the house of life') the day in question, the 19th of July,[190] was the ideal new year's day.[191] In the ninth year of Ptolemy III's reign, in 239/8, this day coincided with the first of Payni in the civil calendar. In order to ensure that this festival celebrated at the morning rising of Sothis would fall on the same day in the future so that neither the calendar year nor the festivals should move through the seasons, every four years a sixth intercalary day was to be added to the five epagomenal days in the Egyptian year of 365 days. This intercalary day was to be celebrated as a festival of the Theoi Euergetai.[192]

This calendar reform of 238 meant that for the first time in history a leap year of 366 days was, by decree, to be inserted every four years. The return of Sothis after a period during which the star was not visible was also a sign for Egyptians of the beginning of the Nile inundation. Since the festival of the royal couple was celebrated at this same time, the two came to be seen as guarantors of the Nile flooding and of the land's fertility. This image was quite in keeping with the ancient conception of the pharaoh. Berenike, who at the time was already beginning to be identified with Isis, could consequently also appear as Isis-Sothis. The reform of the calendar would have meant that the conjunction of all these important events – a matter of significant religious and ideological consequences – would have recurred each and every year. The reform, however, failed; the attempt to impose Greek rationalism on a priesthood which, for its part, sought to maintain a thousand-year-old tradition could not succeed. Not until the Alexandrian calendar of the Roman period, which was instituted on 29 August 22 BC did the practice of inserting an intercalary day every four years gain official acceptance.

While the synod of the priests were in progress, the princess Berenike (see Stemma 1), known from birth as 'queen' (Βασίλισσα), died while still a child. The second part of the Canopus Decree describes the cultic honours conferred upon her.[193] The death of the princess occurred at the beginning of the month of Tybi, just after the festival of Osiris which was celebrated in the month of Khoiak. As a result of this, the rites of mourning performed by the priests and other related ceremonies were taken to be a continuation of the festival of Osiris. The princess was laid to rest in the temple of Osiris erected by her parents at Canopus[194] and rituals pertaining to the cult of the dead were performed for her; these last corresponded to the deification rites of the sacred bulls Apis and Mnevis. Like Arsinoe II before her, the dead princess Berenike was thereby explicitly[195] elevated to the rank of a goddess in the Egyptian pantheon. In all of Egypt, golden images of her were placed in the inner sancta of the *r-pr* sanctuaries (of the first and second rank) bearing the inscription 'Berenike, mistress of the virgins'.[196] This image was now also to be carried at every procession of the gods.

The goddess Berenike was associated above all with Osiris both because of where she was laid to rest and owing to her inclusion in future Khoiak-festivals throughout Egypt.[197] Since her death had taken place in the month of Tybi, she also came to be linked with Hathor-Tefnut, whose festival was celebrated at that time. The principal theme of the festival of Hathor-Tefnut was the myth of her disappearance and eventual return to the gods. Since Berenike shared a similar fate, a festival in her honour was set up at the same time of the year. As part of the proceedings of this new festival, priestesses offered the first ripe ears of corn before her statues[198] and so Berenike came to be associated with Isis-Renenutet (the Greek Isis-Demeter) in relation to the fertility of the land.

This second part of the Canopus Decree detailing events after Berenike's death describes the process in which a member of the royal dynasty is deified in strict accordance with ancient Egyptian rituals, just as in the case of Arsinoe II. In this latter case the priests of Mendes were on their own, while in this instance the high clergy from all of Egypt were present and this provided the Ptolemies with a valuable opportunity to further the goals of their religious policy. The priests became the targets of Ptolemaic propaganda and, at the same time, they were the ones who in the future would propagate its message to participants in the religious festivals. The ritual from the cult of the dead, customarily performed for Apis and the king in the Serapeum of Memphis,[199] was now being performed for a princess who had died in her childhood. This meant that the divinity of the king was not something confirmed through great deeds as in the case of the Hellenistic basileus; instead, it was thought to be an innate quality of the royal family and was confirmed by the entire Egyptian priesthood.

Henceforth, the charisma of the Ptolemaic family, which in the Alexandrian dynastic cult was apparent in the automatic deification of every ruling couple, began to be interpreted and elaborated on the basis of Egyptian religious themes. The intrinsic divinity of the royal family, which the Canopus Decree now officially corroborated, assured the fertility of the land and hence the happiness and prosperity of the inhabitants. This claim was of course strengthened by the relation of the royal family to Sothis and the flooding of the Nile as well as by their connection to Osiris and the produce of the fields. These traditional views of the pharaoh as provider of plenty represent the logical counterpart to the tryphé ('luxury') of the Ptolemaic basileus. The Canopus Decree clearly indicates how the dynasty attempted by means of traditional festivals and cults to introduce a Ptolemaic cult into the local temples, but it was a cult which went far beyond the standard forms of the Egyptian cult of the king from which it had originated. The actual success of the cult for the young Berenike is hard to evaluate in comparison with the

popular response which the goddess Arsinoe enjoyed. In the end, both phenomena may perhaps be viewed as special cases in the development of the
Egyptian cult of the Ptolemies.

Aside from what was prescribed in the Canopus Decree, other monuments
also indicate that distinct changes within the Egyptian cult of the king took
place under Ptolemy III. These were developments analogous to those taking
place in the Alexandrian dynastic cult.[200]

The first item to be mentioned are the scenes of ancestor-worship found
on temple reliefs from Ptolemy III to IX which are a continuation of an
ancient Egyptian tradition, which we know particularly from the New Kingdom period. In these scenes the deceased royal couples, beginning with Ptolemy II and Arsinoe II,[201] are worshipped as those who pass on a hereditary
royal power with rites including incense-burning, libations or a sacrificial
animal. In this way, the divine powers of the dead king or of the deceased
royal couple are passed on to the new ruling pair. Other representations
associated with these scenes of the transferral of power are meant to show
that the gods countenance what has transpired. In these illustrations, the
years of his reign are written for the ruling king by a deity on a palm frond
following an ancient tradition; the act of transferral is testimony to the fact
that the powers at work in the royal pair (their ka's) may be addressed as
'divine'.[202] The sacrifice before the ancestors, who from time to time are
characterized as 'co-gods' (z3w.n.sn = θεοὶ σύνναοι) and this representation
is found even in the inner sanctum in Edfu.

Accordingly, from the rule of Ptolemy III, the divinity of the Ptolemies is
sometimes represented by including them among the ancient Egyptian gods.
Thus, on the gate of Euergetes in Karnak,[203] the first and second Ptolemaic
couples are attached as σύνναοι to the two processions of the gods worshipping the moon. We also find deceased and living Ptolemies among the gods
displayed on the upper fields of the stele from Kom-el-Hisn (the Canopus
Decree)[204] (Fig. 3.6).

It is clear that the erection of statues of the Ptolemies in Egyptian
temples[205] is in itself not sufficient proof of a change in the Egyptian cult of
the king. Nevertheless, the numerous titles of local priests from all Egypt,
but in particular of the high priest of Ptah in Memphis, indicate that a
new ruler worship had been instituted in Egyptian sanctuaries, reminiscent
of Alexandrian dynastic cults. This ruler worship was a further development
of the existing cults for ancient Egyptian pharaohs[206] and, beginning with
Ptolemy III, was based on the Egyptian cult of statues. The relevant priestly
titles indicate that the priest not only was in service to one or more Egyptian
deities, he also administered the cult of the ruling Theoi Euergetai;[207] in
addition, the ruling Ptolemaic couple were added to the title as Theoi
Philopatores, Epiphaneis, etc. until the end of the Ptolemaic period. The
series of titles was thus formed in a similar fashion to that of the priests of
Alexander.[208] Occasionally, precedence was given to the Theoi Adelphoi as
the first couple, who were already being worshipped in the native Egyptian

religious environment.[209] The practice of this local dynastic cult, whose origins lay in the daily and festival cultic activities for the statues of the Ptolemies, was attached to the synods of the priests, certainly as a result of pressure from the government. Accordingly, the Canopus Decree includes the resolution that all wᶜb priests had to be called 'wᶜbw of the Theoi Euergetai';[210] later decrees[211] prescribed the addition of the living royal couple.[212] In contrast with the Alexandrian dynastic cult, where the dead Alexander was the origin and focal point of the cult, the Ptolemies were made synnaoi of the local gods in native sanctuaries all over the country. Alexander, on the other hand, was always excluded there. An Alexander cult in the chora is attested only from the second century.[213]

## *The ideological connection between the Hellenistic and ancient Egyptian figures of the king*

The evolution of the Egyptian Ptolemaic cult, which developed along parallel lines to the Alexandrian dynastic cult, leads us to conclude that it became successful with the aid of the Egyptian priesthood who made the divinity of the dynasty acceptable not only in Greek but also in Egyptian circles.

The task of combining the many ideal characteristics of the basileus with the image of the pharaoh, who was defined by his religious functions and mythical role, was easy enough. On the one hand, the traditional qualities of the pharaoh had to be interpreted in a Greek manner. In this regard, Theocritus (*Id.* XVII) lauded Ptolemy II as a pharaonic conqueror of foreign countries. As such Ptolemy III bears the title of 'Great King' (βασιλεὺς μέγας)[214] on a propagandistic inscription from Adulis; addressing him by this title, an Egyptian wishes the king world domination in a written petition.[215] The same term is found again in Greek versions of the most common Egyptian royal title, that is in the title 'king of Upper and Lower Egypt' (nswt bjtj), first attested in the Raphia Decree of 217.[216] In his hymn to Delos (IV.160–195), Callimachus appropriates the ideas behind the Egyptian royal titulary for his own poetic purposes: he places Ptolemy II and Apollo in close relation to each other and so casts the victorious Horus-King in the role of the triumphant Apollo. In this way, he attempts to synthesize Egyptian and Greek concepts and rituals.[217]

Conversely, the Greek cult names of the Ptolemies were also translated into Egyptian and could be understood in terms of the pharaoh's traditional cultic role.[218] *Soter* could thus refer to the 'saving' and 'protecting' aspects of the Horus-King. Similarly, *Euergetes* touched upon the ancient Egyptian idea of 'euergetism' which in the Canopus Decree is defined as the care of the temples and the gods.[219] Arsinoe II bore the name *Philadelphos* perhaps already during her lifetime and certainly she received it as a cult title after her death; its use as a title for Ptolemy II is attested only from the second century. Among members of the Ptolemaic dynasty, this title was assigned for the first time to Arsinoe II and was later taken up by other Hellenistic royal families. It served to communicate to the subjects the high moral worth of sibling affection, loyalty and harmony, all of which the royal house claimed to uphold.[220] In the case of the second Ptolemaic couple,[221] the title *Philadelphos* made reference to the sibling-marriage which itself was most often apostrophized with the cultic title of *Theoi Adelphoi*. It was the court's propagandist aim[222] that the marriage remind the Greeks of Zeus and Hera; from an Egyptian point of view this was a clear reference to Isis and Osiris and to the exemplary bond of love and matrimony between the two. It is worth noting, however, that although sibling-marriages did occur at the ancient Egyptian court, there is no evidence from that time of a royal marriage between full brother and sister.[223] The marriage between Ptolemy II and Arsinoe II, therefore, represented for the Egyptians a purer imitation of Isis and Osiris than that of their predecessors at the ancient Egyptian court. As we have seen in the previous section, beginning with Ptolemy III at the latest, the names given to the Ptolemaic couples were genuine cult titles, widely current even in the native Egyptian milieu.[224]

This overview of the religious policy of the Ptolemies shows us that they at once followed ancient Egyptian and Greco-Hellenistic traditions and attempted to synthesize the two. The Hellenistic cult of Sarapis was the natural result of such an attempt. Despite the great importance of the Alexandrian Serapeum, Sarapis never became an imperial god of the Ptolemies. Instead, further financing of the cult was terminated after Ptolemy IV because of its limited appeal to the native Egyptian population. Initiatives independent of those of the dynasty were responsible for the worldwide fame of the religion of Isis and Sarapis.

It thus remains the case that the kingship was for all peoples of the kingdom the only element of unity in all areas of culture and religion. For this reason, the kingship was given an exalted religious status and, in fact, became the focal point for all initiatives in religious policy. As a means of strengthening this elevated position, the king supported the cults of the gods, ancient Egyptian as well as Greek (especially the cult of Dionysos but also of Aphrodite), because of their ideological connection with the kingship.

## Notes

1  On the more than ten generations of the family of the high priest of Memphis which are attested from Ptolemy I to Augustus: Quaegebeur (1980); Reymond (1981); Thompson, D. J. (1988), 138–146.
2  See p. 90f. (Hephaistion and Ptolemy I).
3  On this see provisionally T. Holm-Rasmussen, 'Some monuments of the last pharaoh viewed in the light of contemporary ideology', *Hafnia* 10, 1985, 7–23.
4  The halting of Persian preparations for an invasion of Egypt in 359 could also be viewed as a triumph of Nectanebo.
5  An interesting side-comment is that the sarcophagus of Nectanebo II (today in the BM) in which the king was probably never buried, had at one time been revered as the tomb of Alexander the Great; it was situated in Alexandria in

the mosque of Athanasius. It is unknown whether the sarcophagus had truly served for a time as the dead Alexander's resting place. On this see E. D. Clarke, *The Tomb of Alexander the Great*, Cambridge 1805 (*non vidi*); H. Jenni, *Das Dekorationsprogramm des Sarkophages Nectanebos II*, Geneva 1986.

6 With regard to the legend of Alexander as the son of Nectanebo II, one may note the interesting detail that the oldest son of this last native pharaoh returned to Egypt after the turmoil had passed and still lived in Iseion (Behbeit el-Hagar, Delta) as an esteemed person at the start of the Ptolemaic period; cf. J. J. Clère, 'Une statuette du fils aîné du roi Nectanebô', *REg*, 1951, 135–156; Huß (1991, 1), 57.

7 The royal names discussed here and their parallels found in past Egyptian history can be seen in Beckerath (1984); id.: LÄ III. 1980, 542–556 (s.v. königsnamen); D. Kurth, LÄ IV.1982, 1193–1196 (s.v. Ptolemaios). On the development of the titulature of Alexander cf. Burstein (1991).

8 Cf. Kuhlmann (1988), 152. Similar conclusions can also be made for the throne name of Dareios I, 'beloved of Amun-Re': Dareios also had great need of legitimization from the gods.

9 See p. 83f.

10 Ramses VII, Sheshonk I, Osorkon II.

11 See p. 110.

12 L. Koenen, *ZPE* 54, 1984, 11, note 12.

13 Bresciani (1969), 561f.

14 Satrap Stele, l.3–4 = Urk. II.14.7–11.

15 Pithom Stele, l. 11–15 = Urk. II.91–94. The provenance of the Pithom Stele is the biblical Pithom now identified as Tell el-Mashuta in Wadi Tumilat (on this see p. 56 with note 114); it was erected in the city's temple of Atum in the twenty-first year of Ptolemy II evidently on the occasion of his coronation jubilee. The stele itself: see Kamal (1904–5), no. 22183; Urk. II.81–105; Roeder (1959), 108–128 (trans.); Grzybek (1990), 67–112. See the other references to the stele in the third index to this book.

16 Canopus Decree, l.6 = Urk. II.128f.; OGIS I.54.20–22 (see p. 71 with note 73).

17 See p. 111.

18 Raphia Decree, l.21–22, following Thissen (1966), 17, 60; on the decree see p. 162.

19 Orth (1977), 19.

20 Kamal (1904–5), no. 22182; Urk. II.11–22; Roeder (1959), 97–106 (trans.); U. Kaplony-Heckel, in *Texte aus der Umwelt des Alten Testamentes*, ed. O. Kaiser, I, Gütersloh 1982–5, 613–619; Goedicke (1985); Winnicki (1991, 1), 164–185.

21 See index three s.v Satrap Stele.

22 See p. 5, note 1 as an introduction. Arses (according to Goedicke's reading, last note) was the son and successor of Artaxerxes III Ochos; he ruled from about November 338 to June 336.

23 The stele: Kamal (1904–5), no. 22181; Urk. II.28–54; Roeder (1959), 168–188; H. de Meulenaere, P. MacKay, Mendes II, Warminster 1976, 174–177, 205f. (no. 111), pl. 31; the passage mentioned: lines 6–10 = Urk. II.36–38. The stele at one time stood in the temple of the ram god of Mendes and was made after 264 BC on the occasion of the instalment of a new ram.

24 Pithom Stele, lines 6–10 = Urk. II.88–90; on its meaning see G. Hölbl, *Tyche* 7, 1992, 119f.

25 Mendes Stele; l.19–20 = Urk. II.46f.

26 Urk. II.30.6; Ph. Derchain, Une mention méconnue de Ptolémée 'le fils', *'ZPE* 61, 1985, 35f.

27 On the royal titulatures of queens and divine spouses see Beckerath (1984); Troy (1986).

28 Quaegebeur (1978), 254f.

29 On construction in Thebes under Alexander: M. Abd El-Raziq, *Die Darstellungen und Texte des Sanktuars Alexanders des Großen im Tempel von Luxor*, Mainz 1984; Ph. Martinez, 'A propos de la décoration du sanctuaire d'Alexandre à Karnak: réflexions sur la politique architecturale et religieuse des premiers souverains lagides', *Bulletin d la Société d'Égyptologie*, Genève, 13, 1989, 1–7–116; Cl. Traunecker, 'La chapelle de Khonsou du mur d'enceinte et les travaux d'Alexandre', in *Cahiers de Karnak III*, 1982–85, 347–354. See also the summary of the monuments of Alexander the Great in W. Helck, LÄ I.1975, 132 (s.v. Alexander, 'der Große').

30 Horus is falcon-headed but accompanied by Isis, therefore her son. On the temple see A. Fakhry, *The Egyptian Deserts, II: Bahriyah and Farafra Oases*, Cairo 1974, 99–103. Also worthy of mention is that a second priest of equal rank appears offering behind Alexander who is evidently the local governor of the oasis. His position is reminiscent of that of the oasis king of Siwah (see p. 74, note 129), who alone, however, – at any rate according to evidence prior to Alexander – faces the gods. Conversely, the contemporary Egyptian king Nectanebo II appears outside of the context of the same relief wall; cf. Kuhlmann (1988), pl. 31a.

31 SIRIS I.

32 S. Snape, D. Bailey, *The Great Portico at Hermopolis Magna: Present State and Past Prospects*, London 1988.

33 The monuments of Alexander IV are, naturally enough, few in number; cf. M. Atzler, 'Ein ägyptisches Reliefbruchstück des Königs Alexander IV', *Antike Kunst* 15, 1972, 120f., pl. 38; O. Koefoed-Petersen, *Catalogue des bas-reliefs et peintures égyptiens*, Copenhagen 1956, 48f.; further, on the burial of a mother of Apis in June 308, that is, posthumously under his name: Smith, H. S. (1972), Table 5.

34 Overview in Ph. Derchain, *Zwei Kapellen des Ptolemaios I Soter in Hildesheim*, Hildesheim 1961; Swinnen (1973), 118–121; See Cauville, *BIFAO* 89, 1989, 45.

35 J. Yoyotte, 'L'Amon de Naukratis', *R.Eg.* 34, 1982–83, 129–136. The pylon dates to Ptolemy II.

36 Kom el-Ahmar: W. Wessetzky, *MDIK* 33, 1977, 133–141, pl. 44–47; W. Schenkel in *Problems and Priorities in Egyptian Archaeology*, J. Asmann *et al.* (ed.), London 1987, 149–173; L. Gestermann *et al.*, GöttMisz 98, 1987, 28–34; 104, 1988, 53–56; L. Gestermann, 'Neue Spuren des Ptolemäischen Tempels am Kom al-ahmar at Šaruna, *MDIK* 48, 1992, 11–35. There are also reliefs of Ptolemy II extant there – Oxyrhynchos: *Cleopatra's Egypt* (1988), 100f.

37 Urk. II.116.9–13. On the donation of the Dodekaschoinos see p. 162, 189.

38 Haeny (1985), 207, note 2.

39 See p. 167f.

40 H. Junker, *Das Kloster am Isisberg*, Vienna 1922, 13.

41 S. Sauneron, *La porte ptolémaïque de l'enceinte de Mout à Karnak*, Cairo 1983; one may also find cartouches of Ptolemy III here.

42 C. de Wit, *Les inscription du temple d'Opet à Karnak*, III, Brussels 1968, VII (= Bibliotheca Aegyptiaca, XIII).

43 Daumas (1958), 83; also see p. 272. On the development of the so-called birth houses (also called Mammisis) as well as on the cult practised there see pp. 263–267.

44 W. Helck: LÄ VI.1986, 463 (s.v. Theadelphia). On this temple see p. 296, note 56.

45 Bresciani (1980), 51.

46 Situated on the east end of the sphinx alley leading to the Serapeum, east of the pyramid complex of Teti; on this construction see D. G. Jeffrey, H. S. Smith, *The Anubieion at Saqqâra, I: the settlement and the temple precinct*, London, 1988, esp. 50.

47 H. G. E. White, J. H. Oliver, *The Temple of Hibis in El Khargeh Oasis*, New York 1938, 49f., no. 7.

48 Haeny (1985), 211; Published report: H. Junker, E. Winter, *Das Geburtshaus des Tempels der Isis in Philä*, Vienna 1965.

49 I. Philae, I., no. 4.

50 E. Bresciani *et al.*, *Assuan*, Pisa 1978.

51 Cauville, Devauchelle (1984), 32f.; Publication of the temple: *Edfou I-XIV* (see bibliography).

52 See pp. 106–110.

53 see p. 72, note 91.

54 The memorial stele found in Karnak with a building inscription to a brick-retaining wall around a temple of Month I attribute to Karnak-Nord and not to Medamud as per M. Saleh, *MDIK* 37, 1981, 417–419. My opinion follows that of Cl. Traunecker, 'Une stele commémorant la construction de l'enceinte d'un temple de Montou', in *Karnak* V, 1970–1972, Cairo 1975, 141–158. On the gate also mentioned here see H. Sternberg-El Hotabi, *Der Propylon des Month-Tempels in Karnak-Nord*, Wiesbaden 1993 (= Göttinger Orientsforschungen, IV series, vol. 25).

55 PM V.143; F. Gomaà: LÄ III, 1980, 1252 (s.v. Medamud). On the Ptolemaic construction of the temple of Month see p. 270.

56 Bernand (1970), 236f. (no. 7) (= OGIS I.60).

57 Turner: *JEA* 60, 1974, 239–242 (see p. 29, note 11).

58 D. Hagedorn, 'Ein Erlaß Ptolemaios' I. Soter?', *ZPE* 66, 1986, 65–70; K. J. Rigsby, 'An edict of Ptolemy I', *ZPE* 72, 1988, 273f.

59 PSI IV.328 (257 BC); Pestman (1980), 188–194 (no. 50).

60 For all problems in the relation between the cult of the king and the sacred beasts, see Kessler (1989). On the Apis burial see R. L. Vos, *The Apis Embalming ritual, P. Vindob. 3873*, Leuven 1993.

61 On these various topics cf. Otto, W., I–II (1905–8); Quaegebeur (1979), W. Clarysse, 'Egyptian estate-holders in the Ptolemaic period', in *State and Temple Economy in the Ancient Near East, II*, Leuven 1979, 731–743; J. H. Johnson, 'The role of the Egyptian priesthood in Ptolemaic Egypt', in *Egyptological Studies in R. A. Parker*, ed. L. H. Lesko, Hannover and London 1986, 70–84.

62 The temple organization sketched here mostly follows Kessler (1989), *passim*, esp. the outlines after p. 48.

63 See p. 27; as well as Kessler (1989), 195.

64 Thompson, D. J. (1988), 110 (Anemhor II).

65 Quaegebeur (1979), esp. 714; D. Meeks, 'Les donations aux temples dans l'Égypte du Ier mill. a. J.-C.', in *State and Temple Economy in the Ancient Near East*, II, Leuven, 655 (on Petosiris); S. Cauville, 'La chapelle de Thot-Ibis à Dendera édifiée sous Ptolémée I par Hor, scribe d'Amon-Rê', BIFAO 89, 1989, 43–66, pl. II-VI.

66 P. Goukowsky, 'Basileus Alexandros', in Will *et al.* (1990), 323–331.

67 To this must be added the different systems of reckoning (Macedonian and Egyptian) the years of kingship of both Soter and Philadelphos: see pp. 20–22 with note 48 as well as p. 67, note 2.

68 On Macedonian tradition in the Ptolemaic and Seleukid kingdoms see Hammond (1989), 281–288. The nature and ideology of the Hellenistic king has been treated in countless works; cf. Gehrke (1990, 165f. and the bibliography on pp. 238–240. See, in particular, H. Heinen (1978) and H.-J. Gehrke, 'Der siegreiche König', *Archiv für Kulturgeschichte* 64, 1982, 247–277; further, see Cl. Préaux, 'L'image du roi de l'époque héllenistique', in *Images of Man in Ancient and Medieval Thought*, FS G, Verbeke, Leuven, 1976, 53–75; P. Lévêque, 'Idéologie et pouvoir sous les deux premiers Lagides', *AttiCAntCl* 10, 1978–79, 99–122; Préaux, I (1978), 181–238; Samuel (1989), 67–81; Will *et al.* (1990), 441–444.

69 On the grain donations see p. 41 with note 34, p. 53; the benefactions to Delos see Bruneau (197), 516–531.

70 Cf. Merkelbach (1981), 27–35.

71 Guéraud (1931–32).

72 The largest public demonstration of Ptolemaic tryphé known to us is represented by the pompé of Philadelphos; see p. 38f.

73 Heinen (1983).

74 The literature on Hellenistic ruler cult is immense and therefore I will mention only a few: Habicht (1956); Taeger, I (1957); Préaux, I (1978), 238–271; Walbank in *CAH* VII.I.87–99; F. W. Walbank, 'Könige als Götter, Überlegungen zum Herrscherkult von Alexander bis Augustus', *Chiron* 17, 1987, 365–382; H. Hauben (1989), 441–467; Gehrke (1990), 152, 167; L. J. Sanders, 'Dionsyius I of Syracuse and the origins of ruler cult in the Greek World', *Historia* 40, 1991, 275–287.

75 Goukowsky, I (1978), 204f.

76 Leschhorn (1984), 204–212.

77 Ibid., 227–229. The oldest source is perhaps I.Philae.I, no.20 (118/116 BC).

78 German translation in Walbank, *Chiron* 17, 1987, 374f.

79 The view that the Rhodians used the cult title 'Soter' for Ptolemy I, as Pausanias claims, seems doubtful in view of the silence of the other sources, particularly the documents of the Rhodian priests; see Hazzard (1992). It seems that one cannot confirm whether or not Ptolemy I used the name 'Soter' in his lifetime, either as a cult title or simply as an epithet. The demotic evidence for 304 BC in Deir el-Bahari (Bresciani, MDIK 39, 1983, 103–105) is questionable on paleographic grounds: W. Clarysse, 'Greek loan-words in Demotic', in S. P. Vleeming *et al.*, *Aspects of Demotic Lexicography*, Leuven 1987, 30, note 78.

80 Syll.I³, 390, l.28, 48f.; cf. Bruneau (1970), 531f. Ptolemy bears the cult title of 'Soter' in these circumstances; since the inscription is undated but at any rate

after Ptolemy's death, the cult title would not necessarily have existed already in 287/6; see Hazzard (1992), 56, note 35.

81  See p. 41, 52f. with notes 31 and 98 respectively.

82  Kienast (1987), 322–324.

83  Kessler (1989), 185–189.

84  G. Grimm, 'Die Vergöttlichung Alexanders d. Gr. in Ägypten und ihre Bedeutung für den ptolemäischen Königskult', in *Ptol. Äg.* (1978), 103–112 (with the important observation by Derchain on p. 111 that the link between Amun and Osiris/Dionysos is first attested to in the Ptolemaic period). On the connection between Ptolemy I and Dionysos: *Kyrieleis* (1975), 7f.; M. Donderer, 'Dionysos und Ptolemaios Soter als Mcleager- zwei Gemälde des Antiphilos', in *Zu Alexander d. Gr., FS G*, Wirth, W. Will (ed.) II, Amsterdam 1988, 781–799. On the connection with Pan: H. P. Laubscher, 'Hellenistische Herrscher und Pan', *AM* 100, 1985, 346.

85  Goukowsky, II (1981), 79–83.

86  Idealized beardless busts bearing ram's horns and other stylistic influences taken from the representations of Alexander the Great as well as other Hellenistic rulers proliferated widely; cf. J Leclant, G. Clerc: *Lexicon Iconographicum Mythologiae Classicae*, I, Zurich 1981, 683f. (s.v. Ammon); in addition, the beautiful Alexander-Ammon from Utica or Carthage in Copenhagen, Nationalmuseet, Inv. Abb 97 (copy of Severan date). During the Roman times (Clem.Al.*Protr.*IV.54.2), it was thought that statues of Alexander as the son of Ammon with ram's horns had been made at the king's personal behest.

87  Ijsewijn (1961); Clarysse, Van der Veken (1983); Peremans (1973), 60f.

88  Clarysse, Van der Veken (1983), 4, no. 7; PP III.5196.

89  The earliest, securely dated sources for Ptolemy I bearing the title of 'Soter' appear only from the year 263/2: Hazzard (1992), 56, note 35.

90  SEG XXVIII 60, l. 55–64 (Kallias Decree; see p. 68, note 13 and 69, note 34); also, REG 94, 1981, 396f.; with a somewhat different interpretation of the sources: Hazzard (1987), 150; cf. Hauben (1992), 159.

91  See p. 38f.

92  Cf. p. 40 on the encomium of Theocritus.

93  H. Volkmann, *RE* XXIII, 2, 1959, 1578–1590 (s.v. Ptolemaia); for Athens see p. 52.

94  IG XI.4.1038.17; 1043.14; Bruneau (1970), 531f. The league festival must be distinguished from other festivals celebrated on Delos which were also called 'Ptolemaia', which the Ptolemaic kings themselves sponsored: so-called Ptolemaia I (probably celebrated from 279 to honour Ptolemy I, II and III (on this see p. 45 and p. 98); on all three Bruneau (1970), 519–525.

95  The first 'priest of Alexander of the theoi adelphoi' was Kallikrates of Samos, high-commander of the Ptolemaic royal fleet for two decades from the 270s to the 250s: PP VI.14607; Mooren (1975), 58–60 (010); Hauben (1970). On the question of the chronological ordering and contribution of Arsinoe II in the context of when she died: Hauben (1992), 160f. with the literature cited here.

96  The changes in the title of the priest of Alexander during the course of its history: cf. Ijsewihn (1961), 119–121; Pestman (1967), 134–157 (for the demotic versions); see also pp. 171, 285–288.

97  See p. 49 with note 77.

98  See p. 287.

99    See pp. 101–104.

100    See p. 71, note 83.

101    SEG IX.12; Bartson (1982), 480f.

102    P. M. Fraser, 'Inscriptions from Cyrene', *Berytus* 12, 1956–58, 101–108; Fraser (1972), I, 233; Laronde (1987), 424f.

103    A Phoenician: PP VI.15014; Michaelidou-Nicolaou (1976), 29, A 2; Bagnall (1976), 71f.; Parmentier (1987), 408; J. Teixidor, 'Ptolemaic chronology in the Phoenician inscriptions from Cyprus', *ZPE* 71, 1988, 188–190; Hauben (1992), 164.

104    P. Brun, 'Les Lagides à Lesbos: essai de chronologie', *ZPE* 85, 1991, 99–113 (no. 1).

105    IG XII.3.443 = SIRIS 137. The *Basilistai* are known to us from the third century in both Greek or Hellenized communities of the Egyptian chora (see on this p. 301, note 171) as well as the office of ἱερεὸς τοῦ βασιλέως in the local gymnasia of Egypt in the Ptolemaic period; cf. E. Van 't Dack, 'Notice au sujet de SB I 1106', in *Atti del XVII Congr. intern. di Papirologia*, Naples 1984, 1325–1333 (= Van 't Dack, 1988, 85–95).

106    Cf., for example, B. J. Borchhardt, 'Zum Naos des Ptolemaios von Limyra', in *Akten des 3. Österreichischen Archäologentages Innsbruck*, 1987, P. Scherrer (ed.), Vienna 1989, 31–38; id. *et al.*, in *Götter, Heroen, Herrscher in Lykien*, Vienna 1990, 79–84, 182f.; id., 'Ein Ptolemaion in Limyra', *RA* 1991, H.2, 309–322; id. 'Zur Bauskulptur am Naos des Ptolemaions von Limyra', in *Die epigraphische und altertumskundliche Erforschung Kleinasiens: Hundert Jahre Kleinasiatische Kommission der Österreichischen Akademie der Wissenschaften, Akten des Symposiums vom 23–25. Okt., 1990*, G. Dobesch, G. Rehrenböck (ed.), Vienna 1993, 71–84; id., Die Steine von Zemuri, Vienna 1993, 79–93.

107    I. Cret.III.4.4 = Syll.I³. 463; Habicht (1956), 121f.; Bagnall (1976), 121.

108    See p. 50 with note 81.

109    Financed by Artemidoros of Perge: PP VI.15188; Bagnall (1976), 134.

110    Wace *et al.* (1959), 4–11; Fraser (1972), I.234, II.384, note 356.

111    On this topic see Tondriau (1948, 2).

112    Kyrieleis (1975), 166 (B1); for Ptolemy III as Herakles see ibid., 38, 170 (C 17). On the glorification of Philadelphos as Herakles in the 'Herakliskos' of Theocritus, see Koenen (1977), 79–86.

113    OGIS I.54.4–5.

114    A. Alföldi, 'From the Aion Plutonios to the Ptolemies in the Saeculum Frugiferum of the Roman emperors', in *Greece and the Eastern Mediterranean in Ancient History and Prehistory, Festschrift für Schachermeyr*, K. H. Kinzl (ed.), Berlin 1977, 1–10; W. Huß, 'Ptolemaios III as Sarapis?', *JNG* 26, 1976, 31–36.

115    Fraser (1972), I.226, 236; for Cyprus e.g. SIRIS 352.

116    Cf. Tondriau (1950) and id. (1953).

117    Swinnen (1973), 128f.

118    For a summary see W. Hoepfner, 'ΦΙΛΑΔΕΛΦΕΙΑ. Ein Beitrag zur frühen hellenistichen Architektur, AM 99, 1984, 353–364, pl. 53f. For Samothrake see J. R. McCredie *et al., The Rotunda of Arsinoe*, text, plates, Princeton 1992 (= *Samothrace* 7) (of Arsinoe II; the rotunda was evidently sponsored only after her marriage to Ptolemy II, cf. 238); A. Frazer, *The Propylon of Ptolemy II*, text, plates, Princeton 1990 (= *Samothrace* 10).

119 See p. 117, note 94.

120 See p. 10* with note 6.

121 Similarly, modern scholarship can no longer decide whether he was the son of Zeus or of Ammon: Kienast (1987).

122 Cf. the text in M. Lichtheim, *Ancient Egyptian Literature*, II, Berkeley 1976, 64–69.

123 See on the Hephaistion p. 92. At a festival of Dionysos in Ekbatana in 324, Alexander had himself crowned as the son of Ammon: Ephippos: FGrHist. 126 F 5.2abs.

124 See p. 12 with note 14.

125 See p. 93.

126 Cf. p. 4; UPZ I, no. 1.

127 On this complex see p. 89 and pp. 281–283.

128 Cf. Kessler (1989), 57–84.

129 On the name see G. Mussies, 'some notes on the name of Sarapis', in Hommages à M. J. Vermaseren, M. B. De Boer, T. A. Edridge (eds), II, Leiden 1978, 821–832.

130 On Manetho see p. 29; the cult legend is also in Tac.*hist*.IV.83–84; cf. Fraser (1972), I.246–251.

131 The solar aspects of Apis-Osiris appear only later.

132 L. Castiglione, 'Nouvelles données archéologiques concernant la génèse de Sarapis', in *Hommages à Vermaseren* (see note 130), I.208–232, pl. XIX-XXVII.

133 See p. 86.

134 They also appear as such in the dedicatory inscriptions mentioned on pp. 96–97 with note 115.

135 G. Grimm, 'Zum Ptolemäeraltar aus dem alexandrinischen Sarapieion', in *Alessandria*, I (1983), 70–73.

136 Rowe (1946); Wild (1981), 29–34, 167f. On the Serapeum as an academic institution see p. 64.

137 A statue of Ptolemy III is mentioned in P. Haun.6.fr.1, l.21 (cf. ZPE 39, 1980, 4f.).

138 Cf. the overview in G. Hölbl:LÄ VI.1986.920–969 (s.v. Verehrung ägyptischer Götter im Ausland, esp. Greco-Roman period).

139 It was the 'priests of the king' on the island of Thera who endowed the temple treasury in the sanctuary of the Egyptian gods during the reign of Philadelphos; see p. 118, note 105; a votive tablet was also found in the same sanctuary dedicated to Arsinoe Philadelphos (IG XII.3.462); on this tablet see p. 104. For Cyprus: Dunand (1973), III, 120.

140 Lines 12–14; On the Mendes Stele see p. 84 with note 23, p. 69, note 29.

141 I.e. the god of Mendes.

142 in Greek: Θεὰ φιλάδελφος.

143 On her posthumous, pharaonic titulary see p. 85.

144 Quaegebeur (1971, 1), esp. 242f.

145 Cf. Fig. 3.3 (p. 84).

146 We know of other equally excessive examples from the ancient pharaonic kingdom dating to Ramses II who, for example, offers to his own name image over the entrance gate of Abu Simbel; cf. L. Habachi, Features of the Deification of Ramses II, Glückstadt 1969; Quaegebeur (1978), 259, 261 (ill. N).

147 Quaegebeur (1971, 2).

148  Quaegebeur (1988), 47, Fig.17.
149  Citations from Thompson, D. J. (1988), 127, note 116.
150  PP IX.5361; Quaegebeur (1980), 65; Reymond (1981), 60–70 (no. 3).
151  Quaegebeur (1971, 1), 262–270.
152  Pithom Stele, lines 20–21 = Urk. II.100; Roeder (1959), 124f.; Grzybek (1990), 74, note 17.
153  Documents, for ex., from Sais (Urk. II.80.10), Memphis: Quaegebeur (1971, 1), 242, 246–248.
154  Thompson, D. B. (1973), 67, 70, 74.
155  See p. 59; on Arsinoe as nome-goddess: Rübsam (1974), 17–19; on the name of the nome capital see p. 75, note 153. In Philadelphia an Arsinoeion and a shrine of the Theoi Adelphoi stood near one another: PCZ 59169.
156  Cadell (Ch. 2, note 29), 3. See the list in Clarysse, Van der Veken (1983), 7–39 which goes to the end of the second century.
157  Tondriau (1948, 1).
158  Fraser (1972), I.239f., 568–571; Hauben (1983), 111–114.
159  The name 'Philotera' is here in the cartouche: Reymond (1981), 62; on Nesisty II, see pp. 101–102 with note 150.
160  PP III.5524 (see also IX); on the familial tie see Thompson, D. J. (1988), 129.
161  On 'Arsinoe' and 'Philotera' as well as other places mentioned, see index 2.
162  *Kyrieleis* (1975), 78–80; W. Cheshire, 'Zur Deutung eines Szepters der Arsinoe II Philadelphos', *ZPE* 48, 1982, 105–111. The statuary also depicts Arsinoe II as a goddess; cf. *Kyrieleis* (1975), 82–94; Brunelle (1976), 10–29; M. Prange, 'Das Bildnis Arsinoe II Philadelphos', *AM* 105, 1990, 197–211, pl. 38–46.
163  Revenue Laws Papyrus, col. 23–37; see p. 62 with note 152 as well as Bingen (1978), 17f.; C.Ord.Ptol., no. 17–18; K. Maresch, 'Steuerobjectsdeklaration' in *Kölner Papyri* 7, M. Gronewald and K. Maresch (eds), Opladen 1991, 79–85.
164  Probably after the deified daughter of Ptolemy III; see p. 108f.; on this topic see Thompson, D. J. (1988), 132f.
165  Fraser (1972), I.232; see the compilation of the documents from the Zenon archiv in Pestman (1981), II.514.
166  P.Oxy.XXVII, no. 2465; Fraser (1972), I.229f. (with the important passages translated); *Kyrieleis* (1975), 142.
167  E.g. a sanctuary for Arsinoe and a festival honouring the Theoi Adelphoi are attested in Cilician Arsinoe; see the literature cited on p. 72, note 86. On this topic see M. Segre, 'Il culto di Arsinoe Filadelfo nelle città greche', *BArchAlex* 31, 1937, 286–298.
168  A Phoenician woman: H. Donner, W. Röllig, *Kanaanäische und aramäische Inschriften,* I–III, 3rd edn, Wiesbaden 1969–1971, no. 40, l.2–3; Michaelidou-Nicolaou (1976), 32 (A 24); PP VI.15016; Teixidor, loc. cit (here note 104), 189. Cf. also PP VI.15026 = Michaelidou-Nicolaou (1976), 94 (039), a gymnasiarch as priest of Arsinoe, first half of the second century.
169  Bruneau (1970), 528–530; on the office of the Nesiarch see p. 60 with note 137.
170  Bruneau (1970), 533f. Perhaps this is sanctuary A of Kynthos which evidently was a temple of Agathé Tyche from the second century; ibid., 539–541.
171  IG XII.3.1343; F. Hiller v. Gaertringen, *Stadtgeschichte von Thera*, Berlin 1904, 96 (= *Thera*, 3).

172 A. Hermary, 'Le culte d'Aphrodite à Amathonte', RDAC 1988, 2, 102 (in the temple of Aphrodite at Amathus); SIRIS 270 (Halikarnassos, reign of Ptolemy II); for Thera see note 138.

173 In the Aegean basin one should include the following: Miletus, Samos, Lesbos, Paros, Ios, Amorgos, Paphos, Delos, Thera (see p. 119, note 137) and Eretria (*BCH* 114, 1990, 809; K. Reber: *AntK* 33.2, 1990, 113); References to all the finds: L. Robert, 'Sur un décret d'Ilion et un papyrus concernant des cultes royaux', *AmStP* 1, 1966, 175–211 (= *Opera minora selecta* VII, 1990, 599–635); Bruneau (1970), 544 with note 4; also, I. Louvre, no. 9.

174 Cf. the parallel development of the king's spouse into a female pharaoh: see p. 85f.

175 See p. 64.

176 Mentioned in Fraser (1972), I.729f., I.1021–1026, notes 100–109; see also S. West, 'Venus Observed? A note on Callimachus, frg. 110,' *ClQ* 35, 1985, 61–66.

177 G. Nachtergael, 'Bérénice II, Arsinoé III et l'offrande de la boucle', *ChronEg* 55, 109–110, 1980, 240–253.

178 On this topic: Th. Hopfner, *Plutarch. Über Isis und Osiris*, I, Prague 1940, Darmstadt 1967, 44; J. Hani, *La religion égyptienne dans la pensée de Plutarque*, Paris 1976, 54f.; G. Nachtergael, 'La chevelure d'Isis', *AntCl* 50, 1981, 584–605; E. Bernand, Isis déesse de la chevelure', *ZPE* 45, 1982, 103f.

179 P. A. Pantos, 'Bérénice II Déméter', *BCH* 111, 1987, 343–352.

180 P. J. Parsons, 'Calllimachus: Victoria Bereniccs', *ZPE* 25, 1977, 1–50; Cl. Meilleir, 'Papyrus de Lille; Callimaque, Victoria Berenices (supp.hell. 254–258), éléments de commentaire sur la divinité de Bérénice', *CRIPEL* 8, 1986, 83–87.

181 Guérard (1931–32), no. 13.3; Rübsam (1974), 134.

182 Rübsam (1974), 22, cf. also p. 211.

183 See p. 170.

184 As per the Canopus Decree: Urk. II.143.1. When no particular site had been chosen for the synod, such as Memphis, then the priests would have to travel to Alexandria.

185 Huß (1991, 2) provides an overview of the evidence for all the known synods during the Ptolemaic period as well as the decrees resulting from the synods together with an overview of the sources and a detailed bibliography. There is evidence for possibly two synods during Philadelphos' reign (Huß, ibid, no. 1–2); besides the Canopus Decree, perhaps three other decrees can be placed in the reign of Euergetes I (Huß, ibid., no. 3 = (?) 6, 4 and perhaps 13; also see J. Schwartz, 'Décrets de prêtres sous Ptolémée III Evergète,' ZPE 91, 1992, 83f.). For the Greek text in Huß (1991, 2), no. 3a (end of 243) see now I. Louvre, no. 2 and J. Bingen, 'Le décret du synode sacerdotal de 243 avant notre ère', ChronEg 67, 134, 1992, 319–327. On Huß (1991, 2), no. 3b see Bernand (1989), no. 1 and id. (1992), no. 11.

186 Urk. II.124–154: hieroglyphic and Greek version of the Tanis copy; Spielberg (1922): demotic text of the stelae from Kom el-Hisn and Tanis with a German translation of the hieroglyphic version; Bernand (1970), 989–1036 and id. (1992), no. 9–10: Greek text with a translation of the Tanis copy and the Elkab fragments; I. Louvre, no. 1: Greek text of the Cairo fragment; Roeder (1960),

143–166: translation of the hieroglyphic version (with mistakes). For linguistic questions see Daumas (1952).

187  See p. 81 with note 16.

188  See p. 49 with note 79.

189  On the concept *r-pr* and the wᶜb priests who carried out their service their see Kessler (1989), 46–55, 149f. and *passim*.

190  Following Skeat (1969)'s tables.

191  Urk. II.138.4.

192  The entire passage in Urk. II.137–142.

193  Urk. II.142–153; Onasch (1976), 144–147; Heinen (1978), 197f.; Dunand (1980, 2).

194  See p. 87 with note 56.

195  Urk. II.143.9; 144.10; 147.5.

196  This passage is reminiscent of the measures for Arsinoe II although, according to the Mendes Stele (Urk. II.41.11) she received cult images in the 'houses of the god' of the temple precinct which were legally independent of the pharaoh (ḥwt ntr) while in Berenike's case the royal cult institutions are named; on the organization of the temples see the schematic representation in Kessler (1989), following p. 48.

197  The detailed measures for this and the roles ascribed to the daughters of the priests as well as to other girls and priestesses, cannot be treated in full here; for a fuller treatment see Dunand (1980, 2).

198  Urk. II.150.7–151.4.

199  See p. 89.

200  On this topic see Winter (1978); Quaegebeur (1989, 1); Lanciers (1991).

201  The oldest scene of ancestral worship known to me appears already on the Pithom Stele (Fig. 3.1; p. 82) in the upper field left, where Ptolemy II offers an udyat to 'his father' (Urk. II.83.1–6); this 'father', namely Ptolemy I, is at the same time likened to 'father Atum'. I do not, however, accept the thesis of Grzybek (1990), 69–80 according to which the 'Atum' on this stele is to be interpreted throughout as Ptolemy I.

202  Particularly emphasized by Quaegebeur (1989, 1), 97.

203  PM II², 225 (*Propylon*, 1–2).

204  See note 184.

205  See p. 88f. It was a very regular practice at the latest beginning with Ptolemy III; cf. Winter (1978), 156; P. Gallo, 'Quelques monuments royaux provenant de Behbeit el-Hagar', *BIFAO* 90, 1990, 226–228.

206  Cf. PP IX.5351, 5352, 5359.

207  PP III.5584, 5588, 5587; see also the evidence in note 207.

208  A cursory search through PP revealed an amazingly large number of such priests: PP III or IX.5351, 5352, 5358, 5359, 5363, 5480, 5485, 5486, 5502d, 5527, 5561, 5571, 5584, 5585, 5588, 5597, (5638), 5652, 5653, 5655, 5700, 5720, 5721, 5734, 5752, 5759, 5764, 5767, 5800, 5809, 5818, 5829a, 5850, 5870, 5871, 5881, 5887, 5908–5911, 5911a, 5913 (= 5865a), 5915, 5917, 5919, 5945, 5952, 5968, 5992, 6323, 6397, 6415, 6416, 6419, 6420, 6428, 6445, 6463, 6497, 6512–6515, 6537, 6586, 7737, 7739, 7746, 7748a, 7751, 7761, 7773, 7776, 7827, 7839, 7840, 7842b. Further examples can be found in Lanciers (1991). On a comparison with the title of the priest of Alexander see p. 287f.

209 This already occurs in the oldest example: PP IX.5379a (document from 19 October 227). On the early worship of the Theoi Adelphoi in Egyptian communities see note 222.

210 Urk. II.133.10–134.2.

211 Preserved on the Rosetta Stone (Urk. II.196.4–8) and in Philensis I (Urk. II.212.6–9).

212 In spite of the many examples mentioned in note 206 it can be seen that these decrees were not complied with in a cohesive way.

213 On the cenotaph of Alexander the Great in Kom Madi see p. 289; on this native priest of Alexander in *c.* 160 BC see Ray (1976), 102f. (no. 31a, 1–2).

214 OGIS I.54.1; see p. 48f. with note 73.

215 PSI V.541.

216 See p. 162f.

217 Koenen (1983), 174–190; W. H. Mineur, *Callimachus, Hymn to Delos*, Leiden 1984.

218 On the following see Koenen (1983), 152–170; on *Soter* see p. 116, note 79.

219 Urk. II.128.1–3.

220 Criscuolo (1990).

221 As well as in the case of the twelfth Ptolemaic couple; see p. 223.

222 See p. 36.

223 Cf. S. Allam in LÄ II.1977, 568–570 (s.v. 'Geschwisterehe'); W. Seipel in LÄ III.1980, 465 (s.v. 'Königin').

224 But the placing of statues of the second Ptolemaic couple in the Arsinoieon as mentioned in the Pithom Stele was effected under the title of 'brother and sister loving gods': Urk. II.100.8; see p. 101. The Egyptian Theoi Adelphoi were still worshipped later as independent gods: *Cleopatra's Egypt* (1988), 103f. (no. 14) (reign of Ptolemy V).

Part II

# Change and decline of the Hellenistic state of the Ptolemies

Foreign policy and dynastic
history from Ptolemy IV to
the 'Day of Eleusis' (221–168)


PTOLEMY IV PHILOPATOR (221–204) AND THE
FOURTH SYRIAN WAR (219–217)

After Euergetes I had established Ptolemaic supremacy in the eastern Mediterranean basin, the phase marking the expansion of the empire was at an
end. The reign of the fourth Ptolemy represents a change from the period of
growth under the first three Ptolemies to a situation – arising after the death
of Philopator – marked by crises affecting the dynasty and its interests
abroad. Henceforth, the crucial issue was to try to maintain the gains made
on an international level, partially by deft diplomacy and partially by the
deployment of forces, even in the face of painful losses. This was especially
true during the transition from the third to the second century when the
Ptolemaic kingdom had to reassert its interests in the face of a new political
scenario, not least the increasing influence of Rome. The real weakness of the
kingdom's government as early as Ptolemy IV is most apparent in the
continuous rebellions in Egypt (Chapter 5).

At the beginning of 221, we find the eldest son of Ptolemy III and
Berenike II on the throne at approximately 20 years of age. He was probably
crowned pharaoh in accordance with the proper Egyptian ceremonial rites.[1]
From the outset, if not while his father was still alive, he bore the epithet of
philopator (the 'father-loving' one), which is soon attested as his cult title.[2]
Sometime between his accession to throne and the autumn of 220, Ptolemy
IV married his sister Arsinoe III.[3]

Already at the beginning of his reign, the king was under the sway of the
most powerful man at court, the Alexandrian Sosibios.[4] He was one of the
most intelligent and unprincipled figures of the Hellenistic age; for decades
he proved himself a match for all court intrigues. From his early youth
Sosibios had close ties to Greece and was a victor at several games including
the Isthmian, Nemean and Panathenaic games. It was clearly as a result of
these victories that sometime around 240 Callimachus composed the elegy
Σωσιβίου νίκη (fr. 384 Pf.); at the same time, the Delians honoured him in
a decree and the Knidians even erected a statue in his honour at an unknown
date. In 235/4, under Euergetes I, Sosibios held the distinguished post

of priest of Alexander. After the accession of Philopator, Sosibios had the most important members of the royal family murdered (Plb. V.34.1; 36.1; XV.25.1–2): Lysimachos, the brother of Euergetes I, Magas the younger brother of Philopator, and finally the mother of the king, Berenike II, who had evidently placed Magas in a very influential position with the army (Plu. *Cleom.* 33.3).[5] In this way, Sosibios eliminated any possible opposition at court which might influence the king and diminish his own powers. 'The murdered is well-disposed' (εὔνους ὁ σφάκτης) became a saying in Alexandria with regard to these murders (Paroem. I., Zen. III. no. 94 and suppl. III a., no. 46).

Sosibios also moved against the Spartan king Kleomenes who at the time was living in exile in Alexandria (Plb. V.38–9; Plu. *Cleom.* 36–7). By means of intrigue, he managed to make the king suspicious of Kleomenes and so Kleomenes was placed under watch. But once Ptolemy IV had left for Canopus, the Spartan king succeeded in deceiving his guards and escaping with his friends. This group went through the streets of Alexandria calling on the people to rise up, but no one responded. Their plan to break into the fortress and free those imprisoned there also failed. Kleomenes and his followers thereafter committed suicide, probably in the spring of 219.

Acting behind the scenes and in collusion with Sosibios was Agathokles of Samos.[6] He was probably a boyhood friend of Philopator and we encounter him in 216/15 as priest of Alexander. Agathokles almost certainly benefited from the influence his sister Agathokleia[7] had on Philopator in her role as royal mistress (Plb. XIV.11.5).

Around 220, kings as young as Philopator ruled in the other two great Hellenistic monarchies. In Macedonia, Philip V, who was about 17 years old, came to the throne in 221. As for the Seleukid kingdom, from the reign of Seleukos II (246–226/5), it had been weakened by a war on two fronts, in the east against the Parthians and in Anatolia against the Galatians; Seleukos III Soter (226/5–222) continued to suffer under the burden of these campaigns. A new era commenced for the kingdom in 222 with the accession to the throne of Antiochos III, one of Seleukos III's younger brothers who was about 20 at the time. The young Seleukid king aimed to restore the empire as far as possible to its size under Seleukos I and he also planned to pursue Seleukid claims – left neglected in the past – to Ptolemaic possessions.[8]

But first the Seleukid kingdom suffered serious blows: in Asia Minor, a relative of the king (perhaps a cousin) named Achaios was *de facto* the ruler, while in the eastern satrapies the viceroy, Molon, rose up against Antiochos. Antiochos was persuaded in the crown council to undertake personally the reconquest of Ptolemaic Coele Syria and to send his generals against Molon (Plb. V.42). Antiochos III thus marched in the summer of 221 into the Beqaᶜ valley and attacked Ptolemaic forces in the strongholds of Gerrha and Brochoi. The commander-in-chief in Coele Syria, the Aetolian Theodotos,[9] however, had arrived before the Seleukid king and had erected a blockade with a rampart and trenches. After severe losses, Antiochos was forced to give up the attempt to break through this blockade, particularly once he learned that in the meantime Molon had defeated his generals (Plb. V.45.7–46.5). Molon consequently assumed the title of king and even had his own coins minted; at this point, he had united under his rule an area ranging from eastern Iran to Babylon. Thus, the precarious situation of its opponent bought the Ptolemaic administration a reprieve from the war. Antiochos riposted with unwonted energy, finally defeating the usurper at the beginning of 220; the latter then committed suicide. In the same year, Achaios was acclaimed as king in the west with a dominion that was limited to Asia Minor. In these circumstances, co-operation with the Ptolemaic kingdom was obviously the next step and no doubt was initiated soon thereafter.

As part of a strategic plan aimed both against Achaios as well as Ptolemaic 'Syria and Phoenicia', Antiochos thought it best first to acquire the naval stronghold of Seleukia in Pieria, which Euergetes I had occupied 27 years earlier;[10] the city fell into Seleukid hands in the spring of 219 (Plb. V.59.1–61.2) by an act of betrayal. Thus began the Fourth Syrian War (219–217)[11] which represented a struggle for supremacy in the eastern Mediterranean, where the Ptolemies dominated by means of their strong fleet.

Antiochos had originally planned a campaign against Achaios (Plb. V.61.6) after taking the city of Seleukia but he was forced to change his plans owing to unexpected circumstances. The Ptolemaic strategos, Theodotos, had fallen into disfavour owing to court intrigues in Alexandria. In a pre-emptive move against the Ptolemaic government, he decided on betrayal and so offered to deliver the province of Coele Syria to the Seleukid king (Plb. V.40.1–3). As soon as Antiochos was apprised of the situation, he travelled south and took the cities of Tyre and Ptolemais (Ake) without a struggle; the 40 naval ships which lay there represented a welcome addition to the strength of the Seleukid fleet (Plb. V.61.3–63.3). The traditional course of action for an Asiatic ruler in such a situation would have been to march against Pelusion. But when he caught wind of the sweeping defensive measures being prepared by the Alexandrian court, Antiochos was quick to abandon those plans. It was more important for him to extend his control over Palestine; but here his cause did not meet with the support which he had expected. Antiochos had to lay siege to a series of cities over a long period of time (Plb. V.62.4–6) and he did not succeed in capturing the coastal cities of Dora (Plb. V.66.1) and Sidon. At the end of 219, when the parties agreed to a cease-fire of four months, the military situation in Coele Syria must have been very unclear and confused. Theodotus' betrayal had paid off, since he now exercised high command over Seleukid occupation troops in Coele Syria (Plb. V.66.5).

The Ptolemaic government concluded the cease-fire, because as yet it had nothing with which to counter the invasion of Syria; the Seleukid king, on the other hand, hoped to acquire the Ptolemaic province without a struggle. The counsellors of the king, Sosibios and Agathokles, led the Ptolemaic committee in this crisis with remarkable ability. The diplomatic activities carried out before and during the cease-fire were initiated by them to gain time and from the beginning had not been meant in earnest. To this end, they had asked numerous Greek states, Rhodes, Byzantium, Kyzikos and the Aetolian League to act as mediators in the negotiations (Plb. V.63.5–6; 67.11). The foreign envoys were always received in Memphis, since the government wanted to keep its preparations for war in Alexandria a secret and thereby keep Antiochos ignorant of its true objectives. The main negotiations took place during the winter of 219/18 in Seleukia (Pieria) where the historical arguments on who was entitled to the possession of Coele Syria were exchanged. Only one point mattered to Antiochos; namely, that after the victory at Ipsus in 301 Seleukos had been granted all of Syria and, therefore, the fact that he had now broken his recent agreement with the Ptolemaic kingdom by conquering Coele Syria was of no legal consequence, since he was only taking back what belonged to him (Plb. V.67.4–8). The Ptolemaic side presented historical events from their point of view and also insisted upon the inclusion of the opposing Seleukid king, Achaios, in the peace treaty; Antiochos absolutely refused to negotiate on this point (Plb. V.67.9–13).

As a significant part of the preparations taking place in Alexandria (Plb. V.63.8–65.11), soldiers were gathered from all of the foreign territories and were recruited in a variety of places, including in particular Crete, Greece, Thrace and Galatia. Thus officers of exceptional ability[12] could be enlisted for the campaign which was being prepared by the Ptolemies. In conjunction with these efforts, important military reforms were enacted: the units were arranged according to place of origin and age while the individual sections were each issued the same arms; the soldiers were drilled and psychologically prepared for the upcoming battle. Whereas, in the past, Egyptian contingents of significant size had served only occasionally in the Ptolemaic imperial army,[13] a regular force of Egyptian troops was now mustered and armed in the Macedonian style. This phalanx, numbering some 20,000 men, was personally commanded by Sosibios (Plb. V.65.9; 82.6; 85.9).

It appears that in actual fact Antiochos was not fully aware of the scale of the military preparations on the part of the Ptolemies. As long as the army and navy remained unfit for action, Ptolemaic leadership avoided any decisive action and even ceded further victories to the Seleukid king. In the spring of 218, following the end of the cease-fire, Antiochos again went on the offensive. In a combined land and naval battle near Berytos, he succeeded in breaking the Ptolemaic blockade; whoever was able to escape from the slaughter fled to Sidon. Antiochos now attempted to conquer southern Coele Syria from his eastern flank but was not quite able to achieve his aim in the war: the strongholds of Gerrha and Brochoi in the southern Beqaᶜ, together with Damascus and Sidon,[14] remained in Ptolemaic hands. Antiochos then managed to conquer Philadelphia (Rabbat ᶜAmmôn), though with much effort and with the help of his Nabataean allies; it had become a strong centre of Ptolemaic resistance.[15] Finally he led his troops to their winter quarters in Ptolemais (Ake) (for the year 218: Plb. V.68–71).

The year 217 was a decisive one (Plb. V.79–86; Just. XXX.1.6f.). Ptolemy IV marched northwards from Pelusion and arrived near Raphia, southwest of Gaza. Antiochos was already there. Both sides displayed impressive armies: on the Ptolemaic side, there were 70,000 infantry, 5,000 cavalry and 73 African elephants ready for battle; on Antiochos' side, there were 62,000 infantry, 6,000 horsemen and 102 Indian elephants. The phalanx equipped with Macedonian-style weapons formed, however, the core of both armies.[16] The resources of Asia were at the Seleukid king's disposal; his Medes and Persians were reminiscent of the armies of the Achaemenid Great Kings; also taking part were 10,000 Nabataeans and members of different Arabic tribes. The significant revenues being collected from the people as well as the inclusion of the Egyptians in the army were factors that strongly influenced domestic developments in the years to come. Discussion of the actual circumstances and repercussions of these changes had already started in Polybius' day and to this day, no agreement has been reached.

The kings joined battle at Raphia on 22 June 217[17] (Plb. V.84–86); at Ptolemy's side stood his sister and wife Arsinoe (Plb. V.83.3; 84.1; 87.6). Already from the beginning, the African elephants in the Ptolemaic army were intimidated and fled into their own ranks, causing much disarray. Meanwhile, Antiochos was able to overcome the left flank of his opponent's army with his right wing and, confident of victory, he neglected what was happening on other fronts. We are told that: 'Suddenly Ptolemy, who earlier had retreated under the protection of his phalanx, came on the scene in the middle of his ranks and showed himself to both armies, spreading fear among his opponents and powerfully reviving the courage and lust for battle on his own side.' In this passage (V.85.8),[18] Polybius depicts, for the last time in history, a pharaoh doing battle in Asia following the ancient Egyptian model. The Ptolemaic phalanx with its large contigent of Egyptians finally brought about victory for Philopator. Antiochos was forced to admit defeat and retreated to Antioch; perhaps because he feared a revolt and now saw Achaios as a threat, he wanted a quick peace settlement (Plb. V.87.1–2).

Philopator sent the cunning Sosibios to Antioch to negotiate. The king himself reorganized matters in reconquered Coele Syria, where more than ever before the people's sympathies lay with the Ptolemies (Plb. V.87.5–6). Late in the summer of 217, Ptolemy IV invaded Seleukid Syria, plundering a few cities there, probably to put pressure on the negotiations taking place at that time.[19] We can discern in the treaty that followed, though its details remain unknown to us, the consummate statecraft of the Ptolemies and their long-term policy of a balance of power. Their victory was used only to secure for themselves the Ptolemaic province of 'Syria and Phoenicia'. Presumably, the Seleukids even regained Seleukia in Pieria; the city could only be maintained as an enclave by means of costly defences and, at any rate, it was to be of secondary importance in future relations between the great powers.[20] The king returned in triumph to Egypt and he rewarded the victorious army with 300,000 pieces of gold.[21] On the occasion of the victory celebrations in

Memphis, the most important priests of the country gathered for a large synod and they passed a decree on 15 November 217.[22]

By its great efforts in the war, the Ptolemaic kingdom had achieved a purely defensive aim and for the future Philopator could devote himself to the leisure which he sought. Antiochos III, on the other hand, was just beginning his activities. He recovered very swiftly from his defeat and from 216 to 213 concentrated his efforts on taking action against Achaios. As the latter's position became threatened, the Ptolemaic government attempted to support him (215/14 and 214/13) in various ways including military assistance from soldiers levied in Aetolia, but they were too late to help. With the fall of Achaios, Ptolemaic foreign policy also suffered a setback.[23]

The passivity of Philopator allowed Antiochos to achieve spectacular successes in the eastern satrapies from 212 to 205. Even the Maurya prince, Sophagasenos, and the Parthian king, Arsakes II, recognized Seleukid supremacy in the area. Antiochos now assumed the Achaemenid title of Great King (μέγας βασιλεύς) and, reminiscent of Alexander, was named 'Antiochos the Great'.

In order to be prepared for future clashes with the Seleukid kingdom, the Ptolemaic government avoided war on other fronts by promoting peace in areas where it was threatened. Sosibios tried to maintain relations with Greece[24] as they had been since the time of Euergetes I. To this end, Ptolemaic diplomats always attempted to intervene there as arbitrators. In the war known as the War of the Allies (220–217) where war broke out between the Hellenistic League under Macedonian leadership and the Aetolian League, Ptolemy IV, along with delegates from Chios, Rhodes and Byzantium, succeeded in bringing about the Peace of Naupaktos (Plb. V.100.9). During the First Macedonian War (215–205) between Rome and Philip V of Macedonia, Philopator's emissaries together with representatives from other neutral states attempted to mediate between the two warring sides. These attempts at negotiation took place on three occasions between 210 and 207, though the chronological details remain unclear (Plb. XI.4.1; Liv. XXVII.30.4–12; XXVIII.7.13f.).[25]

From the time Euergetes I had come to the aid of the Rhodians in 227/6, the friendship between the Ptolemies and the island state had developed further. Philopator was honoured with a statue there.[26] The Ptolemaic king made himself popular in other Greek cities as well by means of donations. In the city-sanctuary of Oropos in Boeotia, statues were erected in honour of Philopator and Arsinoe III.[27] The cities of Tanagra and Orchomenos even honoured Sosibios directly with a proxenos decree, since the latter had been responsible for a policy favourable to the Boeotians.[28] Philopator favoured the city of Gortyn on Crete (Str. X.4.11) with the construction of a city-wall there. As for the Ptolemaic foreign territories themselves, they remained untouched during the reign of Philopator.[29]

Philopator kept a neutral position in his relations with Rome and Carthage during the Second Punic War – unlike the Siwah oasis where the last priest-king known to us pursued his own political interests and in 207 was a general in the service of the Carthaginian army (Silen. XV.672f.).[30] Philopator, however, did grant asylum to the distinguished leader of the pro-Roman party from Capua, Decius Magius; Hannibal had sent him to Carthage after he had marched into Capua but his ship was driven on to the coast off Cyrene (Liv. XXIII.10.3–13). In 210, Roman ambassadors arrived at the Egyptian royal court wishing to renew their friendship with the Ptolemies and bringing gifts for the royal couple (Liv. XXVII.4.10). Rome was in serious difficulty at this time owing to the ravages wrought by Hannibal in Italy. It may be the same embassy which Polybius claims (IX.11a) had been sent by Rome to ask for grain. Whether or not the king granted their request is not known.

Relations between the Ptolemies and Hieron II of Syracuse (275/4–215) had always been fairly close. Hieron had formerly changed the name of his luxury ship from Συρακοσία to Ἀλεξανδρίς and had loaded it with grain and presented it to one of the Ptolemaic kings – perhaps Ptolemy III – as a gift (Athen. V.206d–209e). Syracuse was caught between two great powers, Rome and Carthage, and so had to secure support, if it was to maintain its independence. Hieronymos (215–4), the successor of Hieron II, entered into a coalition with Carthage and openly attempted to bring the Ptolemaic kingdom over to its side (Plb. VII.2.2.; Liv. XXIV.26). Philopator was given a way out of this awkward position when Hieronymos fell victim to a conspiracy in 214.[31]

As far as the character of Ptolemy IV is concerned, Polybius' portrait of the king (V.34; XIV.12) depicts him as responsible for the decline of his empire because of his neglect of administrative duties and his insatiable appetite for festivities. Polybios' verdict is based on the '*Histories*' of Phylarchos (FGrHist. 81), *the 'stories about Philopator'* by Ptolemy of Megalopolis (FGrHist. 161)[32] and the biography of Arsinoe by the elder Eratosthenes (FGrHist. 241F 16).[33] In all these accounts, we see a negative attitude toward court life – a milieu where the ideal of *tryphé* expected of the Ptolemaic ruler and the lavish lifestyle which was bound up with the worship of Dionysos increasingly held sway.[34] The palace ship of Philopator, yet another of those sensational luxury items which were meant to impress the rest of the world (Kallixeinos: FGrHist. 627F 1), is also worth mentioning in this regard.[35]

Like his predecessors, Philopator also showed a strong interest in literature. It is said that he himself composed a tragedy called '*Adonis*' and his minister, Agathokles, wrote the accompanying commentary (Schol. Ar. *Th.* 1059). Because of his love of Homer, the king financed a temple dedicated to him together with a cult in his honour in Alexandria (Ael. *VH* XIII.22).[36] There is evidence for a festival of the Muses in Alexandria under Philopator. The royal couple, moreover, were also special patrons of the Muses' festival celebrated in the valley of the Muses at the Boeotian city of Thespeia.[37]

In the spring or summer of 204,[38] Ptolemy IV died at almost 40 years of age. He left behind a son who was barely six years old and who had become 'co-regent' soon after he was born (9 October 210).[39]

Under Ptolemy IV, the kingdom could still display a brilliant façade stemming from its supremacy in the foreign politics of the eastern Mediterranean. The victory at the battle of Raphia, however, marked the close of a glorious era, the end of the 'century of the Ptolemies'. In the later years of Philopator's reign, the Ptolemaic empire began to totter on its feet like a colossus unsure of its step. The high costs of the Fourth Syrian War, the insurrections in southern Egypt and the establishment of a Theban pharaonic state (Chapter 5) had no doubt taken their toll on the vitality of Egypt's economy; the extent of the damage that these caused is still the subject of debate.[40] Following the death of Philopator, the Hellenistic state of the Ptolemies, in a dramatic decline, lost its pre-eminent rank in the world through domestic crises and aggression from abroad. Finally, by 169/8, it had been shaken to its roots.

## PTOLEMY V EPIPHANES (204–180) AND THE LOSS OF THE EASTERN MEDITERRANEAN EMPIRE

### Tutelary governments and foreign policy until the eve of the Fifth Syrian War

It is quite likely that Philopator's wish was that Arsinoe III take up the regency for the young king. The two most powerful men in the kingdom, Sosibios and Agathokles, who earlier had *de facto* run the administration of the empire, prevented this from occurring by having the queen murdered in secret. Thus passed away a highly educated Macedonian woman who had gazed aghast at her husband's Dionysian excesses (Eratosth.: FGrHisto. 241F 16) and eventually had been supplanted by his mistress Agathokleia. With only a child as king, the royal dynasty was no longer able to act. The rulers were paying dearly for the murders committed upon the accession of Philopator.

Sosibios and Agathokles summoned the Macedonian court-troops stationed at Alexandria for a military council held in the largest court of the royal palace. The council was composed of bodyguards and the palace guard together with infantry and cavalry officers (Plb. XV.25.3).[41] The death of the royal couple was announced to the group and in their presence, the royal child was adorned with the diadem and declared king. They then read the royal will which Polybius probably correctly judges to be spurious. It alleged that Philopator had made Sosibios and Agathokles guardians (ἐπίτροποι) of the young Ptolemy V. The youth was entrusted to the care of Agathokleia and her mother Oinanthe[42] who was still alive.

Sosibios died soon after this event. His exceptional ability as an organizer and diplomat had made him one of the most important political figures of the third century. The cold-blooded murders which he had instigated together with the intrigues devised by him represent a type of conduct that was quite characteristic of those involved in the power-struggles of the Hellenistic age. Agathokles was now the sole guardian of Ptolemy V; from the beginning, he had made himself hated and now he was held to be responsible for the murder of Arsinoe who had been much loved in Alexandria (Plb. XV.25.3–12).

Men who owing to their importance were held to be a potential threat by Agathokles were sent on diplomatic missions. Pelops,[43] who had been strategos of Cyprus from 217 until 204/3, was sent to negotiate with Antiochos III in Asia Minor. There the Seleukid king was pursuing his former ambition[44] of making territorial gains in the region. It mattered little to him whether these gains were made in areas of Attalid (Teos),[45] Antigonid (Alinda[46] in Karia) or Ptolemaic influence. Because of the crisis of government in Alexandria, Antiochos was able to add several Ptolemaic sites in Karia to his possessions without any risk, including Amyzon in the spring of 203.[47] Pelops is said to have protested against these acts and to have reminded the king of the terms of the agreement reached after Raphia and of the obligations of φιλία that these imposed (Plb. XV.25.13).

A son of the famous Sosibios, Ptolemy, travelled to see Philip V at Agathokles' behest to negotiate a dynastic union which had already been planned under Philopator. He was also to ask for Macedonian assistance should Antiochos III undertake a large offensive against the Ptolemaic empire (Plb. XV.25.13). Ptolemy of Megalopolis,[48] who was later (from 197 to 180) to become the strategos of Cyprus, had the task of announcing in Rome the change of government in Egypt and probably to make the senate privy to Antiochos the Great's mobilization in Asia Minor.

The diplomatic missions to Philip and Antiochos were not successful. On the contrary, the two came to a secret agreement in the winter of 203/2 to divide up the Ptolemaic empire; this meant, at the very least, that they would seek to acquire the foreign territories of the Ptolemies and to eliminate Ptolemaic hegemony in the eastern Mediterranean (Plb. III.2.8; XV.20; XVI.1.9 and 10.1; Liv. XXXI.14.5; App. *Mac.* 4.1; Just. XXX.2.8). Since ancient times, there has been much speculation concerning the actual contents of this agreement.[49]

In Alexandria, under the leadership of the strategos of Pelusion, Tlepolemos, there was growing opposition to the unscrupulous Agathokles. The 'Macedonian' troops were incessantly being drawn into court intrigues and invoked as legal authority. At the end of 203,[50] Agathokles was ousted and with his entire family was horribly murdered in the stadium by a mob of Alexandrians. Oinanthe, who had fled to the Thesmophoreion, i.e. to the temple of Demeter, was dragged out, led naked on a horse to the stadium and brutally killed (Plb. XV.25.20–XV.33). It was not uncommon in Alexandria for interested parties to induce the mob to vent its anger and to satisfy its lust for sensational events through such violent executions.[51]

Tlepolemos[52] took on the position of regent and along with the son of Sosibios, also named Sosibios,[53] became the guardian of Ptolemy V. After a short time, however, the younger Sosibios was stripped of this position. But soon there was general dissatisfaction with the remaining regent, since he was more interested in the pleasures of life than in the duties of the state (Plb. XVI.21–22). For this reason, already in 201 an earlier follower of Agathokles named Aristomenes[54] was able to take his place as guardian and regent; the fate of Tlepolemos is unknown.

## From the beginning of the Fifth Syrian War to the marriage at Raphia (202–194/3)

### *The end of Ptolemaic rule in Syria, Anatolia and Thrace*

Probably following the secret agreement with Philip V of Macedonia, Antiochos III gave up plans for any further activity in western Asia Minor and early in 202 (or in the early summer of 202) he began what is known today as the Fifth Syrian War.[55] He marched southwards staying to the east of Antilebanon and first conquered Damascus (Polyain. IV.15). It seems that once the government in Alexandria – then headed by Tlepolemos – learned of Antiochos' offensive it sent an embassy to Rome asking for support ( Just. XXX.2.8).[56] In the course of the year 201, Antiochos occupied large parts of Palestine without much difficulty and finally, after much resistance from the Ptolemaic garrison there, he also took Gaza. The coastal cities of Phoenicia remained in the hands of the Ptolemaic kingdom. The Ptolemaic governor, Ptolemaios, son of Thraseas, went over to the Seleukid side, probably because he was perturbed by the political instability in Alexandria. Inspired by the example of Theodotus in 219, he had reasonable hopes that he could thereby retain his holdings and position in the province. He was not disappointed by Antiochos; from 201, the former Ptolemaic commander-in-chief went by the title of strategos of the Seleukid province of 'Coele Syria and Phoenicia'.

In the winter of 201/200, the Ptolemaic general, Skopas,[57] succeeded in taking back almost all of the territory that had been lost along with Jerusalem (Plb. XVI.39.1; Porph.: FGrHist. 260 F 45–46). Damascus, on the other hand, remained Seleukid; this allowed Antiochos to launch his second offensive in 200 and to defeat Skopas' army at Panion (later known as Caesarea Philippi on the southern slope of Mt Hermon) in the summer of the same year (Plb. XVI.8–19, 22a, 19). Skopas retreated with 10,000 men to Sidon where he was besieged in the winter of 200/199. The Ptolemaic government was no longer able to come to his assistance with relief-troops or with a naval detachment and so he capitulated in 199 (perhaps at the beginning of the year or in the summer) and was allowed to depart unharmed. Henceforth, Sidon remained in Seleukid hands. Upon his return to Alexandria, Skopas was sent with considerable funds to Aetolia where he was to recruit troops and send them to Egypt in case of an invasion by Antiochos (Liv. XXXI.43.5–7). The Seleukid king, however, was quite content to look after matters in the province which he had just acquired and in the first half of

198 he turned his attention to extending his control over the rest of the former Ptolemaic province of 'Syria and Phoenicia' (Liv. XXXIII.19.8). For the local inhabitants, this did not represent much of a change, since the current and former governor, Ptolemaios, guaranteed a continuity in policy.

Philip V's offensive against Ptolemaic territories was closely connected with his undertakings in the Aegean and with the developments leading up to the Second Macedonian War (200–197). In 201, Philip was openly at war with Attalos of Pergamon and with the Rhodians; at the same time, he conquered the island of Samos which was an important naval base for the Ptolemaic fleet (Plb. III.2.8; XVI.2.9; Liv. XXXI.31.4; App. *Mac.* 4.1). Before 197, Macedonian occupying forces had to retreat when Ptolemaic forces reconquered the island.[58] Soon thereafter Samos regained its freedom through the intervention of the Rhodians (Liv. XXXIII.20.12).

In the autumn of 201, envoys from Pergamon and Rhodes arrived at Rome and issued complaints against Philip. In response, the senate sent an embassy of three men[59] to the east. Their first task was to go to Greece and to supervise the formation of a coalition against Macedonia. They were then to enquire into imminent developments in Syria and Egypt. In April/May, Athens joined the military coalition against Philip.[60] The Macedonian king paid no heed to a first ultimatum issued by Rome and so at the end of the spring/summer of 200 he went on to conquer Ptolemaic Thrace; Kallipolis (modern Turkish Gelibolu), Kypsela (modern Turkish Ipsala), Ainos and Maroneia were among the places taken (Liv. XXXI.1.3–6a). The *comitia* in Rome responded by declaring war against Philip should he refuse to comply with a new ultimatum which was to be presented to him by M. Aemilius Lepidus. Lepidus had just been in Rhodes with the three-man embassy and now in the autumn of 200 he travelled to Abydos on the Dardanelles, which Philip was besieging, to deliver the ultimatum (Plb. XVI.34). The Romans demanded that all hostilities against Greek states cease and that the Ptolemaic territories be left untouched (Plb. XVI.34.3).[61] Since it was apparent from the beginning that Philip would reject such an ultimatum, the Roman army landed practically at the same time (in October 200)[62] in Illyria; the Second Macedonian War had begun.

After fulfilling their duties with regard to Philip, the Roman embassy of 200 went to Alexandria and also paid Antiochos a visit. Although they were supposed to broker a peace between the two kingdoms should the possibility present itself (Plb. XVI.27.5), in Alexandria they only exchanged amicable words with their hosts (Liv. XXXI.2.3f.)[63] and, when they saw Antiochos, their efforts were directed at preventing him from forming an alliance with Philip against Rome. The Romans thus did nothing to further the cause of Ptolemaic Egypt; on the contrary, Antiochos could take advantage of the war between Philip and Rome and once again pursue Seleukid claims to Asia Minor.[64]

Soon after completing the annexation of Coele Syria in 198, the Seleukid king commenced his great campaign in Asia Minor in the spring of 197

(Plb. XVIII.39.3; Liv. XXXIII.19.8–20); starting from Cilicia he moved westwards with his army and navy. In Cilicia, according to our historical sources (Liv. XXXIII.20.4; Porph.: FGrHist. 260 F46), he conquered Mallos, Zephyrion, Soloi, Aphrodisias, Anemurion, Selinus and Korakesion. We know nothing of the situation in Pamphylia at this time, but it was certainly already Seleukid territory.[65] Lycia, as a whole, was still Ptolemaic, but it is said that now the following cities passed from Ptolemaic to Seleukid control: Korykos, Andriake, Limyra, Arykanda, Patara/Arsinoe and Xanthos (Porph.: FGrHist. 260 F46; Agatharchides: FGrHist. 86 F16). Even Telmessos fell into Antiochos' hands; under the sovereignty of the Ptolemies, the successors of Lysimachos had ruled there since the time of Ptolemy III.[66]

The Rhodians arrived in Karia before Antiochos (Liv. XXXIII.20.11–12); the land lay directly in their sphere of interest since part of it already belonged to the Rhodian Peraia. The Rhodians managed to obtain by negotiation the freedom of Kaunos, which they bought from the Ptolemaic state for around 200 talents (Plb. XXX.31.6), as well as of Myndos and Halikarnassos.[67]

Antiochos therefore turned to Ionia but had only limited success there. Philip V had already taken Miletus from the Ptolemies in 201; immediately after the Macedonian rule, the city gained its independence. In the autumn of 197, the Seleukid king was able to conquer the city of Ephesos, a powerful and well-garrisoned Ptolemaic base which was transformed into his winter headquarters for that year (Plb. XVIII.40a; Liv. XXXIII.38.1; Porph.: FGrHist. 260 F 46).

As we have already seen, at the beginning of the Second Macedonian War, Rome represented the interests of the Ptolemaic kingdom in negotiations with Macedonia. At the conference of Nicaea in November 198, T. Quinctius Flamininus required of Philip that he return all cities taken from the Ptolemies from the time of Philopator's death (Plb. XVIII.1.14; Liv. XXII.33.4). In 197, Flamininus defeated Philip at Kynoskephalai in Thessaly and sought a quick settlement, no doubt because Seleukid gains in Asia Minor were becoming a matter needing urgent attention. In the peace of 196 between Rome and Macedonia, the Thracian cities were no longer part of the negotiations since Flamininus had given them their freedom. In the meantime, Antiochos III had left Ephesos and had arrived on European soil in the spring of 196. The Seleukid empire had risen to become the greatest power in the Hellenistic world.

In Alexandria, on the other hand, there was growing frustration with the weakness of the Ptolemaic kingdom; it seemed of vital importance to restore the power of the kingship. The leading man at court was still Aristomenes. In 197, Polykrates of Argos[68] arrived in the capital. He was an officer whose mettle had already been tested at Raphia and who in recent years (203–197) had proven himself as strategos and archiereus of Cyprus. He was also the one who in 197 organized the so-called Anakleteria to celebrate the coming

*Figure 4.1* Miniature alabaster head of the young Ptolemy V with double crown and lock of childhood. Height 10 cm; from Egypt. Berlin, Staatliche Museen Preussischer Kulturbesitz, Agyptisches Museum Inv. 14568; Kyrieleis (1975), E 1 (p. 54, 172), pl. 41

of age of the young Ptolemy who at the time was barely 13 years old. On that occasion, he gave the king a large sum which he had obtained through careful management of Cyprus (Plb. XVIII.55.3–6). In Memphis on 26 March 196, the high priest of Ptah crowned the young Ptolemy V Epiphanes pharaoh[69] (Fig. 4.1). Quite in keeping with the unstable conditions of court-life at the time, Polykrates now supplanted Aristomenes as the leading figure at court and came to acquire much property (Plb. XVIII.55.7). The latter fell in disfavour with the king in the following years (196 and 192) and was eventually compelled to take poison (Diod. XXVIII.14; Plu. *Mor.* 71 c–d).

Probably at the close of 197, the Alexandrian government had lodged its complaints in Rome concerning the conquests of Antiochos III (App. *Syr.* 2). In 196 on the occasion of the Isthmian games, Flamininus made a public announcement granting freedom to the Greek states. The Roman senate then sent a man of consular rank, L. Cornelius Lentulus, east to put an end to the conflicts between Antiochos III and the Ptolemaic kingdom (Plb. XVIII.49.2–3; Liv. XXXIII.39.1). Lentulus, together with three members of a Roman commission of 10 men set up to promote peace in Greece, brought the list of Roman demands to the Seleukid king in Lysimacheia on the Hellespont in the autumn of 196 or at the beginning of 195 (Plb. XXVIII.49–52; Liv. XXXIII.39.1–41.3; App. *Syr.* 3). Among these conditions was the stipulation to 'evacuate the cities subject to Ptolemy which he had recently acquired for himself in Asia' (Plb. XVIII.50.5). Since this was clearly a peacemaking mission, the return of the conquered territory will have been meant quite literally. The Romans represented Ptolemaic interests in negotiations with Antiochos, just as they had with Philip, at the request of the Alexandrian court. To be sure, while the Romans did negotiate on behalf of Egypt, they were not really looking after its interests. What is clear is that at the turn of the third century the Ptolemaic kingdom entered slowly and imperceptibly into the Roman sphere of influence.

Antiochos, in his turn, had prepared a diplomatic manoeuvre in Lysimacheia which was a stroke of genius. He announced that he was just about to conclude a pact of friendship with Ptolemy and that a marriage-tie between the two had been planned (Plb. XVIII.51.10; Liv. XXXIII.40.3). How far these particular negotiations between the Seleukid and Alexandrian courts had progressed remains unclear; it is evident, however, that the Romans had been unaware of their existence. Suddenly a false rumour of the death of Epiphanes arrived in Lysimacheia and this brought a halt to the proceedings of the peace conference. Antiochos even attempted to capitalize on the element of suprise and take the island of Cyprus in the confusion that ensued; he was not successful, however, because of a stormy sea (Liv. XXXIII.4.1; App. *Syr.* 4).

In the following year, 195, however, the daughter of Antiochos III, Cleopatra, was engaged to Ptolemy Epiphanes. The wedding was celebrated in the winter of 194/3 in Raphia (Liv. XXXV.13.4; Porph: FGrHist. 260 F47). The 16 year-old king was now wedded to Cleopatra I, a bride of approximately 10 years old who was called 'the Syrian' (ἡ Σύρα; App. *Syr.* 5) because of her background and natural allegiance to the Seleukids.

In view of these events, the Romans no longer concerned themselves with the claims of the Ptolemies, probably because the Alexandrian administration had given up their possessions in Asia as part of the peace settlement with Antiochos (195).[70] The loss of the Anatolian territories as well as of Coele Syria (particularly the trade centres of Tyre and Sidon) was to have serious economic consequences for the Ptolemaic kingdom. As a result, efforts were made from the end of the 190s (from 192/1) to have Cyprus fill the role of the lost Coele Syria. Since Paphos was easily reached from Alexandria, it followed Salamis as a new administrative centre for all of Cyprus.[71]

## Foreign policy and the royal house in the last years of Epiphanes' reign

Toward the end of the 190s, the Ptolemaic administration attempted to renew ties with Rome. Following their declaration of the freedom of the Greek cities, which was promulgated at the Dardanelles, the Romans intervened in the disputes between Greek cities that had flared up on account of the war against Antiochos III (known as the War of Antiochos: 192–188). A Ptolemaic embassy in Rome (191) offered financial support and even offered to send an army to Aetolia;[72] the senate refused (Liv. XXXVI.4.1–3). After the Roman victory at Thermopylae in 191, envoys from the Egyptian royal couple went to Rome again, this time to offer congratulations and to demonstrate their willingness to support Rome in the war in every way (Liv. XXXVII.3.9–11). The Romans once again did not respond to their overtures. The final result was that the two great Hellenistic kingdoms remaining had fooled only themselves. In spite of the dynastic union, Antiochos III did not succeed in persuading the Ptolemaic court to maintain a neutral position regarding events in Asia Minor. The Ptolemies, for their part, had failed for a second time in their efforts to preserve their own interests in Asia by associating themselves with Rome in the war against Antiochos. Thus, in 188, when Rome concluded the peace of Apameia with Antiochos, the issue of Ptolemaic claims in Asia Minor was not even raised. The city of Ephesos, which formerly had been in Ptolemaic hands, and a major part of Seleukid Asia Minor west of Tauros, were awarded to the kingdom of Pergamon. Lycia and Karia south of the Meander which had previously belonged to the Ptolemies went to Rhodes (Plb. XXI.45.8; Liv. XXXVIII.39). Pergamon and Rhodes had energetically supported the Romans.

The Ptolemaic government now had again to devise an independent policy to regain its supremacy in the eastern Mediterranean and more specifically in Coele Syria. In the middle of 187, Antiochos the Great was killed while plundering a temple of Bel near Susa by the outraged inhabitants of the area. He was succeeded by a weak king, Seleukos IV, who ruled from 187–175.

In 185, we find Aristonikos[73] the eunuch, a friend of Epiphanes from early childhood (σύντροφος) (Plb. XXII.22), in Greece recruiting soldiers. He is the first palace eunuch to play an active role in the history of Ptolemaic Egypt. Before this, he had already had a career as a diplomat, as a priest of Alexander in 187/6 and even as a cavalry commander. Before the middle of 182, Aristonikos led a naval expedition to Syria, more specifically to the area surrounding Apameia and to the island of Arados. From there he is said to have returned with an abundance of booty.[74] This expedition presented the concrete motive for the Syrian War planned by Epiphanes.

Meanwhile, the Ptolemaic administration went about making friends in Greece; most importantly, it renewed former treaties with the Achaean League and even sent monetary gifts in 185 (Plb. XXII.3.5–9; XXII.9). A few years later, Ptolemy V promised the league ten fully equipped groups of fifty rowers. In 180, envoys of the league were nominated to go to Egypt and receive this gift; among them was Polybius who was around 20 years old at the time. But the embassy was prevented from setting off on its journey, because news had arrived of the death of Epiphanes (Plb. XXIV.6).

Since the king lacked the means to finance the reconquest of Coele Syria, it is said that he had been intimating that he would lay claim to the income of his friends for this purpose. In reaction to these veiled threats, his generals poisoned him in the spring of 180[75] (Diod. XXIX.29; Porph.: FGrHist. 260 F48).

Epiphanes died at about 30 years of age. We are told that he showed an interest in athletic games (Plb. XXVII.9.7) and was even capable himself of great physical accomplishments in hunting, riding and fencing (Plb. XXII.3.8–9). It is said that after the death of Aristomenes the king's character grew increasingly worse (Diod. XXVIII.14).[76]

In about 186,[77] Cleopatra I had given birth to her eldest son who later would be Ptolemy VI Philometor. The birthdates of the two younger siblings, namely of the future Ptolemy VIII Euergetes II as well as of Cleopatra II, are not clear. Sharing the fate of Arsinoe III, Cleopatra I, who was around 24 years old at the time, found herself alone as queen of her land with two children who were underage.

During the reign of the fifth Ptolemy, the kingdom underwent a fateful development. The first decade was characterized by the complete crippling of the royal house owing to the young age of Epiphanes and to the fact that he had been placed in the custody of guardians who were unscrupulous and changed in quick succession. Thus it is quite clear that it was the most influential families who steered the fate of the kingdom under the fourth and fifth Ptolemies. This aristocracy which came to exercise great power in the state apparatus came from the most diverse regions of the Greek world. They were, therefore, not intimately bound to their new homeland but for the same reason were all the more beholden to the royal house and to the state machinery. The relations between the king and the upper classes determined the court hierarchy, which had begun to take shape from the time of Epiphanes and could be best discerned in the titles indicating a person's rank at court. Egyptian families succeeded in entering court society only from the late second century.[78]

During the first decade of Ptolemy V's rule, the empire lost the majority of its foreign possessions in Asia and Europe; all that remained was Cyprus, Cyrenaica and the Aegean bases of Itanos, Thera and Methana.[79] The Alexandrian court had gambled away Rome's willingness to intercede on its behalf – which was already half-hearted in itself – by its hasty alliance with Antiochos the Great. The increasing number of uprisings taking place within Egypt and the loss of the Thebaïd (Chapter 5) must certainly have been factors contributing to the kingdom's weakness abroad. Although the situation at court after the death of Epiphanes was comparable to conditions after Philopator passed away, the decline of the royal house had progressed so far that the prospect of reversing this trend had now vanished for good.

## THE FIRST YEARS OF PTOLEMY VI PHILOMETOR AND THE SIXTH SYRIAN WAR (180–168)

After the death of his father, the six-year-old prince, Ptolemy VI, was easily accepted as king by the Alexandrian elite; his mother, the royal widow Cleopatra I, succeeded in assuming his guardianship as well as being officially established as regent. This is attested in papyri dating to the early 170s; in the dating formulae Cleopatra I is named before her son as 'Θεὰ Επιφανής', her son, on the other hand, still lacks the title of 'θεός'.[80] As regent she was permitted to have coins minted which bore her name. The success of Cleopatra stands in marked contrast to the unhappy fate of Arsinoe III, who had been murdered in the transition from the fourth to the fifth Ptolemy. As regent, Cleopatra, who was friendly to the Seleukids, immediately put an end to the preparations for war against her brother Seleukos IV.

The death of Cleopatra I in the spring of 176[81] was a severe setback for the Ptolemaic kingdom and engendered a catastrophic change of policy. From the ranks of court members, two incompetent candidates emerged as the guardians and leaders of the state: a former Syrian slave named Lenaios and the eunuch Eulaios who probably was also of eastern descent. The latter had been assigned as a kind of nurse to the sixth Ptolemy when the royal heir was in his early youth (Porph.: FGrHist. 260 F49). Eulaios obviously had the higher rank of the two guardians, since he was the main counsellor of the young king (Plb. XXVIII.20.5.21.1); he did not even hesitate to put his name on copper and silver coins.[82]

Both regents immediately tried to strengthen the authority of the royal child entrusted to them in order to increase the importance of their own positions. It was quite clear to them that under constitutional law their own political status rested on very shaky ground. They granted him the title of a god[83] while the princess Cleopatra II appeared as the 'basilissa' or 'queen'.[84] Soon afterwards (still before 15 April 175)[85] the marriage of the two under-age siblings was celebrated.

With their foreign policy aimed at the reconquest of Coele Syria, Eulaios and Lenaios eventually brought the state to the brink of destruction. In the Seleukid kingdom, Antiochos IV Epiphanes (175–164), the brother of Seleukos IV and Cleopatra I, ruled from the autumn of 175. Not long after his accession to the throne, he was represented by an envoy, the Milesian Apollonios, on the occasion of a great festival in Alexandria (between 174 and 172). This envoy was able to observe the new attitude at the Alexandrian court which was now clearly hostile to the Seleukids. Antiochos IV immediately introduced the necessary security measures and positioned troops in the border area between Syria and Palestine (II Macc. 4.21f.). Moreover, at the beginning of 173 he sent the same Apollonios to Rome with an embassy[86] to request a renewal of the *societas et amicitia* which had arisen between them with the peace of Apameia in 188. The Seleukid king was greatly in arrears in paying the indemnities imposed on him by Rome and so he sent an especially large sum with the embassy in 173. Clearly he wished to secure favourable diplomatic relations between himself and Rome in the face of an impending clash with the Ptolemaic kingdom. Confronted with Egypt's intentions to go to war, he may have increasingly come to hope that he would emerge out of this conflict as the leader of the Ptolemaic kingdom. No doubt he was encouraged in this by the fact that the Egyptian kingdom was in a lamentable state under the leadership of the underage royal couple; equally encouraging was the fact that he happened to be their uncle.

In Macedonia, King Perseus succeeded Philip V in 179. The new king soon attempted to break his political isolation by means of diplomatic manoeuvres and to establish finally a large Hellenistic coalition against Rome (Plb. XXIX.4.7–10; Liv. XLII.26.8; XLIV.24).[87] In response, in 173/2 Rome sent out embassies to the east to find out what conditions were like in Macedonia and Greece and to test the mood in Pergamon, Syria and Egypt (Liv. XLII.6.4–5) regarding the upcoming clash between Rome and Macedonia. For Rome, this also meant renewing existing *amicitiae* everywhere possible or, at the very least, obtaining a guarantee of neutrality. In Alexandria, the Roman envoys received assurances of support but they also noticed the preparations for war against Antiochos IV undertaken by the two guardians of the king (Liv. XLII.26.8; 29.7). They did not attempt to interfere in these. Obviously, a war between Egypt and Syria would have been welcome to the senate given the prospect of war with Perseus. Soon thereafter the Third Macedonian War (171–168) began.

At the same time, the developments leading to the Sixth Syrian War (turn 170/69–168) pursued their course.[88] Without having taken the necessary military preparations, the regents seem to have promised the Alexandrians at a mass assembly (Diod. XXX.16) the swift acquisition of Coele Syria and perhaps even of the entire Seleukid empire. As part of the propaganda of their operation, they proclaimed between 5 October and 12 November of 170 the common rule of the three Ptolemaic siblings, that is of Ptolemy VI Philometor, his sister-wife Cleopatra II and of their younger brother Ptolemy VIII. Official reckoning of the king's reign had to be changed because of this new development; the year in progress was no longer taken to be the twelfth year of Philometor's rule but the first year of joint-rule.[89] Soon thereafter, the Anakleteria was celebrated in honour of the coming of age of Philometor (Plb. XXVIII.12.8–9).

The remaining chronology of events of the winter of 170/69 is unclear. During this period, Seleukid as well as Ptolemaic envoys were sent to Rome on goodwill missions (Plb. XXVIII.1; Diod. XXX.2). Antiochos' representatives complained about the war started by Ptolemy and insisted that the Seleukid kingdom was entitled to Coele Syria by virtue of Antiochos' conquest.

The Ptolemaic envoys were sent with the express purpose of observing the negotiations of the opposing party and were even predisposed to arrange a peace between Rome and Perseus. From this latter goal, at any rate, they were urgently dissuaded by the *princeps senatus* of the time, M. Aemilius Lepidus.[90] The senate in the end tried to placate both parties without committing himself unduly. Rome's forces were now bound to the war with Perseus.

During these negotiations, it was assumed that the war had already begun and that Egypt was the aggressor. In actual fact, the Egyptian army probably marched against Syria only after these events.[91] Antiochos was better prepared; he even had a navy and elephants (I *Macc.* 1.17) and this despite the fact that both of these weapons of war had been forbidden to the Seleukid kingdom since Apameia (Plb. XXI.42.12f.). He was the first to cross his borders and defeated the Ptolemaic army between Pelusion and Mount Kasios (Porph.: FGrHist. 260 F 49a). After his victory and a brief cease-fire, Antiochos was able to take the fortress of Pelusion by a ruse (Plb. XXVIII.18).

The fate of the incompetent regents, Eulaios[92] and Lenaios, was thereby sealed. Komanos and Kineas[93] took their place as the advisers of Philometor and the leading figures at court. Komanos in particular had proved his worth during the domestic clashes which erupted in the reign of Epiphanes.[94] The king's council was convened and it was decided that a deputation, made up of the envoys then present in Alexandria from the various Greek states, be sent to see Antiochos together with representatives from the Ptolemaic government (Plb. XXVIII.19).

In the meantime, Antiochos had occupied a large part of Lower Egypt and attempted to win over with gifts the inhabitants there, especially the Greeks from Naukratis. He discussed the problem of Coele Syria with the mixed embassy from Alexandria from the historical perspective of the Seleukids. He cited the acquisition of the land by Antigonos Monophthalmos, its legal status after the battle of Ipsos (301) and its conquest by Antiochos III in the Fifth Syrian War. He also rebutted the version promulgated at that time by the Alexandrian court alleging that Cleopatra I had brought Coele Syria to Egypt as part of her dowry in her marriage to Ptolemy V.[95] He let it be known that he would make his decision only after the envoys which he had sent to Alexandria had returned. Subsequently, he moved toward the capital to keep the pressure on the government there (Plb. XXVIII.20).

The Syrian envoys in Alexandria managed to negotiate a meeting between the two kings; so great was the trust which Philometor and his advisers had come to have in Antiochos IV. The young Ptolemy went to his uncle's camp where an agreement was reached, the contents of which are not known. Antiochos now posed as the protector of Philometor, all the while, as it is said, deceiving him in the most blatant fashion (Plb. XXX.26.9; Diod. XXX.18.2).[96]

But Alexandria yielded neither to the terms of Philometor's agreement nor to Seleukid power. The Alexandrians once again acclaimed his younger brother king (Plb. XXIX.23.4; Porph.: FGrHist. 260 F 2.7) and thereby replaced the rule of the three siblings with a new regime; the nominal position as 'queen' of the 11- to 12-year-old Cleopatra II remained unchanged (cf. Liv. XLIV.19.9 and 12). This stubborn resistance gave Antiochos the opportunity to besiege the Mediterranean metropolis under the guise of representing Philometor's interests. Despite the vast quantity of supplies in warehouses and the possibility of obtaining provisions from overseas contacts, the city must have soon been faced with shortages.

The Alexandrian court then sent an embassy to the Roman senate in the summer of 169 to try its luck at persuading the Romans to intervene (Liv. XLIV.19.6–12). Once again, the Ptolemaic government had been compelled to move in a direction which would later bring it under the controlling influence of Rome.[97] The senate perhaps then assigned to T. Numisius the task of negotiating between the two warring parties, though no results came of this (Plb. XXIX.25.3–4). Rome was still involved in the war against Perseus and Antiochos probably knew that for the time being there was no danger of Roman military intervention in Egypt.

Alexandria was lucky. The effects of the Nile inundation in the Delta must have slowly become perceptible and caused difficulties for all military operations. The defence of the city was, moreover, excellently organized. Antiochos attempted an assault which the Alexandrians were able to fend off (Liv. XLV.11.1; Porph.: FGrHist. 260 F 49b). Antiochos had to return to Syria in the autumn of 169, evidently on account of domestic difficulties in Syria or Palestine.[98] He had left behind the elder Ptolemy in Memphis hoping that he would continue the campaign against his brother. Antiochus also continued to keep Pelusion under siege (Liv. XLV.11; Diod. XXXI.1).

The way was now open for a reconciliation between the three Ptolemaic siblings. Contrary to the expectations of the Seleukid king, the elder Ptolemy went to Alexandria and joint rule was re-established along with the practice of reckoning dates on the basis of the reign of the three siblings. Since they were certainly expecting another invasion from the Seleukids, the Ptolemaic government turned to the Achaean League for help. But because of the objections of the pro-Roman party, the league contented itself with sending delegates to mediate (Plb. XXIX.23–25). Perhaps at this time, envoys from Egypt had just arrived in Rome (Just. XXXIV.2.7–3.1). Following the chronology of Livy (XLIV.19.1), however, the Alexandrian embassy from the summer of 169 was still in Rome in January of 168 and it brought its requests before the *curia*. In response, the senate sent a deputation east under the leadership of C. Popilius Laenas to observe events and to make a decision regarding the Syrian-Egyptian conflict which would be in Rome's favour and would not provoke a new war for the Romans (Liv. XLIV.19.13f.).[99]

Antiochos obviously took the reconcilation between the Ptolemaic siblings as a breach of the agreement which he had forced on Philometor. He refused the treaty of alliance offered by Perseus in the winter of 169/8 (Liv. XLIV.24), since he did not want to lose Rome's favour completely. Instead, he rushed to take the Ptolemaic kingdom by surpise, before matters between Rome and Macedonia could be settled.

Antiochos IV moved against Egypt in the spring of 168. He sent part of his infantry accompanied by a naval escort to Egypt while a fleet together with some land-forces was dispatched to Cyprus. The Cypriot venture was completely successful (Plb. XXIX.27.10; Liv. XLV.11.9). After having capitulated, the Ptolemaic strategos, Ptolemy 'Makron',[100] handed over the island to the Seleukids and went into their service (II Macc. 10.12f.). The Ptolemaic administration sent a deputation to the borders of Egypt to confer with the Selukid king himself concerning his conditions for peace. Antiochos IV probably had Rome in mind when he asked only for Cyprus, Pelusion and the land around it (Liv. XLV.11.10f.); he was well aware that Rome would have opposed any effort to unite the two Hellenistic empires. The Ptolemaic side rejected his ultimatum, since it would have left to Egypt only a formal independence from the favour of the Seleukid king.

Although Antiochos must have been well aware of what he could now expect from Rome, he quickly occupied the northern part of Egypt (at least the Delta and Fayum) and moved into Memphis without a battle. There the local organization was entrusted to one of his men who perhaps now acted as governor.[101] There were also some raids, as the partial destruction of a temple of Ammon in the Fayum attests.[102] Acting as basileus, Antiochos imposed a *prostagma* on the kleruchoi in the Fayum[103] and thus showed that toward the end of the spring of 168 he was the *de facto* ruler of the Egyptian chora. Somewhat problematic is the account (Porph.: FGrHist. 260 F49a–b) which represents Antiochos IV as having received the kingdom in Memphis 'following the Egyptian custom' (*ex more Aegypti*); this would mean that on this occasion he was crowned pharaoh. It seems more likely that Antiochos tried to establish a Seleukid protectorate over Egypt and did this officially in the name of his nephew Ptolemy VI.[104] This arrangement would then have been made legitimate through some kind of agreement with the priests of Memphis. Whatever the case may be, Antiochos IV now approached Alexandria with his armed forces for the second time.

On the Roman front, C. Popilius Laenas had taken up quarters on the island of Delos. There he received the news of the Roman victory at Pydna over Perseus of Macedonia (22 June 168) as well as Antiochos' march on Alexandria. The situation was ideal for Popilius Laenas to intervene in this conflict and so a Roman embassy made its way to Egypt (Liv. XLIV.29.1; XLV.2–3). It met with Antiochos at Eleusis, a suburb of Alexandria (see Map 3), and there, at the beginning of July 168 on what is now known as 'the day of Eleusis', a scene was played out which was to be made famous in the works of numerous authors (Plb. XXIX, 27; Liv. XLV, 12; Diod. XXXI, 2 among others).[105] Popilius refused to acknowledge Antiochos' greeting and presented him with the Roman ultimatum which was very straightforward in its demand: the immediate cessation of the war and complete withdrawal from Egypt in the shortest time possible. When Antiochos asked for time to consider, Popilius drew a circle with a stick around the king and 'bade him to give his answer to the note within the circle' (Plb. XXIX.27.5). The humiliated Seleukid king agreed to the ultimatum and acted accordingly.

An ostrakon informs us that Antiochos departed from Egypt on 30 July 168, crossing the sea from the city of Pelusion.[106] We are further told that Popilius also settled domestic matters in Egypt by exhorting the sibling kings to maintain the peace. It was clear to the Roman diplomat that the joint rule of the three Ptolemies contained the seeds of future strife. After-wards, the Roman envoys went to Cyprus and enforced the removal of the Syrian army from the island.

The arrogant and humbling measures taken by Popilius Laenas in Eleusis became the stuff of history. His course of action made the best of the element of surprise and was in fact extremely shrewd. If he had been given time to deliberate, the king might have rejected the ultimatum and Rome was certainly not interested in starting a war against the powerful Seleukid army in Egypt or Syria.[107] Thus a mere Roman delegation, emboldened by the victory at Pydna, managed to save the Ptolemaic kingdom in 168. Although the Ptolemaic kings went on to rule as independently as they had done prior to the Sixth Syrian War, the power of Rome had become so strong that henceforth their help was sought in conflicts and even in internal dynastic matters. In the future, the Ptolemaic kingdom would be as much under Roman sway as the rest of the Hellenistic world.

As a follow-up to the Roman embassy of Popilius Laenas, an Alexandrian deputation was sent to Rome to relay the thanks of the Ptolemaic kings to the senate. The embassy was led by a well-known man named Numenios[108] (Plb. XXX.16.1; Liv. XLV.13.4–8); he was one of the philoi of the kings bearing the title of archisomatophylax and in 165/4 was an eponymous priest for the cult of Ptolemy I Soter in Ptolemais. The report of his trip to Rome in a demotic text written ten years later (158) represents the oldest reference to the city of Rome in an Egyptian text.[109]

## Notes

1 The distinction between accession to the throne and coronation ceremony is strictly maintained in the liturgy of Edfu under Ptolemy IV; see M.-Th. Derchain-Urtel: LÄ VI, 1986, 532.

2 See p. 168 and SEG VII, 326 [probably from 219, cf. Lanciers (1988, 2), 31]; concerning the name 'Philopator' for the crown prince, cf. Huß (1976), 264.

3 Lanciers (1988, 2).

4 PP I and VIII.48; III and IX.5272; VI.17239; Mooren (1975), 63–66 (018); Huß (1976), 242–251.

5 See p. 54 with note 101.

6 PP VI.14576; Mooren (1975), 67f. (020).

7 PP VI.14714.

8 See pp. 129–130, cf. 145. On the programme and politics of Antiochos the Great: Schmitt (1964), 85–107; on the date of his accession to the throne see p. 72, note 101.

9 PP VI.15045.

10 See p. 48, 51.

11 Huß (1976), 20–83; Will, II (1982), 29–40; Grainger (1991), 90–97.

12 PP II.2150, 2160, 2161 (= VI.15204), 2165, 2172 (= VI.15065: Polykrates of Argos; see p. 138, 157), 2178, 2182.

13 E.g. at Gaza and in the Chremonidean War; see p. 25, 18 with notes, 76, 33 respectively. Concerning the question of Egyptians in the army and the concept of machimoi cf. Goudriaan (1988), 121–125; J. K. Winnicki, 'Das ptolemäische und das hellenistische Heerwesen', in *Egitto* (1989), 213–230.

14 Grainger (1991), 95.

15 F. Zayadine, 'La campagne d'Antiochos III le Grand en 219/217 et le siège de Rabbatamana', in *Akten des XIII. Internationalen Kongresses für Klassische Archäologie, Berlin 1988*, Mainz 1990, 433f.

16 The Ptolemaic phalanx was made up of 25,000 'Macedonians', 20,000 Egyptians and 3,000 Libyans; on the structure of both armies cf. Huß (1976), 60–62.

17 Raphia Decree, l.11,37: Thissen (1966), 15, 22f., 53.

18 On the source used by Polybius for the description of the battle of Raphia which is favourable to the Ptolemies cf. Marasco (1979–80), 176f. and Huß (1976), 8–20; on the image of the pharaoh at the battle of Raphia see also the Raphia Decree, lines 10–15: Thissen (1966), 13f., 53–57.

19 Raphia Decree, ll.23–25: Thissen (1966), 19, 60–63; Huß (1976), 74–77.

20 In 204/3 the city is attested as being Seleukid: P. Herrmann, 'Antiochos der Große und Teos', *Anadolu* 9, 196, 40, l.103.

21 Raphia Decree, ll.27–30; Greek version, A, ll.1–22: Thissen (1966), 20f., 64f.

22 See p. 162f.

23 Huß (1976), 88–94.

24 For a summary of the Greek policy of the Ptolemies under Philopator: Huß (1976), 103–131.

25 Cf. Gruen (1984), 677; Hammond, Walbank (1988), 403.

26 IG XII.1.37.

27 IG VII.298.

28 IG VII.507 (Tanagra), 3166 (Orchomenos).

29 Most of the sources dating to Philopator come from Lesbos. For Lesbos cf. P. Brun, 'Les Lagides à Lesbos', *ZPE* 85 (1991), 99–113.

30 Kuhlmann (1988), 97, 106.

31 Huß (1976), 173–175.

32 Concerning Ptolemy of Megalopolis see p. 135.

33 Cl. Préaux, 'Polybe et Ptolémée Philopator', *ChronEg* 40.80, 1965, 364–375; Marasco (1979–80).

34 See p. 171.

35 F. Caspari, 'Das Nilschiff Ptolemaios' IV', *JdI* 31, 1916, 1–74; Grimm (1981), 17.

36 Cf. Fraser (1972), I.611; II.862, note 423. There were also shrines dedicated to Homer in the Greek world: ibid., I.313.

37 Fraser (1972), I.313,316; II.467, note 55.

38 The last document dated by Philopator: 22 July 204; cf. G. Casanova, 'Una datazione tardiva di Tolemeo IV e il banchiere Protos di Crocodilopolis', *Aegyptus* 68, 1988, 13–18. Philopator may have been already dead for some time at that point since his death was kept secret for a long time (Just. XXX.2.6). The

'taking over of his father's kingship' by Ptolemy V on the 17th Mecheir (end of March) mentioned in the Rosetta Stone should be placed, in my opinion (as well as that of Koenen (1977), 73–75), with the coronation of 196 and not with the accession to the throne of 204 (following Abel (1983)). The first text dated by Epiphanes is from 8 September 204: UPZ 1, no. 112; Samuel (1962), 111–114.

39  Cf. Pestman (1967), 36; Will, II (1982), 110. The birthday of Ptolemy V (30th of Mesore) is found in the Rosetta Stone: Urk. II.194.1.

40  E. Lanciers, 'Ägyptisches Brot (k$^c$k$^c$) in UPZ I 149 und die wirtschaftliche Lage zur Zeit Ptolemaios' IV. Philopator', *ZPE* 82, 1990, 89–92.

41  The court troops in Alexandria (οἱ Μακεδόνες) perhaps mostly derived from descendants of Macedonian-born men but will have already been supplemented by men of other origins; cf. Hammond (1989), 284; see also p. 58.

42  P.P. VI.14731; Oinanthe was the mother of both Agathokles and Agothokleia – on the power structure at court following the death of Philopator cf. the model found in Mooren (1985), 216.

43  P.P. VI.15064; Michaelidou-Nicolaou (1976), 96f. (Π 18); Bagnall (1976), 252f.

44  See p. 128.

45  Herrmann, loc. cit. (p. 308, note 20), 29–160.

46  J. and L. Robert, *Fouilles d'Amyzon en Carie, I, Paris* 1983, 146–154.

47  Ibid., 132–137; on Antiochos in Karia: Schmitt (1964), 245f.

48  PP VI.15068, 16944; Michaelidou-Nicolaou (1976), 103 (Π 59); Bagnall (1976), 45, 255f.; on Ptolemy as a historian see p. 133.

49  Cf. Schmitt (1964), 237–261; Walbank II (1967), 471–473; Klose (1972), 84f.; Will, II (1982), 114–118; Hammond, Walbank (1988), 412.

50  Abel (1983), 283–286.

51  Cf. A. Jähne, 'Politische Aktivität der Bevölkerung Alexandreias am Ende des 3 Jh. v. u. Z. (nach Polybios)', *Klio* 58, 1976, 405–423.

52  PP I.50; VI.14634.

53  Sosibios II: PP I.12; Mooren (1975), 75f. (035).

54  PP I.19; III.5020; VI.14592; Mooren (1975), 76f. (036); id. (1977), 51–61. Aristomenes was the priest of Alexander in 204/3 and a somatophylax in 203.

55  Still a basic source: Holleaux (1908); further: Will, II (1982), 118–121; Gera (1987); Grainger (1991), 99–104.

56  Heinen (1972, 1), 644; according to Gruen (1984), 679 the passage is uncertain. Ptolemy of Megalopolis (see p. 135) had possibly already sought assistance from Rome: Will, II (1982), 111, 120.

57  Aetolian general who served under the Ptolemies after his third time as strategos (205/4): PP II.2177; VI.15241; On his fate (condemned in Alexandria and executed in prison): Plb. XVIII.53–55.1.

58  Schmitt (1964), 257f.

59  The evidence for this embassy can be found in Knibbe (1958), 23.

60  Habicht (1982), 142–150.

61  Cf. D. Golan, 'Autumn 200 BC: The events at Abydos', *Athenaeum*, n.s. 63, 1985, 389–404.

62  As per Will, II (1982), 134.

63  In a series of later historiographical documents (although not in Polybios nor in Livy) mention is made of a guardianship (*tutela*) which M. Aemilius Lepidus

is said to have undertaken at that time for Ptolemy V. It may perhaps be a family legend of the Lepidi stemming from the mid-first century BC. On this much discussed issue: Otto (1934), 27–29; Heinen (1972,1), 647–650; Huß (1976), 168–170; Gruen (1984), 680–682; A. R. Meadows, 'Greek and Roman diplomacy on the eve of the Second Macedonian War', *Historia* 42, 1993, 40–60 (argues for the historicity of the *tutela*).

64 Will, II (1982), 120; Gruen (1984), 682.

65 See p. 50 as well as Schmitt (1964), 279.

66 See p. 38 as well as Huß (1976), 192f.

67 This also applies to Samos, see p. 137, cf. A. Mastrocinque, 'Osservazioni sull'attività di Antioco III nel 197 e nel 196 a. C.', PP 31, 1976, 307–322, esp. 317.

68 See note 12; Bagnall (1976), 253–55; Michaelidou-Nicolaou (1976), 99f. (Π 34); Ptolemy of Megalopolis succeeded him as strategos of Cyprus, see p. 135; on the significance of the family of Polykrates in administration: Mooren (1981).

69 Rosettana: Urk. II.183.5. 194.3. The date is determined, in agreement with Koenen (1977), 73–75, by giving preference to the demotic version (17 Mecheir of the ninth year = 26 March 196) over the date in the hieroglyphic version (17 Paophi = 26 November 197) because in practice the demotic text would be the one that was read.

70 Will, II (1982), 190f.

71 F. G. Maier, V. Karageorghis, 'Paphos', Nicosia 1984, 230; O. Mørkholm, A. Kromann, 'The Ptolemaic silver coinage on Cyprus 192/1–164/3 BC,' *Chiron* 14, 1984, 149–173.

72 The Aetolians were allied with Antiochos while the Achaeans were allied with Rome.

73 PP I.2152, 2194; III.5022; VI.14895, 15187; Mooren (1975), 146–149 (0191).

74 Reported in a priest's decree of July 182: Daressy (1911 & 1916/7) = Huß (1991, 2), no. 15; further: Daumas (1952), 260f.

75 Last dated document is from the 20 May; Samuel (1962), 139.

76 Cf p. 157f., the mismanagement of the revolt in Sais.

77 The setting of the birth day of an Apis to January 186 (after Ray (1978), 117–120 among others) is, however, not relevant: see p. 281 with note 126.

78 On the whole cluster of problems see Mooren (1974); id. (1977); id. (1981).

79 See p. 43.

80 Cited in Volkmann (1959), 1703; see also Pestman (1967), 46.

81 Pestman (1967), 46d; Ray (1976), 79.

82 Otto, W. (1934), 24, note 3; the two: PP VI.14602, 14612.

83 Attested from 22/23 February, 175 in the title of the Egyptian w$^c$b priests: Lanciers (1988, 2), 28.

84 I. Philae, I. no. 11.

85 Walbank, III (1979), 323.

86 It remains fundamentally unclear whether Apollonios was in Egypt before or after the accession; the sequence presented here seems more likely; cf. Walbank III (1979), 323f.

87 On the politics of Perseus see Hammond, Walbank (1988), 490–497, 532–37.

88 For the sources and facts see Otto, W. (1934), 23–81; Mooren (1979); Will, II (1982), 311–325; Gronewald (1982).

89　T. C. Skeat, '"The twelfth year which is also the first": the invasion of Egypt by Antiochus Epiphanes', *JEA* 47, 1961, 107–112. Sources for this first year: C. H. Roberts, E. G. Turner, *Catalogue of the Greek and Latin papyri in the John Rylands Library IV*, Manchester 1952, no. 583 (12 November 170); Ray (1976), no. 12, p. 125 (12 December 170 but only written after 168). The beginning of the new era, however, was not noticed in large parts of Egypt.

90　He was in Egypt in 200 as an envoy, see p. 137 with note 63.

91　On this see Walbank, III (1979), 324; Gruen (1984), 655.

92　Eulaios had even persuaded Philometor to seek protection in the sanctuary of Samothrace; whether he actually arrived there or was prevented from going remains unclear: Plb. XXVIII.21.

93　PP II & VIII. 1926; VI. 14610.

94　See p. 138, 140; PP I. 270; II & VIII.1833; IV. 10087a; VI.14611; Mooren (1975), 82–85 (042); id. (1977), 74–80; Thomas (1975), 112.

95　On the question of the dowry: Will, II (1982), 192.

96　On this widely discussed topic: Gruen (1984), 653, note 199.

97　On this matter see Gruen (1984), 690.

98　A Babylonian cuneiform text reports on the fifth Babylonian month of the 143rd year of the Seleukid era (= second half of August and first half of September 169) that 'king Antiochos travelled victoriously through the cities of Egypt . . .'; A. J. Sachs, H. Hunger, *Astronomical Diaries and Related Texts from Babylonia, II*, Vienna 1989, 474 (Text no. 168 a.15).

99　Gruen (1984), 657f.

100　Actually he was 'Ptolemy, son of Ptolemy, son of Makron'. He was strategos from about 180–168; after being in Antiochos' service for five years, he was accused of treason and committed suicide; PP VI.15069; Mooren (1975), 187f. (0350); Bagnall (1976), 256f.; Michaelidou-Nicolaou (1976), 105 (Π 65).

101　Ray (1976), 14–29 (no. 2, recto 9–10, verso 11f.; no. 3 verso 13f.), 127.

102　Rübsam (1974), 123. On this temple, see also p. 181.

103　C. Ord. Ptol., no. 32; on its dating to 168 see Mooren (1979), 84.

104　Habicht in: CAH VIII.344. On the facts treated here and their problematic nature see Mooren (1979).

105　Further citations can be found in Volkmann (1959), 1710.

106　Ray (1976), 14–29 (no. 2, recto 5–7, verso 11f.; no. 3 verso 13f.), 127.

107　E. Badian, 'Hegemony and independence. Prolegomena to a study of the relations of Rome and the Hellenistic states in the second century BC', in *Proceedings of the VIIth Congress of the International Federation of the Societies of Classical Studies, I,* Budapest 1984, 397–414; cf. also E. Paltiel, 'Antiochos Epiphanes and Roman Politics', *Latomus* 41, 1982, 229–254.

108　PP I.196; II.1966; III.5213; VI.14617; see also VIII and IX; Mooren (1975), 70 (024), 88f. (049), 220 (050); Clarysse, Van der Veken (1983), 46, no. 126 bis; see p. 176, note 70.

109　Ray (1976), 20–29 (no. 3 verso 21f.), 128.

# 5   Domestic resistance and the Pharaonic state in Thebes (206–186)

The Egyptian uprisings against Ptolemaic rule[1] are best understood as something that grew out of a background of social tension. This underlying social unrest must have grown in proportion to the government's increasing exploitation of its country's resources and its manpower, among other things, to advance the goals of its foreign policy and to finance court life. It was Philadelphos who instigated this course of events and eventually, when the expenses incurred by the Third Syrian War became too much of a burden, this development led to the very first uprising of local Egyptians against the Ptolemaic regime.[2]

It remains difficult to assess the extent to which this opposition to the Ptolemies was a revival or perhaps even continuation of Egyptian resistance to their former masters, the Persians. One can see that, in fact, with the advent of Ptolemaic rule, belief in the cultic relevance of the ruling king dwindled or disappeared altogether in certain areas of ancient Egyptian religion, such as in the cult of the falcon of Edfu or in the rituals of the birth houses.[3] The document known as the Demotic Chronicle, which reflects the anti-Persian sentiment prevalent in the fourth century, prophesies in its present version (dating to the late third century) that a native king from Herakleopolis would rise to break up the supremacy of the Greek kings. Here we have an explicit formulation of the view that the Ptolemaic regime of the time did not correspond to Maat.[4] It is evident, nevertheless, that the high-priesthoods of the entire country, and especially those from Memphis, came to terms with the royal house and through the native dynastic cult were even closely associated with it. Thus, at least at the end of the third century, the fact that the Egyptian revolts occurred on a national scale cannot be explained by pressure from the influential priesthoods; it must be attributed, rather, to a widespread discontent among the mass of working people. Finally, the native Egyptian ideal of pharaonic rule was taken up by a very successful group from the south of Egypt and they managed to establish a state in Thebes which lasted almost 20 years, partially with the military assistance of Nubia.

The tremendous expenses incurred by the Fourth Syrian War must have imposed a significant burden on the lower classes. In addition, approximately

20,000 Egyptians were required to undergo training for military service and to be armed in the Macedonian style. Though they could be proud in their claim that they had made a significant contribution to the victory at Raphia, their service in the army also brought them first-hand experience of the extravagance of court-life and, when they returned to their villages, the poverty of the Egyptian farmers must have been all the more appalling. It remains questionable whether Polybius (V.107.1–3) was correct in seeing a direct connection between the battle of Raphia and the Egyptian uprising which occurred not long after it.[5] Certainly, the conditions arising after this battle were fertile ground for the outbreak of such a revolt.

In the years following 217, some men of the new military class led a revolt against the Ptolemaic regime in the northern part of the country. Their intentions were not to gain satisfaction on certain minor issues, but, rather, to establish a lasting independent power under a leader who would immediately distinguish himself (Plb. V.107.1–3). Philopator, who was a slave to court-life, was forced to engage in a true partisan war, complete with all of its most gruesome aspects and in which the usual Hellenistic style of warfare was of no avail (Plb. XIV.12.4). In 213, Antiochos III and Philip V offered the Ptolemaic king their assistance probably to deal with these internal difficulties (Plb. XV.20.1).[6]

A papyrus dating to the end of the third century,[7] probably still during Philopator's reign, describes how Egyptian bandits attacked a military post and a temple precinct; the attackers came from an area outside the village community. This is obviously an example of the well-known phenomenon of anachoresis in which individuals would seek refuge in the deserts and Delta marshes as a result of the intensive exploitation of the Egyptian peasantry. Such indigents gathered together and plundered wherever there was something to be had; it was of no concern to them whether the owners were Greeks, Egyptians or even Egyptian priests. From the Rosetta Stone[8] we also know that, at the end of Philopator's reign, civil war raged in the Delta. In light of the fact that the 'enemies' even attacked sanctuaries, this war should be viewed as a rebellion of the lower classes inspired by social injustice. This uprising in Lower Egypt dating to the last years of Philopator's reign represented a growing movement which would be completely quashed only in 185.[9]

The chaotic situation in the north obviously came as a boon to the uprising in the south just mentioned. Construction and ornamentation of the temple of Edfu was pursued with great energy under Philopator, no doubt with the aim of binding the influential local priests to the dynasty. Later, as a building inscription states, 'unrest broke out, after unknown rebels in the south had interrupted the work on the throne of the gods (= temple of Horus of Edfu); the uprising raged in the south until the 19th year of the king . . . Ptolemy V.' (= 187/6).[10] The revolt probably began in the area between Thebes and Syene.[11]

The chronology of this major revolt in southern Egypt against the Ptolemies (lasting from 206 to 186) can be determined more precisely from another group of documents, in particular from certain demotic sources.[12] After their initial victory, the rebel forces elevated their leader, Herwennefer, to pharaoh in Thebes. An ostrakon from Karnak, bearing his name and dated 11 November 206, represents the oldest evidence for this event. The Ptolemaic troops could not have been immediately driven from their headquarters in Thebes, since, in Epiphanes' first year (summer until the beginning of October 204), soldiers still departed from there to go to the southern nomes that were in revolt.[13] But then Thebes itself fell completely to the rebels.

Herwennefer ruled from 206 until 200. A graffito from the temple of Abydos, which attests to the fact that he bore a Greek name (Hyrgonaphor) there in 202/1, is especially important for assessing the extent of his dominion.[14] It is a very interesting monument written in the Egyptian language but with Greek letters. Herwennefer was succeeded by Ankhwennefer, attested as Chaonnophris in Greek,[15] ruling from 200 until 186. The relationship between the two remains unclear.

The names of the two kings are meant as an official declaration of the resurrection of the mythical kingdom of Osiris in the form of Wennefer (Onnophris). To judge by their titulary[16] 'loved by Isis,[17] loved by Amun-re, the king of gods, the great God', next to Isis (obviously of Philae), Amun-Re of Thebes must have been the most important patron-god of both Egyptian pharaohs of the Theban state. This fact was meant, among other things, to underline their ideological opposition to Ptah of Memphis, whose high priest worked very closely with the Ptolemies. The priesthood of Amun-Re at Thebes officially recognized Herwennefer and Ankhwennefer as pharaohs and perhaps also officiated at their coronation ceremonies. The fact that the demotic sources name both native kings but do not mention the Ptolemaic kings or the eponymous priests of the Ptolemaic cult, reveals how nationally minded the movement was.

As in Edfu, construction work on the temples had to be stopped everywhere in southern Egypt. While the Meroitic kings were increasing their influence in the northern part of Lower Nubia (12-mile district) and even began appearing as pharaohs in temple reliefs there, Herwennefer and Ankhwennefer could not turn their attention to building projects. A constant struggle for survival marked the period of their rule. Soon after Herwennefer's death, Ptolemaic troops were able to achieve some victories once again. A siege of Abydos, mentioned in one of the demotic sources, probably took place in August of 199.[18] For a short time even Thebes came under Ptolemaic control, as is shown by documents dated by Epiphanes' reign in the autumn of 199 and winter 199/8.[19]

At this time, the Ptolemaic army also made considerable headway in the Delta. In 197, the rebels had entrenched themselves in the Lower Egyptian city of Lykopolis, which was in the Busirite nome but whose exact location remains unkown. The Ptolemaic forces cut off their water supply, besieged the fortress for a short time and finally stormed the site and subjugated it (Plb. XXII.17.1). The leaders of the insurrectionists were brought to Memphis and executed on the occasion of the coronation feast of Epiphanes (26 March 196).[20]

This did not put an end to the uprisings in the north or in the south; the two were probably connected in some way. At this time, Ankhwennefer was receiving military aid from Nubia, presumably official relief contingents from the Meroitic king. According to a demotic graffito in the temple of Isis at Aswan,[21] in 196/5 invaders from Nubia occupied the city of Syene and remained there until 187. In concord with this event, Ankhwennefer was able to regain Thebes; he is attested as pharaoh here in the seventh year of his reign (autumn 195). Following this victory, he was able, as far as we know, to extend his influence much further north than his predecessor. The followers of Ankhwennefer obviously had to fight bitter battles in the nome of Assiut; in one of these, the majority of the inhabitants of a village were killed.[22]

From the beginning of the 180s, Ankhwennefer's rule probably began to suffer serious set-backs. In 187, the Nubians abandoned Syene and, from the spring of 187, in Deir el-Medina dates were once again reckoned in accordance with Epiphanes' reign. At the same time (end of spring/summer 187), there is evidence that supplies for Ptolemaic troops were being sent as far away as Syene; the commanding general Komanos had set up his headquarters in Akoris, in the Middle-Egyptian nome of Hermopolis.[23] Evidently, the priests who had sympathized with the rebels fled to Nubia at that time; they were granted immunity and asked to return.[24]

The final battle took place approximately one year later in the nome of Thebes: Ankhwennefer no doubt led the Egyptians himself, since the sources explicitly tell us that his son commanded the Nubian relief contingents. At the end of August in 186, Komanos defeated both in battle; Ankhwennefer was imprisoned while his son was killed.[25]

A few days later, priests were summoned to a synod held in Alexandria[26] and there Ankhwennefer was branded as an enemy of the gods;[27] he had defied official ideology which maintained that the Ptolemaic pharaoh was the sole legitimate king of Egypt. The renegade king's prospects were no doubt damaged by the fact that the Theban kings had been compelled to gather every conceivable kind of supply from the people and the temples in what was, for all intents and purposes, a hopeless fight for survival. Advantage could be taken of these circumstances in drafting the priestly decree by branding the measures of the freedom-fighters as crimes against men and gods. Nevertheless, some sort of compromise was proposed in priestly circles; they requested pardon for Ankhwennefer and Epiphanes consented to this.[28] Hence, an attempt was clearly made to placate Egyptian opposition in the south; the ancient pharaonic ideology which it represented pointed directly at Thebes and was perceived as dangerous. The Ptolemaic king, it is said, spared no expense in equipping the temples with all the necessary supplies.[29]

Probably on New Year's Day of his 20th year of rule (9 October 186), Epiphanes published his great Amnesty Decree (φιλάνθρωπα: 'benefactions').[30] Heading the enactment is a demand that all fugitives return to their homes; they would be absolved of all their crimes with the exception of premeditated murder and temple theft. The administration was attempting to deal with the phenomenon known as anachoresis,[31] namely the flight of farmers from their villages. Anachoresis had already occurred in pharaonic Egypt during the late New Kingdom. Then, just as in the current Ptolemaic era, the main cause of this situation was excessive taxation and the intransigent manner in which it was executed. During the years of civil war, the condition of the peasantry must have become so unbearable that many sought to escape from the grasp of the authorities. There were several possible alternatives for the fugitive: he could disappear in Alexandria or in another village or even seek refuge in one of the sanctuaries that could grant the right of asylum. In conjunction with the Amnesty Decree of 186, a general amnesty was enacted which included crimes committed up until the month of Mesore of the 19th year (4 September until 3 October 186), and the reduction of debts among other things. Ptolemy V thus announced that his kingdom had been revived by the re-establishment of order, that the want of his subjects was at an end and that this was a new beginning for all. Many such amnesty decrees (philanthropa decrees) were issued in the course of Ptolemaic history.[32]

The rebels in the Delta, however, fought on. Polykrates of Argos, who had many successes behind him, finally stamped out the rebellion for good in 185 and probably promised the leaders a pardon. Whether he deceived them in this or whether Epiphanes double-crossed him is not known. The leaders of the rebels, called δυνάσται of the Egyptians by Polybios, went in good faith to Sais and were treated there in the most reprehensible manner (October 185): harnessed naked to carts they were forced to pull them through the streets of the city and then were tortured to death (Plb. XXII.17.3–7).[33]

As part of the measures enacted as a result of the great Upper-Egyptian revolt, the Alexandrian government settled Greek soldiers in Egyptian communities.[34] Furthermore, the office of epistrategos was created with the new officer residing in Ptolemais and exercising over-arching control over military and civil administration in the entire chora; the first epistrategos was probably Komanos (from 187).[35] Later[36] the office was usually combined with that of the strategos of the Thebaïd and during the first century this became the regular practice. A possible result of this was that the epistrategos came to lose his authority outside of the Thebaïd and this was the office eventually absorbed into the Roman administration.

Owing to the military support which the rebels received from the Nubians, political relations between the Ptolemaic and Meroitic kingdoms became quite strained; the names of the Meroitic king Ergamenes II were mutilated on the temple of Arensnuphis at Philae or adapted for Epiphanes.[37]

## Notes

1 On the revolts in general: Préaux (1936); Peremans (1978).
2 On the situation during the reign of Philadelphos see p. 62 with notes 151f.; on the revolt under Euergetes I, see p. 49.
3 See, pp. 267, 273.
4 On the so-called Demotic Chronicle in the papyrus Bibliothèque Nationale Paris 215 see P. Kaplony: LÄ I, 1975, 1056–1060 (s.v. Demotische Chronik); the interpretation presented here: J. H. Johnson, 'Is the Demotic Chronicle an Anti-Greek tract?', in *Grammata Demotica*, FS E. Lüddeckens, Würzburg 1984, 107–124; cf. also Huß (1991, 1), 58f.; on Maat as representing the pivotal value of the Egyptian worldview see above p. 1.
5 On this question: Peremans (1975).
6 Cf. Huß (1976), 84f.
7 Goudriaan (1988), 112f., 141 (Doc. 109); cf. Préaux (1936), 529f.
8 Urk. II.183.1–2; Roeder (1960), 181. In a decree of priests, where the Egyptian world order is aligned with the Ptolemaic king as pharaoh and whose enemies are, therefore, enemies of the gods (see p. 156f.), one should place little value on such statements. Such a message, however, is confirmed by papyrological documents for various Egyptian revolts (see here note 6 and p. 181).
9 See p. 157.
10 Cauville-Devauchelle (1984), 35f.
11 The fragmentary Elephantine-Papyrus P. 23641 cannot unfortunately be dated with certainty. It mentions a Herwennefer who 'has come south while he is revolting in Elephantine (?)'. It may be referring to the aforementioned native king. I would like to thank Prof. Dr K.-Th. Zauzich for elucidating this passage to me in correspondence; cf. Zauzich (1983), 424.
12 On the pharaonic state in Thebes and on source material: Alliot (1951); id. (1952); Pestman (1965); Clarysse (1978); Vandorpe (1986).
13 UPZ II, no. 162, col. 5, 27–30; Pestman (1965); Clarysse (1978); Vandorpe (1986).
14 Pestman (1977), no. 11; K.-Th. Zauzich, 'Neue Namen für die Könige Harmachis und Anchmachis', GöttMisz 29, 1978, 157f.; Vandorpe (1986), 300.
15 Clarysse (1978). Both kings were read until recently as 'Harmachis' and 'Anchmachis'; on this: ibid.; F. de Cenival, P. dém.Lille 97 verso, *Enchoria* 7, 1977, 10f.; Zauzich, loc. cit. (note 14).
16 Gauthier (1916), 426–428.
17 In a graffito from Abydos the expanded form 'loved by Isis and Osiris . . .' appears: Zauzich, loc. cit. (note 14).
18 Pestman (1977), II.111f.
19 Pestman (1965), 167.
20 Rosettana: Urk. II.180–183; Roeder (1960), 180f.
21 E. Bresciani, in E. Bresciani *inter alios*, *Assuan*, Pisa 1978, 141–143 (no. 43). The graffito is dated 7 March 187 BC.
22 Clarysse (1978), 245f.
23 H. Hauben, 'Des bateaux de Diospolis Mikra? A propos de SB VI 9367 VII et VIII', in *Proceedings of the XVIII Intern. Congr. of Papyrology, 1986*, Athens 1988, II, 243–253; id, 'The Barges of the Komanos family', *AncSoc* 19, 1988, 207–211.
24 Zauzich (1983), 424; according to the Elephantine papyrus, P. 15527.

25 Described in the priest decree Philensis II: Urk. II. 217. 6–10; 223. 9–224.2; Sethe (1917), 34, 44, 46; Müller, W. M. (1920), 60f., 74–76; Alliot (1951), 435–438; id. (1952). The date of the battle is read as either 27 or 28 August 186.

26 Philensis II (see previous note): Urk. II.214–230; Sethe (1917); Müller, W. M. (1920), 57–88, Tables 21–40; Daumas (1952), 257–260; Török (1986), 233f. (doc. 47a); Huß (1991.2), no. 11 a–b.

27 The hieroglyphic texts also express this clearly by magically changing Anch-wennefer's name to Ḥr-wn-nfr ('enemy of Wn-nfr (i.e. of Osiris)'); cf. E. Winter, in *Temple und Kult*, ed. W. Helck, Wiesbaden 1987, 71; Clarysse (1978), 246–250.

28 Our interpretation of the passage in Urk. II.224.4–6 follows Sethe (1917), 46 and Alliot (1951), 440f.; Müller, W. M. (1920), 75 presents a different view.

29 Urk. II.223.6–8; Sethe (1917), 45; Alliot (1951), 440.

30 Koenen (1957); LC. Ord. Ptol. no. 34; Marcsch (1991).

31 G. Posener, 'L'ἀναχώρησις dans l'Egypte pharaonique', in *Le monde grec, Hommages à Cl. Préaux*, ed. J. Bingen *et al.*, Brussels 1975, 663–669; Dunand (1980, 1) provides a good overview of the phenomenon of anachoresis in Ptolemaic Egypt; see also p. 154.

32 See p. 166 (Rosetta Stone) and p. 201f. (peace decree of 118); C. Ord. Ptol. no. 41–43, 53–55, 71; T. Tibiletti, 'Frammento di ordonanze reali', *Aegyptus* 63, 1983, 28–33.

33 Walbank (1980).

34 It seems most probable to me to interpret the passage in Urk. II.222.10–223.5 as a security measure. Greek soldiers of this kind would gradually become a part of the Egyptian population, as the still unpublished archive of a family illustrates who had lived in Syene during the second century; see Zauzich (1983), 433f.

35 Mooren (1975), 82f. (042 B); H. Hauben, AncSoc. 19, 1988, 209; on Ptolemaic epistrategoi generally: Thomas (1975); Van 't Dack (1988), 247–271, 288–313.

36 From 135 in the case of Boëthos (see p. 189): Vandorpe (1988); for the late Ptolemaic period cf. Bingen (1970).

37 Winter (1981), 512. Cf. also the fate of the stele of Adikhalamani on the island of Philae: p. 173, note 14.

# 6 The sacred kingship from Ptolemy IV until the early years of Ptolemy VI

## EGYPTIAN BUILDING AT THE TIME OF PHILOPATOR AND EPIPHANES

Ptolemy IV's reign of approximately 15 years (until the Upper-Egyptian revolt of 206) was the last period in the life of the empire during which Ptolemaic rule still enjoyed an image of well-balanced sovereignty. The dynasty's prominence in foreign affairs, its display of splendour and its pharaonic building projects all complemented each other in presenting a healthy picture of the Ptolemaic kingship.

The royal house naturally cultivated close relations with the religious centres of the north. Unfortunately, the archaeological remains of the Delta from every period of Egyptian history are more difficult to interpret than those from the desert areas of Upper Egypt. This is, of course, due to the condition of the soil there and the modern-day practice in the area of re-using ancient stone blocks. As we know, the Serapeum and the temple of Ptah in Memphis were always at the centre of Ptolemaic religious policy; for example, the east gate in the precinct of Ptah is from the time of Ptolemy IV.[1] In addition to these monuments, we should also mention Tanis, the famous residence of the twenty-first and twenty-second dynasties with its royal cemetery in the large precinct of Amun. Adjoining it to the south is the precinct of Muth, where Philopator is attested as the Egyptian patron of building because of his programme to rebuild the Naos. Its foundation plaques tell us much about the relation between the dynasty and the world of the gods, since on these the king is described as loved not only by Muth and Khonsu but also by the Theoi Adelphoi, the Theoi Euergetai and even the Theoi Philopatores (the last would, of course, include Ptolemy Philopator himself).[2]

In Middle-Egyptian Qusae (al-Qūṣīja), a temple of Hathor was erected during Philopator's reign; the foundation plaques, written in Egyptian and Greek, liken the goddess (as per Ael. NA X.27) to Aphrodite Urania.[3] In general, the work began under Euergetes I was continued; among these were the decorations in the temple of the Theban triad of Qasr Gueida (Kharga), the reliefs on the great gate of the temple of Month in North Karnak, the work on the third-century Month sanctuary in Medamud and the ornamentation of the temple of Isis of Aswan.[4] The budding tensions which finally led to the uprising of 206 will have furnished a pretext for increased activity in the south. The monolithic chapel of Khonsu-Neferhotep was thus erected under Philopator west of the alley of the ram-sphinxes leading to the temple of Khonsu in Karnak.[5] In Deir el-Medina (West Thebes) the king had the small temple for Hathor and Maat constructed and reliefs inserted in the inner area.

At the forefront of the construction policy was the temple of Horus of Edfu (Figs. 9.5, 9.6). The sanctuary and surrounding chapels were constructed during a period of 25 years, beginning in 237. Afterwards the foundation ceremonies were celebrated for a second time in August of 212, perhaps this time in connection with the inner hypostyle (Fig. 9.6D). In the sixteenth year of Philopator's reign (207/6), the entire naos including all rooms and an inner hypostyle (Fig. 9.6.A–G, I–XIV) was finally completed and decorations were added which, for the most part, were done in the name of the fourth Ptolemy.[6]

The inscriptions, especially those in the most sacred rooms of the temple interior, laud the pharaoh as a most feared war-hero and a ruler over the entire world and, particularly, as the 'ruler of *fnḫw* (Syria)'.[7] These distinctions fitted him best, because he had fulfilled his 'world-preserving' cultic-role through his victory at Raphia. It is important to emphasize, however, that the Ptolemaic king in Edfu only received and held his divine office as king – his role in ritual aside – by analogy to the actual heavenly as well as earthly king, Horus of Edfu. During the course of the coronation ritual at the New Year's Festival, the god Horus himself received the symbols of rule (crowns, various sceptres) as tokens of the transferral of the kingship to him from his fathers Re and Osiris; a chapel next to the inner sanctum was reserved for these ceremonies called the 'throne of the gods' (Fig. 9.6.IV). In a corresponding ritual, the king, always 'played' by a 'priest of the king',[8] received his divine office in the chapel of Re-Horus, also known as the 'throne of Re' (Fig. 9.6.XI). The ceremonies represent the *raison d'être* of the cult of Edfu: a periodic and festive renewal of the kingship in order to ensure a preservation of world order under divine rule.[9] In 206, work here had to be abruptly suspended.[10]

Construction in the ancient pharaonic style was also financed in the cataract area and in the Dodekaschoinos before these lands were lost. Blocks from a small temple on the island of Sehel bear incriptions of Ptolemy IV.[11] On the island of Philae, where Ptolemies II and III distinguished themselves as patrons of building projects, Philopator initiated the first building phase of the temple of the Meroitic god, Arensnuphis (Fig. 9.1.R).[12] Most important, however, is the reconstruction of the temple of Thoth of Dakke which was started by Philopator and is testimony that his sovereignty extended up to the southern border of the 12-mile district.

The Meroitic king, Ergamenes II (Arqamani), was able to occupy this stretch of land (i.e. northern Lower Nubia) in 207/6 or shortly thereafter, because of a power vacuum in the area. The Meroitic king continued the building projects begun under Ptolemy IV on the temple of Arensnuphis of Philae and on the temple of Thoth of Dakke; in Dakke, this went as far as having the inscriptions which had been drawn up for Philopator re-inscribed with the name of Ergamenes. The uprising in Upper Egypt presented Ergamenes II with the opportunity of appearing in Philae and Dakke in the guise of an Egyptian pharaoh.[13] His successor, Adikhalamani, erected the first chapel of the temple of Amun of Dabod, 15 km south of Philae. The Meroitic court cultivated close relations with the priesthood of Philae; clearly, it respected the so-called gift of the 12-mile district to Isis of Philae.[14]

The Ptolemaic renewal in the last years of Epiphanes' reign barely reached beyond Philae; there the Meroitic kings suffered *damnatio memoriae*.[15] It was perhaps on the occasion of a voyage of the royal family in 185 that the temple of Imhotep was established on the island (Fig. 9.1.P); the Greek dedicatory inscription to Asklepios (=Imhotep) also mentions the son of the royal couple, the one to two-year-old Ptolemy VI.[16] Further work was done on the temple of Arensnuphis (Fig. 9.1.R) and a new naos was constructed. Up until the political catastrophe of 169/8, the general situation made it impossible to go ahead with the projects in progress on the same scale as before.[17] On the temple of Horus at Edfu only two inscriptions bearing the name of Epiphanes were added to its ornamentation. Despite this, in a decree dating to the late 180s, the priests of Theban Amun emphasized the excellent state of the old cult buildings as well as of the city of Thebes. The priests thereby implicitly praised the rebel kings to whose following they had attached themselves. At the same time, they paid lip-service to the re-established Ptolemaic regime by lauding the construction efforts of the ruling king.[18] In fact, in Karnak only the restoration of a relief on the enclosure wall of the great temple of Amun can be attributed to Ptolemy V and Cleopatra I with any certainty.[19]

From an ideological point of view, Memphis was of great significance to Epiphanes precisely as the Egyptian counter-weight to Thebes. The Ptolemaic king was, therefore, crowned there at the time of the uprisings in 196. The new decoration of the Apieion, which stood in the southwest corner of the temple of Ptah and held the cult image of Apis, was counted at that time among the pious deeds of the king.[20] In Saqqara, the Anubieion underwent a new construction phase during the rule of Ptolemy V.[21]

## PRIESTLY DECREES AND WORSHIP OF THE PTOLEMIES IN THE EGYPTIAN COMMUNITY

As previously mentioned,[22] a synod of priests was held in Memphis during the great celebrations of the victory at Raphia on 22 June 217. Their decree, known as the Decree of Raphia, dates from 15 November of the same year. The resolution was, as usual, composed in hieroglyphic, demotic and Greek.

Three fragmentary stelae recording the decree are still extant,[23] with the largest portion of the surviving text in demotic.[24]

The representations on the upper field of the stelae are noteworthy: Philopator rides on horseback and wears a double crown; with a long lance he lays low the enemy – probably Antiochos III – crouched before him. On the stele from Memphis (Fig. 6.1) the king is clad in Egyptian style, whereas on the Pithom Stele he is wearing Macedonian armour. The latter portrayal recalls earlier depictions of the Achaemenid Great Kings in which elements of both Egyptian and Persian garb are combined.[25] In each case, Arsinoe III

*Figure 6.1* Section of the Raphia Decree, stele from Memphis, 15 November 217 BC. Philopator fells Antiochus III (not preserved) with a lance. Arsinoe III stands behind with the head-dress of an Egyptian goddess. Beneath are lines of the hieroglyphic text of the priestly decree; on the left are 29 lines of the demotic version; and below is a short part of the Greek version. Height: 32 cm; Cairo, Egyptian Museum, Cat Gén. 31088.

is wearing the head-dress of an Egyptian goddess and stands behind the king who is on horseback. The image of the equestrian pharaoh represents an innovation in official Egyptian art.[26] The priests had expressly resolved to include the king on the stele and had even described his comportment 'as he strikes a figure, lance in hand'[27] in the body of the text.

As mentioned above,[28] from the time of the Canopus Decree (238) to that of the Rosetta Stone (196) one can clearly detect a development in the relationship between the Ptolemaic king and the Egyptian priesthoods; the Hellenistic ruler's predominance in 238 has been reduced by the time of the Raphia Decree to a more evenly balanced and reciprocal relationship between king and clergy. After his victory, the king heaped benefactions on the temples and priests in keeping with ancient tradition.[29] Through his victory at Raphia, Philopator had fulfilled the pharaoh's duty of maintaining or, as in this case, of restoring order in the world. He thereby legitimized his cultic kingship and gave the best possible proof of its authenticity. This glorious deed was now interpreted in a mythical way:[30] just as in the ancient Egyptian *Königsnovelle*, the gods of Egypt had announced victory to him in a dream and assured him of their assistance. At the decisive moment, he killed his enemies as Horus, son of Isis, had once done. After careful consideration, the king returned to Egypt on the birthday of this god (on the second Epagomenal day) and like a new Horus travelled by ship downstream at the time of the Nile flooding[31] (probably from Memphis to Alexandria).

To honour the royal pair, it was decreed that a statue of the king with the name 'Ptolemy Horus who protects his father and whose victory is beautiful' would be placed in the large courts of all the temples of Egypt; an image of the queen was always to stand next to his statue.[32] In the final analyis, the victory of Philopator was understood as the victory of Horus over Seth. These constant allusions to the myth of Horus as avenger and protector of his father (Osiris) were a means of giving the cultic title 'Philopator' a distinctly Egyptian connotation.[33] The Greek translation of the third part (the golden-name) of the king's titulary, of which the Raphia Decree is the oldest known testimony, betrays a similar intent.[34] This version of the golden-name describes the king in the role of the victorious Horus as Ἀντιπάλων Ὑπέρτερος' ('superior in battle'). Even the formula 'loved by Isis' at the end of Ptolemy IV's proper name (fifth part of the titulary) emphasizes the fact that in his office the king takes on the role of Horus; this part of the titulary reads 'loved by Ptah' in the proper names of the succeeding Ptolemies.

To all the statues of the royal couple, which were to be made in accordance with the conventions of Egyptian art, was to be added a sculpture of the patron god of the city. This god was to be represented in the act of delivering the sword of victory to the king. The priests decreed that every day cultic ceremonies should be performed in the Egyptian sanctuaries in front of the three statues.[35] They thus bestowed cultic honours on the royal pair in the manner of Egyptian religious tradition. Following the example of the festivals of the Theoi Euergetai,[36] in the future, a five-day festival was to be held honouring the Theoi Philopatores and in memory of the victory at Raphia.[37] The text of the Raphia Decree thus praised the pharaoh's (Ptolemy Philopator) ability to triumph in battle which was according to ancient Egyptian tradition and in harmony with the myth of Horus. This cultic ability to produce victory was also consistent with the ideology of the victorious basileus.

When the Egyptian priests gathered again in Memphis on 27 March 196 to pass a decree on the day after the coronation of Epiphanes, 20 years had elapsed since the Raphia Decree had been issued. Since then, the international standing of the Ptolemaic empire had diminished considerably and the domestic order had also been severely shaken. For the government in Alexandria, now marked by unrelenting crises, the need finally to place a recognized king at their head became a question of survival. The court relied more than ever upon the co-operation of the Egyptian clergy, since it could not count on being vindicated by a victorious king returning home to receive religious honours for his great deeds. Instead, a 14-year-old youth faced the prospect of redeeming eight years of chaos and restoring 'order' in fulfilment of his cultic obligations. Given this state of affairs, there was not in 196 that reciprocal freedom of action which hitherto had proven so fruitful for both government and clergy. The young king was crowned, took on the cultic role of an ancient Egyptian pharaoh and donned all the trappings of the royal ideology which was being propagated at the time. The priests associated with the royal cult concomitantly granted themselves a series of advantages which were to be counted among the benefactions of the king. This shows us the extent to which relations between the king and the priesthoods in the third and early second centuries were determined by the political realities of the empire and the dynasty; a phenomenon which is clearly reflected in the priestly decrees of 238, 217 and 196.

The priests' decree of 196 survived on the Rosetta Stone and in fragmentary form in other sources.[38] The Rosetta Stone, of course, is that famous monument which led to the decipherment of hieroglyphics by Jean-François Champollion in 1822,[39] an event which initiated the modern discipline of Egyptology. The stone was found by the French in 1799 in a fortification which they called Fort Julien near el-Rashid (Rosetta) at the mouth of a Nile tributary; it is possible that the stone originally stood in the temple of the city of Sais which was located further upstream.

In keeping with developments in the Ptolemaic cult at Alexandria, the Athlophoros of Berenike II, the Kanephoros of Arsinoe Philadelphos and the Hiereia of Arsinoe III, respectively, appear in the prescript behind the king – with his five-part titulary – and the priest of Alexander.[40]

Honours bestowed upon the king follow in the second part of the main text and they include numerous measures which are meant to present the monarch as a benefactor as much of the Egyptian gods as of his subjects. The income of priests associated with the royal cult was not only confirmed but their various duties to the throne were reduced.[41] The general public received a reduction of taxes and an amnesty for certain crimes, especially for collabora-tion in the recent domestic unrest.[42] Hence, an amnesty decree is included.[43] In addition, special emphasis is placed on promoting the cult of the bull-gods, Apis and Mnevis, as well as other animal cults.[44] These measures were attributed to the 14-year-old king and conferred legitimacy upon him for having re-established the rightful order after a long period of disorder. These measures then led him to be compared with Thoth 'the twice Great'.[45]

In this last section, the allusions to the uprisings raging in Egypt contribute to a picture of recent historical events which was meant to depict the king as a leader in warfare following the model of the ancient Egyptian pharaoh. At the same time, this portrayal is also closely linked to the ideology of the king which was propagated at the coronation of the young Ptolemy. One event mentioned in this connection is the seizure of Lykopolis in 197 with the help of the Nile – stylized in ritual form. Ptolemy V was thus likened to Horus and Re and, because of his victory over enemies of the gods, was now worthy of becoming king. The second relevant event is the execution of the ringleaders by the triumphant Horus-king as part of the coronation ceremony, that is, at the 'festival where he received the kingship from his father'.[46] In the ritual, Philopator, who had long since been dead, hands over to his son the rule of the kingdom or, more specifically, the insignia of rule. The divine status of the young Ptolemy who as king is 'the image of Horus, son of Isis and Osiris' is already clearly established in the preamble to the whole decree.[47]

Through the coronation, the Greek cult-titles already bestowed on Ptolemy V at an earlier date took on a disinctly Egyptian connotation: he was now truly an Epiphanes, in Egyptian *ntr prj*, that is, 'the god who has become manifest' or, more specifically, the 'manifest god'. Analogously, the second cult title Eucharistos is rendered in the hieroglyphic texts as 'Lord of Good-ness' (*nb nfrw*) and by a similar formula in the demotic texts.[48] In the Rosetta Stone, both epithets are consistently added to the cartouche of Ptolemy V and thus could be interpreted by Egyptians as corresponding to the ancient, royal adjective *ntr nfr* ('the perfect' or more specifically 'the present god').[49]

The actual honours resolved upon[50] are not unrelated to what we have already seen in the Canopus Decree and the Raphia Decree, consisting of the establishment of cult statues and festivals for the king in all the Egyptian sanctuaries. In this case, private indivuals are also advised to practise the Egyptian cult of the king established in the decree by putting up shrines in their houses.[51]

On the whole, the Rosetta Stone gives us the picture of a king who has the power to enact ritual and whose sovereignty enjoys the sanction of mythical tradition; as a result of the weaknesses of the dynasty at the time, however, he has to submit to the wishes of the priests.

Two councils of priests took place following the defeat of the opposition in the domestic revolts and the re-acquisition of the Thebaïd. Their resolu-tions were carved on the eastern exterior wall of the birth house at Philae

(Fig. 9.1.F) in hieroglyphic and demotic script (known as the Philae Decrees). Unfortunately, the decrees suffered serious damage from the large areas of reliefs and inscriptions with which they were covered in the time of Ptolemy XII.

Cleopatra I is already mentioned in Philae Decree II[52] which was passed in the nineteenth year of Epiphanes' rule on 6 or 12 September 186.[53] The priest of Alexander, Aristonikos, announces the victory over the rebel Ankhwennefer.[54] According to this decree, victory was the result of a favour granted to the royal couple by 'all the gods and goddesses of Egypt' as a reward for the benefactions they bestowed on the temples and cults.[55] The priests assembled in Alexandria resolved, therefore, to establish honours for the royal couple which were very similar to those in the decrees of 217 and 196. Additional statues of the royal couple and of the relevant city-god were to be placed in all the sanctuaries of the country and to receive their own cult; in the future, the day of the battle and the day of the announcement of victory (also the day of the synod's resolutions) were to be observed as feast-days in the temples.

In the autumn of 185, a revised version of the decree was put on display at Philae together with Philensis I.[56] At that time, in the twenty-first year of Epiphanes' reign, the priests gathered together once again in Memphis on the occasion of the enthronement of an Apis. The meeting was perhaps a 'diplomatic' preparation for the journey of the royal family to Upper Egypt. To this end, the duties in arrears of sanctuaries subordinate to the state administration were waived and the priesthoods of the cult of Arsinoe Philadelphos and of the Theoi Philopatores, which had disappeared during the uprisings, were reinstated. Above all, the priests elevated the queen to the cultic status of her spouse by extending to her the honours which are granted to Epiphanes in the Rosetta Stone. In addition to the name appearing in her cartouche, the queen bore the cult name of 'manifest goddess' (*ntrt pr{t}*)[57] which is a translation of the Greek θεά Ἐπιφανής. Like Berenike II[58] before her, she received a royal Horus-name as 'female Horus' (*Ḥrt*), which is attested in Edfu.[59]

The reason that the priests' decrees are the most important historical sources – with the exception of the literary tradition of classical antiquity – for the specific period of Ptolemy V's reign is because the royal court at the time was severely hampered by financial pressures. This is quite clear in the account of the death of Epiphanes. Evidently it seemed necessary to have the sanction of the Egyptian priesthoods when the government proposed action of any significance in both domestic and foreign[60] affairs. The priests, for their part, were well aware of their strong position and occasionally used it to oust their own rivals.

The priests of Elephantine suffered a serious setback as a result of the so-called gift of the Dodekaschoinos to the temple of Isis at Philae.[61] As the ministers of the cult of the cataract gods Khnum and Satet, they had enjoyed a dominant position in the border region to the south of Egypt from time immemorial. Perhaps they saw an opportunity, precisely in the last years of Epiphanes' reign, to capitalize on Philae's open collaboration with the Meroitic kings. The so-called Famine Stele,[62] an inscription carved into the living rock on the island of Sehel at the first cataract, could date from this period. Here there is a description of the seven-year famine which occurred in the reign of King Djoser of the third dynasty; according to the stele, Djoser had at that time handed over the Dodekaschoinos to the temple of Khnum on the island of Elephantine. This, of course, comprised its agricultural yields, a tenth of the animals hunted on this land as well the transit tolls and mineral rights. On the basis of this alleged grant of land in ancient times, the priests of Khnum laid claim to the entire income from the Dodekaschoinos. They were not successful, since the kings who followed confirmed anew the gift of the Dodekaschoinos to Isis of Philae.

This overview of the decrees[63] issued by the priests has shown that at their synods decisive steps were taken with regard to the cultic worship of the ruling king or royal couple. The series of titles for the Egyptian priests associated with the Ptolemaic cult was inspired by the title of the priests of Alexander.[64] But the deification of the Ptolemies in the native Egyptian milieu was essentially carried out independently of the Alexandrian dynastic cult. The fourth Ptolemaic couple, for example, was already added to the list of titles of such (wᶜb) priests either at the time of the wedding or shortly thereafter[65] – there is testimony of this for the autumn of 220. Before the battle of Raphia, the form *ḥm*-priest of 'the father-loving gods' (*ḥm nṯrwj mrjw jt*) was added to the title of the high-priest of Ptah in Memphis.[66] Moreover, in the Raphia Decree the honours proclaimed were expressly for the Theoi Philopatores, although they had not yet been added to the title of the priest of Alexandria. Thus, on Egyptian monuments both members of the royal couple – as 'father-loving gods' – received from the gods a confirmation of their rule and in their lifetime were depicted as being 'alike in their divinity' to the other gods.[67] Arsinoe III appears in sacrifice-scenes next to her husband and of equal rank, like Berenike II[68] before her.

As we have seen, the Greek cult titles of the Ptolemies (Soter, Philadelphos, Euergetes, Philopator, Epiphanes, Eucharistos) were constantly interpreted in the light of the ideology of the ancient Egyptian pharaoh; this was especially true at the synods of priests. In the first years of Ptolemy VI's reign, the royal mother, Cleopatra I, was together with her child the head of state; the cult name Philometor ('mother-loving') is a direct reference to this. According to Egyptian mythology and Egyptian royal dogma, this arrangement could only be an instance of Isis appearing with the child Horus. To an Egyptian this could also have suggested the traditional representation of the king as *Kamutef* ('bull of his mother').[69] The highly complex Kamutef theology of the New Kingdom implies that a god (Min or Amun) causes a goddess or queen to become both his wife and mother in the act of procreation because the begetter is then reborn as the 'son'. The notion of Kamutef expresses the essential unity of the divine father and the divine son and especially of a ruling king and his predecessor, both of whom had played the same role of Horus.

A petition[70] of the priests of Isis from Syene to the strategos of the Theban nome (dating to 17 September 170) provides us with an interesting example of the Egyptian cult dedicated to the living members of the Ptolemaic family; in the petition 'sacrifices and libations' (col. II, ll.5–6) for the 'pharaoh, his sister and his brother' are mentioned. Since the sister is here marked with the determinative of godhead but the brother is not, it is clear that 'the ruling Theoi Philometores' refers to the wedded sibling-couple, Ptolemy VI and Cleopatra II, and not the three siblings who went on to form a joint-rule. Ptolemy VIII is, however, already included in the sacrifices.

In the relationship between ruler and religion, there is a clear divergence in the way that both 'aspects' of the king – i.e. the Hellenistic and ancient Egyptian one – evolve with the decline of the dynasty following the death of Ptolemy IV. While the cult of the Ptolemies is officially continued without interruption in Alexandria and Ptolemais (see next section), the divinity of the basileus becomes less and less credible. Indeed, the Hellenistic ruler, as he had come to be known in the third century, slowly disappears. The pharaoh Ptolemy, on the other hand, gradually assumes the role prescribed in the ancient Egyptian ideology of the king and as a consequence the priests gain influence as his representatives. Although the domestic revolts could be quashed physically by military intervention, on the spiritual and ideological plane the return to ancient Egyptian ways continued to spread unchecked.

## GREEK CULTS OF THE PTOLEMIES AND DYNASTIC GODS

The development of the Greek cult of the Ptolemies can be traced step by step in the period of just over 50 years with which we are now dealing. As previously mentioned, Ptolemy IV is attested as Theos Philopator soon after his accession to the throne and the royal couple are referred to as 'father-loving gods' in a demotic text.[71] Nevertheless, the Theoi Philopatores were first added to the cult of Alexander only after the meeting of priests at Memphis (i.e. after 15 November in 217) and the addition is attested to for the autumn of 216.[72]

Significant innovations were introduced on the occasion of the Ptolemaia festivals of 215/14 and 211. While the first Ptolemaic couples had been buried in individual graves near the sema of Alexander the Great, Philopator had a new, collective sema constructed for both Alexander and the Ptolemaic kings; it had a pyramidal superstructure and was located in the palace precinct at Alexandria (Zen. III.94 = Paroem. I. p. 81; Str. XVII.1.8).[73] This magnificent shared mausoleum was probably dedicated during the Ptolemaia of 215/14. This was now Alexander's third grave.[74] At the same time, the king had the Theoi Soteres joined to the cult of the Ptolemies and Alexander and thereby gave the dynastic cult in Alexandria its final form.[75] Presumably in the same year 215/14, Ptolemy IV established in Ptolemais (Upper Egypt) in addition to the cult of Ptolemy, the founder of the city, an eponymous cult of this same Ptolemy and of the ruling king or, more specifically, the ruling couple. This meant that during the lifetime of Ptolemy IV the cult was in honour of Theos Ptolemaios and the Theoi Philopatores as his σύνναοι.[76]

An athlophoros ('contest-prize bearer') for the murdered mother of the king, Berenike II, (ἀθλοφόρος Βερενίκης Εὐεργέτιδος) was added to the ranks of the eponymous priests of Alexandria (priest of Alexander, Kanephoros for Arsinoe Philadelphos) on the occasion of the Ptolemaia of 211/10; in the preamble to official documents, this athlophoros was inserted just before the kanephoros of Arsinoe II. In this way, the new state cult for Berenike II enjoyed priority even over that of Arsinoe Philadelphos. Philopator may have had a temple constructed for Berenike II as σῴζουσα ('saviour') in the coastal area near Alexandria (Zen. III.94 = Paroem. I, p. 81); the attribute is best understood as a link to Isis in her role as patroness of sea-travellers.[77]

By establishing a collective burial site for Alexander and the Ptolemies and through the innovations in the state cults of the Ptolemies at Alexandria, Ptolemy IV evidently wished to display to the world the ascendancy of his dynasty. This was all the more important given the shaky foundations upon which this pre-eminence rested in the course of his reign.[78] After his victory over Antiochos III, Philopator established a royal cult for himself in Jaffa. In addition, there are inscriptions from Coele Syria in honour of the victor of Raphia in which he is referred to as 'Theos Philopator' and his sister-spouse Arsinoe III as 'Thea Philopator'.[79] From Rhodes we now have evidence of a cult in honour of the third Ptolemaic couple, which had probably been established while Euergetes was still alive; perhaps just after he had given aid to Rhodes in 227/6.[80] Moreover, there are indications from within and outside of Egypt that the crown prince and 'co-regent' was associated with the cult of the Ptolemies while still a child.[81]

Philopator had a fondness for certain dynastic gods. During the early years of his reign, he added a small shrine dedicated to Harpocrates next to the naos for Sarapis in the Alexandrian Serapeum. According to bilingual (hieroglyphic–Greek) foundation tablets, the shrine had been made as the fulfilment of a command (πρόσταγμα) from Sarapis and Isis.[82] After Philopator's reign, there is no evidence for building activity on the hill of Rhakotis during the Ptolemaic period. Even personal interest in the cult of Sarapis dwindled in the years that followed. In the chora, however, the cult took on more and more significance, particularly among inhabitants of mixed Greek descent in the second and first centuries.

The god Dionysos was of paramount importance to Philopator, although the Ptolemies had been closely associated with him from the beginning. Through him they had forged a direct bond to Alexander and, at the same time, the god best represented the ideal of Tryphé which required that a ruler bestow wealth and good fortune on his kingdom.[83] Philopator incorporated into the proceedings of his government a programme dedicated to Dionysos:[84] he established various festivals and ceremonies honouring Dionysos, in which he himself took part 'carrying the tympanon' (Eratosth.: FGrHist. 241 F16). At his court, he established a community devoted to the cult of Dionysos. The first phyle of Alexandria was named Dionysia and its demes were given Dionysian names. Within the first six years of his rule (before 215/14), the king issued a prostagma ordering that certain worshippers of Dionysos, presumably the priests who initiated newcomers into the mysteries, must register within three weeks in Alexandria.[85] The edict shows not only that the monarch had a great interest in the cult but also that he was attempting to impose some control on its obscure mystery rites. Philopator was the first Ptolemy who received at least unofficially – the epithet of Νέος Διόνυσος (Euphronios: Powell, Coll. Alex., 176; cf. Clem. Al. *Protr.* IV.54.2) which attributed to him the god's characteristics.[86] The same conception is expressed in the frequent examples from iconography in which the king is likened to Dionysos.

During the reign of Ptolemy V,[87] the first innovations to the state cult of the Ptolemies were probably implemented at the Ptolemaia of 199/8. This had obviously not been possible at the previous Ptolemaia in 203/2 on account of the internal crises in connection with the overthrow of Agathokles. According to our sources, Ptolemy V was added to the Alexandrian dynastic cult as of 199/8; this meant that he was inserted into the title of the priest of Alexander, after Alexander the Great and previous Ptolemies, as Theos Epiphanes Eucharistos. At the same time, an eponymous priestess was established for Arsinoe III who had been killed during the change of government (ἱέρεια Ἀρσινόης Φιλοπάτορος). The state cult of the Ptolemies in Alexandria thus attained that state of development which is described in the prescript of the Rosetta Stone.[88]

One may assume that after 206, with the revolt of Thebes, the cult of the Ptolemies was interrupted in Upper-Egyptian Ptolemais. In the autumn of 199, Alexandrian troops temporarily controlled Thebes[89] and this explains why there is evidence there (from 199/8) that the title of the eponymous priest was changed to include Ptolemy V. He becomes 'Priest of Theos Ptolemaios and King Ptolemaios, Theos Epiphanes Eucharistos'.

After the marriage of the royal couple in 194/3, Cleopatra I was also incorporated into the dynastic cult. This meant that Theos Epiphanes Eucharistos was replaced by the Theoi Epiphaneis in the last part of the title of the Alexander-priest. After the Thebaïd had been recovered, there was also a kanephoros for Arsinoe Philadelphos in Ptolemais (attested from 185/4).

On the island of Cyprus, the cults were already put under the control of the central authority of the strategos in the first years of Epiphanes' reign. Hence the strategos also bore the title of archiereus from the time of Polykrates of Argos.[90] This made him the highest official of the state cult of the Ptolemies on the island – there is explicit evidence of this for Ptolemy of Megalopolis.[91]

All these measures show us that, despite or perhaps precisely on account of the weakness of the dynasty, the political propaganda of the Ptolemaic cult was stubbornly upheld or, more accurately, was bolstered as much as possible. Conversely, the general image of the king's divinity suffered a general decline in the private sphere from the second century onwards. The Ptolemies appear in votive inscriptions more rarely as gods or deities to whom an altar has been consecrated; just as in the time before Euergetes I, their names are generally distinguished by the preposition ὑπέρ from the gods, who are named in the dative case.[92] Thus, there is a clear discrepancy between the official claim of the state cult and the attitude of the common people, as evinced by these documents, who no longer detected any element of divinity in their ruler.

In view of this, the following remarks on the development of the state Ptolemaic cult during the early years of Ptolemy VI are meant only as a supplement to what has already been said on the subject. In the first two years confusion still reigned in the testimonia for the dynastic cult, but, by the third, 'King Ptolemaios Philometor' (without the epithet 'Theos') was added to the title of the Alexander-priest (179/8). Shortly after the time of our earliest source attesting to his deification,[93] the king is worshipped as Theos Philometor as part of the Alexandrian dynastic cult (attested from 5 March 175, about one year after the death of Cleopatra I).[94] After Ptolemy VI and Cleopatra II married, the Theoi Philometores appear at the end of the title of the priest of Alexander: this term included all three royal siblings once their threefold rule began; this situation lasted until autumn 164.

The eponymous priesthoods of Ptolemais, which also had authority in the whole Thebaïd, were beset by confusion during the 170s. Contrary to the practice established by Philopator, after the death of the fifth Ptolemy the priest for Ptolemy Soter and Ptolemy Epiphanes was retained just as he was. Following the death of Cleopatra I, a certain Kineas, who was perhaps the well-known adviser of Philometor,[95] assumed the office of priest of Ptolemy VI and of his mother for the rest of the decade. By 172/1, two other priesthoods appear in the documents of Upper Egypt, one for Cleopatra II and an additional one for Ptolemy VI. In about 170, therefore, there were five eponymous priesthoods in Ptolemais.[96]

We should like to conclude this chapter with the observation that during the first two decades of the second century the fusion of basileus and pharaoh which had long been the aim of the dynasty was no longer a viable objective. This was despite the fact that the meetings of the priests were intended as a means of elaborating a Ptolemaic ideology of the king which would help foster such a fusion. The Egyptian priests, however, manipulated the image of the Ptolemaic pharaoh according to their own interests. Thus, the Ptolemaic king is portrayed differently in the various influential religious centres of the country; these local discrepancies become quite evident, if we compare, for example, the cult of the king in Memphis with that of Edfu. The Ptolemaic empire was no longer led by a victorious basileus as in the third century. As a substitute, an attempt was made to propagate the charisma of the dynastic family, but it found little credence.

## Notes

1  W. M. Fl. Petrie, *Memphis, I*, London 1909, 14, plate XLV.
2  J. Ries, *Théologies royales en Égypte et au Proche-Orient ancien et Helléllenisation des cultes orientaux*, Louvain-La-Neuve 1986, 39; Quaegebeur (1989, 1), 101.
3  SEG XVI.860; Fraser (1972), II. 332, note 50.
4  On these projects see p. 87f.
5  PM II², 224.
6  On the construction history of Edfu under Philopator cf Cauville, Devauchelle (1984), 33–35, 44.
7  On the epithets of Ptolemy IV in Edfu: Götte (1986).
8  See p. 89.
9  On the cult and theology of Edfu: Alliot (1949–54); M. E. A. Ibrahim, *The Chapel of the Throne of Re of Edfu*, Brussels 1975; S. Cauville, *La théologie d'Osiris à Edfou*, Cairo 1983; Cauville (1987); F. Labrique, *Stylistique et théologie à Edfou, le rituel de l'offrande de la campagne; étude de la composition,* Louvain 1992 (on the reliefs from the period 145/2 to 88/80).
10 See p. 154f. It is possible that the pre-Ptolemaic colossal temple of Min of Achmim (Upper Egypt) which Herodotos (II.91.2) had already described, was given its large hypostyle (pronaos) under Ptolemy IV; the temple was described by Arab writers as one of the wonders of the world and was destroyed in the fourteenth century; the building material was re-used; cf. Kl. P. Kuhlmann, *Materialien zu Archäologie und Geschichte des Raumes von Achmim*, Mainz 1983, 25–49; Arnold (1992), 174–176. On Qau el-Kebir see p. 271.
11 L. Habachi, *JEA* 37, 1951, 17.
12 Haeny (1985), 220.
13 On this whole problem see Winter (1981).
14 On this topic see p. 86f. and p. 189 with note 38. On the relations of the two Meroitic kings with Philae, cf. L. Török, 'Geschichte Meroes', in *ANRW* II.10.1, Berlin 1988, 273; furthermore, the stele of Adikhalamani of Philae on which this king offers to the gods of Philae and the cataract god Khnum-Re: A. Farid, 'The stele of Adikhalamani found at Philae', *MDIK* 34, 1978, 53–56, plate 9. The stele was later used as a filling underneath the pavement floor of the pronaos.
15 See the fate of the stele of Adikhalamani (previous note) and p. 157.
16 I. Philae, I. no. 8.
17 On this see Lanciers (1986 and 1987).
18 G. Wagner, 'Le décret ptolémaïque du dromos de Karnak', BIFAO 70, 197, 1–21; id., 'Un décret ptolémaïque trilingue du dromos de Karnak (fragments grecs)', in Akten des XIII. International Papyrologenkongresses, Marburg, Lahn 1971, ed. E. Kießling, H. A. Rupprecht, Munich 1974, 439–445.
19 PM II². 130 (no. 476); Lanciers (1986), 91f.
20 Urk. II.186.3–4; Kessler (1989), 61f.
21 See p. 87 with note 47.
22 See p. 131 as well as the historical facts mentioned in connection with the Raphia Decree together with notes 18 and 20.

23  On all three Raphia stones: Huß (1991,2), no. 8 a–c (with bibliography). Copy from Memphis: Kamal (1904–5), no. 31088a (p. 218f. plate LXXIV); Spiegelberg (1904), no. 31088 (pp. 14–20, plate II); Bernand (1992), no. 13. Copy from Pithom/Tell el-Mashuta: Gauthier, Sottas (1925); Spiegelberg (1932), 20–26; Bernand (1992), no. 14. Copy from et-Tôd: Bernand (1989), no. 2 and id. (1992), no. 12 (text, translation and commentary of the Greek version on this copy).

24  The most important discussion of the contents and translation of the demotic version: Thissen (1966); the lines cited here are taken from the text presented there (pp. 11–25).

25  Cf. the statue of Dareios the Great from Susa: CahDelFrIran 4. 1974 or a coin of Artaxerxes III where the Great-King is represented in Persian national garb with an Egyptian double crown: H. Luschey, 'Archäologische Bemerkungen zu der Darius-Statue von Susa', in *Akten des VII. Internationalen Kongresses für Iranische Kunst, München 1976*, Berlin 1979, 212 (= AMI, Erg.-vol. 6).

26  Cf. the commentary on the cultural and art-historical content by Thissen (1966), 71–73.

27  Raphia Decree, ll.35–36; Thissen (1966), 23.

28  See p. 106.

29  Raphia Decree, ll. 28–30; Thissen (1966), 21, 81f. On the topos of the return of the statues of the gods see p. 81 with note 18.

30  On the following passages mentioned from the decree (ll.9–10, 12, 26, 27) cf. Merkelbach (1963), 23f.; Thissen (1966), 52, 55, 63f.

31  This can be assumed because in 217 the new year's festival was celebrated on the ideal new year's day in the year of Sothis (19 July): L. Koenen, 'Calendar problems', in Proceedings of the XVIII International Congress of Papyrology 1986, Athens 1988, II. 209. The king returned therefore on 15 July (second epagomenal day in the Sothis year); cf. Merkelbach (1963), 24, 30; Thissen (1966), 63f.

32  Raphia Decree, ll. 32–33; Thissen (1966), 63f.

33  Koenen (1959), 109f.; Thissen (1966), 68. On linking historical with mythical events cf. U. Luft, *Beiträge zur Historisierung der Götterwelt und Mythenschreibung*, Budapest 1978, 185.

34  Thissen (1966), 27–42. On the Greek interpretation of the Egyptian royal titulary see also p. 111 esp. the designation Μέγας Βασιλεύς as a component of the *njswt-bjtj* name. Ptolemy IV and Arsinoe III are also known as 'Great-King' and 'Great-Queen' in dedicatory inscriptions from Coele Syria after the battle of Raphia: Huß (1976), 71–74; this designation probably refers to the regained rule in Asia; we prefer to leave open the question of the tradition behind it (Egyptian concept of a world ruler or Near Eastern Great-King).

35  Raphia Decree, ll. 33–34; Thissen (1966), 69–71.

36  See p. 107.

37  Raphia Decree, ll. 36–37; Thissen (1966), 73–75. This victory festival is attested in Alexandria for the first anniversary of the battle of Raphia: Spiegelberg, Otto (1926).

38  1. On the extant text: OGIS I. 90 (Greek); Urk. II.166–198 (Hierogl., Dem., Gr.); Spiegelberg (1922), 38–65 (Dem., Hierogl.,), 77–86 (Greek, translation of the Demotic and Hieroglyphic texts); Roeder (1960), 167–190 (translation of the Hieroglyphic text); Quirke, Andrews (1988) (copy, transcription of the Hieroglyphic and Demotic text; translations of all three versions); Bernand (1992), no. 16 (Greek with translation). On the fragments from Elephantine:

D. Devauchelle, 'Fragments de décrets ptolémaïques en langue égyptienne conservés au Musée du Louvre', *REg* 37. 1986, 45–47; Bernand (1989), no. 241; id. (1992), no. 18; I. Louvre, no. 3. On the fragment from Tell el-Jahudija (Leontopolis): SEG XVIII.634; Bernand (1992), no. 17.

   2. Secondary Sources: Daumas (1952); Bergman (1968), 99–106; Onasch (1976); G. Pugliese Caratelli, 'Il decreto della stele di Rosetta', PP 38, 1983, 55–60; H.-J. Thissen: LÄ V, 1984, 310f. (s.v. Rosette, stein von); Huß (1991, 2), no. 10 a–c. Moreover, mention should be made of the Nobaireh Stone (near Damanhur on the Canopic branch of the Nile). The beginning of this decree which was passed on 29 April 182 was for some reason joined with the text of the Rosetta Stone: Kamal (1904–5), no. 22188; used in Urk. II.166–168 as well as as by Spiegelberg (1922) and Roeder (1960), see this note; Huß (1991, ?), no.14.

39  J.-F. Champollion, *Lettre à M. Dacier . . .*, Paris 1822.
40  On these eponymous priestesses see p. 103 and p. 170f.
41  Urk. II.176–178.1; 183.9–184; on this see also p. 121, note 184 and Kessler (1989), 53.
42  Urk. II.174.7–176.1; 179.1–5.
43  See p. 157 with note 32.
44  Urk. II.185–186; see also p. 162 and Kessler (1989), 54.
45  Urk. II.178.2–8.
46  Urk. II.183.5; cf. Koenen (1977), 74; on this see pp. 155–156 with note 20; on the role of Horus assumed by Ptolemy I see p. 80.
47  Urk. II.174.1
48  Vittmann (1981), 21.
49  Koenen (1983), 157, 168.
50  Urk. II.174.1.
51  Urk. II.196.9–197.6. A comparable passage can be found on p. 167 in the Philensis I decree discussed there: Urk. II.212.10–213.5.
52  Chronologically reverse numbering of the decrees goes back to Lepsius: LD IV.20, VI.26–34 (both decrees); on Philensis II cf. the sources mentioned in note 26, p. 159.
53  On the various readings of the date: Sethe (1917), 37; Müller, W. M. (1920), 57.
54  On the historical statements see p. 156f. with notes 25–29; on Aristonikos: p. 141 with note 73.
55  Urk. II.221–224.
56  Urk. II.198–214; Müller, W. M. (1920), 31–56; Huß (1991, 2), no. 12 a–b.
57  See Urk. II.208.5.9.
58  See p. 85.
59  Edfou I.517; Beckerath (1984), 119, 289; Troy (1986), 179 (P. 7).
60  Cf. p. 141 with note 73.
61  See p. 86f.
62  P. Barguet, *La stèle de la famine à Sehel*, Le Caire 1953; G. Roeder, *Urkunden zur Religion des alten Ägypten*, Jena 1915, repr. Düsseldorf 1978, 177–184 (translation); K. Zibelius: LÄ III.1980.84 (s.v. Hungersnotstele); Lichtheim (1980), 94–103 (translation with commentary); A. Schlott-Schwab, *Die Ausmaße Ägyptens nach altägyptischen Texten*, Wiesbaden 1981, 75f.; Török (1986), 15, 231f. (doc. 47).

63  Apart from the overview presented here see also Chapter 3 (pp. 105–112).
64  See p. 112.
65  In P. Vatic. dem. 2037b: Lanciers (1988, 2).
66  Anemhor II, died 8 June 217: PP IX.5352; Quaegebeur (1980), 65f. (no. 6); Reymond (1981), 71–77 (no. 4).
67  Quaegebeur (1978), 255; *Cleopatra's Egypt* (1988), no. 15.
68  See p. 84f.
69  Koenen (1983), 168.
70  Pap. BM e.g. 10591 verso col. I–II: H. Thompson, *A family archive from Siut from papyri in the British Museum*, Text and plates, Oxford 1934, 50f., plate XI; see also Lanciers (1988, 1), 405. The strategos mentioned here is called Numenios and is probably the same as the Numenios sent to Rome (see p. 148 with note 108).
71  See p. 127 with note 2, p. 168 with note 65.
72  Lanciers (1988, 2), 28.
73  Fraser (1972), I.16 with notes 80, 83, pp. 221, 225.
74  On the first two graves of Alexander see p. 15.
75  See p. 95. On the problem that the theoi soteres were often also in the future omitted from the title of the Alexander priest, cf. J F. Oates, 'Theoi Soteres', *EtP* 9, 1971, 55–72.
76  Ijsewijn (1961), 123; Pestman (1967), 136.
77  See p. 105.
78  The over 3 m high Alexandrian statue of Arsinoe Philadelphos seems also to be a part of this programme: A. Krug, in Alessandria, I (1983), 192–200, pl. XXXVIII.1–4.
79  Huß (1976), 71f.
80  Habicht (1956), 110; Huß (1976), 115.
81  Bernand (1970), 1036f. (no. 2: Kom el-Hisn, NW-Delta); IG XII. supp. 115, see also Bagnall (1976), 162 (Methymna on Lesbos).
82  Rowe (1946), 55; Wild (1981), 167. On the construction by Euergetes see p. 100, on the cult group of the fourth Ptolemaic couple ibid. with note 137.
83  On τρυφή see p. 92.
84  Tondriau (1946), 149–156; id. (1948, 2), 132; id. (1950), 293–301; id. (1953), 457f.; Dunand (1986).
85  C. Ord. Ptol. no. 29; G. Zuntz, 'Once more: The so-called 'Edict of Philopator on the Dionysiac Mysteries (BGU 1211)', Hermes 91, 1963, 228–239; E. G. Turner, 'The Ptolemaic royal edict is to be dated before 215/214 BC' in Papyrus Erzherzog Rainer, FS zum 100jährigen Bestehen der Papyrussammlung der Österreichischen Nationalsbibliothek, Wien 1983, 148–152.
86  Nock (1928), 30–38.
87  On the changes in the state cult of the Ptolemies discussed here see Ijsewijn (1961), 119f., 123, 127; Pestman (1967), 137–139; Clarysse, Van der Veken (1983).
88  See p. 166.
89  See p. 156.
90  See p. 138 with note 68.
91  See p. 135 with note 48.
92  On these dedicatory formulae see p. 96.

93  See p. 143 with note 83.
94  Lanciers (1988, 2), 28.
95  PP III.5169; see p. 145 with note 93.
96  Clarysse, Van der Veken (1983), 44f. (119 bis).

Part III

# The Ptolemaic kingdom under the shadow of Roman power

# 7 History of the kingdom and dynasty from the withdrawal of Antiochos IV to the interlude of Ptolemy XI (168–80)

## PTOLEMY VI PHILOMETOR (UNTIL 145)

### The situation in Egypt after the Sixth Syrian War

After Antiochos IV had been forced to retreat by C. Popilius Laenas at the end of July in 168, the Ptolemaic kingdom was ruled jointly for a few years (until the autumn of 164) by the three Ptolemaic siblings, Ptolemy VI, Cleopatra II and Ptolemy VIII. But even during this period Egypt was not to be at peace. At latest around 165, a courtier (philos) by the name of Dionysios Petosarapis,[1] who was quite probably an Egyptian, attempted to use the discord existing between the two brothers to his own advantage. But the intrigue was not successful and he was forced to leave Alexandria and flee to Eleusis, where he nonetheless succeeded in inciting the soldiers stationed there to a revolt. His troops of about 4,000 men were, however, defeated and he fled to the chora. There he acquired a large following on account of his popularity among the native population. The final fate of this rebel remains unknown (Diod. XXXI.15a).

On the other hand, there is testimony from the Fayum of very serious clashes occurring there around 164 on account of social conditions. Even the Egyptian priests suffered in these conflicts. The Ammonion of Myeris near Krokodilopolis had been rebuilt after its destruction during the invasion of Antiochos IV,[2] 'but afterwards the Egyptian rebels attacked it', tore apart the stone building, damaged all the gates and caused parts of the roof to cave in.[3] The reason for this destruction of a sanctuary for kleruchs who had settled in the region was that the latter, together with the local priests, had obviously collaborated with the dynasty. 'Egyptian rebels' who burned the property deeds of a priest are also mentioned in a papyrus from Soknopaiou Nesos (Dime) dating to the period 169–164.[4]

At this time or shortly after the revolt of Petosarapis, an uprising broke out in the Thebaïd. Oracular announcements preserved on a few ostraka from the archive of Hor, an Egyptian 'scribe' and $w^cb$-priest, are addressed by him to the three ruling Ptolemies: Hermes Trismegistos (i.e. Thoth) had announced to him that the (rebellious) Egyptians would be defeated and that the king (i.e. Philometor) would soon come to the Thebaïd.[5] Clearly the same revolt is being referred to here as the one mentioned by Diodorus (XXXI.17b): afterwards, Philometor easily subjugated the Thebaïd, although he took the city of Panopolis (Achmim) only after a long siege.[6]

The agricultural situation and the condition of the rural population must have worsened drastically in those turbulent times. Burdened by taxes, many farmers left their villages; the well-known phenomenon of anachoresis[7] was once again on the rise. The government attempted to counter the problem with a royal prostagma 'On Agriculture' dating from August/September 165.[8] The ordinance was published in both Greek and demotic and referred to the devastation of the land and to the water shortage resultant on insufficient low flooding. The gist of the law was that farmers would now be compelled to lease abandoned lands at a reduced price and those owning livestock would have to make them available for the cultivation of royal land. Complaints soon appeared throughout the country about the rigorous execution of the prostagma by the civil administrators and they finally ended up in the office of the dioiketes; the guard stationed in Alexandria and the Egyptian soldiers of a low social standing, known as the Machimoi, complained the most about the measures, knowing full well that they were in a position of strength. The dioiketes clarified the prostagma in circulars from 21 September and 23 October 164[9] stating that the parcels of land would only be allotted to each in accordance with his capabilities. The Machimoi were to be completely exempt from the forced leasing, since they even had to borrow money in winter to ensure that their lots of land could be tilled. Only those who were capable of fulfilling what was required would be treated with an exemplary severity. The prostagma 'On Agriculture' represents the first example of a forced tilling of the land on a large scale. Such compulsory cultivation is first attested to in the early years of Philopator's reign and, above all, it was a custom that became widespread on account of conditions arising from the armed clashes of the second century.

At this time the government was compelled to establish a new branch of financial administration called the Idios Logos ('special account') with an official at its helm bearing the same name.[10] It was this new official's responsibity to make a profit from estates that were without an owner or had been confiscated; many of these properties had fallen into the state's possession as barren land, since often it proved impossible to lease or sell them. During the Roman period, the office would become an important equestrian procuratorship in Egypt.

Many of the fugitives gave themselves over to the protection of sanctuaries. Such people are mentioned in a considerable number of papyri (dating from the period of 169–152)[11] from the Serapeum of Memphis and are referred to as 'katochoi', 'recluses (of the god)'. They performed various tasks in the sanctuaries of this great precinct and thus came to enjoy a certain religious relationship to the god whom they were serving; their condition was called κατοχή or '(religious) detention by the (god)'.[12] Katochoi are also found outside Egypt in the cult of Sarapis in Priene in about 200 BC and Smyrna in AD 211, although in both cases the institution was no longer what it had been in Memphis.[13]

Some men were all too willing to shirk their domestic responsibilities in this fashion. For example, a certain Hephaistion, who was most probably a soldier in the Sixth Syrian War, had been able to disappear in the Serapeum of Memphis at an opportune moment. When all of his comrades had already returned home, he preferred to stay in the Serapeum – much to the despair of his wife – and no longer concerned himself with the needs of his family.[14] Quite the reverse happened when an Egyptian woman formed a tie with a Greek soldier and incited him to kill her husband; although the latter was able to escape by swimming across the river, he died soon after. The twin daughters then fled to the Serapeum where they found their place as priestesses. A group of 42 papyri dating to the late 160s deal with these twins who at that time were playing the role of Isis and Nephthys in the cult of Osiris-Apis.[15]

## The strife between brothers in the house of the Ptolemies (164–154) and the independent reign of the sixth Ptolemaic couple (163–145)

The establishment of the joint rule of the three siblings made disputes between the two Ptolemaic brothers inevitable and matters finally came to a head in the autumn of 164.[16] Philometor had to cede the field. He went to Rome as a simple traveller, accompanied only by a eunuch and three slaves. There he put up at the house of a Greek acquaintance from Alexandria to whom he had done a favour at a previous date (Diod. XXXI.18). Philometor wished to impress upon the senate his pathetic attire and retinue. The senate did in fact excuse itself for not having received the king suitably (V. Max. V.1.1.). It is unknown what decisions it reached in this matter. Philometor then went to Cyprus. It is possible that Cyprus had remained in the hands of supporters of Philometor and that Cleopatra II had gone there upon the expulsion of her brother-husband; in 164/3, Ptolemy VIII was ruling in Alexandria without his sister.[17]

In the Alexandrian dynastic cult, Ptolemy VIII had until that time been subsumed under the title 'Theoi Philometores'. In order to distance himself from his older brother and at the same time to express his ties with his great predecessor, Ptolemy III, he assumed the title of 'Euergetes'[18] and retained it until his death in 116. His tyrannical rule, however, rapidly made him unpopular and soon the Alexandrians were calling for his older brother's return from Cyprus (Diod. XXXI.17c; Plb. XXXI.18.14). Between the middle of July and 13 August 163, Philometor was reinstated as king in Alexandria. Despite his stronger position, he brought about a reconciliation with his younger brother through a division of the kingdom between the two of them, which was solemnized with great festivities: Ptolemy VIII Euergetes II became king of Cyrene, while Philometor was to rule over the rest of the kingdom. It is not known whether or not the Roman envoys who were present in Alexandria at this time had a hand in arranging circumstances to suit Rome's interests (Plb. XXXI.10.4–5). Nonetheless, it is important to point out that, on account of Philometor's visit to Rome, the Roman senate had been brought into the strife between the two brothers from the beginning. Moreover, it had contributed towards a resolution of this conflict, because of the obligations of its international stature.[19]

So began, in the summer of 163, the independent government of Ptolemy Philometor, who was now about 23 years old, and of his sister and spouse, Cleopatra II. This period lasted until the death of Ptolemy VI in 145 and it was the first time in Ptolemaic history – apart from the exceptional period of threefold rule before it – that the royal couple ruled jointly. There is evidence for this in the preambles of documents dating to this time, where the 'pharaohs Ptolemy and Cleopatra, his sister, . . .' are regularly mentioned together.[20]

Immediately after his accession to power, Philometor tried to rectify the deplorable state of domestic affairs in Egypt. Through an amnesty decree, he pardoned certain offences and deliberate crimes that had been committed before 17 August 163. On 22 September, he wrote a letter to the strategos of the district of Memphis explicitly urging him to carry out this ordinance. He warned that when he came as king to Memphis he did not want to receive any legal complaints from anyone with regard to this matter.[21]

At the beginning of the next Egyptian year (October 163), the royal couple were in Memphis for the celebration of the new year. It seems that Philometor made a habit of taking up his residence in the Serapeum of Memphis at the beginning of the year.[22] The royal couple lived there in the palace beside the temple of the dead (Fig. 9.12, no. 3, near the east temple)[23] and personally received petitions through the window designated for royal appearances.[24] The presence of the royal couple in the Serapeum created many security problems, since it was so close to the common people. Thus, in October of 163, the Astarteion inside the precinct of the Serapeum was searched for weapons, but none were found. Unfortunately, the agents of the state abused the special authority invested in them and so used this search as an opportunity to rob the sanctuary and the katochoi living in it. The latter, for their part, brought a petition (ἔντευξις) directly to the royal couple asking for help.[25]

During his stay in Memphis, Philometor visited the temples and made offerings there. He thereby performed the duties of a pharaoh and this was no doubt perceived as a most appropriate course of action in this time of crisis. In the documents of his archives, the Egyptian priest, Hor, is frequently emphatic in pointing out the legitimacy of Philometor's rule (cf. Fig. 7.1).[26] The fact that a synod was held in the summer of 161 also reflects the king's eagerness to gain the support of the clergy.[27]

*Figure 7.1* Granite head of Ptolemy VI as pharaoh with royal fillet and double crown (of which the upper part is broken) with Uraeus on the front part; the royal cartouche preserved on the remains of the column; from the sea near Aegina (i.e. near the Ptolemaic base of Methana); height 49 cm; Athens, National Museum, Inv. ANE 108; Kyrieleis (1975), F 1 (pp. 37, 59–62, Table 47, 1–3).

Such promising developments could not go on unimpeded, since Euergetes II was not satisfied with his rule over Cyrene. At the passage of the new year (163/2), he therefore resorted to the same course of action previously taken by Philometor and appeared in person before the Roman senate: he wanted 'the partition of power with his brother to be annulled on the grounds that he did not enter into the agreement of his own will, but had consented to the arrangements which had been drawn up under compulsion and because of the pressure of circumstances at the time. Thereupon, he asked the senate to give him Cyprus' (Plb. XXXI.10.2–3). Philometor's case was represented in Rome by an embassy led by a certain Menyllos. The majority of the senators opted in favour of the younger brother's request; an embassy was to depart immediately entrusted with the task of reconciling the two brothers and obtaining Cyprus for the younger without recourse to violence (Plb. XXXI.10).

Polybius includes in his account of these events an explanation of why the senate acted as it did. In his opinion, the senate agreed to the request of the younger brother because the new division of power would weaken what was still a large empire and thereby further Rome's imperial designs. Whether he knew of the senate's actual intentions or simply came to this conclusion with hindsight remains an open question. What we can establish as fact is that the senate came to a decision regarding a dispute within the dynastic family of the Ptolemies and that he tried to implement it without violence and by purely diplomatic means.

It is necessary to insist emphatically on this last point. For when Ptolemy VIII had with all haste recruited soldiers in Greece and rushed to the Rhodian Peraia from where he intended to move on to Cyprus, he was persuaded there by the Roman embassy to give up his military plans, to discharge his soldiers and to proceed to the Libyan-Egyptian border and await the results of the negotiations. Nevertheless, while he was on Crete during the return voyage, he recruited 1,000 soldiers and then proceeded to Apis (Umm el-Raḥam, 30 km west of Marsa Matruh). There he had waited impatiently for news of his brother's answer to the Roman embassy for a period of 40 days, when suddenly the people of Cyrene revolted under the leadership of Ptolemy Sempetesis[28] whom Euergetes II had left behind to govern in his absence. Although Euergetes II had the 1,000 Cretan soldiers with him, he suffered a defeat. According to Polybius, the people of Cyrene, like the Alexandrians one year before, no longer wanted to submit to a tyrant and were willing to fight for their freedom (Plb. XXXI.17–18). After the revolts of 313/2, c. 304/300 and 249/8–246, this was now the fourth attempt by the Cyreneans to shake off their Ptolemaic overlords.[29] We do not know the final outcome of the insurrection of 162.

In the meantime, Philometor had been very deft at prolonging the negotiations with the Roman emissaries in Alexandria. When news reached Alexandria that Euergetes was having the greatest difficulty in maintaining his sovereignty over Cyrenaica and thus could no longer devote himself to the acquisition of Cyprus, Philometor made it clear to the Roman embassy that he would respect their original agreement and then eased them out of his presence. Philometor had understood very well to what extent the Romans were ready to intervene in the strife between the two brothers of the royal house.

After things had settled down in Cyrene, Euergetes II sent an embassy to Rome conveying a bitter message of complaint. Finally, in the winter of 162/1, his emissaries[30] along with Philometor's representatives (again led by Menyllos) were given a hearing in the senate. This time, the senate decided on harsher measures: it banished Menyllos from Rome and broke off diplomatic relations with Philometor. From that moment, Euergetes II alone enjoyed the distinction of being the *amicus et socius* of Rome. With this decree of the senate, which was delivered to him in Cyrene, Euergetes II saw his claims clearly recognized by Rome and so once again began to enlist soldiers for the conquest of Cyprus (Plb. XXXI.20). The details of these events remain unknown. At all events, Rome was not ready to provide military assistance and the younger Ptolemy could not achieve his objectives by relying solely on his own forces.

In 156/5, an attempt was made on Euergetes' life[31] possibly by Cyreneans who wanted him deposed. Using this attempt as a pretext, he immediately set in motion a series of manoeuvres designed to induce the Romans to help him keep his power and aid him in pursuing his secret ambitions. He drew up a will favouring Rome, the so-called will of Euergetes, and early in 155 he published an abbreviated version of it on a stele[32] which was found in the temple of Apollo at Cyrene in 1929. In a reference to the attempt on his life, the younger Ptolemy, which is actually what he called himself (Πτολεμαῖος ... ὁ νεώτερος), promises to leave the Romans his kingdom (without specifying what exactly what this might be), if he should die without a legitimate heir. He also makes a solemn proclamation that he has upheld irreproachably his friendship and alliance with Rome and, at the same time, he entreats Rome to come to his assistance, should his realm be subject to attack. He invokes in his 'will' a number of gods as witnesses, among them Jupiter Capitolinus, and proposes that copies of the will be kept in Rome and in the temple of Apollo at Cyrene.

For the modern historian, the importance of the 'will' lies in the fact that for the first time a Hellenistic ruler made the Roman people his beneficiary in the case of his dying without leaving behind a legitimate heir. This fact underlines the type of relationship which existed between Rome and the Hellenistic kingdoms at that time. The most important case of this sort appeared a little more than 20 years later (133) when Attalos III of Pergamon bequeathed his kingdom to the Romans. The Romans, in turn, were able to transform it into one of their richest provinces within only a few years (already by 129).

In this particular instance, Euergetes II was using his will primarily to frighten his political opponents at home, since it implied the threat of military intervention by Rome. The Romans evidently did not attach much importance to the 'will'; Euergetes was barely 30 years old and thus it was not very likely that he would not leave a legitimate heir behind. For this reason, the 'will' did not find its way into the literary sources; this omission is very telling in Polybius' case, since he is otherwise very detailed in his account of Rome's involvement through Euergetes II in the affairs of the Ptolemaic empire.

The younger Ptolemy was able to make effective use of the assassination attempt in his conflict with Philometor. In 154 he appeared before the senate in person for the second time and laid the blame on his brother for his misfortunes. 'By making an open display of the scars left behind by his wounds and then lodging a vehement complaint for what he had endured, he elicited pity from those present' (Plb. XXXIII.11.1–3). The senate then intervened on behalf of the younger Ptolemy more energetically than before; it did not hold an audience with Philometor's embassy and expelled them. Euergetes, conversely, was allotted five legates who were to escort him to

Cyprus. The senate gave them five quinquiremes to provide a modest show of naval strength and authorized their allies in Greece and Asia to support the campaign (Plb. XXXIII.11.4–7). All of this was of course no more than a show of support for Euergetes; it was understood that if military action were to become necessary, he would have to proceed on his own. The Romans could not and did not want to involve themselves any further; they were sufficiently preoccupied with the wars in Spain and the imminent conflict with Carthage. Ptolemy VI was also quite aware of this situation and thus saw no reason to yield to Rome's will.

The younger Ptolemy was in fact able to take up his position on Cyprus and acquired a stronghold in the city of Lapethos. Nevertheless, he still fell into his brother's hands. For his part, Philometor was supported by the league of Cretan cities as is made clear by a Delian inscription in which the Cretans decree honours for Ptolemy VI.[33] No doubt as a favour to the Romans, Philometor was lenient with his brother. In spite of his victory, he left the latter the Cyrenaica and also promised him his daughter, Cleopatra, in marriage; she was later known as Cleopatra Thea (Plb. XXXIX.7.6; Diod. XXXI.33). At the time, the girl was no more than ten years old. With this wedding project, Ptolemy VI obviously wished to prevent certain political developments which his younger brother's will of the preceding year might bring about; the marriage, however, did not take place.

The Roman envoys returned home from Cyprus empty-handed. One of them was L. Minucius Thermus. He would later – the exact date is not known – be sharply attacked in a speech by M. Porcius Cato, the famous censor, for corruption, deceit and other offences. In this speech titled *De Ptolemaeo minore contra Thermum* (Cato: ORF 8 F 177–181), Cato lauded a certain Ptolemaic king as *rex optimus atque beneficissimus* (Cato: ORF 8 F 180). In view of the extraordinarily good reputation of Ptolemy VI in the ancient sources, especially in Polybius (Plb. XXXIX.7), it is generally assumed that Cato meant Philometor.[34] The younger brother seems to have maintained relations with the Roman aristocracy. It is even said that, after the death of Ti. Sempronius Gracchus in about 152, he asked for the hand of the famous Cornelia, mother of the two great tribunes of the people, Tiberius and Gaius Gracchus (Plu. *Tib. Gr.*1.7). Apparently, Cornelia, in strict obedience to the *mos maiorum*, declined the offer and thus refused a share of his kingdom. Of course, there is some doubt as to the historicity of these events.[35]

In the end, Ptolemy VIII had to be content with Cyrenaica for the remainder of his brother's rule. Ptolemy I had extended the western borders of the Ptolemaic kingdom to Euphrantas Pyrgos, but in the meantime they had been pushed back to the site of the legendary 'altars of the Philainoi' (φιλαίνων βωμοί) (Plb. III.39.2). In Cyrene, where the younger Ptolemy resided from 162–145, the king attempted to revamp his poor image and to prove himself as 'Euergetes'. He assumed the office of priest of Apollo and gave incredibly lavish feasts as a display of Ptolemaic *tryphé*. On these occasions, the priests of Apollo, in particular, returned home showered with gifts. As a complement to these efforts, the king initiated a large-scale building programme in Cyrene. It is possible that a gigantic mausoleum west of the city of Ptolemais was intended for him, since at this time he could hardly have hoped to rule in Alexandria.[36]

It is certain that, shortly after the uprising in the Thebaïd had been put down in the late 160s, the Ptolemaic government had once again become active in Nubia. The procession representing the Nubian district depicted on the first pylon of the temple of Isis at Philae is clearly connected with this policy.[37] What comes to the fore in this representation is its idealized claim to sovereignty over all of Nubia as well as Napata and all its gold. Other monuments of the period, however, show that it was in fact possible that at that time Ptolemaic rule had been re-established in Lower Nubia. In this regard, the Dodekaschoinos Stele in front of the second pylon of the temple of Isis of Philae deserves special mention (Fig. 9.2); in it, Philometor confirms (in September of 157 towards the end of his 24th year) his grant of the tax revenues from the 12-mile district to the temple of Isis of Philae.[38] Approximately ten years later, in a Greek inscription,[39] the priests of Mandulis of Philae asked for the tribute (wheat, wine and wool) which the leader of the Nubians (ἔπαρχος), i.e. of the native population, had to render to them. Also of interest is a votive inscription, dating from the last years of Philometor's reign (between 152 and 145), in which the strategos, Boëthos, is depicted as the founder (κτίστης) of the cities of Philometoris and Cleopatra in the 30-mile district (Triakontaschoinos); this region includes all of Lower Nubia between the first and second cataract. The two settlements just mentioned have not yet been identified.[40] Boëthos is attested 'strategos of the Thebaïd' from 149; he later also held the title of epistrategos under Ptolemy VIII in 135.[41]

Under Ptolemy VI, the Jews of Egypt grew in importance. Of the settlements dating to the pre-Ptolemaic period, the Jewish military colony on the island of Elephantine (fifth century) is particularly well known on account of three Aramaic archives. Sources report (J. *AJ* XII.3–9; *Ap.* 1.208–211; Ps. Aristeas 12–14, 22–25) that Ptolemy I took Jerusalem by a ruse on the Sabbath during one of his campaigns in Palestine, perhaps in the spring of 311 in the course of events following the battle of Gaza. As a result, he supposedly took a large number of Jews back to Egypt. Some of these he incorporated into his army by assigning them to military garrisons. The rest became slaves and were later freed by Ptolemy II. Papyrological and epigraphic sources show that Jews did, in fact, serve in the Ptolemaic army from the third century.

Alexandria already had a considerable Jewish community by the third century and its traditions harked back to Alexander the Great (J. *BJ* II.487f.). Synagogues are attested in Egypt from the reign of Ptolemy III.[42] With the passage of time, the number of Jews in Egypt grew ever larger; the Ptolemies received increasing numbers of Jewish immigrants, especially after Coele Syria had been lost. Jewish communities of considerable size arose in various places in the Delta, in Memphis, in the Fayum (especially in the nome capital of Krokodilopolis), in Oxyrhynchos and in the Thebaïd. The Jews were recognized as a separate ethnic group possessing a distinct nationality and religion. For this reason, they were organized into *politeumata* and enjoyed the privileges accorded to these groups.

In the Seleukid empire, on the other hand, after the Sixth Syrian War Antiochos IV proceeded brutally against the Jews on account of his policy of Hellenization. As a result of the decrees of 167, Jerusalem was converted into a Greek polis, the cult of Yahweh was forbidden and the temple consecrated to Zeus Olympios. The priestly family of the Hasmoneans provoked a national and religious war of liberation against these measures; this was the great Maccabean revolt. After several campaigns, Judas Maccabeus succeeded in conquering Jerusalem and re-establishing the cult of Yahweh in 164; the new Seleukid king, Antiochos V Eupator (164–162), yielded to the change.

Of significance to the history of the Ptolemies is the fact that Onias IV[43] arrived in Egypt at the end of the 160s with a large following (J. *ant Iud.* XII.387). He was the son of Onias III, the high priest who had been deposed in 175/4. Philometor allowed him and his people to settle in Leontopolis in the Delta and to erect a temple to Yahweh on the site of an abandoned temple of Bastet (J. *BJ* VII.427–430; *AJ* XIII.65–68, 70–71); the area became known as the 'land of Onias' (J. *AJ* XIV.131; *BJ* I.190) in the sources. The temple of Yahweh of Leontopolis (today known as Tell el-Jahudija 'hill of the Jews') remained an important centre for the Jewish community in Egypt even in Roman times, until the Romans destroyed it a year after the great Jewish War of AD 66–70.

It was not long before Onias IV and his follower Dositheos received from the king very high positions of command in the Ptolemaic army. But it is a case of biased exaggeration on the part of Josephus Flavius (*Ap.* II.49) when he writes that Philometor and Cleopatra II had entrusted the two with the administration of the whole kingdom and the control of the armed forces. Also enjoying the favour of the Ptolemaic court were the two sons of Onias, Chelkias and Ananias, both of whom still held high-ranking military positions under Cleopatra III at the end of the second century.

Because bitter clashes[44] had been frequent in Judaea ever since the accession of Demetrios I Soter (162–150), the number of Jews in Alexandria grew sharply during the reign of Ptolemy VI. On account of this fact and Philometor's personal interest in the Jews (cf. J. *AJ* XIII.74–79),[45] it is quite likely that the Jewish community in Alexandria benefited from some kind of formal organization at that time. The first writer to mention the special status of the Alexandrian Jews as a community that enjoyed partial autonomy was Strabo (in J. *AJ* XIV.117) in the Augustan period. The Jews resided in a separate area of Alexandria which was reserved for them; an ethnarch presided over them whose function was like that of the highest magistrate (archon) of an independent state (politeia).[46]

On average, the Jews of Alexandria had a relatively high level of education. Jewish literature from Alexandria in the third and second centuries BC demonstrates the great extent to which Greek culture was adapted by Jewish communities. One of the most important intellectual achievements of the Hellenistic Jews was the translation of the Pentateuch into Greek. Legend has it that the initiative for this work originated in the court of Philadelphos (Ps. Aristeas 35–40) but the only tangible evidence of such a project known to us, the Septuagint, can be approximately dated to the middle of the second century.[47] The development of Jewish-Alexandrian literature was fostered especially by Ptolemy VI. One of the most important representatives of the Jewish intelligentsia was the philosopher Aristobulos who dedicated an exegesis of the book of Moses to Philometor.[48]

Despite their open-minded culture, the Jews of Alexandria remained in essence a closed community. Their growing influence in all areas of life and the tensions with the Greek population of Alexandria that arose from this laid the groundwork for later anti-Semitism. It could easily be discerned in the course of the first century and, during the Roman period, anti-Semitism in Alexandria reached a high point with the local Jews being treated in a brutal and bloody manner for the first time. We can discern here the roots of what in later history became a widespread phenomenon and from which we still suffer today.

We turn now to Greek-Alexandrian scholarship. From the second century, scholarly activity devolved upon Greeks born in Alexandria[49] and the result was that the level of erudition quickly sank in all areas of the sciences. In philology, however, two great scholars are known from the second century. The first was Aristophanes of Byzantium, who had already spent his childhood in Alexandria and became the successor of Eratosthenes as director of the library in the Museion. Above all, he produced new critical editions of Homer, Hesiod, and Pindar among others. Since he died in 180, he belongs to the period of Ptolemy V. The work of Aristophanes was continued by his student Aristarchos of Samothrake who was also primarily concerned with Homer. As director of the library he was also the royal tutor at the court of Ptolemy VI.

Relations with Greece at the time are best understood if we keep in mind the three Ptolemaic bases in the Aegean: Thera, Itanos and Methana (cf. the find spot of the royal head in Fig. 7.1). At the very beginning of his sole rule in August 163, Philometor attended to the organization of Ptolemaic troops on Thera.[50] The island remained the headquarters of the Ptolemaic navy in Greek territory until the Ptolemies finally pulled out of the Aegean following the death of Philometor in 145.

The reputation of the Ptolemies in Athens reached its high point in the mid-second century. The Ptolemaia festival was celebrated with extraordinary pomp and circumstance and Philometor was probably the Ptolemy who received a bronze equestrian statue on the acropolis next to the temple of Athena Polias.[51]

The question of a successor became a matter of serious concern for Philometor, especially since he had obviously decided to exclude his brother from the throne in Alexandria. The oldest son of Philometor, Ptolemy Eupator ('of distinguished lineage'),[52] was probably born on 15 October 166 (?); in 158/7, at approximately eight years of age, he was already the eponymous priest of Alexander. In the spring of 152, he was made nominal co-regent by his father and given the title of basileus;[53] in a demotic document dating to 5 April 152, he is named 'pharaoh Ptolemy, the oldest son, god Eupator' and is mentioned after the royal couple.[54] After a few months of this joint rule, Ptolemy Eupator died suddenly; from 31 August 152, the name of Theos Eupator appears in the title of the Alexander-priest as the last member of the Ptolemaic house to pass away before the ruling Theoi Philometores.

The eldest daughter, Cleopatra, later given the epithet Thea, was undoubtedly born not long after Eupator. The younger daughter of Philometor is known as Cleopatra III. Toward the end of the king's reign (before 15 December 146), a 'priestess of the daughter of the king' was appointed for her worship in Ptolemais. This was an unprecedented event in which an eponymous cult was established for a daughter of the royal family who was not a queen.[55] Perhaps this was an attempt to nip in the bud any hopes that Euergetes II might have been harbouring of assuming power in Alexandria, should both members of the royal couple die prematurely. Cleopatra III could thus be accepted more easily as regent for the second son of Philometor who was still underage. Scholars who have counted this second son as Ptolemy VII are certainly mistaken.[56]

## Syrian policy in the last years (150–145)

Soon after Philometor had finally managed to keep his brother in check, he became aware of the Ptolemaic kingdom's newly acquired strength. He now directed his attention towards the Seleukid kingdom and the former Ptolemaic territory, Coele Syria. Demetrios, a cousin of Antiochos IV, had been a hostage in Rome but in 162, following the advice of Polybius, he was able to escape. He was then energetically supported by the envoy of Philometor, Menyllos, who was in Rome at the time (Plb. XXXI.11–14). After Antiochos V had been ousted, he ascended the Seleukid throne as Demetrios I (162–150). Attalos II of Pergamon championed a man of low birth named Alexander Balas as rival of Demetrios for the kingship of the Seleukid realm. This second king was declared to be a son of Antiochos IV.

Ptolemy VI[57] now became involved in the struggle for the Syrian throne by sending troops to help Alexander Balas. These forces took part in the decisive battle of Antioch in 150, where Demetrios I fell. The new Seleukid king, Alexander Balas (150–145), then asked the Ptolemaic king for his elder daughter's hand. In 150/49, Philometor personally accompanied his daughter to Ptolemais (Ake) in Phoenicia to participate in the wedding celebrations;[58] he also contributed a rich dowry in gold and silver (I Macc.

10.54–60). The coins struck in the Phoenician cities at this time testify to the close relations which existed between Alexander Balas and Philometor. They were imitations of Ptolemaic currency and showed the Ptolemaic eagle on the reverse of the coins.

Demetrios II, the eldest son of Demetrios I, was 15 years old when (in 147) he took up the battle against Alexander Balas for his right to accede to the throne as the legitimate heir of the royal house. This in turn caused Philometor to go to Phoenicia with a strong army and naval force, purportedly as his son-in-law's ally but obviously with the intention of regaining Coele Syria. Without regard for Alexander Balas, the Ptolemaic king placed garrison troops in the Syrian cities and even the high priest Jonathan came to meet him in Joppa (Jaffa) in pomp and splendour (I Macc. 11.6–7). In Ptolemais, where Philometor even had coins minted in 146, an attempt was made to assassinate him, supposedly by a confidant of Alexander Balas. Philometor demanded that the perpetrator be handed over to him and duly punished, but Alexander refused. His refusal was the pretext which Philometor needed to reverse his official policy and to pursue his objectives with the help of the opposing claimant to the throne, Demetrios II. He probably hoped to have more influence with Demetrios who was still very young and was willing to use his elder daughter to this end. He therefore called her back from the court of Alexander Balas. When the coastal cities as far as Seleukia in Pieria went over to the Ptolemaic king, he allied himself officially with Demetrios II and gave him his daughter, Cleopatra, as his bride. Used as a pawn to further the ambitions of the dynastic houses, she became the Syrian queen for the second time under the name of Cleopatra Thea.

Matters then came to a head. Two ministers of Alexander Balas in Antioch, who rejected both the Seleukid kings, arranged for Philometor to be received in the city. In a ceremony, Ptolemy VI was officially given the Seleukid kingdom; on that occasion, he wore two diadems, one of 'Egypt' and one of 'Asia' (J. *AJ* XIII.113; I Macc. 11.13; Diod. XXXII.9c). With these developments, it seemed as if the clock had turned back to Ptolemy III's reign. At the end of the spring of 145, Philometor began to have dates reckoned on the basis of his rule in both kingdoms. Two dates began to appear on documents, year 36 of his reign in Egypt and year 1 of his dominion over Asia.[59] Philometor probably wished to underline that the acquisition of the Seleukid kingdom marked the beginning of a new era. But it soon became clear to the Ptolemaic king that, in view of Rome's authority in the Mediterranean, such a situation could not be sustained, especially at a time when Carthage and Corinth had just fallen to the Romans. Philometor thus refused the crown of Asia in order not to offend the Romans (J. *AJ* XIII.114) and in a second popular assembly he persuaded the people of Antioch to accept Demetrios II. He then concluded a treaty with his son-in-law in which he awarded himself only the former Ptolemaic territory of Coele Syria and conceded to Demetrios dominion over the rest of Syria. Probably at this time, Philometor gave instructions to revoke the system of dating according to the years of his rule in both kingdoms; in Alexandria a coin-type was minted at this time on which there was mention only of the 36th year of his reign in Egypt.[60]

Ptolemy VI had fulfilled the main aims of Ptolemaic foreign policy. But it was to be a dream of short duration. Alexander Balas moved against Antioch with an army. Although Alexander was defeated by troops of Philometor and Demetrios at the river Oinoparas not far from the city, the Ptolemaic king fell from his horse and sustained fatal injuries. Alexander Balas fled to an Arabian sheik who had him killed. Philometor survived long enough to look upon the head of his murdered foe when it was brought to him; a few days later, in the summer of 145, he died at approximately 41 years of age and in the 36th year of his reign. He had led an incredibly tumultuous and, in the end, very successful life.[61]

If Philometor had not met his end at this juncture, Coele Syria would once again have become Ptolemaic. In one fell swoop, Demetrios II had been relieved of his rival to the throne, Alexander Balas, as well as his newly acquired protector. The Ptolemaic army returned home and Coele Syria remained Seleukid.

The positive image that we have of Ptolemy VI Philometor is based on Polybius' obituary of him (XXXIX.7). While this does tend to idealize his portrayal of Philometor, it is, for the most part, confirmed by the Egyptian texts.[62] Special emphasis should be placed on Polybius' observation that Philometor never pronounced the death sentence on anyone. Such humane conduct stands in stark contrast to the almost casual manner in which members of the court resorted to murder throughout the third century and to the negative image of Ptolemy VIII in the ancient sources.

## PTOLEMY VIII EUERGETES II AND HIS TWO QUEENS CLEOPATRA II AND III (145–116)

### The reign of Ptolemy VIII until 132

After Philometor died in Syria in the middle of July 145, it soon became evident that there was no reasonable alternative to Ptolemy VIII Euergetes II. He was brought back from Cyrene by envoys (Just. XXXVIII.8.2–3; Diod. XXXIII.13) and was in power after a three-week interregnum in Alexandria.[63] A little later he married Cleopatra II, his brother's widow.

The change in rulers had engendered certain tensions, since literary sources indicate that Ptolemy VIII began his rule with brutality and injustice. First, he had the followers of the young son of Philometor killed and he then had the boy himself killed in the arms of his mother during the celebrations of his marriage to Cleopatra (Just. XXXVIII.8.4). The Jewish troop commanders, Onias and Dositheos, supposedly also set themselves against him and this resulted in severe reprisals against the Jews (J. *Ap.* II.50–55).[64] At the same time, many of the Greek intellectuals were driven out of Alexandria; among them was the director of the Museion library, Aristarchos of Samothrake, who died in Cyprus in 144. The king's title was changed by the Alexandrians from 'Euergetes' to its opposite 'Kakergetes' (Menekles of Barke: FGrHist. 270 F 9). It was not long before the pejorative nickname of Physkon ('fatso') was coined for him (Str. XVII.1.11; Plu. *Coriol*.11.2)

While Euergetes II was harsh in his persecution of those who opposed his accession to the throne, he sought to win over the people of the Ptolemaic kingdom with amnesty decrees that date from the 26th year of his rule (145/4, when reckoned from 170/69!);[65] in addition, the Egyptian temples and priests received a guarantee of their rights and revenues.[66] An agreement was reached with Cleopatra II; she was allowed to retain her position as official co-regent, a status which had been granted to her by Philometor. The dating formulae in documents once again included 'the pharaohs Ptolemy and Cleopatra . . .' and the cult title of the royal couple was 'theoi Euergetai' from 145/4.[67] In Tod there are inscriptions in which the royal couple are referred to as 'the two Horus', 'rulers of the two lands' or 'the two rulers of Egypt'. From the time of Berenike II, the king's wife had appeared next to the king as a priestess on temple reliefs, but now she was depicted as a ruler of equal status in a joint monarchy.[68]

Shortly after his accession to the throne, Euergetes II recalled the troops from the last three Ptolemaic bases in the Aegean (Itanos, Thera and Methana).[69] From now on, with the exception of strongholds in the Red Sea, the Ptolemaic kingdom would only encompass Egypt with at least the northern part of Lower Nubia as well as Cyprus and the Cyrenaica.

In 144, a son was born to the royal couple at about the same time as the coronation festival[70] in Memphis (Diod. XXXIII.13); for this reason, he is known in the literary sources as 'Memphites'. Towards the end of the 140s, he was depicted alongside his parents as 'Ptolemy, son of Ptolemy' on two reliefs on the outer walls of the naos of Edfu; in one case, he is explicitly named crown prince ('successor of the king') and bears the cult title of his father ('God Euergetes').[71]

Soon after Ptolemy Memphites was born, Euergetes II is said to have begun intimate relations with Cleopatra III, the younger daughter of his sister and wife who was thus his own niece and step-daughter (Liv. *Per.* LIX; Just. XXXVIII.8.5; among others). In 141/40, he also married Cleopatra III in due form[72] and like Cleopatra II elevated her to the rank of queen. It is thus evident that the agreement reached with Cleopatra II upon his accession to the throne was only for the sake of appearances. With this act, the king deeply injured his sister and at the same time caused mother and daughter to become the fiercest of rivals. A second marriage of this sort was without precedent in the Hellenistic world. Legally, the two women were placed on the same level; they were mentioned in official documents next to their husband as 'queen' (βασίλισσα). Cleopatra II, however, was known as 'the sister' (ἡ ἀδελφή) to distinguish her from Cleopatra III, 'the wife' (ἡ γυνή).[73]

All three members of this unique matrimonial arrangement were included in the term 'Theoi Euergetai', although Cleopatra III replaced her mother as Thea Euergetis (or *t3ntrt mnḫt*) in the preambles.[74] The hatred between the two women that ensued on the king's actions, and for the renewal of hostilities between Ptolemy VIII and Cleopatra II, had dire consequences for the dynasty and the empire.

It is clear that in his attempt to oust Ptolemy VIII Galaistes could already count on the support of Cleopatra II. Galaistes[75] was born the son of a king of the Athamanians (in Athamania, a part of Epiros) and, after the battle of Pydna in 168, he came to the Alexandrian court as an officer. In 150 and 145, he commanded expeditionary forces in Syria as a *philos* of Ptolemy VI. Soon after the accession of the new king, he fell into disfavour with Euergetes II. The property which he had received from Philometor was confiscated around the turn of the year 145/4. He fled, therefore, to Greece and gathered around him many other exiles from Egypt. A little later he announced that Ptolemy VI had entrusted to him a son of Cleopatra II whom he was to raise as the successor to the throne. Finally, Galaistes crowned the youth and attempted to invade Egypt, probably shortly after Euergetes II's marriage to Cleopatra III. The Ptolemaic mercenaries were already preparing to go over to Galaistes when the strategos, Hierax,[76] paid their outstanding wages out of his own pocket; he thus put an end to the mercenaries' insurrection and undermined Galaistes' undertaking.

The victory against Galaistes clearly strengthened Euergetes II's position. In February 139, he again confirmed the revenues and rights of the Egyptian priests in an effort to solidify his rule by gaining the support of the native Egyptians.[77] The royal trio maintained outward appearances and continued to appear together.

Most probably in 139, a Roman embassy arrived in Alexandria led by the younger Scipio, P. Cornelius Scipio Aemilianus, the destroyer of Carthage (Diod. XXXIII.28b; Poseid.: FGrHist. 87 F6; Just. XXXVIII.8.8–11 *inter alios*).[78] The task of the legates was to visit the Eastern states allied to Rome and to arrange matters to the advantage of Roman policy (Plb. frg. 76, Büttner-Wobst). This last objective was probably also directed at the Ptolemaic kingdom, although when the envoys arrived Ptolemy VIII had again become master of the situation in Egypt. Euergetes II welcomed the distinguished Romans at the harbour and accompanied them to the palace – it is said he could barely keep up with them owing to his girth and effeteness. At that point, the king was a perfect example of the Ptolemaic ideal of tryphé in his clothing and behaviour. From a Roman point of view, he made himself look ridiculous. The literary accounts of this senatorial embassy sharply contrast the revolting weakness of the flagging Euergetes (the negative view of *tryphé*) with the manly and disciplined *mos maiorum* of the Romans.[79] The envoys visited the sights of Alexandria, including the famous Pharos lighthouse, the pharos and then headed for Memphis. Impressed by the fertility of the Nile country and the density of the population, they then returned to Alexandria and thence travelled to Rhodes, Cyprus, Syria and finally Pergamon.

## Civil war and reconciliation in the royal family (132–116)

Conflicts among the ruling trio were certainly intensified during the 130s, although all three always appear together in the dating and votive formulae. Soon after the start of the 39th year of rule (before 11 November 132), civil war[80] broke out between followers of Euergetes II and partisans of Cleopatra II. It seems that Euergetes had the upper hand in Alexandria for a year, since he was still having coins minted at Alexandria in the 40th year of his reign which began on 25 September 131.[81]

Matters then came to a head (Just. XXXVIII.8.11–15; Liv. *Per.* LIX) when the royal palace was set on fire. Euergetes could no longer think of resistance; he secretly fled to Cyprus with his second wife Cleopatra III. There he planned to reconquer Egypt with the soldiers stationed there who were still loyal to him as well as with newly recruited soldiers. He had read the situation. He also realized that the main danger to him was that his eldest son by Cleopatra II, Ptolemy Memphites, would be acclaimed king. The boy was in Cyrene and Ptolemy VIII now had him brought to Cyprus.

In response, Cleopatra II was acclaimed sole queen in Alexandria. Euergetes was stripped of his royal powers and his statues were destroyed. In order to make a clean break with the past, Cleopatra II started a new era by counting the year 132/1 as 'year 1'.[82] A reckoning of dates solely on the basis of a woman's rule represented an extremely audacious innovation in the Ptolemaic period. It recalled the reigns of Hatshepsut and Tauseret in the Egyptian New Kingdom. At the same time, the ruler cult was used especially for reasons of political propaganda. Cleopatra II had been included in the cult titles 'Theoi Philometores' (until 145) and 'Theoi Euergetai' (from 145/4) and before the marriage betwen Euergetes II and her daughter Cleopatra III she was even explicitly called 'Thea Euergetis'. As the sole Ptolemaic queen she deliberately assumed a cult name – Thea Philometor Soteira – which would link her to the past. In this way, she evoked the period of good governement under her first husband, Ptolemy Philometor, and, at the same time, she cast herself as a female counterpart to the dynastic founder, Ptolemy I. The Theoi Euergetai were removed from the title of the priest of Alexander and during the years 131 to 127 the title ended with: . . . καὶ θεοῦ Φιλομήτορος καὶ θεᾶς Φιλομήτορος Σωτείρας.[83]

From his Cypriot exile, Euergetes II avenged himself in a most atrocious manner. He had his own son murdered before his eyes. His son, Ptolemy Memphites was 14 years of age at that time and obviously had completely trusted his father. The exiled king had his head, legs and hands cut off and then sent his son's remains to Alexandria. These were delivered to Cleopatra II the night before her birthday celebrations. She, in turn, put the mutilated limbs of the murdered crown prince on display in Alexandria in order to arouse the people's wrath (Diod. XXXIV/XXXV.14; Just. XXXVIII.8.13–15).

Cleopatra II's main support came from the Greeks and Jews of the capital as well as from the Greek and Jewish population in the chora. She never succeeded, however, in bringing all of Egypt under her sway, since the native Egyptians in particular remained on Euergetes' side because of the favour he had always shown them. The most important of these was the Egyptian Paos who was the strategos of all the nomes of the Thebaïd (attested from 15 January 130).[84] By virtue of his position, he was the head of the civil and military administration. Hence Euergetes had placed an entire army, including the Greek soldiers and officers, under the command of an Egyptian; in addition, the entire administrative body, from the lowest Egyptians to the highest Greek civil servants, were obedient to him. It is clear that in January of 130 the followers of Euergetes were in control at Thebes, since Paos was preparing to put down a revolt in Hermonthis just south of the city.[85] Paos would later be rewarded for his loyalty by being promoted to epistrategos of the Chora (attested for July 129) as well as receiving the highest court rank of συγγενής (blood relative).

At this critical moment in Ptolemy VIII's reign, Egyptians thus finally succeeded for the first time in becoming members of the elite.[86] The upper class of the Ptolemaic kingdom was responsible for administering the state and was organized on the basis of court ranks. This policy, which opened up to Egyptians the possibility of promotion to the highest levels of the administration was continued and extended towards the end of the second century and into the first. Since many high-ranking Greeks were increasingly under the command of Egyptians, with time this no doubt engendered important changes in attitude. A notable instance of Euergetes' favourable policy towards native Egyptians was the marriage (in 122) between the high priest of Ptah, Psenptah II, to a Berenike who was close to the royal house and probably a relation.[87]

In 131/30, the Egyptian element gained prominence in another way also. Once again, an Egyptian, Harsiese,[88] tried his luck at being pharaoh. In the summer or autumn of 131, he succeeded in coming to power for a short time in Thebes. A copy of a letter from the files of the royal bank in Thebes, dated by Euergetes II (10 November 131)[89] revealed that a large amount of money had been paid out to the 'enemy of the gods, Harsiese' and attempts were now being made to cover up any traces of this transaction. According to the document, Harsiese had just been driven out of the city again, perhaps by Paos and his troops. The rebel king was cursed as an enemy of the gods, just as Ankhwennefer had been in the second Philae Decree.[90] After fleeing from Thebes, Harsiese managed to retreat to the area of el-Hibeh in Middle Egypt and he remained there for about a year. A marriage contract dating from the second year of his reign (15 September 130) refers to him as 'pharaoh, son of Isis, son of Osiris'.[91]

Harsiese is, to be sure, one rebel among many. But his historical position is unique in one respect: after Herwennefer and Ankhwennefer, he is the only Egyptian mentioned in the sources to have claimed the title of pharaoh during the Ptolemaic period. He is, as far as we know from our evidence, the last ancient Egyptian who bore the title of pharaoh. Perhaps his swift downfall was the direct result of Euergetes II's policy of favouring the native Egyptians.

As a postcript to the episode involving Harsiese, it is worth mentioning the 'Oracle of the Potter' known to us from Greek sources. It belongs to that kind of literature which foretells a saviour-king after a period of great misfortune; here the prophecy is revealed in the apocalyptic visions of a potter who represents the god Khnum. The existing versions have a long textual tradition and probably belong to the years 130–116. They express disappointment over Harsiese's defeat.[92]

Let us return to the conflicts between the members of the Ptolemaic family. In the autumn of 131 at the latest, Euergetes left for Cyprus. Soon afterwards he no doubt returned to Egypt with an army, since in the spring of 130 the dating system in Memphis is based on his and Cleopatra III's reign. In a document of 28 May, the eponymous priests of the ruler cult are listed with an addition that suggests that Euergetes II had appointed counter-priests.[93] Until at least 127, there were two priests of Alexander; one in Alexandria with Cleopatra II bearing the title which we just mentioned[94] and the other, 'in the king's camp' (ἐν τῶι τοῦ βασιλέως στρατοπέδωι).[95] This unusual arrangement reveals once again the extent to which the ruler cult served as a tool for political propaganda.

The creation of a new eponymous priesthood was also part of of political history. This new priest was known as 'Hieropolos' and served the deified Cleopatra III who was now portrayed as 'Isis, the great one, mother of the gods' (ἱερὸς πῶλος ᾿Ισιδος μεγάλης μητρὸς θεῶν).[96] This innovation elevated Cleopatra III over the Thea Philometor Soteira of the opposing party. The supremacy of the former's position was expressed in the dating formulae of documents. In these, the new priest was inserted directly after the priest of Alexander and so before the priestesses of the apotheosized queens (the athlophoros of Berenike Euergetis, the kanephoros of Arsinoe Philadelphos and the hiereia of Arsinoe Philopator).

The fact that there is a great quantity of documents from 130 and 129 which are dated by Euergetes' reign indicates that the king's cause made swift progress. In Thebes, Euergetes' rule was firmly established from 21 January 130.[97] The city of Hermonthis, which was situated not far from Thebes, defied the punitive expedition of Paos[98] for quite some time and at the end of October was still in Cleopatra II's hands. For years, however, Euergetes could not succeed in his efforts to take Alexandria. The Mediterranean metropolis had incredible resources at its disposal, just as when Antiochos IV had attacked in 169 and 168, and it was also able to use overseas trade to its own advantage. This time, the Romans did not intervene, although a debate took place in the senate concerning Egypt in 130, in which mention was made of the murder of Memphites (Liv. *Per.* LIX).

The Seleukid king, Demetrios II, was now presented with an opportunity to interfere in Egypt's affairs. He had previously married Ptolemy VI's daughter, Cleopatra Thea,[99] and thus was Cleopatra II's son-in-law. Although Demetrios had been captured by the Parthian king Mithridates I in 139, he became king again when his brother and rival, Antiochos VII Sidetes, died in a battle against the Parthians in 129. At that time, Cleopatra II was completely isolated in Alexandria. For this reason, she offered the Egyptian throne to her Seleukid son-in-law in exchange for military assistance (in 129: Just. XXXVIII.9.1; XXXIX.1.2–4). What the Seleukid kings had long dreamed of was now being offered to Demetrios. But in the Egyptian campaign that followed, he managed to get only as far as the border stronghold of Pelusion with his troops, where he encountered Euergetes. Because of a revolt of his troops, he was forced to give up his plans in the spring of 128.[100] Cleopatra II's situation in Alexandria had now become hopeless; she fled to Syria taking the Ptolemaic state treasure with her.

Euergetes was as clever in his political manoeuvres as he was brutal. He now attempted to use the resentment of the Syrians against Demetrios II to his own advantage. When the latter had already left for Egypt, Euergetes evidently incited the city of Antioch to rise against the Seleukid king. Soon other Syrian cities joined in the revolt. As early as 129/8, Euergetes II appointed a man of low birth named Alexander Zabinas as a rival to Demetrios II for the kingship; he tried to confer legitimacy on this usurper by announcing that he was the adopted son of Antiochos VII Sidetes (Just. XXXIX.1.4–8; J. *AJ* XIII.267–8).[101] In 126, Euergetes sent Alexander Zabinas with a large army to Syria where he defeated Demetrios II at Damascus. Soon after this battle, Demetrios was murdered; one of the many rumours in circulation alleged that Cleopatra Thea had been responsible for the deed.[102]

Thus, with the success of his foreign policy, Euergetes II snatched away the support which Cleopatra II had hoped to get from Syria. He probably took Alexandria in 127/6. From 126 there was only one priest of Alexander there, with the same title that he had borne before Euergetes' flight to Cyprus. The re-establishment of ties between Alexandria and the Egyptian chora had important effects on the economy of the eastern Mediterranean world. Even the many Italian merchants on Delos, the Ῥωμαῖοι, profited from renewed relations between the two. A group of them dedicated a statue to a certain Lochos, who is attested as strategos of the Thebaïd at the time,[103] out of gratitude for the benefactions shown them 'when Alexandria was taken by King Ptolemy Theos Euergetes'.[104]

After Alexandria had been conquered, the king took his revenge by meting out punishment with remarkable brutality. Among other reprisals, he is said to have had the gymnasium surrounded and set on fire while a great many ephebes were inside. Many of them were killed (V. Max. IX.2. ext.5).

In 124, the dating formulae indicate that, at least officially, the two Ptolemaic parties had been reconciled and the bizarre triple monarchy was continued. The title 'Theoi Euergetai' again included Ptolemy VIII and his two wives, Cleopatra II and III, just as it had previously from 140–131. It is unknown why Euergetes II suddenly made peace with his defeated sister and wife, but it may have had something to do with his Syrian policy.

In the Seleukid kingdom, Cleopatra Thea soon had her elder son killed; he had become the successor of Demetrios II as Seleukos V (126) (App. *Syr.* 69; Eus. I.257, Schöne; Just. XXXIX.1.9). She was now the sole representantive of the legitimate Seleukid dynasty, whereas Alexander Zabinas was a candidate for the kingship only because of the machinations of Euergetes. Her coins in Ptolemais (Ake) dating from 126/5 still portray her alone; thereafter, she appears with her younger son Antiochos VIII Grypos ('hooked nose')[105] as his guardian and co-ruler. Ptolemy VIII completely reversed his Syrian policy in 124/3. He abandoned his protégé Alexander Zabinas and now supported the party which had gathered around Cleopatra Thea and Antiochos VIII; he even wed his daughter Tryphaina, whose mother was Cleopatra III, to the young king (Just. XXXIX.2.3). Thanks to Egyptian military assistance, Alexander Zabinas was decisively defeated in 123 and executed by Antiochos Grypos.

The Ptolemaic queen in Syria, Cleopatra Thea, showed by her ruthless pursuit of power and her willingness to murder even her own son, Seleukos V, that she was very much like the rulers of the late Ptolemaic period, particularly her mother and sister, Cleopatra II and III. It is said that in 121/20, having become concerned with her own position, she offered a cup of poison to her son, Antiochos Grypos, and that he then forced her to drink it (App. *Syr.* 69; Just.XXXIX.2.7f.). Her unrestrained ambition led to her doom. Her mother Cleopatra II, for her part, was again elevated to the rank of queen of Egypt in 124.

The senseless civil war and the military intervention in Syria resulted in a new age of decline for Egypt. After a period of progress in the last years of Ptolemy VI's reign, the condition of the lower classes must have deteriorated significantly once again. Just as in previous times of crisis, the phenomenon of anachoresis was once again on the rise. Even after the Ptolemaic triple monarchy had been re-established, a general climate of uncertainty prevailed in Egypt. The situation demanded comprehensive and radical solutions. Euergetes II attempted to redeem the recent past by means of reforms and ordinances granting pardons.

The generous Amnesty Decree[106] issued by the Ptolemaic trio in 118 is still extant thanks to rather careless copies on papyrus fragments which were used for crocodile mummies; they were found in the nekropolis of Umm el-Baragât. Of these, the most important texts come from the archive of a village scribe from Kerkeosiris – the longest consists of 264 lines arranged in ten columns.[107]

Like the decree issued by Epiphanes in 186,[108] this proclamation also begins with a general amnesty. With the exception of murder and temple theft, all crimes committed before 28 April 118 were to be pardoned. Fugitives from their land were to return. All the kleruchic land which was legally held – in particular the small lots belonging to the machimoi – was confirmed. Taxes in arrears were waived and the duty was reduced on goods arriving by way of the harbour of Alexandria. In general, the administration sought to implement measures which would improve the legal and economic situation of the working population, particularly farmers of crown land.[109] In the interest of the state, this latter group could neither be enslaved nor imprisoned for debt of any kind.[110] If their property was seized, they had to be left sufficient means to subsist and carry on with their work. Very significant was the new assignment of the respective jurisdictions of the Greek and Egyptian courts (χρηματισταί and λαοκρίται) made their jurisdiction according to the language of the document which was being contested.[111]

The higher and lower priesthoods were to receive still greater advantages. Those who had bought the office of priest were allowed to retain it, but they could not transfer it to others on their own authority. The immunity and freedom of temple land was upheld and the right of the temples to grant asylum was confirmed. Renovation of temple precincts and sanctuaries was encouraged. As a devout pharaoh in the ancient Egyptian style, Euergetes II promoted the animal cults. Most importantly, it was decided that the costs of burying the sacred animals Apis and Mnevis would be met by royal funds. The concern of the king for the sacred animals is a common motif in the decrees of the priests issued in the period spanning the reigns of Ptolemy III and Ptolemy V.

It is true that this decree, like the earlier amnesty decrees issued by the Ptolemies, was inspired by the political necessities of the day, but it is important to remember that it had its precedents in the ancient Egyptian tradition. General amnesties, including the release of prisoners, the reinstatement of lost property and the ordering of fugitives back to their land as well as decrees enacted to support temples and cults are all attested from the New Kingdom and the late Egyptian period. Amnesty decrees listing the benefactions of a ruler stem from the beginnings of the pharaonic state and represent an important feature of the ancient Egyptian royal ideology.[112]

The group of decrees enacted in 118 were part of a large-scale programme designed to bring about peace and stability. Other amnesty decrees followed in the same year.[113] The creation of a new dynastic god, however, represents the high point in the attempt to bring about a reconciliation between the members of the Ptolemaic family. This new god, bearing the cult-title of Neos Philopator, appears in the title of the priest of Alexander between the title of the deceased Theos Philometor and of the ruling Theoi Euergetai and is attested as early as 22 May 118. Neos Philopator became part of the list of Ptolemaic kings shortly after the great peace decree of 28 April 118, making the relation between the two events quite clear. One must assume that a crown prince murdered by Euergetes II was subsequently rehabilitated, analogously to the inclusion of the former co-regent Ptolemy Eupator in the dynastic cult. It was previously thought that the new god was in fact the son of Philometor who had been killed at the wedding of Ptolemy VIII and Cleopatra II and has come to be known as Ptolemy VII. There are good reasons, however, for identifying Neos Philopator as Ptolemy Memphites, the most notable victim of the dynastic war who as the 'father-loving one' allegedly forgave his murderer posthumously.[114]

After the murder of Memphites, the later Ptolemy IX Soter II was made crown prince; the ancient texts (Just. XXXIX.3.1; Paus. I.9.1–3; Porph.: FGrHist. 260 F 2.8) all confirm that he was the elder son of Cleopatra III. This identification should not be cast in doubt on account of the dating of the marriage between Ptolemy VIII and Cleopatra III to 141/40. Despite his epithet 'distinguished because of his birth together with the living Apis', there is no need to align his birth with that of Apis in 142.[115] A much more likely date of birth is 140/39. Shortly before his father's death in about 117, he received the office of governor-general of Cyprus (Paus. I.9.1) at his mother's urging and along with this position he was given many titles including strategos, nauarch, and archiereus.[116] Cleopatra III, who was not fond of him, obviously had him sent away in order to pave the way for his younger brother, later known as Ptolemy X Alexander I, to succeed to the throne.

Apart from these two sons, Ptolemy VIII and Cleopatra III also had three daughters. The oldest was probably Tryphaina who married Antiochos VIII Grypos in 124/3. Despite the fact that none of the ancient sources attribute to her the name 'Cleopatra', she is still referred to as 'Cleopatra Tryphaina' in modern sources. The second daughter, Cleopatra IV, was married to her brother Ptolemy IX at a very young age. The youngest daughter was named Selene. Aside from these offspring, Ptolemy VIII also had an illegitimate son called Ptolemy by a concubine. Euergetes had planned in his will that this Ptolemy, given the epithet of Apion, would rule Cyrenaica as an independent kingdom (Just. XXXIX.5.2), but he is attested as king in Cyrene only from 100.[117]

Alexandrian scholarship went through a second rather significant period of decline during the reign of Eueregetes II; the expulsion of Greek intellectuals from Alexandria when control of the city changed hands again in 145 and the brutal conduct of the king after the metropolis was retaken in 127/6 were milestones in this development. It should be emphasized, however, that these actions were motivated by purely political reasons. Ptolemy VIII was himself an enthusiastic philologist and even wrote a critical study of Homer, perhaps together with Aristarchos of Samothrake before the fateful year of 145. In addition, Euergetes II wrote 24 books of *Hypomnemata*, treating various topics, from which a rather large number of fragments have survived (FGrHist. 234); among the subjects discussed in this work are the animals found in Libya, the birds in the Alexandrian zoo, the mistresses of Ptolemy II and the habits of the Numidian king, Massinissa, whom Euergetes had visited at one point during his rule in Cyrene (162–145).[118]

The final years of Euergetes II's reign marked a new era in the development of trade with India. During the course of the second century, the Greeks explored the west coast of India more and more exhaustively and thereby came to the realization that the ocean was framed by East Africa, Arabia and India. At the court of Ptolemy VIII, the commercial implications of this new knowledge were quite clear. As early as about 117 under Euergetes II, Captain Eudoxos of Kyzikos was sent to India for the first time; after the death of Ptolemy VIII, he was sent there once again (Poseid.: FGrHist. 87 F28.4–5).[119] During the decades which followed, trade relations between India and Egypt became closer; presumably a shorter route was found by taking advantage when possible of the seasonal monsoons. As trade with the east intensified, the Nabataeans evidently tried to intervene. It is reported (Just. XXXIX.5.5–6) that King Aretas II (*c.* 120–96) undertook a series of plundering campaigns against the Ptolemies and Seleukids. The office of 'strategos of the Red and Indian Sea', however, was first created under Ptolemy XII, perhaps in the early 70s.[120]

A building inscription from Edfu[121] informs us that Ptolemy VIII Euergetes II died on 28 June 116. One of the most brutal and at the same time shrewdest politicians of the Hellenistic age had passed away. He bears comparison with the minister of Ptolemy IV, Sosibios. The classical sources emphasize, above all, his faults in comparison with the virtues of his elder brother Philometor. To complete the picture, it should be mentioned that the amnesty decrees show us that he did also show some concern for good government and the welfare of the country.[122] There can be no doubt that the internal dynastic disputes under Ptolemy VIII wrought terrible consequences on all of Egypt.

## DYNASTIC POWER STRUGGLES AT THE TURN OF THE CENTURY: PTOLEMY IX, X AND XI (116–80)

### The first reign of Ptolemy IX Soter II (116–107)

The extraordinary measures taken by Ptolemy VIII in his will regarding his successors show that he was no longer a match for the difficult familial situation. Clearly influenced by Cleopatra III, he left the kingdom of Egypt to her and to 'whomever of the two sons she would choose' (Just. XXXIX.3.1). He had intended that Cyrenaica should be ruled by Ptolemy Apion as an independent kingdom (Just. XXXIX.5.2). What he had planned for Cyprus is unclear; either the island was to continue to be ruled from Alexandria or it was to be a broadly autonomous territory under the control of the son who was not ruling in Alexandria. The fact is that by handing over all power to his younger wife, Euergetes II disregarded the normal practice of conferring direct succession on the eldest son.

Cleopatra III wanted to make her younger son Ptolemy X Alexander I co-regent but was thwarted by her mother and rival, Cleopatra II. The army and people installed the elder Ptolemy as king with the result that Cleopatra III was forced to accept him as co-pharaoh (Paus. I.9.1–3; Just. XXXIX.3.2; Porph.: FGrHist. 260 F 2.8).[123] At the same time, Cleopatra II asserted her own right to rule as one of the co-regents of Egypt. This new triple monarchy is documented in a demotic source[124] from 29 (?) October 116; the two women pharaohs, both bearing the name Cleopatra, are mentioned first in the document followed by the pharaoh Ptolemy bearing the cult name Philometor Soter. This title is a masculine version of the one Cleopatra II assumed during the civil war against Ptolemy VIII; it must, therefore, have been the older queen who imposed this form of continuity.

Before the year 116 had come to a close, Cleopatra II died. Documentary evidence indicates that from then on Cleopatra III ruled with Ptolemy IX (116–107). They counted the years of their reign from the death of Ptolemy VIII and propagated an image of dynastic solidarity by means of their cult title – individually they were known as Philometor Soteira and Philometor Soter and together as the Theoi Philometores Soteres. Cleopatra III also occasionally appeared as Thea Euergetis, her title from the reign of the eighth Ptolemy.[125] The king, who was dependent on his mother, soon received the nicknames Lathyros ('chickpea') and also Physkon ('fatso') which had already been attached to his father Euergetes II.

As far as Cyrenaica is concerned, a series of inscriptions dating from the end of the second century indicate that Ptolemy IX was in power there at that time. Evidently Ptolemy Apion was not able to accede to the throne for some time yet.[126]

After Euergetes II died in 116, Ptolemy X Alexander I replaced Soter II, his older brother, as strategos of Cyprus. When Soter II had been appointed strategos of the island in 117, a certain Helenos who had previously held the post naturally had to resign. Now he appeared as tropheus ('caretaker', 'helper' *vel sim*) of the strategos Ptolemy Alexander. The latter proclaimed himself 'king' of Cyprus in 114/13 and henceforth reckoned the years of his reign as of that date. Helenos once again became strategos (114–106).[127]

From the beginning, Ptolemy IX sought to establish himself as the religious representative of the country. To this end, every year from 117 to 107 he assumed the office of priest of Alexander and as such supervised the cult of the Theoi Philometores Soteres which had been established for himself and his mother.[128] The political propaganda of the Ptolemaic cult was intensified, especially in regard to the rule of Cleopatra; three new eponymous priests were created for the queen mother who now took on certain attributes of the goddess Isis.[129]

In the month of Mesore in 115 (from 17 August), Ptolemy IX journeyed south to offer sacrifices to the 'Great God Nile' on the island of Elephantine. The occasion was the festival celebrating the flooding of the Nile when it reached a level beneficial to agriculture.[130] This shows us the extent to which the king, who evidently had come alone,[131] personally observed his duties as pharaoh. The priests of Khnum were granted certain privileges at this event. The documents drawn up for this purpose (a royal letter and a decree) as well as other recent texts (the oldest dating from after the end of Ptolemy VIII's reign) were displayed on the memorial stele erected on the occasion of the king's visit.[132]

The royal documents on this stele as well as other texts from the period 117–107 clearly reveal the official hierarchy within the triple monarchy. Although the king's wife is sometimes named 'queen Cleopatra, the sister', neither the king alone nor the royal couple headed the administration or represented the state. Instead, the royal couple at the head of the kingdom was now composed of the mother – who was always named first – and her son. One can trace the increasing prominence of women in the dynasty in the course of the second century. Cleopatra I was the first woman to succeed in taking over the guardianship of a young king and in being officially recognized as the regent (180–176). From 170, Cleopatra II was an equal participant in the rule by two and even three Ptolemaic monarchs. Under Ptolemy VIII, one or two of the Cleopatras – depending on political circumstances – was always placed after the king in the royal decrees as an equal representative of the royal will. When she ruled alone at the time of the civil war, Cleopatra II took matters one step further but only for a limited time. After the death of Euergetes II, the rival queens no longer wished to step down. The options available to them were no longer limited to the guardianship of an underage king or to an almost equal partnership with the king. The female element, in the guise of the mother, had supplanted the king in the administrative documents and sometimes even the pharaoh in the temple reliefs.[133] This development later culminated in the person of the great Cleopatra.

A sister and spouse of Soter II is mentioned in passing in a document of late summer 115, but it remains unclear who exactly she was. It is said that, shortly after the beginning of his reign, he had been compelled by his mother to divorce his sister, Cleopatra IV (Just. XXXIX.3.2). He then married his younger sister, Selene, who from then on appeared as Cleopatra Selene and is now numbered by scholars as Cleopatra V.

After her divorce, Cleopatra IV intended to marry the Seleukid Antiochos IX Kyzikenos (114/3–95) who from 113 was at war with his half-brother Antiochos VIII Grypos (125–96). So as not to make an appearance empty-handed, Cleopatra IV went first to Cyprus, collected an army under the very eyes of the Ptolemaic strategos Ptolemy Alexander and his 'helper' Helenos and then set off with her troops for Syria as the future Seleukid queen (Just. XXXIX.3.3). But she was not to enjoy good fortune as the wife of Antiochos IX; Cleopatra IV was besieged by Grypos in Antioch and after the city had been conquered in 112, she was murdered at the behest of her own sister Tryphaina, the wife of Antiochos VIII (Just. XXXIX.3.4–11). But a little later in 111 after Antiochos IX had defeated Grypos, Tryphaina was herself captured and executed (Just. XXXIX.3.12: 'He sacrificed her to the *manes* of his wife (scil. Cleopatra IV)').

The Romans remained interested in the fertile land on the Nile river. In the summer of 116, a group of four Romans came to visit Philae; they left behind two inscriptions[134] which are the oldest Latin inscriptions from Egypt so far discovered. It is not known whether the group formed part of a delegation sent to Egypt after the death of Euergetes II.

The Roman senator, L. Memmius, made an official voyage to Egypt in 112. Details of the trip are known from a copy of a letter (dated to 5 March 112) sent by one Hermias, who was perhaps dioiketes in Alexandria, to a lower-level civil servant at the finance department in the Fayum.[135] The letter was occasioned by Memmius' journey from Alexandria to the Arsinoite nome. It particularly emphasizes that the senator is to be attentively received everywhere; at certain places, his accommodations were to be neatly arranged rooms and it was also envisaged that the senator would be given guest-gifts at the landing stages of his lodgings. Part of the programme included attractions such as the feeding of the crocodile-god Petesuchos and the other sacred crocodiles as well as visiting the so-called labyrinth, i.e. the pyramid-temple of Amenemhet III at Hawara from the twelfth dynasty. Provisions were also to be made for votive offerings and the performance of a sacrifice. L. Memmius may well have been sent by Rome as an observer, but his trip through the Fayum was in actual fact a sight-seeing tour; he is often cited as an early example of Roman tourism in Egypt.[136]

In Alexandria, dynastic struggles for power were soon to begin again (Just. XXXIX.4.1; Paus. I.9.2; Porph: FGrHist. 260 F 2.8). Cleopatra III succeeded in rousing the Alexandrians against the king. She spread the rumour that Soter II was planning an attack against her. In autumn of 107 he was compelled to flee from Alexandria; his sister and wife Selene and their two sons had to stay behind. While these events were taking place, Ptolemy X Alexander I left Cyprus where he had ruled from 114/3 and travelled to the Egyptian border. Cleopatra fetched him from Pelusion and brought him back to Alexandria where she elevated him to the throne of the Egyptian kingdom as her co-regent and the successor of Ptolemy IX. Just as in the case of Soter II, this political procedure of Cleopatra II was expressly referred to in the hieroglyphic titulature of Ptolemy X Alexander I.[137]

## Ptolemy X Alexander I (107–88)

It was, in fact, a revolutionary step for a woman at the head of the state to banish one son and then have another son hold office as a puppet co-regent. Cleopatra III now officially established a twofold system of reckoning of the years of their reign; her eleventh year in power was now mentioned alongside the eighth of Alexander I. The period of co-rule started at the beginning of November 107[138] and ended with the queen's death toward the beginning of September 101.[139] The supremacy of the queen mother was underlined by the fact that she had ruled for a longer time and her name was always mentioned first in the dating formulae. For the last time in Ptolemaic history, the dynastic cult was to display its effectiveness as a means of political propaganda; with the creation of yet another priesthood,[140] there were now five priesthoods dedicated to the living Cleopatra III in the dynastic cult at Alexandria. From 107 to 105, Ptolemy X took over the position of priest of Alexander from his banished elder brother.[141] Next, Cleopatra III's lust for power led her to commit an incredible act: for the year 105/4, she took over as a woman the title of priest of Alexander. By assuming this supremely Hellenistic title, which hitherto had been reserved for men, she flouted the very essence of the Ptolemaic tradition of sovereignty.[142]

After Soter II was expelled from Alexandria in 107, he fled to Cyprus but was pursued by Cleopatra III's troops. From there he went to Seleukia in Pieria where yet another attack on him was attempted. Soter II's forces, however, remained intact. From Syria he was able to reconquer Cyprus and ruled the island from that time on (106/5–88) as an independent sovereign ruler. Just as in 116, the Ptolemaic brothers had once again exchanged places between Cyprus and Alexandria (Just. XXXIX.4.1–2; Diod. XXXIV/XXXV.39a). Interestingly enough, Alexander I continued to mint coins for Cyprus out of Alexandria; we know of only very few tetradrachms of Soter II originating from the Cypriot mints of Paphos and Salamis.[143]

After his banishment from Alexandria, Soter II was also able to retain control of Cyrenaica until about the end of the second century.[144] He also succeeded in consolidating his position in Cyprus, as is evidenced by the fact that he would soon intervene in Syria with his troops; the area was in turmoil after 113 on account of the civil war in progress between the Seleukid half-brothers, Antiochos VIII and Antiochos IX.

When Soter II was reigning in Alexandria, he had sent Antiochos IX Kyzikenos 6,000 soldiers in about 109/8 for a campaign against the Jews led by the Hasmonean, Hyrkanos I (J. *AJ* XIII.278). Hyrkanos' successor was Aristobulos I who held the office of high priest in 105/4 and at the same time declared himself king. By 104/3, the king and high priest of the Jews was Alexander Iannaios who during the following decades succeeded in expanding his empire, at the expense of the shattered Seleukid dynasty and its neighbours, as far as the Palestinian coast and eastern Jordan.

In the war that followed from 103 to 101 (J. *AJ* XIII.324–364),[145] the estranged Seleukid half-brothers kept their distance for the most part. When the Jewish king Alexander Iannaios prepared to conquer Ptolemais (Ake) toward the end of winter in 103, the inhabitants appealed to Soter II in Cyprus for help. The latter was on the spot immediately, but the citizens of Ptolemais had changed their minds in the meantime and now refused his support. Fearing Soter II, Iannaios broke off his siege of Ptolemais and moved against Soter II with a new army. Ptolemy Soter then captured the city of Asochis in Galilee, crossed Jordan, defeated the army of Iannaios at Asophon and overran Judaea in a murderous campaign of plunder.

In her own realm, Cleopatra III was counting on the Jewish generals, Chelkias and Ananias (the sons of Onias IV), and had already secretly negotiated with Iannaios.[146] Soter II's advance on Egypt caused the queen to attack. Prior to this she had brought her grandchildren, who would later be the kings Ptolemy XI, XII and Ptolemy of Cyprus, together with a large portion of her treasure, to the Asklepieion on the island of Kos for safety. She had done this anticipating a period of great political turbulence within Egypt (J. *AJ* XIII.349; App. *Mithr.*23).[147] Cleopatra III then sent her son Alexander with a fleet to Phoenicia late in the summer of 103; Alexander then succeeded in advancing as far as Damascus.[148] She herself travelled by land to Ptolemais with all of her infantry troops; she was denied entry and so besieged the city in about September 103.

Since so much of the army was being deployed outside Egypt, Soter II saw the chance to regain his sovereignty in Egypt and marched on Pelusion in the autumn of 103. But Ptolemy Alexander was swifter; he succeeded in driving back Soter II, who then spent the winter of 103/2 in Gaza. Alexander stationed his army in Pelusion and kept watch over the Egyptian borders.[149] The only option left to Soter II was to return to Cyprus where afterwards he lived peacefully and ruled until 88.

The city of Ptolemais evidently had to surrender to Cleopatra III's troops at the commencement of 102. The Egyptian general Petimuthes recounts the capture of the city in the autobiography on his statue in Karnak.[150] The king of the Jews, Alexander Iannaios, then went to Ptolemais to pay homage to Cleopatra. Some of her philoi even suggested making Judaea a Ptolemaic province. Once again, the Ptolemaic kingdom was close to regaining a part of Coele Syria. But then the Jewish general of Cleopatra, Ananias, warned of the hatred of the entire Jewish people and the suggestion was dropped. Cleopatra probably also took into consideration how the Romans would react, for Judaea had become Rome's ally in 161. Cleopatra thus concluded a treaty with Iannaios (J. *AJ* XIII.353–355). After these events, the queen returned to Egypt. She left behind her troops in Ptolemais until the end of September 102, probably to discourage Soter II from further action in Syria. Alexander Iannaios was now able to resume his conquest of Palestine without hindrance by the beginning of 101.

The weakness of the Seleukids is clearly indicated by the fact that in the war lasting from 103 to 101 a dynastic conflict of the Ptolemies was played out on Seleukid territory. The Jews and their king, Alexander Iannaios, were also implicated in the war, but the Seleukid kings had been neutralized by their own internal disputes. Cleopatra III had already taken up Antiochos VIII's side before the war broke out in 103. She had provided him with material aid and had sent him her daughter Selene to be his wife (Just. XXXIX.4.4); the latter had been left behind by Soter II when he had fled from Alexandria.[151]

Before the second century had come to a close, a clash arose between Ptolemy X and Cleopatra III. Either before or after the Syrian war, the king managed to escape from his mother but soon let himself be persuaded to return. Late in the summer of 101, he had her killed.[152] With Cleopatra III's death, one of the most domineering of the Ptolemaic women passed away. She had been the equal of her mother, Cleopatra II, in every way.

Ptolemy X Alexander I then married Cleopatra Berenike III, the daughter of his brother from the latter's first marriage to Cleopatra IV. Cleopatra Berenike became the new co-regent; the queen was now named after the king in documents from that time[153] and the couple jointly bore the cult title of Theoi Philometores Soteres.[154] A daughter was born from this union whose name and fate are not known (Porph.: FGrHist. 260F 2.8).

In 100, a law on piracy (*lex de piratis persequendis*) was passed in Rome which, among other things, exhorted the three friendly Ptolemaic kings in Alexandria, Cyprus and Cyrene[155] as well as the two Seleukid monarchs to carry out certain measures against the pirates. In this law, Greek Libya is named as an independent kingdom with its seat of power in Cyrene. By this time, Ptolemy Apion had finally obtained control of Cyrenaica, as Euergetes II had intended in his will. Perhaps this had occurred in about 102 with the help of Cleopatra III who wished to remove the Cyrenaica from Soter's sphere of influence. Ptolemy Apion died in 96, after he had made over his dominion to the Romans. The senate was content to take the Ptolemaic crown land into its possession and declared the Greek cities free (Liv. *Per.* LXX; Cic. *Agr.* II.51). Thus, Ptolemaic rights to the crown land and, more importantly, all the revenues from that land were transferred to the Romans. For the moment, the Romans preferred not to burden themselves with the task of organizing the land into a province, since this would have required a considerable amount of administrative work.[156] The Roman province of Cyrene, therefore, was formed only in 75/4.

Rome had thereby acquired the oldest foreign territory of the Ptolemies; it had been conquered by Ptolemy I in 322. For various reasons, Cyrenaica had been among the most important foreign territories of the Egyptian empire. It was a very large country with many trade connections and, most importantly, it shared a border with the Egyptian heartland. From its position of supremacy in the Mediterranean basin during the third century, the Ptolemaic kingdom now, at the beginning of the first century, could count only Cyprus as a foreign possession. Rome had advanced directly to the Egyptian borders.

The autumn of 91 brought news of unrest in southern Egypt. Followers of a 'rebel' had attacked landholdings in the two neighbouring nomes, Latopolites (around Esna) and Pathyrites.[157] Thebes itself was no doubt quick to join the uprising while the city of Pathyris, lying south of Thebes on the west bank, remained loyal to the Ptolemaic regime. The resistance of the city of Pathyris to the insurrection in the Thebaïd was even led by an Egyptian and Egyptian priests.

# The second reign of Ptolemy IX in Egypt (88–81)

Soter II was evidently able to profit from the unrest and deplorable state of affairs in Egypt at the beginning of the second decade of the first century. At the beginning of 88, Ptolemy X Alexander I was ousted as a result of a military revolt and an uprising of the Alexandrians. Apparently the Alexandrians had become incensed with his friendliness towards the Jews (Porph.: FGrHist. 260 F2.9); a clear sign that Alexandria was rife with anti-Semitism already at the beginning of the first century BC (cf. Jord. *Rom.* 81).[158] The Alexandrians called for Soter II's return and he was thus able to join Cyprus and Egypt into one Ptolemaic realm once again.[159]

The first political task facing the king at home was to quell the uprising in the Thebaïd. He had hardly arrived in Memphis when he sent his general Hierax south with a considerable number of troops. The strategos Platon communicated this to the inhabitants of Pathyrites in a letter dating to 1 November 88 and urged them to hold out.[160] Shortly thereafter, the Theban rebellion was crushed with the utmost severity only three years after it had broken out (Paus. I.9.3) – its dates are therefore about 90–88. Ptolemaic rule over Lower Nubia was lost during the uprising and only a very small fraction of it was re-established. Evidence for Ptolemy XII's reign here can only be found as far as Debod, 15 km south of Philae.[161] At the time when Roman rule was established the land was Meroitic.

After being driven out of Alexandria, Ptolemy X Alexander I began recruiting soldiers but was defeated in a sea battle. Barely escaping with his life, he fled with his wife and daughter (the son was, of course, still on Kos) to Myra in Asia Minor. There he prepared for a campaign against Cyprus and apparently had to borrow money from the Romans in order to pay his soldiers. As a kind of surety he probably made over his kingdom to the Romans should he pass away (Cic. *Agr.* I.1; II.41–42).[162] There was no lack of precedents for a deal of this kind, notably that of his father Ptolemy VIII. The dynastic clashes of the Ptolemies once again took on an international dimension. In attempting to take Cyprus, Ptolemy X was defeated for the second time and lost his life (Porph.: FGrHist. 260 F 2.8–9; Paus. I.9.3; Just. XXXIX.5.1).

The will of Ptolemy Alexander and the question which it raised concerning the benefits or disadvantages of making Egypt a Roman province no doubt left their mark on political life at Rome in the 60s and 50s. The bequest placed Rome in an awkward situation, since there were those in the senate who were opposed to extending the responsibility and power of the provincial governor. In their opinion, a proconsul in Egypt would have posed a great threat to the republic. Hence, Rome left the question of the Egyptian succession pending. This situation allowed Soter II to deal with Egypt's external affairs in peace and tranquillity for the rest of his life (88–81); naturally enough, he had to be tactful and diplomatic when dealing with any issue touching Roman interests.

After he returned, Soter II evidently had himself crowned for a second time in Memphis by the priest of Ptah.[163] It was the thirtieth year since he had acceded to the throne; it was a happy coincidence that in ancient Egyptian times it was precisely after so many years of rule that a jubilee celebration was held, called the Sed-festival, which marked the renewal of a king's sovereignty. Soter II suppressed any memory of his mother; henceforth, his cult name would simply be Soter instead of the earlier Philometor Soter.[164] Soter II did not remarry; he now appeared alone as king in the documents. He did, however, make his daughter Cleopatra Berenike III co-regent. She was the widow of his brother Ptolemy X Alexander I and now had returned from exile. Ptolemy X obviously underwent a moderate sort of *damnatio memoriae*, since subsequently he appears neither in the title of the priest of Alexander nor in other lists of the Ptolemaic kings.[165]

Since Cleopatra III had brought her grandchildren to Kos in 103, these children became implicated in the expansionist policy of Mithridates VI Eupator, king of Pontos. Soon after the First Mithridatic War (89–84) broke out between Rome and the Pontic king, Mithridates, justifiably confident of his military strength, quickly conquered a large part of Anatolia, including the Roman province of Asia, and occupied the island of Kos in 88. There he was able to capture the Ptolemaic princes along with the state treasure of the Ptolemies. The king had the princes brought up at his own court; two of them, the future Ptolemy XII and Ptolemy of Cyprus, even became engaged[166] later to Mithridates' daughters (App. *Civ.* 102; App. *Mithr.* 23.111). Mithridates was probably planning eventually to gain the support of the Ptolemaic kingdom in his anti-Roman policy.

In 87, Sulla took up the war against Mithridates, with L. Licinius Lucullus serving under him as quaestor. In the winter of 87/6, Sulla dispatched Lucullus as proquaestor to Crete, Cyrene, Alexandria and further into the Levant to raise a fleet. Cyrene was at that time a free polis. Lucullus, naturally, was especially interested in building up support for Sulla's army. Consequently, he set himself the task of organizing the muddled state of affairs in Cyrene and so imposed a constitutional order on the city (Plu. *Luc.* 2.4–5). On his way to Alexandria, Lucullus became embroiled in clashes with the pirates who were on Mithridates' side; as a result, he lost most of his ships which were already few in number and he himself barely escaped from the pirates through diversionary tactics (Plu. *Luc.* 2.6).

When the summer of 86 began, Lucullus arrived in Alexandria (Plu. *Luc.* 2–3; App. *Mithr.* 33)[167] and thereby put Soter II in an awkward position. The Ptolemaic king could not afford to offend the Romans, since his brother's will was now in Rome's possession. But once Sulla had travelled east, Marius and Cinna had begun their reign of terror against the Optimates at Rome and so the fate of Sulla was still very uncertain. Soter II decided to receive Lucullus magnificently in Alexandria and so proved himself to be a friend to the Romans. Lucullus was given his lodgings in the royal palace and was invited to the royal table. The Roman proquaestor behaved modestly; he refused the gifts offered to him by the king and even took part in philosophical discussions (Cic. *Ac.* 1.II.11). Ptolemy IX did not, however, send any ships; this seemed to him too risky, in view of the confused political situation in Rome and perhaps also the threat of Mithridates (cf. Plu. *Luc.* 3.1). Lucullus then travelled on to the Syrian harbour-cities. He was loaded with presents from Soter II and was escorted by Ptolemaic ships as far as Cyprus; the Egyptian ships went no further.

The negotiations between Sulla and Mithridates which took place in 84 also had an impact on the development of Ptolemaic history. During these negotiations, one of the Ptolemaic princes, who would later be Ptolemy XI Alexander II, managed to escape to Sulla's side. After peace had been concluded, Sulla took the prince back to Rome. Sulla's personal relationship with the Ptolemaic youth gave him insight into the workings of the Ptolemaic dynasty and he began to contemplate the possibility of intervening in Egypt at the next change of government.

Ptolemy IX Soter II's last years were spent peacefully on the political front. The dynastic struggles for power had, nonetheless, left their mark on the social and economic life of Egypt. An uprising and its subsequent quelling (90–88) are only the tip of the iceberg. As the second century ended and the first century began, the abandonment of land (anachoresis) and the resultant fallow land reached alarming proportions. An actual report dating from 83/2 shows that most of the inhabitants of a village in Herakleopolites (Middle Egypt) had abandoned it on account of economic difficulties and oppressive taxation.[168] This was not an isolated incident.

At the end of December 81,[169] Ptolemy IX Soter II died and left his daughter Cleopatra Berenike III alone on the throne.

## Cleopatra Berenike III and Ptolemy XI Alexander II (80)

After the demise of Soter II, Cleopatra Berenike III became the sole monarch (Porph.: FGrHist. 260 F 2.10). In memory of her father, she probably took on the cult title of Thea Philopator at this time and after her death was referred to by this name in official lists of the Ptolemies; she was inserted between Ptolemy IX and the succeeding Ptolemaic couple.[170]

Barely six months had passed when Ptolemy XI Alexander II, who at the time was in Rome, was recalled to Alexandria. Obviously, Cleopatra Berenike III's attempt to rule alone had met with opposition. (Porph.: FGrHist. 260 F 2.10–11). Ptolemy XI was the son of Ptolemy X Alexander I by an unknown woman.[171] He now married Cleopatra Berenike III, his step-mother, and shared the throne with her. Appian (*civ.* I.102) is no doubt correct in claiming that Sulla was largely responsible for having the joint rule established, because he wished to have influence over Egypt and its resources by means of his client.

Sulla was immediately given a taste of the type of conduct that was possible within the Ptolemaic dynasty. After 18[172] or 19[173] days (sometime in June 80),[174] the king murdered Berenike III. Since she had been very popular with the Alexandrians, the outraged masses dragged Alexander II from the palace and killed him in the gymnasium (Porph.: FGrHist. 260 F 2.10–11; App. *Civ.* I.102; Cic. *Alex.* fr. 9).[175] Ptolemy XI Alexander II suffered *damnatio memoriae*; he is not attested in the hieroglyphic texts.

## Notes

1  Mooren (1975), 70f. (026).
2  See p. 147.
3  Préaux (1936), 540; Rostovtzeff, II (1955), 571f.
4  Mitteis, Wilcken, I. no. 9; Goudriaan (1988), 144 (doc. 115).
5  T. C. Skeat, E. G. Turner, 'An oracle of Hermes Trismegistos at Saqqâra', *JEA* 54, 1968, 199–208; Ray (1976), 1–6; Goudriaan (1988), 124f. (DOC 111b); on the archive see p. 148 with note 109; on Hor, who discharged his service at the Hermaion of Ibis-Thoth in Saqqara: Kessler (1989), 110–112.
6  A papyrus fragment in which a 'revolt of Egyptians' is mentioned from the area around Edfu may possibly refer to these same events; SB 9681; F. Uebel, 'ΤΑΡΑΧΗ ΤΩΝ ΑΙΓΥΠΤΙΩΝ', *ArchPF* 17, 1962, 147–162; Goudriaan (1988), 143 (DOC 114).
7  See p. 154, 157.
8  SB 12821; L. Migliardi Zingale, in *Atti del XVII Congresso Internazionale di Papirologia, III*, Napoli 1984, 889–900.
9  UPZ I. no. 110; Rostovtzeff, II (1955), 569–573; C.Ord.Ptol., all. 39; Thompson, D. J. (1988), 254f.; Goudriaan (1988), 124 (on the Machimoi; on this topic see also p. 43).
10  Securely dated documents are extant from 162; cf. Rostovtzeff, II (1955), 715, III (1956), 1262, note 128, 1326, note 186; O. Montevecchi, in *ANRW* II.10.1, 432–435.
11  UPZ I. no. 2–105.
12  UPZ I. p. 52–77; H.-J. Thissen: LÄ III.1980, 366f. (s.v. Katochoi); Thompson, D. J. (1988), 216–231.
13  SIRIS 291, l. 29; 306; Dunand (1973), III.168f.
14  UPZ I. no. 59–60; Thompson, D. J. (1988), 230f.
15  UPZ I. no. 17–58; Lewis (1986), 79–85; Thompson, D. J. (1988), 233–245; Kessler (1989), 100.
16  The joint rule of three is still attested in the month of Thoth of the seventh year (beginning 3 October 164); the first known document for the sole rule of the eighth Ptolemy is dated to 7 December 164; cf. Lanciers (1988, 1), 410–412.
17  Cf. ibid., 413, 420f.
18  Lanciers (1988, 1).
19  Cf. Gruen (1984), 794–698.
20  Pestman (1967), 50. The examples for 'the pharaoness Berenike (II)' in the dating formulae represent exceptional cases; see p. 85.
21  UPZ I.111; C.Ord.Ptol., no. 35.
22  This is already attested for the period of the threefold rule in October 164, and further for the years 163, 162 and 158; cf. UPZ I. p. 247, 250; Thompson, D. J. (1988), 151, 215; Lanciers (1988, 1), 411f.

23 See p. 89, 100.

24 Cf. UPZ I. no. 14, col. I; 41.4–5; 42.4; Kessler (1989), 125.

25 UPZ I. no. 6; Thompson, D. J. (1988), 215f.; cf. W. Clarysse, 'UPZ I 6a, a reconstruction by Revillout', *Enchoria* 14, 1986, 43–49.

26 M. C. Betrò *et al.*, 'Mito e propaganda in età tolemaica', *Egitto e Vicino Oriente* 5, 1982, 35–39; on Hor see p. 181f.

27 This is confirmed by a poorly preserved priests' decree: E. Lanciers, 'Die Stele CG 22184: Ein Priesterdekret aus der Regierungszeit des Ptolemaios VI. Philometor', *GöttMisz* 95, 1987, 53–61; Huß (1991, 2), no. 16.

28 PP VI. 5071.

29 On these events see Laronde (1987), 439f.

30 The embassy was led by the general and statesman Komanos who is known from the civil war (186) and the Sixth Syrian War: see p. 145 with note 94 and p. 156 with note 23.

31 SEG IX.7, ll. 6–11.

32 SEG IX.7 (with extensive bibliography); Winkler (1933), 50–59; Otto, W (1934), 97–116; Bartson (1982), 540–543; Gruen (1984), 702–705; Laronde (1987), 440–442.

33 OGIS I.116; M. Holleaux, 'Décret des auxiliaires crétois de Ptolémée Philométor, trouvé à Délos', *ArchPF* 6, 1913, 9–23 (= id., *Études d'épigraphie et d'histoire grecques, III*, Paris 1942, 77–97).

34 This identification is, nonetheless, not certain because diplomatic relations with Philometor had been broken off at that time, while Euergetes was in Rome's favour.

35 Günther (1990).

36 On this topic see Laronde (1987), 442–444.

37 Placed in the gate room of the West Tower during the last two decades of Philometor; cf. Junker (1958), 263–277; Török (1986), 236–238, no. 51.

38 On the 'gift' of the Dodekaschoinos see p. 86f.; on the stele: LD IV.27b; PM VI.229–231 (241); A. Giammarusti, A. Roccati, *File, storia e vita di un santuario egizio*, Novara 1980, 104f. The stele is dated to the last months of the Macedonian year (Peritios) which at that time was adapted to the Egyptian year (beginning with Dystros = Thoth); cf. Pestman (1967), 8.

39 I. Philae, I. no. 12 bis; Török (1986), 238f., no. 52; Bernand (1992), no. 19 (from February/March 148). On the problem of the Mandulis chapel on Philae: Haeny (1985), 222.

40 Bernand (1989), no. 302; I. Louvre, no. 14 (perhaps from Sehel); the two 'cities' are either rather small military garrisons or 'new foundations', i.e. not much more than a renaming of previously existing settlements; for this latter case, one is mostly reminded of Buhen and Dakke; cf. Török (1988), 274f. On the question of Ptolemaic rule in Lower Nubia south of the 12-mile district the fortifications of Qasr Ibrîm constructed about 100 BC cannot unfortunately be included although the excavators considered them to be Ptolemaic (W. Y. Adams *et al.*, 'Qasr Ibrim 1980 and 1982', *JEA* 69, 1983, 57–59; W. Y. Admas, 'Primis and the "Aethiopian" frontier', *JARCE* 20, 1983, 93–104); cf. M. Horton, 'Africa in Egypt: new evidence from Qasr Ibrim', in *Egypt and Africa. Nubia from Prehistory to Islam*, ed. W. V. Davies, London 1991, 268, 273.

41 On Boëthos see p. 157 with note 36; also: PP I, II & VIII.188, 1869; Thomas (1975), 91–94; Mooren (1975), 90f. (053); id. (1977), 115f.

42 I. Fay. 1; Griffiths (1987), On the relations between the Jews and Ptolemy I and II cf. Winnicki (1991, 1), 147–164.

43 PP III.5399; A.-P. Zivie: LÄ IV, 1982, 569–572 (s.v. Onias).

44 Between Jewish-Hellenists who sought support from the ruler and the Hasmonaeans; cf. J. A. Soggin, *Einführung in die Geschichte Israels und Judas*, Darmstadt 1991, 237f.

45 On this see Fraser (1972), I.285f. with note 793.

46 Augustus established a Gerusia (council of elders) in the Jewish community of Alexandria in AD 12; it is not clear whether the ethnarch was abolished as a result of the reform or perhaps presided over the new administrative body; cf. Kasher (1985), 253–255.

47 Kasher (1985), 4–6. On Egyptian influences see M. Görg, 'Ptolemäische Theologie in der Septuaginta', in *Ptol. Äg.* (1978), 177–185.

48 II Macc. 1.10 names him 'teacher of king Ptolemy'; on this topic cf. Fraser (1972), I.687–716.

49 In contrast, during the third century, the best scholars from all over the world had been summoned to the Museion; see p. 63f.

50 C.Ord.Ptol., no. 33 (from 13 August 163). On the three Ptolemaic bases in the Aegean see p. 42f.

51 IG II².983; Thompson, M. (1964).

52 PP III & IX.5246; VI.14549; Pestman (1967), 52, plus note e; Ray (1978), 119 (on the date of birth); Vittmann (1981); Clarysse, Van der Veken (1983), 28 (no. 133); Van 't Dack (1983, 2), 'P. Schubert, Une attestation de Ptolémée Eupator régnant?', *ZPE* 94, 1992, 119–122.

53 The elevation to co-ruler came after 3 February 152. Three statue bases from Cyprus honour Eupator as basileus: OGIS I.125–127; T. B. Mitford, 'The Hellenistic Inscriptions of Old Paphos', *BSA* 56, 1961, 22f. (no. 56); id., *The inscriptions of Kourion*, Philadelphia 1971, 86f. (no. 39).

54 See the sources in note 52.

55 Chauveau (1990), 157f.

56 Chauveau (1990 and 1991).

57 Primary sources for Philometor's policy in Syria in the period 150–145: I Macc.10.51–89; 11.1–19; Diod. XXXII.9c–d; XXXIII.3; Liv. *Per.* LII; J.A.J.XIII.80–119; App. *Syr.*67 *inter alios*. Secondary sources: cf. Otto, W. (1934), 123–131; Amantini (1974); Will, II (1982), 377–379; Grainger (1991), 122f.

58 On this voyage of the king see K.-Th. Zauzich, Enchoria 7, 1977, 193; Winnicki (1991, 2), 92.

59 Chauveau (1990 and 1991) summarizes the problems associated with this topic.

60 Until recently, modern scholarship had assumed that the beginning of the new reckoning of years next to the old was meant to announce the elevation of the younger son of Ptolemy VI to co-ruler and that this son was for a short time the sole representative of the kingdom as Ptolemy VII after the death of his father in the summer of 145. This conclusion cannot be sustained in the light of the abandonment of double dating in Philometor's lifetime as well as on chronological grounds; cf. Chauveau (1990 and 1991).

61 Last document preserved which dates to Ptolemy VI is on 15 July 144; cf. Lanciers (1988, 1), 422.

62 Ray (1976), 129f.

63 The first extant document which is dated by Ptolemy VIII and Cleopatra II is a demotic papyrus from the Fayum of 13 August 145: Lanciers (1988, 1), 422f. (erroneously 14 Aug.); on all questions of the change of monarch cf. Chauveau (1990 and 1991). Since this is not the place for a review of the numeration of the Ptolemaic kings that has been accepted by scholars for decades, Euergetes II remains here the eighth Ptolemy although I am aware that there was no independent ruler between him and Ptolemy VI Philometor.

64 The same passage also relates a legend about Ptolemy IV (III Macc.5–6) in which the king wished to set drunken elephants upon the Jews but owing to divine intervention the beasts had turned upon his own people instead. The legend seems to fit in better with the historical context of Ptolemy VIII.

65 C.Ord.Ptol. no. 41–42; F. Piejko, 'An act of amnesty and a letter of Ptolemy VIII to his troops on Cyprus', *AntCL* 56, 1987, 254–59.

66 C.Ord.Ptol., no. 43.

67 Lanciers (1988, 1), 423, 428.

68 Grenier (1983).

69 See p. 43, 191. The last epigraphic evidence of Ptolemaic rule on Thera dates from 145: Van 't Dack (1973), 84–89 (no. 6).

70 On this Bergman (1968), 108f.

71 Cauville, Devauchelle (1984), 51.

72 The latest consensus in a long discussion places the date of the marriage between 8 May 141 and 14 January 140: P. W. Pestman, *The Archive of the Theban Choachytes (second century* BC*)*, Leiden 1994 (?), 80–82 (no. 14), 85f. (no. 15). (I would like to thank the author for sending me a draft of the afore-mentioned pages in the spring of 1993).

73 Otto, Bengtson (1938), 31–33; Mooren (1988), 436.

74 Pestman (1967), 60, 62.

75 PP II.2155; IV.10070a; VI.14595; Mooren (1975), 71f. (027); W. Schäfer, in *Kölner Papyri 5*, edited by M. Gronewald *et al.*, Opladen 1985, 199–214 (no. 223–4); L. Criscuolo, 'L'archivio di Philô (P. Köln V, 222–225) e la confisca dei beni di Galaestes, l'Atamano (Diod. XXXIII.20), *ZPE* 64, 1986, 83–86.

76 PP I.264; II.2163.

77 C.Ord.Ptol., no. 47.

78 Knibbe (1958), 194–200.

79 On the topic of *tryphé* during the visit see Heinen (1983).

80 Otto, Bengtson (1938), 45-112; Will, II (1982), 429–436.

81 On the chronology: Mooren (1988), 436, note 10; on the coinage: Mørkholm (1975), 11.

82 This must have been retrospective by a year but the chronology is still uncertain. Some scribes used both reckonings for clarity; see Otto, Bengtson (1938), 47, note 1.

83 Ijsewijn (1961), 120.

84 Mooren (1975), 91f. (054), 116 (0120); Thomas (1975), 94–96; Vandorpe (1988), 48.

85 Mitteis, Wilcken, I, no. 10.

86 In the period 130/29 we still know of two Egyptian officers with the court title of one of τῶν πρώτων: Mooren (1975), 154f. (0213), 159 (0226); in the period 115–110 there was also one Egyptian epistrategos: ibid., 94f. (058); cf. also Mooren (1974).

87  Reymond (1981), 116f. (no. 16), Quaegebeur (1980), 69; Huß (1990), 199–202.
88  Secondary literature on Harsiese: Koenen (1959); Pestman (1967), 58–62;
    Beckerath (1984), 122; R. S. Bagnall, 'An unrecognized date by the rebellion
    of 131 BC', *ZPE* 56, 1984, 58–60; R. Bogaert, 'Un cas de faux en écriture à la
    banque royal thébaine en 131 avant J.-C.', *ChronEg* 63, 125, 1988, 145–154.
89  UPZ I., no. 199.
90  See p. 156, 166.
91  E. Lüddeckens, Ägyptische Eheverträge, Wiesbaden 1960, 176–180 (no. 11 D
    + Z).
92  L. Koenen, 'The prophecies of a potter: a prophecy of world renewal becomes
    an apocalypse', in *Proceedings of the 12th Intern. Congress of Papyrology*, ed. D. H.
    Samuel, Toronto 1952, 249–254; Koenen (1983), 181, 184, 186; L. Koenen,
    'A supplementary note on the date of the oracle of the potter', *ZPE* 54, 1984,
    9–13; Huß (1991, 1), 59f.
93  P. Leiden 373a: Lüddeckens, op. cit., 92–95 (no. 37); according to the transla-
    tion offered here 'welche mit Pharaoh ist' the addition can linguistically only
    refer to the 'priestess of Arsinoe'. It is generally assumed (Otto, Bengtson
    (1938), 70; Volkmann (1959), 1731; Ijsewijn (1961), 120, note 11), however,
    probably with justification that the appointment of all the counter-priests
    preceded the date of the document.
94  See here p. 197.
95  Mitteis, Wilcken, I. no. 107 (127 BC); Ijsewijn (1961), 120.
96  Attested for the first time in the same document dated to 28 May 130 and, for
    this reason, undoubtedly created for Cleopatra III; see here above note 93; on
    the hieropolos see p. 286.
97  Pestman (1967), 58, 60.
98  See p. 198.
99  See p. 193.
100 Following A. Houghton, G. Le Rider, 'Un premier règne d'Antiochos VIII
    Epiphane à Antioche en 128', *BCH* 112, 1988, 410.
101 Will, II (1982), 435.
102 Grainger (1991), 135. Cleopatra Thea had been married to Antiochos VII
    Sidetes during the Parthian imprisonment of Demetrios II; see Stemma 3. Her
    relations with Demetrios during 129–126 remain unclear.
103 Mooren (1975), 92–94 (055); Thomas (1975), 115–117.
104 OGIS I, 135; Rostovtzeff, II (1955), 727; Fraser (1972), II.217, note 242.
105 Houghton, Le Rider, loc. cit. (note 100), 402–411.
106 C.Ord.Ptol., no. 53, 53 bis, 53 ter.
107 Ibid., no. 53; the summary of the contents which follows is taken from this text.
108 See p. 157.
109 On this topic see p. 25.
110 Cf. this passage with p. 63 above together with note 155, an enactment by
    Philadelphos.
111 On this passage in C.Ord.Ptol., no. 53, ll. 207–220: P. W. Pestman, 'The
    competence of Greek and Egyptian Tribunals according to the decree of 118
    BC', *BAmSocP*, 1985, 265–269; Goudriaan (1988), 96–100; P. W. Pestman,
    *The New Papyrological Primer*, Leiden 1990, 85f. (no. 8).
112 H. S. Smith, 'A note on amnesty', *JEA* 54, 1968, 209–214.
113 C.Ord.Ptol., no. 54–55.

114 Chauveau (1990), 154–156.
115 See p. 281 with note 126.
116 Bagnall (1976), 45, 261; Michaelidou-Nicolaou (1976), 105 (Π 67).
117 See p. 210.
118 Fraser (1972), I.311, 515; Volkmann (1959), 1736.
119 On Eudoxos: PP VI.16258. Perhaps he was fortunate enough to sail around Africa for a second time in about 110; see W. Huß, 'Die antike Mittelmeerwelt und Innerafrika bis zum Ende der Herrschaft der Karthager und der Ptolemäer', in *Afrika. Entdeckung und Erforschung eines Kontinents*, ed. H. Duchhardt *et al.*, Köln 1989, 16.
120 L. Mooren, 'The date of SB V 8036 and the development of the Ptolemaic maritime trade with India, 'AncSoc 3, 1972, 127–133; Bernand (1984), no. 49 (from 74/3?), cf. Ricketts (1982/3); I. Philae, I, no. 52 (dating to 62).
121 Edfou VII.9.3–4; Cauville, Devauchelle (1984), 40f.; on this see p. 267 with note 38.
122 Cf. the visit of the royal couple in 144/3 to the Fayum: C. Balconi, 'Un papiro tolemaico inedito della collezione dell'Univ. Catt. di Milano (P.Med. Bar.4 verso)', in Proceedings of the XVIII Intern. Congress of Papyrology, 1986, Athens 1988, II.41–48. Reference has already been made to the golden age of the city of Cyrene during 162–145 when he resided there: see p. 188.
123 The official agent, even under constraint, was Cleopatra III. Accordingly, part of Ptolemy IX's hieroglyphic titulature (as well as later that of Ptolemy X) includes the phrase 'his mother makes him to appear on the throne of his father'; Beckerath (1984), 292, N 1; Cauville, Devauchelle (1984), 49.
124 P. Rylands dem. III.20; see Pestman (1967), 64, 66.
125 The assumption that Cleopatra III is meant here is indicated by the Classical sources and not, as Cauville, Devauchelle (1984), 48–50, a continuation of Cleopatra II's rule, is discussed by Thompson, D. J. (1989).
126 Laronde (1987), 445f.; Paci (1989), 590.
127 On the development on Cyprus: Mooren (1975), 195–197 (0356); Bagnall (1976), 260f.; Michaelidou-Nicolaou (1976), 57 (E5), 103f. (Π 60).
128 Clarysse, Van der Veken (1983), 34, 36.
129 See p. 287.
130 Bernand (1989), no. 244, ll. 1–14; id. (1992), no. 24, ll. 1–14. What is meant here is the so-called signal festival (σημασία) which is known from numerous documents from the Roman period; cf. D. Bonneau, 'Les fêtes de la crue du Nil', Reg 23, 1971, 58f.
131 Cf. SEG XXVIII. 1479, ll. 7–9; Van 't Dack *et al.* (1989), 20.
132 C.Ord.Ptol., no. 57–60, 89, all. 76–77; Bernand (1989), no. 244, ll. 15–75; id. (1992), no. 24, ll. 15–75.
133 Cf. two examples in which the mother (Cleopatra III) is rendered performing cultic rites preceding the king (Ptolemy IX): Sacrificial relief on the southern outer wall of the temple of Deir el-Medineh: PM II², 1972, 407, (34), 2; Temple of Khonsu at Karnak, first hypostyle, door lintel of the north gate, end of the left series of gods: PM II², 1972, 235, (36) a–b = The epigraphic survey, the temple of Khonsu, II, Chicago 1981, pl. 190.
134 SEG XXVIII.1485 (26 August 116); XXX.1750; Van 't Dack (1983, 3), 393–397; H. Devijver, 'La plus ancienne mention d'une tribu romaine en Égypte', *ChronEg* 60, 1985, 96–101; Van 't Dack *et al.* (1989), 23.

135 P.Teb.I.33: Mitteis, Wilcken, I, no. 3; Olshausen (1963), 6–11; Sonnabend (1986), 23, 121.

136 Sonnabend (1986), 121.

137 Beckerath (1984), 292 (10, H).

138 Last known date according to Soter: 23 October; first date of the joint rule with Alexander: 15 November; cf. Maehler (1983), 12, note 12.

139 On the chronology of this double-dating: Boswinkel, Pestman (1982), 67f.; Van 't Dack *et al.* (1989), 21f., 110–114.

140 See pp. 287–288.

141 Clarysse, Van der Veken (1983), 36, no. 184 b–185.

142 Ibid., no. 186.

143 Michaelidiou-Nicolaou (1976), 106.

144 R. S. Bagnall, 'Stolos the admiral', *Phoenix* 26, 1972, 358–368.

145 Van 't Dack *et al.* (1989).

146 See p. 190.

147 This was to some extent traditional, as she probably had also brought her own children to Kos and put them in the custody of 'one of the first Philoi' at the time of the civil war between Ptolemy VIII and Cleopatra II: OGIS I.141, 4–5; PP VI.14604; Mooren (1975), 207 (0383).

148 Van 't Dack *et al.* (1989), 50–61 (doc. III.3.1.19).

149 Cf. ibid., 83f. (doc. IV.1).

150 Quaegebeur, in ibid., 88–108. The statue is evidence for the fact that Cleopatra III had taken with her not only Jewish but also Egyptian high-ranking military officers on her campaign; on the Ptolemaic army of Soter II and Cleopatra III, cf. ibid., 128–136.

151 The later life of Cleopatra V Selene is probably characteristic of a royal lady of that time: when Antiochos VIII Grypos was killed in 96, she married his rival Antiochos IX Kyzikenos; after the latter also met a violent end (95), she joined herself to Antiochos X Eusebes, the son of her third husband (see Stemma 3) in a fourth marriage. Since the latter was probably killed in a Parthian campaign in 92, Cleopatra Selene remained a widow for more than two decades until she was killed by the Armenian king Tigranes in 69.

152 See pp. 207–208 with note 139.

153 C.Ord.Ptol., no. 62–63.

154 Pestman (1967), 72, 156.

155 SEG III.378.B.l.8f.

156 Laronde (1987), 455, 467; Paci (1989).

157 W. Spiegelberg, 'Eine neue Erwähnung eines Aufstandes in Oberägypten in der Ptolemäerzeit', *ZÄS* 65, 1930, 53–57. On the insurrection and resistance of the city of Pathyris cf. Préaux (1936), 549f.

158 On the slow rise of anti-Semitic sentiment during the course of the first half of the first century, cf. Fraser (1972), I.88, II.168, note 337.

159 According to the sources from the Egyptian chora the return of Soter II was known there at the latest by 21 May 88, although uncertainties as to the ruling king still occur among scribes until the autumn of that year; cf. Van 't Dack *et al.* (1989), 136–150.

160 Mitteis, Wilcken, I. no. 12; Van 't Dack *et al.* (1989), 147–149.

161 See p. 271 with note 63.

162 Following the most probable meaning of the relevant sources as per Badian (1967); Van 't Dack *et al.* (1989), 150–161.

163 Edfou VII.9.5–8; H. Brugsch, *ZÄS* 24, 1886, 32f. (Serapeum stele from the 31st year); Cauville, Devauchelle (1984), 52; Cl. Traunecker, *BIFAO* 79, 1979, 430.

164 Pestman (1967), 74, 76.

165 Ijsewijn (1961), 121; Müller, W. (1966); Winter (1978), 156.

166 These engagements have generally been dated (and probably rightly so) to the late 80s (after 84, since one hears nothing of Ptolemy XI who had managed to go over to Sulla in that year; see pp. 213–214): Seibert (1967), 120f.; 134; Will, II (1982), 480; Van 't Dack *et al.* (1989), 155. B. C. McGing, *The Foreign Policy of Mithridates VI Eupator, King of Pontus*, Leiden 1986, 139, on the other hand, interprets the engagements as an expression of a diplomatic measure by Mithridates in 74 directed at the ruling kings in Alexandria and Cyprus prior to the outbreak of the Third Mithridatic War with Rome.

167 On the Egyptian mission of Lucullus: Olshausen (1963), 12–21; A. Keaveney, *Lucullus*, London 1992, 23f.

168 BGU XIV.2370, col III.37–46; see also Maehler (1983), 6 with note 47; cf. Rostovtzeff, II (1955), 715f.

169 Following now A. Bernand, 'Une inscription de Cléopâtre Bérénice III', *ZPE* 89, 1991, 145.

170 Ijsewijn (1961), 121; Müller, W. (1966).

171 On this lineage cf. Van 't Dack *et al.* (1989), 150–155.

172 P. Oxy. 2222.

173 Following the literary tradition.

174 Following A. Bernand, *ZPE* 89, 1991, 146.

175 *Scholia in Ciceronis orationes Bobiensia*, ed. P. Hildebrandt, Leipzig 1907 (Stuttgart 1971), 32.

# 8 The final period: Egypt in the political designs of Roman leaders (80–30)

## PTOLEMY XII NEOS DIONYSOS (80–51)

### From his accession to the throne until his banishment from Alexandria (80–58)

After Ptolemy XI had been murdered, the Alexandrians had to act quickly if they wished to impose their choice of king. Roman intervention was a genuine concern for them since if his family line were wiped out the possibility became very real that the Romans would hold the Alexandrians to the terms of Alexander I's will. Cleopatra V Selene was the only remaining legitimate offspring of the Ptolemaic family. At the time, she was living in Cilicia as the widow of the Seleukid king, Antiochos X. On behalf of her two sons from that marriage (one of whom later became Antiochos XIII Asiaticus), she now laid claim to both Seleukid and Ptolemaic rights of succession (cf. Stemma 3).[1] From a Greek point of view, with the exception of Cleopatra Berenike III who had just been killed, the children of Ptolemy IX were seen as illegitimate (Paus. I.9.3; Cic. Agr. II.42). In cases where the mother is unknown and no proof exists that the royal offspring had later been acknowledged as legitimate, there is always the possibility that they had arisen from a marriage between their father and an Egyptian woman of high rank (perhaps from the family of the high priest of Memphis).[2]

Trying to take the initiative in the negotiations, the Alexandrians immediately recalled both sons of Ptolemy IX.[3] who were probably still at the court of Mithridates VI. One of the two princes, Ptolemy XII, was declared king of Egypt by them while the other was made 'king of Cyprus'. This was the first time that a Ptolemy was given the legal right to rule Cyprus as a separate kingdom (80–58).[4] The Alexandrians probably hoped that the Romans would be more disposed to accept an independent successor to the throne if Cyprus were officially separated from Egypt.

Ptolemy XII's reign was reckoned directly from the end of Soter II's last year in power; this meant that the short period of rule by Berenike III and Alexander II was now officially ignored. Soon after taking the throne, the king married his sister Cleopatra VI Tryphaina; Berenike IV issued from this union.

Ptolemy XII's cult title ʽΘεὸς Φιλόπατορ καὶ Φιλάδελφος' is attested from 79.[5] The epithet Philadelphos was used not only by Ptolemy XII and Cleopatra VI Tryphaina but also by Berenike III. It may have been given by Soter II to all of his children as an expression of his desire for harmony among all the siblings.[6] Because his mother had not been a member of the royal dynasty, Ptolemy XII probably felt it was necessary to strengthen his ties to his father Soter II by adopting this title. The royal couple appeared jointly as the Θεοὶ Φιλοπάτορες καὶ Φιλάδελφοι.[7]

By the time of his Egyptian coronation, if not before, Ptolemy XII bore the title of Νέος Διόνυσος ('New Dionysos') – the only Ptolemy to have done this in an official capacity![8] In conjunction with this new epithet, Ptolemy was also given the nickname of 'Auletes' due to his fondness for accompanying choruses on the flute. He even held contests in the royal palace in which he took part as a flute-player (Str. XVII.1.11; Athen. V.206d).

In 76, Ptolemy XII named the 14-year-old son of the recently deceased priest of Ptah in Memphis as the latter's successor. The fact that this young priest, Psenptah III, was selected to crown Ptolemy XII as pharaoh in Memphis may well have been related to the difficulties the young monarch was experiencing in getting the much-coveted recognition of Rome. Thanks to the funerary stele of Psenptah[9] we are well informed about the events of the coronation and what followed. The high priest then travelled to Alexandria and was named 'prophet of the pharaoh' while the king made frequent visits to Memphis to fulfil his pharaonic duties there. Since Psenptah's grandmother was a lady of high standing at the Ptolemaic court,[10] it follows that there were close relations between the royal dynasty and the most important priestly family of Egypt. It was a political necessity on both sides to foster these connections.

It may have been for this purpose that the king entered into what to Greek eyes was an illegitimate union with a woman who came precisely from these circles of the Egyptian elite. Cleopatra VII, who was born at the turn of 70/69, and the other children of Ptolemy XII may well have issued from a union of this kind.[11] Shortly after Cleopatra was born, the sister and spouse of the king, Cleopatra VI Tryphaina, fell into disfavour (69/8);[12] the reliefs depicting her on the great entranceway to the pylon of Edfu were now carefully covered over.[13] Cleopatra VI Tryphaina reappeared on the stage of history after her brother and husband had been deposed in 58/7.[14]

It may be that from the beginning the Romans were using the will of Alexander I to put pressure on Ptolemy XII and extort revenues from him. Nonetheless, the situation remained relatively calm until about the mid-60s. From then on, the question of Egypt and its abundant resources was hotly disputed by rival political leaders at Rome and it was a constant source of strife in the senate.[15] In 65, one of the two censors, M. Licinius Crassus, who would later form part of the first triumvirate, proposed the annexation of Egypt as a Roman province (Plu. *Crass.* 13.2), but the proposal collapsed owing to the objection of the other censor, Q. Lutatius Catulus. The part which one of the aediles of the year 65, a certain C. Iulius Caesar, played in these proceedings is not clear. Suetonius' statement (*Jul.* 11.1) that Caesar had attempted through a plebiscite to obtain an extraordinary *imperium* for the annexation of Egypt is highly doubtful. Suetonius' account, however, clearly illustrates that at the time ambitious Roman politicians began to see in Egypt a wonderful opportunity for advancing their careers. The efforts of Crassus and other members of the senatorial elite to lay claim to Egypt evidently gave rise to Cicero's intervention in 65 in his speech *De rege Alexandrino* of which unfortunately only a few fragments have been preserved.[16] The *optimates*, along with Cicero, energetically opposed the annexation plans.

Ptolemy XII now launched a campaign of handing out generous bribes to Roman officials from the different political parties at Rome – a course of action which was to prove quite successful. His goal was to be recognized as king by Rome. Whatever our opinion of Ptolemy XII's character, his policy of bribing members of the different political factions at Rome was the only way he could ensure that the dynasty would continue to exist and that Egypt would retain some degree of sovereignty.

Ptolemy XII was especially counting on support from Pompey. When the latter was in Damascus as part of his victory campaign in the east, the Ptolemaic king had a heavy gold crown sent to him (App. *Mithr.* 114; J. *AJ* XIV.35). Pompey had just ended the Third Mithridatic War (74/3–63) and had done away with the Seleukid kingdom. In 63, he reorganized Pontus, Syria and Cilicia into new Roman provinces. Ptolemy XII offered to support 8,000 of Pompey's cavalrymen as the latter began (also in 63) a military campaign in Judaea (Plin. *Nat.* XXXIII.136).

The king had to finance the high costs of his policy by raising taxes and cutting back on administrative costs. This meant that the situation of the working population in Egypt deteriorated once again. The fact that Ptolemy XII had to ask Pompey for help in putting down a revolt – precisely at the time when the Roman general was in the east – no doubt testifies to this. Pompey refused (App. *Mith.* 114), even though he was given the unique opportunity of being the first Roman to take the much coveted kingdom of Egypt by military intervention. Pompey was probably well aware of what would be the consequences in Rome of a direct intervention in Egypt. Such a course of action would have seriously hampered his attempt to gain official recognition of his other accomplishments in the east. Despite Pompey's refusal, Ptolemy XII apparently sent equipment for an entire army to Pompey and thus exhausted the Ptolemaic crown revenues. For this reason, Ptolemy XII was eventually compelled to borrow money from Roman lenders, particularly from the knight and powerful banker, C. Rabirius Postumus.

Crassus' followers, who had been hoping Rome would intervene in Egypt, were not satisfied with the defeat of their cause in 65. At the end of 64, the tribune of the people, P. Servilius Rullus, proposed an agrarian law which was to grant a commission of decemviri full powers over the Roman *ager publicus* both within and outside Italy. Roman farmers without property could thus obtain land through the sale of *ager publicus* in the provinces (Cic. *Agr.* II.38).

The associates of Catiline may well have been behind the proposed law,[17] but Crassus and Caesar would also have profited greatly from it. Already on the first day of his consulship Cicero opposed the proposal (1 January 63 following the pre-Julian, Roman calendar) by giving his first speech *De lege agraria* in the senate and a few days later his second such speech in the popular assembly. He delivered two more short speeches on the topic (Cic. *Att.* II.1.3), one of which is still extant. It is possible to infer from Cicero's remarks that certain influential circles in Rome entertained hopes of including Egypt into the law planned by Servilius Rullus by appealing to the will of Ptolemy Alexander. With regard to the question of the Egyptian inheritance, Cicero feared that Rullus and his ten men would act in a completely arbitrary fashion.[18] Although other areas such as Bithynia and Mytilene (Cic. *Agr.* II.40) are mentioned by Cicero, Alexandria and Egypt are at the heart of his argument. Cicero and his followers feared that a Roman aristocrat in Egypt could establish an independent power-base from which it could then succeed in destroying the Roman *res publica*. Cicero's speech evidently succeeded in winning over the people and Rullus dropped his proposal.

The political situation within Egypt worsened. Heavy taxation resulted in strikes such as the one by the crown farmers in a village of the Middle Egyptian nome of Herakleopolis, datable to 61/60.[19] In addition, the Alexandrians were well aware of the incredible sums their king had taken from Egypt and then simply handed over to the Romans. Direct intervention on the part of the Romans remained a constant threat and this meant that both throne and people anxiously saw to it that no disputes arose from their contact with Italians in Egypt so as not to provide the Romans with a pretext for acting. Diodorus (I.83.8–9) described the tense situation and had even visited Egypt around the year 60 before Ptolemy XII had been recognized as king and *amicus* by the Romans. While discussing the rites associated with the Egyptian animal cult, Diodorus also mentions that a person could have been lynched on the spot by an enraged mob for having unintentionally or intentionally killed an ibis or a cat (cf. Hdt. II.65.5). He himself had witnessed a Roman being slaughtered after he had inadvertently killed a cat and had seen agents of the crown standing by helplessly, even though it was their duty to put an end to such actions. Religious fanaticism was possibly also a welcome pretext for the people to kill a hated Roman.

Ptolemy XII had previously set his hopes primarily on Pompey, when the latter was active in the east. Now, in order to counteract the attempts to annex Egypt by the *populares* gathered around Crassus and Caesar, he was forced to focus on Caesar in the year of the first triumvirate (60). The king now promised Caesar and Pompey 6,000 talents as payment for being recognized as the legitimate king, a sum which roughly represented the entire annual revenues of Egypt (Suet. *Jul.* 54.3 among others). This time Ptolemy XII was not disappointed. As consul for the year 59, Caesar soon cleared up the situation and saw to it that Ptolemy XII was confirmed as king by a *senatus consultum*. In addition, Caesar introduced the *lex de rege Alexandrino* making the Ptolemaic king an *amicus et socius populi Romani* in gratitude for the help he gave to the Roman army in Syria (Caes. *Civ.* III.107; Cic. *Rab. Post.* 3; Cic. *Att.* II.16.2). Theoretically, Ptolemy XII had now achieved the goal for which he had long been striving through an extensive campaign of bribing Roman officials. He thus deflected the sword of Damocles which had been hanging over Egypt in the form of Alexander I's will. Caesar's *lex agraria* of 59 did not mention Egypt. It was no doubt on this occasion that the king issued an amnesty decree – datable to this period – which also guaranteed anew the hereditary character of kleruchic land.[20]

Recognition of his status as king was to bring the twelfth Ptolemy less fame than he had thought. From 80 onwards, Cyprus had been an independent kingdom, but it had also been included in the will of Alexander I. In the agreements between Rome and Ptolemy XII, it appears that Cyprus was ignored. P. Clodius Pulcher, the notorious tribune of the people in 58 and Caesar's henchman, then proposed and passed a law making the Cypriot kingdom into a Roman province. The alleged justification for this law was that the king of Cyprus had been assisting pirates during their operations on the Cilician coast.[21] At the same time, the *lex Clodia* provided for the confiscation of the Cypriot crown treasury and the removal of M. Porcius Cato from Rome under honourable circumstances. Cato, as dedicated a republican as Cicero, represented the senatorial aristocracy and to him was given the assignment of carrying out the annexation of Cyprus as *quaestor pro praetore* (Plu. *Cat.* 34.4–7; Liv. *per.* CIV among others). Ptolemy XII should have objected at the time, but he feared the Romans and was not interested in a confrontation with them. In the meantime, Cato sought to persuade Ptolemy of Cyprus to hand over the island by means of envoys while he remained at Rhodes and offered him the priesthood at the temple of Aphrodite in Paphos in exchange. Ptolemy of Cyprus chose suicide by poisoning as the honourable alternative and thus made Cato's task that much easier. After Cato's mission (58/56), Cyprus was joined to the province of Cilicia. Cyprus' status as a Roman province lasted approximately ten years until Caesar gave the island back to Cleopatra in the summer of 48.

The Alexandrians viewed Rome's annexation of Cyprus as an attack on Egypt since they themselves had once placed the brother of their king on the Cypriot throne. They were incensed with the passive Ptolemy XII, not least because of his wasteful bribery policy (D.C. XXXIX.12). For this reason, the leading members of the Alexandrian court forced the king to leave Egypt (sometime late in the summer of 58)[22] (D.C. XXXIX.12; Plu. *Pomp.* 49.7; Porph.: FGrHist. 260 F2.14).

There was only one possibility left for the Ptolemaic king: to turn to the Romans. First, he betook himself to Cato who at that time was staying on the island of Rhodes. Cato was certainly at odds with the leading men of

Rome and the meeting between Cato and Ptolemy XII as reported by Plutarch
(*Cato* 35.4–7) should be understood in the light of this fact. After the king
had made known to Cato his intention to go to Rome, Cato pointed out to
him the corruption and greed of the Roman aristocracy, whose main interests
lay in the economic exploitation of Egypt.[23] Cato is said to have offered the
king his support in the eventuality of his return to Alexandria but, in
reality, Ptolemy XII could not expect to obtain any real assistance from him.
In the end, the king could only find help of any substance in the capital. In
the course of 57, he arrived at Rome and Pompey received the 'New Dionysos,
present on earth' in his villa in the Alban hills (Str. XVII.1.11; D.C.
XXXIX.14.3). The king was to remain away from Egypt until the spring
of 55.

## Berenike IV (58–55) and the return of Ptolemy XII

The children of Ptolemy XII had remained in Alexandria; perhaps they
had even taken a position against their father. Cleopatra VI Tryphaina had
been eliminated from political life for over ten years. The Alexandrians now
put Ptolemy XII's eldest daughter, Berenike IV, together with her mother,
Cleopatra VI, who was now back in the public eye, on the throne.[24] The
daughter named herself Cleopatra Berenike, evidently following the example
of the third Berenike and also of previous female members of the dynasty.[25]
With the accession of both queens,[26] there the system of reckoning the years
of rule of the Ptolemaic sovereign was, naturally enough, started anew, with
58/7 counting as year one. Cleopatra VI Tryphaina, however, died before the
end of 57.[27]

The Alexandrians could expect the Romans to contest the latest developments in Egypt and at home there was sure to be some resistance to the new
regime headed by a woman. Accordingly, a husband was sought for Berenike
IV (Porph.: FGrHist. 260 F 2.14; Str. XVII.1.11; D.C. XXXIX.75.1–2).[28]
At first, two Seleukid princes were viewed as likely candidates; one died,
however, and the other was prevented from coming to Egypt by A. Gabinius,
the Roman proconsul in Syria. A third named Seleukos, nicknamed Kybiosaktes
('saltfish-trader'),[29] who claimed likewise to be a Seleukid, managed to reach
Alexandria. Berenike, however, was said to be so outraged at the base character of her spouse that she had him strangled after a few days. Finally, a
certain Archelaos,[30] who put forth that he was the son of Mithridates VI
Eupator, gained wide acceptance as her future husband. In fact, he was the
son of a general of Mithridates named Archelaos; Pompey had granted him
the office of high priest in the Pontic city of Komana in 63. The new situation in Egypt from the spring of 56 until the spring of 55 is described by
papyrological sources dating to 'year two, which is also year one'.[31]

In Rome, Ptolemy XII had found a supporter in his host, Pompey, who
brought the concerns of the king to a debate in the senate. The 'Egyptian

question'[32] concerning the reinstatement of Ptolemy was to become a highly complicated matter. In the end, the king's ability to pay off his huge loans to his Roman creditors, who naturally had a vested interest in Ptolemy's success, depended on whether or not he could return to Egypt.

The Romans were soon to discover how a Ptolemaic king usually handled his political opponents (D.C. XXXIX.13–14; Str. XVII.1.11; Cic. *Cael.* 23 and 51). An embassy composed of a hundred men arrived in Rome from Alexandria with the purpose of countering Ptolemy XII's accusations. The deposed king sent hired assassins to head them off in Puteoli. Most were killed there, some of those who survived were murdered in Rome and the rest were silenced through intimidation and bribery. Even the leader of the embassy, the philosopher Dion of Alexandria,[33] was poisoned in his host's home. The incidents were hushed up as much as possible and the investigation proposed by the senate never took place. Ptolemy XII had received money from Roman bankers in 57, while he was staying in Rome, and this represented a huge risk for the bankers; the latter therefore became implicated in the king's cause.

The 'Egyptian question' was dragged out painfully in several sessions of the senate and the popular assembly, where proposals and counter-proposals produced a stalemate. The opponents of Roman involvement in Egypt eventually fabricated an oracular pronouncement designed to further their cause. The statue of Jupiter Latiaris on the Alban hill was said to have been struck by lightning and the ensuing consultation of the Sibylline books revealed that, although it was necessary to uphold Rome's friendship with the Egyptian king, the Romans should refrain from reinstating him by means of military force (D.C. XXXIX. 15.1–3). As a result, Ptolemy XII had to surrender his hopes and left for Ephesos at the end of 57 (D.C. XXXIX.16.3; cf. Cic. *Fam.* I.1.1).

In reality, Pompey wanted to be forced to carry out a military campaign in Egypt. In the course of the first six months of 56, copies of a letter supposedly written by Ptolemy XII were distributed in the forum and at the entrance to the senate in which the king wished he had Pompey as his commander-in-chief (Plu. *Pomp.* 49; Cic. *Q.fr.* II.2.3). The consul in 57 and later also governor of Cilicia, L. Cornelius Lentulus Spinther, was the most likely candidate for such a task, since in 57 he had already received this assignment by decree of the senate (Cic. *Fam.* I.1.3; D.C. XXXIX.12). In the summer of 56, Cicero advised him in a letter (*Fam.* I.7) to take possession of Alexandria and to put the Ptolemaic king back on the throne. Given the complex and problematic nature of the situation, Lentulus distanced himself from any involvement in it.

Only during the consulship of Pompey and Crassus was the problem finally resolved. After Ptolemy XII had again either spent large amounts of money for bribes or had promised such sums,[34] he was able to obtain letters of support from Pompey which were addressed to the proconsul of Syria,

A. Gabinius. In the letters, Pompey exhorted Gabinius in a most high-handed fashion to lead the king back to Alexandria (the whole expedition is described in D.C. XXXIX.55–58; cf. Str. XVII.1.11). C. Rabirius Postumus was one of the most prominent supporters of the campaign, since his entire income was on the line; he had advanced money to Ptolemy time and time again and had even hidden it from others in order to finance the king's loan (Cic. *Rab. Post.* 4; 6; 25; 38; 43). Disregarding the question of the legality of his actions, Gabinius thus set off for Egypt by marching through Palestine. The Jewish High Priest, Hyrkanos II, and the Idumean, Antipatros, father of Herod the Great, offered money, arms and supplies for the campaign (J. *BJ* I.175; *AJ* XIV.99). M. Antony, who was heading the expeditionary corps as general of the cavalry, reached Pelusion with his troops and brought the garrison under his command (Plu. *Ant.* 3.4–7). Before Alexandria, Archelaos was completely defeated in a battle on two fronts led by Antony and Gabinius. After a second battle by the Nile river, Gabinius was able to hand over the land to Ptolemy XII; in the meantime, Archelaos had met his death (Str. XII.3.34; Plu. *Ant.* 3.10). Ptolemy XII is attested once again as the king of Egypt from 15 April in the year 55.[35] For the first time in history, a Roman army had taken hold of Egypt.

## Ptolemy XII's second reign (55–51)

Ptolemy XII had barely returned before he had his daughter Berenike IV as well as many of her supporters killed (D.C. XXXIX.58.3). He was desperately in need of money in order to pay off the huge loan he had taken out at Rome. Rabirius Postumus secured for himself the supervision of Ptolemaic finances, thus receiving the title of dioiketes (Cic. *Rab. Post.* 22–28; 38–45).[36] The Roman used his position to collect his money and he went to such extremes that the king eventually had to place him in special police custody to protect him from the Alexandrian people; he was then allowed to escape.

In the meantime, Gabinius had arrived in Rome as a civilian in the autumn of 54, where he was charged *de maiestate* (for transgressing the bounds of his authority as governor) and *de repetundis* (on account of gains made illegally). He was acquitted on the first charge but fined 10,000 talents for the second – presumably the sum promised him by the Ptolemaic king. Cicero had conducted his defence under compulsion from Pompey, but lost the case. Gabinius was unable to pay the fine and had to go into exile. Likewise, when Rabirius returned to Rome at the end of 54, he too was charged *de repetundis*. Cicero defended him in his speech *Pro C. Rabirio Postumo*; the outcome of the trial is unknown.

Back in Egypt, some Roman troops had been left behind to protect the king. These troops, known as the Gabiniani,[37] also included Gallic and Germanic cavalrymen (Caes. *Civ.* III.4.4) and they were to leave their mark on history there. They were deployed on numerous occasions to counter insurrections by native Egyptians, but eventually they adopted the local mores and married local women (Caes. *Civ.* III.110.2). In this way, they gradually lost their ties to Rome and eventually formed the core of the army which would fight against Caesar in the *Bellum Alexandrinum*.

After a long period of decline and stagnation under Ptolemy XII, intellectual life in Alexandria underwent a renaissance, no doubt as a result of the king's personal support. The physician, Apollonios of Kition,[38] dedicated his Hippocratic commentaries to a king Ptolemy, i.e. either to Ptolemy XII or Ptolemy of Cyprus. More importantly, several new philosophical schools developed during the course of the first century in Alexandria. For example, philosophical eclecticism was mainly an Alexandrian phenomenon before moving on to Rome where Cicero made it famous and bequeathed it to posterity.[39]

After Ptolemy XII had his eldest daughter, Berenike IV, killed in 55, he had left only his four younger children, offspring by another mother:[40] Cleopatra VII (born in 70/69), Ptolemy XIII (born in 61), Ptolemy XIV (probably born in 59) and Arsinoe (IV) whose date of birth is uncertain. Their father conferred on them the title of Θεοὶ Νέοι Φιλάδελφοι which was confirmed on 31 May 52.[41] Although the notion of θεός had become a mere formula devoid of meaning, the term 'philadelphos' still implied, as it did a generation before,[42] the father's hope of a peaceable succession to the throne.

In view of the illegitimacy of his children (from a Greek point of view), it was important for Ptolemy XII to assure the continuity of his dynasty. Hence, at the end of his life, he made his daughter Cleopatra co-regent (perhaps 52 until the beginning of 51); she is represented as such in the crypt of the temple of Hathor of Dendera behind her father.[43] Her age alone (perhaps 18 at the time of her father's death) made her the only possible candidate in the royal family to take control of the monarchy. The will of Ptolemy XII, however, in keeping with tradition, placed the elder brother of Cleopatra VII at her side in a joint rule. The old king also called on the Roman people, by invoking the gods and the *foedera* (treaty of 59) he had made with Rome, to see to it that the terms of his will were carried out (Caes. *Civ.* III.108.4–6; *B. Alex.* 33.1f.; Luc. X.92–99; D.C. LXII.35.4; Porph.: FGrHist. 260F 2.15). A copy of the will remained in Alexandria while a second copy, which was to have been kept in the aerarium at Rome, was actually kept by Pompey in his house. Since Ptolemy XII had been his guest, the two were bound together by a *hospitium* (guest-friendship relationship). The most important provision in the will was the one whereby the shrewd king made Rome responsible for protecting the continuity of his dynasty.[44]

Soon after 51 had begun, Ptolemy XII Neos Dionysos died. His clever policies had given Egypt a certain autonomy but had also decisively influenced the level of Rome's involvement in Egypt. The Ptolemaic kingdom had now dwindled almost to the borders of that satrapy which Ptolemy I had once taken over upon the death of Alexander the Great.

## CLEOPATRA VII PHILOPATOR (51–30)

### Cleopatra and Caesar

On 22 March 51, a new Buchis bull was enthroned. This event is dated by the burial stele of the bull[45] to the first year of a king who is not named and 'a female ruler, mistress of both lands (empty cartouche), the goddess Philopator'. This indicates that Ptolemy XII had just died and Cleopatra ruled, at least nominally, with one of her brothers, as had been determined by her father. The sibling marriage between Cleopatra VII and Ptolemy XIII, which following Ptolemaic tradition (D.C. XLII. 35.4) was probably one of the provisions of the will, may never have taken place.[46]

A series of documents[47] makes it clear that, shortly after their accession to the throne, Cleopatra VII expelled her brother from the joint kingship and ruled alone for approximately 18 months. Evidently to propagate dynastic continuity[48] and perhaps also to cut her brother out of the kingship completely, Cleopatra had documents from the first half of 51 dated to the 30th year of Ptolemy XII's reign and her first year of rule.[49] The cult title of *Thea Philopator*, which she had borne from the beginning, made clear that she would continue the administration and policies of her father and it also served to distinguish her from Cleopatra VI Tryphaina who had fallen into disfavour.

By the autumn of 50 at the latest, supporters of Ptolemy XIII had gained the upper hand. This is shown by a prostagma of 27 October[50] in which the basileus is mentioned at the head of the document and the basilissa is named only after him. The decree gives us a good indication of the situation in Egypt at the time. It orders the sellers of grain and legumes in Middle Egypt to transport all their goods to Alexandria upon pain of death; the authorities wished, in this way, to counteract the hunger riots which were looming large in Alexandria. Other documents also show how difficult the economic situation had become in the last years of Ptolemy XII's reign and in the early years of Cleopatra VII's government. The collection of taxes, in particular, appears to have been carried out rather stringently. The resulting anachoresis almost entirely depopulated certain villages at this time; occasionally, only the priests in their sanctuaries had stayed behind and they were no longer able to fend off thieves.[51]

Later in the third year (attested from June 49), there emerges on documents a twofold dating system in the form 'year 1, which is also year 3'.[52] One may assume that Ptolemy XIII had begun a dating system based on the years of his own reign and that this number was placed first because of his prominence by this time.[53]

A group of powerful men at court, above all the eunuch Potheinos,[54] assumed responsibility for Ptolemy XIII's position; the king was about 12 years of age at the time. Already during Ptolemy XII's lifetime, Potheinos had asserted his influence as *nutricius* ('nurse') of the thirteenth Ptolemy. By the spring of 48, he held the office of dioiketes. Together with an Egyptian named Achillas,[55] he acted in an official capacity as guardian of Ptolemy XIII. The third most important man in the group was Theodotos of Chios,[56] one of the young king's teachers.

When Caesar crossed the Rubicon on the night of 10/11 January 49 (pre-Julian calendar), the Roman civil war began. Soon afterwards, Pompey withdrew from Italy in order to build up armed forces in the east against Caesar. The dynasties allied to him were also to take part in the war. In the spring/summer of 49, Pompey's eldest son, Cn. Pompey, arrived in Alexandria to ask for military support (Plu. *Ant.* 25.4; Lucan. II.636). Cleopatra's charm will already have made itself felt. The Ptolemaic court was bound by duty to assist Pompey, since Ptolemy XII had cultivated with him a relationship of *hospitium* and *amicitia*. The Roman general thus emerged as a *patronus* of the Ptolemaic dynasty. Livy (Liv. *Per.* CXII) and the other relevant sources (Sen. *Ep.* 4.7; Luc. VIII.448f. among others) even refer to Pompey as the guardian of Ptolemy XIII,[57] but probably only in insofar as the latter's dealings with Rome were concerned. One should recall, however, that Ptolemy XII had made the Romans the guarantors of the terms of his will.

The Ptolemaic court supplied Cn. Pompey with 500 Gallic and Germanic cavalry from the Roman troops of the Gabiniani (Caes. *Civ.* III.4.4.; App. *Civ.* II.49). In addition, he was given 50 warships which were instrumental in his victories off the Epirote coast in the spring of 48 (Caesar. *Civ.* III.40; D.C. XLII.12).

Before the summer of 49 had ended, the men around Ptolemy XIII succeeded in having Cleopatra ousted from the throne.[58] At first, she retreated into the Thebaïd (Malalas, IX.279) but somewhat later, perhaps at the beginning of 48,[59] she was compelled to leave Egypt and head for Syria. From there, she hoped to regain the throne (App. *Civ.* II.84; Str. XVII.1.11).

In the autumn of 49, the Roman counter-senate held its own meeting in Thessaloniki. There, the high command was given to Pompey for the upcoming year and allies who had distinguished themselved were awarded honours. As part of these honours, Ptolemy XIII was officially recognized as king and legitimate ruler of Egypt upon the recommendation of Pompey (Luc. V.58–64). Cleopatra was excluded from the throne in this resolution and this meant that the Roman faction in Thessaloniki, feeling hard pressed by difficult circumstances, had chosen to ignore the will of Ptolemy XII and confirm the *status quo*.

After his defeat at Pharsalos, Pompey travelled to Egypt with 2,000 armed men and headed for Pelusion. The city was close to where Ptolemy XIII and his army opposed Cleopatra VII who was attempting to secure her reinstatement by military means. Pompey asked for the king's assistance through an embassy referring to the good relations he had cultivated with the Ptolemaic court. Although the philoi and guardians of the king sent back a message to Pompey that they would receive him, they had already decided to have him killed. In this way, they could prevent Pompey from turning Egypt into a base for his campaigns against Caesar and they could endear themselves to the victorious Caesar; their main objective was to keep Egypt out of the Roman civil war. Thus, they sent to Pompey's ships Achillas and a Roman military tribune from the Gabiniani troops who was a personal acquaintance of Pompey from the days of the wars against the pirates. Because of his acquaintance with the latter, Pompey was easily persuaded to board the barge carrying the emissaries and was then murdered while on board (July 48 Julian calendar)[60] (Caes. *Civ.* III.104; *inter alios*). Part of Pompey's fleet was able to escape while the rest was captured by the Egyptians who had prepared for this manoeuvre in advance. Ptolemy XIII had appeared in full regalia on the shore lending his full support to the operation.

Caesar had quickly taken up the pursuit of Pompey and was on the scene only two days after his rival had been murdered in front of Alexandria. So as not to waste any time, he had taken with him only two very small legions of about 3,200 infantry and 800 cavalry on a small fleet of warships (Caes. *Civ.* III.106.1–2; *B. Alex.* 17.3; 29.4).[61]

Before Caesar had landed, Theodotos of Chios brought him the head and signet ring of Pompey the Great; it was assumed that this would satisfy Caesar and persuade him to continue his journey. Instead, Caesar reacted with a tearful lament of the fate of his son-in-law, Pompey, and gave orders to land. He entered the city accompanied by his lictors as a Roman consul with military *imperium* and set up his quarters in the royal palace (Caes. *Civ.* III.112.8).

Caesar thus embarked on an adventure fraught with uncertainties. He would be detained in Egypt for quite some time, even though the civil war was far from over. He completely misjudged the situation and viewed the murder of Pompey exclusively as a show of support for his side, forgetting the desire for independence of both the administration and the people of Egypt. Caesar's behaviour was viewed as an insult to the sovereignty of the state and to royal dignity; from the beginning, he and his soldiers faced great discontent in the streets of Alexandria (Caes. *Civ.* III.106.4). Caesar nonetheless remained in Egypt, presumably because he wished to employ the country's resources for his own purposes and, at the same time, wanted to seize this opportunity to settle the dynastic dispute to his own advantage.

Caesar therefore ordered reinforcement troops from Asia (Caes. *Civ.* III.107.1) and generally gave the impression of being an educated and peaceful visitor. He visited the sights of the city, especially the tomb of Alexander the Great and took part in philosophical discussions (e.g. App. *Civ.* II.89; Luc. X.14–19).

Drawing a parallel with his first consulship during which he had secured recognition for the twelfth Ptolemy, Caesar explained that since he was again consul it was his duty to settle the dispute between the two royal siblings. He therefore ordered Ptolemy XIII and Cleopatra VII to dismiss their armies and to appear before him (Caes. *Civ.* III.107.2). Ptolemy XIII came to Alexandria, but his supporters thought it would be best if he retained his

*Figure 8.1* Marble head of Cleopatra VII with a royal diadem in her hair; obtained from art dealer; H.: 29.5 cm; Berlin, Staatliche Museen Preußischer Kulturbesitz, Antikenmusuem, Inv. 1976.10; Smith, R. R. R. (1988), 169, cat. no. 68.

army. Cleopatra asked to defend her position before Caesar in person and secretly.

Thus began the dramatic love story which would be rendered in countless works of world literature. Since the matter was to be kept secret, Cleopatra had herself hidden in a coverlet in which she was carried past the guards, into the palace and finally to Caesar (Plu. *Caes.* 49). Here these two remarkable people, both of whom were characterized by their political genius, their determined ambition and a sense of adventure, met as man and woman. Caesar was 52 years old, Cleopatra not yet 22. Although she was admired in the sources for her beauty (D.C. XLII.34.3–5; Plu. *Ant.* 27.3; cf. Fig. 8.1), Cleopatra was particularly remarkable for her intelligence, *esprit*, culture and irresistible charm. With these talents she won Caesar over to her side in that one night. Caesar was now prepared to re-establish her on the throne in a joint reign with her brother Ptolemy XIII. Through her incredible skill, the queen had managed to involve Caesar in her political ambitions without having the kind of power that might have been of use to him. The Roman consul had given no thought to how few supporters Cleopatra had and the extent to which the people favoured Ptolemy.

On the next day, as Cleopatra's brother appeared in the palace and realized what had transpired, he rushed forward to the crowd of people waiting outside and cried out that he had been betrayed, tearing the diadem off his head. The dramatic scene, whether spontaneous or carefully staged by Cleopatra's great adversary, Potheinos, had the desired effect; the people threatened to storm the palace. Caesar was able to intervene in a reassuring manner; he read aloud the will of Ptolemy XII in a meeting of the people and confirmed the two estranged siblings as rulers of Egypt (D.C. LXII.35.1–5).

With Caesar acting as intermediary, Rome paid a very high price to secure peace in the royal house. This was done essentially for the sake of Cleopatra. The Roman consul established the younger sibling couple, which consisted of the fourteenth Ptolemy and Arsinoe, as rulers of Cyprus. Thus, the valuable island was taken out of Roman control after only ten years as a Roman province and restored to the Ptolemaic kingdom (D.C. XLII.35.5–6). It remained a Ptolemaic possession until Roman rule was finally re-established on the island after the battle of Actium.[62]

Cleopatra's true opponent was Potheinos who restrained himself in Caesar's presence. He stirred up disapproval of the Roman presence in Egypt quite vigorously, he attempted to block the policy of reconciliation and he initiated the so-called Alexandrian War. Potheinos was justifiably confident of Caesar's weakness and therefore summoned the royal army to Alexandria. The army of about 20,000 men, the core of which was formed by the Gabiniani, was still near Pelusion close to the Kasian promontory and was under Achillas' command (Caes. *Civ.* III.110.1–2).[63]

When news of the approaching army reached Caesar, he was taken completely by surprise. Given the small number of troops at his disposal, he could not afford to enter into a battle outside the city. After an attempt to stop the enemy by means of an embassy had failed, Caesar took Ptolemy XIII into custody as a hostage. Achillas' army was enthusiastically received by the people and it occupied most of the city. The war against Caesar developed into an Alexandrian, national movement of protest against the threat of Roman rule over Egypt. A formal people's militia was organized, slaves were armed and every person capable of bearing arms was levied from all parts of Egypt (*B. Alex.* 2–3).

Caesar hastily requested that overseas troops be sent to him, but for the time being he had to remain content with closing off the palace district in Alexandria; he also managed to occupy the island on which the Pharos[64] lighthouse stood as well as the lighthouse itself and was able to keep the large harbour open. He had the ships docked in the harbour set on fire to prevent his opponents from making use of them. The fire spread quickly, burning not only the fleet and the dockyards but also most of the Museion library which lay in the palace district near the coast. Approximately 400,000 papyrus rolls went up in flames late in the summer of 48. Although Antony later bestowed on Cleopatra a large part of the works from the Pergamon library and so partially made up for the loss, henceforth the Serapeum library which had hitherto been the second centre of learning in Alexandria would become the heart of Alexandrian scholarship.[65]

Meanwhile, Arsinoe, the younger sister of Cleopatra, escaped from the royal palace with her tutor, the eunuch Ganymedes.[66] She joined Achillas' army and there was acclaimed queen (D.C. XLII.39.1). The new queen was not meant as a rival to Ptolemy XIII, who was also hostile to Caesar, but as the opponent of Cleopatra VII. She was subsequently referred to as Arsinoe (IV). At any rate, she and Achillas soon quarrelled over how the war should be conducted; Potheinos sent messengers to announce that he supported Achillas. Caesar intercepted these envoys and had Potheinos executed (Caes. *Civ.* III.112). His survival now depended solely on whether or not he could hold out until reinforcements arrrived. In the other camp, Ganymedes, who was the driving force behind Arsinoe (IV), brought about Achillas' downfall (*B. Alex.* 4) and so Caesar was rid of his most serious adversaries, Potheinos and Achillas.[67]

Ganymedes himself took charge of the war against Caesar and demonstrated the greatest zeal in carrying out this task. His methods bore a resemblance to modern, chemical warfare as he attempted to contaminate the drinking water in the palace quarter: the subterranean canals were closed off and large amounts of sea water were pumped into those parts of the city which were at higher elevations; from there the salt water was made to flow into the pipes which normally carried drinking water into the district of the city occupied by Caesar (*B. Alex.* 6). Caesar responded by having new springs dug and managed to get sufficient fresh water (*B. Alex.* 8–9).

After these actions, the battle reached new levels of intensity as Caesar concentrated all his forces on bringing the island of Pharos and the causeway leading to it, the so-called Heptastadion (see Map 3), under his control. Caesar suddenly found himself in the greatest danger. When all of his people had fled and his own ship had been stormed by a crowd of people, the 53-year-old man jumped into the brackish water of the Alexandrian harbour, which had nearly reached winter temperatures, and swam for his life to ships lying further off (*B. Alex.* 17–21; App. *Civ.* II.90; D.C. XLII.40.3–4). Even under those extreme circumstances, Caesar never thought of handing over Cleopatra, who was sitting in the palace, to establish a provisional peace. His actions were obviously inspired by a genuine romantic attachment.[68]

On the other hand, Caesar did release Ptolemy XIII because this action promised him negotiations for peace. Ptolemy had scarcely reached the army before taking up the war with renewed vigour, much to Caesar's disappointment (*B. Alex.* 23–24; D.C. XLII.42).

But Caesar's general, Mithridates of Pergamon, was now approaching Pelusion with his troops which had been stationed in Asia Minor. There he may even have obtained reinforcements from the former troops of Cleopatra. In addition, the Nabataean king, Malchos I (60–30), had sent a contingent of cavalry from Petra (*B. Alex.* I.1) and 3,000 Jews under the command of Antipatros also joined the campaign (J. *BJ* I.187–192; *AJ* XIV.127–136).[69] Pelusion was taken by storm. Afterwards, Caesar joined his forces with those of Mithridates and was then able to defeat the Egyptians decisively. Ptolemy XIII perished in the encounter. At the beginning of 47 (Julian calendar),[70] Caesar entered Alexandria as the glorious victor and the people submitted themselves to his authority (*B. Alex.* 26–32; D.C.. XLII.43). The day was later included in the Roman calendar of festivals.

After his victory, Caesar once again regulated the succession to the crown by invoking Ptolemy XII's will. In reality, he handed over complete control to Cleopatra but placed at her side her younger brother, Ptolemy XIV, who was then 12 or 13 years old, in place of the deceased Ptolemy XIII. This male counterpart to Cleopatra was meant as a concession to tradition (*B. Alex.* 33.1–2; Suet. *Jul.* 35.1; App. *Civ.* II.90; D.C. XLII.44.1–2[71] among others). The couple took on the name *Theoi Philopatores Philadelphoi*,[72] which was probably the cult title which Cleopatra shared with Ptolemy XIII (though this is not attested), to maintain the appearance of continuity. Some hiero-glyphic inscriptions in Koptos evidently take account of the new regime, Cleopatra is now described as 'wife of the king' and appears in conjunction with Ptolemy (sc. Ptolemy XIV) for whom, for simplicity's sake, the car-touches of Ptolemy XII were used.[72a] Arsinoe (IV) had officially led the army against Caesar and was thus brought back to Rome by him to be led in his triumph dating to the year 46. Afterwards, she was banished to Ephesos and lived there in the temple of Artemis (J. *AJ* XV.89; D.C. XLIII.19.2–3; erroneously Miletus in App. *Civ.* V.9). Perhaps Caesar wished to keep the princess alive as a legitimate heir to the throne should the need arise in the future.

Cleopatra's unpopularity provided Caesar with a welcome pretext for leaving behind three legions as a garrison. These were left under the command of the son of a freedman, the experienced and trustworthy officer named Rufio (*B. Alex.* 33.3–4; Suet. *Jul.* 76.3).[73] One can see how these arrangements anticipated those of the imperial period, when the administration of Egypt was given to an equestrian prefect who was directly answerable to the *princeps*. After Caesar's assassination, there were four legions in Egypt (Cic. *Fam.* XII.11.1) and this meant that in the meantime their numbers had been increased. The occupation troops on the Nile allowed Caesar to keep other options open. It is important to remember, however, that for all intents and purposes Egypt was a Roman protectorate in the period from 47 to 44.

The new arrangement suited the interests of Rome and Caesar and even those of Cleopatra, although she was now politically dependent on Caesar. The romantic liaison between the two prevented Egypt from becoming a Roman province, but the first signs of the arrangement later espoused by Antony were already visible. Finally, Cleopatra's firm establishment as monarch and the re-acquisition of Cyprus probably improved the financial and economic situation of Egypt.[74]

During this time, perhaps even before the royal sibling-couple had ascended the throne, Caesar and Cleopatra took a voyage on the Nile for the purposes of leisure and culture (Suet. *Jul.* 52.1; App. *Civ.* II.90; D.C. XLII.45.1). No doubt, Caesar was also motivated by a political objective: he wished to make direct contact with this newly acquired land which was now so immediately bound to his own person.[75]

After remaining probably close to nine months in Egypt (App. *Civ.* II.90), Caesar set off in the spring of 47 to lead a campaign against Pharnakes, the son of Mithridates VI (victory at Zela: 'veni, vidi, vici'), before proceeding with the civil war.

When Caesar departed, Cleopatra was in the seventh month of her pregnancy (cf. Plu. *Caes.* 49.10). According to a demotic Serapeum stele,[76] '*pharaoh Caesar*' was born on 23 June 47; the text is said to have been written on his birthday. By giving the child the title of 'pharaoh' and naming him 'Caesar', Cleopatra was propagating the message that the future pharaoh had been born and that he was, at the same time, Caesar's heir. As son and heir of the dynasty, the child's first name was *Ptolemaios*, hence we say *Ptolemaios XV Caesar*, which agrees with the most common form of his birth name in the hieroglyphic titulary 'Ptolemaios named Caesar . . .' (*Ptwlmjs ḏd.tw-n.f. Kjsrs*) as well as with the Greek nomenclature Πτολεμαῖος ὁ καὶ Καῖσαρ'.[77] Since Caesar was one of Ptolemy XV's official names, he could also be called by that term alone.[78] Cicero, for example, mentioned him as 'that Caesar' (*Caesar ille*) in a letter dated 11 May 44 (Cic. *Att.* XIV.20.2). In Egypt, hieroglyphic monuments publicly announced[79] that Caesar was the father of the child[80] (as of 43) and the Alexandrians also expressed his paternity with the now-famous patronymic 'Caesarion' ('son of Caesar') (Plu. *Caes.* 49.10). In Rome, however, Caesar mentioned him only in the closest circle of friends with extreme discretion (Suet. *Jul.* 52.1–2). His relationship with Cleopatra had not yet been made legal. This was obviously to take place after a law had been passed which would allow the dictator to have more than one legal marriage for the purpose of begetting male heirs (Suet. *Jul.* 52.3). Caesar's marriage to Calpurnia had, until that time, remained without issue. The question of Caesarion's paternity later took on special political and propagandistic significance in the clash between Octavian and Antony. Given Octavian's own position as Caesar's adopted son, he had to discredit the claim emphatically upheld by the opposition that Caesarion was Caesar's legitimate son.

In July of 46, Caesar celebrated a fourfold triumph over Gaul, Egypt, Pontus and Mauretania. About this time, Cleopatra and Ptolemy XIV arrived in Rome as invited guests[81] and set up quarters in the gardens of one of Caesar's villas on the other side of the Tiber. They received the title of *reges socii et amici populi Romani* (D.C. XLIII.27.3; Cic. *Att.* XV.15.2; Suet. *Jul.* 52.1).

Among the most important events of that period was the Julian calendar reform which was inspired by the Egyptian calendar. On the first of January of the year 45, the Julian calendar was introduced in Rome and it was based on the calculations of the Alexandrian mathematician and astronomer, Sosigenes. As part of the new calendar, the Roman lunar year was replaced by a year of 365¼ days. The idea which had been publicized in the Canopus Decree of 238 had finally come to fruition.[82]

Cleopatra's effect on Caesar is not to be underestimated. Influenced by his relationship with her, he began to act more and more like a Hellenistic ruler, especially with regard to his religious policy.[83] For this very reason, the presence of the queen in Rome was extremely distasteful to the republicans, as Cicero's correspondence after the death of Caesar clearly indicates (Cic. *Att.* XIV.8.1; XV.17.2). Cleopatra was probably partially to blame for the fact that the opposition moved quickly to assassinate the dictator.

A month after Caesar had died, the royal couple journeyed back home. During her stay in Rome, Cleopatra had not accomplished her political goal of having Caesarion confirmed as Caesar's only male heir.[84] Soon after their return to Alexandria, the queen had her brother Ptolemy XIV killed (Porph.: FGrHist. 260 F 2.16–17; J. *AJ* XV.89; J.*c.Ap.*II.58) and immediately thereafter probably had her three-year-old son, Ptolemy XV Caesar, established as a nominal co-regent. He was officially recognized as such in 43 by P. Cornelius Dolabella who was fighting in the east against the assassins of Caesar (D.C. XLVII.31.5). Cleopatra was thereby attempting to secure at least the Egyptian succession for Caesarion. In the preamble of official documents, the mother appears before her son, just as formerly in the case of Cleopatra III;[85] the son bears the cult title θεὸς Φιλοπάτωρ καὶ Φιλομήτωρ,[86] epithets which link him directly to his parents Caesar and Cleopatra.

## Cleopatra and Mark Antony

The 40s were characterized by famines in Egypt because of the low levels of flooding of the Nile river. Already in 48 the flooding was extremely poor (Plin. *Nat.* V.58: only 5 cubits) and apparently none took place at all in 43 and 42 (Sen. *Nat.* IV.2.16).[87] We know that during the Roman civil war following Caesar's death there were widespread famines and plagues in Egypt (App. *Civ.* IV.61 and 108); a detailed report of them was made by the court physician Dioskurides Phakas[88] ('the warty one'). Cleopatra had grain from the crown warehouses distributed to the citizens of Alexandria. Since the Jews of Alexandria had not been granted citizenship, they were passed over (J. *Ap.* 60).

The chora, especially Upper Egypt, was essentially left to its own devices. During the late Ptolemaic and Augustan period, many native Egyptians were appointed as strategoi of nomes in this area.[89] In the south, the family of a certain Kallimachos, who is attested in many inscriptions,[90] was very influential. He appears as strategos (74/3–39) and epistrategos (62–39) of the Thebaïd, as 'strategos of the Red and Indian Seas'[91] and bore the court title of *syngenes*. The priests and the people of Thebes issued a decree in his honour sometime between 44 and 39; it has been preserved on a royal stele from Karnak which originally bore an inscription dating from the New Kingdom.[92] The decree was composed in both Greek and demotic scripts and it gives an account of a catastrophe which lasted two years but which fortunately local residents survived. With the help of the gods, Kallimachos had as 'Saviour of the city' come to the rescue in a time of need; for this accomplishment, he now received honours like the ones conferred on kings in the decrees of the priests. On his birthday, images of him were to be displayed in public and festivals were to be celebrated in his name. In the final part of the text it was provided that the decree was to be published on a stone in both Greek and Egyptian.[93] The successful strategos, Kallimachos, had thus attained the same status as a beneficent king in the minds of the people.

In view of her past involvements, Cleopatra, who was very much interested in foreign affairs, could only be on the side of the Caesarians in the civil war. She concluded a treaty of alliance with P. Cornelius Dolabella in order to obtain from him an official recognition of Ptolemy Caesar's status as the legitimate king of Egypt. She sent him the four legions stationed in Egypt, but, defying her orders, the commander of the legions led his troops to one of Caesar's assassins, C. Cassius, who at the time was fighting Dolabella in Syria (Cic. *Fam*. XII.11.1; App. *Civ*. III.78; IV.59 and 61; V.8).[94] An Egyptian fleet stationed in Cyprus together with the Ptolemaic governor of the island, Serapion,[95] also went over to Cassius' side. They had chosen to disregard Cleopatra's policy favouring the followers of Caesar. The queen probably wished to become involved personally in the civil war, since she set out westwards from Alexandria in command of her own fleet. She headed into a storm on the Libyan coast and then turned back to Alexandria since she was also ill at the time (App. *Civ*. V.8). Her attempt to become involved in the Roman civil war had ended in failure.

In the autumn of 42, Antony defeated Brutus and Cassius, Caesar's murderers, at Philippi. After the battle, the various responsibilities of power were divided among the *triumviri* and Antony was given the task of organizing the east. It was to prove a fateful event for Cleopatra that precisely this man had been given authority in the east. Like Caesar, he was an adventurous politician and, even more importantly, he was particularly receptive to the splendours of oriental luxury. Through his victory at Philippi he was legitimized as ruler according to Hellenistic ideology. In 41, he summoned Cleopatra to Tarsos where she was to justify herself in light of the support which Cassius had received from the Ptolemaic kingdom (Plu. *Ant*. 25.1–4). This was only the official pretext for her visit; Antony's real purpose was to assure himself of the support of the Ptolemaic queen in the impending Parthian war.

Cleopatra obeyed the summons and arrived in Tarsos, having come with a specific purpose in mind (Plu. *Ant*. 25–26; D.C. XLVIII.24). Her intention was to conquer the Roman general by a display of Ptolemaic *tryphé* and through her feminine charms. Once, with Caesar, she had been a highly educated and charming woman but still only a woman; this time she appeared as the seductive Aphrodite-Isis surrounded by royal luxury and an example of perfect refinement. This diplomatic coup was later wonderfully dramatized by Shakespeare in his play 'Antony and Cleopatra'.[96] The queen was 28 years old and at the height of her beauty; she won over the 42-year-old Antony on the first evening. With this victory over Mark Antony and the power that it put at her disposal, it was now easy for her to avenge herself on all her enemies. At her bidding, Antony ordered the murder of Arsinoe (IV), who in the meantime had been living in the Artemision of Ephesos (J. *AJ* XV.89).[97] The ex-strategos of Cyprus, Serapion, who had taken refuge in Tyre after the defeat of Brutus and Cassius, was now deported and paid with his life for his support of Caesar's enemies (App. *Civ.* V.9; D.C. XLVIII.24.2).

After their meeting in Tarsos, Cleopatra returned to Alexandria; Antony came a little later and spent the winter of 41/40 there as her guest (Plu. *Ant.* 28–29; App. *Civ.* V.11). They enjoyed a lifestyle full of splendour and lavish festivities. Once again, Cleopatra sought to impress Antony with a show of royal tryphé. Of their unbridled pursuit of pleasure in Alexandria many anecdotes have survived.

The queen probably attempted to bind the Roman general to her person in a permanent way. In 40, she gave birth to twins fathered by Antony, whom she named Alexander and Cleopatra. Clearly, Cleopatra attempted to further the same political objectives in her relationships with Caesar and Antony. By her liaison with both men, she attempted to ensure the continued existence of the Ptolemaic dynasty and to re-establish as much as possible the kingdom's past glory. It was, therefore, absolutely imperative that she bear children by both men.

Antony probably added Roman Cilicia to Ptolemaic Cyprus during his first stay in Alexandria; both lands had been united as one Roman province before 48. The new organization is attested in an inscription from Cypriot Salamis dating from 19 November 38. In it there is reference to the Ptolemaic 'strategos of the island and of Cilicia'.[98]

In September of 40, the treaty of Brundisium was signed and the *triumviri* officially delineated their areas of authority. Antony received the east from Greece to the Euphrates. In addition, he agreed to marry the sister of Octavian, Octavia, who from now on would be Cleopatra's rival. It was Octavia who prevented a war between her brother and her spouse. The treaty of Tarentum, which was signed in the summer/early autumn of 37 and renewed the triumvirate for another five years, was also very much due to her efforts.

This finally allowed Antony to concentrate his efforts on the Parthian war, a struggle which he could not undertake without Egypt's assistance. He did not bring Octavia with him as he headed east (D.C. XLVIII.54.5). After he had arrived in Antioch in the autumn of 37, Antony had Cleopatra summoned to his side and they then spent the winter of 37/6 together. During this time, Antony acknowledged the twins, Alexander and Cleopatra, as his own offspring. The children were then four years old and had been brought along to Antioch. They also received epithets that linked them with the sun and moon and which were meant to evoke the cosmic nature of the Ptolemaic dynasty and kingdom. From then on they were called Alexander Helios and Cleopatra Selene (Plu. *Ant.* 36.5).[99]

During the winter of 37/6, Antony was busy with the reorganization of the entire Near East (Plu. *Ant.* 36.3–4; D.C. XLIX.32.1–5). He reduced the number of Roman provinces from five to three; these were now Asia, Bithynia and Syria. The position of the Ptolemaic kingdom was greatly enhanced. To Cleopatra went the kingdom of Chalkis in Lebanon whose king had just died (Porph.: FGrHist.260 F 2.17), the rich balsam and date groves of Judaea near Jericho along with the neighbouring regions of the Nabataean kingdom (J. *AJ* XV.94–96 with erroneous chronology), estates on Crete and the city of Cyrene. A third status was granted to various client-kingdoms such as Galatia, Cappadocia, Pontus and Judaea where Antony established new rulers. Among these was Herod the Great, who would later lease from Egypt the areas of Judaea given to Cleopatra. It is no longer the opinion of modern scholarship that these so-called gifts to Cleopatra were the acts of an unrestrained lover. Instead, they are now seen as a 'balanced and clear-sighted reorganization of the administration of the east which won over to Antony's cause capable figures and powerful dominions'.[100] Antony had restored the Ptolemaic kingdom to its original historical stature; it was to form the heart of a great eastern empire which he hoped to rule. In Rome, however, these 'gifts' to Cleopatra were met with much disapproval. Octavian would later make use of this ill-will in his propaganda against Antony.

Cleopatra saw the increased size of the Ptolemaic kingdom as marking the beginning of a new era. Thus, (Porph.: FGrHist. 260F 2.17), in the sixteenth year of her reign (37/6), a new system of counting dates beginning with 'year 1' was established alongside the old one. In the future, all documents were to be dated on the basis of both the old and new systems, hence such entries as 'year 17 which is also year 2'.[101] Another boy was born, now the third child of Antony and Cleopatra, and he received the name of Ptolemy Philadelphos. His epithet was a deliberate attempt to link Egypt's position at this time with the glorious epoch of Ptolemy II.

The extent to which the orient was now viewed as *one* domain under *one* ruling couple is illustrated in various ways by the numismatic evidence. From 37/6, Antony, who was acting as a Roman magistrate, had silver tetradrachms minted in Antioch with the portrait of Cleopatra on the reverse. Cleopatra had bronze coins struck, with the image of Antony on the reverse, in many cities of Coele Syria (Arados, Damascus, Ptolemais [Ake], Askalon, etc.) as well as in Cyrene.[102] Egyptian supremacy over Cyrene, which had been newly re-established, was in fact only nominal. Other coins from this area indicate that it continued to be managed by Roman administrators who were acting as the representatives of Cleopatra but had been placed there by Antony.[103]

In 36, despite massive preparations, Antony's Parthian campaign ended in utter disaster (Plu. *Ant.* 37–52; D.C. XLIX.24–31).[104] Before the Median capital of Phraaspa, the Armenian auxiliary troops retreated and this contributed to the failure of the campaign. For this reason, King Artavasdes of Armenia could be blamed for the disastrous outcome. The general retreat to the Armenian borders resulted in the deaths of 20,000 infantrymen, the equivalent of five legions, as well as 4,000 cavalry; in the ensuing march through Armenia – where it had just snowed – as far as the Mediterranean coast, a further 8,000 men lost their lives. Cleopatra arrived with her fleet on the Libyan coast, bringing money and clothing for the exhausted soldiers who had survived. By the beginning of 35, she was together again with Antony in Alexandria.

After Sextus Pompey and Lepidus had been eliminated in 36, east–west rivalries gradually intensified. Plutarch's dramatic account (Plu. *Ant.* 53) describes the conflict from the perspective of the women involved. Out of gratitude for the ships which Antony had sent for the battle against Sextus Pompey and to counteract Cleopatra's aid, Octavia apparently sent Antony a small army of 2,000 elite soldiers from Italy for a new Parthian war. On the basis of the treaty of Tarentum, Antony was entitled to reinforcements.

In 35, Antony had just set off on a new campaign against Artavasdes. In order to be able to proceed with the Parthian war, first he had to create a secure Roman base in Armenia. When he learned that Octavia was approaching with reinforcements, he turned back and delayed the campaign until the next year (D.C. XLIX.33.3). According to Plutarch's account (*Ant.* 53), Cleopatra was with Antony in Syria at the time. When she learned of Octavia's attempts to bring Antony assistance, the queen apparently despaired and began to act the part of a languishing, suffering and wounded woman. At her bidding, Cleopatra's sycophants allegedly succeeded in persuading Antony to decide once and for all in favour of Cleopatra; he wrote to Octavia in Athens, saying that while he was happy to accept the reinforcements he would not allow her to join him (cf. D.C. XLIX.4). Whether Cleopatra was actually in Syria at the time is somewhat doubtful; at any rate, Octavia would have been obliged to return to Rome, since she could hardly have accompanied Antony on his campaign. In Plutarch's version, Cleopatra is said to have been responsible for Antony's decision because of her show of wounded love. Plutarch's narrative was obviously influenced by Octavian propaganda which attempted to portray Cleopatra as a skilled seductress. Octavian managed to provoke a feeling of outrage in Rome by drawing attention to Antony's mistreatment of his sister; his sister, Octavia, who was very popular in Rome, and his wife, Livia, were granted special rights, among which was the inviolability usually conferred on tribunes of the people (D.C. XLIX.38.1).

In the spring of 34, Antony moved against Armenia. He took the unfortunate king, Artavasdes, prisoner and brought him back to Alexandria to lead him in his 'triumph' (autumn 34). This triumph resembled a Dionysiac procession more than anything else: cast as a second Alexander[105] and displaying the attributes of the god Dionysos, Antony went to the temple of Sarapis where Cleopatra waited for him sitting on a golden throne (Plu. *Ant.* 50; D.C. XLIX.40; Vell.II.82.4).

Soon afterwards, the ruling couple's vision of a great Egyptian and Hellenistic empire was made public in the Gymnasium of Alexandria (D.C. XLIX.41; Plu. *Ant.* 54).[106] Cleopatra was confirmed as ruler of Egypt and Cyprus and was distinguished with the title 'queen of kings'. In this regard, the 13-year-old Ptolemy XV Caesar received the corresponding title of 'king of kings' (D.C. XLIX.41.1);[107] at the same time, he was explicitly identified as the son of Caesar and Cleopatra. Antony's main purpose was to compromise the situation of Caesar's adoptive son, Octavian, who day by day grew more powerful in Rome. Alexander Helios received Armenia, Media and all the land on the other side of the Euphrates which was left to conquer; his twin sister Cleopatra Selene received from Antony Cyrene and neighbouring Libya as her own kingdom. He gave the youngest son, Ptolemy Philadelphos, Phoenicia and Cilicia as well as the Syrian territories up until the Euphrates.

This spectacular division of the east did not make any fundamental changes to the *status quo* of the administration. The area under Cleopatra's control remained just as it was in 36. The vassal-rulers retained their positions, as did Herod the Great, although Cleopatra would have liked to have his land. The Roman proconsul continued to administer Syria while Armenia and Cyrene remained garrisoned by Roman legions. Media Atropatene came into the hands of the ally Artavasdes I of Media; Alexander Helios had become engaged to the Median king's daughter during the Armenian campaign. Parthia represented a future prospect.

Although Antony saw his status elevated in a religious sense based on the ideology surrounding the Hellenistic basileus,[108] as *triumvir*, his position from a legal point of view remained the same. In order to bolster his imperial vision, in 32 Antony had a silver denarius minted by his itinerant mint in Asia Minor, the obverse of which depicted his head with the legend *Antoni Armenia devicta*, while the reverse showed the bust of queen Cleopatra with the legend *Cleopatrae reginae regum filiorum regum* ('to Cleopatra, queen of kings and (her) sons, who are kings').[109]

Probably as part of the festivities of 34, Antony and Cleopatra had their union made legal by marriage (Sen. *Suas.* 1.6; Plu. *Comp. Dem&Ant.* 1.5; 4.2; Suet. *Aug.* 69.2 among others). As long as Antony was still not divorced from Octavia, the marriage remained a second marriage and so was not recognized by Roman law, though it was quite acceptable in the tradition of the Hellenistic rulers. On a bronze coin from the city of Dora in Phoenicia, an area under Cleopatra's control, the queen and Antony are depicted together as a married couple on the obverse with him behind her.[110]

The final phase of the Ptolemaic kingdom began in 33 as the political tensions between east and west grew and eventually developed into a real propaganda war (Suet. *Aug.* 69; Plu. *Ant.* 55; D.C. L.1). Octavian's attacks were mostly aimed at the gifts bestowed on the Ptolemaic kingdom, especially those favouring Antony's children by Cleopatra.[111] He also directed his criticism at Antony's marriage to Cleopatra and was especially vehement in his condemnation of the fact that Ptolemy Caesar had been acknowledged by Antony as Caesar's son; the latter gesture had put into question Octavian's status as the heir of the great Caesar. The self-indulgent lifestyle of the pair – facts as well as stories – provided Octavian with still more ammunition in his attempt to discredit Antony. The fact that a great number of papyrus rolls had been brought to Alexandria from the Pergamon library was censured as an unjust act of discrimination (Plu. *Ant.* 58.9);[112] it had probably been done in compensation for losses incurred during the fire in the Alexandrian war. Another easy target was the divine rulership of Antony and Cleopatra, a theme which had been inordinately played up by them.[113] For his part, Antony had numerous friends in Rome who acted on his behalf and even his legal wife Octavia tried to intervene in his favour.

Towards the end of 33, Antony gathered together his forces in Anatolia. At the beginning of 32, he was in Ephesos with Cleopatra. Antony had 800 ships at his disposal; of those, 200, most of which were supply ships, had been contributed by Cleopatra together with 20,000 talents for the war fund and the maintenance of the entire army (19 legions in all) in western Asia Minor. Financially, Antony was deeply dependent on Cleopatra and so was compelled to grant her permission to stay with him in his military headquarters. The followers of Octavian condemned this scandalous behaviour (Plu. *Ant.* 56.1–6). Octavian's propaganda became more and more insistent on depicting Cleopatra as the true adversary.

On 31 December 33, the triumvirate legally expired; Octavian and Antony now retained the *imperium consulare* only in the realm of *militiae*.[114] The consuls of 32, Cn. Domitius Ahenobarbus and C. Sosius, were both friends of Antony. When Octavian openly attacked them in the senate (D.C. L.2.5–6), they left Rome accompanied by some three to four hundred senators and joined Antony in Ephesos where they formed their own senate (D.C. L.2.6–7; Plu. *Ant.* 56.3; Suet. *Aug.* 17.2).

Sometime in April of 32, Antony and Cleopatra moved their headquarters to Samos where once again magnificent festivals were held with various performances in honour of Dionysos (Plu. *Ant.* 56.6–10). In May/June, the two set up their headquarters in Athens (Plu. *Ant.* 57.1–2). Antony was probably swayed by Cleopatra to send Octavia a letter of divorce and finally assume the full consequences of a separation from her. Octavian could now view this gesture as an insult to his sister and an open declaration of war (D.C. L.3.2; Plu. *Ant.* 57.4–5; Liv. *Per.* CXXXII). When he learned from certain traitors that Antony's will was kept in Rome, he defied all human and divine statutes by forcing the document to be delivered to him. He read it aloud before the senate and the people: in his will, Antony once again acknowledged Caesarion as the son of the great Caesar, upheld the measures he had enacted in 34 and also gave instructions that his body was to be brought to Alexandria and laid next to Cleopatra's, should he die in Rome (D.C. L.3.3–5; Plu. *Ant.* 58.4–11; Suet. *Aug.* 17.1).

The contents of the will elicited much disapproval in Rome and people began to believe that Antony would move the capital from the Tiber to the Nile, if he should be victorious against Octavian (D.C. L.4.1). From now on, Romans saw Cleopatra as a 'ruinous monster' (*fatale monstrum*: Hor. *Carm.* I.37.21) and a 'calamitous danger' (*tristissimum periculum*)[115] – an image of the queen which Augustan poetry rendered most effectively. With the depiction of Cleopatra as a danger to Rome and the world, the groundwork was laid for the ideology of the later principate in which Augustus was portrayed as the *vindex libertatis*.

In mid-32, resolutions of the senate and people deprived Antony of the consulship for 31 and revoked his military *imperium*. Octavian, on the other hand, retained his *imperium* and took up his third consulship on 1 January of the year 31. Antony did not accept the decisions. The imminent war increasingly resembled a personal feud between Octavian and Antony (*inimicitia*). Cleopatra, for her part, was declared an enemy of the state (*hostis*) at the end of the summer/autumn of 32 (D.C. L.4–5; 6.1; 26.3–4; Plu. *Ant.* 60.1).[116] Octavian thus cleverly manipulated the people's outrage and channelled it against Cleopatra who was blamed for having brought Antony, a Roman, under her power by practising witchcraft on him. It was even said that she was planning an attack on Rome using every means available to her. The civil war between Octavian and Antony was thus transformed into a war between Rome and the Ptolemaic kingdom.

Antony and Cleopatra spent the winter of 32/1 in Patras. In the spring of 31, war broke out. Cleopatra's influence was considerable in every aspect; she was probably to blame for Antony's failure to attack Octavian in Italy despite his superior military force. Cleopatra favoured a defensive tactic that was to be implemented from Cyrene all the way to the Ionian Sea and was to prevent an invasion by Octavian; in her mind, the decisive battle was to be fought at sea. This strategy clearly indicates that Cleopatra was primarily concerned with Egypt and obviously was not interested in marching on Rome as Octavian's propaganda had alleged (Hor. *Carm.* I.37.6–8).

Octavian's outstanding general and admiral, M. Vipsanius Agrippa, succeeded in taking the island of Corcyra in a surprise attack. With about 80,000 men Octavian crossed over to Epiros where approximately 100,000 of Antony's men – including auxiliary units from numerous eastern dynasties – awaited him. Antony's fleet lay in the Gulf of Ambracia which is mainly enclosed by the promontory of Actium. In the course of the summer, Agrippa's naval blockade managed to prevent many of the supplies from reaching Antony's enormous army and thereby undermined the morale of many legionary commanders. Cleopatra once again cast the decisive vote in the war council in favour of trying to break through the naval blockade. On 2 September 31, the naval battle of Actium was fought (D.C. L.31–35; Plu. *Ant.* 65–68).[117] Cleopatra succeeding in breaking through with 60 fast-sailing ships while Antony was embroiled in a battle which resulted in heavy casualties; Octavian and Agrippa had clearly been apprised of their plans by traitors from within Antony's camp.[118] It seems that the infantry was also a victim of treachery, since the 19 legions were forced to capitulate after only a few days. The naval battle was an unmitigated disaster; Macedonia, Greece and Asia Minor were lost to Antony and his system of vassal-states fell apart.

Cleopatra immediately returned to Egypt, while Antony went to Cyrenaica to organize a counter-attack against Octavian; but the governor, L. Pinarius Scarpus, who had been put into office by Antony, refused him and went over to Octavian's side (D.C. LI.5.3–6; Plu. *Ant.* 69.1–3). Antony then returned to Alexandria.

In keeping with ancient pharaonic tradition, Cleopatra had entered the harbour accompanied by victory songs and garlanded ships, but she was unable to suppress the news of the defeat at Actium. As a result of her father's expenditures and her own extravagant foreign policy, the Ptolemaic royal treasury had almost been emptied. She now attempted in every possible way to fill the royal coffers once again. It is said that she resorted to confiscations and special taxes and even looted the temple treasuries (D.C. LI.5.5; 17.6; J.*AJ* XV.90–91; *Ap.* II.58).When one considers what wealth later fell into Octavian's hands, her efforts must have been very effective.[119]

But ill-tidings were quick to follow: the governor of Syria had gone over to Octavian and following also Herod the Great. Many changed sides hoping that Octavian would reward them once Egypt had fallen. With these changes of alliance, the way was now open in both the east and the west for Octavian to take his offensive as far as the borders of Egypt. Under these circumstances, Cleopatra prepared to flee to Arabia or even India (D.C. LI.7.1; Plu. *Ant.* 69.3.5): she had ships brought to the Red Sea and they were loaded with treasure. The Nabataeans, however, who were hostile to the queen not least because they had been forced to cede territory to her in 37/6,[120] burnt her ships and thwarted her plans.

Cleopatra then tried to prepare Egypt for a defensive stand (Plu. *Ant.* 69.5). She had Ptolemy XV Caesar registered in the lists of ephebes and declared that he was now of age and fit to assume the succession to the throne (D.C. LI.6.1; Plu. *Ant.* 71.3). There was also a flurry of diplomatic activity with Octavian during which Cleopatra even offered up her own royal insignia in return for the guarantee that the kingship would remain in the hands of her children (D.C. LI.6–8;[121] Plu. *Ant.* 72.1).

In the spring of 30, Octavian's armies in the east and west moved against Egypt (D.C. LI.9–10; Plu. *Ant.* 74–75); he himself came from Syria. Pelusion fell surprisingly quickly and C. Cornelius Gallus, who was later to be the first *Praefectus Aegypti*,[122] advanced from Libya and caught Paraitonion unawares. East of Alexandria near the hippodrome, another battle ensued in the course of which Antony was able to beat back Octavian's cavalry. The following day, as Antony positioned himself for the last battle, his fleet and cavalry went over to Octavian's side. The suspicion that Cleopatra had betrayed

Antony was never dispelled (D.C. LI.10.4; Plu. *Ant.* 76.1–3). On 1 August 30 (according to the Roman calendar in use at the time),[123] Octavian entered Alexandria and officially brought an end to the Ptolemaic kingdom.

Cleopatra went to her mausoleum and had Antony notified that she was dead; in reaction to the news, he attempted to commit suicide but then learning that Cleopatra was still alive, he had himself brought to her in order to die in her arms. That is the tragedy of Mark Antony, who not so long ago had been raised to the heavens, and now ended his life at the age of 52 (D.C. LI.10; Plu. *Ant.* 76–77). It is possible that Cleopatra cleverly drove him to suicide so as to leave herself open for other opportunities (D.C. LI.10.5–6). According to Plutarch, however, she lamented the dying Antony and was overcome with grief (Plu. *Ant.* 77.5).

After Octavian learned of the death of his adversary, he made Cleopatra leave the mausoleum by means of a ruse. He wanted her to be the crown of his triumph in Rome and therefore had her kept under close watch (D.C. LI.11; Plu. *Ant.* 78–79). The children she had with Antony were also taken into custody and treated generously. Caesarion, on the other hand, had been provided with treasures by Cleopatra and sent south to escape Octavian's forces. According to Plutarch, he was heading for India (Plu. *Ant.* 81.4). It was, however, in Octavian's best interests to have him eliminated; he could not have Caesar's innocent son and the legitimate king of Egypt put on display in his triumph, since this would elicit much protest. After Cleopatra's death, Caesarion was captured and brutally murdered (D.C. LI.15.5; Plu. *Ant.* 82.1; Suet. *Aug.* 17.5).

Octavian allowed Cleopatra to bury the dead Antony with royal honours and let her live in the palace. Her own deepest wish was to avoid offering herself as a spectacle to the Roman people in Octavian's triumph. She therefore attempted to starve herself to death; her personal physician, Olympos, was there and wrote an account of Cleopatra's last days (FGrHist.198) which later served as the basis for Plutarch's version. Octavian threatened her with reprisals against her children and so once again put an end to her plan (Plu. *Ant.* 82). He visited her in the palace and in the ensuing conversation (D.C. LI.12; Plu. *Ant.* 83) Cleopatra had to acknowledge that she had not been able to receive any guarantees with regard to her own fate or the succession to the throne. She then had Octavian believe that she was only interested in prolonging her own life and 'he left believing that he had deceived her while he, in fact, was the one deceived' (Plu. *Ant.* 83.7). After the meeting, Cleopatra arranged her death, probably on 10 August 30 following the Roman calendar (most probably 12 August by our own calendar). Plutarch's account of her death (*Ant.* 85.2–8) was to become renowned in world literature:

> After her bath, she went to the table and made a sumptous meal. Meanwhile, a fellow from the country brought a little basket. When the guards asked what he had brought, he opened it and lifted up the leaves and showed them that the vessel was full of figs. When they admired

the largeness and beauty of the figs, he smilingly invited them to take some. They then allowed him to enter without being suspicious of him. After the meal, Cleopatra sent a letter, which she had written and sealed, to Caesar; sending everyone out except for her two women, she shut the doors. As Caesar opened the letter and read Cleopatra's prayers and entreaties that she might be buried in the same tomb with Antony, he immediately understood what had transpired. At first, he wanted to go himself in all haste to save her life, but then he sent others to hurry to the queen and investigate the matter. But the matter had progressed too quickly for them. The messengers rushed to the monument and found that the guards were not aware that anything had happened; when they opened the door, they found Cleopatra already dead and lying upon a bed of gold in her royal ornaments. One of her two women, Eiras, lay dying at her feet, and the other one, Charmion, was already swaying and in a daze, adjusting the diadem on the head of the queen. When one of the guards said angrily: 'A fine state of affairs, Charmion!', she answered, 'Certainly, extremely fine and as becomes the descendant of so many kings.' She spoke no more but instead sank down by the side of the bed to the floor.[124]

Although it remained a mystery whether or not Cleopatra had died from a snake bite (ἀσπίς), as in Plutarch's account (Plu. *Ant.* 86; cf. Str. XVII.1.10), this became a common assumption later on. Octavian had an image of Cleopatra carried in his triumphal procession of 29 in which she was depicted with snakes (Hor. *Carm.* I.37.26–28; Prop. III.11.53–54; Verg. *A.* VIII.697). Thus, Octavian officially proclaimed that Cleopatra's death was due to a snake bite.[125] The exemplary loyalty of the two servants, Eiras and Charmion, who probably took poison, became proverbial in Alexandria.[126]

Cleopatra died at 39 years of age (Plu. Ant. 86.8) after a short but incredibly turbulent life. She evidently gave little thought to domestic affairs. The strategos of Thebes, Kallimachos,[127] was a perfect illustration of the fact that 'God helps those who help themselves'. Roman intervention together with Ptolemy XII's policy of handing out generous bribes had hopelessly weakened Egypt, though it was still a land that was rich in resources. Under Cleopatra, economic resources were placed at the disposal of the navy and they were also to be used by Antony in his Parthian campaign and in his other projects.

The queen's true talent lay in imperial politics which more than any other member of her family she transformed into world politics. In this way, she rose to become one of the most remarkable women of the ancient world and in modern times came to be known as 'Cleopatra the Great'. Her knowledge of the Egyptian language and culture was exceptional, perhaps because of her mother;[128] Plutarch (*Ant.* 27.4–5) portrays her as a linguistic genius altogether. She was quite receptive to the model of sovereignty of the ancient Egyptian pharaoh linking her to former queens of ancient Egypt such as

Hatshepsut and Tauseret. She also dreamed of the victory of Hellenism throughout the world, first with Caesar and then with Antony. While the two Roman men were merely ahead of their time in this regard (the Augustan principate is characterized by ancient Roman customs and ideals), Cleopatra, by espousing this ideal, went against the very grain of history in Ptolemaic Egypt. Although she made the greatest use of her intellectual and physical capacities to further this dream, she was not able to restore in any lasting manner the conditions of the third century.

Modern assessments of the queen differ greatly from the characterization of her in Octavian's propaganda and the later Roman tradition[129] where occasionally she is even referred to as a royal whore. Treatments of her by her Roman contemporaries, for example Horace (*Carm.* I.37), are less given to caricature and so still mention some of her historical and political accomplishments. Horace acknowledges without reserve the queen's lofty character which led her to choose death over shameful exposure in Octavian's triumphal procession (*Carm.* I.37.32: *non humilis mulier*).

By right of conquest Octavian made himself the ruler of Egypt. The country was officially annexed not upon Cleopatra's death but on the day he entered Alexandria (1 or 3 August 30); this was the beginning of the history of the Roman province of *Aegyptus*. This day was declared a holiday in Rome by a *senatus consultum* and was fixed as the date from which the years of the new ruler should start to be counted (D.C. LI.19.6). Accordingly, a dating system was established in Egypt on the basis of the Καίσαρος κράτησις θεοῦ υἱοῦ (the seizure of power by Caesar, son of the god = Octavian as son of the deified Caesar). The system at the same time marked a break between the old and the new regimes.[130] On hieroglyphic monuments, however, tradition could not simply be ignored and so the beginning of the new era had to wait until the next new year's day for full acknowledgement (29 August, probably our 31 August, of the year 30). The reckoning of the years on the basis of the *kratesis* was only later brought into line with the traditional system.[131] On the political front, C. Cornelius Gallus, a friend of Octavian's who had fought alongside him, took over the administration of the land as the first *praefectus Aegypti*.

Rather appropriately, Cleopatra was laid to rest at Antony's side. No harm came to the children they had had together. They accompanied the image of their dead mother in the triumph of 29 in Rome; afterwards, Octavia took them in and raised them together with her own children by Antony (D.C. LI.15.6–7; Plu. *Ant.* 87; Suet. *Aug.* 17.5). Nothing more is known of Alexander Helios and Ptolemy Philadelphos. Of Cleopatra Selene, however, we do know that Augustus had her betrothed to Juba II, king of Mauretania, in about 20 BC. Coins from that region portray Cleopatra Selene as a queen (20 – *c.* 4 BC) very much conscious of her power in the tradition of the Ptolemaic family. Juba II eventually transformed his residence Caesarea (Cherchel) into a little Alexandria with an important library that became a centre of culture and learning. To foster family history, Egyptian art was transported to the region and we can infer from the Ptolemaic portrait busts found there that a sort of gallery of ancestors was set up there.[132] The marriage of Juba II with Cleopatra Selene produced Ptolemy of Mauretania, who ruled the kingdom as his father's successor from AD 23 to 40. He was executed by Caligula because the emperor had begun to suspect him (D.C. LIX.25.1); Suet. *Cal.* 35.1). With this action, the Ptolemaic line was finally extinguished 363 years after the death of Alexander the Great.

## Notes

1 On Cleopatra V Selene see p. 220, note 151. She emphasized the claims of both of her sons to the Egyptian crown after the coronation of Ptolemy XII (in 76) by sending them both to Rome. There, however, they were put off by the senate and returned empty-handed after two years (Cic. Ver.II.4.61–68).
2 Huß (1990), 203.
3 See p. 212 with note 166.
4 Michaelidou-Nicolaou (1976), 20, 102f. (Π 58).
5 Bloedow (1963), 83.
6 Criscuolo (1990), 95
7 Ijsewijn (1961), 121.
8 On this see the passage on the Harris stele p. 283; on the ideology linked with the title see p. 289f.
9 See p. 283f.
10 See p. 198 with note 87.
11 Huß (1990).
12 The last monument on which she is named dates from 7 August 69 while she is absent from a document from 25 February 68; cf. Huß, esp. 196; Quaegebeur (1989, 2), 604.
13 Quaegebeur (1989, 2).
14 See p. 227.
15 On what follows: Bloedow (1963), 35–46; Sonnabend (1986), 27–30.
16 Scholia . . . (loc. cit.: p. 325, note 175), 29–32; Havas (1977), 41 argues, however, for the year 56.
17 Havas (1977).
18 Cic.leg.agr.II.43: 'If Rullus desires to be the friend of the people, he will award the kingdom to the Roman people. And so too, by virtue of his law, he will sell Alexandria, he will sell Egypt, and we shall discover that he is the judge, the arbiter, the owner of a most wealthy city and of the most beautiful country – in fine, the king of a most flourishing kingdom. Oh but he will not take so much for himself, he will not be greedy: he will decide that Alexandria is the king's, he will decide that it is not the Roman people's.' (translation: John H. Freese, *The Speeches of Cicero*, Cambridge, Harvard University Press, 1961.)
19 BGU VIII.1815; Bloedow (1963), 30.
20 C.Ord.Ptol. no. 71. The hereditary nature of kleruchic land is already known from the amnesty decrees of Ptolemy VIII; cf. ibid., p. 199.
21 On the annexation of Cyprus by Rome as well as on the pertinent sources: Olshausen (1963), 38–44; Michaelidou-Nicolaou (1976), 20f.
22 Bloedow (1963), 51–53.

23  Sonnabend (1986), 31.
24  According to Porph.: FGrHist. 260 F 2.14 both queens were daughters of Ptolemy XII. Since, however, Strabo XVII.1.11 does not know one daughter, Cleopatra Tryphaina, and one may conclude from the reliefs in Edfu that the wife of Ptolemy XII had not died, the queens of 58/7 must have been mother and daughter; cf. Huß (1990).
25  Quaegebeur (1989, 2), 605; see Thissen, note 26 here below, 17.
26  Both queens are referred to in BGU VIII.1762: cf. Skeat (1969), 37; Maehler (1983), 6 with note 48.
27  Noteworthy are the double-datings by both Berenike IV and Ptolemy XII; dem.Pap.Louvre 3452, col. 14.6: 'Written in year two of the queen (*ß Pr-ꜥ3t*) which is the 25th year of the king (*Pr-ꜥ3*)'; the reverse order (year 26 = year 3) is found in H. J. Thissen, *Die demotischen Graffiti von Medinet Habu*, Sommerhausen 1989, no. 43, l.1.
28  Bloedow (1963), 68–71; Will, II (1982), 524f.
29  PP VI.14567.
30  PP VI.14496.
31  From the time between 7 March and 16 April, 56; cf. Gauthier (1916), 408f.; Samuel (1962), 156; Pestman (1967), 80f.; Skeat (1969), 39.
32  Bloedow (1963), 61–67; Olshausen (1963), 45–63; Shatzman (1971); Sonnabend (1986), 30–33.
33  PP VI.16749.
34  Supposedly also 10,000 talents to Gabinius: Plu. *Ant.* 3.4; Cic. *Rab. Post.* 21.
35  Quaegebeur (1991), 56; On the reinstatement of Ptolemy see Bloedow (1963), 72–74.
36  On the position of Rabirius Postumus cf. E. Van 't Dack, in *Studia P. Naster oblata, II*, Leuven 1982, 326 (= id., 1988, 181); H. Heinen, *BiOr* 47, 1990, 664.
37  Heinen (1966), 48–52; Van 't Dack (1983, 1).
38  PP VI.16580; Fraser (1972), I.362f., 371f.
39  Fraser (1972), 484–486.
40  See p. 223.
41  OGIS II.741; Fraser (1972), II.428, note 682; Criscuolo (1990).
42  See p. 223.
43  Quaegebeur (1989, 2), 605; id. (1991), 50, 60f., 66.
44  On the will cf. Heinen (1966), 9f.; Criscuolo (1989), 337f.
45  Selected literature: R. Mond, O. H. Myers, *The Bucheum*, London 1934, II.11–13, no. 13, pl.XLIII. O. Koefoed-Petersen, *Les stèles égyptiennes*, Copenhagen 1948, 43–45, no. 58 (with an erroneous name for the month); Crawford (1980), 11; Thompson, D. J. (1988), 125.
46  Criscuolo (1989).
47  Ricketts (1980), 12–21; on this I. Fay.205 (= I. Louvre, no. 21) from 2 July, 51; on this stele see pp. 280–281 with note 121.
48  To which her own joint rule had already paid lip service; see p. 204.
49  Ricketts (1980), 11–21; Huß (1990), 197, note 27; Chauveau (1991), 134.
50  C.Ord.Ptol., no. 73.
51  Maehler (1983), 7.
52  SB 9065, l.2; 9764, l. 6f.; BBU VIII.1839, l.5.
53  Cf. Heinen (1966), 23–32, 185f.; Ricketts (1980), 21–28, 91; Criscuolo (1989), 326.

54 PP VI.14620; Mooren (1975), 72f. (028).

55 PP II.2154; VI.14594; Mooren (1975), 73f. (029).

56 PP VI.14603; on this figure: Heinen (1966), 36–45.

57 Heinen (1966), 11–23.

58 Heinen (1966), 32f.; Criscuolo (1989), 328f.

59 According to Caes.*Civ.* III.103.2 a few months before Caesar's arrival in Alexandria.

60 Sources provide us with a pre-Julianic date of 28 September 48. On converting dates to the Julianic calendar, see G. Radke, *Fast Romani*, Münster 1990, esp. tables on p. 77. On the flight and death of Pompey: Heinen (1966), 60–68; P. Greenhalgh, *Pompey, the Republican Prince*, London 1981, 256–269, 291.

61 A third legion arrived later: *Bell.Alex.* 9.3; cf. Van 't Dack (1983, 1), 20.

62 Heinen (1966), 91, note 2; Michaelidou-Nicolaou (1976), 22; E. Van 't Dack, 'Notices cypriotes' in *Studia P. Naster oblata*, II, Leuven 1982, 321–326 (= id., 1988, 175–184); *contra* continuous Ptolemaic rule from 48: Bicknell (1977).

63 Heinen (1966), 92–142 is a basic source for the Bellum Alexandrinum.

64 The lighthouse pharos was not located on the island of Pharos but rather on another small island: see Map 3 as well as Heinen (1966), 106, note 5. On the battle for the island of Pharos see pp. 235–236.

65 Cf. Fraser (1972), I.334f.; sources on the burning of the library: ibid., II, 493f., notes 224–5; on the Serapeum library see p. 64.

66 PP II.2156.

67 On this development: Heinen (1966), 111–120.

68 Heinen (1966), 160f.

69 This had already taken place in 55: see p. 229. On the composition of the relief troops: Van 't Dack (1983, 1), 21f.

70 Transmitted by the sources as 27 March; see Heinen (1966), 141 with note 1; on its conversion see Radke, loc. cit. (p. 327, note 60).

71 Only Dio states that Caesar ordered that Cleopatra was to marry her second brother. This generally accepted (Heinen (1966), 143; Volkmann (1959), 1759; Sonnabend (1986), 46) marriage between siblings has also recently been cast into doubt: Criscuolo (1989).

72 Heinen (1966), 177–179; Geraci (1983), 24; Criscuolo (1989), 327, note 6.

72a C. Traunecker, *Coptos, hommes et dieux sur le parvis de Geb* (Leuven 1992) 271–293, 320–324.

73 On Rufio: PP VI.16093. It remains uncertain to what rank Rufio had actually been promoted; Geraci (1983), 26, note 69.

74 Maehler (1983), 7. On the issue of the rush of new appointments to administrative offices in the wake of the constant changes in the power structure of the royal house from the return of Ptolemy XII cf. L Criscuolo, 'Guerre civili e amministrazione tolemaica. Il caso degli strateghi dell'Herakleopolites', *AncSoc* 22, 1991, 229–234.

75 On the voyage: Geraci (1983), 34–36.

76 Louvre 335: Heinen (1969), 182–186; E. Grzybek, 'Pharao Caesar in einer demotischen Grabschrift aus Memphis', Mus.Helv 35, 1978, 149–158 (unsustainable hypothesis); Geraci (1983), 36–40.

77 Gauthier (1916), 412f. (VI, VIII), 417f.; Beckerath (1984), 295, E 4–5.

78 Gauthier (1916), 413 (VII = Harris stele, see p. 284); Beckerath (1984), 295, E 2, 6–7; Heinen (1969), 185f.

79 See p. 276 with note 88, p. 290 with note 208.

80 The topic has been much discussed since antiquity; in my view, the historical circumstances allow for no doubt on the matter.

81 Cf. E. Van't Dack, 'La date de C.Ord.Ptol. 80–83 = BGU VI 1212 et le séjour de Cléopâtre VII à Rome', AncSoc I, 1970, 53–67 (= Van 't Dack, 1988, 229–246); on the reasons for the voyage: Geraci (1983), 40–46.

82 On this see p. 107f. Since Caesar had already started his reform in 49, his stay in Alexandria cannot have been the catalyst for the project. In order for 1 January 45 to be fixed correctly in astronomical terms, the outgoing consular year of Caesar and Lepidus had to be lengthened by 90 days (Cens.XX.8); cf. G. Radke, loc. cit (p. 327, note 60), 62–68.

83 See p. 290f.

84 Whether or not she took Caesarion with her to Rome seems to be uncertain; Geraci (1983), 40, note 146.

85 See p. 206, 209.

86 Pestman (1967), 82; C.Ord.Ptol., no. 75–75 (= Bernand (1992), no. 45); cf. also OGIS I.194 from 43/2.

87 On this chronology: Bonneau (1971), 231; cf. however Hutmacher (1965), 29.

88 PP VI.16595; Fraser (1972), I, 367, 372.

89 H. De Meulenaere, 'Les stratèges indigènes du nome tentyrite à la fin de l'époque ptolémaïque et au début de l'occupation romaine', *RivStOr* 34, 1959, 1–25; Mooren (1974), 150 with note 74; Rickets (1980), 70–89. Egyptians as strategoi bearning the title of syngenes: see in Mooren (1975), 117–122 (0123–4, 0127–9), 125–128 (0137–8; Augustan period).

90 PP I & VIII.194; VI.16273, 17147; Hutmacher (1965); Bingen (1970); Mooren (1975), 96f. (061); Thomas (1975), 106–108, Ricketts (1982/3).

91 See p. 203f. with note 120.

92 SB 8334; SEG XXIV.1217; Hutmacher (1965); Bernand (1992), no. 46.

93 On this cf also the structure of the decrees of priests pp. 106f., 162–168.

94 Cf. Van 't Dack (1983, 1), 20f.

95 PP VI.15077; Michaelidou-Nicolaou (1976), 109f. (Σ 7).

96 On the relation between Plutarch and Shakespeare see Pelling (1988), 37–45; on this encounter: 186f.

97 Cf. H. Thür, 'Arsinoe IV, eine Schwester Cleopatra VII, Grabinhaberin des Oktogons von Ephesos? Ein Vorschlag', *Öjh* 60, Hauptblatt, 1990, 43–56.

98 PP VI.15040a; Mooren (1975), 197f. (0358); Michaelidou-Nicolaou (1976), 53 (Δ 44); Bagnall (1976), 262; Van 't Dack, loc. cit. (p. 328, note 62), 323, 326.

99 On account of the recognition of the children, the marriage between Antony and Cleopatra has commonly been dated to the winter of 37/6. The sources, however, seem to indicate 34 as a more likely date; see p. 244 with note 110.

100 Christ (1984), 448.

101 The double dating is also found in coinage from Berytos; in addition, there are also coins from Berytos, Tripolis, Orthosia and Alexandria which are dated only by the new era: Ricketts (1980), 40.

102 Ricketts (1980), 36, 40f.; M. H. Crawford, *Coinage and Money Under the Roman Republic*, London 1985, 253; Smith, R. R. R. (1988), 133.

103 Following G. Perl, 'Die römischen Provinzbeamten in Cyrenae und Creta zur Zeit der Republik', Klio 52, 1970, 338–342; 354.

104 Pelling (1988), 220–243; Reinhold (1988), 55–63; Chamoux (1989), 279–288.
105 Cf. D. Michel, Alexander als Vorbild für Pompeius, Caesar und Marcus Antonius, Brussels 1967, 126–132. On the 'triumph' of Antony in Alexandria: Reinhold (1988), 76.
106 Geraci (1983), 55–59, 69f., 79; Pelling (1988), 249–251.
107 The inscription fragment CIL III.7232 from Delos may be supplemented in such a way that a 'king of kings, son of Cleopatra' is mentioned. It is clear, therefore, that Plutarch (*Ant.* 54.7) wrongly asserts that only the sons of Cleopatra and Antony bore the title of 'king of kings'.
108 See pp. 231–234.
109 L. P. C. Kent *et al.*, *Die Römische Münze*, Munich 1973, pl. 29, no. 111; M. Crawford, *Roman Republican Coinage, I*, London 1974, 539, no. 543.
110 H. R. Baldus, 'Zur Münzprägung von Dora/Phönizien zu Ehren Kleopatras VII und Mark Antons', *Chiron* 19, 1989, 477–480. On the discussion concerning the marriage beween Antony and Cleopatra see also Reinhold (1988), 220–222.
111 The re-organization of the east by Antony was incomprehensible to the Italo-Roman mind.
112 It is scarcely to be believed that the entire contents (*c.* 20,000 rolls) of the library would have been brought to Alexandria.
113 Cf. p. 293 Octavian's speech before the battle of Actium.
114 Kl. M. Girardet, 'Der Rechtstatus Oktavians im Jahre 32 v. Chr.', *RhM* 133, 1990, 322–350. See Reinhold (1988), 85–101 for the events of the year 32.
115 Thus is she described in the Roman calendar of festival on the day of Octavian's seizure of Alexandria; on this topic: Geraci (1983), 47–81.
116 Reinhold (1981/2).
117 Bengtson (1977), 230–243; Chamoux (1989), 332–349 provide clear descriptions of the battle; cf. also Reinhold (1988), 113–116.
118 Cleopatra, on the other hand, did not betray Antony; the theme of her betrayal is post-Augustan: Pelling (1988), 284.
119 Geraci (1983), 108f.
120 See pp. 241–242. Horace (*carm.*I.37.23f.) views Cleopatra's attempt to escape as a rumour which he dismisses.
121 Dio depicts the queen here as a traitor.
122 Primary and secondary sources on him: *ANRW* II.10.1, 474f., 159.
123 Probably corresponds to our 3 August; cf. Geraci (1983), 159.
124 Translation by Tina Saavedra (based loosely on Dryden's translation).
125 The death of Cleopatra has caused a large body of secondary sources to be formed: cf. among them, W. Spiegelberg, 'Weshalb wählte Kleopatra den Tod durch Schlangenbiß?' in *Ägyptologische Mitteilungen, SbMünchen*, 2, H., part 1, 1925, 3–6; Griffiths (1961) as well as *JEA* 50, 1964, 181f. and 51.1965, 209–211; Becher (1966), 150–173; Geraci (1983), 113–117; Pelling (1988), 318–323.
126 *Plutarchi de proverbiis Alexandrinorum*, ed. O. Crusius, Tübingen, 1887, no. 45 (= Corpus Paroemiographorum Graecorum, supp. IIIa).
127 See p. 239.
128 See p. 223.
129 Becher (1966).

130  Geraci (1983), 119f., 158–163; Reinhold (1988).

131  T. C. Skeat, 'The Augustan era in Egypt', *ZPE* 53, 1983, 241–244.

132  Cf.: '*Die Numider, Reich und Könige nördlich der Sahara*', ed. H. G. Horn, B. Rüger, Cologne 1979, 69–72, 221f.; Kl. Fittschen, 'Zwei Ptolemäerbildnisse in Cherchel', in *Alessandria* I (1983), 165–171.

# 9 Religious culture and divine kingship from Ptolemy VI to Cleopatra VII

## THE PHARAOH AND THE EGYPTIAN SANCTUARIES

### The golden age of temple building under Ptolemy VI and VIII

The periods of crisis experienced by the Ptolemaic kingdom from the end of the third century to the 160s resulted in changes to the composition of the monarchy. The governance of Egypt in co-operation with certain priesthoods led increasingly to a balanced collaboration and a fruitful exchange between the dynasty and the Egyptian elite. From the time of Ptolemy VIII onwards, Egyptians were able to rise to the highest offices in the administration. With the greater participation of the native Egyptians in the government of Egypt, the kings gained increasing support in their attempts to portray themselves as solicitous and beneficent rulers by means of philanthropa-decrees.[1] In pursuing this objective, the Ptolemaic rulers sought to bring their regime in line with the ancient Egyptian royal ideology of the king. The arrangement between dynasty and priesthoods also led to the last allocations of property to the temples under Ptolemy VI.[2]

The widespread construction of sacred monuments that took place after the devastating crises in Ptolemy VI's early years was, in spite of the destructive dynastic clashes under Ptolemy VIII, one of the most significant phenomena in the development of Egyptian culture. According to the temple reliefs from the time of Philometor and Euergetes II, these kings belong to the series of the great pharaonic builders of ancient Egypt. To be sure, temple reliefs and inscriptions must not always be taken at face value; though official acknowledgements might indicate otherwise, it is not safe to assume that the initiative and funding[3] for monuments always came from the king. It was the priests who carefully directed the temple ornamentation on the basis of the situation within the ruling family at any given time. Moreover, quite in keeping with ancient Egyptian religious tradition, the priests also made sure that the historical person of the king was officially represented in such a way that it showed him acting in fulfilment of his cultic obligations. It is important not to forget that, as a result of the specific way in which the Ptolemaic monarchy developed, the spouse(s) and later on even the royal

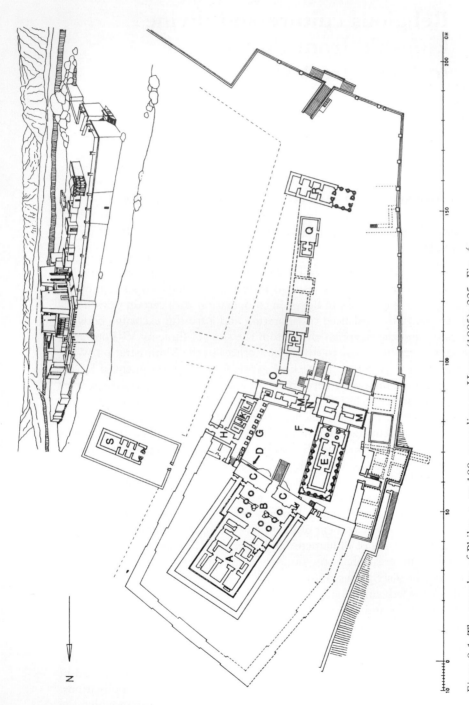

*Figure 9.1* The temples of Philae, *c.* AD 100, according to Haeny (1985): 225, Fig. 4.
A Temple of Isis of Ptolemy II; B Pronaos and Peristyle; C Second Pylon; D Dodekaschoinos Stele; E Birth House; F Wall with Philensis Decrees; G East Colonnade; H 'Gate of Tiberius'; I Library; J Cleaning Room; K Courtroom; L Laboratory; M First Pylon; N Gate of Nectanebo I; O Gate of Philadelphos; P Temple of Imhotep; Q Small Temple; R Temple of Arensnuphis; S Temple of Harbor (symbols for architectural elements are my own).

mother became important elements of royal ideology. However we may choose to characterize the building programmes of later Ptolemaic history, it remains a fact that the ruling house espoused a policy which led to the flourishing of temple architecture.

Turning to the area of Lower Nubia which was retaken during the reign of Philometor, we will first deal with Ayuala (near Kalabsha). There is reference here to Ptolemy VI on a stele fragment from the temple of Mandulis, a monument dating to the Ptolemaic-Roman period.[4] Ptolemy IV had started construction of the temple of Thot at el-Dakka and it was pursued by Ergamenes II during the revolt in the Thebaïd at the turn of the century;[5] in the period currently under consideration, a pronaos with two frontal columns was built and its façade was decorated in the name of Euergetes II.[6] In Dabod as well, work begun in the Meroitic period was continued:[7] the chapel for Amun (and the Isis of Philae) erected by King Adikhalamani was expanded into a temple under Ptolemy VI and decorated under Euergetes II with work still continuing into the early Imperial period; a naos made of rose-granite which was found in the temple bears the names of Ptolemy VIII and one of the two Cleopatras.[8]

On the island of Philae (Fig. 9.1), the comprehensive building project around the temple of Isis which was started under Philadelphos was continued and completed by Philometor.[9] The placing of the Dodekaschoinos Stele of 157 on the granite rock in front of the second pylon (Fig. 9.1 C–D; Fig. 9.2) shows that the framework of the great hypostyle hall, which is attached to this second pylon in unfinished form, was already complete at that time; likewise, the first pylon (Fig. 9.1 M) was erected under Philometor, as the inscription in the passageway to the west tower indicates.[10] Cartouches of the sixth Ptolemy are also found on the gates of the birth house which is directly beside this passageway. Euergetes II had the colonnaded hall of the temple of Isis (Fig. 9.1 B) decorated. During his reign, the birth house (Fig. 9.1 E) was expanded by the addition of a third room behind the old sanctuary which now closed off the space between the pylons on the west side; this expansion represents an important step in the larger development of birth houses from small subsidiary sanctuaries to actual temples.[11] In the course of this enlargement the columns of the ambulatory, which stood at the former rear wall, were pushed back and additional columns were installed in the place made available along the side-walls. The decoration of three rooms in the birth house was completed in the reign of Ptolemy VIII. At the same time (under Euergetes II), as a complement to this architectural complex, a colonnade was erected – with rooms behind it – directly across from the birth temple (Fig. 9.1 G–L). The space between the pylons was now also closed off in the east. The upper frieze of the so-called gate of Tiberius (Fig. 9.1 H) which leads outside the complex, also bears the cartouches of the eighth Ptolemy. The great platform in front of the first pylon was given its present appearance through the construction of supporting walls in the last years of Euergetes II. The priests placed two granite obelisks here out of gratitude

*Figure 9.2* Philae, temple of Isis, view of the second pylon with scenes of the king with the cartouches of Ptolemy XII sacrificing before deities. Main image on the left: king, who is obscured by the rear part of the birth house, before Osiris-Onnophris and Isis. Main image on the right: king before Horus and Hathor. At the base of the right gate tower is the Dodekaschoinos Stele of 157.

for the benefactions bestowed upon them by Euergetes II; the eastern obelisk stands today in the gardens of Kingston Hall in Dorset, England.[12]

Aside from the work done on the temple of Isis, the temple of Hathor (Fig. 9.1 S) on the eastern bank of the island was founded and partially decorated in the reign of Philometor. While early construction phases of the temple of Arensnuphis (Fig. 9.1 R) are associated with Ptolemy IV, Ergamenes II and Ptolemy V, Ptolemy VI continued the project and also dedicated a naos. Probably under Euergetes II, both buildings were expanded by the addition of one room – just like the birth house mentioned above – behind the sanctuary; its rear wall was clearly taken down for this purpose.[13]

The New Kingdom temple of Satet on the island of Elephantine had already begun to be demolished at the time of the Sixth Syrian War. On 4 February 164 BC the foundations of the new building were laid.[14] We may assume that Ptolemaic religious policy was attempted to create a certain equivalence between the rival priesthoods of Philae and Elephantine.

During the reign of Euergetes II, scenes and inscriptions were added to the temple of Isis of Aswan which dates from the reigns of Ptolemy III and Ptolemy IV. The cartouches, which normally included the individual names of the king, remained empty.[15]

Approximately 45 km north of Aswan lies Kom Ombo (in Greek, Ombos) which, as of the reign of Philometor, became the administrative centre of the first nome of Upper Egypt (Ombites). The impressive temple of Haroeris and Sobek was part of a new and large-scale building project under Philometor. The cult and theology[16] associated with the temple are unique because two male divinities – who originally were not linked together and who had their proper divine family – shared the sacred structure: the one is Haroeris, 'the elder Horus' or 'Horus the powerful' which is an aspect of the celestial god in the form of a falcon (quite distinct from Harsiese or Horus in his role as the son of Isis); the other is the crocodile god Sobek. Next to Haroeris are his partner, Tasenetnofret ('the good sister') and the child-god Panebtawi ('lord of the two lands'); another triad is formed by Sobek with Hathor and Khons. As was always the case in Egypt, numerous other divinities were worshipped in the temple, such as Amun of Thebes, Ptah of Memphis, a form of Khnum, the gods in Osiris' circle (Osiris, Isis, Nephthys, Harsiese), Min of Koptos and Thoth. In the theological system of the temple, the main gods appear to be assimilated to the gods of Heliopolis, i.e. Haroeris is assimilated to Shu and Sobek to Geb, Tasenetnofret to Tefnut and Hathor to Nut.

The twin sanctuaries set up for the twofold cult of the two principal gods (Fig. 9.3) and were intended for; in the inner part are two sanctuaries next to each other, of which the northern one is for Haroeris and the southern one for Sobek. The rooms in front of the sanctuaries ('hall of the Ennead', offering hall, a room called the 'large palace',[17] and the inner and outer colonnaded halls) were common to both Haroeris and Sobek, but each sanctuary has its own axis with a double gateway leading from one room to the other. The temple house (Fig. 9.3 A–E) was erected during the reign of Philometor[18] and its interior was decorated as far as the 'large palace'; the ornamentation of the inner hypostyle ('Hall of the Appearance') and the erection of a large part of the birth house – the building stands in front of the temple and lies perpendicular to its axis – belong to Euergetes II's reign. Of particular interest is the fact that the decoration of the sanctuary of Haroeris was undertaken by the troops stationed in Ombos. A Greek dedicatory inscription,[19] dating from the time of Ptolemy VI and Cleopatra II (163–145), records this act. Because we are here dealing with a sanctuary of central importance which was part of a large-scale building project, this inscription is of special significance with regard to the larger question of the relationship between royal religious policy and private initiative in the construction of temples. It confirms that neither the king nor the local priesthoods[20] always paid for 'pharaonic' building enterprises.[21]

The so-called temple monographs preserved in approximately 50 inscriptions in Kom Ombo merit some comment. They represent the basis of the theology of Kom Ombo and, at the same time, inform us about the temple and its cult; they tell us about such sacred themes as cult sites or the form and appearance of the gods, they record myths and legends and explain such

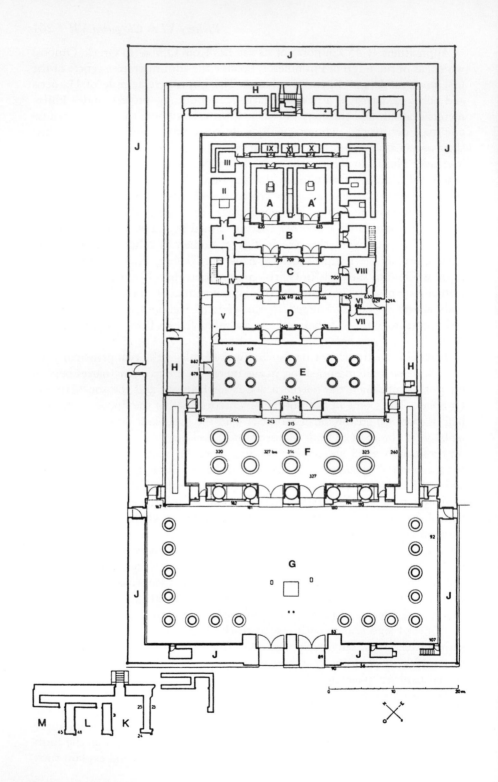

things as the order of the world, the nature of heaven and the origin of the gods. Familiar themes are often treated in various different ways and always in original versions. Specific to Kom Ombo is, for example, the creation of Osiris by the united gods Shu and Geb; there are even several versions of this myth.[22]

In the birth house (Mammisi) of Kom Ombo, the different mother goddesses and child-gods converge in the figure of one mother with a child. Of particular importance is a relief in a chamber directly in front of the sanctuary (Fig. 9.3 M) which depicts Ptolemy VIII in a boat in a thicket of reeds before the god Min (Fig. 9.4). The scene and the accompanying inscriptions present the king in conjunction with the gods as guarantors of abundance for Egypt and illustrate the purpose of the rituals associated with the birth house. These rites served to renew the cycle of nature as well as to restore the child god of the temple together with the king who acted as his counterpart (i.e. those of the king's powers which were active in the cult).[23]

In contrast to Kom Ombo, the building inscriptions from Edfu[24] provide us with fairly precise information on all the important stages in the completion of this sacred edifice – it remains the best preserved monumental temple from the Ptolemaic period (Figs. 9.5, 9.6). The inscriptions also tell us that its erection was dependent on local political events; the latter prevented any sort of construction from taking place on the sanctuary between 206 and 186.[25] As a result, apart from small details on the gates which date to Cleopatra I's lifetime, work was taken up again only in 152/1 under Ptolemy VI. By then, the worst of the crises in dynastic, domestic and international affairs had been resolved. The rooms annexed to the inner hypostyle were now decorated: these included the laboratory, the Nile room and the treasury (Fig. 9.6 E–G); as the inscriptions explicitly state,[26] the reliefs were painted and coated with gold.

About ten years later, work had advanced so far that it was possible to dedicate the entire inner temple complex together with the inner hypostyle. Two texts describe the operation up to the 18th day of the fourth month of the Shemu season in the 28th year of Euergetes II's reign (= 10 September 142). At this time, the dedication festival took place 'in the course of which the house of eternity was given to its masters by the king of Upper and Lower Egypt (heir to the Theoi Epiphaneis . . . ), i.e. the son of Re (Ptolemy

*Figure 9.3* (opposite) The twin temple of Kom Ombo, according to A. Gutbub: LÄ III, 1980, 677f. (symbols are from Gutbub).
A Sanctuary of Haroeris; A′ Sanctuary of Sobek; B 'Hall of the Ennead'; C Offering hall; D 'Large palace'; E 'Hall of the Appearance'; F Pronaos; G Courtyard; H Inner enclosure wall; J Outer enclosure wall; K, L, M Birth house (contains the relief of Ptolemy VIII on a barge, our Fig. 9.4); Roman numerals: I so-called New Year's court; II Wabet ('pure room'); III 'Throne of Re'; IV Stairs on a right angle going to the roof; V Room through which the offerings are brought; VI Nile room; VII Laboratory; VIII Room facing upright stairs.

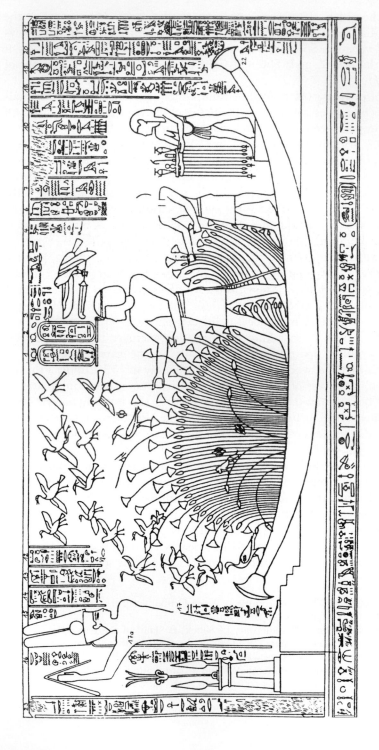

*Figure 9.4* Relief in the birth house of Kom Ombo: Ptolemy VIII offering geese and reeds to the god Min; the king stands in a boat in a reed bush and grips the reed stem, around him are countless geese and other water birds, behind the king are two divine companions; taken from W. Wettengel, loc. cit. (see p. 294, note 23), Fig. 4.

*Figure 9.5* Southern view of the temple of Horus at Edfu. In the foreground lies the birth house situated at right-angles to the main temple; the façade of the pylon is dominated by the colossal reliefs which depict the king defeating his enemies.

VIII) together with his wife, the queen and mistress of the two lands (Cleopatra II), also known as the Theoi Euergetai. This made it 95 years from the time when the measuring rope was stretched[27] until the 'entrance festival'.[28] The way the text is phrased implies that perhaps the royal couple had themselves gone to Edfu. Other documents describe the consecration festival as a great popular celebration which was enthusiastically attended by the people living in the city and the surrounding regions. The lovely coronation scenes of Ptolemy VIII on the eastern and western outer walls of the inner hypostyle are worthy of mention.

Between 142 and 139, the kiosk was built on the roof.[29] From this point onwards, the culmination of the new year's festival would take place here in the form of the ritual of 'the union with the solar disc', for it was this ritual which engendered the periodic renewal of the gods and the king when their statues were exposed to the rays of the sun.[30]

Inscriptions dating from 2 July 140 give accounts of the rites celebrating the foundation of the pronaos.[31] This was the first great colonnaded hall which was completed in 124 (Fig. 9.6 H); work on the roof is reported to have come to an end on 5 September and then decoration of the great hypostyle was begun and continued until the death of Euergetes II.

During these years (between 124 and 116), the birth house (Fig. 9.5) was built in front of the main temple.[32] In contrast to the birth house in Kom

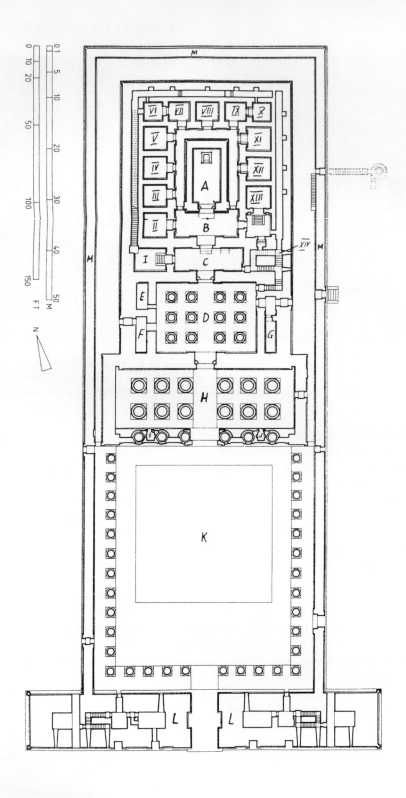

Ombo, it was given a colonnaded ambulatory, something which in Philae was there from the beginnning. This sort of ambulatory would henceforth be characteristic of birth temples. The construction work carried out on the birth houses in Egypt under Ptolemy VIII indicates that the rituals of birth, rearing and enthronement of the child god[33] had greatly increased in significance. The more belief in the charismatic powers of the earthly king declined, the more elements of the religious kingship were transferred onto the gods; this was particularly true of the ritual kingship of the divine falcons of Edfu and Philae[34] but also of the divine child of the birth houses who was crowned as the ideal ruler of the world. As a direct correlate of the latter notion, there also emerged the conception of an ideal earthly king as the central figure of Egyptian religion. In the reliefs on the birth house, the historical cartouches represent the king together with the child god and they even treat the two as identical. The portrayal of Ptolemy VIII in Edfu receiving the divine kingship is a good example of this.[35] A similar image of the king is to be found in the epithets of Euergetes II in the main temple; they describe him as a solicitous father of the country who ensures the fertility of the fields and the maintenance of the people.[36]

At the end of Euergetes II's reign, the monumental pylon of Edfu had just been erected (Fig. 9.6 L) and decoration of it had begun; the inscription relating the death of Ptolemy VIII[37] also reports that construction of the courtyard and the enclosure wall (Fig. 9.6 K and M) had ended.[38]

On the road to Thebes approximately 20 km north of Edfu lies Elkab, the city of the vulture goddess Nechbet. A Ptolemaic temple at the edge of the desert and partially built into the cliffs was dedicated to that goddess; here as well as in the nearby desert temple of Amenophis III, where restoration work was carried out under Ptolemy VIII, cartouches of the latter have been found. A further 30 km north stands the very charming Roman hypostyle of the great temple of Khnum. The rear wall of the colonnaded hall was formed by the façade of the Ptolemaic temple and it bears inscriptions and illustrations of the sixth Ptolemaic couple. Given that an architrave and a base inscription dating to the period of the reign of triple monarchy were found here together with cartouches of Ptolemy VI, VIII and Cleopatra II, it is quite possible that construction of the temple had already commenced under Epiphanes.[39] In Tod (*c.* 20 km south of Luxor) stands the temple of the god

*Figure 9.6* (opposite) Temple of Horus at Edfu, after S. Sauneron, H. Stierlin, *Die letzten Tempel Ägyptens, Edfu und Philae*, Zurich 1978, 36f.
A Sanctuary with the naos of Nectanebo II; B 'Hall of the Ennead'; C Offering hall; D 'Hall of Appearance'; E Laboratory; F Nile room; G Treasury; H Pronaos; I Purification room; J Library; K Courtyard; L Pylon; M Enclosure wall; Roman numerals: I Room in front of straight stairway; II–XII Ambulatory with chapels around the sanctuary (IV 'throne of the gods', VIII 'chapel of Horus of Lower Egypt, XI 'throne of Re'), XIII wabet ('pure room', in front of it is the New Year's court), XIV Stairway on a right-angle leading to the roof (the symbols for the architectural features are my own).

Month which dates from the Middle Kingdom. This solar god of the Theban nome is usually represented with a falcon's head and his main cult site, the great Month temple, was in Armant (Hermonthis) on the other side of the Nile. During the reign of Ptolemy VIII, the ancient sanctuary of Tod – a structure which was completely destroyed – was expanded by a large porch (consisting of several rooms and a hypostyle).[40]

In Thebes, which always tended to rebellions, there is evidence for construction in numerous places dating to the mid-second century. On the site of the temple of Karnak, of which the building history is unusually complicated, cartouches of Ptolemy VI have been found in such locations as the entrance to the temple of Harpara in the precinct of Month and the first gate of the temple of Ptah. Reliefs and inscriptions dating from the reign of Ptolemy VI and the reign that followed his have been found on the inner sides of the gate in the second pylon; Euergetes II is well attested in the temple of Khons. The most important structure here is the temple directly adjacent to the precinct which was dedicated to the mother goddess Opet (Ipet) who was depicted as a hippopotamus. The naos of this temple has survived and is a product of a new construction phase under Ptolemy VIII.[41] The theology of the temple is interesting, since this temple was viewed as the site of the creation of Osiris; consequently, Osiris assumes epithets which portray him as the child-god. The Theban divine triad (Amun-Re, Mut and Khons) were equated with the family of Osiris (Osiris, Isis, Horus) in the sanctuary. In Karnak, the east temple of Ramses II for Amun-Re-Harakhty should also be mentioned. According to the dedication inscription on it, the central gate between the two hypostyles belong to the reign of Euergetes II.[42]

On the west side of Thebes, the temple in Deir el-Medina constructed under Philopator[43] is certainly the most important: the anteroom, which was decorated under Philometor, contains a relief dating to the joint monarchy of the three siblings (170–164) which depicts them one behind another with their cartouches (Fig. 9.7).[44] Ornamention of the interior was completed under Euergetes II.

In terms of the history of Egyptian religion, the so-called sanatorium[45] on the third terrace of the temple of Hatshepsut was significant from the time of the eighth Ptolemy. There a cult was maintained for two popular holy men from Egyptian tradition who had been elevated to healing gods: one was Amenophis, son of Hapu, architect from the time of King Amenophis III, and the other was Imhotep, the architect of Djoser from the third dynasty, whose main cult site was connected with his grave in Saqqara and who in like manner to Asklepios was a healing god.[46] By the beginning of the Ptolemaic period at the latest, Amenophis, son of Hapu, was being worshipped in the ancient bark hall of the temple of Hatshepsut;[47] this room was the foremost of the two rooms which were both completely carved into the cliffs of the original sanctuary. During the period of the joint reign of Ptolemy VIII and his two wives, Cleopatra II and Cleopatra III, a third room was carved into the cliffs and fitted with well-wrought reliefs which present

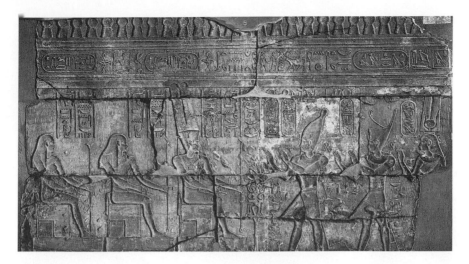

*Figure 9.7* Relief of the triple monarchy (170–164) from the antechamber of the temple at Deir el-Medina: Ptolemy VI, VIII and Cleopatra II before Amun-Re of the small temple of Medinet Habu (see Fig. 9.10) as well as Amun and Amaunet (the last two as members of the the eight primeval gods of Hermopolis); Berlin, Staatliche Museen Preußischer Kulturbesitz, Ägyptisches Museum, *Inv. 2115*.

the two healing gods in conjunction with numerous other deities. Furthermore, the Greek visitor inscriptions in the room name the Greek healing goddess Hygieia. A kiosk with six pillars, which had been built on the floor of the uppermost terrace of the old temple, sheltered the entrance to the small sanctuary probably from the time of Euergetes II. The new cult room mainly served as an oracle where the deified holy men acted as intermediaries between worshippers and the great celestial gods. It also served as the so-called sanatorium, presumably a place where the convalescent sought recovery by praying to the healing gods and by sleeping in the temple.[48]

In Medinet Habu stood the so-called small temple from the eighteenth dynasty, which was dedicated to the primeval Amun and the eight original gods of Hermopolis. The small temple lay within the fortress-like precinct of the great temple of the dead of Ramses III. It had already undergone much renovation and reconstruction during the late Egyptian period and under Euergetes II the central entrance and, above all, the bark hall (Fig. 9.10 A) were completely restored.[49] In addition, Euergetes II had the small temple of Thoth built in Qasr el-Aguz approximately 200 m south of Medinet Habu. In keeping with changes to the monarchy, the pharaoh appears in the reliefs at times with Cleopatra II and at other times with Cleopatra III and in one representation is acompanied by both queens. The dedicatory inscriptions are composed in the name of all three members of the monarchy.[50] Thoth was worshipped in the sanctuary as an oracular god next to the healing gods,

*Figure 9.8* View of the temple of the birth of Isis at Dendera; the preserved naos with an entrance on the north side dates from the Augustan period and rests upon foundations of the cella of Nectanebo I. Its north-south axis runs parallel to that of the main temple of Dendera; the low-lying Ptolemaic porches (the four-column chamber of Philometor directly next to the naos and the hypostyle of Ptolemy X with entrances from the east side – on the left side of the picture) are built along an older temple axis from the time of Ramses II whose orientation, not quite on a right angle, follows a roughly east-west direction; a false door 'connects' the fore-temple to the Augustan naos.

Amenophis, son of Hapu, and Imhotep. This indicates that there was a sharp increase in the significance of oracles and healing gods in the course of the Ptolemaic period.

Another large-scale temple building project was undertaken with the construction of the temple of Month of Medamud (9 km north of Luxor) – possibly in the last years of Epiphanes.[51] The temple house (sanctuary, ambulatory with radial chapels and antechambers), however, was completely destroyed. Cartouches of Ptolemy VI are found north of the building in the courtyard. Numerous reliefs of Ptolemy VIII are well preserved as are the five columns which are still standing at the magnificent portico in front of the façade.

Continuing north, the following should be briefly mentioned: In Dendera the temple of the birth of Isis (Fig. 9.8) was given its first four-column chamber under Philometor. The cella of the temple dates to Nectanebo I and gave way to a new building only in the Augustan period; a small bark chapel north of the sacred lake as well as the propylaea of the older birth

house were decorated under Euergetes II.[52] Approximately 45 km north of
Dendera lay the Ptolemaic temple of Hiw (Diospolis Parva) which was at
least partially decorated during the reign of the sixth Ptolemy.[53] In Athribis
(at Sohag) the main temple in honour of the lion-headed goddess Repyt
(Triphis) dates from the time of Euergetes II.[54] According to a Greek dedicatory inscription, the temple of the falcon god Nemti (*nmtj*) in Qaw el-Kebir
(Antaiupolis) received a new pronaos that had three rows of six columns
with palm capitals under Ptolemy VI;[55] in the sanctuary of the temple stood
a 4 m high naos of Ptolemy IV which was made of granite. The temple was
restored during the high Roman empire but was washed away by the Nile
between 1813 and 1821.

The monuments mentioned above – even if they are fragmentary – reveal
an incredibly lavish and complex programme of temple construction in
Upper Egypt in the six and a half decades spanning the reigns of Ptolemy VI
and Ptolemy VIII. Building projects in the Nile Delta are hardly worth
mentioning, since buildings in that area generally perished (this is true of all
periods of Egyptian history to varying degrees).[56]

We do know of many private endowments in the Fayum owing to Greek
dedicatory inscriptions. Various parts of sanctuaries are named, in particular,
monumental entrances (propyla).[57] In 155/4, a few soldiers together with
their commander dedicated a pronaos in Karanis;[58] during the period 163–
145 three Egyptians even financed a temenos for Arsinoe Philadelphos in
Narmouthis.[59]

## Pharaonic building projects in the late Ptolemaic period

In the Lower Nubian site of Kalabsha (50 km south of Philae), the oldest
architectural monuments reconstructed come from the time of Ptolemy IX;
they probably date, as a whole, from his first reign in Egypt.[60] A small
chapel next to the northern enclosure wall of the large Augustan temple of
Mandulis has been preserved and is today re-erected in New Kalabsha (by
the Aswan dam) in its original position.[61] The gods worshipped are regional
ones: above all Mandulis in his old and young forms but also Osiris, Isis,
Horus, Arensnuphis as well as the cataract gods Khnum, Satis and Anukis.
In addition, when the great temple was disassembled in 1962, over 200
blocks were uncovered which had been used as filling in the sanctuary
walls.[62] From these blocks, approximately half of a chapel could be reconstructed which today stands on the southern point of Elephantine; there are
reliefs of Ptolemy IX on the inside and some of Augustus on the outside.[63]

The latest evidence of a Ptolemaic pharaoh south of Philae is probably a
monolithic granite naos of Ptolemy XII in the temple of Amun in Dabod.[64]

On the island of Philae, hardly[65] any building activities are associated
with the names of Ptolemy IX and X; reliefs may belong to their reigns
which were later given the cartouches of the twelfth Ptolemy, probably as in
the case of the pylon of Edfu.[66] On Philae, the cartouches of Ptolemy Neos

Dionysos are blazoned on the colossal reliefs of the pylon (Fig. 9.1 C and M); Ptolemy is here depicted purely as a ritual king carrying out sacrifices or defeating enemies. The claim that he would 'destroy the Haunebu with his club' in accordance with ancient tradition – during the Ptolemaic period this would have meant 'the Greeks' – may well have drawn a smile from the educated.[67] The subordinate role of the historical ruler is well illustrated by the reliefs on the side walls of the first pylon over the large middle gate. They portray a ceremony that took place there in the presence of the people in which a living falcon was crowned king; as such he was viewed as the Ba of Re (soul of the sun god) and worshipped in the temple for the rest of his life (Strab. XVII.1.49).[68] Furthermore, the two Philensis Decrees of Ptolemy VI in the birth house (Fig. 9.1 F) were now covered with large reliefs and inscriptions and so were severely damaged. Probably during this period, the kiosk of Nectanebo I at the southern end of Philae was rebuilt.[69] On the neighbouring island of Bigga, which was closely associated with Philae in cult, inscriptions in the outer hall of the temple of Osiris contain cartouches of Ptolemy XII.[70]

Kom Ombo is also poor in reliefs from the turn of the century.[71] It remains unclear when the great outer hypostyle (pronaos; Fig. 9.3 F) was built; this hall and the southern gate (at the modern entrance to the archaeological site) were decorated with reliefs under Ptolemy Neos Dionysos. Afterwards, an inner enclosure wall (Fig. 9.3 H) was constructed which continues the side walls of the pronaos; on its eastern side are found six chapels, the decoration of which was commenced under Ptolemy XII and remained unfinished. A few reliefs found there are interesting because they depict Cleopatra VII executing pharaonic cultic ceremonies (e.g. the performance of Maat) and facing the divinities alone.[72] The large courtyard surrounded by colonnaded halls and the outer enclosure wall (Fig. 9.3 G and J) date to the principate.

In Edfu, ornamentation was continued during the reigns of Ptolemy IX and X. This is especially true of the reliefs on the enclosure wall (Fig. 9.6 M).[73] A wide-ranging series of depictions of myths and inscriptions[74] on the inner walls both reveal the conceptual and imaginary world of the theologians of Edfu and give us insight into the ceremonial proceedings at the great annual festivals. They were completed towards the end of the first reign of Ptolemy IX (i.e. in the years before 107). It should be mentioned that the names of the king in the inscriptions reflect the dynastic confusion around 107. Many of the cartouches remained empty or deliberately struck a neutral tone leaving open the question of which Ptolemy was meant.

The cosmogonical texts and representations[75] illustrate in various versions how the creation of the world was conceived and incorporate also a mythical history of the origin and development of the Egyptian temple, or, more specifically, of the different kinds of temples in Egypt. In this way, the origin of the temple of the falcon was linked with the appearance of land from the primeval water: a reed stem grows out of the water and two creation gods plant it firmly; Horus-Re flies by as a falcon and alights on the reed; this place becomes the original domain of the falcon of Edfu, whose cult was established by Thoth. After creation is complete, the foundation of the sun temple ensues.

Five relief cycles provide various versions of the battle of Horus against Seth (the so-called Horus myth). Among them is the 'legend of the winged solar disc'[76] on the western longitudinal wall: Horus of Edfu fights in many scenes against Seth, who appears in numerous guises, and against his followers; his opponents are, in fact, the enemies of his father who is depicted as the king of Egypt, Re-Harakhty. After the final victory, Horus of Edfu takes his place in all the sanctuaries of Egypt in the form of a winged sun. This aetiological myth explaining why Horus appears as a winged sun may perhaps have been performed in the cult of Edfu.

The large relief panels directly below these scenes undoubtedly illustrate a dramatic cult performance called 'the triumph of Horus'[77] which may have been executed as part of an annual festival on the sacred lake. Five scenes make up the first act which follows the prologue. These scenes recount a harpoon ritual already known to us from the first dynasty. Two boats are seen on each panel – one for Horus as Lord of Lower Egypt and another for him as Lord of Upper Egypt – and from each boat the god mortally wounds Seth who is represented by a hippopotamus; the earthly representative of Horus is the pharaoh depicted with his cartouches and who looks on from the shore. In the second act, the ceremonial ship of Horus with a billowing sail makes its first appearance; Isis kneels at the bow and passionately spurs on the young harpoonists ( helpers of Horus). In the next scene, the victorious Horus receives the insignia of the monarchy from Thoth and is crowned. The earthly king is absent, since the crowned Horus is identical to him; on the other hand, the queen stands on the shore – she is explicitly called 'female regent . . . (Cleopatra) mother of the gods . . . (Ptolemy, etc.)' – and shakes the sistra. The third act brings together the closing ceremonies with the ritual dismembering of the hippopotamus. The main theme of the mythical cycle is the kingship, meaning the periodic renewal of the victorious power of the earthly king whose force sustains the world of the cult and who in the play is the same as the celestial king. The performance of the cult is attested in citations from several inscriptions, even in the oldest part of the Edfu temple; the text is probably based on a compilation dating to the late New Kingdom. We can be certain, however, that the performance was updated to match conditions at the end of the second century BC.

In the centre of the northern inner wall (rear wall) of the enclosure wall are reliefs and inscriptions which describe the festival in which the sacred falcon was crowned king.[78] In the course of the ceremonies, the statue of Horus of Edfu was taken from the inner sanctum of the great temple and brought to the temple of the falcon which was probably situated in the southeast corner of the square in front of the large pylon. There the statue of Horus itself selected the falcon from a row of candidates; after having been

*Figure 9.9* Relief on the pylon of the temple of Horus at Edfu, east side of the
west tower, over the middle gate (cf. Fig. 9.5): enthronement of the sacred falcon
by Horus at Edfu in the presence of the earthly ritual king.

chosen, the bird was then crowned king (cf. Fig. 9.9) and presented to the
people. While in Philae the falcon remained on the throne for life, in Edfu
the process was repeated in an annual festival with a new bird. In the festival
calendar of Edfu, the ceremonies bear the descriptive title of 'festival of the
inauguration of the ruling year of Horus of Edfu, son of Re, loved by man'.[79]
This festival also had to fulfil another aim. During the Ptolemaic period the
renewal of the royal powers was evidently seen as crucial; by putting together
in a performance the divine world-ruler (Horus of Edfu), the ritual animal
crowned king and the pharaoh who is represented by a priest, the festival
achieved this renewal on a cultic level. This ritual clearly shows that as the
ruling monarch lost his credibility as the central figure of Egyptian religion,
the god took over (once again)[80] the office of the king; a royal cult which had
been taken out of the hands of human rulers was now to ensure the welfare
of the country. This development occurred despite the fact that there is testimony showing that the later Ptolemies tried to fulfil their cultic duties even
in the south.[81]

The ornamentation on the side walls and columns of the courtyard was
completed at the end of the 80s. The court was well suited to serve as a
mythical site (Fig. 9.6 K) where the annual festivals for Hathor and Sokar took
place and a cult for the solar god Re was maintained. The Hathor festival is
depicted in detail on the base of the southern walls of the courtyard (rear

side of the pylon tower).[82] Hathor of Dendera came in her bark to Edfu for the 'lovely festival of Behedet'. Here together with her divine spouse Horus of Edfu she visited the necropolis of the divine ancestors (the sacred precinct of Behedet). The festivities surrounding the procession by water and land became a two-week-long celebration for the inhabitants of the nome of Edfu. The annual rejuvenation of Horus and Hathor as well as the renewal of royal power were tied to agricultural fertility by means of the sacrificial rites to primeval and creation gods.

The giant reliefs on the pylon (Fig. 9.5) were probably adorned with cartouches of Ptolemy XII in the 70s.[83] The illustrations leave an impression similar to the one conveyed by the scenes on the first pylon of Philae, both are marked by dominating images of the king defeating the enemy. The depiction of the enthronement of the falcon (Fig. 9.9) can be found, just as in Philae, over the large gate. On the pylon, the figure of the king is equated with that of Horus of Edfu, even though as a historical personage Ptolemy XII could hardly have defeated an enemy and was only too happy if he could find lodgings in the house of Pompey. This identification was meant to underline royal legitimacy and the ascendancy of the god over Egypt.

On 7 February 70, the temple of Edfu as a whole was dedicated in the Egyptian manner and given over to its lord, Horus of Edfu.[84] No doubt it took several more years to perfect its ornamentation. Around the mid-50s, work was so advanced that it was possible to move the workshop to Dendera. According to the cosmogony depicted on its temple walls, Edfu represented, in its finished state, the completion and the coronation of the world and so was where the god-king of the universe resided. At the same time, the structure was a grandiose manifestation of the celestial kingship which periodically was renewed by the festival cult; it was during the festivities that mythical events were re-enacted (new year's festival, coronation of the falcon, triumph of Horus and the festival of Behedet). In Memphis, the Ptolemaic king, through his visits to the site, had remained until the end of the kingdom an integral part of the cultic rites performed there. In Edfu, on the other hand, a human monarch was no longer necessary in the late period; his cartouches had probably often remained empty in view of the confused situation in Alexandria at the turn of the century.

Continuing north, only the most important construction work from the late Ptolemaic period will be mentioned. The Ptolemaic Hemispeos of Elkab is of interest mainly because of the depictions of Cleopatra III — beside the exit on the cliff wall — which portray her alone performing a cultic act (holding sistra in front of Nekhbet).[85] Facing Esna, the inner hall of the temple of Isis in el-Hella (Contra-Latopolis) was decorated during the reign of Cleopatra III and Soter II.[86]

The temple of Month in Armant (Hermonthis) was mentioned above[87] and today almost nothing dating from the Ptolemaic period is visible. It is worth pointing out, however, that precisely this late Ptolemaic–Roman epoch represented the high point of the cult of the so-called bull of Buchis, the sacred bull of the god Month. Like Apis in Memphis and Mnevis in Heliopolis, the Buchis of Hermonthis also leads a 'ceremonial life'; many Buchis stelae in museums throughout the world inform us of the birth, enthronement and death of the bulls from the reign of Nectanebo II through that of Alexander the Great and of almost all the Ptolemaic kings and even of many Roman emperors, until the fourth century AD.

In terms of the history of religion and ideology, the birth house in Hermonthis dating from the reign of Cleopatra VII and Ptolemy Caesar is significant, though only drawings of the building have been preserved.[88] Harpre ('Horus, the sun god'), son of Month and Rat-tawi ('female sun of the two lands'), was the child-god in the small temple; the birth of the child-god corresponded in this case to the birth of the sun. In the cartouches of the large frieze inscription on the southern outer wall of the cella, the young pharaoh bears the throne name (Ptolemaios) and also his personal name (Caesar) etc.;[89] this means that for anyone able to read hieroglyphics it was being clearly and openly announced that on his mother Cleopatra's side the king was a new Caesar and heir of the great Caesar; the fifteenth Ptolemy bore in the same inscription a cult title which referred to his parents ('father-loving and mother-loving god').[90] Cleopatra herself appeared in the ritual scenes of the birth house of Hermonthis, generally alone or in front of the male king.

For the most part, the late Ptolemaic pharaohs left behind few traces in Thebes. Reliefs with offering scenes and texts from the time of Ptolemy X are found, for instance, in Karnak[91] on the first gate of the temple of Ptah, while those linked to Ptolemy XII are found in the same temple on the first and third gate as well as at the entrance to the hypostyle of the temple of Opet; the chapel of Osiris of Koptos was erected from older blocks under Neos Dionysos. The reliefs of Cleopatra III and Ptolemy IX (behind her) in the temple of Khonsu as well as on the temple at Deir el-Medina were mentioned above.[92] Cartouches of the king-god scenes on the gate of the enclosure wall of the temple of Deir el-Medina were filled in with the names of the twelfth Ptolemy.

The small temple of Medinet Habu was at the centre of building activities in western Thebes during the late Ptolemaic and Roman periods.[93] Under Ptolemy X Alexander I, the gallery of the twenty-fifth dynasty (between the peripteros and the pylon) was replaced by a hypostyle with two rows of columns (Fig. 9.10 D); to the peripteros itself was added a room on both the northern and southern ends (Fig. 9.10 B–C). The first pylon (from the Saitic hypostyle) and the portico lying in front of it (Fig. 9.10 G–H) mainly go back to Ptolemy IX. The portico was dedicated on 24 September 77 in the presence of the strategos.[94] During the principate the portico was enlarged and a spacious courtyard was placed in front of it; these last renovations were associated with the name of Antoninus Pius.

Apart from Dendera, late Ptolemaic construction to the north of Thebes merits only brief mention. Two pylons from the temple in Qus (Apollinopolis

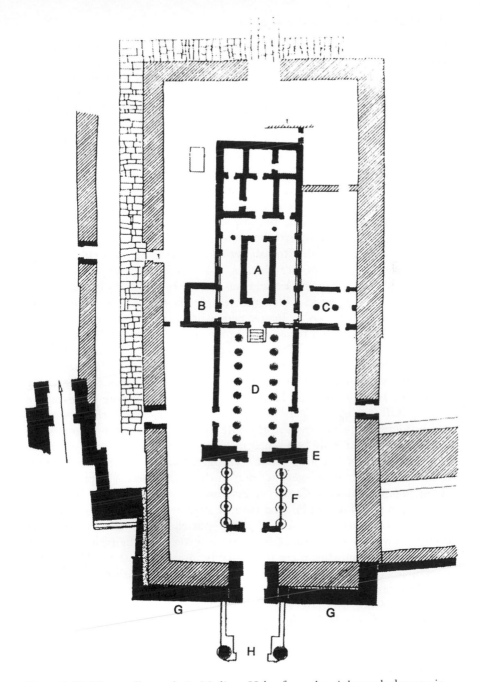

*Figure 9.10* The small temple in Medinet Habu from the eighteenth dynasty in the late Ptolemaic period, after W. J. Murnane, *United with Eternity, a Concise Guide to the Monuments of Medinet Habu*, Chicago 1980, 79, Fig. 65.
A Bark hall; B, C Annexes to the peripteros; D Hypostyle of Ptolemy X;
E Pylon from the twenty-fifth dynasty; F Portico of the twenty-sixth dynasty;
G Late Roman pylon; H Late Roman portico.

Parva, 10 km south of Koptos) date from the reign of Ptolemy X;[95] under Ptolemy XII, three kiosks were erected[96] in front of the Month temple in Medamud and a monumental birth house was added at right-angles to the large temple of Repyt at Athribis (Sohag);[97] in Koptos, a chapel bore cartouches of Cleopatra VII and Caesarion as well as the cartouches of Ptolemy XII used – obviously – for Ptolemy XIV.[98]

In Dendera, work on the Ptolemaic temple complex dedicated to Isis was continued.[99] Under Ptolemy X, an outer hypostyle (Fig. 9.8) was set up before it and the entire building were surrounded by a colonnaded ambulatory. As a result, the building now resembled other birth houses from that period. The pre-Augustan naos had scenes typically found in a birth house and they corresponded to the purpose of the temple. It may be that the temple was in origin a real birth house for Harsiese ('Horus son of Isis') and that by the beginning of the Roman period it became a special cult place for the birth of Isis by her mother Nut.

The temple of Hathor in Dendera was closely tied to Edfu because of the festival cult.[100] Just as in Edfu, the temple in Dendera was completely demolished because it was no longer pertinent to its time. After the temple of Horus in Edfu was completed during the second period of Ptolemy XII's reign, a last large-scale Ptolemaic project was begun which was carried out with incredible vigour during the 20-year reign of Cleopatra VII. According to a hieroglyphic building inscription, construction of the temple house lasted from 16 July 54 until 22/1 BC.[101] The crypts still bore the names of Ptolemy XII and his co-regent Cleopatra. In the naos itself, the cartouches remained empty in every case; in the cult scenes, either a king appears alone or a queen, who can only be Cleopatra VII, is behind him and is given the title 'ruler, lady of the two lands'. The great reliefs on the back of the temple[102] are admired by every tourist; in them Cleopatra is depicted twice behind her son Ptolemy Caesar in a symmetrical arrangement before the gods of Dendera (Fig. 9.11). The two are depicted as a couple performing cultic acts. Cleopatra's head-dress, which was the usual one for Ptolemaic queens and was the head-gear of Isis-Hathor, gives her a divine look. During the first year of Augustus' reign (presumably in summer 30 BC), Hathor was ceremonially led into her temple and this meant that the cult was established in the new temple.

We should not overlook Ptolemais in Upper Egypt. Directly after the Theban insurrection had been put down, several sacred buildings were dedicated (in 85/4), among them an Iseum; this may have been intended to mark the re-establishment of peace in the Thebaïd.[103] In 46, the strategos Kallimachos had just erected a sanctuary to Isis.[104]

Private individuals also devoted themselves to sanctuaries in the Fayum and, as always, mainly financed temple gates (propyla), as, for example, in Theadelphia,[105] Karanis[106] or Tebtunis.[107]

An attempt to assess the historical significance of the construction of temples in Egypt during the Ptolemaic period will always remain incomplete

*Figure 9.11* Rear side (southern outer wall) of the temple of Hathor at Dendera. Left half: Ptolemy XV Caesar and Cleopatra VII (left in the picture) performing rituals before the gods (Harsomtus as a child-god, Isis, falcon-headed Harsomtus, Osiris-Onnophris, Horus of Edfu, Isis with a double crown). Far right: the head of Hathor (frontal view, crowned by cow-horns with a solar disc) in the centre of the temple wall.

because of the loss of monuments. The monuments still remaining in Upper Egypt or those for which there is some kind of testimony must arouse our admiration, especially if we consider these as evidence of the incredible consistency, determination and tenacity with which the priesthoods pursued their agendas. This was not a simple building programme serving an ossified religion – an erroneous view all too often adopted in the past; rather, in many cases, monumental architecture was a means of developing cult and theology. In this regard, religious culture in Egypt would reach a new high point during the Roman principate. One need only recall the great hypostyle of Esna where the theology of Khnum was further developed and promulgated by means of a reformed and markedly pictorial hieroglyphic script.

## The Ptolemaic kingship and the Egyptian priesthoods

The nature of the relationship between the pharaoh and the priesthoods, in periods during which a foreign dynasty ruled, depended in part on the extent to which the ruler, who was not firmly rooted in Egyptian religion, was willing to fulfil the duties of a pharaoh. It was also dependent on the extent to which the priests were willing to integrate the ruler into the religious world of the temples. Such an integration required that the priests provide the ruler with legitimizing titulatures and depictions and, indeed, foster a royal cult in his honour. A cult of this kind could be incorporated into Egyptian tradition only by means of the most strenuous efforts. In actual fact, the behaviour of the priests varied from a slavish adherence to whichever monarch was in power to attempts to emancipate themselves from his influence by distributing the king's functions among the gods and priests – the latter became the norm outside of Egypt where one did without the figure of the king.[108]

Examples of the accomplishment of pharaonic duties in the south during the period currently under discussion are the performance – if we can believe the texts – of dedicating the temple in Edfu by Ptolemy VIII and Cleopatra II (142)[109] or the sacrifices performed by Ptolemy IX at Elephantine (115).[110] It is possible to infer from the formulation of a Buchis Stele[111] that Cleopatra VII was personally present at the ceremonies surrounding the induction of a new Buchis bull in 51.

At opportune moments, some priesthoods in key positions managed to persuade the king to grant them privileges. Three documents which are reproduced on the base of the Philae Obelisk at Kingston Hall indicate that this was the case.[112] They report that the priests of Philae, who were also entrusted with the native dynastic cult, were granted their request and thus no longer had to provide for civil servants and troops passing through Philae.[113] The inscription is dated to the period 124–117, a time when Ptolemy VIII was doing everything to maintain peace within the country. When the priests of Khnum on Elephantine got hold of Ptolemy IX in 115, they were also able to procure some favours to their own benefit.[114]

Among the most conspicuous examples of a Ptolemaic ruler being integrated into the cultic world of the priests are the above-mentioned[115] representations of the pharaoh on the pylons at Philae and Edfu; both bear the cartouches of Ptolemy XII. On the other hand, the priests were confronted with a real task in their attempts to depict the Ptolemaic queen in power at the time. In Tod, such terms as 'the two Horus' or 'the two rulers of Egypt' or the like[116] had already been coined for the joint rule of Ptolemy VIII and Cleopatra II.

In contrast to past tradition, the queen mothers and queens, Cleopatra III and VII, appeared preceding their shadowy co-regent[117] in numerous temple reliefs as true actors in the performance of the cult and were also depicted alone before the divinities.[118] Cleopatra III is depicted in the latter function at Elkab bearing the pharaonic titulature 'strong bull, female Horus, lady of the two lands'.[119] Moreover, just like Hatshepsut, who once ruled as pharaoh, and in analogy to the goddesses Hathor and Isis, she is often called Rait ('female sun').[120]

An uncommonly complex titulary has been attested for Cleopatra VII. An example from it is the title 'queen of Upper and Lower Egypt' in an abnormal form.[121] Thus it comes as no surprise when on a stele that was produced at an earlier date, probably during the reign of Ptolemy XII, a Greek inscription associates the name of Cleopatra VII with the image of a male pharaoh wearing the royal loin-cloth and the double crown.[122] The examples just cited referring to Cleopatra III and VII in the role of pharaoh illustrate that temple reliefs and titulatures (likewise those of Caesarion)[123] were occasionally adapted to fit historical circumstances, even if Egyptian tradition was violated. The large ornamental reliefs on the southern outer wall at Dendera are not instances of such radical departures from tradition.[124]

As far as the Egyptian priesthoods are concerned, the royal house was most closely connected to the clergy of Memphis. As we have pointed out on several occasions, the high priests of Ptah functioned as representatives of the Egyptian clergy in general; on the whole, they were the deputies of the local dynastic cult and were viewed as being responsible for the image of the Ptolemaic pharaoh in theology.[125] The theological relationship between the king and Apis – the birth of the king being analogous to that of the Apis bull[126] – is emphasized in the Horus name from the time of Ptolemy VI onwards by means of various epithets. This is true of all the ruling Ptolemaic kings whose hieroglyphic titulature is attested (Ptolemy VI, VIII, IX, X, XII).

The visits of the Ptolemaic kings to Memphis, especially Philometor's at the beginning of the year, have already been mentioned.[127] Ptolemy X Alexander I and Cleopatra Berenike III were also in Memphis in 99 at the beginning of the Egyptian year in the month of Thoth (17 September until 12 October).[128] The Serapeum was at the heart of these events; it was a central site in the Egyptian cult of the king and its palace was where the royal couple usually resided (Fig. 9.12, no. 3).[129]

Even before the Ptolemaic period, this district had been a place where Greeks and Egyptians could encounter each other. From the early third century, the elite of the Greek civil service participated in the religious life of the Serapeum and, in particular, were very much involved in financial matters.[130] In this way, the Serapeum of Memphis also became a centre of Greek-Alexandrian scientific and literary culture, as numerous papyrological finds dating from the second and first centuries attest.[131] At some time in the first decade of Philadelphos' reign, a Greek had financed construction of a chapel in the Greek style (Fig. 9.12, no. 6) which was built with its entrance opening directly on to the dromos between the east temple and the burial site of the bulls.[132] Immediately beside it stood an Egyptian-style chapel with a statue of Apis dating to the thirtieth dynasty (Fig. 9.12, no. 7). It is possible to infer from these facts that the dromos was of a mixed Egyptian and Greek character from the early Ptolemaic period onwards.

The date of the semi-circular exedra (Fig. 9.12, no. 2) which stands in front of the east temple by the dromos is much disputed. In the exedra are located Greek statues of poets and philosophers (Pindar, Hesiod, Homer, Protagoras, Thales, Heraclitus, Plato) as well as of other unidentified figures which could include Alexander the Great and some of the Ptolemies. Apparently, at the same time as the so-called philosophers' circle was laid out, the

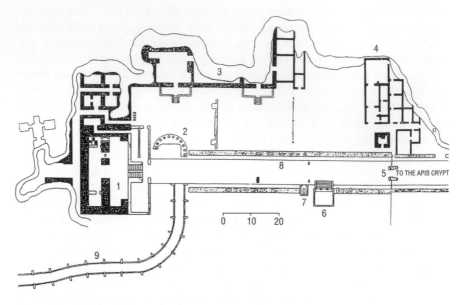

*Figure 9.12* East temple and dromos in the Serapeum district of Memphis, taken from Kessler (1989), Fig. 5 (following p. 58) with his numbering system (Map after Mariette).
1 East temple of Nectanebo II; 2 Semi-circle (so-called Philosophers' Circle);
3 Palace area; 4 Area of the Pastophoria; 5 Gate and lion statue of Nectanebo I;
6 Small Greek temple of Sarapis; 7 Egyptian sanctuary with statue of Apis;
8 Dromos area with groups of Dionysiac statues and Egyptian statues; 9 The sphinx alley leading to the Anubieion.

dromos was furnished with Dionysiac reliefs which stood on the low stone walls marking off the dromos (Fig. 9.12, no. 8). They mainly consisted of statues of animals upon which rode the boy Dionysos and they included a female panther, two peacocks spreading their tails, a lion and a cerberus (or a lion-gryphon). In addition, there were also two seated, winged female sphinxes of the type found in Greece, two sirens (women's heads on the body of a bird) as well as a falcon with the bearded head of a man and a double crown.[133]

Since the statue of Pindar bears an artist's signature which was visible from the dromos, the figures on the exedra and the Dionysiac sculptures must be dated to the period between the second half of the second century and the first century BC[134] In our view, the motivation for such an artistic project must have come from particular aspects of the king's relationship with the priests of Memphis. As far as the theme of Dionysos is concerned, it recalls the Dionysiac *tryphé* of Ptolemy VIII,[135] but, more probably, it was meant as a reminder of Ptolemy XII Neos Dionysos' preference for the god in connection with his close ties to the high priest of Memphis. Hence, the above-mentioned sculptures could possibly have been created on the occasion of Ptolemy XII's coronation in 76.

In view of the Dionysiac character of the Hellenistic cult of the Ptolemies, the purpose of this site was no doubt to foster the Egyptian cult of the king. That is, the Egyptian statue cult here practised on the statues of the king was combined with the Hellenistic notion of the deified ruler. The philosophers and poets who were recognized as divine were linked to this phenomenon.[136] If Alexander and some of the Ptolemies were in actual fact displayed in the exedra, then it would be clear that the dromos was meant to illustrate Alexander's campaign of conquest which traditionally was identified with the triumph of Dionysos in India. The hypothetical date of the site (70s BC) suggests that Ptolemy XII, who had been crowned pharaoh, appeared as the concrete incarnation of the young Dionysos returning to earth.[137] This would seem to be the best explanation for the imposing representations of the youth Dionysos riding on animals. In any case, this complex in front of the east temple represents a synthesis of the Egyptian and Greek cult of the king and it served the purpose of clarifying Egyptian rituals to the Greek population.

The so-called Harris Stele is real evidence of the relations between the royal court and the high priest of Ptah in Memphis during the late Ptolemaic period. It is the funerary stele of the high priest Psenptah III and no doubt comes from his grave chapel in Saqqara.[138] The stele was executed with great care and its text was composed in the script of the great temples with the phonetics characteristic of this period. From a historical point of view, it is the most significant hieroglyphic monument[139] of the late Ptolemaic period and also the most important source for a Ptolemaic coronation in Memphis.

After stating his date of birth (4 November 90) and mentioning his appointment as high priest (76), Psenptah reports that he himself performed the ceremonial coronation of Ptolemy XII and, as part of the ceremonies, led the purification rites by which the newly crowned king was born anew as the sun child.[140] In the following section, which deals with Psenptah's voyage to Alexandria, Ptolemy XII's cartouche contains epithets which are known to us from his Greek titulary: 'the father-loving and sibling-loving God, the young Osiris' (θεὸς Φιλοπάτωρ καὶ Φιλάδελφος Νεός Διόνυσος). In the Egyptian translation which equates Dionysos with Osiris (like Hdt. II.42.2), Neos Dionysos is understood as the young god, probably the youthful Dionysos.[141] The king performed cultic acts in a temple of Isis,[142] then crowned the head of the 14-year-old high priest and named him 'his prophet', i.e. the priest of the living pharaoh Ptolemy XII in the Egyptian cult at Memphis.

In the text that follows, Psenptah states that the king had come to Memphis for ceremonial reasons and had undertaken journeys to inspect the whole country. This meant that according to Psenptah's report he had fulfilled his pharaonic duties in an exemplary fashion. During his visits to Memphis, he resided in the royal palace in the Serapeum district,[143] just as his predecessors had done,[144] and thus had a direct view of the group of Dionysiac statues in the dromos. He had brought with him his court, 'his wives',[145] the royal children and the whole baggage train.

Following Psenptah's appointment as royal priest of Ptolemy XII, he was provided with temple revenues from all of Egypt.[146] He could, thefore, conclude his historic report by saying that he was 'a distinguished man, rich in all things' and could boast of a 'beautiful harem'. He died on 14 July in 41 at a time when – a point explicitly mentioned in the text – Cleopatra was ruling jointly with her son Caesar.[147]

The ties of the Memphis priests to Alexandria should not be overestimated. Nevertheless, Psenptah III's visit to the capital reminds us that two statues of his great-grandfather, the high priest of Memphis Psenptah I (late third to the early second century), were found in the Serapeum of Alexandria.[148]

With regard to the Egyptian cult of the Ptolemies from the time of Ptolemy VI to the reign of Ptolemy XII, it is sufficient to point out what we already know. Scenes of ancestor worship were often placed in Egyptian temples, particularly under Ptolemy VIII, and they depict the ruling king burning incense and making offerings before deceased Ptolemaic couples.[149] There are many examples from Edfu, some from Qasr el-Aguz and one from Tod. It is worth noting that Euergetes II makes offerings in the presence of the second to the fifth Ptolemaic couples but not in the presence of Philometor with whom he always had strained relations. The relief in Tod where Ptolemy VIII and Cleopatra II make offerings to all the gods of the dynastic cult (including Philometor and Eupator) is an exception.[150]

In keeping with the measures announced in the decrees of the priests,[151] the priesthoods increasingly refer to themselves as priests also connected to the dynastic cult. This was true, for instance, of the priests of Khnum from Elephantine who together with the garrison commander of Syene dedicated the well-known[152] Boëthos Inscription (152/145) and also of those priests who received privileges from Ptolemy IX in 115.[153] As mentioned above,[154] the priests of Philae who had the obelisks erected in front of the temple of Isis in 124/117 also emphasized their connection to the dynastic cult. From the festival calendar of Kom Ombo we learn that as part of the procession of the gods the statues of the royal ancestors and of the living royal couple left the temple after the main god Haroeris.[155] Under Ptolemy XII, in Dendera there were chapels for members of the royal family and a special 'prophet' (*ḥm-nṯr*) for the cult practised therein.[156] These chapels with the cult statues are represented in the reliefs in the new temple (in the passageway around the inner sanctum).[157]

In general, we are left with the impression that the political goal pursued during the late Ptolemaic period of promoting a rapprochement between the state monarchy and the native element was reflected in the various expressions of religious culture. To the latter belong the numerous decrees granting asylum (or the right of immunity) to sanctuaries in the Fayum from the 90s to the 50s.[158] Even some synagogues received the right of asylum. A case is known in which Cleopatra VII and Ptolemy Caesar renewed the right of asylum of a synagogue which originally had been granted by a certain King Euergetes (Ptolemy VIII?).[159] The asylum decrees show that the kings wanted to appear as benefactors of the cults and sanctuaries.

## THE HELLENISTIC KING AND THE OFFICES OF THE EPONYMOUS PRIESTS FROM PTOLEMY VI TO THE LAST YEARS OF PTOLEMY IX

We have already encountered the ideal of tryphé as a characteristic feature of the Hellenistic ideology of the king in Ptolemaic Egypt.[160] In the second century, it was Ptolemy VIII, first in Cyrene and then in Alexandria, who cultivated the image of a ruler as someone who makes a show of his abundant wealth. In this way, he also tried to form a link to his famous great-grandfather, the third Ptolemy. From 164/3 onwards he named himself 'Euergetes' like his predecessor of the same name. The king grew soft from his tryphé and earned only mockery from the members of the Roman embassy of 139.[161] Perhaps towards the end of 133,[162] Euergetes II took on the supplementary epithet of 'Tryphon', in imitation of Ptolemy III; accordingly, he named his eldest daughter 'Tryphaina'.

Under Ptolemy VI, the offices of the eponymous priests in Alexandria remained as they were. Eupator appeared as a co-regent in the title of the Alexander priest, i.e he was mentioned after the ruling royal couple. After his death, he was placed before the couple in the same title as the most recently deceased Ptolemy.[163]

In contrast, Philometor reformed the offices of the dynastic priests in Ptolemais which had gradually become confused since 165/4. As a consequence, toward the end of the 50s there was a priest for each of the deceased Ptolemies (including Eupator) as well as for the ruling Philometor; to these were added three offices of priestesses for Arsinoe II (already from 185/4), Cleopatra I and II (the latter from 172/1).[164] The 'priestess of the king's daughter', created in 146 for Cleopatra III, has already been mentioned.[165]

The measures carried out by Philometor in Ptolemais were essentially retained by Euergetes II. The title of the priest for the ruling Ptolemy VIII – which was repeated in a variety of ways – was meant to produce a pompous effect: the king is described as a just judge sitting on the throne of the gods and is given the most florid series of epithets (Euergetes, Great King, Eucharistos).[166] After Ptolemy VIII's marriage to Cleopatra III in 141/40, a new priestess was created for her ('Cleopatra, the wife'); the 'priestess of Cleopatra, the daughter' who had existed since 145 was retained. Afterwards, the cult for Cleopatra III was duplicated in the Upper Egyptian polis in order to enhance her status in comparison with her mother Cleopatra II.[167] At least as far as we know, at the end of these developments (confirmed as of the fall of 139) there existed five offices of priestesses of the dynastic cult in Ptolemais: the kanephoros for Arsinoe Philadelphos as well as the priestesses for 'Cleopatra, the mother' (= Cleopatra I), for 'Cleopatra, the sister' (= Cleopatra II), for 'Cleopatra the wife' and for 'Cleopatra the daughter' (probably Cleopatra III in both cases)[168]. After Ptolemy VIII, the eponymous priesthoods of the Thebaïd no longer appear in the records.

In the Alexandrian dynastic cult, the changes in the title of the Alexander priests reflect the history of the Ptolemaic family and the domestic policy shaped by it. The facts have already been mentioned: from Euergetes II's 26th year (145/4, i.e. some time after his accession to the throne in his 25th year) the theos Philometor and the theoi Euergetai are named at the end of the title of the Alexander priest; Cleopatra III was included from 141/40; between 131 and 127, the theoi Euergetai were replaced by the Thea Philometor Soteira and a second rival group of 'Alexandrian' eponymous priests appeared as a result of the expulsion of the king from Alexandria (130–127); From 126 onwards, there is again only one priest of Alexander with the title he bore before 131; in 118 the new dynastic god Neos Philopator was inserted in the title before the ruling Ptolemies.[169]

As already mentioned,[170] when the rival priest was established in 130, a *hieropolos* was created at the same time for Cleopatra III. We can recognize in the title of this priest a further step in the elevation of Ptolemaic queen to the status of a goddess: the queen's individual name is left out of this title and she is now seen as Isis, here identified with the mother goddess of Asia Minor, Cybele; this means that the living queen is addressed as a real goddess without any mortal elements to her name. Also worthy of note is the fact that a male priesthood was created for a female goddess.

Regarding these developments, it is important to point out that the cult titles for members of the royal house, the increasingly complicated development of the dynastic cult and the growing divinity of the living queen all reflect political propaganda. This propaganda which was shaped partially by individual family members and partially by the ruling house as a whole was meant to produce a certain effect on the subjects of the kingdom. Euergetes II desperately tried to evoke the splendour of the old Ptolemaic kingdom by associating himself with the generosity of the earlier kings (especially Ptolemy III) in elevated language. The administrative branches, particularly the army, participated in this propaganda by setting up dedicatory inscriptions for the ruling theoi of the dynastic cult and for other gods.[171] The appointment of so many new priests and the excessive language of the epithets used to describe them must increasingly have left the people indifferent. Among those in power, the fact that the propaganda of these dynastic cults was not producing the desired results became apparent only later towards the end of the second century.

The usual cult title borne by the ruling couples from 116–88 – Cleopatra III with Ptolemy IX (116–107) and then Ptolemy X (107–101), and finally the latter with Cleopatra Berenike III (101–88)[172] – was always *Theoi Philometores Soteres*. Behind this lay a desire to maintain a sense of dynastic continuity. The office of priest of Alexander was enhanced by the fact that the king himself took over the position annually from 116/15. By holding this office, he became the highest priest of the state cult dedicated to maintaining the 'charisma' of the Ptolemaic family: on account of their victories, the early Hellenistic kings (Alexander the Great to Ptolemy IV) had endowed the royal family with a charismatic appeal which was upheld by later Ptolemaic rulers.[173] Because the king was named with his mother at the end of the title of the priest of Alexander (in the form of various cult names), it can be said that he was actually performing the cult for himself as well. The illustration on the Mendes Stele which fictively shows Arsinoe II making offerings to herself, which was extremely rare in former Egyptian reliefs,[174] now actually became manifest reality in Alexandria. To this must be added the astounding fact that Cleopatra III took over the office of the priest of Alexander in 105/4.[175]

Although the scribes varied the now complicated title in many ways and even omitted parts of it, it seems useful to state the complete form which was used during the reign of Cleopatra III and Ptolemy IX; the following version is common in Lower Egypt and in it the name of Cleopatra II, the great adversary of her daughter Cleopatra III, is suppressed:[176]

ἱερεὺς Ἀλεξάνδρου καὶ θεῶν Σωτήρων καὶ θεῶν Ἀδελφῶν καὶ θεῶν Εὐεργετῶν καὶ θεῶν Φιλοπατόρων καὶ θεῶν Ἐπιφανῶν καὶ θεοῦ Εὐπάτορος καὶ θεοῦ Φιλομήτορος καὶ θεοῦ Νέου Φιλοπάτορος καὶ θεοῦ Εὐεργέτου καὶ θεῶν Φιλομητόρων Σωτήρων.

Priest of Alexander, of the Theoi Soteres (Ptolemy I and Berenike I) of the Theoi Adelphoi (Ptolemy II and Arsinoe II), of the Theoi Euergetai (Ptolemy III and Berenike II), of the Theoi Philopatores (Ptolemy IV and Arsinoe III), of the Theoi Epiphaneis (Ptolemy V and Cleopatra I), of Theos Eupator (Ptolemy Eupator), of Theos Philometor (Ptolemy VI), of Theos Neos Philopator (Ptolemy Memphites [?]), of Theos Euergetes[177] (Ptolemy VIII) and of the Theoi Philometores Soteres (Cleopatra III and Ptolemy IX).

Since eponymous priests are no longer named in the sources from the turn of the century, we know of hardly any other Alexander priests after this point; the last one is Ptolemy IX Soter II who is attested for 84/3.[178]

As a result of the predominance of the queen/royal mother, the propaganda of the dynastic cult began to focus increasingly on the special eponymous priesthoods for Cleopatra III identified with Isis. Although the hieropolos acted on her behalf from 130 onwards and was directly subordinate only to the priest of Alexander in rank, she also created, as previously mentioned,[179] three priestesses for herself: a *stephanephoros* (garland bearer), a *phosphoros* (light bearer) and a *hiereia* ('priestess') – each for 'Cleopatra Philometor Soteira Dikaiosyne Nikephoros'.[180] The last three epithets ('saviour', 'justice', 'bringing victory') represent, now in the person of a woman, the ideal characteristics of the basileus. As a goddess, Cleopatra III then became 'queen Isis'.

After the change of government in Alexandria from Ptolemy IX to Ptolemy X (107), for the last time an eponymous priest was created to administer a cult in honour of the living ruler. The strategos of Cyprus, Helenos,[181] is attested in this role for the year 107/6 with the title 'priest during the lifetime (ἱερεὺς διὰ βίου) of the queen Cleopatra, the goddess Aphrodite and Philometor'.[182] In demotic texts, Aphrodite is replaced by Hathor as a consequence of the Egyptian translation of the title.

At the height of the eponymous priesthoods in the last years before the turn of the century, nine such priesthoods are found in Alexandria, five of which were in honour of the living Cleopatra III. Their official listing, which generally was not respected, could have been the following:[183]

> the priest of Alexander (from 290),
> the priest during the lifetime of the queen/king . . . (from 107/6),
> the hieropolos (from 130),
> the stephanephoros of queen Cleopatra (from 116),
> the athlophoros of Berenike Euergetis (from 211/0),
> the phosphoros of queen Cleopatra (from 116),
> the kanephoros of Arsinoe Philadelphos (from 269?),
> the hiereia of queen Cleopatra (from 116),
> the hiereia of Arsinoe Philopator (from 199).

From the end of the second century onwards, the dating formulae which had become impossibly complicated were shortened by omitting the names of individual priests and replacing them with general set phrases. For this reason, we do not know if there were developments in the dynastic cult during the first century – both in Alexandria and in Ptolemais- and we have the names of only a few of those who held this office during this period. The latest evidence for a hieropolos dates to 4 September 104;[184] there are two references to the ἱερεὺς διὰ βίου of Ptolemy IX from the 80s.[185] The king himself was the priest of Alexander at that time.[186]

Worship of the Ptolemies was generally upheld in the foreign territories throughout the second century. The strategos of Cyprus was also the archiereus and, in this function, was certainly responsible for the state cult of the king;[187] under Philometor, the commander of the city of Kition is also attested as priest of the third Ptolemaic couple.[188] The city of Salamis on Cyprus dedicated a statue of Ptolemy X – the base of which has been found – in their temple of Zeus.[189] The situation in Cyrene in the spring of 108 was quite interesting, since there had been a break between Cleopatra III and Soter II. The city of Cyrene[190] resolved in a decree that certain ceremonies and sacrifices should be carried out for the royal family every year; Ptolemy IX and his sister and wife Cleopatra V Selene are referred to by name as the Theoi Soteres and a son is also mentioned. The name of Cleopatra III is omitted.

The existence of a cult in honour of Alexander in the Egyptian chora during the second century has already been mentioned.[191] The cult chapel (cenotaph) for Alexander the Great in Kom Madi at Medinet Madi/Narmouthis has been dated to the end of the century.[192] It is an expression of the political and religious propaganda which was aimed at the mixed Egyptian-Greek population of the Fayum. In a series of paintings in the court of the chapel, Alexander was rendered in a Dionysiac guise, obviously in a triumphal scene of the god Dionysos. Hellenistic themes were here expressed through the medium of traditional Egyptian painting. The theme of the cella is more Egyptian, even if the death bed is a Macedonian motif.

## DIVINE RULE UNDER CLEOPATRA VII

From the point of view of its development up to the period under consideration, the royal ideology under Ptolemy XII seems to lose all contact with reality: the victorious Horus king on the temple pylons bears his names;[193] the dioiketes Hephaistion praises him in 59 as 'Great King Ptolemy, God Neos Dionysos, Philopator and Philadelphos';[194] in the temple of Isis on Philae, the epistrategos Kallimachos set an act of veneration (προσκύνημα) for the twelfth Ptolemy who went under the name 'Kyrios Basileus, God Neos Dionysos Philopator Philadelphos'.[195]

The difference between this later ideology and the propaganda of the dynastic cult in the second century is due to the peculiar intellectual and spiritual climate of the first century. Increasingly, people hoped for salvation at the hands of a 'new Dionysos' on earth and the Hellenistic kings were able to use this new trend to their benefit by presenting themselves in the god's role. This was particularly true of the Seleukid king Antiochos XII and of Mithridates VI Eupator who established his Hellenistic empire as Neos Dionysos.[196] In the Ptolemaic kingdom, this spiritual development reached its peak under Ptolemy XII; the nickname of 'Auletes' reveals the prominence which the Dionysiac court thiasos (the court group bound through their participation in Dionysiac festivities) had gained.[197] Emulating the tendency of the early Ptolemies, especially Ptolemy I, III and IV (cf. Fig. 3.4),[198] to equate themselves with the god in artistic works, Ptolemy XII often had himself depicted as Dionysos.[199] We know from the Harris Stele, however, that by means of this practice the gap was narrowed between Hellenistic-Greek and Egyptian ideas: the king now appeared as the incarnation of the young Osiris-Dionysos.[200]

The divine rule of the great Cleopatra was given its special historical significance through her ties with Caesar and Antony. Already in 48 upon his arrival in Ephesos, Caesar was hailed as 'the theos Epiphanes descended from Ares and Aphrodite and the common saviour of mankind' by the cities and peoples of Asia Minor.[201] Moreover, from a Roman point of view, a general on campaign in the east could think of himself as a new Alexander and so, because of the close link between the Alexander and the Dionysos myths, could easily come to be regarded as a New Dionysos.

Already in 79 after returning from Africa, Pompey arrived in Rome with elephants in imitation of Dionysos' triumph over India (Plin. *Nat.* VIII.4). Caesar's fourfold triumph in the summer of 46 was strongly reminiscent of the procession of Philadelphos[202] – a public banquet was held at 22,000 tables and exotic animals were led along in the triumphal march; there were giraffes and many elephants, some of which carried torches, and at the end of the festivities they escorted Caesar to his house (D.C. XLIII.19–24; Plu. *Caes.* 55; Suet. *Iul.* 37–39).

Thus, Caesar took on the appearance of Dionysos in his triumph. It is also reported (Serv. *ecl.* V.29) that he allowed the Hellenistic mysteries of Dionysos to be celebrated in Rome. Caesar therefore used the popularity of the cult of Dionysos to foster his own political myth; no doubt the international character of this cult corresponded nicely to his personal view of the world.[203]

He did not need to be concerned by the fact that his soldiers mocked his love for Cleopatra at his triumph and on other occasions (D.C. XLIII.20.2). According to Ptolemaic family tradition, Cleopatra represented the goddess Isis. Coins of the queen with the epithets and head-dress of Isis are attested from 47/6.[204] Caesar was able to turn this to his advantage by linking the figure of Cleopatra as Isis to his triumph. At the end of his victory celebrations, he dedicated the Forum Iulium which had been constructed in 54, in the centre of which was erected the temple of Venus Genetrix which he had pledged at the battle of Pharsalos. The triumph was thereby converted into a religious and political spectacle; the goddess of the Julians appeared as a deity who granted victory. Caesar had a gold statue of Cleopatra placed next to the cult statue of Venus (D.C. LI.22.3; App. *civ.* II.102). He thus publicly acknowledged the divinity of Cleopatra and associated her with the ancestral mother of his family.

To the informed observer, this meant that Venus Genetrix of the Julians was assimilated to Isis-Aphrodite and *Isis regina*; moreover, the earthly manifestation of the latter was Cleopatra who was now living in Caesar's house in Rome. Caesar himself played the part of the victorious ruler, a much lauded Soter and Euergetes (App. *civ.* II.144)[205] of divine descent, and was even acknowledged as a (future) state god from the end of 45.[206] The discrepancy between the partnership of Caesar[207] and Cleopatra and the traditional Ptolemaic royal couple must have seemed slight indeed from an Egyptian viewpoint. As was already mentioned above,[208] the hieroglyphic titulary of their son, Ptolemy XV, described him as the New Caesar and his father's successor. One particular form of his throne name was taken from Ptolemy XII and was obviously meant to evoke the political programme which Cleopatra had associated with her journey to Rome: Ptolemy XV was the 'heir of Theos Soter, etc.';[209] at that time in the east there was only one man who was generally acknowledged as '*Soter*, or more precisely, *Theos Soter* and that was Caesar.

Mark Antony, who was in many ways the true successor of Caesar, cultivated his philhellenism and even had himself initiated into the mysteries (probably the Eleusinian) (Plu. *Ant.* 23.2). Above all, he adopted Dionysiac themes for his own political purposes and so in 41 was hailed as Dionysos Χαριδότης ('bringer of joy') and Μειλίχιος ('benefactor') upon his arrival in Ephesos. This greeting meant that the dignity of a 'new Dionysos' was already ascribed to Antony at that time – a dignity which placed him in line with the Hellenistic kings and which let him slip into the Ptolemaic ruler ideology. Accordingly, when Cleopatra arrived in Tarsos in 41, she announced that 'Aphrodite had to come to feast with Dionysos for the good of Asia' (Plu. *Ant.* 26.5). When Antony stayed in Athens with Octavia, he named himself 'Neos Dionysos', had himself addressed by this title and asked to be honoured with statues and games (Socrates of Rhodes: FGrHistt. 192F2; D.C. XLVIII.39.2; Sen. *suas.* I.6–7).[210]

In conjunction with the territorial gains made in Coele Syria and Cyrene (37/6), which Cleopatra had marked as the beginning of a new era,[211] a measure of some religious significance was enacted: coins were issued in Syria and Cyrene depicting the queen on one side as 'Thea Neotera' with Antony on the reverse.[212]

During his 'triumph' of 34, Antony dressed in the gold-embroidered gown of Dionysos, made his way through Alexandria, holding the thyrsos stick in his hand and wearing cothurnes on his feet; again he called himself Neos Dionysos (Vell. II.82.4).[213] Antony had long cultivated his own unique image which combined a propensity to imitate Alexander and a tendency to portray himself as the equal of Dionysos. As such, he fitted in well with the Ptolemaic tradition of sovereignty in Egypt's capital. The Egyptian form of Dionysiac ideology (i.e. pertaining to Osiris-Dionysos), which Ptolemy XII had once claimed for himself, was now transferred to the person of Antony. The assimilation of the elements of this ideology by Antony became even more apparent when Cleopatra appeared in the garb of Isis in the ceremony which took place in the gymnasium after the 'triumph' of 34. In the future, she would present herself as such in public and had herself named the 'New Isis' (Plu. *Ant.* 54.9; cf. Serv. *A.* VIII.696).

The ceremony just mentioned which was held to celebrate the division of the east in 34[214] was purely an act of political ideology. It only concerned the Ptolemaic dynasty and the areas it was to control in the future. Although the sons of Antony and Cleopatra appeared as the direct successors of the Seleukids, the ceremony laid the ideological basis for creating a kingdom which would unite Achaemenid and ancient pharaonic traditions. To this was added a synthesis of the Hellenistic and Roman themes of triumph and victory in battle.

The encompassing Egyptian and Asiatic background can be best observed in the titles 'queen of kings' and 'king of kings' which Cleopatra and her co-ruler assumed at the time. The origin of these titles or others like them lay in the religious domain of both Egypt and the Near East; in the religious traditions of these areas, these titles were first used of the gods and then of the kings and pharaohs as an expression of their sweeping claim to power.[215] Following the ancient Persian Great Kings, the Ptolemies (II–IV) bore the title 'king of kings' in Coele Syria as did the late Hellenistic kings in Asia, especially the Parthian king.[216] When Cleopatra was also named 'queen of kings' and Ptolemy Caesar 'king of kings', they were expressing their sovereignty over the newly acquired lands in Asia and also publicizing a claim to future acquisitions in the area. In Egypt, given the success of the cult of Isis and Osiris in the late period, Osiris was now cast as the embodiment of the kingship. Osiris appears on more than one occasion as the 'ruler of rulers' (ḥq3ḥq3w) or 'king of kings' (*nswt nswjw*)[217] particularly in Philae. Ptolemy XII also bore this latter title as a pharaoh performing cultic acts in a representation of him on the first pylon at Philae.[218] An Egyptian could thus establish a direct connection to the young Osiris Ptolemy of the Harris Stele as well as to the titles which were handed out in Alexandria in 34.

Antony's elevation to the divine sphere unquestionably turned him into a Hellenistic ruler, though he was not a basileus. A Neos Dionysos (cf. Plu. *Ant.* 60.5) and a Nea Isis probably viewed themselves in this latest elevation of their status as incarnations of the divinity.[219] It is said that Antony represented himself with Cleopatra in images and statues in which he appeared with the traits of Osiris and Dionysos and she with those of Selene and Isis (D.C. L.5.3; cf. Plu. *Ant.* 60.5). Octavian is said to have denounced such things in his speech before Actium, charging that Antony depicted himself as Osiris and Dionysos and Cleopatra named herself Selene and Isis (D.C. L.25.3–4). Statues of both in their divine forms stood on the Athenian acropolis and they were said to have fallen down into the theatre because of a stroke of lightning which was one of the evil omens before the battle of Actium (D.C. L.15.2). When Antony and Cleopatra established their headquarters in Patras in the winter of 32/1,[220] the city struck coins which depicted the queen as Isis.[221]

It was certainly soon after the events of 34 that Cleopatra ordered the erection of a temple for Antony near the coast in the centre of the large harbour of Alexandria (see Map 3).[222] A monumental square was situated behind this cult enclosure and, in the middle of the square Cleopatra had a great obelisk raised following the example of the obelisk standing in the Arsinoeion[223] located more to the west. Her obelisk is now in St Peter's Square in Rome.[224] Immediately after Octavian entered Alexandria, he assigned his comrade-in-arms, Cornelius Gallus, the task of completing the square under the name of the *Forum Iulium*; a few weeks later, the Latin dedicatory inscription on the obelisk already announced that the assignment had been carried out and thus served to record Rome's supremacy and its sovereignty over Egypt. The temple of Antony was only half-finished and was later completed as the Sebasteion or more precisely the Caesareum (Suda, s.v. ἡμίεργον). Near the temple was found a statue base which a follower of Antony had dedicated on 28 December 34 BC to 'Antony, the Great, the Inimitable[225]. . . . God and Euergetes'.[226]

The so-called Tazza Farnese, the dating of which is much disputed, merits mention. A cameo made of sardonyx, the Tazza Farnese is of Alexandrian provenance and is now in the archaeological museum of Naples:[227] on the left we see a half-naked, bearded god with a cornucopia, either Nile or Pluto or more precisely Aion Plutonios; in the foreground is Isis-Demeter with ears of corn in her hand which she stretches out to a beardless, Egyptian sphinx; behind her appears Triptolemos/Horus who carries a bag of seed and the ploughshare. The picture represents the Nile flood bringing forth crops as well as the renewal of the land and its kingship associated with the flood – for Isis wears a royal diadem in her hair, and is, therefore, the *Isis regina*. In my view, the assignment of the Tazza to the events of 34 seems highly appealing; it would serve to mark the beginning of a golden era of a queen who is both Isis-Demeter and *Isis regina*.[228] By this interpretation, the cameo would also represent Ptolemaic tryphé.

The golden age of Cleopatra and Antony was a short-lived dream. The death of the queen from a cobra's bite[229] is open to a wide variety of interpretations. The term 'aspis' refers to a snake capable of puffing up its neck into a shield; it was the Egyptian uraeus and meant to be a symbol associated with Egypt.[230] The cobra is an outward shape of Isis, especially of Isis as the 'great magician' (*wrt ḥk3w*). According to Cleopatra's ideology, she herself would have been identical with the snake; the earthly Isis Cleopatra would then have experienced rebirth as the celestial *Isis regina*. The image shown at Octavian's triumph which depicted the queen with two cobras (Verg. *A.* VIII.697), referred to the double cobra of the Egyptian royal crown.[231] Assuming this interpretation is valid, one could say that Cleopatra eluded her enemies with the help of this pharaonic instrument of power and, in death, triumphed over them. We may conclude, therefore, that either Cleopatra herself staged her death from a snakebite – however it actually occurred- or this version of her death was spread by her closest followers of Egyptian descent because it seemed most suited for Cleopatra as pharaoh and the earthly *Isis regina*.

Cleopatra attemped to synthesize her Hellenistic kingship with her conception of the office of pharaoh by appearing as Isis and thereby uniting the divine powers of the pharaoh with the authority of the Hellenistic ruler cult. Also of use was the fact that, in Cleopatra's day, Isis was being interpreted more and more often as a universal ruler, as a queen both of the gods and of the earth. While the theological doctrine of the pharaoh and his divine status would later be transposed on to the Roman emperors and these emperors could appear as being endowed with the powers of a divine pharaoh on their occasional trips to Egypt, the attempt by Antony and Cleopatra was, despite their failed ambitions and extravagant fantasies in Egypt, the last as well as the most extreme manifestation of political and religious unity – a unity upon which was based the entire history of Egypt until that point, with the exception of the Assyrian and Persian periods.

## Notes

1 Cf. the amnesty decrees from the reigns of Ptolemy V–VIII above, pp. 157, 184, 195, 201f.
2 D. Kessler: *LÄ* VI, 1986, 371 (s.v. Tempelbesitz).
3 See p. 261 together with note 19.
4 E. Otto: *LÄ* I, 1975, 112 (s.v. Ajuala).
5 See p. 161f.
6 *PM* VII, 43f. (It is indeed a pronaos and not a vestibule.)
7 See p. 162.
8 On Dabod: W. Schenkel: *LÄ* I, 1975, 997; Gauthier (1916), 322 (LIV), on the latter see PM VII, 5 (23); according to the Greek inscription on the cornice, the second gate was dedicated to 'Isis and the synnaioi' under Ptolemy VI: OGIS I, 107; Török (1986), 235f. (Nr. 50).
9 On the history of construction at Philae cf. in general Haeny (1985); on the relief ornamentation: E. Vassilika, *Ptolemaic Philae*, Leuven 1989 (= *Orientalia Lovaniensa Analecta*, 34); On Mandulis and his chapel at Philae cf. p. 189 with note 39.
10 See p. 189 with note 37.
11 The site of Dendera is ideal for research into the entire architectural development of birth houses on account of the very early date of a birth house from the reign of Nectanebo I and the late date of one from the Roman period. For all related issues see Daumas (1958).
12 See pp. 279–280, 283–284.
13 Haeny (1985), 212, 220, 222, 230.
14 G. Vittman, 'Das demotische Graffito vom Satettempel auf Elephantine', *MDIK* 53 (1997) 263–281, pl. 37.
15 E. Bresciani *et al.*, *Assuan*, Pisa, 1978, 109–111.
16 On what follows and all related questions see A. Gutbub, *Textes fondamentaux de la théologie de Kom Ombo*, I-II, Le Caire 1973 (=*Bibliothèque d'Etude*, 47).
17 This hall represents an addition to the so-called canonical arrangement of rooms of the Ptolemaic temples of Edfu and Dendera; the traditional distribution of rooms in a temple is otherwise respected at Kom Ombo.
18 Whether a single block of stone with the cartouche of Ptolemy V indicates that the temple of Kom Ombo was already begun at the end of the eighties of the second century remains an open question; cf. A. Gutbub, 'Kom Ombo: les textes et leur étude' in *Textes et langages de l'Egypte pharaonique*, 3, Le Caire, 1974, 241.
19 Bernand (1989), Nr. 188.
20 See p. 90 together with note 63.
21 The best example of this fact is provided by the inhabitants of the city and district of Dendera who in early Roman times dedicated – and probably also financed – the east gate in the wall of the temenos (first century AD) which leads to the temple of Isis and, even more importantly, the large hypostyle (between 32 and 37 AD): Bernand (1984), Nr. 25, 28.
22 Detailed account in Gutbub, op. cit. (note 15).
23 W. Wettengel, E. Winter, 'Der Text der Kom Ombo-Szene von der Fahrt im Papyrusdickicht', in *Religion und Philosophie im alten Ägypten*, Festschrift für Ph. Derchain, ed. V. Verhoeven et E. Graefe, Leuven 1991, 363–374.

24 For the architectural history of Edfu cf. always Cauville, Devauchelle (1984).

25 See p. 154f.

26 Cauville, Devauchelle (1984), 37.

27 At the foundation festival under Ptolemy III on 23 August 237; see p. 87f.

28 According to *Edfou* IV, 9, 1–3 = Cauville, Devauchelle (1984), 37f., A; the second text: *Edfou* VII, 7, 6–8 = ibid., 38, B.

29 Cauville, Devauchelle (1984), 41f.

30 Cauville (1987), I, 239.

31 These inscriptions in Cauville, Devauchelle (1984), 39f.

32 Ibid., 44. The general reconciliation of the Theoi Euergetai after 124 is illustrated in a historically interesting relief in which the crown prince (the later Ptolemy IX Soter II) is portrayed with Euergetes II along with Cleopatra II and III; E. Chassinat, *Le mammisi d'Edfou*, Le Caire 1939, 14f., plate XIII (tableau A s. 1d III).

33 See p. 87.

34 See pp. 272–273 and pp. 273–275 together with Fig. 9.9; on this subject see G. Hölbl, 'Wer ist König in der Endphase der ägyptischen Religion?', in *Akten des 4. Intern. Ägyptologenkongresses*, München 1985, ed. S. Schoske, 3, München 1988, 261–268.

35 Chassinat, op. cit., 18, plate XIII (tableau A s. 2d. II and III).

36 Götte (1986). This description stands in contrast to the political descriptions of the victorious Philopator (see p. 161) and in agreement with the birth house reliefs of Euergetes II in Kom Ombo: p. 263f. with Fig. 9.4.

37 On this inscription see p. 204 with note 121, but a better translation in Kurth (see next note).

38 D. Kurth, 'Das 53. Regierungsjahr Ptolemäus' XII', in *Edfu: Studien zu Ikonographie, Textgestaltung, Schriftsystem, Grammatik und Baugeschichte*, ed. D. Kurth, Wiesbaden 1990, 76–83.

39 PM VI, 116; cf. Lanciers (1988, 1), 419.

40 J.-Cl. Grenier, *Tod, les incriptions du temple ptolémaïque et romain*, I, Le Caire 1980; Arnold (1992), 107.

41 C. de Wit, *Les inscriptions du temple d'Opet à Karnak*, I-III, Bruxelles 1958–68 (see p. 86 with note 42); on what follows in the text see Otto, E. (1964), 87; on Opet see D. Meeks: LÄ III, 1980, 172–176 (s.v. Ipet). On the creation of Osiris cf. p. 263 (Kom Ombo). The representation of the child Osiris is a late phenomenon; one such illustration can be found on Handrian's gate at Philae: H. Junker, *Das Götterdekret über das Abaton*, Wien 1913, 42, Fig. 10 a–b.

42 cf. for example R. A. Schwaller de Lubicz, *Les temples de Karnak*, Vol. 2, Paris 1982, 163, plate 225.

43 See p. 161.

44 LD IV, plate 28; PM II$^2$, 403 (15), I.

45 E. Laskowska-Kursztal, *Le sanctuaire ptolémaïque de Deir el-Bahari*, Varsovie 1984 (= Deir el-Bahari, 3).

46 On the similarity between the two gods see p. 162 with note 16; on the two holy men see D. Wildung, *Imhotep und Amenhotep, Gotterwerdung im alten Ägypten*, München 1977. The two healing gods are also present at the temple of Deir el-Medina: PM II$^2$, 402 (8–9).

47 J. Karkowski et al., *Amenhotep, Son of Hapu, and Imhotep at Deir el-Bahari*, MDIK 39, 1983, 93–105.

48  Laskowski-Kusztal, op. cit., 106–113.

49  PM II², 469f.; W. J. Murname, *United with Eternity, a Concise Guide to the Monuments of Medinet Habu*, Chicago 1980, 79f.

50  PM II², 527–530; J. Quaegebeur: LÄ V, 1984, 40f. (s.v. Qasr el-Aguz).

51  Lanciers (1986), 90; on the temple of Medamud see PM V, 137–143; Arnold (1992), 160–162.

52  S. Cauville, 'Le temple d'Isis à Dendera', *BSFE* 123, 1992, 31–48; ead., *Le temple de Dendera, guide archéologique*, Le Caire 1990, 4, 89, 93.

53  W. M. Fl. Petrie, *Diospolis Parva*, London 1901, 54–56; Arnold (1992), 168.

54  Arnold (1992), 177.

55  Arnold (1992), 177f.

56  We might mention in this connection the dedication of the temple of Xois (Sacha) in the late 140s; Ptolemy VIII and Cleopatra are referred to: Heinen (1974).

57  I. Fay. 4 (end of the 180s): propylon in Krokodilopolis; I. Fay. 133 (between 175 and 163?): propylon for Premarres (the deified Amenemhet III) in Euhemeria; I. Fay. 105 (145–116); propylon and peribolos for the god Heron in Theadelphia on the part of an Egyptian family; I. Fay. 107 (from 137): first pylon and dromos of the temple of Pnepheros in Theadelphia on the part of an Alexandrian (on exhibit in the garden of the Greek and Roman Museum in Alexandria); I. Fay. 151 (from 118): propylon among other things for the god Heron in Magdola on the part of a certain cavalry commander.

58  I. Fay. 83.

59  I. Fay. 155.

60  See p. 211f. H. De Meulenare, 'Ptolémée IX Soter II à Kalabcha', *Chron Eg* 36, 71, 1961, 98–105.

61  H. De Meulenare, M. Dewachter, 'La chapelle ptolémaïque de Kalabcha', fasc. 1–2, Le Caire 1964–70 (Collection Scientifique).

62  On this find: D. Arnold, *Die Tempel von Kalabsha*, Kairo 1975, 6; recently it has been discovered that the so-called Kalabsha door, now re-erected with some of these blocks in the Egyptian Museum, Berlin (Charlottenburg), and which carries early Augustan cartouches, indeed comes from a temple precinct dating to the reign of Ptolemy VIII (I thank Prof. D. Wildung, Director of the Egyptian Museum, Berlin, for this information).

63  G. R. H. Wright, *Kalbasha III: The Ptolemaic Sanctuary of Kalabsha, its Reconstruction on Elephantine Island*, Mainz 1987.

64  Gauthier (1916), 401 (XXX); PM VII, 5 (23).

65  Of interest, however, is a relief in the chamber of the east tower of the first pylon [Junker (1958), 172, Fig. 100], where Ptolemy IX is shown followed by two Cleopatras; who the two women are cannot be determined, since we do not know whether the relief refers to the triple monarchy of 116 or to a later regime – before or after the divorce of Cleopatra IV.

66  See pp. 274–275 together with note 84.

67  Junker (1958), 32, l. 4, Figure 13; E. Winter, in *Ptol. Äg.* (1978), 49f.

68  H. Junker, 'Der Bericht Strabos über den heiligen Falken von Philae im Lichte der ägyptischen Quellen', *WZKM* 26, 1912, 42–62; id. (1958), 73–75, 77f., Figures 38, 40.

69  Haeny (1985), 224, 228. It follows that the building was displaced for a second time in the twentieth century.

70  A. M. Blackman, *The Temple of Bigeh*, Le Caire 1915.

71  There is testimony of Soter II in the inner hypostyle; also, the columns in the birth house bear his name.

72  J. de Morgan *et al. Catalogue des monuments et inscriptions de l'Egypte antique*, 1$^{ère}$ sér., III, 2, Vienne 1909, Nr. 915, 916, 927, 1063, 1067 (on the basis of the references and according to the opinion of Ph. Derchain, *Elkab I: Les monuments religieux à l'entrée de l'Quady Hellal*, Bruxelles 1971, 49, note 4).

73  Extensive sources for the reign of Alexander I as pharaoh can only be found here on the enclosure wall of Edfu.

74  Cf. overview of the arrangement in Cauville (1987), 169 (Fig. 49); Fig. 50 (between 170 and 171). On the chronology: A. Egberts, 'A note on the building history of the temple of Edfu', *Reg* 38, 1987, 55–61.

75  Works of fundamental importance are: E. A. E. Reymond, *The Mythical Origin of the Egyptian Temple*, Manchester 1969; R. Finnestad, *Image of the World and Symbol of the Creator*, Wiesbaden 1985; J. C. Goyon, *Les dieux-gardiens et la genèse des temples*, Le Caire 1985; D. Kurth, 'Über den Ursprung des Tempels von Edfu', in *Religion, etc.* (op. cit.: p. 331, note 22), 189–202.

76  H. W. Fairman, 'The Myth of Horus at Edfu – I', *JEA* 21, 1935, 26–36.

77  Alliot (1954), 677–822; H. W. Fairman, *The Triumph of Horus*, London 1974.

78  Alliot (1954), 561–676.

79  *Edfou* V, 399, 7; Alliot (1954), 561.

80  See p. 77.

81  Page 265 (Ptolemy at the temple of Edfu), 205–206 (Ptolemy IX on Elephantine), 231, 279–280 (Cleopatra VII at the consecration of the Buchis bull in Hermonthis.

82  These reliefs also probably belong for the most part to the time before Ptolemy XII; cf. Quaegebeur (1989, 2), 606f. For an explanation of this festival: D. Kurth, 'Die Reise der Hathor von Dendera nach Edfu', in *Ägyptische Tempel – Struktur, Funktion und Programm*, ed. R. Grundlach, M. Rochholz, Hildesheim 1994, 211–216 (= *Hildesheimer Ägyptologische Beiträge*, 37).

83  The reliefs themselves were for the most part certainly already there before the reign of Ptolemy XII. On the pylon cf. Cauville (1987), 189–202.

84  *Edfou* VIII, 67, 6; Cauville, Devauchelle (1984), 42.

85  PM V, 187 (5–6); Derchain, op. cit. (note 71 in this chapter), 49, plate II A.

86  PM V, 171; Arnold (1992), 106.

87  See p. 268.

88  LD IV, 59 c–65.

89  LD IV, 65a.

90  On this subject see p. 239 with note 86.

91  For what follows in the text on Karnak: PM II$^2$, 196 (1 c–e, g), 197 (3), 207, 246 (12). On the work in the temple of Opet under Ptolemy XII cf. also de Wit (op. cit., p. 295, note 41), III, see VII, 101 (Linteau, 2).

92  P. 219f., note 133.

93  On this temple see p. 268f.

94  H.-J. Thissen, *Die demotischen Graffiti von Medinet Habu*, Sommerhausen 1989, 18–29 (Nr. 44), 214; the strategos in question is Pamonthes: Mooren (1975), 122 (0129); on Ptolemy X in this temple cf. also Murnane, op. cit. (p. 296, note 49), 80f.

95  H. G. Fischer: LÄ V, 1984, 72 (s. v. Qus).

96  PM V, 139.

97  Arnold (1992), 177; on the temple see pp. 271–272.

98  R. Weill, 'La titulature pharaonique de Ptolémée César et ses monuments de Koptos', *RecTrav* 34, 1912, 77–86; C. Traunecker, *Coptos, hommes et dieux sur le parvis de Geb*, Leuven 1992, 271–293, 320–324.

99  On this temple complex see p. 272 and Cauville, loc. cit. (p. 296, note 52, first entry).

100  See p. 275.

101  H. I. Amer, B. Morardet, 'Les dates de la construction du temple majeur d'Hathor à Dendera à l'époque gréco-romaine', *ASAE* 69, 1983, 253–258; E. Winter, 'A reconsideration of the newly discovered building inscription on the temple of Denderah', *GöttMisz* 108, 1989, 75–85; the year in question, the ninth year of Augustus, is 22/1 BC and not 21/0 as given in the quoted literature. For further information on the history of the construction of the temple of Dendera see J. Quaegebeur (1991). For the best overview of the entire site of Dendera see Cauville, 'Le temple de Dendera', op. cit. (see p. 296, note 52). Publication of the temple: E. Chassinat, F. Daumas, 'Le temple de Dendara', Iff., Le Caire 1934ff.

102  PM VI, 79 (257–260, bottom section).

103  L. Criscuolo, 'OGIS 52 e il culto de Iside a Ptolemais', *ZPE* 61, 1985, 37–42.

104  C.Ord.Ptol., No. 67, cf. also Bernand (1992), No. 36 (with dating that is no longer valid).

105  Again a gate at the temple of Pnepheros donated by a rich komoqrammateus between 107 and 101: G. Wagner, Chr. Leblanc, 'Dédicace d'un propylone au dieu Pnepheros', *BIFAO* 83, 1983, 335–341, plates LV-LVI; a propylon for the god Heron dedicated by an Egyptian family on 27 September, 67: I. Fay. 115.

106  A propylon for the crocodile gods Pnepheros and Petesuchos along with their synnaoi on the part of an Egyptian on 20 August, 95: I. Fay. 84.

107  Dedication of an Iseum in the years 80–68 on the part of an officer of an Egyptian battalion: I. Fay. 145 – Dedications at uncertain locations in the Fayum: propylon for the goddess Thoeris in the time of Ptolemy X on the part of common people: H. Heinen, 'Thoeris und heilige Fische', in *Hellenistische Studien, Gedenkschrift f. H. Bengston*, München 1991, 41–53; a propylon for Herakles Kallinikos between 88 and 80: I. Fay. 203.

108  Hölbl, loc. cit. (p. 295, note 34).

109  See p. 265.

110  See p. 205.

111  See p. 231.

112  See p. 261.

113  E. Iversen, *Obelisks in Exile*, II, Copenhagen 1972, 62–85; I. Philae, No. 19; Bernand (1992), No. 22; C.Ord.Ptol., No. 51–52; Haeny (1985), 218 with note 1; on the persons mentioned: a) PP I & VIII, 195; Mooren (1975), 92–94 (055) (Lochos, strategos of the Thebaïd); b) PP I, 2; IV, 10092; Mooren (1975), 170f. (0269) (Numenios).

114  See p. 206f. with note 132.

115  See pp. 271–273, 275.

116  See pp. 194–195.

117  See p. 206 with note 133 and also p. 276.

118  See p. 275f.

119 Derchain, op. cit. (p. 297, note 72), 49, plate II A.

120 A. Gutbub: LÄ V, 1984, 87–90 (s. v. Rait): D. Devauchelle, 'Le titre Rait', REg 40, 1989, 190.

121 In Hermonthis: cf. Gauthier (1916), 417 (XVIII, F); D. Kurth: LÄ IV, 1982, 1195; Quaegebeur (1991), 64, note 60 (*nsjt-n-tȝ-šmᶜ bjtjt-n-tȝ-mḥw*).

122 *Cleopatra's Egypt* (1989), cat. 78; it is the stele from 2 July 51 mentioned on p. 252, note 47.

123 See p. 278.

124 See p. 278f. with Fig. 9.11.

125 See pp. 78, 80f., 110.

126 This analogy applies to Ptolemy VI, VIII, IX (see p. 203) and X, from which it becomes clear that it is absolutely false to postulate a birth date for these kings that is at the same time as the birth of an Apis bull; see Kessler (1989), 80.

127 See p. 184 with note 22 and also p. 223.

128 UPZ 1, No. 106 = C.Ord.Ptol., No. 62.

129 See p. 89.

130 G. Hölbl, 'Aussagen zur ägyptischen Religion in den Zenonpapyri', *Papyrologica Lupiensia* 2, 1993, 1–30.

131 H. Maehler, 'Poésie alexandrine et art hellenistique à Memphis', *ChronEg* 63, 125, 1988, 113–136, especially 115.

132 Fraser (1972), I, 253, II, 402, note 498, 404, note 512.

133 Bibliography on the Greek sculptures: J.-Ph. Lauer, Ch. Picard, *Les statues ptolémaïques du Serapeion de Memphis*, Paris 1955; Fraser (1972), I, 253, 255, II, 402, notes 498, 404 and 512; W. Hornbostel, *Sarapis*, Leiden 1973, 408–417; M. Pietrzykowski, *Rzezby greckie z Sarapeum memfickiego*, Warszawa 1976; Thompson, D. J. (1988), 28; Kessler (1989), 126f.; A. Schmidt-Colinet, 'Exedra duplex', *HefteABern* 14, 1991, 58–60.

134 According to information in a letter which I received from Dr Michael Donderer, Erlangen, in the post-archaic period artists' signatures appear again on the statues themselves only in the late second century. The suggested dates for these Greek sculptural ornamentations extends from as early as Ptolemy I to the period of the Roman empire; see bibliography in note 132 (I must thank Dr Donderer for several references in this list).

135 See p. 285.

136 Cf. Kessler (1989), 125–128.

137 According to the titulature of the king on the Harris Stele; see what follows.

138 Stele BM 1026 (886), formerly in the Harris collection, Alexandria. For more recent literature: Bergman (1968), 112–120; P. Munro, *Die spätägyptischen Totenstelen*, I–II, Glückstadt 1973, 165, 341, plate 63; J. Quaegebeuer, 'Inventaire des stèles funéraires memphites d'époque ptolémaïque', *ChronEg* 49, 97, 1974, 70 (No. 25); Wildung, op. cit. (p. 258, note 45), 65–67; plate XI, 1, XII; Reymond (1981), 138f. This stele is completed by fragments of a demotic stele of the same Psenptah in the Ashmolean Museum, Inv. 1971/18, on which the historical section, however, has been lost – assuming there was one. Published in Reymond (1981), 150–164 (No. 19) plate XI.

139 On the historical section see p. 223.

140 According to the text in Reymond (1981), 148f.: (l. 8) 'I was the one who placed the ceremonial collar of Uraeus on the king [or according to the interpretation

in K. Sethe, *Beiträge zur ältesten Geschichte Ägyptens*, Leipzig 1905, reissued Hildesheim 1964, 135: '{who} laid the Uraeus ornament on the head of the king'] on the day on which the two lands were united for him and who carried out all the rites in the house of the jubilee festival in his name. I was the one who performed all the secret functions. I was the one who gave instructions for the purification of the god on the occasion of the divine birth of Re in the gold house.'

141  This is certainly within the range of meaning of the Greek νέος: cf. Nock (1928), 149 (in reissue). On the equation Dionysos = Osiris see p. 291f., p. 117 with note 84; on the child Osiris see p. 268 with note 42.

142  There is here also a relationship to Memphis, for Isis is defined as the 'mistress from *ʒt-wḏʒt*', a place which was in the former 21st Upper Egyptian district and which in the Ptolemaic period belonged to Memphis; see J. Yoyotte: *REg* 13, 1961, 93.

143  *r-pr*, the institution charged with the royal cult within a precinct of the gods can here only be the complex consisting of the temple of the dead and the palace.

144  See p. 281 with notes 127–129.

145  *ḥmwt.f* (plural): Is the reference to the two wives of the king at the end of the 70s?

146  Which did not affect the royal household in the least.

147  On this point see p. 253 with note 78.

148  Rowe (1946), 9; Quaegebeuer (1980), 55–59, 68, 77f.

149  On these scenes and their meaning see p. 110.

150  Winter (1978), 151; Grenier (1983). Otherwise, the first Ptolemaic couple, which up to the time of Philopator had been excluded from the Alexandrian dynastic cult, almost never appears in the Egyptian cult of the Ptolemies. The suppression of Philometor represents an individual feature in the temple reliefs of ancestor worship; in the eponymous cult of Alexandria and Ptolemais he is retained as dynastic god.

151  See p. 111 with notes 210, 211.

152  See p. 189 with note 40.

153  See p. 206f. with note 132 and also pp. 280–281.

154  See p. 280 with note 113.

155  De Morgan (op. cit.: p. 297, note 72), No. 597 (the time of Philometor).

156  Quaegebeuer (1989, 1), 101.

157  See Cauville, 'Les statues cultuelles de Dendera d'après les inscriptions pariétales', *BIFAO* 87, 1987, 107f.; Quaegebeuer (1989, 1), 101. ≬

158  I. Fay. 112–114, 116–118, 135–136, 152; C.Ord.Ptol., No. 64–66, 68, 69, 72; Bernand (1992), No. 30, 32–34, 36–39, 42–44; J. Bingen, in *Egitto* (1989), 24–30. C.Ord.Ptol., No. 64 [=Bernand (1992), No. 30] is a decree in three languages from Athribis in the Delta dating to 96; for the hieroglyphic version see P. Vernus, *Athribis*, Le Caire 1978, 196–198.

159  Mitteis, Wilcken, I, No. 54; J. Bingen, 'L'asylie pour une synagogue', *CIL* III suppl. 6583 = CII 1449, in *Studia P. Naster oblata*, II, ed. J. Quaegebeur, Leuven 1982, 11–16; Griffiths (1987), esp. note 42; Bernand (1992), No. 23.

160  See p. 92.

161  See p. 196.

162  Heinen (1983), 120, note 14.

163 See p. 192 and p. 286f.

164 On this situation: Clarysse, Van der Veken (1983), 46–50.

165 See p. 192 with note 55.

166 Otto, Bengston (1938), 41f.; Ijsewijn (1961), 125 (m); Pestman (1967), 147 (β).

167 Very enlightening on this issue is Chauveau (1990), 159, note 96.

168 That 'Cleopatra the daughter' should already mean Cleopatra IV in the autumn of 139 [thus Pestman (1967), 149; Clarysse, Van der Veken (1983), 51] hardly seems right in terms of family history.

169 The phases of this development: see p. 195 with note 67, p. 196, p. 197 with note 83, p. 199 with note 93 and pp. 101, 200, 203 with note 114.

170 See p. 199 with note 96.

171 For Ptolemy VI: Bernand (1989), No. 242, 302 (see p. 215, note 40); for Ptolemy VIII: ibid., No. 190, 243, 315, 316, 318, 320. On this type of dedicatory inscription see p. 97 with note 115. Also worth mentioning are the 'basilistae' who derived their designation from the royal cult and assembled on the island of Sehel (the 'island of Dionysos'): Bernand (1989), No. 303 (late 140s; to the health of Ptolemy VIII and Cleopatra II); cf. the numerous improvements in H. J. Thissen, 'Zwischen Theben und Assuan, onomatische Anmerkungen', *ZPE* 90, 1992, 292–296. On the basilistae see also p. 96 with note 105.

172 See p. 205, 210 with note 154; Pestman (1967), 150, 153, 156.

173 On this development see p. 95.

174 See p. 101 with note 148.

175 See p. 208.

176 Following Pestman (1967), 150.

177 Upper Egyptian documents render this as . . . *of the theoi Euergetai* (Ptoleny VIII and Cleopatra II): Pestman (1967), 151 (1), d.

178 Clarysse, Van der Veken (1983), 38 (No. 207).

179 See p. 205.

180 Otto, Bengston (1938), 150f.; Ijsewijn (1961), 122; Pestman (1967), 152; Clarysse, Van der Veken (1983), 35, 37.

181 See p. 205 with note 127.

182 E. Van't Dack, in id. *et al.* (1989), 20, note 18.

183 According to Ijsewijn (1961), 122.

184 Thompson, D. J. (1989), 699, note 16.

185 PP III and IX, 5220a, 5221.

186 Clarysse, Van der Veken (1983), 38.

187 See pp. 171–172.

188 PP VI, 15120; Michaelidou-Nicolaou (1976), 80 (M10).

189 J. Leclant: *Orientalia* 36, 1967, 218 (6, g).

190 SEG IX, 5; XVI, 865; Bagnall (1976), 30; Paci (1989), 589.

191 See p. 111 with note 213.

192 E. Bresciani, *Kom Madi 1977 e 1978. Le pitture murali del denotafio di Alessandro Magno*, Pisa 1980.

193 See p. 272, 275.

194 SEG VIII, 468.

195 I. Philae, I, No. 52 (already cited on p. 219, note 120 in relation to another topic).

196 Tondriau (1953).

197  Tondriau (1946), 156–160; on the Dionysiac cult circle at court under Ptolemy IV see p. 171 with note 85.

198  See p. 93, 171.

199  Cf. a bronze bust from Alexandria in *Cleopatra's Egypt* (1989), cat. 58.

200  See p. 293.

201  Syll. II³, 760.

202  See p. 39f.

203  On this theme: R. Turcan, 'César et Dionysos', in *Hommage à la mémoire de J. Carcopino*, Paris 1977, 317–325.

204  Ricketts (1980), 39.

205  SEG XIV, 121 (Megara, 48 BC), 561 (Chios, 48 BC), 762 (Pergamon, 48 BC), IG XII, 2, 151 and 164c (Mytelene), 5, 556 (Keos); Syll. II³, 759 (Athens, 47 BC). In these examples 'Soter' and 'Euergetes' may not bear implicit references to the charisma of the kings; cf. Taeger, II (1960), 55f. Conversely, except for the inscription cited above (note 200) in IG XII, 5, 557 (Keos, 46 BC), Caesar appears as a divine saviour (god, autocrat and saviour of the oikumene). In Rome, Caesar's image as a victorious safeguarder must be entirely understood from a Roman perspective; cf. G. Dobesch, *Caesars Apotheose zu Lebzeiten und sein Ringen um den Königstitel*, Wien 1966, 11f., 16. He proved himself to be a 'Euergetes' through the distribution of enormous quantities of produce to the common people and the soldiers; we are reminded of the same measures taken by Philopator after the battle of Raphia, see p. 131 with note 21.

206  Dobesch, op. cit. (note 204); G. Dobesch, 'Wurde Caesar zu Lebzeiten in Rom als Staatsgott anerkannt?', *ÖJH* 49, Beiheft, 1971, 20–49. For discussion cf. the article in *Römischer Kaiserkult*, ed. A. Wlosock, Darmstadt 1978, 329–374.

207  In Rome the 'partnership' was concealed as much as possible; on this subject see the above, p. 238, account of the planned law on the basis of which Caesar could have entered into an additional marriage with Cleopatra.

208  See p. 276 with note 89.

209  Cf. Weill, loc. cit. (p. 298f., note 98).

210  On this subject see IG II², 1043, ll. 22–23. Cf. Tondriau (1948, 2), 139f.

211  See p. 242f.

212  Rickets (1980), 39f. It remains unclear why the name 'Thea Neotera' ('newer' or 'younger goddess') is used in the case of Cleopatra. To see here simply a connection to Cleopatra Thea who had formerly ruled over Syria (as Ricketts), is, in my opinion, far too restricted in view of the coins from Cyrene. Cf. J. T. Milik, 'Recherches d'épigraphie proche-orientale', I, Paris 1972, 418–423; G. Hölbl, 'Das Neotera-Problem', in *Die orientalischen Religionen im Römerreich*, ed. M. J. Vermaseren, Leiden 1981, 182f.

213  See pp. 243–244.

214  On this subject see pp. 243–244.

215  J. G. Griffiths, 'βασιλεὺς βασιλέων: remarks on the history of a title', *ClPhil* 48, 1953, 145–154.

216  W. Huß, 'Der 'König der Könige' und der 'Herr der Könige', *ZDPV* 93, 1977, 131–140: Sullivan (1989), 273f., 280, 297f., 304; G. Hölbl, 'Zum Titel ḥqꜣḥqꜣw des römischen Kaisers', *GöttMisz* 127, 1992, 49–52.

217  Wb passages in II, 328, 7; in III, 171, 13.

218  Junker (1958), 214, l. 5.

219 As indicated (p. 283) I attribute this designation already to Ptolemy XII in contrast to earlier assimilations to the god; see p. 93, p. 171 with note 85. Incidentally, there are no contemporary inscriptions attesting to the title 'Neos Dionysos' und 'Nea Isis' being applied to Antony and Cleopatra.'

220 See p. 246.

221 Dunand (1973), II, 21.

222 On what follows see Alföldy (1990), 38–54.

223 See p. 103.

224 Or at least planned to set it up.

225 Cf. the 'company of the inimitable livers' which Antony and Cleopatra had founded in the winter of 41/40 at Alexandria in a spirit of carefree revelry: Plu. *Ant.* 28, 3.

226 OGIS I, 195; Alföldy (1990), 46.

227 More recent literature: D. B. Thompson, 'The Tazza Farnese reconsidered', Ptol. Äg. (1978), 113–122; Koenen (1983), 171–173; La Rocca (1984).

228 La Rocca (1984).

229 See p. 249 with note 125.

230 That the ancient Egyptian monuments depict Uraeus as a snake spewing venom while here there is mention of a snake bite is certainly of no consequence: on the types of snakes in Egypt cf. L. Störk: LÄ V, 1984, 644–652, on Uraeus as a snake spewing venom: 646.

231 Griffiths (1961).

# Epilogue: Fundamentals of the development of the Ptolemaic kingdom

The historical development of the Ptolemaic kingdom can be divided into three periods to which the three parts of this book correspond. The first period, the beginning and the golden age of Ptolemaic rule, begins with Alexander the Great and ends with the death of the third Ptolemy (332–222). The historical significance of this period was that it saw the formation of a kingdom which would become the foremost power in the eastern Mediterranean basin.

The initial phase of this period is characterized by the conflict between attempts to maintain Alexander's empire and the individual interests of the successors; among this latter goup, one of the most significant figures is Ptolemy I. During his clash with the various opposing forces (Perdikkas, Antigonos Monophthalmos, Demetrios Poliorketes), Ptolemy I is able to establish himself in his own satrapy, Egypt; he annexes Cyrenaica (322) and makes, in his first attempts, to take Syria (319/18, 312/11), Cyprus (313–306, Asia Minor (Karia, Lycia: 309) and the Aegean (309–303). The political consequence of these early years in the history of the successors is the establishment of the Hellenistic kingdoms (306). After the defeat of Antigonos in 301 at Ipsos, western Syria (Coele Syria) passes over to the Ptolemaic kingdom for about a hundred years; as a result of what is seen as a legally questionable annexation, several wars are fought during the third and second century.

Conflicts arise between the Hellenistic empires when they are in the process of being formed and also when they have become established. During this formative period, i.e. the last phase of the history of the successors (from Ipsos to Kurupedion: 301–281), Cyprus passes into Ptolemaic hands (295/4) for good. During the early 280s, by heading the Island League, Ptolemy is able to establish Ptolemaic hegemony in the Cycladic area.

During the golden age of the empire under Ptolemy II and III (282–222), areas of disagreement develop among the established Hellenistic monarchies; these are the Ptolemaic, Seleukid and Macedonian kingdoms, although all three kingdoms are headed by Macedonian dynasties. The general balance of powers that arises during the Hellenistic period is scarcely avoidable despite great and costly wars – wars which are carried out at the expense of the working people as is the case in all periods of history.

At any rate, at the very beginning of his reign, Ptolemy II succeeds in strengthening Ptolemaic supremacy in the coastal areas of southern and western Anatolia and thus in greatly expanding the empire (280/79). During the 260s (in the Chremonidean War: 267–261), his strategos Patroklos is able to establish strongholds of Ptolemaic rule in the Aegean (especially Itanos on Crete, the island of Thera and Methana on the Saronic Gulf across from Athens). Under Ptolemy II, Ptolemaic power in the eastern Mediterranean basin is largely based on naval rule (thalassocracy) and is for that reason highly vulnerable (e.g. at Ephesos and Kos in the 250s). The Third Syrian War (246–241) which occurs under Ptolemy III results in the largest territorial expansion of the Ptolemaic empire: the control already achieved by Ptolemy II over southern Anatolia is further strengthened; in the west, Ionia (with the very important base of Ephesos, which had already been Ptolemaic in the late 60s and early 50s) together with the Dardanelles are added; the acquisition of southern Thrace is also very significant. With this expansion, the third Ptolemy has supplemented the thalassocracy he inherited from his predecessor with a widely unified territorial control of the coastal lands of the eastern Mediterranean basin (from Thrace to Libya). In this way, he secures Ptolemaic supremacy for a further four decades.

The second phase in the history of the Ptolemies has been described as a period of transition (under Ptolemy IV) and decline (from Ptolemy V to the Day of Eleusis). Political crises both within and outside of the Ptolemaic kingdom are initiated by the excessive strains resulting from the manner in which the Fourth Syrian War (219–217) is conducted – a war which nonetheless ends in victory for the Ptolemies at the battle of Raphia.

Nevertheless, this second period is characterized by two different motifs. First, the successful ventures of Philip V of Macedon and of Antiochos the Great who leads the Seleukid kingdom to the splendour which it formerly enjoyed under Seleukos I. In the end, gains are made at the expense of the Ptolemaic kingdom. Secondly, there is the rise of the imperial power of Rome which gradually results in the elimination of the two powerful Hellenistic kingdoms and, in the end, leaves the weakened Ptolemaic kingdom to its own devices.

Decisive factors for the decline of the Ptolemaic kingdom are, in part, the struggles within Egypt together with the last triumph of the Egyptian people in the pharaonic state in Thebes (206–186) as well as the dynastic crises in Alexandria. After the death of Ptolemy IV in 204, Ptolemy V, who is barely six years old, is left behind as heir to the Egyptian kingdom; tutelary governments come and go and the foreign possessions in Syria, Anatolia and Thrace are lost.

After the death of the fifth Ptolemy, the situation repeats itself: three children are left behind but for the first time in Ptolemaic history, a woman, Cleopatra I, succeeds in ruling the kingdom for a few years (180–176) as guardian of her children. The successive guardians manoeuvre the kingdom into the Sixth Syrian War (170/69–168), resulting in Antiochos IV of Syria gaining control over all of Egypt (with the exception of Alexandria) and even issuing royal decrees. Immediately after defeating Perseus of Macedon (at the battle of Pydna at the end of the Third Macedonian War), a Roman embassy led by C. Popilius Laenas appears in Antiochos' camp before Alexandria; Popilius Laenas orders the Seleukid king to leave the Ptolemaic kingdom (Egypt and Cyprus) without delay; this event takes place on the so-called Day of Eleusis at the beginning of July in 168. Antiochos obeys; Rome has saved the Ptolemaic kingdom.

This milestone marks the beginning of a third phase in which Roman authority is a key factor in the development of the Mediterranean states; for the Ptolemaic kingdom, this is the period from 168–30. Ptolemy VI wears himself out in strife with his brother, Ptolemy VIII; Rome is increasingly asked to intervene. It is the family disputes within the dynasty which will now characterize Ptolemaic history and wear out the kingdom. During the reign of Ptolemy VIII, he fights for power with his sister and first wife, Cleopatra II. The strife is picked up by his sons for the 15 years of Cleopatra III's rule (116–101). Interventionist actions in Syria, especially by Ptolemy VI (150–145) and Cleopatra (103–101), are in the end not successful. The Alexandrians are able to come to the foreground as makers and ousters of kings (88, 80, 58). In the meantime, the Romans become the heirs of the Ptolemies in Cyrenaica (96/74) and Cyprus (58). At this time, Egypt becomes an important element in the political designs of Roman leaders because of its much-admired economic resources. Pompey, Caesar and Antony pursue personal policies with regard to Egypt. Both of the last two Ptolemies, Ptolemy XII and Cleopatra VII, attempt to win over these representatives of Roman power. Their attempts are motivated by their own concerns, a desire to secure the existence of the dynasty and kingdom and even to realize a new vision of Roman–Ptolemaic joint rule in the eastern Mediterranean basin. The idea fails; Octavian establishes the Roman province of *Aegyptus* and thus permanently secures the economic resources of Egypt for Rome.

Relations within Egypt are primarily formed by the heterogeneity of its people: on the one side, we find the dominant Greek class of officials and merchants; on the other, there is the mass of Egyptian farmers and workers supplemented by a small elite of highly educated Egyptians. A middle position is occupied by the mixed Greek–Egyptian population which is particularly characteristic of the Fayum. There are, moreover, other ethnic groups in Ptolemaic Egypt of varying importance (Karians, Jews, Syrians, Phoenicians among others) but whose presence in Egypt generally goes back further. The relation of the Egyptian masses to the Ptolemaic administration and their officials nevertheless determines the course of domestic affairs and indirectly affects foreign policy as well. This is already the case with the first Egyptian revolt in 245 which compels Ptolemy III to break off his grandiose eastern campaign during the Third Syrian War.

Pressure from the Egyptian community comes to the surface after the Fourth Syrian War. Since regular Egyptian troops have been created, an Egyptian military class has also been permanently established; the victory at

Raphia strengthens their confidence. Soon after the battle at Raphia, roused by social tensions which have deepened as a result of the Fourth Syrian War, the Egyptian troops revolt and clearly express their secessionist aims. They receive support from the exploited agricultural class living in rural regions so that eventually a civil war based on social strife rages in the Delta at the end of Philopator's reign. In the course of the uprising, the insurgent Egyptians even plunder the temples. It is only in 197/6 that the monarchy succeeds in delivering the first major blow to the movement.[1]

The opposition in the south is able to benefit from the unrest in the north and, partially supported by Nubia, establishes a native pharaonic state in the Thebaïd (206–186). The Egyptian kings Herwennefer and Ankhwennefer are continually involved in a struggle for survival. Ankhwennefer is defeated in battle in the summer of 186 but he is pardoned – presumably because the movement is viewed as being extremely dangerous. From this point on, the chora is assigned to an epistrategos possessing complete civil and military power who resides in Ptolemais. In contrast to the balanced result in the south, the northern revolt in the Delta is brutally put down in 185 and the ringleaders are tortured.

We assign the next series of disturbances to the 160s: the rebellion of Petosarapis at the Alexandrian court, socially motivated battles in the Fayum and a revolt in the Thebaïd. While the Ptolemaic family war between Ptolemy VIII and Cleopatra II is being played out, at the same time in Thebes a native called Harsiese attempts to exploit this situation: in 131–130, he is the last attested Egyptian to take on the title of pharaoh. Individual Egyptians, however, make their way into the civil service and from the time of Ptolemy VIII even attain the highest offices; the best-known example is the epistrategos Paos.[2]

In this same period, the forces driving the political resistance of the Egyptians slowly come to a halt: in 88, Soter II puts down with great severity a Theban revolt which has lasted three years; in 63, Ptolemy XII asks Pompey in vain for his help in ending a revolt. After 55, the Roman Gabiniani are eventually deployed several times against the inhabitants of Egypt. These events are to be interpreted as a revolt against exploitation by the elite. The Thebans undertake a last attempt at self-assertion after the Roman province has been established in 29; the prefect, C. Cornelius Gallus has to conquer five 'cities' in Upper Egypt and fight two battles.[3] One conclusion to be drawn from the history of Ptolemaic Egypt is that the capacity for political resistance of the native Egyptians is slowly but surely crushed.

The development of Egyptian culture and religion runs its own course, although occasionally it converges with the political history of the native population. Its formation is decisively marked by the clever attempt to adapt the ancient Egyptian royal ideology to the court of the Ptolemies. Darius the Great had already advanced this measure with great success; it is revived by Alexander the Great and by his representative and his successor. Since construction work on the sanctuaries in Egypt has always been seen as one of the basic requirements for the legitimacy of a pharaoh, Ptolemaic religious policy which makes possible such aims is to be viewed as an integral component of the history of the Ptolemies. This policy also presents an opportunity – one which is quickly seized – to develop Egyptian religious culture. The grandiose temple building projects, the rich development in theology in various religious centres as well as the creation of a new hieroglyphic writing system (to be used by those very centres) all equally express the cultural activity and creativity of the Egyptian upper classes of that period.

Under Ptolemy II, the new construction of the temple of Isis of Philae is begun. During the reign of Ptolemy III, the first foundation rites for the temple of Horus of Edfu (237) take place – a self-contained project which is dedicated in 70 and is completely finished about 15 years later. Edfu, with its stylistic unity, is the classic example of Ptolemaic architecture and is today the best preserved ancient Egyptian temple. The new temple of Thoth in Dakke (Lower Nubia) is begun by Ptolemy IV. Under Ptolemy VI most of the twin temple of Haroeris and Sobek in Kom Ombo is constructed together with the temple of Khnum of Esna (of which today, however, only the Roman hypostyle is preserved). Around the mid-first century Dendera is constructed and becomes the last large-scale project of the Ptolemaic period. It must also be emphasized that most of these large undertakings are carried out at the same time as many smaller projects. Precisely during the turbulent years of Ptolemy VIII, work at Philae, Kom Ombo and especially Edfu is driven forward with great energy.

In an inquiry into the historical contribution of the Ptolemaic epoch, we must certainly consider the achievements of Ptolemaic religious policies to be among the most significant. Certainly, the policy of Augustus takes this point into account: the great temple of Kalabsha is erected in Nubia, where, after the clashes with Meroe, the fostering of religious culture is especially important; but Augustus is also identified as pharaoh in many other sanctuaries throughout the land. This process continues as long as the resources exist,[4] meaning for the most part until Trajan, Hadrian and Antoninus Pius.

The most important feature in the history of Ptolemaic ideology is the fact that the king like the people of his kingdom has two faces: one that is pharaonic and another that is Greek-Macedonian. As a Hellenistic ruler the king becomes a cult figure. Alexander the Great sees himself as the son of Zeus-Ammon. Ptolemy I further fosters the divinity of Alexander and creates the cult of Alexander in Alexandria. Although the cult is founded on purely Greek principles, in Egypt it has its precedents in ancient Egyptian tradition. The cult of Alexander is supplemented from the second Ptolemy onwards by the cult of the living and deceased Ptolemies and thus develops into a Ptolemaic dynastic cult. The fame of the Ptolemies is so great in the third century that several of them are worshipped in a cult outside of Egypt and festivals are celebrated in honour of the dynasty such as the so-called Ptolemaia. Worship of the Ptolemies is not limited to Ptolemaic territories; Delos, Rhodes, Byzantium, Athens among others also take part. The eponymous priests and priesthoods in Alexandria and Ptolemais are included in documentary preambles during the third and second centuries. The divinity of the queen presents a distinct development. Particularly prominent is the divinity of Arsinoe II decreed by Ptolemy II after her death. This meant she was an independent goddess in the Egyptian and Greek communites and was also identified with Isis(-Hathor) and Aphrodite. In addition, one may note the gradual increase of the divinity of the reigning queen in the course of her assimilation and then identification with Isis. The high point is reached in the person of Cleopatra VII together with the representation of the male ruler as Neos Dionysos or, more precisely, Osiris.

The priestly decrees represent a search for an ideology which can unite the two aspects of the king (pharaonic and Hellenistic). Of these, the most important date from the period spanning the reigns of Ptolemy III to V.[5] In these decrees, there is an attempt to bring the king into the temple cult by means of the authority of the clergy. A clear testimony to this attempt are the statues of the king erected in sanctuaries and the festivals established to honour the royal couple. The local priesthoods foster the Egyptian cult of the Ptolemies, especially the high priest of Ptah in Memphis.

One of the major problems, if not the most important one, of religious culture in Egypt during the late period (Ptolemaic and Roman) is the discrepancy between the cultic-religious functions assigned to the king and the varying capabilities of the actual ruler to fulfil them. Since the cultic obligations of the king are at the heart of ancient Egyptian religion, one can discern throughout a struggle to maintain and regain a kingship of cultic relevance. Possibilities for solving the dilemma range from an automatic projection of the role of pharaoh onto every ruler to an actual transferral of the king's functions to gods and priests. We can count among the latter the crowning of the falcons at Edfu and Philae and the enthronement of the respective child-god as world ruler in the birth houses; Isis is increasingly thought of as a universal ruler and, as such, becomes ever more prominent. In the cult, there are constant efforts to renew the royal powers which grant fertility and victory; the historical names of the ruling monarch are then added but in the late Ptolemaic period the cartouches often remain empty (particularly in Dendera). As a compensatory measure, the earthly king is often compared to the god/king (in the birth house, in the play *Triumph of Horus* at Edfu, etc.) and from time to time a human and a divine king are identified.[6]

After the Roman province of *Aegyptus* is formed, the Roman emperors are very soon adopted as pharaohs into the world of temple reliefs. In some cases, Ptolemaic innovations must once again yield to older traditions.[7] During this process, gradual changes take place in the cult of the king and in the religious organizations of Egypt. This is especially true of the family of the high priest of Ptah in Memphis: Imuthes/Petubastis IV,[8] the son of that Psenptah III who crowned Ptolemy XII in 76, was high priest of Ptah from 39 (when he was barely seven years of age) and held the position of 'prophet of the (living) pharaoh' for Cleopatra VII; two days before the fall of Alexandria in 30, he died. Octavian evidently had grave misgivings from the beginning about leaving the family of the high priest in Memphis in office. The family disposed great influence over the entire country and had been closely associated with the Ptolemaic royal house. It is, however, precisely this family and their circle who perform important services to effect Augustus' transformation into a pharaoh within the cultic fiction of the Egyptian temple; the pharaonic titulature of Augustus and the concomitant 'hieroglyphic' ideology of the emperor-pharaoh are created within the ambit of the high priest of Ptah.[9] A provisional agreement is reached: during Augustus' third year (28/7 BC), Psenamun II[10] is finally named high priest of Ptah; at the same time, he takes on the position of 'prophet of Caesar' with his mother, Tnepheros.[11] Augustus' decision was however to be valid only during this initial phase when the province was in the process of being established. After the death of Psenamun II (after 23 BC), the office of high priest of Memphis is no longer filled.

The dynastic cult in Alexandria which was organized by the state is discontinued with the Roman conquest, but the cult of Alexander as the founder of the city (ktistes) continues.[12] Similarly, certain cults of the Ptolemies which had taken root among the people are preserved. For example, the cult of Theos Soter in Ptolemais which had a subsidiary sanctuary in Koptos is frequently attested as late as the third century AD.[13] The excavations in Hermopolis Magna indicate that the great temple together with the cult statues of the Theoi Euergetai and Theoi Adelphoi remain untouched into the late Roman period. Afterwards, the foundations and construction materials are used for the early Christian basilica built on the same spot.[14]

In particular, it is the famed Cleopatra the Great who lives on as a cult figure; her statues are spared while those of Antony are destroyed (Plu. *Ant.* 86.9). The existence of a much visited Cleopatreion not far from Alexandria is confirmed for AD 4/5.[15] We know of a cult of Cleopatra who is identified with Aphrodite dating to the reign of Alexander Severus (222–235).[16] As late as AD 373, we find a priest on the island of Philae who has a statue of Cleopatra gilded.[17] Given the fame and tradition of the last Ptolemaic queen, it is easy to see why Zenobia in AD 270 should represent herself as (new) Cleopatra, when she joined Egypt to her kingdom at Palmyra by military force (H.A., *trig.tyr.* 27.1; 30.2; 30.19; Claud. 1.1.; Aurel. 27.3; Prob. 9.5).

The most significant contribution made by the religious policy of the Ptolemies to the general history of religion is the creation of a cult of Sarapis in Alexandria. The divine couple Isis and Sarapis are enthusiastically worshipped during the high principate throughout the whole Roman empire. It was precisely the Alexandrian Serapeum which was to become a bastion of ancient religion during the late Roman period and it was there that the clashes between paganism and Christianity reached their bloody culmination. As a result of this confrontation, the temple fell into ruin.

The history of the Ptolemies constitutes a distinct epoch during which Egypt evolved from a Persian satrapy to a Roman province: in place of a large-scale, oriental kingdom and a Persian king far away in Susa, Egypt was now under the control of the Roman empire and the emperor in Rome. The conquest of Egypt became a theme of fundamental importance in the ideology of the principate. From the perspective of Roman ideology, the establishment of the Roman province of *Aegyptus* meant fortune and prosperity for the world; coins bearing the legend *Aegypto capta* convey this message from 28 BC onwards.[18] Such notions had no meaning for the Egyptian people: Roman rule not only intensified class differences, but through its legal institutions it made social rank dependent on a person's ethnic background.[19]

The Ptolemaic period has provided us with a great cultural legacy in the form of the impressive temples and Alexandrian scholarship which we still enjoy today.

## Notes

1 Reported in the Rosetta Stone: p. 156 with note 20.
2 See p. 198 with notes 84–86.
3 I.Philae.II, no. 128.
4 Cf. p. 294, note 21.
5 See pp. 105–111, 169–173.
6 E.g. Ptolemy VIII in the birth house of Edfu; see p. 267 with note 35.
7 The queen, for example, disappears again from the reliefs even though she appeared as a priestess of equal rank next to the pharaoh during the Ptolemaic period (see p. 84f.); on the transition cf. E. Winter, 'Das Kalabsha-Tor in Berlin', *JbPreussKul* 14, 1979, 59–71. This Ptolemaic practice only reappears again slowly shortly before the end of the practice of Egyptian relief sculpture, namely with Sabina, the wife of Hadrian, and Julia Domna, wife of Septimius Severus; cf. H. Gauthier, *Les livre des rois d'Égypte, V: Les empereurs romains*, Cairo 1917, 135 (LXXI, B), 197 (LXV, A).
8 PP IX.5372; Quaegebeur (1980), 71, no. 35; id. (1989, 1), 107.
9 J.-Cl. Grenier, 'Le protocole des empereurs romains', *REg* 38, 1987, 81–104; id., *Les titulatures des empereurs romains dans les documents en langue égyptienne*, Brussels 1989.
10 PP IX.5375 a; Quaegebeur (1980) 71, no. 36; see also the note which follows.
11 PP IX.5843b; on the mother and son see Reymond (1981), 223–231 (no. 29 and 31).
12 Leschhorn (1984), 204–212.
13 Leschhorn (1984), 227f.
14 See p. 96 with note 108. I am not at all certain if the great oracle statue Berlin, no. 7996 (east section of the Egyptian museum) from the villa of Hadrian truly refers to Arsinoe II; cf. W. Iwas, 'Moderne Analysemethoden für antike Plastik', Urania 56, 1980, H.3, 24–27.
15 SB 647; Becher (1966), 180; Bernand (1970), 505, pl. 15.3.
16 Mitteis, Wilcken, I, no. 115.

17  Quaegebeur (1978), 276; id. (1988), 41.
18  On this topic see H. Bellen, 'AEGVPTO CAPTA. Die Bedeutung der Eroberung Ägyptens für die Prinzipatsideologie', in Politische Ideen auf Münzen, Festschrift zum 16. Deutschen Numismatikertag, Mainz, 1991, R. Albert (ed.), Speyer 1991, 33–59.
19  Goudriaan (1988), 119.

# Bibliographical supplement

## Selected literature on the history of the Ptolemaic empire from 1990 to 1999

Abd El Ghani, M. 'Zenon in Syria and Palestine', in *Alessandria e il mondo ellenistico-romano, Atti del II. Congr. Intern.* Italo-Egiziano, Alessandria 1992, Roma 1995, 12–21.

Abdullatif, A. A. 'Cleopatra and Caesar at Alexandria and Rome', in *Roma e l'Egitto nell'Antichità Classica, Atti del I Congr. Intern. Italo-Egiziano*, Cairo 1989, Roma 1992, 47–61.

Al Hamshary, M. 'Nabateans reactions towards Alexandrians trade activity in the Ptolemaic period', in *Alessandria e il mondo ellenistico-romano, Atti del II. Congr. Intern. Italo-Egiziano, Alessandria 1992*, Roma 1995, 26–35.

Alexandria and Alexandrinism. Papers delivered at a Symposium organized by the J. P. Getty Museums, etc., April 1993, Malibu 1996.

Bacchielli, L. 'Berenice II: la regina della riunificazione fra Egitto e Cirenaica', in *Vicende e figure femminili in Grecia e a Roma*, R. Raffaelli (ed.), Ancona 1995, 239–245.

Bailey, D. M. 'The canephore of Arsinoe Philadelphos: What did she look like?', *ChronEg* 74, 147, 1999, 156–160.

Balconi, C. 'Rabirio Postumo dioiketes d'Egitto' in P. Med. inv. 68.53?, Aegyptus 73 (1993) 3–20.

Barry, W. D. 'The crowd of Ptolemaic Alexandria and the riot of 203 BC', Echos du Monde Classique, *Classical Views* 37, 1993, 415–431.

Bennet, C. 'Cleopatra V Tryphaena and the genealogy of the later Ptolemies', *AncSoc* 28, 1997, 39–66.

Bernand, A. *Alexandrie des Ptolemées*, Paris 1995.

Bilde, P. and others (eds) 'Ethnicity in Hellenistic Egypt', *Aarhus* 1992 [many relevant articles].

Bilde, P. and others, *Aspects of Hellenistic Kingship*, Aarhus 1996.

Bingen, J. Les ordonnances royales *C.Ord.Ptol.* 75–76 (Héracléopolis, 41 av. J.-C.), ChronEg 70, 139–140, 1995, 206–222.

Bingen, J. 'Cléopâtre VII Philopatris', *ChronEg* 74, 147, 1999, 118–123.

Brambach, J. *Kleopatra*, München 1995.

Brodersen, K. and others, *Historische griechische Inschriften in Übersetzung, III: Der griechische Osten und Rom (250–1 v. Chr.)*, Darmstadt 1999.

Caccamo Caltabiano, M. (ed.) *La Sicilia tra l'Egitto e Roma, la monetazione siracusana dell'età di Ierone II*, Atti del Seminario di Studi Messina 2–4 Dic. 1993, 1995 [many relevant articles].

Caccamo Caltabiano, M. 'Berenice II. Il ruolo di una basilissa rilevato dalle sue monete', in *La Cirenaica in età antica. Atti del convegno intern. di studi Macerata. 18–20 maggio 1995*, E. Catanni, S. M. Marengo (eds), Macerata 1998, 97–112.

Cadell, H. and Le Rider, G. *Prix du blè et numéraire dans l'Egypte lagide de 305 à 173*, Bruxelles 1997.

Carney, E. D. 'Arsinoe before she was Philadelphus', *The Ancient History Bulletin* 8, 1994, 123–131.

Casson, L. 'Ptolemy II and the hunting of African elephants', *TransactAmPhilAss* 123, 1993, 247–260.

Chauveau, M. 'Ères nouvelles et corégences en Égypte ptolémaïque', in *Akten des 21. Intern. Papyrologenkongresses, 13.–19.8. 1995*, B. Kramer and others (eds), Stuttgart 1997, 163–171 (= APF. Beihefte, 3).

Chauveau, M. *L'Égypte au temps de Cléopâtre 180–30 av. J.-C.*, Paris 1997.

Clauss, M. *Kleopatra*, München, 1995.

Criscuolo, L. 'Guerre civili e amministrazione tolemaica. Il caso degli strateghi dell'Herakleopolites', *AncSoc* 22, 1991, 229–234.

Della Monica, M. *Les derniers pharaons*, Paris 1993.

Dietze, G. 'Der Streit um die Insel Pso', *AncSoc* 26, 1995, 157–184.

Dietze, G. 'Philae und die Dodekaschoinos in ptolemäischer Zeit', *AncSoc* 25, 1994, 63–110.

Dreyer, B. 'Der Beginn der Freiheitsphase Athens 287 v. Chr. und das Datum der Panathenäen und Ptolemaia im Kalliasdekret', *ZPE* 111, 1996, 45–67.

Dreyer, B. 'Zum ersten Diadochenkrieg. Der Göteborger Arrian-Palimpsest (ms Graec 1)', *ZPE* 125, 1999, 39–60.

Duttenhöfer, R. 'Ptolemäische Urkunden aus der Heidelberger Papyrus-Sammlung (P. Heid. VI)', Heidelberg 1994.

Erskine, A. 'Culture and power in Ptolemaic Egypt: the museum and the library of Alexandria', *Greece and Rome* 42, 1995, 38–48.

Fleischer, R. 'Kleopatra Philantonios', *IstMitt* 46, 1996, 237–240.

Grimm, G. *Alexandria, Die erste Königsstadt der hellenistischen Welt*, Mainz 1998.

Grimm, G. 'Der Ring des Aristomenes', *Antike Welt* 28, 6, 1997, 453–469.

Grimm, G. 'Verbrannte Pharaonen? Die Feuerbestattung Ptolemaios' IV. Philopator und ein gescheiterter Staatsstreich in Alexandria', *Antike Welt* 28. Jg., H. 3, 1997, 233–249.

Habicht, Chr. 'Athens and the Ptolemies', *ClAnt* 11, 1992, 68–90 (= id., Athen in hellenistischer Zeit. Gesammelte Aufsätze, München 1994, 140–163.

Haiying, Y. 'The famine stela: a source-critical approach and historical-comparative perspective', in *Proceedings of the 7th Intern. Congress of Egyptologists, Cambridge 3–9 Sept 1995*, Leuven 1998, 515–521.

Hallof, Kl. and Mileta, Chr. 'Samos und Ptolemaios III. Ein neues Fragment zu dem samischen Volksbeschluß' AM 72 (1957) 226 Nr. 59, *Chrion* 27, 1997, 255–285.

Heinen, H. 'Der Sohn des 6. Ptolemäers im Sommer 145. Zur Frage nach Ptolemaios VII. Neos Philopator und zur Zählung der Ptolemäerkönige', *ArchPF, Beih.* 3, 1997, 449–460.

Heinen, H. 'Ein griechischer Funktionär des Ptolemäerstaates als Priester ägyptischer Kulte', in *Hellenismus*. Akten des internationalen Hellenismus-Kolloquiums 1994 in Berlin (Tübingen 1996) 339–354.

Herz, P. 'Die frühen Ptolemäer bis 180 v. Chr.', in *Legitimation und Funktion des Herrschers. Vom ägyptischen Pharao bis zum neuzeitlichen Diktator*, R. Gundlach and H. Weber (eds), Stuttgart 1992, 51–97.

Herz, P. 'Hellenistische Könige, zwischen griechischen Vorstellungen vom Königtum und Vorstellungen ihrer einheimischen Untertanen', in *Subject and Ruler. The Cult of the Ruling Power in Classical Antiquity*, A. Small (ed.), Ann Arbor 1996, 27–40.

Hose, M. 'Der alexandrinische Zeus. Zur Stellung der Dichtkunst im Reich der ersten Ptolemäer', *Philologus* 141, 1997, 46–64.

Huss, W. 'Das Haus des Nektanebis und das Haus des Ptolemaios', *AncSoc* 25, 1994, 111–117.

Huss, W. *Der makedonische König und die ägyptischen Priester. Studien zur Geschichte des ptolemaiischen Ägypten*, Stuttgart 1994.

Huss, W. 'Die römisch-ptolemaiischen Beziehungen in der Zeit von 180 bis 116 v. çhr.' in *Roma e l'Egitto nell'Antichità Classica, Atti del I Congr. Intern. Italo-Egiziano*, Cairo 1989, Roma 1992, 197–208.

Huss, W. 'Memphis und Alexandreia in hellenistischer Zeit', in *Alessandria e il mondo ellenistico-romano, Atti del II. Congr. Intern. Italo-Egiziano, Alessandria 1992*, Roma 1995, 75–82.

Huss, W. 'Ptolemaios der Sohn', *ZPE* 121, 1998, 229–250.

Huss, W. 'Ptolemaios Eupator', in *Proceedings of the 20th International Congress of Papyrologists*, Copenhagen 1994, 555–561.

Jacob, Chr. and de Polignac, F. (eds) Alexandrie III$^e$ siècle av. J.-C. Tous les savoirs du monde ou le rêve d'universalité des Ptolémées, Paris 1992 [many relevant articles].

Jähne, A. 'Maroneia unter ptolemäischer Herrschaft', in *Stephanos nomismatikos. E. Schönert-Geiss zum 65. Geburtstag*, U. Peter (ed.), Berlin 1998, 301–316.

Johnson, C. G. 'Ptolemy V and the Rosetta decree: The Egyptianization of the Ptolemaic kingship', *AncSoc* 26, 1995, 145–155.

Johnson, J. H. (ed.) *Life in a multi-cultural society. Egypt from Cambyses to Constantine and beyond*, Chicago 1992 [many relevant articles].

Jones, A. 'On the reconstructed Macedonian and Egyptian lunar calendars', *ZPE* 119, 1997, 157–166.

Kessler, D. 'Der Serapeumsbezirk und das Serapeum von Tuna el-Gebel', in *Lingua restituta orientalis*, FS J. Aßfalg, R. Schulz and M. Görg (eds), Wiesbaden 1990, 183–189.

Koenen, L. 'The Ptolemaic king as a religious figure', in *Images and ideologies. Self-definition in the Hellenistic World*, A. Bulloch and others (eds), Berkeley 1993, 25–114.

Kosmetatou, E. 'Pisidia and the Hellenistic kings from 323 to 133 BC', *AncSoc* 28, 1997, 5–37.

Köthen-Welpot, S. 'Die Apotheose der Berenike, Tochter Ptolemaios'III', in *Wege öffnen, FS Gundlach*, Wiesbaden 1996, 129–132.

Kügler, J. 'Priestersynoden im hellenistischen Ägypten. Ein Vorschlag zur sozio-historischen Deutung', *GöttMisz* 139, 1994, 53–60.

Lampela, A. *Rome and the Ptolemies of Egypt. The development of their political relations 273–80 BC.*, Helsinki 1998.

Laubscher, H. P. *Ptolemäische Reiterbilder*, AM 106, 1991, 223–238, pl. 46–51.

Laubscher, H. P. 'Zur Bildtradition in ptolemäisch-römischer Zeit', *JdI* 111, 1996, 225–248.

Locher, J. 'Die Schenkung des Zwölfmeilenlandes in der Ergameneskapelle von Dakke', *ChronEg* 72, 144, 1997, 242–268.

Marasco, G. 'Cleopatra e gli esperimenti su cavie umane', *Historia* 44, 1995, 317–325.

Maresch, K. 'Das königliche Indulgenzdekret vom 9. Oktober 186 v. Chr.', in *Kölner Papyri* 7, bearb. v. M. Gronewald and K. Marsch, Opladen 1991, 63–78.

Mastrocinque, A. 'Guerra di successione' e prima guerra di Celesiria: un falso moderno e una questione storica, *AncSoc* 24, 1993, 27–39.

Mehl, A. 'Griechen und Phöniker im hellenistischen Zypern – ein Nationalitätenproblem?', in *Hellenismus*. Akten des internationalen Hellenismus-Kolloquiums 1994 in Berlin (Tübingen 1996) 377–414.

Mehl, A. 'Militärwesen und Verwaltung der Ptolemäer in Zypern', *RculClMedioev* 38, 1996, 215–260.

Mehl, A. 'Zypern und die großen Mächte im Hellenismus', *AncSoc* 26, 1995, 93–132.

Melaerts, H. (ed.) 'Le culte du souverain dans l'Égypte ptolémaïque au III$^e$ siècle avant notre ère', in *Actes du colloque international, Bruxelles 10 mai 1995*, Louvain 1998 (= *Studia Hellenistica* 34).

Mélèze-Modrzejewski, J. 'Law and justice in Ptolemaic Egypt', in *Legal Documents of the Hellenistic World*, M. J. Geller and others (eds), London 1995, 1–19.

Méléze-Modrzejewski, J. 'Πρόσταγμα περὶ τῆς γεωργίας: Droit grec et réalités égyptiennes en matière de bail force', in *Grund und Boden in Altägypten*, S. Allam (ed.), Tübingen 1994, 199–225.

Merkelbach, R. 'Zur ENKATOXH im Serapeum zu Memphis', *ZPE* 103, 1994, 293–296.

Muccioli, F. 'Considerazioni generali sull'epiteto ΦΙΛΑΔΕΛΦΟΣ nelle dinastie ellenistiche e sulla sua applicazione nella titolatura degli ultimi Seleucidi', *Historia* 43, 1994, 402–422.

Muhs, B. P. *The Administration of Egyptian Thebes in the Early Ptolemaic Period*, Diss. Univ. of Pensylvania, Ann Arbor 1996.

Oates, J. F. *The Ptolemaic Basilikos Grammateus*, Atlanta 1995 [dazu Th. Kruse, Tyche 12, 1997, 149–158].

Perpillou-Thomas, F. *Fêtes d'Égypte ptolémaïque et romaine d'après la documentation papyrologique grecque*, Louvain 1993 (= *Studia Hellenistica* 31).

Pestman, P. W. 'A family archive which changes history', in *Hundred-Gated Thebes*, S. P. Vleeming (ed.), Leiden 1995, 91–100.

Pestman, P. W. 'Haronnophris and Chaonnophris, two indigenous pharaohs in Ptolemaic Egypt (205–186 BC)', in *Hundred-Gated Thebes*, S. P. Vleeming (ed.), Leiden 1995, 101–137.

Pfrommer, M. 'Fassade und Heiligtum. Betrachtungen zur architektonischen Repräsentation des vierten Ptolemäers', in *Basileia. Die Paläste der hellenistischen Könige*. Intern. Symposium in Berlin 1992, W. Hoepfner and G. Brands (eds), Mainz 1996, 97–108.

Pomeroy, S. B. 'Families in Ptolemaic Egypt: continuity, change, and coercion', in *Transitions to empire. Essays in Greco-Roman history, 360–146 BC in honor of E. Badian*, R. W. Wallace and E. M. Harris (eds), London 1996, 241–253.

Pomeroy, S. B. 'Family history in Ptolemaic Egypt', in Proceedings of the 20th International Congress of Papyrologists, Copenhagen 1994, 593–597.

Ravazzolo, C. 'Tolemeo figlio di Tolemeo II filadelfo', in *Studi ellenistici 8*, B. Virgilio (ed.), Pisa 1996, 123–143.

Reger, G. 'The political history of the Kyklades 260–200 BC', *Historia* 43, 1994, 32–69.

Sambin, Ch. 'Une porte de fête-sed de Ptolemée II remployée dans le temple de Montou à Médamoud', *BIFAO* 95, 1995, 383–457.

Samuel, A. E. 'The Ptolemies and the ideology of kingship', in *Hellenistic History and Culture*, P. Green (ed.): Berkeley 1993, 168–210.

Schloz, S. 'Das Tempelbauprogramm der Ptolemäer – die Darstellung eines Rekonstruktionsproblems', in *Ägyptische Tempel – Struktur, Funktion und Programm*, R. Gundlach and M. Rochholz (eds): Hildesheim 1994, 281–286.

Schmidt-Colinet, A. 'Das Grab Alexanders d. Gr. In Memphis?', in *The Problematics of Power*, M. Bridges and J. Ch. Bürgel (eds): Bern 1996, 87–90, Figs. 1–3, pls. 1–2.

Schrapel, Th. *Das Reich der Kleopatra. Quellenkritische Untersuchungen zu den 'Landschenkungen' Mark Antons*, Trier 1996.

Sekunda, N. *The Ptolemaic Army under Ptolemy VI Philometor*, Stockport, 1995.

Sheedy, K. A. 'The origins of the second Nesiotic League and the defence of Kythnos', *Historia* 45, 1996, 423–449.

Siani-Davies, M. 'Ptolemy XII Auletes and the Romans', *Historia* 46, 1997, 306–340.

Stanzel, K. H. *Liebende Hirten. Theokrits Bukolik und die alexandrinische Poesie*, Stuttgart 1995. (= *Beiträge zur Altertumskunde* 60).

Thiers, Chr. 'La stèle de Pithom et les douanes de Philadelphe', *GöttMisz* 157, 1997, 95–101.

Thompson, D. J. 'Egypt, 146–31 BC', in *Cambridge Ancient History IX (The last age of the Roman republic, 146–43 BC)*, 2nd ed, Cambridge 1994, 310–326.

Thompson, D. J. 'Literacy and power in Ptolemaic Egypt', in *Literacy and power in the ancient world*, A. K. Bowman and G. Woolf (eds): Cambridge 1994, 67–83.

Thompson, D. J. 'The high priests of Memphis under Ptolemaic rule', in M. Beard and others, *Pagan Priests. Religion and Power in the Ancient World*, London 1990, 95–116.

Verhougt, A. M. F. W., Vleeming, P. (eds) *The Two Faces of Graeco-Roman Egypt*, Leiden 1998 [many relevant articles].

Vittmann, G. 'Das demotische Graffito vom Satettempel auf Elephantine', *MDIK* 53, 1997, 263–281.

Weber, G. 'Interaktion, Repräsentation und Herrschaft. Der Königshof im Hellenismus', in *Zwischen 'Haus' und 'Staat'. Antike Höfe im Vergleich*, A. Winterling (ed.): München 1997, 27–71.

Weiser, W. *Katalog ptolemäischer Bronzemünzen der Sammlung des Instituts für Altertumskunde der Universität zu Köln*, Opladen 1995.

Wheatley, P. 'Ptolemy Soter's annexation of Syria 320 BC', ClQu, n.s. 45, 1995, 433–440.

Whitehorne, J. E. G. 'A reassessment of Cleopatra III's Syrian campaign', *ChronEg* 70, 139–140, 1995, 197–205.

Whitehorne, J. E. G. 'Ptolemy X Alexander I as 'Kokke's child', *Aegyptus* 75, 1995, 55–60.

Whitehorne, J. E. G. 'The supposed co-regency of Cleopatra Tryphaena and Berenice IV (58–55 B.C.)', in *Akten des 21. Intern. Papyrologenkongresses, 13.-19.8. 1995*, B. Kramer and others (eds), Stuttgart 1997, 1009–1013 (=APF. Beihefte, 3).

Winnicki, J. K. 'Carrying off and bringing home the statues of the gods', *JJurP* 24, 1994, 149–190.

Yoyotte, M. J. *La stèle de Nébireh*, Annuaire du Collège de France 94ᵉ année, 1993–4, 690–692.

# Appendix

## Overview of the events discussed in the history of the Ptolemaic kingdom

| | Political events | Events from the history of ideology and religion | Construction of temples within the Egyptian territory (not in chronological order) |
|---|---|---|---|
| 332 | Towards end of 332: Alexander's invasion of Egypt. | End 332: Alexander's accession as pharaoh. | |
| ALEXANDER THE GREAT | Beginning 331: Foundation of Alexandria. | Beginning 331: Alexander's expedition to Ammoneion (Siwa): royal oracle legitimizes him as pharaoh and confirms Alexander's view of himself as the son of Zeus (-Ammon) and his world empire. | |
| | Spring 331: Alexander departs. | | UNDER ALEXANDER THE GREAT |
| 323 | 10 June 323: Death of Alexander. | | bark shrine in the temple of Luxor; sanctuary in Karnak; ᶜAin el-Tibanija (Bahariya). |

IN THE NAME OF
PHILIP III:

bark shrine in the temple
of Amun at Karnak; large
hypostyle of the temple of
Thoth of Hermopolis.

323: Division of empire at Babylon: The
feeble-minded half brother of Alexander,
Arrhidaios, is acknowledged as king
under the name of Philip, with
Alexander's possible son by the
pregnant Roxane envisaged as joint
ruler; a triumvirate (Krateros,
Antipatros and Perdikkas) is chosen to
rule the empire but Perdikkas, who is
given high command of the royal army
becomes in effect ruler of the whole
empire as the representative of Krateros;
Ptolemy receives the satrapy of Egypt.

322/1: Supporting the oligarchies of Cyrene,
Ophellas wins Cyrenaica for Ptolemy;
Diagramma of Cyrene (321/20)
Coalition of Krateros, Antipatros,
Antigonos, Monophthalmos, Lysimachos
and Ptolemy against the autocratic
Perdikkas.
Ptolemy diverts Alexander's funerary
carriage to Egypt.

321/20: First War of the Successors
(see p. 30, note 27 on the various
chronological stages):
Alliance of Ptolemy with the Cypriot
kings of Salamis, Soloi, Paphos and
Amathus;
Summer 320: Perdikkas loses two
battles in the Nile Delta and is killed
by his officers.

| | Political events | Events from the history of ideology and religion | Construction of temples within the Egyptian territory (not in chronological order) |
|---|---|---|---|
| **PHILIP III ARRHIDAIOS** (Ptolemy as Satrap) | Autumn 320: Settlement of Triparadeisos: Antipatros becomes the new ruler of the empire and names Antigonos as field commander and strategos of Asia; Ptolemy's occupation of Egypt and Libya is confirmed, Seleukos receives the satrapy of Babylon.<br><br>Autumn 319: Death of Antipatros; Successor: Polyperchon.<br><br>319–315: Second War of the Successors: 319/18 Ptolemy annexes Syria and Phoenicia but garrisons are left in only a few cities; 317: Polyperchon is deposed; Kassandros becomes regent; Autumn 317: Murder of Philip III Arrhidaios. | | |
| 317 | | Early years of Ptolemy as satrap: creation of the cult of Sarapis; first Serapeum on the hill of Rhakotis in Alexandria. | |
| **ALEXANDER IV** (Ptolemy as Satrap) | 316: Birth of Arsinoe II.<br><br>315: Seleukos flees to Ptolemy.<br><br>314–311: Third War of the Successors: 314: Ptolemaic garrisons forced to withdraw from Syrian cities.<br><br>313: Acquisition of Cyprus for Ptolemy by Seleukos and Menelaos (brother of Ptolemy). | | IN THE NAME OF ALEXANDER IV:<br><br>gate of the temple of Khnum on Elephantine; small grotto of Speos Artemidos. |

| | |
|---|---|
| **ALEXANDER IV**<br>Ptolemy as Satrap | 312: Nikokreon of Salamis becomes strategos of Cyprus.<br><br>313/12: Revolt of Cyrene.<br><br>312/11: Expedition of Ptolemy and Seleukos to Syria:<br>312: Victory of both in the battle of Gaza over Demetrios, son of Antigonos; Spring 311: Ptolemy forced to withdraw from Syria which is now occupied by Antigonos;<br>August 311: Reconquest of Babylon by Seleukos. | 9 November 311: Satrap Stele: Ptolemy confirms the revenues of the priests of Buto. |
| | Autumn 311: Peace treaty between the allies (Ptolemy, Kassandros and Lysimachos) and Antigonos; Alexander IV remains in Kassandros' custody. | |
| 310/09 | 310/309: Murder of Alexander IV by Kassandros. | |
| **INTERREGNUM**<br>Ptolemy as Satrap | 310: Ptolemaic expedition to 'rough' Cilicia Menelaos becomes strategos of Cyprus and king of Salamis. | |
| | 309: Expedition by Ptolemy to Lycia and Caria: Phaselis, Xanthos, Kaunos, Myndos and Iasos are acquired.<br>309/8: Winter headquarters on Kos; Birth of Ptolemy II (308). | |
| | 309/8: Campaign of Ophellas (governor of Cyrenaica) against Carthage; 308: Murder of Ophellas. | |

| Political events | Events from the history of ideology and religion | Construction of temples within the Egyptian territory (not in chronological order) |
|---|---|---|
| 308: Prolemaic naval expedition to Greece: Corinth, Sikyon, Megara are occupied (but lost again 303). | | |
| 306: Ptolemy loses the naval battle at Salamis (Cyprus) against Demetrios; 306–295/4: Demetrios ruler of Cyprus. | | |
| Summer 306: Antigonos and Demetrios assume the title of king. | | |
| Late summer/autumn 306: Ptolemy assumes the title of king; Seleukos, Kassandros and Lysimachos follow soon after. | | |
| Autumn 306: Campaign of Antigonos and Demetrios in the Nile Delta; Retreat. | | |
| 305/4: Ptolemy supports Rhodes against Demetrios. | January 304: Ptolemy I is crowned pharaoh. Decree to protect Egyptian sanctuaries. 304 Cult of Ptolemy I on Rhodes. | UNDER PTOLEMY I: temple of Hathor in Terenuthis; temple of Amun in Naukratis; temple of Soknebtynis in Tebtynis; temple of Osiris in Kom el-Ahmar/Sharuna; two cult chapels in Tuna el-Gebel near Hermopolis. |
| 304–300: Revolt of Cyrenaica; Magas becomes governor (300). | | |
| 303–301: Fourth War of the Successors: 302/1 Ptolemy acquires Coele Syria (Sidon and Tyros remain possessions of Demetrios); 301: Battle of Ipsos: Death of Antigonos; division of his empire: Seleukos is awarded all of Syria but tolerates Prolemaic rule in Coele Syria. | | |

300: Arsinoe II marries Lysimachos.

297: Ptolemy helps Pyrrhos to regain Epiros. Demetrios of Phaleron comes to Egypt.

295/4: Cyprus finally incorporated into the Ptolemaic empire; henceforth Phoenicians act again as Ptolemaic governors.
Acquisition of Pamphylia (evidence for 278) as well as Sidon and Tyre. Athens unsuccessfully supported against Demetrios by a Ptolemaic fleet (Demetrios conquers the city in the spring of 294).

288–285: Fifth War of the Successors:
287: Ptolemaic troops under the command of Kallias of Sphettos support Athens in their revolt against Ptolemy and Demetrios; Peace between Ptolemy and Demetrios; Ptolemy assumes the protectorate of the Island League.
285: Demetrios is captured by Seleukos; 283.

285/4: Ptolemy II becomes co-regent.

Winter 283/2: Death of Ptolemy I.

From c. 290: Priest of Alexander in Alexandria.

287/6: Divine Honours for Ptolemy on Delos.

284/3: Menelaos becomes priest of Alexander for the fifth time.

PTOLEMY I SOTER

283/2

| Political events | Events from the history of ideology and religion | Construction of temples within the Egyptian territory (not in chronological order) |
|---|---|---|
| 281: Battle of Korupedion: Ptolemy Keraunos murders Seleukos, becomes King of Macedonia and gives up his claims in Egypt. | Beginning of Ptolemy II's reign: Ptolemy I is elevated to *theos soter*. | UNDER PTOLEMY II: naos of the temple of Isis on Philae; Isis sanctuary at el-Qubaniye; Ptolemaic gate in the temple of Mut at Karnak; decorative work in the pre-Ptolemaic temple of Opet in Karnak; expansion of the older birth house in Dendera; temple of Min in Koptos. |
| c. 280: Lighthouse tower Pharos is erected on a small island facing the harbour of Alexandria. | | |
| 280–79: so-called 'Syrian War of Succession': Alliance of Ptolemy II with Meletos, acquisition of Samos, other cities in Caria (Stratonikeia, Amyzon, Halikarnassos), strengthening of Ptolemaic rule in Lycia (Ptolemy of Telmessos). | | |
| 279: Ptolemy Keraunos is killed in a battle against the Celts. | 279: Temple in Pithom dedicated by Ptolemy II. | |
| c. 279: Return of Arsinoe II to Egypt; afterwards (before 274) marriage to Ptolemy II. | From 279/8: Celebration of the quadrennial festival of the Ptolemaia in Alexandria. | *Work on:* temple of Pnepheros in Theadelphia; temple of Isis-Renenutet in Medinet Madi; Anubieion in Saqqara; temple of Isis in Behbeit el-Hagar; temple of Onuris-Shu in Sebennytos; temple of Hibis in the Kharga oasis. |
| early 270s: Magas assumes the title of King in Cyrenaica. | | |
| c. 275: Campaign of Magas against Alexandria: failure owing to the revolt of Libyan nomads; counter-attack by Ptolemy foiled by mutiny of Celtic mercenaries (these subsequently perish on an island in the Nile). | | |

| | |
|---|---|
| Expedition against Lower Nubia. Gold mines of Wadi Allaqi acquired; foundation of Berenike Panchrysos? | c. 275: 'Donation' of the Dodekaschoinos to the temple of Isis of Philae. Winter 275/4: Great pompé in Alexandria on the occasion of the Ptolemaia. c. 274: Priest for Ptolemy I in Lapethos, Cyprus. |
| 274–271: First Syrian War against Antiochos I. 273: First exchange of embassies with Rome. | 272/1: The *Theoi Adelphoi* are added to the cult of Alexander. |
| July 270: Death of Arsinoe II. c. 270/69: Naval expedition of Ptolemy II to the Black Sea to support Byzantium. Canal from the Nile to the Red Sea is re-established; as a result numerous harbour-cities or more precisely bases are founded from the Suez Gulf as far as the Strait of Bab el-Mandeb. | Arsinoe II elevated to a goddess. c. 270/69: Cult for Ptolemy II in Byzantium. |
| August 268: Alliance of the Ptolemaic kingdom, Athens and Sparta at the request of Chremonides in Athens (against Antigonos II Gonatas of Macedonia). 267–261: Chremonidean War: Athens unsuccessfully supported by Ptolemaic fleet under Patroklos' command; establishment of long-lasting Ptolemaic bases in Itanos (east Crete), Thera, Methana/Arsinoe and Keos. | From 269 ? (certainly from 268) kanephoros for Arsinoe II attested in Alexandria. 265/4: Temple in Mendes dedicated by the crown prince, Ptolemy the 'son'. January 264: Pithom stele. After 264: Mendes stele. |

| Political events | Events from the history of ideology and religion | Construction of temples within the Egyptian territory (not in chronological order) |
|---|---|---|
| c. 262: Ephesos (and Lesbos?) become Ptolemaic; spring 261: Capitulation of Athens; the brothers, Chremonides and Glaukon, come to Egypt.<br><br>262–245: Apollonios as Dioiketes; 260–258: Zenon travels through Coele Syria on his behalf; from 256: Zenon administers the Dorea of Apollonios near Philadelpia (Fayyum).<br><br>260–253: Second Syrian War against Antiochus II: 260/59: the successor Ptolemy 'the son' (co-ruler: 267–259) revolts against Ptolemy II in Ionia; 259/8: Antiochos succeeds in obtaining Miletos and Samos; 258: General Inventory of Egypt is drawn up to ascertain its economic potential; 257: Campaign of Ptolemy II against Syria; spring 255 (?): naval battle at Kos; the Ptolemaic fleet commanded by Patroklos is defeated by Antigonos Gonatas; c. 255: Naval battle of Ephesos; the Ptolemaic fleet commanded by Chremonides is defeated by the Rhodians; Ephesos becomes Seleukid (evidence for 254/3). | 263: Large part of the temple quota of produce (apomoira) decreed for the cult of Arsinoe. | |

End of the Ptolemaic protectorate over the Island League.
September 254: Envoys from the Bosporan kingdom and Argos visit the Fayyum.
253: Peace concluded with Antiochus II: Miletos, Samos, Ephesos, Pamphylia and Cilicia become Seleukid.
July 253: Ptolemy II in Memphis to distribute kleruchic land in the Fayyum.
252: Antiochus II of Syria marries Berenike, daughter of Ptolemy II.

251/48: Inscription of King Aśoka (India) mentions diplomatic contacts *inter alia* with Ptolemy II and Magas of Cyrene.

End of the 250s: Ptolemy III is engaged to Berenike, daughter of Magas of Cyrene.

*c.* 250: Death of Magas.
Victory of Ptolemaic fleet over Antigonas Gonatas.

Winter 250/49: Aratos (delegate of Achaian League) comes to Alexandria; receives Ptolemaic subsidies.

250–249/8: Demetrios the Fair (half brother of Antigonas Gonatas) in Cyrene.

249/8–246: Ekdelos and Demphanes (Arcadian legal reformers) in Cyrene.

246: Death of Ptolemy II:
Ptolemy III comes into power and his marriage to Berenike II.
Cyrenaica regained.

255/4: Glaukon is priest of Alexander. Kanephoros is attested for Arsinoe II Kition, Cyprus.

UNDER PTOLEMY III:
birth house of the temple of Isis of Philae (older phase); temple of Isis of Syene;

246

| Political events | Events from the history of ideology and religion | Construction of temples within the Egyptian territory (not in chronological order) |
|---|---|---|
| 246–241: Third Syrian War against Seleukos II: 246: Ptolemy III enters Seleukia in Piera and Antiocheia on the Orontes; his sister Berenike (widow of Antiochos II) and her son murdered; campaign of Ptolemy III as far as the Euphrates. | | foundation of the temple of Horus of Edfu (23 August 237); small temple of Khnum of Esna; gate of Euergetes front of the temple of Khonsu in Karnak; northern gate facing the temple of Month in Karnak-Nord; temple of Osiris in Canopus; temple of Qasr Gueida (Kharga); construction of the Serapeum in Alexandria. |
| 245: First revolt of native Egyptians against the Ptolemaic regime; Ptolemy III breaks off his eastern campaign. | During the Third Syrian War: *Theoi Euergetai* added to the cult of Alexander. | |
| 243: Ptolemy III hegemon of the Achaian League; Ptolemaic subsidies to the league. Acquisitions from the Third Syrian War: in Syria, Seleukia in Pieria and the Ptolemaic base on cape Ras Ibn Hani, the Anatolian areas of Cilicia, Pamphylia (lost again under Ptolemy III), Ionia (especially Ephesos, Lebedos/Ptolemais, Kolophon, Priene and Samos), the Hellespont and southern Thrace (Ainos and Maroneia are confirmed as Ptolemaic) with the island of Samothrake. Ptolemy Andromachos loses the naval battle at Andros against Antigonas Gonatas; is later killed by his Thracian soldiers in Ephesos. Peace with Seleukos II. | 243: Royal Priest in Ainos, Thrace attested. | |
| | 238: Synod of priests in Alexandria and Canopos – Canopos Decree (7 March 238). | |

235/4: Sosibios is priest of Alexander.

From 229/8: Strategoi confirmed as heads of nome administration in Egypt.

229/8: Military alliance between the Aetolian League and the Ptolemaic kingdom.

227/6: Earthquake on Rhodes, the Colossus collapses; together with other dynasties, Ptolemy III sends emergency supplies, money and labour forces.

226/5: Cessation of Ptolemaic subsidies to the Achaean League; instead, support for Kleomenes of Sparta; Ptolemaic guarantees of safety to Athens.

224/3: Cultic honours for the third Ptolemaic couple in Athens; also in Athens, quadrennial Ptolemaia festival celebrated.

Spring 222: Unsuccessful military expedition of Magas, the son of Ptolemy III to Asia; minor support to Attalos I of Pergamon against the Seleukids.

Summer 222: Cessation of aid to Kleomenes; battle of Sellasia; Kleomenes flees to Alexandria.

Turn of 222/1: Death of Ptolemy III.

222/1

After the change in monarchy: marriage of Ptolemy IV to Arsinoe III; murder of Lysimachos (brother of Ptolemy III). Magas (brother of Ptolemy IV) and Berenike at the instigation of Sosibios.

UNDER PTOLEMY IV:
temple of Thoth of Dakke;
temple of Arensnuphis on Philae;
small temple on the island of Sehel;

| Political events | Events from the history of ideology and religion | Construction of temples within the Egyptian territory (not in chronological order) |
|---|---|---|
| Summer 221: Antiochos III invades Beqaᶜ valley; retreat. | | Edfu: completion and decoration of naos; |
| Spring 219: Kleomenes attempts a coup in Alexandria. | | temple of Deir el-Medina; temple of Hathor of Qusae; naos of the temple of Mut in Tanis; |
| 219–217: Fourth Syrian War against Antiochos III: 219: Antiochos III gains Seleukia in Pieria (spring); Betrayal of the Ptolemaic strategos Theodotos; Antiochos III gains most of Palestine (not Dora and Sidon); Winter 219/8: armistice lasting four months; 218: Offensive of Antiochos III; land and naval battle near Berytos; Antiochos III conquers Philadelphia/ Rabbaᵗ ᶜAmmon; 22 June 217: Ptolemy defeats Antiochos III at the battle of Raphia; Coele Syria again becomes Ptolemaic; late summer 217: Ptolemy IV penetrates into Seleukid Syria. | Autumn 217: Victory celebration and synod of priests in Memphis; Raphia decree (15 November). | east gate of the precinct of Ptah in Memphis; naos for Harpokrates in the Serapeum of Alexandria. *Work on:* temple of Isis of Syene; temple in Qasr Gueida; northern gate in front of the temple of Month in north Karnak; Month temple in Medamud. |
| 217: Peace of Naupaktos with Ptolemaic collaboration. | 216: *Theoi Philopatores* are added to the cult of Alexander. | |
| after 217: Revolt in northern Egypt breaks out, led by Egyptian military class. | 216/15: Agathokles is priest of Alexander. | |

215–13: Ptolemaic support of Achaios (relative and counter-king to Antiochos III in Asia Minor) is unsuccessful.

210: Roman envoys in Alexandria. Birth of Ptolemy V (9 October).

210/207: Ptolemaic envoys attempt to intercede between Rome and Philip V three times.

207: The priest-king of Siwa is in the service of the Carthaginian army against Rome.

206: Revolt breaks out in the Thebaïd: 11 November 206: oldest evidence for Herwennefer as pharaoh (ruled 206–200).

204 c. middle of the year: death of Ptolemy IV.

204: Murder of Arsinoe III; Sosibios and Agathokles assume the guardianship of Ptolemy V as well as administrative matters; death of Sosibios.

Spring 203: Antiochus III conquers Ptolemaic sites in Caria.

---

215/4: Dedication of the communal mausoleum for Alexander and the Ptolemies on the occasion of the Ptolemaia;
*theoi soteres* are inducted in the cult for Alexander and the Ptolemies (Alexandrian dynastic cult completed). Eponymous cult in Ptolemais for Ptolemy I and the ruling king. Edict of Ptolemy IV concerning the cult of Dionysos.

211/10: Athlophoros for Berenike II in Alexandria on the occasion of the Ptolemaia.

---

IN THE NAME OF THE MEROITIC KINGS:

Ergamenes II:
work continues on the temple of Arensnuphis on Philae and on the temple of Thoth of Dakke;

Adikhalamani:
first chapel of the temple of Amun of Debod.

| Political events | Events from the history of ideology and religion | Construction of temples within the Egyptian territory (not in chronological order) |
|---|---|---|
| End 203: Fall of Agathokles; Tlepolemos (strategos of Pelusion) becomes guardian and regent (at first together with Sosibios II for a short time). | | |
| Winter 203/2: Secret treaty between Philip V and Antiochus III on the division of Ptolemaic possessions. | | |
| 202/1: The native pharaoh Herwennefer is attested in Abydos under the name of Hyrgonaphor. | | |
| 202–195: Fifth Syrian War against Antiochus III: 202: Offensive of Antiochus III east of Antilebanon; Damascus is captured. 201: Antiochus III occupies large parts of Palestine (not the Phoenician coastal cities); the Ptolemaic strategos Ptolemy, son of Thraseas, goes over to the Seleukid side and retains his position. | | |
| 201: Tlepolemos is deposed; Aristomenes becomes Ptolemy V's guardian and regent. Philip V conquers Samos (the island becomes Ptolemaic again for a short time before 197). Further course of the Fifth Syrian War: 201/200: Skopas reconquers territory which had been lost to Antiochos III but not Damascus. 200: Skopas is defeated by Antiochos III in the battle of Panion. | | |

PTOLEMY V EPIPHANES

200/199: Siege and fall of Sidon; from now on the city becomes Seleukid. Until the spring of 198 the entire Ptolemaic 'Syria and Phoenicia' is under the rule of Antiochos III.

200: Philip V conquers Ptolemaic Thrace. Rome demands that Ptolemaic possessions be inviolable (again in 198). Roman envoys in Alexandria. Ankhwennefer succeeds as pharaoh in Thebes (200–186).

199/8: Ptolemy V is added to the Alexandrian dynastic cult; priestess for Arsinoe III in Alexandria.

199/8: Thebes under Ptolemaic control.

197: Antiochos III conquers the Ptolemaic possessions in Asia Minor: Cilicia, Lycia and Ephesos in Ionia. Rhodes negotiates freedom for the Ptolemaic cities in Caria (Kaunos, Myndos, Halikarnassos). Ptolemaic troops capture the insurrectionist Lykopolis in the Delta.

196/5: Nubian intruders occupy Syene (until 189) Ankhwennefer wins back Thebes. Conference of Lysimacheia: Rome demands that Antiochos III returns the recently captured territories back to the Ptolemaic kingdom; Antiochos, in contrast, announces a pact of friendship and marriage ties with Ptolemy V.

26 March 196: Coronation of Ptolemy V in Memphis and execution of the ringleaders from Lykopolis.

27 March 196: synod of priests in Memphis; Rosetta Stone.

UNDER PTOLEMY V IN THE AREA AROUND MEMPHIS:

decoration of the Apieion in the temple of Ptah; new construction phase in the Anubieion in Saqqara.

| Political events | Events from the history of ideology and religion | Construction of temples within the Egyptian territory (not in chronological order) |
|---|---|---|
| 195: Peace between Ptolemy V and Antiochos III: Engagement between the Ptolemaic king and Cleopatra I, daughter of the Seleukid king. | | |
| Winter 194/3: Ptolemy V marries Cleopatra I in Raphia. | | |
| 191: Two Ptolemaic embassies in Rome. | | |
| 187: Western Thebes (Deir el-Medina) and the south as far as Syene under Ptolemaic control. | 187/6: Aristonikos (eunuch, friend of Ptolemy V) as priest of Alexander. | UNDER PTOLEMY V IN THE SOUTH: temple of Imhotep on Philae; naos in the temple of Arensnuphis on Philae; inscriptions in the temple of Horus at Edfu. |
| August 186: Komanos (first[?] epistrategos of the chora from 187) defeats Ankhwennefer and his son, commander of the Nubian auxiliary troops in the Theban nome. | September 186: Synod of priests in Alexandria; Philensis II decree; Ankhwennefer is pardoned. | |
| 9 October 186: Amnesty Decree of Ptolemy V. | | |
| 185: Polykrates of Argos defeats the rebels in the Delta who are then brutally murdered in Sais. Ptolemaic monetary gifts to the Achaean League. | 185: Synod of priests in Memphis; Philensis I decree. | |
| | 185/4: Kanephoros for Arsinoe II in Ptolemais. | |
| 182: Naval expedition of Aristonikos to Syria (island of Arados, Apamea). | | |
| Spring 180: Ptolemy V is poisoned by his generals. Cleopatra I assumes the guardianship of Ptolemy VI and becomes regent. | | |

180

Spring 176: Death of Cleopatra I; Eulaios (eunuch) and Lenaios (former Syrian slave) become guardians and regents.

Before 15 April 175: marriage between Ptolemy VI and Cleopatra II.

173/2: Roman envoys in Alexandria.

170/169–168: Sixth Syrian War against Antiochos IV:
Autumn 170: joint reign of Ptolemy VI, Cleopatra II and Ptolemy VIII. Winter 170/169: Ptolemaic and Seleukid embassies in Rome; Antiochos IV defeats the Ptolemaic army near Pelusion; Antiochos takes Pelusion and occupies a large part of Lower Egypt; in Alexandria the regents are replaced by Komanos and Kineas; meeting between Ptolemy VI and Antiochos IV. Rival government in Alexandria: Ptolemy VIII is again acclaimed king; Antiochos IV beseiges Alexandria.
Summer 169: Alexandrian envoys ask Rome to intervene.
Autumn 169: Antiochos IV returns to Syria.
Triple monarchy is re-established.
Spring 168: Antiochos IV annexes Cyprus and occupies northern Egypt – perhaps legitimized by the priesthoods in Memphis – and advances towards Alexandria.

179/8: Ptolemy VI is added to the dynastic cult.

c. 170: There is a total of five offices of eponymous priests in Ptolemais.

AT THE TIME OF THE TRIPLE MONARCHY:

relief in the temple at Deir el-Medina (Fig. 9.7); inscriptions in Esna.

| Political events | Events from the history of ideology and religion | Construction of temples within the Egyptian territory (not in chronological order) |
|---|---|---|
| July 168: 'Day of Eleusis': C. Popilius Laenas forces Antiochos IV to leave Egypt and Cyprus. Afterwards, rival embassy of Numenios in Rome (reported in a demotic text from 158; first mention of Rome in an Egyptian document). | | |
| c. 165: Rebellion of Dionysios Petosarapis. Revolt in the Thebaïd. Disturbances in the Fayum caused by social problems. Prostagma 'On agriculture' (compulsory leasing). Creation of the idios logos (positively confirmed from 162). | From 165/4: Gradual reform of the dynastic priesthoods in Ptolemais. | |
| | October 164: The royal couple (perhaps also Ptolemy VIII) in the Serapeum in Memphis for the start of the Egyptian year. | |
| 164/3: Ptolemy VIII rules alone in Alexandria. Philometor, who has been exiled, goes to Rome and then to Cyprus. | End 164: Ptolemy VIII assumes the title of Euergetes. | UNDER PTOLEMY VI: |
| Summer 163: Philometor is called back to Alexandria. Division of the kingdom: Ptolemy VIII becomes king of the Libyan foreign possessions; Ptolemy VI and Cleopatra II rule | | Dakke, temple of Thoth; erection of the pronaos (?); Dabod: chapel of Amun expanded into a temple; |

| | | |
|---|---|---|
| from Alexandria over the rest of the kingdom. Amnesty Decree of Ptolemy VI. | October 163: The royal couple in the Serapeum in Memphis for the start of the Egyptian year. | Philae, temple of Isis: frame of the hypostyle and pylons are constructed; temple of Hathor; temple of Arensnuphis: naos; Elephantine: new construction of the temple of Satet; Kom Ombo: double temple for Haroeris and Sobek: naos is erected and mostly decorated; Esna: naos of the great temple of Khnum; Medamud: construction of the Ptolemaic temple of Month; Dendera, temple of Isis: four-columned hall; Qau el-Kebir: pronaos of the temple of Nemti; private foundations in the Fayum. |
| 163/2: Ptolemy VIII in Rome in order to have the senate allot him Cyprus; the senate decides in his favour but does not involve itself. Revolt of the Cyreneans. | | |
| Winter 162/1: Envoys from both Ptolemies in Rome where the claims of Euergetes II are acknowledged but not supported. | Summer 161: Synod of priests. | *Adornment of:* |
| End of the 160s: Onias IV comes to Egypt with a large number of Jews; a temple of Yahweh is built in Leontopolis. | October 158: The royal couple in the Serapeum in Memphis for the start of the Egyptian year. | Philae: birth house; Edfu: annexes to the inner hypostyle (from 152/1); Karnak: entrance to the temple of Harpre in the Month precinct, first gate of the temple of Ptah, gate in the second pylon; temple at Deir el-Medina: antechamber; temple at Hu. |
| | 158/7: Ptolemy Eupator is priest of Alexander at c. 8 years of age. | |
| | c. September 157: Dodekaschoinos stele on Philae: Philometor confirms the 'gift' of the 12-mile land to the temple of Isis. | |
| 156/5: Assassination attempt on Ptolemy VIII Euergetes II; his 'will' in Rome's favour. | | |

| Political events | Events from the history of ideology and religion | Construction of temples within the Egyptian territory (not in chronological order) |
|---|---|---|
| 154: Euergetes II in Rome; goes afterwards to Cyprus with an escort of Roman ships and falls into the hands of Philometor. Division of empire of 163 reconfirmed. | 153/2: Individual eponymous priests are attested in Ptolemais for each deceased Ptolemy as well as for Philometor and the queens (Arsinoe II, Cleopatra I, and II). | |
| Spring 152: Ptolemy Eupator is co-regent; he dies in the summer. | | |
| 152/145: Boethos inscription on the organization of Ptolemaic rule in the 30-mile district (foundation of the 'cities' Philometoris and Cleopatra). | | |
| 150–145: Philometor's activities in Syria: 150: Ptolemaic troops take part in the battle of Antioch fighting on the side of Alexander Balas against Demetrios I. 150/149: Philometer brings his elder daughter Cleopatra (Thea) to Ptolemais (Ake) to marry Alexander Balas. 147/6: Philometor goes to Syria with an army and navy to support Alexander Balas against Demetrios II. He sets up Ptolemaic garrisons, has coins struck in Ptolemais (146); after the assassination attempt, a shift in politics: Cleopatra Thea marries Demetrios II. Spring 145: Philometor assumes the diadem of Asia in Antioch; begins new reckoning of years (year 36 = year 1); afterwards, he limits his claims to Coele Syria and acknowledges Demetrios II; the double dating is revoked. | Late autumn 146: priestess for Cleopatra III in Ptolemais. | |

| | | UNDER PTOLEMY VIII: |
|---|---|---|
| July 145: Battle at the River Oinoparas: Philometor is mortally wounded; Alexander Balas is defeated and killed; Demetrios II acquires the entire Seleukid inheritance; Coele Syria is lost to the Seleukids. | | Kalabsha: door in the Egyptian Museum, Berlin, Charlottenburg |
| August 145: Ptolemy VIII Euergetes II in power in Alexandria. | From 145/4: the royal pair are added to the dynastic cult as *Theoi Euergetai*. | Philae: the birth house, temple of Hathor and of Arensnuphis are expanded, second east colonnade with rooms attached behind; |
| 145/4: Marriage to Cleopatra II: Euergetes II murders her youngest son by Philometor; brutal actions against the Jews and the Greek intellectuals; Amnesty decrees. Ptolemaic troops withdraw from the last Aegean bases (Itanos, Thera, Methana). | | Kom Ombo: birth house; Edfu: naos is completed (until 142) roof kiosk (142–139), pronaos (from 140), birth house (124/116), frame of the court, pylon and girdle wall; Tod: pronaos in front of the Month temple of the Middle Kingdom; |
| 144: Birth of Ptolemy Memphites in Memphis. | 144: Coronation of Ptolemy VIII in Memphis. | Karnak: Opet temple; Deir el-Bahari: third room of the 'sanatorium' on the third terrace of the temple of Hatshepsut, also a kiosk; Medinet Habu, small temple, renovation of the bark hall; Thoth temple Qasr el-Aguz; Medamud: portico of the Month temple; |
| | 10 September 142: Temple dedicated in Edfu 'by Ptolemy VIII and Cleopatra II'. | |
| 141/140: Euergetes II marries his niece and step-daughter Cleopatra III. | | |
| *c.* 140: Attempted coup by Galaistes. | 2 July 140: Pronaos of Edfu is founded. | |
| *c.* 139: Roman embassy led by P. Cornelius Scipio Aemilianus in Egypt. | From October 139: five eponymous priestesses at the end of the process in Ptolemais: Priestess for 'queen Cleopatra, the sister' (Cleopatra II), for 'queen Cleopatra, the wife' (Cleopatra III), for 'queen Cleopatra, the daughter' (Cleopatra III), for 'Cleopatra, the | |

145

| Political events | Events from the history of ideology and religion | Construction of temples within the Egyptian territory (not in chronological order) |
|---|---|---|
| | mother, the goddess Epiphanes' (Cleopatra I) and the kanephoros for Arsinoe II.<br><br>*c.* 133: Ptolemy VIII assumes the epithet Tryphon. | Athribis (at Sohag): Repyt temple;<br>Xois: dedication of temple; private foundations in the Fayum. |
| 132–124: Civil war between Ptolemy VIII and Cleopatra II:<br>Autumn 132: civil war breaks out between Ptolemy VIII and Cleopatra II.<br>Autumn 131: Ptolemy VIII flees to Cyprus with Cleopatra III and Ptolemy Memphites; Cleopatra II is the sole ruler in Alexandria, a new reckoning of her years of rule (132/1 = year 1); Ptolemy Memphites murdered by his father on Cyprus.<br>Revolt of Harsiese in Thebes (already at the beginning of November he is banished to el-Hibeh; he is attested there on 15 November 130).<br>January 130: The Egyptian Paos is strategos of the entire Theban nome (representative of Euergetes II).<br>Spring 130: Memphis under the control of Ptolemy VIII.<br>129/8: Demetrios attempts an expedition to Egypt; flight of Cleopatra II to Syria. Euergetes II sends Alexander Zabinas to Syria as a rival king in the Seleukid realm.<br>127/6(?): Euergetes II captures Alexandria; bloody trials. | Autumn 131: Cleopatra II assumes the cult title *Thea Philometor Soteira* which replaces the Theoi Euergetai at the end of the title of the priest of Alexander until 127.<br><br>Spring 130: Eponymous counter priests 'with the king' (until 127); office of eponymous priest of Hieropolos for Cleopatra III. | *Adornment of:*<br><br>Dakke: Thoth temple, façade;<br>Debod: temple of Amun;<br>Philae temple of Isis, hypostyle;<br>Syene: temple of Isis;<br>Kom Ombo: inner columned hall;<br>Elkab: Ptolemaic hemispeos, temple dating to Amenophis III;<br>Karnak: gate of the second pylon, temple of Khonsu, central gate in the east temple dating from Ramses II;<br>temple at Deir el-Medina;<br>Dendera: propylaea of the older birth house. |

126: Alexander Zabinas defeats Demetrios II at Damascus; Demetrios II is assassinated.

124: Reconciliation of the Ptolemaic warring factions.

124/3: Ptolemy VIII drops Alexander Zabinas and marries his daughter Tryphaina to Antiochos VIII Grypos. The latter then defeats and executes Zabinas in 123 with the help of Ptolemaic auxiliary troops.

c. 122: The high priest of Ptah, Psenptah II, marries a Berenike who is closely tied to the royal house.

Spring 118: Amnesty Decree of Euergetes II.

c. 117: Ptolemy IX becomes governor-general of Cyprus. Eudoxos of Kyzikos is in India for the first time.

28 June 116: Death of Euergetes II.

Summer 116: Four Romans leave behind in Philae the oldest Latin inscription in Egypt.

Autumn 116: Joint rule of Cleopatra II, III, and Ptolemy IX Soter II. Ptolemy X Alexander I is strategos of Cyprus.

From the end of 116: Joint rule of Cleopatra III and Ptolemy IX.

---

From 126: There is again only one priest of Alexander who bears the title he had prior to 131.

124/117: Ptolemy VIII accords privileges to the priests of Philae.

Spring 118: The dynastic god *Neos Philopator* is created; he is named as the last deceased Ptolemy in the title of the priest of Alexander (Ptolemy Memphites?).

116–107: Ptolemy IX is priest of Alexander.

116: Three new eponymous priestesses for Cleopatra III in Alexandria: stephanephoros, phosphoros, hiereia. The cult title of the ruling Ptolemies now remains *Theoi Philometores soteres* until 88.

---

UNDER PTOLEMY IX AND X:

Kalabsha: chapel next to the temple of Mandulis, chapel constructed from blocks taken from the filling of the

---

PTOLEMY VIII EUERGETES II

CLEOPATRA II AND III AND PTOLEMY IX SOTER II

116

116

| | Political events | Events from the history of ideology and religion | Construction of temples within the Egyptian territory (not in chronological order) |
|---|---|---|---|
| CLEOPATRA III AND PTOLEMY IX SOTER II | *c.* 115: Ptolemy IX is compelled to divorce Cleopatra IV and marry Cleopatra V Selene. | Late summer 115: Ptolemy IX sacrifices to the Nile on the occasion of the so-called signal festival on Elephantine and accords privileges to the priests of Khnum. | sanctuary of the great temple; Edfu: relief cycles on the enclosure walls and court, reliefs on the pylon; Elkab: reliefs of Cleopatra III at the entrance of the hemispeos |
| | 114/3: Ptolemy X Alexander I proclaims himself 'king' in Cyprus. Cleopatra IV musters an army in Cyprus and arrives in Syria with the army. There she marries Antiochos IX Kyzikenos. | | el-Hilla: decoration of the inner hall of the temple of Isis; Karnak: reliefs on the first gate of the temple of Ptah as well as in the temple of Khonsu; Deir el-Medina: relief on the southern outer wall; |
| | 112: Cleopatra IV is captured and murdered by Antiochos VII Grypos in Antioch. The Roman senator L. Memmius journeys through Egypt. | | Medinet Habu, small temple: double-layered hypostyle and annexes to the peripteros, first pylon and portico facing it; Qus: two pylons; |
| | 111: Tryphaina, the wife of Antiochos VIII and elder sister of Cleopatra IV, is captured and murdered by Antiochos IX. | | Dendera, temple of Isis: outer hypostyle, colonnaded ambulatory; private foundations in the Fayum. |
| | *c.* 109/8: 6,000 Ptolemaic soldiers are sent to Antiochos IX for his campaign against the Jews. | | |
| 107 | Autumn 107: Soter II flees from Cleopatra III to Cyprus; Cleopatra III brings Alexander I to Alexandria and makes him co-regent; double-counting of the years of their reign: her 11th year = his 8th year. | Autumn 107–105: Ptolemy X Alexander I is priest of Alexander. | |
| CLEOPATRA III AND PTOLEMY X ALEXANDER I | | Autumn 107: For the queen/king 'priest for life' in Alexandria (for 107/6 Helenos, strategos of Cyprus). | |
| | From 106/5: Soter II rules Cyprus as an independent ruler. | 105/4: Cleopatra III is priest of Alexander. | |

104/3: Cleopatra III takes sides in the Seleukid dynastic war and sends her daughter Cleopatra V Selene to be the wife of Antiochos VIII Grypos.

103–101: War in Syria:

103: Soter conquers Asochis in Galilee, defeats Iannaios, the king of the Jews, at Asophon;

Cleopatra III sends her grandchildren to Cos, sends Alexander I with army and navy to Phoenicia and Damascus. She herself lays siege to Ptolemais (Ake); Soter II attempts to gain a foothold in Egypt, is driven out by Alexander I and returns to Cyprus.

102: Cleopatra III captures Ptolemais and concludes treaty with Iannaios; the latter proceeds with his conquests in Palestine until the beginning of 101.

Late summer 101: Alexander I murders Cleopatra III and marries Cleopatra Berenike III.

100: Ptolemy Apion is attested as king in Cyrene (lex de piratis persequendis).

Early spring 99: The royal couple are at the Serapeum in Memphis for the beginning of the Egyptian year.

96: Death of Ptolemy Apion after he had bequeathed his kingdom to the Romans; the latter then take possession of the crown land and declare the Greek cities to be free (Roman province of Cyrene only in 75/4).

| | Political events | Events from the history of ideology and religion | Construction of temples within the Egyptian territory (not in chronological order) |
|---|---|---|---|
| **PTOLEMY IX SOTER II** — 88 | 91–88: Revolt in the Thebaïd.<br><br>88: Alexander I is driven out of Alexandria; the return of Soter II. Mithridates VI Eupator occupies Cos, takes possession of the Ptolemaic treasure. Alexander I is defeated in a naval battle and goes to Asia Minor. He bequeaths his kingdom to the Romans in the case of his disappearance (will of Alexander). He dies attempting to conquer Cyprus (87). | 88: Soter II is perhaps crowned pharaoh for the second time.<br><br>84/3: Soter II is attested as priest of Alexander. | |
| **CLEOPATRA BERENIKE III AND PTOLEMY XI ALEXANDER II** — 81 / 80 | Summer 86: Lucullus in Alexandria.<br><br>84: Ptolemy XI Alexander II flees from Mithridates to Sulla.<br><br>End of 81: Death of Ptolemy IX Soter II.<br><br>Beginning of 80: Cleopatra Berenike III takes sole control of the throne.<br><br>June 80: Ptolemy XI Alexander II arrives in Alexandria, marries his step-mother Cleopatra Berenike III: after 18 (19) days, he has her killed; for this reason, he is murdered by the Alexandrians. | | |

80: Official division of the Ptolemaic kingdom:
Ptolemy XII accedes to the throne in Alexandria while Ptolemy of Cyprus is 'king of Cyprus'.
The two brothers were probably still at Mithridates' court. They were summoned from there by the Alexandrians.
Ptolemy XII marries his sister Cleopatra VI Tryphaina.

74/3 (?): evidence for the office of a 'strategos of the Red and Indian Seas'.
End of the 70s: Marriage is concluded between Ptolemy XII and a distinguished Egyptian woman?

From 79: The cult title *Theos Philopator and Philadelphos* is attested for the twelfth Ptolemy (in plural for the royal couple).

76: According to the historical passage on the Harris stele:
Psenptah III is named high priest of Memphis; he is 14 years old;
Ptolemy XII is crowned pharaoh;
Psenptah is designated 'prophet of the pharaoh';
*Neos Dionysos* ('the young Osiris') is attested as the official title of Ptolemy XII.

7 January 70: Dedication of the temple of Edfu.

UNDER PTOLEMY XII:
Philae: reliefs on the pylons of the temple of Isis, reliefs on the birth house;
Bigga: inscriptions in the temple of Osiris;
Kom Ombo: pronaos, southern gate, inner girdle wall with chapels on the east side;
Edfu: cartouches on the pylon;
Karnak: chapel of Osiris of Koptos, reliefs on the first and third gate of the temple of Ptah as well as on the entrance to the hypostyle of the temple of Opet;
Deir el-Medina: reliefs on the gate of the girdle wall.
Medamud: kiosks in front of the temple of the Month;
Athribis (near Sohag): birth house (?) for the Repyt temple;
Dendera: temple of Hathor: construction begins on 16 July 54, cartouches in the crypts.

| Political events | Events from the history of ideology and religion | Construction of temples within the Egyptian territory (not in chronological order) |
| --- | --- | --- |
| 70/69: Birth of Cleopatra VII. | | |
| 69/8: Cleopatra VI Tryphaina falls into disfavour. | | |
| 65: The proposal of M. Licinius Crassus to annex Egypt as a Roman province (based on the will of Alexander I) fails; Cicero's speech *De rege Alexandrino*. | | |
| 64/3: Ptolemy XII supports Pompey in the east. | | |
| 63: Cicero prevents Egypt from being included in the Roman *ager publicus* with his speeches *De lege agraria*. | | |
| 61: Ptolemy XIII is born. | | |
| 60: Diodorus is in Egypt. Ptolemy XII promises Caesar and Pompey 6,000 talents to acknowledge him. | | |
| 59: Caesar has Ptolemy XII confirmed as king in Rome as well as designating him as an *amicus et socius populi Romani*. Birth of Ptolemy XIV (probably 59). | | |
| 58/56: Rome annexes Cyprus (M. Porcius Cato); Ptolemy of Cyprus commits suicide (58). | | |
| 58: Ptolemy XII is driven out of Alexandria. Joint rule of Berenike IV and Cleopatra VI Tryphaina (year 1 = 58/7). | | |

| | | |
|---|---|---|
| **BERENIKE IV AND ARCHELAOS** | 57: Ptolemy XII in Rome: 'Egyptian question' in Rome. Death of Cleopatra VI: Search for a husband for Berenike IV. From spring 56: joint rule of Berenike IV and Archelaos. | |
| **55** | Spring 55: A. Gabinius leads Ptolemy XII back to Egypt; Archelaos is defeated and killed. | |
| **PTOLEMY XII NEOS DIONYSOS** | 15 April 55: Ptolemy XII is again attested as the ruling king; Berenike IV is murdered; C. Rabirius Postumus is entrusted with the supervision of ptolemaic finances under the title *dioiketes*; Roman troops ('Gabiniani') remain in Egypt. 54: A. Gabinius and Rabirius Postumus are on trial in Rome. *c.* 52: Cleopatra VII as co-ruler. | 16 July 54: Construction of the temple of Hathor at Dendera commences. |
| **51** | Beginning of 51: Death of Ptolemy XII (Rome is named as guarantor of a joint rule of Cleopatra VII and Ptolemy XIII in his will). | 22 March 51: Cleopatra participates in the installation of the Buchis bull in Hermonthis. |
| **CLEOPATRA VII PHILOPATOR** | 51/50: (probably after a very short joint rule with Ptolemy XIII) Cleopatra VII is sole ruler for 18 months. From autumn 50: Rule of Ptolemy XIII (supported by Potheinos, Achillas and Theodotos of Chios) and Cleopatra VII. | UNDER CLEOPATRA VII: Kom Ombo: reliefs in the chapels on the east side of the inner girdle wall; Armant: birth house of Harpore; |

| Political events | Events from the history of ideology and religion | Construction of temples within the Egyptian territory (not in chronological order) |
|---|---|---|
| 49: Cn. Pompey (son of the great Pompey) in Alexandria; is given 500 Gallic and Germanic cavalry from the Gabiniani for his fight against Caesar. Cleopatra is driven out and goes to the Thebaïd. The Roman counter-senate in Thessaloniki acknowledges Ptolemy XIII as the legitimate ruler (autumn 49). | | Koptos: chapel of Cleopatra and Caesarion; Dendera: naos of the temple of Hathor; Ptolemais Hermaiu: temple of Isis of Kallimachos (46). |
| 48: Cleopatra escapes to the Syrian border area (perhaps at the beginning of the year); from there she attempts to regain the throne. Battle of Pharsalos; Pompey reaches the coast at Pelusion and is murdered (July 48). | | |
| Summer 48: Caesar in Alexandria: Caesar resides in the royal palace. By appealing to the will of Ptolemy XII he attempts to settle the conflict between Ptolemy XIII and Cleopatra VII and summons both to his side; Love affair between Caesar and Cleopatra; Caesar establishes Cleopatra and Ptolemy XIII as joint rulers of Egypt and Ptolemy XIV and Arsinoe as kings of Cyprus (Cyprus is once again Ptolemaic). | | |

48/7: Alexandrian War against Caesar: The Museion Library is set on fire (late summer 48): Arsinoe (IV) is acclaimed queen by the army which is hostile to Caesar.
Start of 47: Caesar and the auxiliary troops under the command of Mithridates of Pergamon) defeat the Egyptians; Ptolemy XIII falls, Arsinoe (IV) is captured. Caesar enters Alexandria.

47: Caesar hands over administration of Egypt to Cleopatra, places Ptolemy XIV at her side and leaves behind three legions in Egypt:
47–44: Egypt is a Roman protectorate.

23 June 47: Ptolemy XV Caesar is born.

Summer 46 until April 44: Cleopatra together with Ptolemy XIV are guests in Rome and reside with Caesar (15 March 44).

44: Cleopatra has Ptolemy XIV killed and takes Ptolemy XV Caesar as her nominal co-regent.

From 47/6: Coins of Cleopatra are attested with the epithets and headdress of Isis.

46: Gold statue of Cleopatra next to the cult image of Venus Genetrix in the latter's temple on the forum Iulium in Rome. The strategos Kallimachos dedicates a sanctuary of Isis at Ptolemais.

| Political events | Events from the history of ideology and religion | Construction of temples within the Egyptian territory (not in chronological order) |
|---|---|---|
| 43: Ptolemy Caesar is officially acknowledged by P. Cornelius Dolabella. Cleopatra sends him four legions from Egypt, which are diverted to C. Cassius; the Ptolemaic governor of Cyprus, Serapion, also goes over to Cassius together with the Egyptian navy. | | |
| 43 and 42: Failure of the Nile flood; famine and epidemic in Egypt. | 44/39: Kinglike honours for the strategos Callimachos as a soter by the priests and people of Thebes. | |
| 41: Cleopatra with Antony in Tarsos. | 41: Meeting in Tarsos is celebrated as the coming together of Aphrodite and Dionysos. Death of the high priest of Ptah, Psenptah III. | |
| Winter 41/40: Antony is Cleopatra's guest in Alexandria; probably at this time Antony adds Roman Cilicia to Ptolemaic Cyprus (attested for November 38). | | |
| 40: Birth of the twins Alexander and Cleopatra. | 39: Petubastis IV (son of Psenptah III) is named high priest of Ptah and 'prophet of the pharaoh' for Cleopatra VII. He is 7 years old. | |

CLEOPATRA VII PHILOPATOR

| | |
|---|---|
| Winter 37/6: Cleopatra with Antony in Antioch; Antony acknowledges the Ptolemaic twins. Re-organization of the Near East: Cleopatra receives the kingdom Chalkis in Lebanon, the balsam and date groves at Jericho, the neighbouring territories of the Nabataean kingdom as well as the city of Cyrene and estates on Crete; Cleopatra now begins a new reckoning of her years of rule alongside the previous system: year 16 = year 1 (37/6). | Winter 37/6: The Ptolemaic twins receive the epithets Helios and Selene. |
| 36: Birth of Ptolemy Philadelphos. Parthian campaign of Antony which ends in disaster. | From *c.* 36: Cleopatra as *Thea Neotera* on coins from Syria and Cyrene. |
| 34: Antony's Armenian campaign. Antony marries Cleopatra (probably as part of the celebrations in the autumn of 34; second marriage is not valid under Roman law). | Autmn 34: Antony enters Alexandria and holds a triumph there during which he goes to the temple of Sarapis as the new Dionysos. Ideological and political ceremony in the gymnasium of Alexandria on the occasion of the creation of a new kingdom joining Achaemenid and ancient pharaonic traditions: Cleopatra, who is presented as *Nea Isis*, becomes the 'queen of kings' while Ptolemy Caesar' is 'king of kings'. The children of Cleopatra and Antony are symbolically given large parts of Asia and Selene, in particular, is given Cyrene as her kingdom. |

| Political events | Events from the history of ideology and religion | Construction of temples within the Egyptian territory (not in chronological order) |
| --- | --- | --- |
| 33: Propaganda war between Octavian and Antony.<br>Antony gathers together military forces in Anatolia.<br>Beginning of 32: Cleopatra with Antony in Ephesos.<br>The consuls Cn. Domitius Ahenobarbus and C. Sosius go to Antony in Ephesos together with 300 to 400 senators.<br>First half of 32: Antony and Cleopatra are first in Samos, then in Athens. (May/June). Antony sends Octavia (sister of Octavian whom Antony had married in 40) a letter of divorce.<br>Octavian forces Antony's will to be opened in Rome; Cleopatra is depicted in highly stylized terms as a danger to Rome and the world.<br>Late summer/autumn 32: Cleopatra is declared an enemy of the state in Rome.<br>Winter 32/1: Antony and Cleopatra in Patras.<br>Summer 31: Agrippa effects a blockade which has a devasting effect on the army of Antony and Cleopatra at Actium. | Turn of 34/3: Construction of a temple to Antony is begun in Alexandria. | |

**ROMAN PROVINCE**
**AEGYPTUS**

2 September 31: Battle of Actium: Antony loses the naval battle; Cleopatra escapes.

1 (or 3) August 30: Octavian takes Alexandria: official beginning of the history of Egypt as a Roman province. In the days which follow Antony commits suicide; Ptolemy Caesar attempts to escape.

10 (or 12) August 30: Death of Cleopatra.

29: Triumph of Octavian over Egypt.

20: Cleopatra Selene marries Juba II of Mauretania.

23 BC – AD 40: Ptolemy of Mauretania.

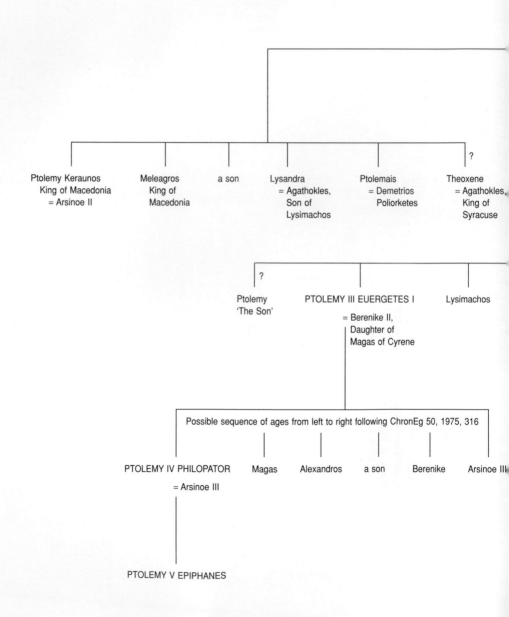

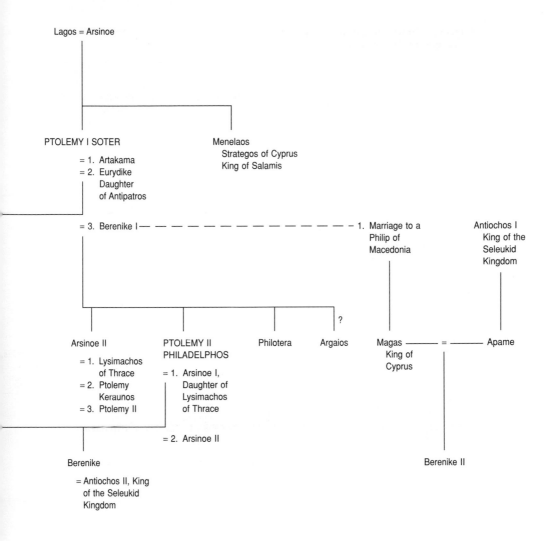

Lagos = Arsinoe

PTOLEMY I SOTER

   = 1. Artakama
   = 2. Eurydike
       Daughter
       of Antipatros

Menelaos
   Strategos of Cyprus
   King of Salamis

= 3. Berenike I — — — — — — — — — — — — — — 1. Marriage to a
                                                 Philip of
                                               Macedonia

Antiochos I
   King of the
   Seleukid
   Kingdom

                                       ?

Arsinoe II

   = 1. Lysimachos
       of Thrace
   = 2. Ptolemy
       Keraunos
   = 3. Ptolemy II

PTOLEMY II
PHILADELPHOS

   = 1. Arsinoe I,
       Daughter of
       Lysimachos
       of Thrace

   = 2. Arsinoe II

Philotera

Argaios

Magas ——— = ——— Apame
   King of
   Cyprus

Berenike

   = Antiochos II, King
   of the Seleukid
   Kingdom

Berenike II

Key:

=   LEGITIMATE MARRIAGE

×   FROM A GREEK VIEWPOINT ILLEGITIMATE UNION

Capital letters: the kings who ruled in Alexandria as well as the queens
if they were regents (while queens not identified primarily as rulers are
written in lowercase letters).

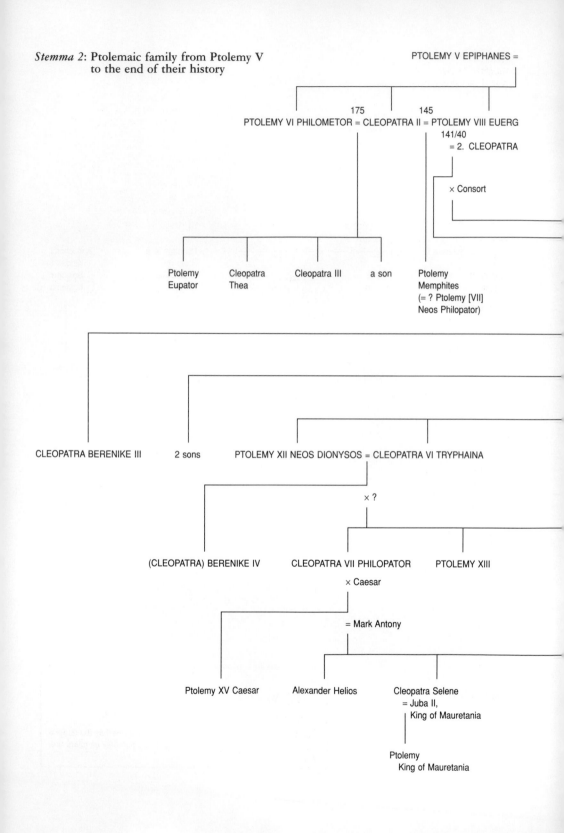

*Stemma 2*: **Ptolemaic family from Ptolemy V**
to the end of their history

PTOLEMY V EPIPHANES =

175    145

PTOLEMY VI PHILOMETOR = CLEOPATRA II = PTOLEMY VIII EUERG

141/40
= 2. CLEOPATRA

× Consort

Ptolemy   Cleopatra   Cleopatra III   a son   Ptolemy
Eupator   Thea                                   Memphites
                                                  (= ? Ptolemy [VII]
                                                  Neos Philopator)

CLEOPATRA BERENIKE III   2 sons   PTOLEMY XII NEOS DIONYSOS = CLEOPATRA VI TRYPHAINA

× ?

(CLEOPATRA) BERENIKE IV   CLEOPATRA VII PHILOPATOR   PTOLEMY XIII

× Caesar

= Mark Antony

Ptolemy XV Caesar   Alexander Helios   Cleopatra Selene
                                                          = Juba II,
                                                             King of Mauretania

Ptolemy
King of Mauretania

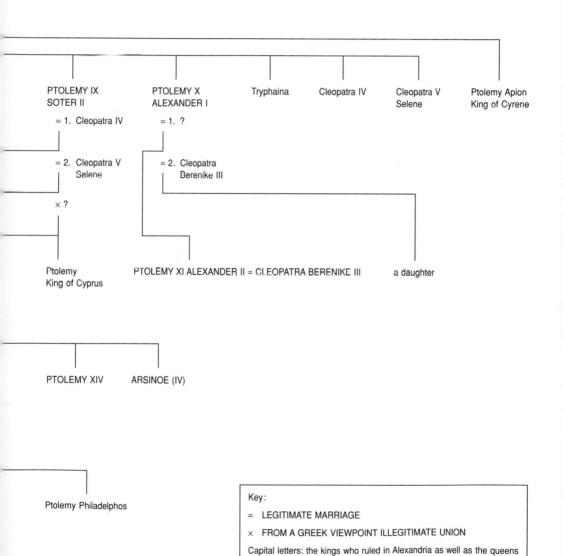

CLEOPATRA I
  Daughter of Antiochos III,
  King of the Seleukid Kingdom

ETES II

III

| PTOLEMY IX | PTOLEMY X | Tryphaina | Cleopatra IV | Cleopatra V | Ptolemy Apion |
| SOTER II | ALEXANDER I | | | Selene | King of Cyrene |

= 1. Cleopatra IV        = 1. ?

= 2. Cleopatra V         = 2. Cleopatra
     Selene                   Berenike III

× ?

Ptolemy            PTOLEMY XI ALEXANDER II = CLEOPATRA BERENIKE III        a daughter
King of Cyprus

PTOLEMY XIV        ARSINOE (IV)

Ptolemy Philadelphos

Key:

= LEGITIMATE MARRIAGE

× FROM A GREEK VIEWPOINT ILLEGITIMATE UNION

Capital letters: the kings who ruled in Alexandria as well as the queens
if they were regents (while queens not identified primarily as rulers are
written in lowercase letters).

*Stemma 3*: **Marriage ties between the Ptolemaic
women and the Seleukid court
beginning in the mid-second century**

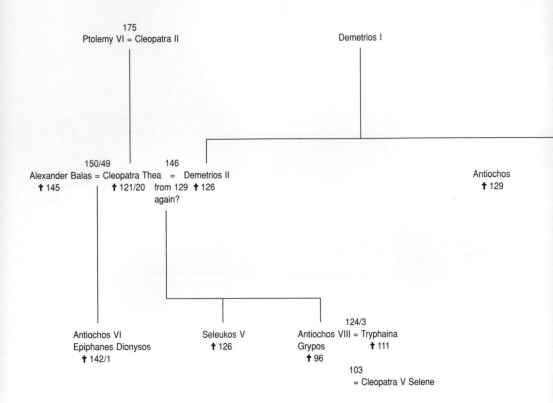

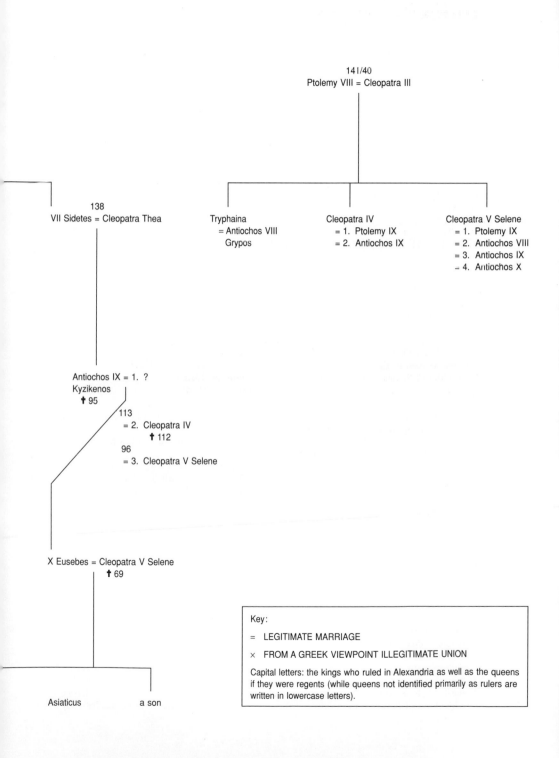

141/40
Ptolemy VIII = Cleopatra III

138
VII Sidetes = Cleopatra Thea

Tryphaina
= Antiochos VIII
Grypos

Cleopatra IV
= 1. Ptolemy IX
= 2. Antiochos IX

Cleopatra V Selene
= 1. Ptolemy IX
= 2. Antiochos VIII
= 3. Antiochos IX
= 4. Antiochos X

Antiochos IX = 1. ?
Kyzikenos
† 95

113
= 2. Cleopatra IV
† 112

96
= 3. Cleopatra V Selene

X Eusebes = Cleopatra V Selene
† 69

Asiaticus          a son

Key:

= LEGITIMATE MARRIAGE

× FROM A GREEK VIEWPOINT ILLEGITIMATE UNION

Capital letters: the kings who ruled in Alexandria as well as the queens
if they were regents (while queens not identified primarily as rulers are
written in lowercase letters).

# Index

## GEOGRAPHIC TERMS

# GENERAL INDEX

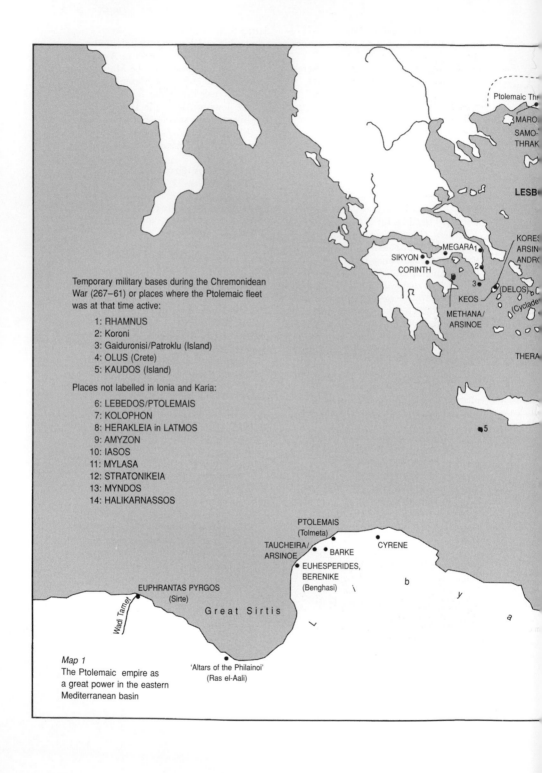

Temporary military bases during the Chremonidean
War (267–61) or places where the Ptolemaic fleet
was at that time active:

1: RHAMNUS
2: Koroni
3: Gaiduronisi/Patroklu (Island)
4: OLUS (Crete)
5: KAUDOS (Island)

Places not labelled in Ionia and Karia:

6: LEBEDOS/PTOLEMAIS
7: KOLOPHON
8: HERAKLEIA in LATMOS
9: AMYZON
10: IASOS
11: MYLASA
12: STRATONIKEIA
13: MYNDOS
14: HALIKARNASSOS

Ptolemaic Thr
MARO
SAMO-
THRAK

LESB

KORES
ARSIN
ANDR

MEGARA1
SIKYON
CORINTH
2
3
(DELOS)
KEOS
METHANA/
ARSINOE
(Cyclade

THERA

5

PTOLEMAIS
(Tolmeta)
TAUCHEIRA/
ARSINOE
BARKE
CYRENE
EUHESPERIDES,
BERENIKE
(Benghasi)
b
y
EUPHRANTAS PYRGOS
(Sirte)
Wadi Tamet
Great Sirtis
a

Map 1
The Ptolemaic empire as
a great power in the eastern
Mediterranean basin

'Altars of the Philainoi'
(Ras el-Aali)

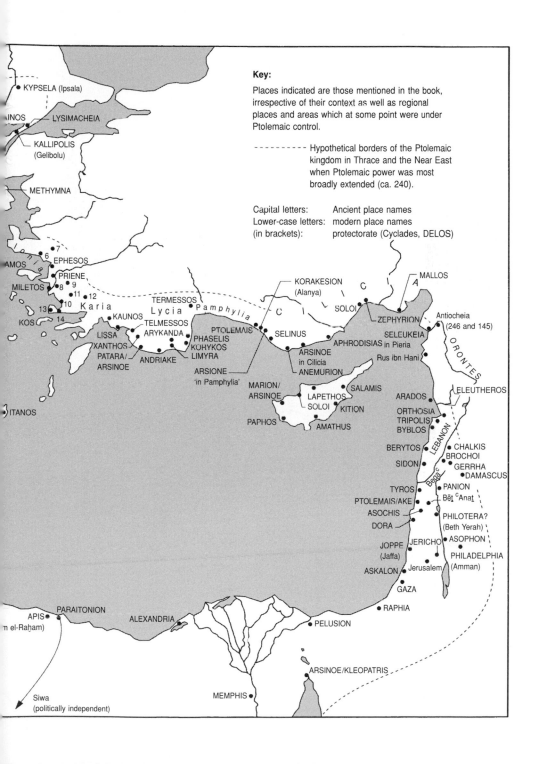

Key:

Places indicated are those mentioned in the book, irrespective of their context as well as regional places and areas which at some point were under Ptolemaic control.

-------- Hypothetical borders of the Ptolemaic kingdom in Thrace and the Near East when Ptolemaic power was most broadly extended (ca. 240).

Capital letters: Ancient place names
Lower-case letters: modern place names
(in brackets): protectorate (Cyclades, DELOS)

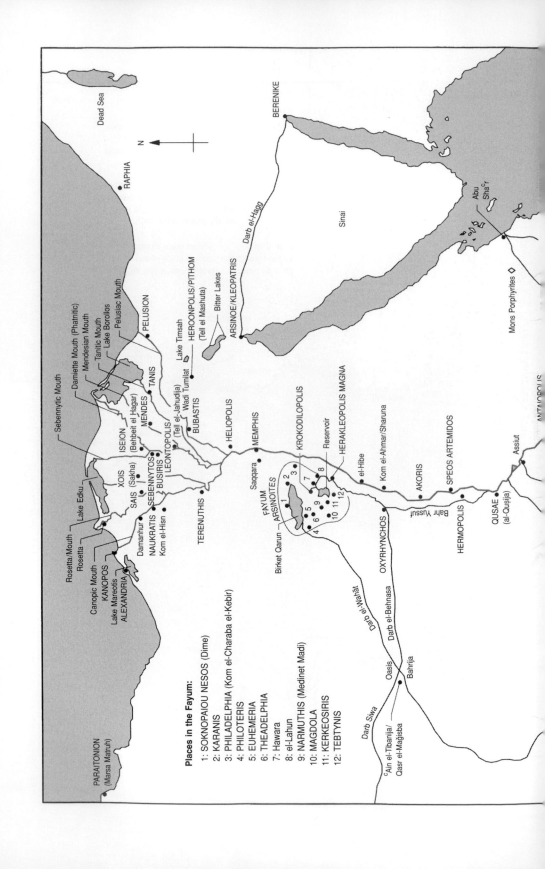

**Places in the Fayum:**

1: SOKNOPAIOU NESOS (Dime)
2: KARANIS
3: PHILADELPHIA (Kom el-Charaba el-Kebir)
4: PHILOTERIS
5: EUHEMERIA
6: THEADELPHIA
7: Hawara
8: el-Lahun
9: NARMUTHIS (Medinet Madi)
10: MAGDOLA
11: KERKEOSIRIS
12: TEBTYNIS

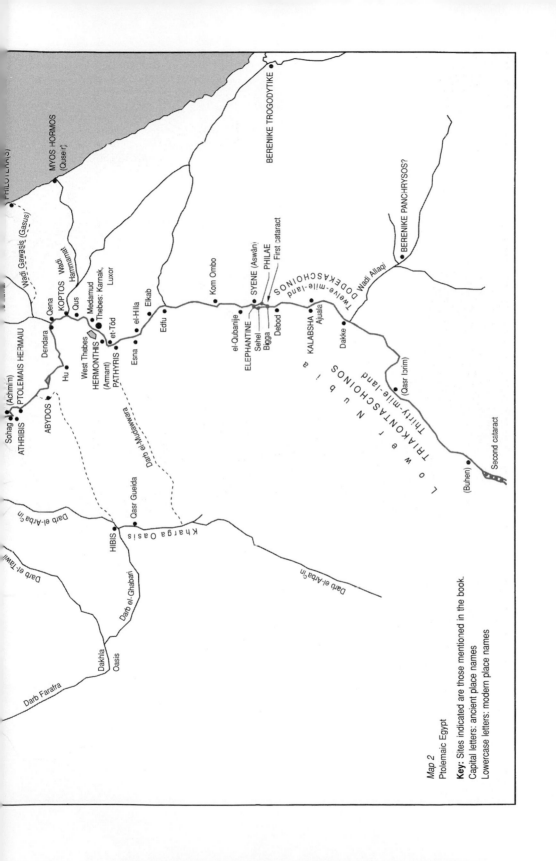

*Map 2*
Ptolemaic Egypt

**Key:** Sites indicated are those mentioned in the book.
Capital letters: ancient place names
Lowercase letters: modern place names

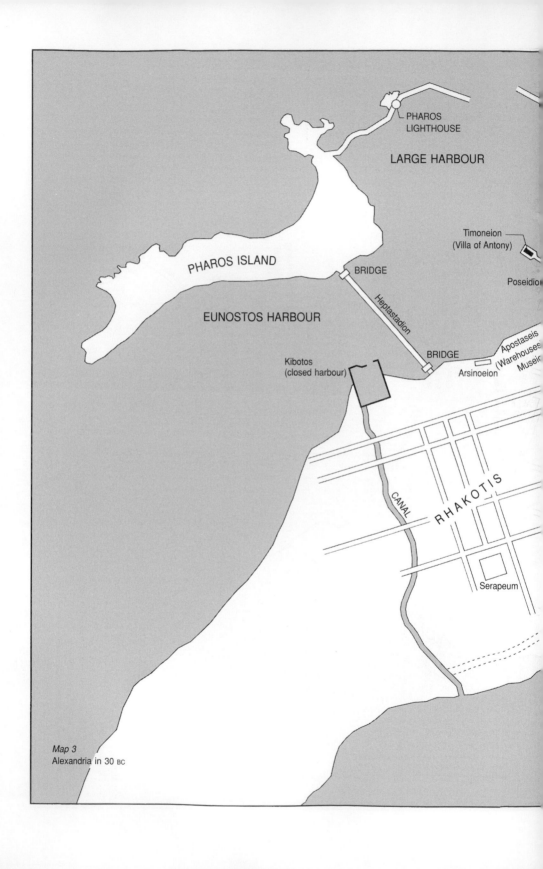

PHAROS
LIGHTHOUSE

LARGE HARBOUR

Timoneion
(Villa of Antony)

PHAROS ISLAND

BRIDGE

Poseidion

Heptastadion

EUNOSTOS HARBOUR

Apostaseis
(Warehouses)

BRIDGE

Museion

Kibotos
(closed harbour)

Arsinoeion

CANAL

R H A K O T I S

Serapeum

Map 3
Alexandria in 30 BC

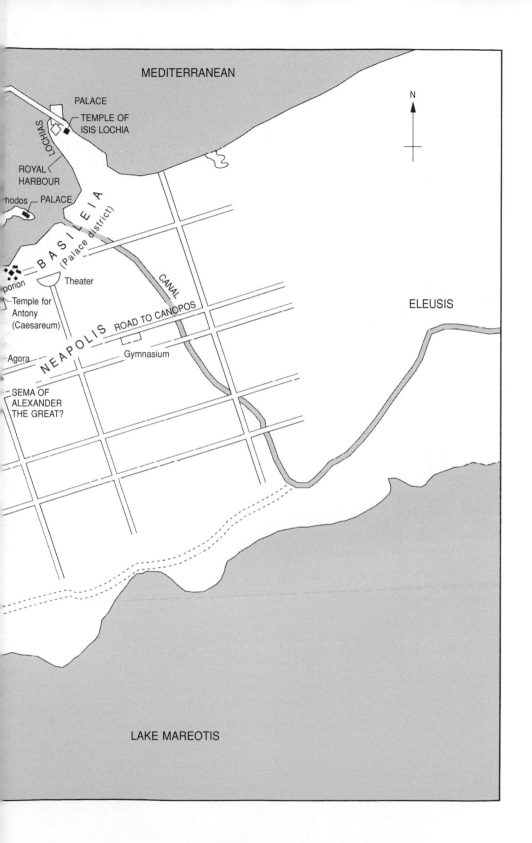

MEDITERRANEAN

PALACE

TEMPLE OF
ISIS LOCHIA

LOCHIAS

ROYAL
HARBOUR

hodos — PALACE

B A S I L E I A
(Palace district)

Theater

porion

Temple for
Antony
(Caesareum)

N E A P O L I S

CANAL

ROAD TO CANOPOS

Agora

Gymnasium

ELEUSIS

SEMA OF
ALEXANDER
THE GREAT?

N

LAKE MAREOTIS